Pearson Scott Foresman Addison Wesley

enVisionMATH™

California

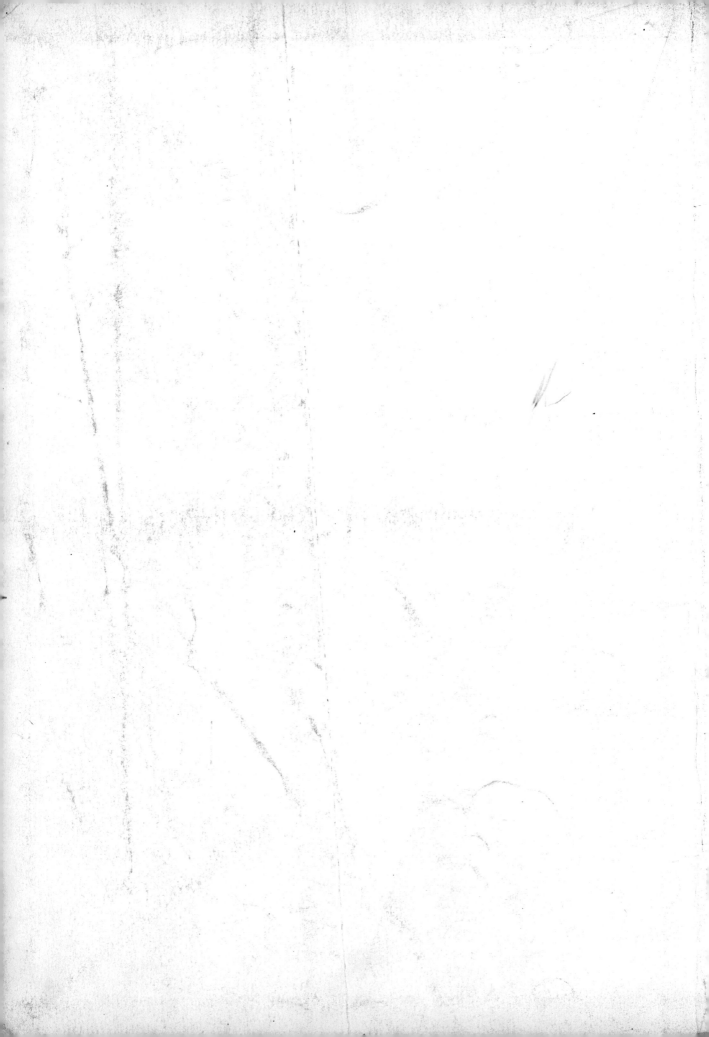

Scott Foresman • Addison Wesley

enVisionMATH™ California

Authors

Randall I. Charles
Professor Emeritus
Department of Mathematics
San Jose State University
San Jose, California

Mary Cavanagh
Mathematics Consultant
San Diego County Office of Education
San Diego, California

Juanita V. Copley
Professor
College of Education
University of Houston
Houston, Texas

Warren D. Crown
Associate Dean for Academic Affairs
Graduate School of Education
Rutgers University
New Brunswick, New Jersey

Francis (Skip) Fennell
Professor of Education
McDaniel College
Westminster, Maryland

Alma B. Ramirez
Sr. Research Associate
Math Pathways and Pitfalls WestEd
Oakland, California

Kay B. Sammons
Coordinator of Elementary Mathematics
Howard County Public Schools
Ellicott City, Maryland

Jane F. Schielack
Professor of Mathematics
Associate Dean for Assessment and
Pre K-12 Education, College of Science
Texas A&M University
College Station, Texas

William Tate
Edward Mallinckrodt Distinguished
University Professor in Arts & Sciences
Washington University
St. Louis, Missouri

John A. Van de Walle
Professor Emeritus, Mathematics Education
Virginia Commonwealth University
Richmond, Virginia

Consulting Mathematicians

Edward J. Barbeau
Professor of Mathematics
University of Toronto
Toronto, Canada

Sybilla Beckmann
Professor of Mathematics
Department of Mathematics
University of Georgia
Athens, Georgia

David Bressoud
DeWitt Wallace Professor of Mathematics
Macalester College
Saint Paul, Minnesota

Gary Lippman
Professor of Mathematics and Computer Science
California State University East Bay
Hayward, California

Editorial Offices: Glenview, Illinois • Parsippany, New Jersey • New York, New York
Sales Offices: Boston, Massachusetts • Duluth, Georgia • Glenview, Illinois
Coppell, Texas • Sacramento, California • Mesa, Arizona

Consulting Authors

Stuart J. Murphy
Visual Learning Specialist
Boston, Massachusetts

Jeanne Ramos
Secondary Mathematics Coordinator
Los Angeles Unified School District
Los Angeles, California

Verónica Galván Carlan
Private Consultant Mathematics
Harlingen, Texas

EL Consultants/Reviewers

Alma B. Ramirez
Sr. Research Associate
Math Pathways and Pitfalls WestEd
Oakland, California

California Reviewers

Martha Borquez
Teacher
Los Angeles USD

Elsa M. Campos
Teacher
Corona-Norco USD

Lynn Cevallos
K-12 Mathematics Consultant
Los Angeles, CA

Jann Edwards
Teacher, GATE Coordinator
Los Angeles USD

Katherine J. Jones
Teacher, District Math Coach
Newark USD

Kevin M. Kazala
Math Specialist K-6
Corona-Norco USD

Karen Jae Ko
Teacher
Long Beach USD

Kristin Leidig-Sears
Teacher
Los Angeles USD

Ariana R. Levin
Teacher
Los Angeles USD

Patrick A. McCormack
Special Education Teacher
Los Angeles USD

Stefani Maida
Teacher
Berkeley USD

Misook Park-Kimura
Professional Development Mentor
Long Beach USD

Elgin Michael Scott
Educator
Los Angeles USD

Doris L. Sterling
Teacher/Math Facilitator
Sacramento City USD

Amy N. Tindell
Math Coach
Los Angeles USD

Rachel M. Williams
Math Curriculum Associate/Teacher
North Sacramento School District

ISBN-13: 978-0-328-27291-4
ISBN-10: 0-328-27291-4

6 7 8 9 10 V057 12 11 10 09
CC: 2

Topic Titles

Topic 1 Numeration

Topic 2 Addition and Subtraction Number Sense

Topic 3 Reviewing Multiplication of Whole Numbers

Topic 4 Division of Whole Numbers

Topic 5 Variables and Expressions

Topic 6 Multiplying Decimals

Topic 7 Dividing Decimals

Topic 8 Shapes

Topic 9 Factors and Multiples

Topic 10 Fractions, Mixed Numbers, and Decimals

Topic 11 Adding and Subtracting Fractions and Mixed Numbers

Topic 12 Multiplying and Dividing Fractions and Mixed Numbers

Topic 13 Length, Perimeter, and Area

Topic 14 Solids

Topic 15 Integers

Topic 16 Solving and Writing Equations

Topic 17 Percent

Topic 18 Equations and Graphs

Topic 19 Graphs and Data

Topic 20 Constructions

Table of Contents

MATH STRAND COLORS

- Number Sense
- Algebra and Functions
- Measurement and Geometry
- Statistics, Data Analysis, and Probability
- Problem Solving

Mathematical Reasoning, which includes problem solving, is infused throughout all lessons.

Problem-Solving Handbook x

Topic 1 Numeration

NS 1.0 Gr. 4, 1.0, 1.1 MR 1.0, 1.1

Review What You Know 3

1-1 Number: Place Value 4

1-2 Number: Comparing and Ordering Whole Numbers 6

Mixed Problem Solving 9

1-3 Decimals: Decimal Place Value 10

1-4 Decimals: Comparing and Ordering Decimals 12

1-5 Problem Solving Look for a Pattern 14

Stop and Practice 17

Topic 1 Test Prep 18

Reteaching 20

Topic 2 Addition and Subtraction Number Sense

NS 1.0, 1.1, 2.0, 2.1, AF 1.2 Gr. 4, 1.1 Gr. 6, MR 1.0, 1.1, 2.1, 2.3

Review What You Know 23

2-1 Number Sense: Mental Math 24

Mixed Problem Solving 27

2-2 Number Sense: Rounding Whole Numbers and Decimals 28

2-3 Number Sense: Estimating Sums and Differences 30

Algebra Connections 33

2-4 Number Sense: Adding and Subtracting 34

Stop and Practice 37

2-5 Decimals: Adding Decimals 38

2-6 Decimals: Subtracting Decimals 40

2-7 Problem Solving Draw a Picture and Write an Equation 42

Stop and Practice 45

Topic 2 Test Prep 46

Reteaching 48

Reviewing Multiplication of Whole Numbers

NS 1.0, 1.1, 1.3, 2.0, 3.3 Gr. 4, AF 1.3 Gr. 6, MR 1.1, 1.2, 2.1

Review What You Know 51

3-1 Multiplication: Multiplication Properties 52

3-2 Multiplication: Estimating Products 54

3-3 Multiplication: Multiplying by 1-Digit Numbers 56

Mixed Problem Solving 59

3-4 Multiplication: Multiplying by 2-Digit Numbers 60

Stop and Practice 63

3-5 Multiplication: Estimating and Multiplying with Greater Numbers 64

3-6 Multiplication: Exponents 66

3-7 Problem Solving Multiple-Step Problems 68

Algebra Connections 71

Topic 3 Test Prep 72

Reteaching 74

Division of Whole Numbers

NS 1.0, 1.1, 2.2, AF 1.1 Gr. 6, MR 2.3, 3.0

Review What You Know 77

4-1 Division: Using Patterns to Divide 78

4-2 Division: Estimating Quotients 80

4-3 Division: Connecting Models and Symbols 82

Stop and Practice 85

4-4 Division: Dividing by 1-Digit Divisors 86

Algebra Connections 89

4-5 Division: Zeros in the Quotient 90

4-6 Division: Dividing by 2-Digit Divisors 92

Mixed Problem Solving 95

4-7 Division: More Dividing by 2-Digit Divisors 96

Stop and Practice 99

4-8 Division: Estimating and Dividing with Greater Numbers 100

4-9 Problem Solving Draw a Picture and Write an Equation 102

Mixed Problem Solving 105

Topic 4 Test Prep 106

Reteaching 108

Topic 5 Variables and Expressions

NS 2.0, AF 1.0, 1.2, 1.3, AF 1.3 Gr. 6, MR 2.0, 2.3

Review What You Know 111

5-1 **Algebra:** Variables and Expressions.... 112

5-2 **Algebra:** Patterns and Expressions 114

Stop and Practice 117

5-3 **Algebra:** More Patterns and Expressions 118

Algebra Connections 121

5-4 **Algebra:** Distributive Property 122

5-5 **Algebra:** Order of Operations 124

Mixed Problem Solving 127

5-6 **Problem Solving** Act it Out and Use Reasoning.................... 128

Topic 5 Test Prep 130

Reteaching.......................... 132

Topic 6 Multiplying Decimals

NS 1.1, 2.1, MR 2.0, 2.1, 2.6

Review What You Know 135

6-1 **Decimals:** Multiplying Decimals by 10, 100, or 1,000...................... 136

6-2 **Decimals:** Multiplying a Whole Number and a Decimal................ 138

6-3 **Decimals:** Estimating the Product of a Whole Number and a Decimal..... 140

6-4 **Decimals:** Multiplying Two Decimals............................ 142

6-5 **Decimals:** Multiplying with Zeros in the Product......................... 144

6-6 **Problem Solving** Reasonableness....................... 146

Topic 6 Test Prep 148

Reteaching.......................... 150

Topic 7 Dividing Decimals

NS 1.1, 2.1, 2.2, MR 1.2, 2.3

Review What You Know 153

7-1 **Decimals:** Dividing Decimals by 10, 100, or 1,000...................... 154

7-2 **Decimals:** Dividing a Decimal by a Whole Number........................ 156

Algebra Connections 159

7-3 **Decimals:** Estimation: Decimals Divided by Whole Numbers 160

7-4 **Decimals:** Dividing a Decimal by a Decimal............................ 162

7-5 **Problem Solving** Multiple-Step Problems 164

Stop and Practice 167

Topic 7 Test Prep 168

Reteaching.......................... 170

Topic 8 Shapes

MG 2.0, 2.1, 2.2, MR 2.4, 3.2, 3.3

Review What You Know 173

8-1 **Geometry:** Basic Geometric Ideas 174

Stop and Practice 177

8-2 **Geometry:** Measuring and Classifying Angles.................... 178

8-3 **Geometry:** Polygons.................. 180

8-4 **Geometry:** Triangles 182

8-5 **Geometry:** Quadrilaterals 184

8-6 **Problem Solving** Make and Test Generalizations.................. 186

Topic 8 Test Prep 188

Reteaching.......................... 190

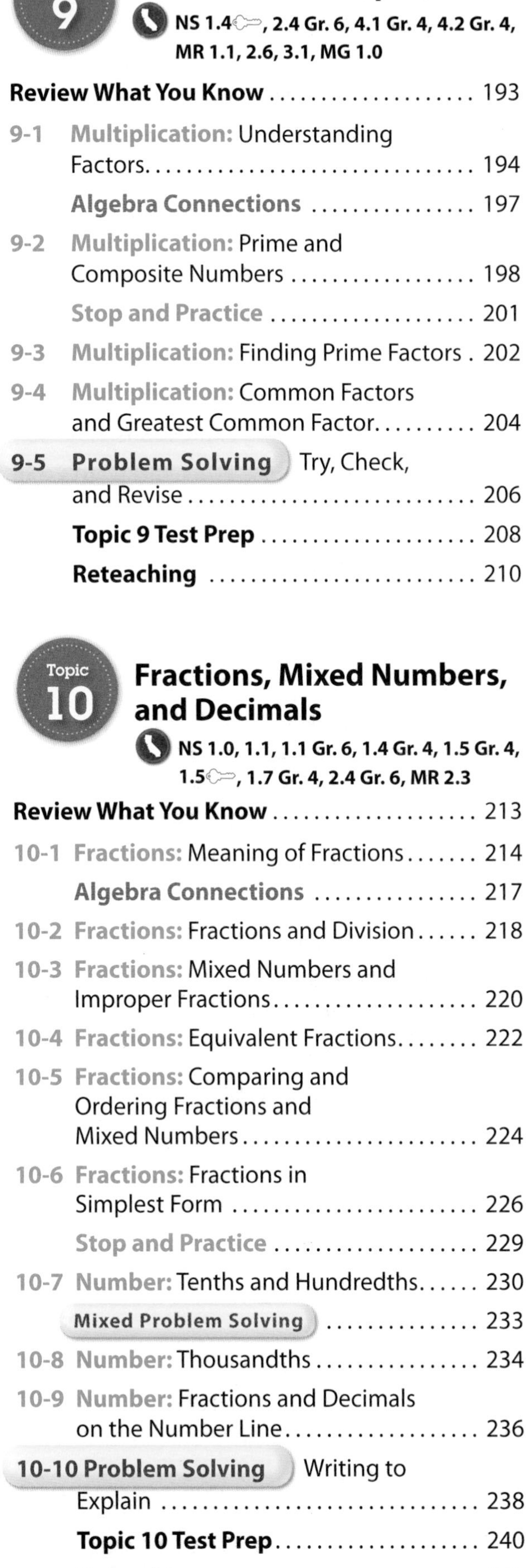

Topic 9 Factors and Multiples

NS 1.4, 2.4 Gr. 6, 4.1 Gr. 4, 4.2 Gr. 4, MR 1.1, 2.6, 3.1, MG 1.0

Review What You Know 193

9-1 Multiplication: Understanding Factors 194

Algebra Connections 197

9-2 Multiplication: Prime and Composite Numbers 198

Stop and Practice 201

9-3 Multiplication: Finding Prime Factors . 202

9-4 Multiplication: Common Factors and Greatest Common Factor 204

9-5 **Problem Solving** Try, Check, and Revise 206

Topic 9 Test Prep 208

Reteaching 210

Topic 10 Fractions, Mixed Numbers, and Decimals

NS 1.0, 1.1, 1.1 Gr. 6, 1.4 Gr. 4, 1.5 Gr. 4, 1.5, 1.7 Gr. 4, 2.4 Gr. 6, MR 2.3

Review What You Know 213

10-1 Fractions: Meaning of Fractions 214

Algebra Connections 217

10-2 Fractions: Fractions and Division 218

10-3 Fractions: Mixed Numbers and Improper Fractions 220

10-4 Fractions: Equivalent Fractions 222

10-5 Fractions: Comparing and Ordering Fractions and Mixed Numbers 224

10-6 Fractions: Fractions in Simplest Form 226

Stop and Practice 229

10-7 Number: Tenths and Hundredths 230

Mixed Problem Solving 233

10-8 Number: Thousandths 234

10-9 Number: Fractions and Decimals on the Number Line 236

10-10 **Problem Solving** Writing to Explain 238

Topic 10 Test Prep 240

Reteaching 242

Topic 11 Adding and Subtracting Fractions and Mixed Numbers

NS 2.0, 2.3, 2.4 Gr. 6, MR 1.1

Review What You Know 247

11-1 Fractions: Adding and Subtracting Fractions with Like Denominators 248

Algebra Connections 251

11-2 Fractions: Common Multiples and LCM 252

11-3 Fractions: Adding Fractions with Unlike Denominators 254

11-4 Fractions: Subtracting Fractions with Unlike Denominators 256

11-5 Fractions: Adding Mixed Numbers 258

11-6 Fractions: Subtracting Mixed Numbers 260

11-7 **Problem Solving** Look for a Pattern 262

Topic 11 Test Prep 264

Reteaching 266

Topic 12 Multiplying and Dividing Fractions and Mixed Numbers

NS 1.4, 2.4, 2.5, AF 1.1, 1.1 Gr. 6, MR 1.1, 2.3

Review What You Know 269

12-1 Fractions: Multiplying Fractions and Whole Numbers 270

12-2 Fractions: Multiplying Two Fractions .. 272

Stop and Practice 275

12-3 Fractions: Dividing a Whole Number by a Fraction 276

12-4 Fractions: Dividing Two Fractions 278

Mixed Problem Solving 281

12-5 **Problem Solving** Missing or Extra Information 282

12-6 Fractions: Multiplying Mixed Numbers 284

12-7 Fractions: Dividing Mixed Numbers ... 286

12-8 **Problem Solving** Draw a Picture and Write an Equation 288

Topic 12 Test Prep 290

Reteaching 292

Topic 13 Length, Perimeter, and Area

NS 1.9 Gr. 4, MG 1.0, 1.1, 1.4 Gr. 4, 1.4, MR 2.0, 2.3

Review What You Know 295

13-1 **Measurement:** Using Customary Units of Length 296

13-2 **Measurement:** Using Metric Units of Length 298

13-3 **Measurement:** Perimeter 300

Stop and Practice 303

13-4 **Measurement:** Area of Squares and Rectangles 304

13-5 **Measurement:** Area of Parallelograms 306

13-6 **Measurement:** Area of Triangles 308

13-7 **Problem Solving** Draw a Picture and Make an Organized List 310

Topic 13 Test Prep 312

Reteaching 314

Topic 14 Solids

MG 1.0, 1.2, 1.3, 1.4, 2.3, 2.4, 3.6 Gr. 4, MR 1.2, 2.2

Review What You Know 317

14-1 **Geometry:** Solids 318

Algebra Connections 321

14-2 **Geometry:** Relating Shapes and Solids 322

14-3 **Measurement:** Surface Area 324

14-4 **Geometry:** Views of Solids 326

14-5 **Measurement:** Models and Volume 328

14-6 **Measurement:** Volume 330

Stop and Practice 333

14-7 **Problem Solving** Use Objects and Solve a Simpler Problem 334

Topic 14 Test Prep 336

Reteaching 338

Topic 15 Integers

NS 1.5, 2.0, 2.1, AF 1.0, 1.2, MR 2.0, 2.3

Review What You Know 341

15-1 **Number:** Understanding Integers 342

15-2 **Number:** Comparing and Ordering Integers 344

15-3 **Number:** Integers and the Number Line 346

15-4 **Number:** Adding Integers 348

Stop and Practice 351

15-5 **Number:** Subtracting Integers 352

15-6 **Number:** Simplifying Expressions 354

15-7 **Problem Solving** Work Backward 356

Topic 15 Test Prep 358

Reteaching 360

Topic 16 Solving and Writing Equations

NS 2.0, AF 1.1 Gr. 6, 1.2, 1.5, MR 1.1, 2.3, 3.0, 3.1

Review What You Know 363

16-1 **Algebra:** Solving Addition and Subtraction Equations 364

16-2 **Algebra:** Solving Multiplication and Division Equations 366

16-3 **Problem Solving** Use Reasoning 368

16-4 **Algebra:** Patterns and Equations 370

Stop and Practice 373

16-5 **Algebra:** More Patterns and Equations 374

16-6 **Problem Solving** Draw a Picture and Write an Equation 376

Algebra Connections 379

Topic 16 Test Prep 380

Reteaching 382

Topic 17 Percent

NS 1.2, 1.2 Gr. 6, MR 1.0, 1.1, 2.3

Review What You Know 385
17-1 Number: Understanding Ratios 386
17-2 Number: Understanding Percent...... 388
17-3 Number: Percents, Fractions, and Decimals............................ 390
17-4 Number: Finding Percent of a Whole Number........................ 392
17-5 **Problem Solving** Make a Table and Look for a Pattern................. 394
Topic 17 Test Prep.................... 396
Reteaching........................... 398

Topic 18 Equations and Graphs

AF 1.4, 1.5, SDAP 1.0, 1.4, 1.5, MR 1.1, 2.3

Review What You Know 401
18-1 **Algebra:** Ordered Pairs................ 402
Stop and Practice 405
18-2 Statistics: Line Graphs 406
Mixed Problem Solving 409
18-3 **Algebra:** Graphing Equations 410
18-4 **Problem Solving** Work Backward............................ 412
Topic 18 Test Prep.................... 414
Reteaching........................... 416

Topic 19 Graphs and Data

NS 1.0, SDAP 1.1, 1.2, 1.3, 3.1 Gr. 6, MR 1.2, 2.2, 2.3, 3.3

Review What You Know 419
19-1 Statistics: Bar Graphs and Picture Graphs........................ 420
Stop and Practice 423
19-2 Statistics: Histograms................. 424
19-3 Statistics: Circle Graphs............... 426
Mixed Problem Solving 429
19-4 Statistics: Make a Graph 430
19-5 Statistics: Mean 432
19-6 Statistics: Median, Mode, and Range 434
19-7 Probability: Outcomes 436
19-8 Probability: Writing Probability as a Fraction 438
Algebra Connections 441
19-9 **Problem Solving** Solve a Simpler Problem...................... 442
Topic 19 Test Prep.................... 444
Reteaching........................... 446

Topic 20 Constructions

MG 2.0, 2.1, MR 2.3, 2.6

Review What You Know 451
20-1 **Geometry:** Constructing Angles....... 452
20-2 **Geometry:** Constructing Lines 454
Stop and Practice 457
20-3 **Geometry:** Constructing Shapes 458
Mixed Problem Solving 461
20-4 **Problem Solving** Use Objects..... 462
Topic 20 Test Prep.................... 464
Reteaching........................... 466

Student Resources

Glossary 468
Credits..................................... 478
Index 479

Problem-Solving Handbook

Use this Problem-Solving Handbook throughout the year to help you solve problems.

Problem-Solving Process xi

Using Bar Diagrams.. xii

Problem-Solving Strategies......................... xiv

Even More Strategies xvi

Writing to Explain.. xviii

Problem-Solving Recording Sheet xx

Don't give up!

Everybody can be a good problem solver!

There's almost always more than one way to solve a problem!

Don't trust key words.

Pictures help me understand!

Explaining helps me understand!

Problem-Solving Process

Read and Understand

What am I trying to find?
- Tell what the question is asking.

What do I know?
- Tell the problem in my own words.
- Identify key facts and details.

Plan and Solve

What strategy or strategies should I try?

Can I show the problem?
- Try drawing a picture.
- Try making a list, table, or graph.
- Try acting it out or using objects.

How will I solve the problem?

What is the answer?
- Tell the answer in a complete sentence.

Strategies

- Show What You Know
  - Draw a Picture
  - Make an Organized List
  - Make a Table
  - Make a Graph
  - Act It Out/ Use Objects
- Look for a Pattern
- Try, Check, Revise
- Write an Equation
- Use Reasoning
- Work Backward
- Solve a Simpler Problem

Look Back and Check

Did I check my work?
- Compare my work to the information in the problem.
- Be sure all calculations are correct.

Is my answer reasonable?
- Estimate to see if my answer makes sense.
- Make sure the question was answered.

Using Bar Diagrams

Use a bar diagram to show how what you know and what you want to find are related. Then choose an operation to solve the problem.

Problem 1

Carrie helps at the family flower store in the summer. She keeps a record of how many customers come into the store. How many customers came into the store on Monday and Wednesday?

Customers

Days	Customers
Monday	124
Tuesday	163
Wednesday	151
Thursday	206
Friday	259

Bar Diagram

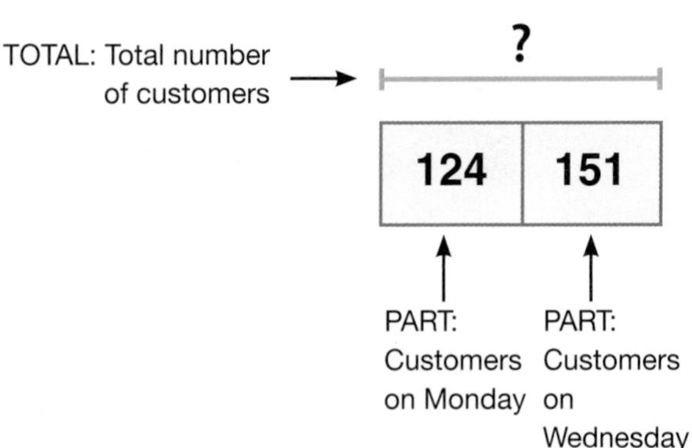

124 + 151 = ?

I can add to find the total.

Problem 2

Kim is saving to buy a sweatshirt for the college her brother attends. She has $18. How much more money does she need to buy the sweatshirt?

Bar Diagram

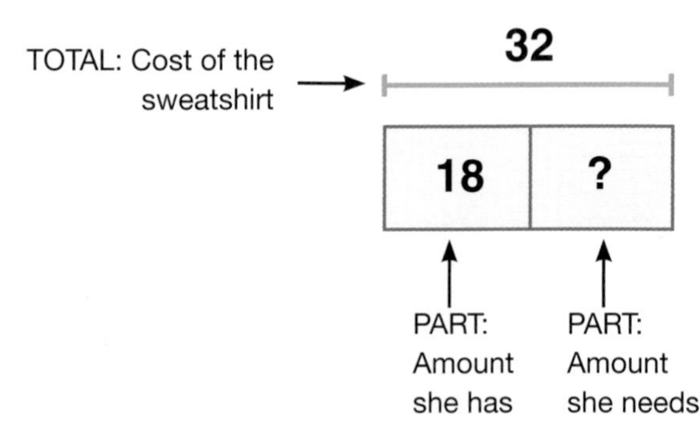

32 − 18 = ?

I can subtract to find the missing part.

Pictures help me understand!

Don't trust key words!

Problem 3

Season tickets to the community theater cost only $105 each no matter what age you are. What is the cost of tickets for four people?

Bar Diagram

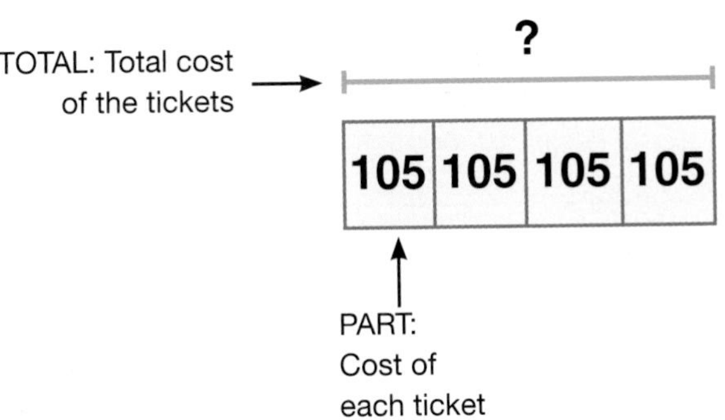

$$4 \times 105 = ?$$

I can multiply because the parts are equal.

Problem 4

Thirty students traveled in 3 vans to the zoo. The same numbers of students were in each van. How many students were in each van?

Bar Diagram

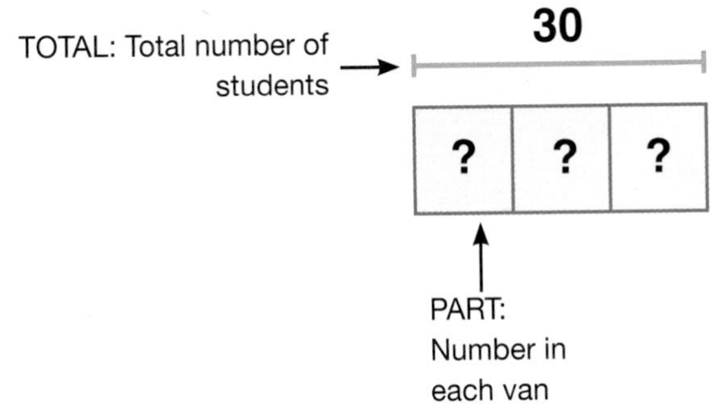

$$30 \div 3 = ?$$

I can divide to find how many are in each part.

Problem-Solving Strategies

Strategy	Example	When I Use It
Draw a Picture	The race was 5 kilometers. Markers were at the starting line and the finish line. Markers showed each kilometer of the race. Find the number of markers used. Start Line — Finish Line Start Line, 1 km, 2 km, 3 km, 4 km, Finish Line	Try drawing a picture when it helps you visualize the problem or when the relation-ships such as joining or separating are involved.
Make a Table	Phil and Marcy spent all day Saturday at the fair. Phil rode 3 rides each half hour and Marcy rode 2 rides each half hour. How many rides had Marcy ridden when Phil rode 24 rides?	Try making a table when: • there are 2 or more quantities, • amounts change using a pattern.
Look for a Pattern	The house numbers on Forest Road change in a planned way. Describe the pattern. Tell what the next two house numbers should be.	Look for a pattern when something repeats in a predictable way.

Rides for Phil	3	6	9	12	15	18	21	24
Rides for Marcy	2	4	6	8	10	12	14	16

3 6 10 15 ? ?

Everybody can be a good problem solver!

Strategy	Example	When I Use It
Make an Organized List	How many ways can you make change for a quarter using dimes and nickels? 1 quarter = 1 dime + 1 dime + 1 nickel 1 dime + 1 nickel + 1 nickel + 1 nickel 1 nickel + 1 nickel + 1 nickel + 1 nickel + 1 nickel	Make an organized list when asked to find combinations of two or more items.
Try, Check, Revise	Suzanne spent \$27, not including tax, on dog supplies. She bought two of one item and one of another item. What did she buy? \$8 + \$8 + \$15 = \$31 \$7 + \$7 + \$12 = \$26 \$6 + \$6 + \$15 = \$27	Use Try, Check, Revise when quantities are being combined to find a total, but you don't know which quantities. **Dog Supplies Sale!** Leash .... \$8 Collar .... \$6 Bowls .... \$7 Medium Beds .... \$15 Toys \$12
Write an Equation	Maria's new CD player can hold 6 discs at a time. If she has 204 CDs, how many times can the player be filled without repeating a CD? Find $204 \div 6 = n$.	Write an equation when the story describes a situation that uses an operation or operations.

Even More Strategies

Strategy	Example	When I Use It
Act It Out	How many ways can 3 students shake each other's hand?	Think about acting out a problem when the numbers are small and there is action in the problem you can do.
Use Reasoning	Beth collected some shells, rocks, and beach glass. **<u>Beth's Collection</u>** 2 rocks 3 times as many shells as rocks 12 objects in all How many of each object are in the collection?	Use reasoning when you can use known information to reason out unknown information.
Work Backward	Tracy has band practice at 10:15 A.M. It takes her 20 minutes to get from home to practice and 5 minutes to warm up. What time should she leave home to get to practice on time? Time Tracy leaves home ? ← 20 minutes ← Time warm up starts ← 5 minutes ← Time practice starts **10:15**	Try working backward when: • you know the end result of a series of steps, • you want to know what happened at the beginning.

I can think about when to use each strategy.

Strategy	Example	When I Use It
Solve a Simpler Problem 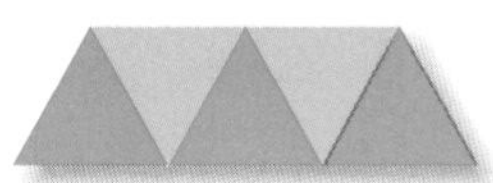	Each side of each triangle in the figure at the left is one centimeter. If there are 12 triangles in a row, what is the perimeter of the figure? I can look at 1 triangle, then 2 triangles, then 3 triangles.  perimeter = 3 cm  perimeter = 4 cm  perimeter = 5 cm	Try solving a simpler problem when you can create a simpler case that is easier to solve.
Make a Graph	Mary was in a jump rope contest. How did her number of jumps change over the five days of the contest? 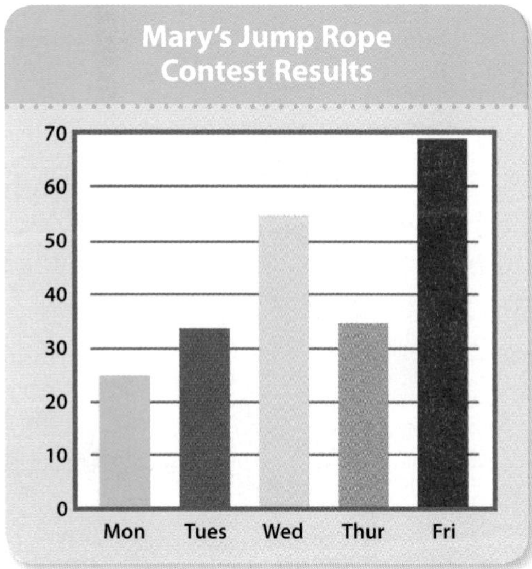 	Make a graph when: • data for an event are given, • the question can be answered by reading the graph.

Writing to Explain

Here is a good math explanation.

Writing to Explain What happens to the area of the rectangle if the lengths of its sides are doubled?

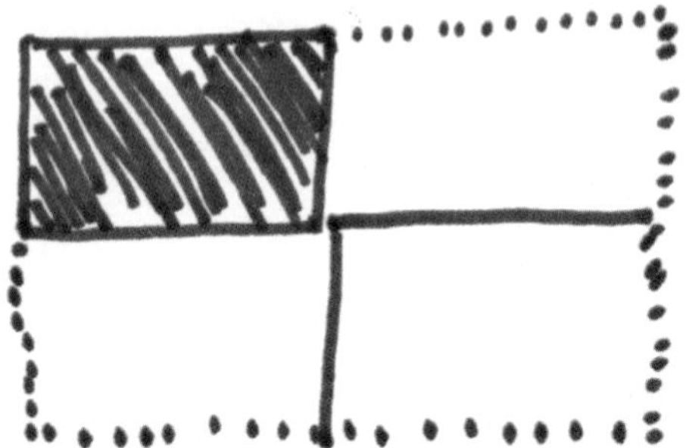

■ = $\frac{1}{4}$ of the whole rectangle

The area of the new rectangle is 4 times the area of the original rectangle.

Tips for Writing Good Math Explanations....

A good explanation should be:

- correct
- simple
- complete
- easy to understand

Math explanations can use:

- words
- pictures
- numbers
- symbols

Explaining helps me understand!

This is another good math explanation.

Writing to Explain Use blocks to show 13 × 24.
Draw a picture of what you did with the blocks.

First we made a row of 24 using 2 tens and 4 ones. Then we made more rows until we had 13 rows. Then we said 13 rows of 2 tens is 13 x 2 tens = 26 tens or 260. Then we said 12 rows of 4 ones is 13 x 4 = 52. Then we added the parts 260 + 52 = 312 So, 13 x 24 = 312.

Problem-Solving Recording Sheet

Name Jane

Teaching Tool 1

Problem-Solving Recording Sheet

Problem:
On June 14, 1777, the Continental Congress approved the design of a national flag. The 1777 flag had 13 stars, one for each colony. Today's flag has 50 stars, one for each state. How many stars were added to the flag since 1777?

Find?

Number of stars added to the flag

Know?

Original flag 13 stars

Today's flag 50 stars

Strategies?

Show the Problem
- ☑ Draw a Picture
- ☐ Make an Organized List
- ☐ Make a Table
- ☐ Make a Graph
- ☐ Act It Out/Use Objects

- ☐ Look for a Pattern
- ☐ Try, Check, Revise
- ☑ Write an Equation
- ☐ Use Reasoning
- ☐ Work Backwards
- ☐ Solve a Simpler Problem

Show the Problem?

50	
13	?

Solution?

I am comparing the two quantities.
I could add up from 13 to 50. I can also subtract 13 from 50. I'll subtract.

$$\begin{array}{r} 50 \\ -\ 13 \\ \hline 37 \end{array}$$

Answer?

There were 37 stars added to the flag from 1777 to today.

Check? Reasonable?

37 + 13 = 50 so I subtracted correctly.

50 - 13 is about 50 - 10 = 40
40 is close to 37. 37 is reasonable.

Teaching Tools • 1

Name Benton

Teaching Tool 1

Problem-Solving Recording Sheet

Problem:

Suppose your teacher told you to open your math book to the facing pages whose pages numbers add to 85. To which two pages would you open your book?

Find?

Two facing page numbers

Know?

Two pages.
Facing each other.
Sum is 85.

Strategies?

Show the Problem
- ☑ Draw a Picture
- ☐ Make an Organized List
- ☐ Make a Table
- ☐ Make a Graph
- ☐ Act It Out/Use Objects

- ☐ Look for a Pattern
- ☑ Try, Check, Revise
- ☑ Write an Equation
- ☐ Use Reasoning
- ☐ Work Backwards
- ☐ Solve a Simpler Problem

Show the Problem?

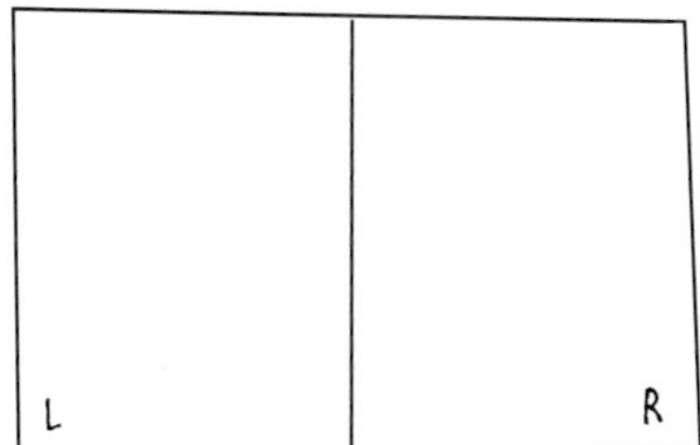

L + R = 85
L is 1 less than R

Solution?

I'll try some numbers in the middle.
40 + 41 = 81, too low
How about 46 and 47?
46 + 47 = 93, too high
Ok, now try 42 and 43.
42 + 43 = 85.

Answer?

The page numbers are 42 and 43.

Check? Reasonable?

I added correctly.
42 + 43 is about 40 + 40 = 80
80 is close to 85.
42 and 43 is reasonable.

Topic
1
Numeration
1
About how many monarch butterflies migrate to the Monarch Grove Sanctuary in Pacific Grove, California, each fall? You will find out in Lesson 1-1.
2
Can you guess the size of a grain of sand? You will find out if you are right in Lesson 1-4.

3 How would you compare the surface area of the Earth to the surface area of the Moon? You will find out in Lesson 1-2.

4 The longest stick insect in the world lives in Borneo. How long is the Borneo stick insect? You will find out in Lesson 1-3.

Review What You Know!

Vocabulary

Choose the best term from the box.

- digits
- period
- place value
- whole numbers

1. __?__ are the symbols used to show numbers.

2. A group of 3 digits in a number is a __?__.

3. __?__ is the position of a digit in a number that is used to determine the value of the digit.

Adding Whole Numbers

Find each sum.

4. 800 + 90 + 2
5. 3,000 + 400 + 50
6. 10,000 + 2,000 + 60 + 1
7. 37 + 85
8. 124 + 376

Comparing

Compare. Use $<$ or $>$.

9. 869 ◯ 912
10. 9,033 ◯ 9,133
11. 1,338 ◯ 1,388
12. 7,325 ◯ 7,321

Place Value

13. **Writing to Explain** In the number 767, does the first 7 have the same value as the final 7? Why or why not?

Lesson

1-1

NS 1.1 Estimate, round, and manipulate very large (e.g. millions) and very small (e.g. thousandths) numbers.
Also **NS 1.0, Grade 4**

Place Value

How can you read and write large numbers?

A place-value chart is helpful in reading and writing a number such as 1,600,000,000. The digits 0, 1, 2, 3, 4, 5, 6, 7, 8, and 9 are used to write numbers. The place of a digit in a number tells you its value.

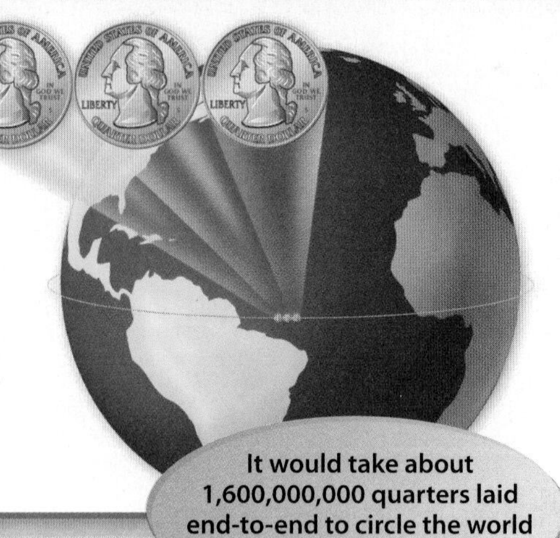

It would take about 1,600,000,000 quarters laid end-to-end to circle the world at the equator one time.

Guided Practice*

Do you know HOW?

In **1** through **3**, write each number in standard form.

1. forty billion, forty-eight million

2. 90,000,000,000 + 5,000,000 + 300

3. six billion, two hundred million, twelve thousand, six

Do you UNDERSTAND?

4. Look at the number in the example at the top. In what place is the digit 6? What is its value?

5. In which period does the 1 occur on the place-value chart? How does the period name help you read a large number?

Independent Practice

Write each number in word form.

6. 7,123 **7.** 18,345 **8.** 10,010,468 **9.** 300,014,000,056

Write each number in standard form.

10. 8,000,000 + 300 + 9

11. 60,000,000 + 10,000 + 20 + 3

12. 114,000,000,000 + 70,000 + 8,000 + 7

13. 50,000,000,000 + 200,000 + 30,000

Write each number in expanded form.

14. 670,200,640 **15.** 1,000,102,200 **16.** 85,000,011,000

What is the value of the underlined digit in each number?

17. 6<u>7</u>,100 **18.** 6,<u>8</u>00,000

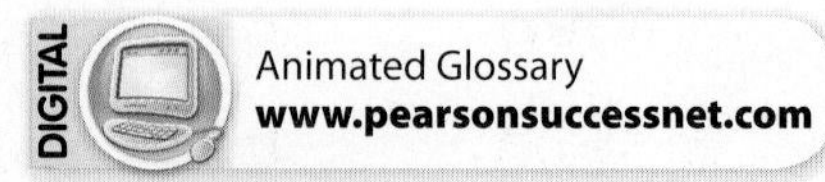

DIGITAL Animated Glossary
www.pearsonsuccessnet.com

For another example, see Set A on page 20.

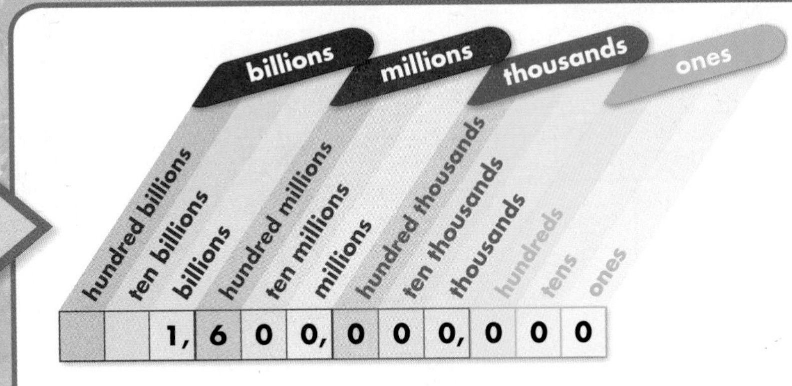

1 is in the billions place.
Its value is 1,000,000,000

Standard form:
1,600,000,000

Expanded form:
1,000,000,000 + 600,000,000

Word form:
one billion, six hundred million

Problem Solving

19. The Milky Way Galaxy has at least two hundred billion stars. Write this number in standard form.

20. Neptune is 4,498,252,900 km from the Sun. Write this number in expanded form.

21. Janet purchased 3 T-shirts and 2 blouses. Each T-shirt cost $12 and each blouse cost $23. What was the total cost of Janet's purchase?

22. **Number Sense** Write three different 10-digit numbers that have a 7 in the millions place.

23. In a recent U.S. Census, California's population was 33,871,648. What is California's population after

a an increase of 100,000.

b an increase of 1,000,000.

c a decrease of 10,000.

24. **Writing to Explain** For the standard form of two billion, three hundred fifty thousand, four, Danielle wrote 2,350,400,000. What error did she make? What is the correct standard form of the number?

25. Each October, millions of monarch butterflies migrate south from as far north as the Canadian Rockies, to locations in California and Mexico. About 65,000 come to stay the winter in Pacific Grove, California. Write 65,000 in word form.

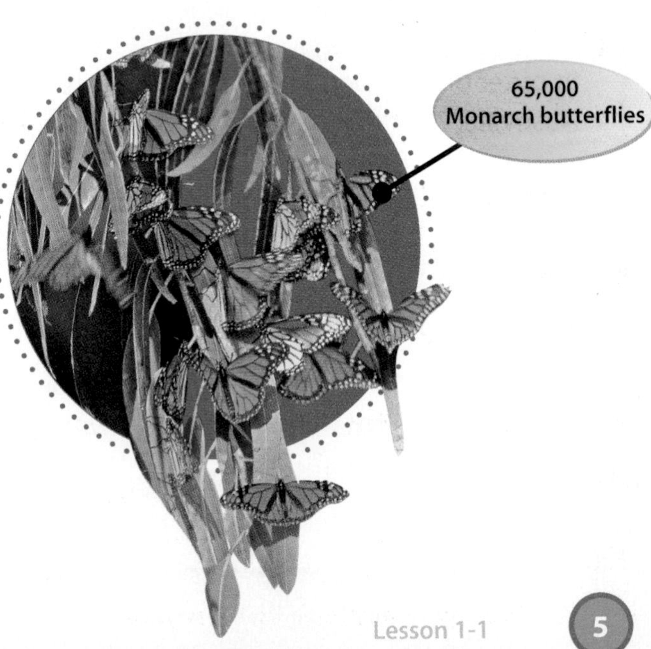

26. What is the value of the underlined digit in 90,80<u>5</u>,001,021?

A 5,000 **C** 500,000

B 50,000 **D** 5,000,000

Lesson

1-2

NS 1.0 Students compute with very large and very small numbers, positive integers, decimals, and fractions and understand the relationship between decimals, fractions, and percents. They understand the relative magnitudes of numbers.

Comparing and Ordering Whole Numbers

How can you compare and order whole numbers?

Which city has the greater population, Charlotte or Nashville?

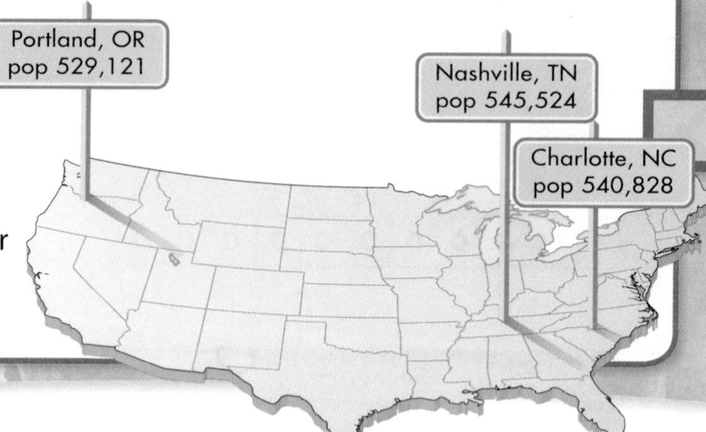

Another Example How do you order numbers?

Order the cities by their populations from greatest to least.

To order whole numbers, line up the digits by place value. Start from the left and compare digits until they are different.

Step 1 Write the numbers. Line up the places. Begin at the left and compare.

545,524 ← greatest
540,828
529,121

Step 2 Look at the two remaining numbers. Compare.

540,828 ← greater
529,121

Step 3 Write the numbers from greatest to least.

545,524 540,828 529,121

In order of their populations from greatest to least, the cities are Nashville, Charlotte, and Portland.

Explain It

1. Explain why 89,010,000 is greater than 89,000,101.
2. How can you order three whole numbers, each with a different number of digits, without comparing digits?

Step 1

Line up the places.

545,524
540,828

Begin at the left.

Compare.

Use > for greater than.
Use < for less than.

Step 2

Find the first place where the digits are different.

545,524
540,828

Compare $5 > 0$

Think 5 thousands > 0 thousands

So, 545,524 > 540,828. Nashville has a greater population than Charlotte.

Guided Practice*

Do you know HOW?

Copy and complete. Write <, > or = for each ◯.

1. 9,445,000 ◯ 10,000,000
2. 496,256,001 ◯ 496,155,001
3. 20,003,888,065 ◯ 20,003,868,001

Do you UNDERSTAND?

4. **Writing to Explain** Why do you compare numbers beginning from the left after you line them up by place value?
5. Long Beach has a population of 491,564 and Fresno has a population of 464,727. Which city has a greater population?

Independent Practice

Copy and complete. Write <, > or = for each ◯.

6. 3,456 ◯ 3,543
7. 9,999 ◯ 10,000
8. 98,325 ◯ 98,325
9. 789,124 ◯ 789,300
10. 4,701,045,756 ◯ 4,701,045
11. 3,000,010 ◯ 3,000,000,010
12. 29,374,087,210 ◯ 28,124,087,210
13. 13,059 ◯ 9,898
14. 6,012,907,000 ◯ 6,012,907,000
15. 8,937,051 ◯ 8,937,501
16. 1,790,023,901 ◯ 1,090,023,901
17. 45,034,521 ◯ 45,034,251
18. 990,148,632,109 ◯ 990,149,632,109

For another example, see Set B on page 20.

Independent Practice

Order from greatest to least.

19. 65,081,127 7,000,128 9,910,001

20. 90,459,012,045 91,459,012,045 90,459,010,045

21. 15,100,000,022 1,510,000,022 10,010,899,002

22. 186,347,987 100,389,120 18,121,817 1,500,987

Problem Solving

23. Number Sense Write three numbers that are greater than 154,000 but less than 155,000.

24. The U.S. Postal Service delivers about 212,000,000,000 pieces of mail every year. Which digit is in the ten billions place?

25. Writing to Explain Here is how Marek ordered three numbers from least to greatest:
870,990; 4,970,070; 1,426,940

What mistake did Marek make? Explain how to correct his mistake.

26. Four brothers each bought a $9 movie ticket and a $4 bag of popcorn. Bottled water cost $2. Together, the brothers had $60. How much was left?

27. Algebra Find all the digits that can replace the missing digit to make this comparison true.

496,☐56,200 > 496,745,310

28. Which of the numbers below is the greatest?
9,781 9,178 9,817
9,187 8,971

A 9,178 **C** 9,781

B 9,817 **D** 8,971

29. Glory Bicycle Company made $589,029 in sales. Right Bicycles made $590,011. Coastal Bikes made more than Glory Bicycle Company, but less than Right Bicycles. How much did Coastal Bikes make?

A $589,020 **C** $590,101

B $589,300 **D** $590,100

30. The surface area of the moon is 37,900,000 square kilometers. Which has a larger surface area?

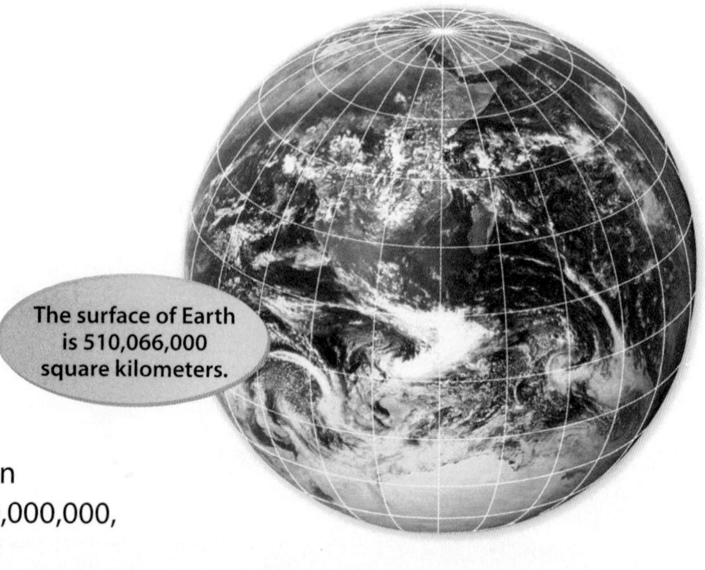

The surface of Earth is 510,066,000 square kilometers.

31. Reasoning If a number is greater than 800,000,000,000 but less than 801,000,000,000, what digit will be in the billions place?

Mixed Problem Solving

For **1** through **4**, use the table at the right.

1. By how much did the United States population increase from 1790 to 1820?

2. What is the difference between the population of the United States in 1850 and 1790?

3. Which decade had the greatest growth in population?

4. Which decade had the least amount of growth in population?

Data

United States Population 1790 to 1850

Census	Population
1790	3,929,214
1800	5,308,483
1810	7,239,881
1820	9,638,453
1830	12,860,702
1840	17,063,353
1850	23,191,876

For **5** through **8**, use the table at the right.

5. Ireland had 143,000 immigrants come to the U.S. before 1790. Which country had more immigrants than Ireland?

6. The table lists the number of immigrants from greatest to least. The number of immigrants from Italy before 1790 was 143,500. Where does Italy belong in the table?

Data

	European Immigrants Before 1790
England	230,000
Ireland	143,000
Germany	103,000
Scotland	48,500

7. How many more immigrants came from Germany than Scotland?

8. Were there more immigrants from Germany and Scotland or from England?

9. **Strategy Focus** Solve using the strategy, Try, Check, and Revise. Jake bought 2 items that cost a total of $24. One item cost $2 more than the other. What was the cost of each item?

Lesson
1-3

NS 1.1 Estimate, round, and manipulate very large (e.g. millions) and very small (e.g. thousandths) numbers.
Also **NS 1.0, Grade 4**

Decimal Place Value

How can you represent decimals?

Jessie bought 2.568 pounds of horned melon. What are some different ways to show 2.568?

Another Example What are equivalent decimals?

Equivalent decimals name the same amount. Name two other decimals equivalent to 1.4.

One and four tenths have 1 and 40 hundredths.

So 1.4 = 1.40.

One and four tenths have 1 and 400 thousandths.

So 1.4 = 1.400.

So 1.4 = 1.40 = 1.400.

1 whole

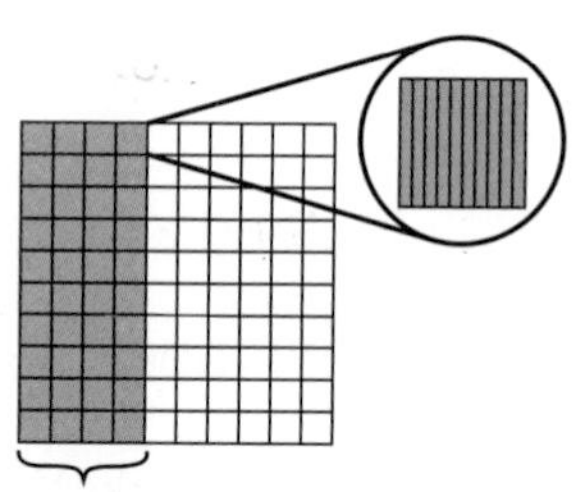

4 columns = 4 tenths
40 small squares = 40 hundredths
= 400 thousandths

Guided Practice*

Do you know HOW?

Write the word form for each number and tell the value of the underlined digit.

1. 4.737 (underlined: 3)

2. 9.806 (underlined: 6)

Write each number in standard form.

3. 6 + 0.6 + 0.03 + 0.007

4. four and sixty-eight hundredths

Write two decimals that are equivalent to the given decimal.

5. 3.700

6. 5.60

Do you UNDERSTAND?

7. **Writing to Explain** The number 3.453 has two 3s. Why does each 3 have a different value?

8. How do you read the decimal point in word form?

9. José finished a race in 2.6 hours and Pavel finished the same race in 2.60 hours. Which runner finished the race first?

*For another example, see Set C on page 21.

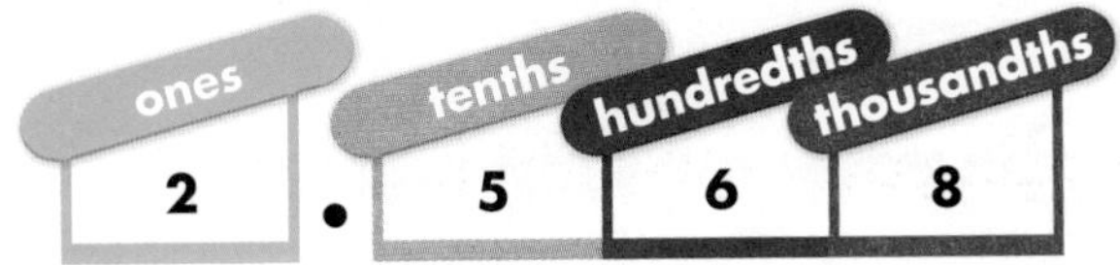

Standard form: 2.568

The 6 is in the hundredths place. Its value is 0.06.

Expanded form: 2 + 0.5 + 0.06 + 0.008

Word form: two and five hundred sixty-eight thousandths

Independent Practice

Write the word form for each number and tell the value of the underlined digit.

10. $2.\underline{3}00$ **11.** $9.\underline{0}27$ **12.** $1.9\underline{8}2$ **13.** $6.\underline{1}7$

Write each number in standard form.

14. two and six hundred thousandths **15.** five and one hundred four thousandths

16. 3 + 0.3 + 0.009 **17.** 9 + 0.2 + 0.04 **18.** 7 + 0.6 + 0.05 + 0.007

Write two decimals that are equivalent to the given decimal.

19. 2.200 **20.** 8.1 **21.** 9.50

Problem Solving

22. **Writing to Explain** Kay is buying juice at the market. She has $9 and each bottle of juice costs $2. Does she have enough money to buy 5 bottles of juice? Explain.

23. Which point on the number line below best represents 0.368?

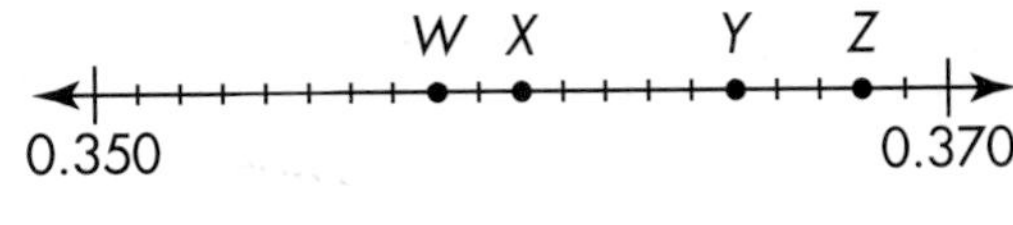

A W **B** X **C** Y **D** Z

24. The Borneo stick insect has a total length including legs, of 21.5 inches. Write 21.5 in word form.

25. Worker leafcutter ants can measure 0.5 inches. Name two decimals that are equivalent to 0.5.

26. **Writing to Explain** Why are 7.63 and 7.630 equivalent?

Lesson
1-4

NS 1.0 Students compute with very large and very small numbers, positive integers, decimals, and fractions and understand the relationship between decimals, fractions, and percents. They understand the relative magnitudes of numbers.

Comparing and Ordering Decimals

How can you compare and order decimals?

Scientists collected and measured the lengths of different cockroach species. Which cockroach had the greater length, the American or the Oriental cockroach? Use these three steps to find out.

Oriental
3.432 centimeters

American
3.576 centimeters

Australian
3.582 centimeters

Another Example How can you order decimals?

Order the cockroaches from least to greatest length. Use the three steps below to help you.

Step 1

Write the numbers, lining up the decimal points. Start at the left. Compare digits of the same place-value.

3.576
3.432
3.582

3.432 is the least.

Step 2

Write the remaining numbers, lining up the decimal points. Start at the left. Compare.

3.576
3.582

3.582 is greater.

Step 3

Write the numbers from least to greatest.

3.432, 3.576, 3.582

In order of their lengths from least to greatest, the cockroaches are the Oriental, the American, and the Australian.

Guided Practice*

Do you know HOW?

Compare the two numbers. Write >, <, or = for each ◯.

1. 3.692 ◯ 3.697 **2.** 7.216 ◯ 7.203

Order these numbers from least to greatest.

3. 5.540, 5.631, 5.625, 5.739

4. 0.675, 1.529, 1.35, 0.693

Do you UNDERSTAND?

5. Write a number that is greater than 4.508 but less than 4.512.

6. Scientists measured a Madeira cockroach and found it to be 3.438 cm long. If they were ordering the lengths of the cockroaches from least to greatest, between which two cockroaches would the Madeira cockroach belong?

*For another example, see Set D on page 21.

Step 1

Line up the decimal points.

Start at the left.

Compare digits of the same place-value.

3.576
3.432

Step 2

Find the first place where the digits are different.

3.576
3.432

Step 3

Compare.

5 > 4

Think 0.5 > 0.4

So, 3.576 > 3.432.

The American cockroach is longer than the Oriental cockroach.

Independent Practice

Copy and complete. Write >, <, or = for each ◯.

7. 0.890 ◯ 0.89 **8.** 5.733 ◯ 5.693 **9.** 9.707 ◯ 9.717

10. 4.953 ◯ 4.951 **11.** 1.403 ◯ 1.4 **12.** 3.074 ◯ 3.740

Order from least to greatest.

13. 2.912, 2.909, 2.830, 2.841 **14.** 8.541, 8.314, 8.598, 8.8

Order from greatest to least.

15. 5.132, 5.123, 5.312, 5.231 **16.** 62.905, 62.833, 62.950, 62.383

Problem Solving

17. **Writing to Explain** Why do you need to line up the decimal points before comparing and ordering numbers with decimals?

18. Judith wants to buy her mother flowers. Judith earns $4 a week doing chores. If each flower costs $2, how many flowers can Judith buy her mother if she saves for three weeks?

19. There are five types of grains of sands: coarse, very coarse, medium, fine, and very fine. A grain of fine sand can have a diameter of 0.125 millimeters.

Which number is less than 0.125?

A 0.5 **C** 0.13

B 0.2 **D** 0.12

Lesson

1-5

MR 1.1 Analyze problems by identifying relationships, distinguishing relevant from irrelevant information, sequencing and prioritizing information, and observing patterns. Also **MR 1.0, NS 1.1**

Problem Solving

Look for a Pattern

There are patterns in decimal number charts. Continue the pattern to label the other squares.

0.01	0.02	0.03					0.08		0.1
				0.15	0.16			0.19	
								0.29	
	0.32		0.34			0.37			

Another Example

In this decimal number chart, what are the patterns in the diagonals?

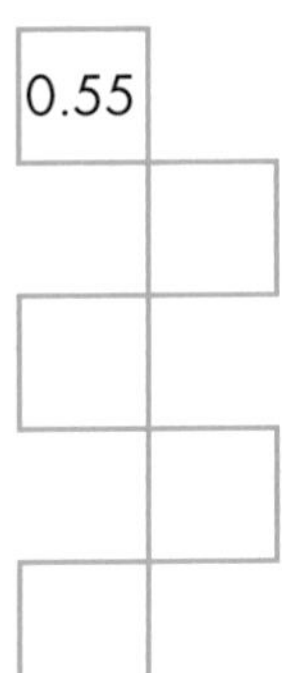

Using the same system as above, you could fill in the diagonals of a decimal number chart.

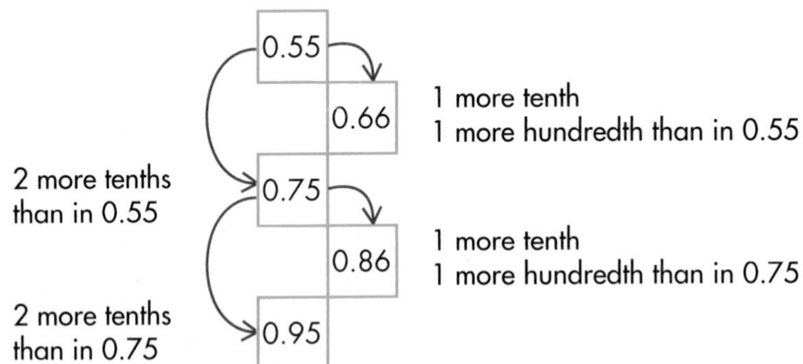

Explain It

1. If the grid above were extended by 2 cells in the same design, what decimals would be used to complete the grid?

What are the missing decimals?

0.01

As you work with vertical columns, you will see the tenths increase by 1 and the hundredths stay the same as you move down.

0.01
0.11
0.21
0.31

What are the missing decimals?

			0.29	

Moving from left to right, tenths are the same in each row except for the last number; the hundredths increase by 1.

0.26	0.27	0.28	0.29	0.30

Guided Practice*

Do you know HOW?

In **1** and **2**, determine the patterns, and then complete the grids.

1.

0.42

2.

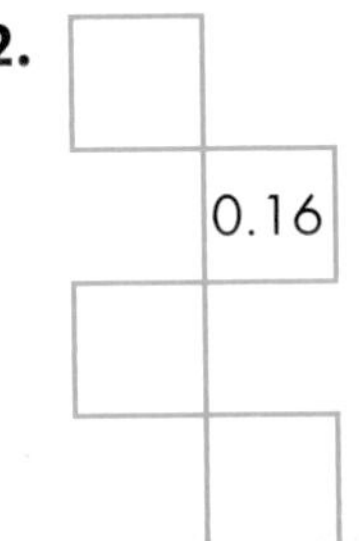

Do you UNDERSTAND?

3. In a completed decimal chart, look at the first row, which begins 0.01, 0.02. If Rene were to create a thousandths table, what two numbers would immediately follow 0.001?

4. Write a real-world problem that you could solve by looking for a pattern.

Independent Practice

In **5** and **6**, determine the patterns, and then complete the grids.

5.

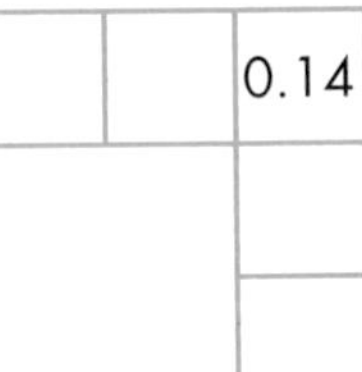

6.

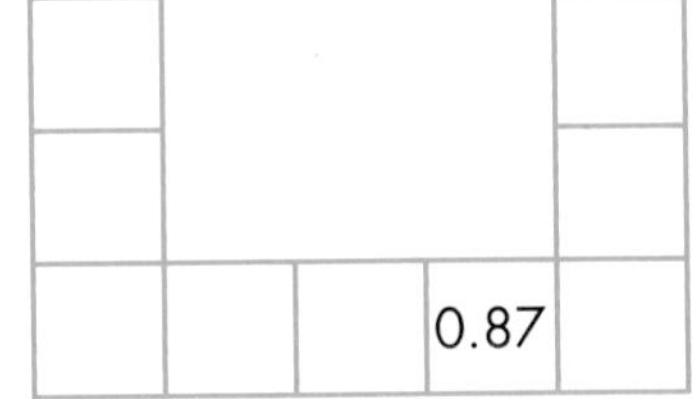

Stuck? Try this....

- What do I know?
- What am I asked to find?
- What diagram can I use to help understand the problem?
- Can I use addition, subtraction, multiplication, or division?
- Is all of my work correct?
- Did I answer the right question?
- Is my answer reasonable?

For another example, see Set E on page 21.

Independent Practice

7. Describe the patterns you should use to complete the following grid, then complete it.

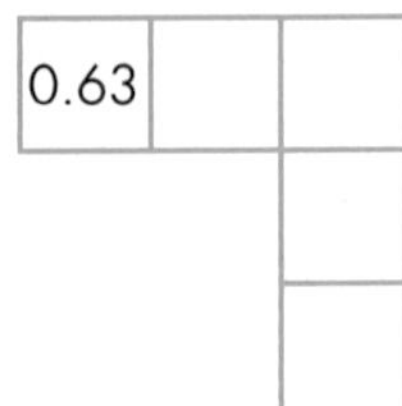

8. Determine the pattern, and then complete the grid.

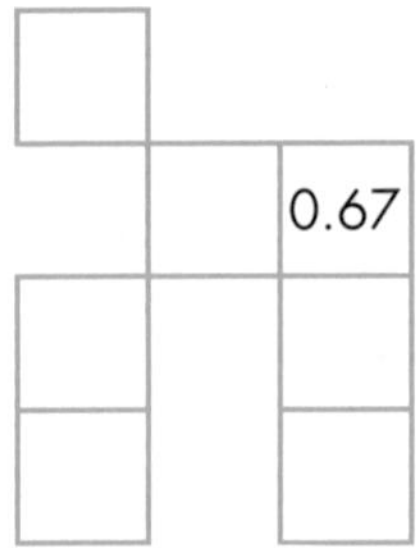

9. Determine the pattern, and then complete the grid.

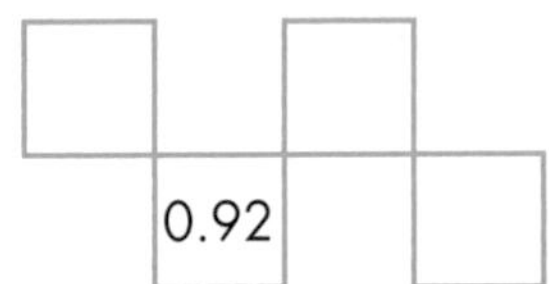

10. What is the missing number in the grid?

	0.27	0.28	0.29

11. Drake drew a grid of five cells in a row. The number 0.75 was in the middle cell. What did Drake's grid look like?

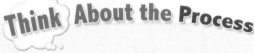

12. Determine the pattern, and then complete the grid.

0.004	0.005	

13. Juan and his family went to a movie. They bought 2 adult tickets for $8 each and 3 student tickets for $5 each. They paid with two $20 bills. How much change did they get?

14. The greatest distance of Mercury from Earth is 136,000,000 miles. Write this number in expanded form.

15. You buy three items costing $0.37, $0.35, and $0.19, and give the clerk $1.00. Which expression shows how to find the amount of change you would get from $1.00?

A $0.37 + $0.35 + $0.19 + $1.00

B $1.00 − $0.37

C $1.00 − ($0.37 + $0.35 + $0.19)

D $1.00 + $0.37 + $0.35 − $0.19

16. If 100 people are waiting in line to buy tickets and only 53 tickets are available, which expression would you use to find how many people won't be able to buy tickets?

A 100 + 53

B 100 − 53

C 100 × 53

D 53 + 53

Find the sum. Estimate to check if the answer is reasonable.

1. $475 + 583$

2. $843 + 27$

3. $673 + 19$

4. $927 + 326$

Find the difference. Estimate to check if the answer is reasonable.

5. $796 - 237$

6. $234 - 99$

7. $705 - 496$

8. $400 - 48$

Find the product.

9. 4×9

10. 6×4

11. 7×5

12. 9×0

13. 5×9

14. 8×3

15. 2×5

16. 3×6

17. 8×2

18. 7×7

Error Search Find each sum or difference that is not correct. Write it correctly and explain the error.

19. $465 - 75 = 410$

20. $503 - 59 = 444$

21. $334 + 39 = 363$

22. $956 + 269 = 1{,}225$

23. $46 - 15 = 61$

Number Sense

Estimating and Reasoning Write whether each statement is true or false. Explain your reasoning.

24. The product of 5 and 7 is 5 less than 30.

25. The sum of 610 and 209 is less than 800.

26. The quotient of 0 divided by 6 is zero.

27. The difference of 619 − 271 is greater than 300 and less than 500.

28. The sum of 196 + 435 is 4 less than 635.

29. The quotient of 7 divided by 1 is 1.

Test Prep

1. About 885,000,000 people speak Mandarin Chinese, the most spoken language in the world. How is 885,000,000 written in words? (1-1)

A eight hundred million, eighty-five thousand

B eight hundred eighty-five million

C eight billion, eighty-five million

D eight hundred eighty-five billion

2. What is eight hundred twenty-five and ninety-two hundredths in standard form? (1-3)

A 825,092

B 825.92

C 825.902

D 825.092

3. About 1,300,000,000 people ride the New York Subway System each year. What is the value of the 3 in 1,300,000,000? (1-1)

A Three hundred thousand

B Three million

C Three hundred million

D Three billion

4. The circumference of a bowling ball must be less than 27.002 inches. Which of the following would be an acceptable circumference for a bowling ball? (1-4)

A 27.02 inches

B 27.2 inches

C 27.004 inches

D 27 inches

5. In a recent year, the number of people who spoke Spanish in the U.S. was 28,100,000. Which of the following is another way to write this number? (1-1)

A 20,000,000 + 8,000,000 + 10,000

B 20,000,000 + 8,000,000 + 100,000

C 2,000,000 + 8,000,000 + 100,000

D 2,000,000 + 800,000 + 10,000

6. The average daily temperatures in July of some cities in the U.S. are shown in the table. Which of the following lists the cities by temperature from the least to the greatest? (1-4)

Data

City	Average Daily Temperature
Atlanta, GA	78.8
Albuquerque, NM	78.5
Omaha, NE	76.9
St. Louis, MO	78.4

A Omaha, St. Louis, Albuquerque, Atlanta

B Atlanta, St. Louis, Albuquerque, Omaha

C Omaha, Atlanta, St. Louis, Albuquerque

D Albuquerque, St. Louis, Omaha, Atlanta

7. Lead melts at 327.46°C. What is the value of the 6 in 327.46°? (1-3)

A 6 hundreds

B 6 tenths

C 6 hundredths

D 6 thousandths

Test Prep

8. Which of the following shows the numbers in order from least to greatest? (1-2)

A 201,008 201,080 201,800

B 201,080 201,800 201,008

C 201,080 201,008 201,800

D 201,008 201,800 201,080

9. A certain machine part must be between 2.73 and 3.55 inches. Which number is greater than 2.73 and less than 3.55? (1-4)

A 3.73

B 3.6

C 2.55

D 2.75

10. Which country listed in the table has the greatest number of cell phones? (1-2)

Data

Country	Cell Phones
Mexico	38,451,100
South Korea	36,586,100
Spain	38,646,800
Turkey	34,707,500

A Mexico

B South Korea

C Spain

D Turkey

11. Which statement is true? (1-2)

A 157,324,113 > 157,323,113

B 157,324,113 < 157,323,113

C 157,323,113 > 157,332,113

D 157,332,113 < 157,324,113

12. Which two decimals are equivalent to 2.5? (1-3)

A 2.050 and 2.500

B 2.50 and 2.500

C 2.50 and 2.05

D 2.005 and 2.500

13. What part of the figure is shaded? (1-3)

A 0.7

B 0.70

C 0.07

D 0.007

14. Lewis is drawing a family tree similar to the one shown. How many boxes would there be for five generations before Lewis? (1-5)

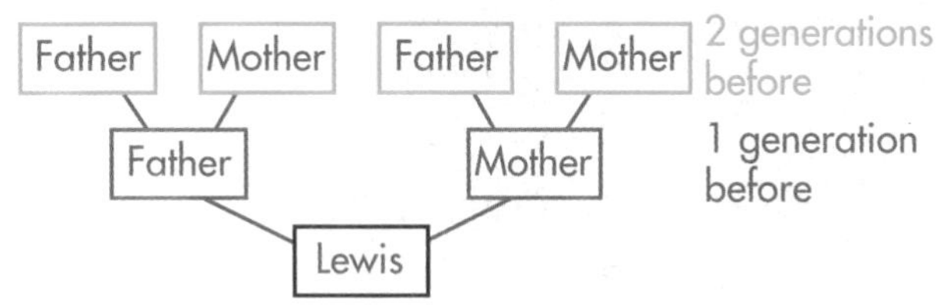

A 10

B 16

C 20

D 32

Reteaching

Set A, pages 4–5

Write the word form and tell the value of the underlined digit for 930,365.

Nine hundred thirty thousand, three hundred sixty-five.

Since the 0 is in the thousands place, its value is 0 thousands or 0.

Write the word form and tell the value of the underlined digit for 65,467,386,941.

Sixty-five billion, four hundred sixty-seven million, three hundred eighty-six thousand, nine hundred forty-one

Since the 6 is in the ten billions place, its value is 60,000,000,000.

Remember that, starting from the right, each group of three digits forms a period. Periods are separated by commas.

Write the word form and tell the value of the underlined digit.

1. 9,000,009
2. 300,000,000,000
3. 25,678
4. 17,874,000,000
5. 4,000,345,000
6. 105,389
7. 876,400,000,000
8. 600,309,470
9. 135,000
10. 2,647,000
11. 4,104,327,894

Set B, pages 6–8

Write <, >, or = for ◯ in

2,876,547 ◯ 2,826,547.

Line up the numbers above one another.

2,876,547
2,826,547

Begin at the left and compare. Notice that the ten thousands are different.

7 ten thousands > 2 ten thousands

So, 2,876,547 > 2,826,547

Remember that lining up place values helps you compare numbers.

1. 9,990 ◯ 9,099
2. 89,128 ◯ 90,000
3. 1,000,000 ◯ 999,999
4. 300,300 ◯ 303,000
5. 6,752,100 ◯ 6,752,000
6. 9,314 ◯ 9,314
7. 17,320 ◯ 17,212
8. 45,006 ◯ 45,060
9. 22,009 ◯ 22,090
10. 145,372 ◯ 147,372
11. 8,374 ◯ 8,374

Set C, pages 10–11

Write the word form and tell the value of the underlined digit for the number $8.7\underline{2}6$.

Write the numbers on a place value chart.

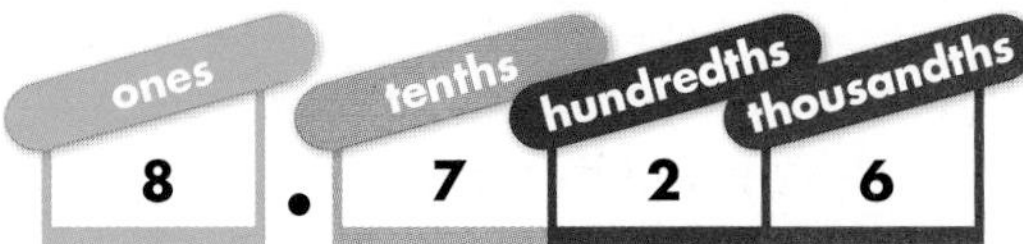

Eight and seven hundred twenty-six thousandths

The 2 is in the hundredths place. Its value is 0.02.

Remember to write the word *and* for the decimal point.

1. $8.\underline{5}9$
2. $2.2\underline{5}1$
3. $7.00\underline{3}$
4. $3.\underline{2}4$
5. $6.8\underline{3}7$
6. $0.63\underline{6}$

Set D, pages 12–13

Write <, >, or = for ◯ in

8.45 ◯ 8.47.

Line up the numbers above each other by the decimals.

$8.4\underline{5}$

$8.4\underline{7}$

5 hundredths < 7 hundredths

So, 8.45 < 8.47.

Remember that equivalent decimals, such as 0.45 and 0.450, can help you compare numbers.

1. 0.584 ◯ 0.58
2. 9.327 ◯ 9.236
3. 5.2 ◯ 5.20
4. 5.643 ◯ 5.675
5. 0.07 ◯ 0.08
6. 3.602 ◯ 3.062

Set E, pages 14–16

The table below shows the number of new members each month for a club. If the pattern continues, how many new members will there be in June?

Jan.	Feb.	Mar.	Apr.	May	June
15	30	60	120		

Pattern: The number doubles each month.

May: $120 \times 2 = 240$
June: $240 \times 2 = 480$

In June, there will be 480 new members.

Remember to look for a pattern.

1. On the board, Andrea's teacher wrote the pattern below. Find the next three numbers in the pattern.

   2, 4, 8, 14, 22, ___, ___, ___

2. Sean bought a rare stamp for $15. He was told that it would increase in value by $11 each year. What will the stamp's value be after 4 years?

Topic 2

Addition and Subtraction Number Sense

1 Lurch is an African Watusi steer. How big around is one of Lurch's horns? You will find out in Lesson 2-2.

2 Golden Gate Park is a very large urban park in San Francisco, California. About how many more acres does this park cover than the number of acres that Central Park in New York City covers? You will find out in Lesson 2-3.

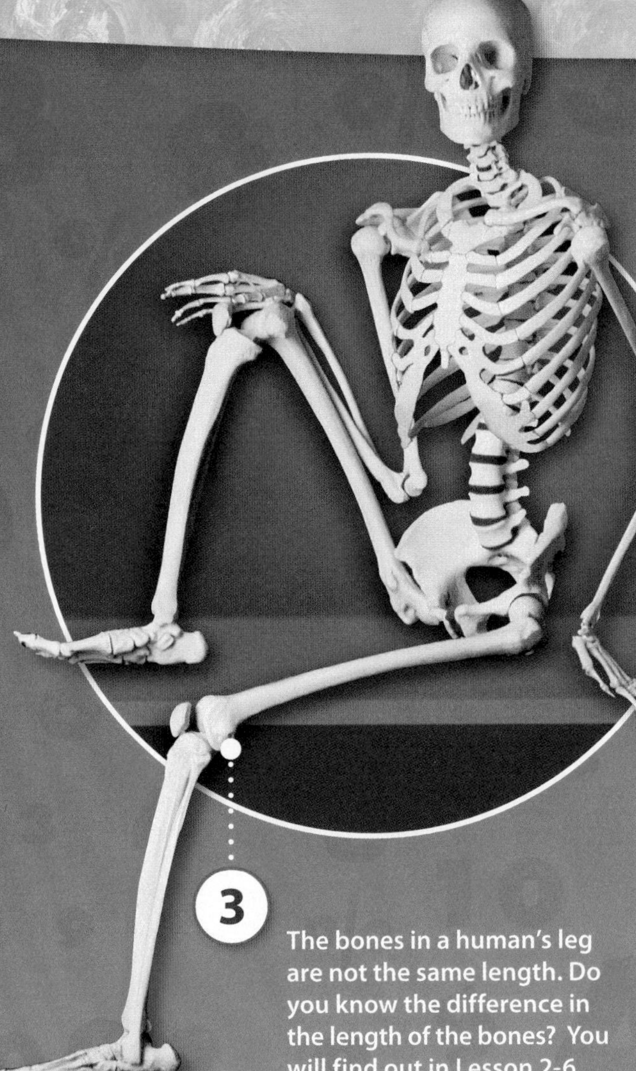

3

The bones in a human's leg are not the same length. Do you know the difference in the length of the bones? You will find out in Lesson 2-6.

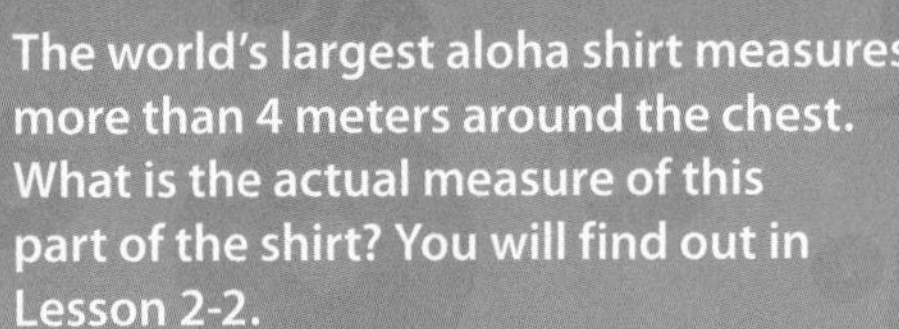

4

The world's largest aloha shirt measures more than 4 meters around the chest. What is the actual measure of this part of the shirt? You will find out in Lesson 2-2.

Review What You Know!

Vocabulary

Choose the best term from the box.

- Associative Property of Addition
- Commutative Property of Addition
- difference
- sum

1. Using the _?_ you can add two numbers in any order.

2. The _?_ is the answer to a subtraction problem.

3. When you can change the grouping of numbers when adding you are using the _?_.

4. The answer in an addition problem is called the _?_.

Rounding

Round each number to the nearest hundred.

5. 748 **6.** 293 **7.** 139

Round each number to the nearest thousand.

8. 3,857 **9.** 2,587 **10.** 2,345

Round each number to the underlined digit.

11. $8\underline{4}.59$ **12.** $2.9\underline{4}8$ **13.** $3.01\underline{2}5$

Estimating

Writing to Explain Write an answer for the question.

14. Explain how to use rounding when estimating.

Lesson

2-1

MR 1.0 Make decisions about how to approach problems.
Also **AF 1.2, Grade 4**, **MR 1.1**

Mental Math

How can you use mental math to add and subtract?

Jon bought 3 items. Properties of addition can help him find the sum of the cost.

Commutative Property: You can add two numbers in any order.

$17 + 9 = 9 + 17$

Associative Property: You can change the grouping of addends.

$17 + (9 + 3) = (17 + 9) + 3$

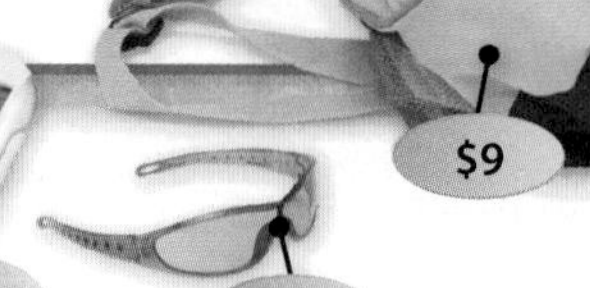
$17
$3
$9

Another Example How can you use compensation to add or subtract?

Sometimes you can change an addition or subtraction problem to make it simpler. With compensation you adjust one number to make computation easier and compensate by changing the other number.

Using compensation to add

Find 39 + 17 mentally.

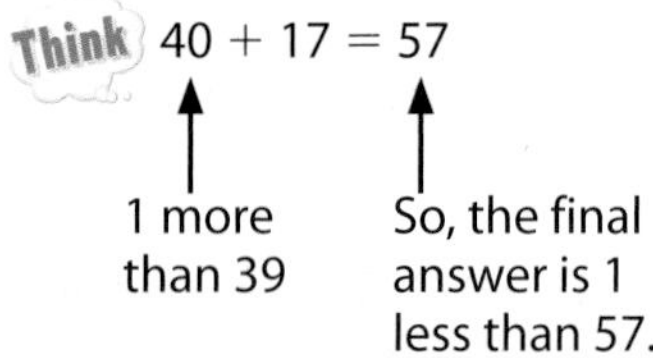
Think 40 + 17 = 57
1 more than 39
So, the final answer is 1 less than 57.

$39 + 17 = 56$

Using compensation to subtract

Find 86 − 19 mentally.

Think $86 - 20 = 66$

1 more than 19

So, the final answer is 1 more than 66.

$86 - 19 = 67$

Explain It

1. In the first example above, why is the answer 1 less than 57? In the second example above, why is the answer 1 more than 66?
2. The equation $0 + 7 = 7$ is an example of the Identity Property of Addition. What is the sum when you add zero to any number?

What You Think

The Commutative and Associative Properties make it easy to add 17 + 9 + 3.

17 and 3 are compatible numbers. These are numbers that are easy to compute mentally.

17 + 3 = 20

20 + 9 = 29

So, 17 + 9 + 3 = 29.

The total cost is $29.

Why It Works

Commutative Property: change the order

17+ (9 + 3) = 17 + (3 + 9)

Associative Property: change the grouping

17 + (3 + 9) = (17 + 3) + 9

Guided Practice*

Do you know HOW?

In **1** through **6**, use mental math to add or subtract.

1. 21 + 9 + 12

2. 35 + 46 + 4

3. 19 + 34

4. 38 + 15

5. 47 − 19

6. 86 − 49

Do you UNDERSTAND?

7. Writing to Explain Which numbers are easier to subtract, 141 − 99 or 142 − 100? Explain.

8. Jim earns $22, $14, and $8 on three different days. How much did he earn in all? Use mental math to find the sum.

Independent Practice

In **9** through **26**, use mental math to add or subtract.

When you add 3 or more numbers, look for compatible numbers.

9. 66 + 18 + 2

10. 97 + 3 + 64

11. 22 + 46 + 4

12. 237 + 195 + 5

13. 39 + 23 + 1

14. 57 + 42 + 3

15. 96 + 73 + 4

16. 299 + 34 + 1 + 6

17. 306 + 199

18. 453 − 98

19. 49 + 87

20. 68 − 29

21. 1,003 + 58

22. 468 − 190

23. 379 + 621

24. 230 + 215 + 70

25. 201 − 99

26. 101 + 17 + 99

For another example, see Set A on page 48.

Problem Solving

27. Writing to Explain Use the Equal Additions Property shown at the right to find each difference mentally. Explain how you found each difference.

a 67 − 29 **b** 456 − 198

Equal Additions Property:

Subtract 369 − 199 mentally.

369 − 199.

+1 +1

↓ ↓

370 − 200 = 170

If the same number is added to each, the difference is the same.

28. The table at the right shows points scored by one team during a football game. Use mental math to find how many points the football team had scored after the first three quarters.

Data

Quarter	Points
1	14
2	9
3	6
4	10

29. On three different days at her job, Sue earned \$27, \$33, and \$49. She needs to earn \$100 to buy a desk for her computer. The cost of the desk includes tax. If she buys the desk, how much money will she have left over?

30. A CD shelf can hold 50 CDs. Jill has 27 CDs. She plans to buy 5 new ones. Each CD costs \$9. After she buys the new ones, how many more CDs will the shelf hold?

31. Three different gymnasts had scores of 8.903, 8.827, and 8.844. Order the scores from greatest to least.

A 8.827, 8.844, 8.903

B 8.844, 8.903, 8.827

C 8.903, 8.844, 8.827

D 8.827, 8.903, 8.844

32. Which shows the Associative Property of Addition?

A 3 + 10 = 10 + 3

B 10 + 0 = 10

C (3 + 10) + 7 = 3 + (10 + 7)

D (3 + 10) + 7 = (10 + 3) + 7

33. André buys 12 apples at \$1 each. He uses a coupon for \$1.50 off the total purchase. How much did André spend on apples?

A \$10.50

B \$11.00

C \$11.50

D \$12.00

34. Which number, when rounded to the nearest ten thousand, is 70,000?

A 6,499

B 7,499

C 64,985

D 74,999

Mixed Problem Solving

1. How much farther is Venus from the Sun than Mercury?

Venus	67,200,000	
Mercury	36,000,000	?

Data

Average Distances from the Sun (in miles)	
Mercury	36,000,000
Venus	67,200,000
Earth	93,000,000
Mars	141,600,000
Jupiter	483,700,000
Saturn	886,500,000
Uranus	1,783,900,000
Neptune	2,795,100,000

2. Is the distance from the Sun to Jupiter greater than or less than the sum of the distances from the Sun to the inner four planets?

3. Which planet has a distance that is closest to 1 billion miles?

4. Neptune is the farthest planet from the Sun. How much farther from the Sun is Neptune than Earth?

5. The diagram below shows about how much of Earth's surface is covered by water. About how much of Earth's surface is NOT covered by water?

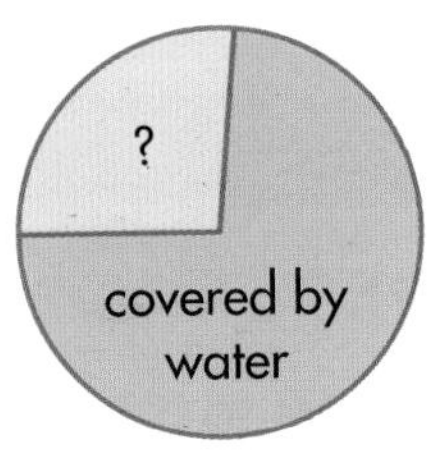

6. A single drop of water doesn't seem like much, but many drips of water from one faucet can quickly add up to several gallons per day. If the number of drips from a faucet is 30 per minute, how many drips is this for 10 minutes? Use repeated addition.

7. **Strategy Focus** Solve using the strategy, Look for a Pattern.
Jack has fish as pets. Every time he buys some new fish, he buys a larger tank to fit them. Jack needs a 1-gallon tank for 3 fish, 2-gallon-tank for 6 fish, and a 3-gallon tank for 9 fish. If the pattern continues, how large of a tank will he need for 27 fish?

Lesson

2-2

NS 1.1 Estimate, round, and manipulate very large (e.g. millions) and very small (e.g. thousandths) numbers.

Rounding Whole Numbers and Decimals

How can you round whole numbers and decimals?

Rounding replaces one number with another number that tells about how many or how much.

Round 634 to the nearest hundred.

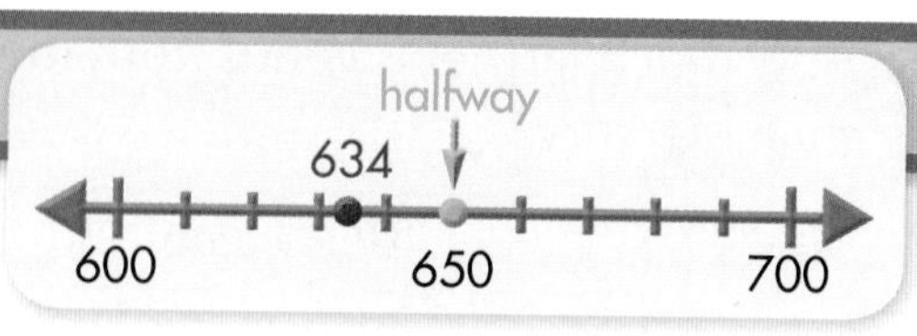

Think Is 634 closer to 600 or 700?

Another Example

How do you round 2.36 to the nearest tenth?

Think Is 2.36 closer to 2.3 or 2.4?

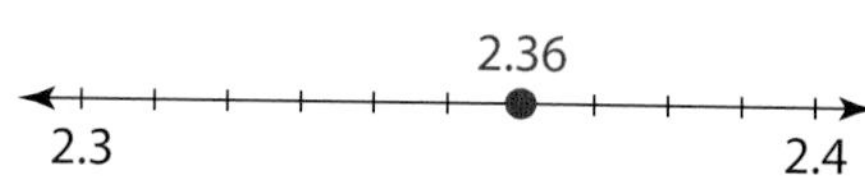

Step 1

Find the rounding place. Look at the digit to the right of the rounding place.

2.3̲6

Step 2

If the digit is 5 or greater, add 1 to the rounding digit. If the digit is less than 5, leave the rounding digit alone.

Since $6 > 5$, add 1 to the 3.

Step 3

Drop the digits to the right of the rounding digit.

2.36 rounds to 2.4

Guided Practice*

Do you know HOW?

In **1** through **6**, round each number to the place of the underlined digit.

1. 1̲6

2. 56̲.1

3. 1.3̲2

4. 42̲7,841

5. 1̲,652

6. 5̲82,062

Do you UNDERSTAND?

7. To round 7,458 to the nearest hundred, which digit do you look at? What is 7,458 rounded to the nearest hundred?

8. A runner is running on a track with markers every 10 meters. If the runner has run 368 meters, is she closer to the 360-meter marker or the 370-meter marker?

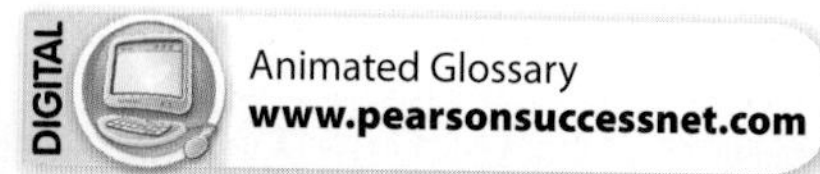

*For another example, see Set B on page 48.

Step 1

Find the digit in the rounding place. Underline this digit.

$\underline{6}34$

Step 2

Look at the digit to the right of the rounding place. If this digit is 5 or greater, add 1 to the rounding digit. If the digit is less than 5, leave the rounding digit alone.

$\underline{6}34 \quad 3 < 5$

Leave 6 the same.

Step 3

Change all the digits to the right of the rounding digit to zeros.

634 rounds to 600.

Independent Practice

In **9** through **16**, round each whole number to the place of the underlined digit.

9. $\underline{6}77$ **10.** $4,5\underline{2}6$ **11.** $12,\underline{0}64$ **12.** $5\underline{7}3$

13. $3\underline{4},739$ **14.** $\underline{5}9,304$ **15.** $93\underline{0},998$ **16.** $74\underline{8},397$

In **17** through **24**, round each number to the place of the underlined digit.

17. $7\underline{5}.8$ **18.** $0.7\underline{5}8$ **19.** $64\underline{3}.82$ **20.** $0.\underline{4}72$

21. $84.\underline{7}32$ **22.** $738.\underline{2}9$ **23.** $5.0\underline{2}8$ **24.** $23.0\underline{0}9$

Problem Solving

25. The world's largest aloha shirt is 4.26 meters around the chest. Round 4.26 to the nearest ones place and nearest tenths place.

26. In the first 3 quarters of a basketball game, a team scored 17, 25, and 13 points. Their final score was 75. How many points did the team score in the fourth quarter?

27. An African Watusi steer's horn measures 95.25 cm around. What is 95.25 when rounded to the nearest tenth? Nearest whole number? Nearest ten?

28. In a recent year, the population of Illinois was 12,653,544. What is that population when rounded to the nearest million?

A 10,000,000 **B** 12,000,000 **C** 12,600,000 **D** 13,000,000

29. The world land speed record set on October 15, 1997, was 763.03 miles per hour. What is this speed rounded to the nearest ones place?

Lesson

2-3

NS 1.1 Estimate, round, and manipulate very large (e.g. millions) and very small (e.g. thousandths) numbers.

Estimating Sums and Differences

How can you estimate sums?

Students are collecting cans of dog food to give to an animal shelter. Estimate the sum of the cans collected in Weeks 3 and 4.

Data

Week	Cans of dog food
1	172
2	298
3	237
4	345
5	338

Another Example How can you estimate differences?

Estimate 22.8 – 13.9.

One Way

Round each addend to the nearest whole number.

$$\begin{array}{r} 22.8 \\ -\ 13.9 \\ \hline \end{array} \longrightarrow \begin{array}{r} 23 \\ -\ 14 \\ \hline 9 \end{array}$$

22.8 – 13.9 is about 9.

Another Way

Substitute compatible numbers.

$$\begin{array}{r} 22.8 \\ -\ 13.9 \\ \hline \end{array} \longrightarrow \begin{array}{r} 25 \\ -\ 15 \\ \hline 10 \end{array}$$

22.8 – 13.9 is about 10.

Explain It

1. Which estimate is closer to the actual difference? How can you tell without subtracting?
2. When is it appropriate to estimate an answer?

Guided Practice*

Do you know HOW?

In **1** through **6**, estimate the sums and differences.

1. 49 + 22 **2.** 86 – 18

3. 179 + 277 **4.** 232 – 97

5. 23.8 – 4.7 **6.** 87.2 + 3.9

Do you UNDERSTAND?

7. Give an example of when estimating is useful.

8. The students in the example at the top collected more cans of dog food in week 4 than in week 3. Estimate about how many more.

For another example, see Set C on page 48.

One Way

Round each addend to the nearest hundred.

$$\begin{array}{r} 237 \\ +\ 345 \\ \hline \end{array} \longrightarrow \begin{array}{r} 200 \\ +\ 300 \\ \hline 500 \end{array}$$

237 + 345 is about 500. The students collected about 500 cans of dog food in Weeks 3 and 4.

Another Way

Substitute compatible numbers. Compatible numbers are easy to add.

$$\begin{array}{r} 237 \\ +\ 345 \\ \hline \end{array} \longrightarrow \begin{array}{r} 250 \\ +\ 350 \\ \hline 600 \end{array}$$

237 + 345 is about 600. The students collected about 600 cans of dog food in Weeks 3 and 4.

Independent Practice

In **9** through **24**, estimate each sum or difference.

9. $\begin{array}{r} 79 \\ +\ 32 \\ \hline \end{array}$ **10.** $\begin{array}{r} 788 \\ -\ 572 \\ \hline \end{array}$ **11.** $\begin{array}{r} 103 \\ +\ 798 \\ \hline \end{array}$ **12.** $\begin{array}{r} 2{,}488 \\ -\ 1{,}320 \\ \hline \end{array}$

13. $\begin{array}{r} 64 \\ +\ 48 \\ \hline \end{array}$ **14.** $\begin{array}{r} 837 \\ +\ 488 \\ \hline \end{array}$ **15.** $\begin{array}{r} 51 \\ -\ 18 \\ \hline \end{array}$ **16.** $\begin{array}{r} 7{,}889 \\ +\ 6{,}455 \\ \hline \end{array}$

17. $\begin{array}{r} 184 \\ -\ 58 \\ \hline \end{array}$ **18.** $\begin{array}{r} 847 \\ -\ 379 \\ \hline \end{array}$ **19.** $\begin{array}{r} 385{,}600 \\ -\ 235{,}700 \\ \hline \end{array}$ **20.** $\begin{array}{r} 7{,}947{,}000 \\ -\ 3{,}119{,}000 \\ \hline \end{array}$

21. 3,205 − 2,812 **22.** 93 − 46 **23.** 1,052 + 963 **24.** 149 − 51

In **25** through **39**, estimate each sum or difference.

25. $\begin{array}{r} 2.9 \\ +\ 3.9 \\ \hline \end{array}$ **26.** $\begin{array}{r} 7.28 \\ -\ 1.32 \\ \hline \end{array}$ **27.** $\begin{array}{r} \$11.33 \\ +\ \$32.43 \\ \hline \end{array}$ **28.** $\begin{array}{r} \$12.99 \\ -\ \$\ 3.95 \\ \hline \end{array}$

29. $\begin{array}{r} 8.1 \\ 3.7 \\ +\ 7.9 \\ \hline \end{array}$ **30.** $\begin{array}{r} 3.8 \\ 4.1 \\ +\ 3.3 \\ \hline \end{array}$ **31.** $\begin{array}{r} 67.9 \\ +\ 81.34 \\ \hline \end{array}$ **32.** $\begin{array}{r} 78.111 \\ +\ 46.032 \\ \hline \end{array}$

33. 77.11 − 8.18 **34.** 35.4 − 7.8 **35.** 89.66 − 27.9 **36.** 99.9 − 27.9

37. 22.8 + 49.2 + 1.7 **38.** 67.5 − 13.7 **39.** \$9.10 + \$48.50 + \$5.99

Problem Solving

40. **Writing to Explain** The cost of one CD is \$16.98, and the cost of another CD is \$9.29. Brittany estimated the cost of these two CDs to be about \$27. Did she overestimate or underestimate? Explain.

41. Martha cycled 14 miles each day on Saturday and Monday, and 13 miles each day on Tuesday and Thursday. How many miles did she cycle in all?

42. One fifth-grade class has 11 boys and 11 girls. A second fifth-grade class has 10 boys and 12 girls. There are 6 math teachers. To find the total number of fifth-grade students, what information is not needed?

A The number of girls in the first class.

B The number of boys in the first class.

C The number of math teachers.

D The number of boys in the second class.

43. On vacation, Steven spent \$13 each day on Monday and Tuesday. He spent \$9 each day on Wednesday and Thursday. If Steven brought \$56 to spend, how much did he have left to spend?

44. Estimate 74.05 + 9.72 + 45.49 by rounding to the nearest whole number. What numbers did you add?

A 75, 10, and 46

B 74.1, 9.7, and 45.5

C 74, 10, and 45

D 75, 10, and 50

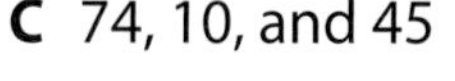

45. Golden Gate Park is located in San Francisco, California. The park covers 1,017 acres and has been compared to the size and shape of Central Park in New York City. Central Park covers 843 acres. About how many more acres does Golden Gate Park cover than Central Park?

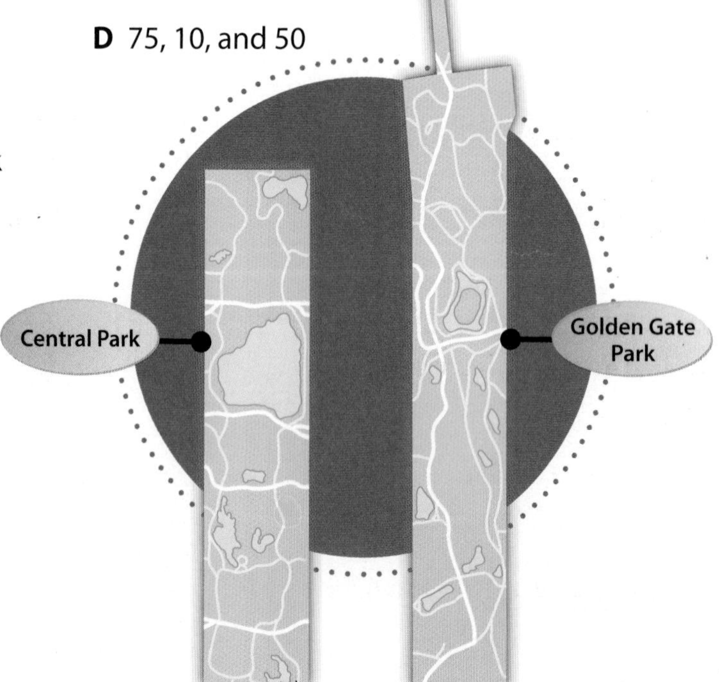

Algebra Connections

Number Patterns

The following numbers form a pattern.

3, 7, 11, 15, 19, …

In this case the pattern is a simple one. The pattern is add 4.

Some patterns are more complicated. Look at the following pattern.

20, 24, 30, 34, 40, 44, 50, …

In this case, the pattern is add 4, add 6.

Example:

What are the next two numbers in the pattern?

24, 29, 28, 33, 32, 37, 36, …

Think The first number is increased by 5. The next number is decreased by 1. I see that the pattern continues.

24, 29, 28, 33, 32, 37, 36, …

+5 −1 +5 −1 +5 −1

To find the next two numbers, add 5, and then subtract 1. The next two numbers are 41 and 40.

Look for a pattern. Find the next two numbers.

1. 9, 18, 27, 36, 45, …

2. 90, 80, 70, 60, 50, …

3. 2, 102, 202, 302, …

4. 26, 46, 66 , 86, …

5. 20, 31, 42, 53, 64, …

6. 100, 92, 84, 76, 68, …

7. 1, 3, 9, 27, …

8. 800, 400, 200, 100, …

9. 20, 21, 19, 20, 18, 19, 17, …

10. 10, 11, 21, 22, 32, 33, …

11. 25, 32, 28, 35, 31, 38, …

12. 5, 15, 10, 20, 15, 25, 20, …

13. The following numbers are called Fibonacci numbers.

1, 1, 2, 3, 5, 8, 13, 21, 34, 55, …

Explain how you could find the next two numbers.

14. **Write a Problem** Write a number pattern that involves two operations.

Lesson
2-4

NS 1.0 Students compute with very large and very small numbers, positive integers, decimals, and fractions and understand the relationship between decimals, fractions, and percents. They understand the relative magnitudes of numbers. Also **MR 2.1**

Adding and Subtracting

How can you add and subtract whole numbers?

What was the total number of motor vehicles made in the United States and Japan in one year?

Choose an Operation
Add to join groups.
Find 11,989,387 + 10,511,518.
Estimate:
12,000,000 + 11,000,000 = 23,000,000

Country	Number of motor vehicles produced in one year
United States	11,989,387
Japan	10,511,518
Germany	5,569,954

Another Example How can you subtract across zeros?

Find 5,002 − 2,684. Since addition and subtraction have an inverse relationship, check your subtraction by adding.

Step 1

Subtract the ones. Think of 5,000 as 500 tens. Regroup.

```
  4  9  9 12
  5, 0  0  2
- 2, 6  8  4
-------------
           8
```

Step 2

Subtract the tens, hundreds, and thousands.

```
  4  9  9 12
  5, 0  0  2
- 2, 6  8  4
-------------
  2, 3  1  8
```

Check

Add the difference to the number you subtracted. The answer checks.

```
  2, 3  1  8
+ 2, 6  8  4
-------------
  5, 0  0  2
```

Explain It

1. Explain the regrouping in Step 1 of the subtraction example above.
2. Why can you check a subtraction problem by adding?

Step 1

Line up numbers by place value. Add the ones, tens, and hundreds.

$$\begin{array}{r} \scriptstyle 1\,1 \\ 11{,}989{,}387 \\ +\ 10{,}511{,}518 \\ \hline 905 \end{array}$$

Step 2

Continue adding. Regroup if needed. Insert commas in the sum to separate periods.

$$\begin{array}{r} \scriptstyle 1\,1\,1\quad 1\,1 \\ 11{,}989{,}387 \\ +\ 10{,}511{,}518 \\ \hline 22{,}500{,}905 \end{array}$$

The sum is reasonable since the estimate was 23,000,000.

In one year a total of 22,500,905 vehicles were made.

Guided Practice*

Do you know HOW?

Add.

1. 5,741 + 31,018

2. 7,110 + 499

Subtract.

3. 9,234 − 2,387

4. 110,652 − 8,600

Do you UNDERSTAND?

5. **Writing to Explain** In Step 2 of the example above, explain how you regrouped the tens place.

6. In the example above, how many cars did the United States and Germany make altogether?

Independent Practice

In **7** through **12**, add.

7. 7,469 + 8,374

8. 19,335 + 24,281

9. 40,742 + 22,597

10. 102,369 + 60,320

11. 18,269 + 109,347

12. 75,977 + 24,683

In **13** through **18**, subtract. Check your answer by adding.

13. 4,002 − 3,765

14. 58,005 − 1,098

15. 113,300 − 1,774

16. 454,900 − 33,870

17. 31,483 − 29,785

18. 103,558 − 64,671

*For another example, see Set D on page 48.

Problem Solving

19. Reasoning Why should you estimate before you find the sum or difference of large numbers?

20. About 66,150,000 households in the U.S. have cats and about 58,200,000 households have dogs. About how many more households have cats than dogs?

21. Write a Problem Use 1,400 and 986 to write a real-world addition problem.

22. Humans are born with 350 bones. Some of these bones fuse together as humans grow. Adults only have 206 bones. How many more bones does a baby have than an adult?

350 bones

?	206

23. Find each sum and difference. Write >, <, or = for each ◯.

a 1,233 + 486 ◯ 2,200 − 481

b 193 + 233 ◯ 309 + 118

c 544 + 4,732 ◯ 2,512 + 1,930

d 9,491 − 6,230 ◯ 7,020 − 3,759

The table at the right shows the amount of time (rounded to the nearest hour) that astronauts have spent in space for several space programs.

24. For the five space programs listed, what is the total number of hours astronauts spent in space?

A 14,608 hours **C** 19,988 hours

B 17,621 hours **D** 20,038 hours

25. How much longer did astronauts in the Space Shuttle program spend in space than all of the other programs combined?

A 631 hours **C** 4,776 hours

B 2,194 hours **D** 12,407 hours

Data

Program	Years	Total Hours
Mercury	1961–1963	54
Gemini	1965–1966	970
Apollo	1968–1972	2,502
Skylab	1973–1974	4,105
Space Shuttle	1981–1995	12,407

26. Lisa has a basket of 17 tomatoes. She makes sauce with 9 tomatoes. If Lisa wants to split up the rest between 3 friends and herself, how many tomatoes does each person get?

27. There are about 44,000 farms in Florida and about 38,000 farms in New York. Are the total number of estimated farms in Florida and New York greater or less than 100,000?

Find each sum. Estimate to check if the answer is reasonable.

1. 5,542 + 7,381

2. 63,805 + 6,597

3. 7,469 + 857

4. 36,247 + 93,312

5. 75,338 + 25,664

6. 16,490 + 3,523

7. 56,080 + 3,920

8. 1,125 + 687

Find each difference. Estimate to check if the answer is reasonable.

9. 291 − 140

10. 9,017 − 939

11. 7,738 − 5,748

12. 44,233 − 16,375

13. 11,111 − 582

14. 36,538 − 14,279

15. 2,010 − 1,355

16. 25,000 − 6,117

17. 76,391 − 68

18. 4,317 − 1,718

Error Search Find each sum or difference that is not correct. Write it correctly and explain the error.

19. 13,643 + 267 = 13,810

20. 56,682 + 39,058 = 95,740

21. 75,350 + 8,926 = 84,176

22. 56,004 − 486 = 55,518

23. 27,033 − 15,834 = 12,199

Number Sense

Estimating and Reasoning Write whether each statement is true or false. Explain your reasoning.

24. The difference of 32,076 and 21,894 is closer to 10,000 than 11,000.

25. The sum of 10,323 and 9,769 is greater than 19,000 but less than 21,000.

26. The sum of 8,242 and 4,031 is less than 12,000.

27. The difference of 6,712 − 3,503 is 3 more than 3,212.

28. The sum of 405 + 319 is 5 more than 719.

29. The difference of 8,764 − 1,843 is greater than 8,000.

Lesson
2-5

NS 2.1 Add, subtract, multiply, and divide with decimals; add with negative integers; subtract positive integers from negative integers; and verify the reasonableness of the results.
Also **NS 2.0, MR 2.1**

Adding Decimals

How can you add decimals?

What was the combined time for the first two legs of the relay race?

Data

Swimmers	Times in Seconds
Caleb	21.49
Bradley	21.59
Vick	20.35
Matthew	19.03

Choose an Operation Add to join groups.

Find 21.49 + 21.59.

Estimate: 21 + 22 = 43

Guided Practice*

Do you know HOW?

In **1** through **6**, add the decimals.

1. 0.82 + 4.21

2. 9.1 + 7.21

3. 9.7 + 0.24

4. 3.28 + 6.09

5. 0.26 + 8.3

6. 4.98 + 3.02

Do you UNDERSTAND?

7. Reasonableness How do you know the total time for the first two legs of the race is reasonable?

8. Writing to Explain How is finding \$4.25 + \$3.50 like finding 4.25 + 3.5? How is it different?

Independent Practice

In **9** through **26**, add the decimals.

9. 1.03 + 0.36

10. 6.9 + 2.8

11. 45.09 + 2.005

12. 2.02 + 0.78

13. 13.094 + 4.903

14. 356.2 + 12.45

15. 4.298 + 0.65

16. 9.001 + 1.999

17. \$8.23 + \$64.10

18. \$44.00 + \$91.46

19. 17.49 + 9

20. 42.89 + 8.2

21. \$271.90 + \$34.22

22. 658.2 + 0

23. 0.922 + 6.4

24. 8.02 + 9.07

25. 13.9 + 0.16

26. 0.868 + 15.973

For another example, see Set E on page 49.

Step 1

Write the numbers. Line up the decimal points.

$$\begin{array}{r} 21.49 \\ +\ 21.59 \\ \hline \end{array}$$

Step 2

First, add the hundredths. Regroup if necessary.

$$\begin{array}{r} \scriptstyle 1 \\ 21.49 \\ +\ 21.59 \\ \hline 8 \end{array}$$

Step 3

Add the tenths, ones, and tens. The decimal point in the sum is aligned with the decimal point in the addends. Check the sum with your estimate.

$$\begin{array}{r} \scriptstyle 1\ 1 \\ 21.49 \\ +\ 21.59 \\ \hline 43.08 \end{array}$$

The total time for the first two legs of the race was 43.08 seconds.

Problem Solving

27. A balloon mural of the Chicago skyline measures 17.6 m on two sides and 26.21 m on the other two sides. What is the perimeter of the mural?

A 38.81 m **B** 48.21 m **C** 55.74 m **D** 87.62 m

28. **Writing to Explain** Juan adds 3.8 + 4.6 and gets a sum of 84. Is his answer correct? Tell how you know.

29. **Think About the Process** Jamie earned $27 taking care of a neighbor's dog for one week. She spent $19.95 on a new DVD. Later, she earned $15 for raking leaves. Which expression shows how to find the money Jamie has left?

A $27 + $19.95 + $15

B $19.95 − $15 + $27

C $27 − $19.95 + $15

D $27 − $19.95 − $15

30. At a flower shop, Teri sees that roses are $3 each, carnations are $4 for 3 flowers, and tulips are $4 for 4 flowers. She buys 3 roses and 3 carnations. She has $20. How much change does Teri get back?

31. Which two cities had the greatest combined rainfall for the period given?

A Caribou and Boise

B Springfield and Macon

C Macon and Boise

D Caribou and Springfield

Data

Location	Rainfall amount in a typical year (in inches)
Macon, GA	45
Boise, ID	12.19
Caribou, ME	37.44
Springfield, MO	44.97

32. What is the typical yearly rainfall for all four cities?

33. Which location had less than 45 inches of rain but more than 40 inches of rain?

Lesson
2-6

NS 2.1 🔑 Add, subtract, multiply, and divide with decimals; add with negative integers; subtract positive integers from negative integers; and verify the reasonableness of the results.
Also **NS 2.0, MR 2.1**

Subtracting Decimals

How can you subtract decimals?

What is the difference in the wingspans of the two butterflies?

Choose an Operation
Subtract to find the difference.

Find 5.92 − 4.37.
Estimate: 6 − 4 = 2

Other Examples

Using 0 as a placeholder

Find 49.59 − 7.9.

```
   8  15
 4 9. 5 9
-   7. 9 0  <- Annex a 0 as a placeholder to show hundredths.
 4 1. 6 9
```

Using 0 as a placeholder

Find 24.6 − 8.27.

```
 1 14  5 10
 2  4. 6  0  <- Annex a 0 as a placeholder to show hundredths.
-   8. 2  7
 1  6. 3  3
```

Subtracting Money

Find $26.32 − $5.75.

```
          12
      5   2  12
 $2   6.  3  2
 -    5.  7  5
 $2   0.  5  7
```

Guided Practice*

Do you know HOW?

In **1** through **8**, subtract the decimals.

1. 16.82 − 5.21

2. 7.21 − 6.1

3. 23.06 − 8.24

4. $4.08 − $2.12

5. 56.8 − 2.765

6. $43.80 − $16.00

7. 22.4 − 10.7

8. $36.40 − $21.16

Do you UNDERSTAND?

9. Reasonableness Explain why 1.55 cm is a reasonable answer for the difference in the wingspans of the two butterflies.

10. In the Other Examples above, is the value of 7.9 changed when you annex a zero after 7.9? Why or why not?

11. Writing to Explain How is finding 9.12 − 4.8 similar to finding $9.12 − $4.80? How is it different?

*For another example, see Set E on page 49.

Step 1

Write the numbers, lining up the decimal points.

$$\begin{array}{r} 5.92 \\ -\ 4.37 \\ \hline \end{array}$$

Step 2

Subtract the hundredths. Regroup if needed.

$$\begin{array}{r} \scriptstyle 8\ 12 \\ 5.\not{9}\not{2} \\ -\ 4.37 \\ \hline 5 \end{array}$$

Step 3

Subtract the tenths and ones. Bring down the decimal point.

$$\begin{array}{r} \scriptstyle 8\ 12 \\ 5.\not{9}\not{2} \\ -\ 4.37 \\ \hline 1.55 \end{array}$$

The difference is reasonable since the estimate was 2.

The difference in the wingspans is 1.55 cm.

Independent Practice

In **12** through **23**, subtract to find the difference.

12. 7.8 − 4.9

13. \$20.60 − \$14.35

14. 43.905 − 7.526

15. 65.29 − 28.038

16. 15.03 − 4.121

17. 13.9 − 3.8

18. 65.18 − 12.005

19. \$52.02 − \$0.83

20. 7.094 − 3.657

21. 34.49 − 12.619

22. 85.22 − 43.548

23. \$10.05 − \$4.50

Problem Solving

24. Writing to Explain Why is it necessary to line up decimal points when subtracting decimals?

25. Reasonableness Sue subtracted 2.9 from 20.9 and got 1.8. Explain why this is not reasonable.

26. The pyramid of Khafre measured 143.5 meters high. The pyramid of Menkaure measured 65.5 meters high. What was the difference in the heights of these two pyramids?

A 68.8 meters

B 69.3 meters

C 78 meters

D 212.3 meters

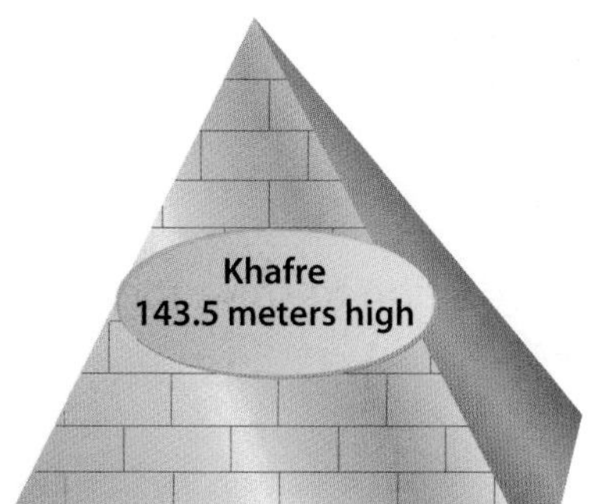

27. An average person's upper leg measures 19.88 in. and the lower leg measures 16.94 in. How much longer is the upper leg than the lower leg?

19.88 in.

?	16.94 in.

Lesson

2-7

AF 1.1 Grade 6 Write and solve one-step linear equations in one variable.
Also MR 1.0, 2.3

Problem Solving

Draw a Picture and Write an Equation

Three friends have music collections. How many more CDs does Susan have than Larry?

Data

Music Collections

	Number of CDs
Susan	42
Chad	17
Larry	26

Another Example

Rori had some balloons and then gave 35 of them away. She now has 21 left. How many balloons did Rori have to begin with?

x

35	21

One Way

Think The total is unknown.

35 were given away and 21 are left.

Write an Equation

$x - 35 = 21$

$21 + 35 = 56$, so 56 is the total.

$x = 56$

Another Way

Think 35 were given away. Rori has 21 left.

The total is unknown.

Write an Equation

$35 + 21 = x$

$35 + 21 = 56$, so 56 is the total.

$x = 56$

Rori had 56 balloons to begin with.

Explain It

1. Why do both ways use addition to solve for x?
2. How can you check if 56 is a reasonable answer?

Read and Understand

What do I know?

Susan has 42 CDs and Larry has 26 CDs.

What am I asked to find?

The difference between the number of CDs from these two collections.

Plan and Solve

Draw a Picture

42 CDs

n	26

Write an Equation

Let n = the number of additional CDs Susan has.

$42 - 26 = n$

$$\begin{array}{r} \overset{3}{\cancel{4}}\overset{1}{2} \\ -\ 2\,6 \\ \hline 1\,6 \end{array}$$

Susan has 16 more CDs in her collection than Larry.

Guided Practice*

Do you know HOW?

Draw a picture and write an equation. Solve.

1. Alec prints digital photos at a camera store. The first order was for 24 prints. The second order was for 85 prints, and the third for 60 prints. How many fewer prints were in the first order than the third order?

Do you UNDERSTAND?

2. What phrase from the above example gives you a clue that you will use subtraction in your drawing to solve the problem?

3. **Write a Problem** Write a real-world problem that uses subtraction and can be solved by drawing a picture and writing an equation.

Independent Practice

In **4**, copy and complete the picture. Then write an equation and solve.

4. Rose needs 22 tacos for a party. She has made 12 tacos so far. How many more tacos does Rose need to make?

	12

In **5**, draw a picture, write an equation in two different ways, then solve.

5. Aryanna is planning to spend a certain number of days on a trip to Florida. If she plans to spend 5 of the days in Orlando, she'll have 16 more days for the rest of her vacation. How many days does Aryanna plan to spend in Florida?

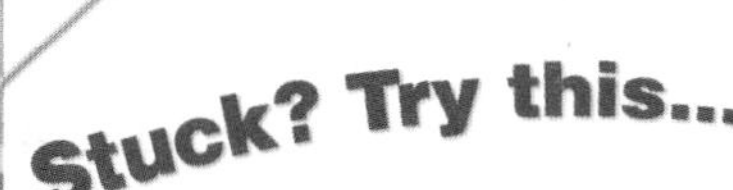

- What do I know?
- What am I asked to find?
- What diagram can I use to help understand the problem?
- Can I use addition, subtraction, multiplication, or division?
- Is all of my work correct?
- Did I answer the right question?
- Is my answer reasonable?

For another example, see Set F on page 49.

Independent Practice

In **6**, use the bar graph at the right.

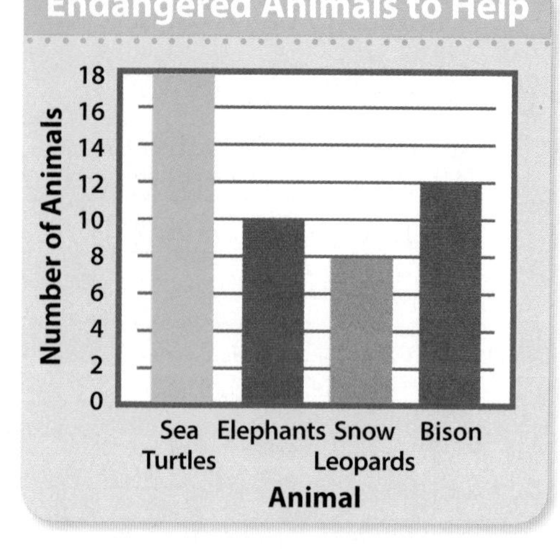

6. Foster Middle School raised money to help care for some endangered animals. The bar graph shows the number of animals they will help with the money raised.

- **a** How many sea turtles and snow leopards can they help?
- **b** What is the difference between the greatest number of animals to be helped and the least number to be helped?
- **c** Show how you can use mental math to find the total number of animals helped.

7. **Writing to Explain** Don is adding 407 and 512. How do you know his sum will be less than 1,000?

8. **Writing to Explain** Is 1,200 a good estimate for the difference of $4{,}725 - 2{,}689$? Explain.

9. A planetarium is 39 miles from Marco's school. The class leaves for the field trip at 8:00 A.M. After driving for 17 minutes and traveling 15 miles, the driver of the bus got caught in traffic. How many more miles are left to travel to the planetarium? Write an equation to solve.

39 miles	
n	15

10. Marlee is taking a class to improve her reading. She began reading a book on Monday and completed 3 pages. Tuesday she read 6 pages, Wednesday, 12 pages. If this pattern continues, how many pages will Marlee read on Friday?

Think About the Process

11. Three fifth-grade classes took a survey and found that 35 students take the bus to school, 25 come by car, 15 walk, and 5 ride their bikes. Which shows how to find how many more students take the bus than walk?

- **A** Subtract 35 from 5
- **B** Subtract 15 from 35
- **C** Add 15 and 35
- **D** Add 35 and 5

12. Darcy brought home 43 seashells from his vacation. Rich brought home *x* shells. Together they brought home 116 seashells. Which equation can you solve to find the number of shells Rich brought home?

- **A** $43 + x = 116$
- **B** $116 + x = 43$
- **C** $116 + 43 = x$
- **D** $x - 43 = 116$

Find each difference. Estimate to check if the answer is reasonable.

1. 133.06 + 79.19

2. 85.19 + 76.82

3. 43.9 + 17.36

4. 0.658 + 0.178

5. 0.375 + 0.92

6. 1.63 + 0.074

7. 724.16 + 3.38

8. 13.92 + 46.3

Find each difference. Estimate to check if the answer is reasonable.

9. 354.1 − 15.8

10. 485.3 − 117.5

11. 64.06 − 15.83

12. 47.6 − 1.53

13. 562.8 − 48.2

14. 1.17 − 0.362

15. 4.9 − 1.003

16. 6.73 − 4.816

Error Search Find each sum or difference that is not correct. Write it correctly and explain the error.

17. 27.02 + 19.89 = 46.81

18. 655.35 + 25.60 = 680.95

19. 4.58 + 13.59 = 18.16

20. 2.05 − 1.831 = 0.221

21. 219.2 − 61.3 = 157.9

Number Sense

Estimating and Reasoning Write whether each statement is true or false. Explain your reasoning.

22. The sum of 56,141 and 3,052 is less than 59,000.

23. The sum of 50.73 and 40.22 is greater than 90 but less than 92.

24. The difference of 63,432 and 21,089 is greater than 41,000 and less than 43,000.

25. The difference of 3,762 – 1,413 is 13 more than 2,362.

26. The sum of 26.96 + 32.25 is 0.04 less than 59.25.

27. The difference of 56.13 and 12.95 is closer to 44 than 43.

Test Prep

1. The Chen family's home has 1,515 square feet downstairs and 625 square feet upstairs. Which of the following is the best estimate of the total square footage in the home? (2-3)

A 2,100

B 2,200

C 2,300

D 2,500

2. What is 2.934 rounded to the nearest hundredth? (2-2)

A 2.90

B 2.93

C 2.94

D 3.00

3. Eduardo is training for a marathon. He ran his first mile in 12.567 minutes and his second mile in 12.977 minutes. What is his combined time for the first two miles? (2-5)

A 24.434 minutes

B 24.544 minutes

C 25.444 minutes

D 25.544 minutes

4. To add 18 + 25 using mental math, Braxton did the following. What is the missing number that makes the statement true? (2-1)

$18 + 25 = 18 + (2 + 23) = (18 + \square) + 23$

A 43

B 25

C 20

D 2

5. Which two trails combined are less than 4 miles? Use estimation to decide. (2-3)

Trails	Red	Blue	Yellow	Green
Miles	2.75	3.5	2.95	1.2

A Red and Yellow

B Blue and Green

C Red and Green

D Blue and Yellow

6. The Thomas Jefferson Memorial is on 18.36 acres of land and the Franklin Delano Roosevelt Memorial is on 7.5 acres of land. How many more acres of land is the Jefferson Memorial on than the Roosevelt memorial? (2-6)

A 9.86

B 10.86

C 11.31

D 17.61

7. The table shows the areas of two islands. How many more square miles is the area of Greenland than the area of New Guinea? (2-4)

Data

Island	Area (square miles)
Greenland	839,999
New Guinea	316,615

A 1,156,614

B 1,145,504

C 587,716

D 523,384

Test Prep

8. In 2005, there were 2,100,990 farms in the United States. Which of the following is 2,100,990 rounded to the nearest thousand? (2-2)

A 2,101,100

B 2,101,000

C 2,100,900

D 2,100,000

9. Which picture represents the problem? Parson's Sporting Goods ordered 56 T-shirts in sizes small, medium and large. If 23 T-shirts are medium and 12 T-shirts are large, how many are small? (2-7)

A

56 shirts in all

23	12	?

B

? shirts in all

23	12	56

C

56

23	?

D

56 + ?

23	12

10. A lecture hall has 479 desk chairs and 216 folding chairs. How many seats are there in all? Use mental math to solve. (2-1)

A 615

B 685

C 695

D 785

11. Parker had a batting average of 0.287 and Keenan had an average of 0.301. How much higher was Keenan's batting average than Parker's? (2-6)

A 0.256

B 0.14

C 0.023

D 0.014

12. April logged the miles she rode on her bicycle in the table shown. Which is the best estimate of the total miles April rode during the first two weeks? (2-3)

Week	1	2	3	4	5
Miles	12.3	7.8	6.2	11.8	9.5

A 19

B 20

C 26

D 38

13. What is 87.25 + 7.69? (2-5)

A 79.56

B 94.2569

C 94.94

D 95.94

14. In the 2004 Presidential Election, 62,040,610 people voted for George W. Bush and 59,028,439 people voted for John F. Kerry. What was the total number of votes for the two men? (2-4)

A 121,069,049

B 121,068,049

C 111,069,049

D 121,169,049

Reteaching

Set A, pages 24–26

Add 53 + 11 + 7 using mental math.

53 and 7 are compatible numbers, and the Commutative Property of Addition allows you to add in any order.

$$
\begin{aligned}
53 + 11 + 7 &= 53 + 7 + 11 \\
&= 60 + 11 \\
&= 71
\end{aligned}
$$

Remember that you can use compatible numbers or compensation to find sums and differences.

1. 67 + 28 **2.** 130 + 470

3. 35 + 14 + 6 **4.** 276 − 99

5. 96 + 234 + 4

Set B, pages 28–29

Round 12.0$\underline{8}$7 to the underlined place.

12.0$\underline{8}$7 Look at the digit following the underlined digit. Look at 7.

Round the 8 to the next higher digit because 7 > 5.

12.087 is about 12.09.

Remember that rounding a number means replacing it with another number that tells about how much or how many.

1. 10.$\underline{2}$45 **2.** 9.1$\underline{4}$5

3. 67,9$\underline{0}$1 **4.** $\underline{9}$9,102

Set C, pages 30–32

Estimate 19.9 + 17.03

$$
\begin{array}{rlr}
19.9 & \rightarrow & 20 \\
17.03 & \rightarrow & +\ 17 \\
\hline
 & & 37
\end{array}
$$

Round to the nearest whole number.

19.9 + 17.03 is about 37.

Remember that you can also use compatible numbers to estimate.

1. 76 + 23 **2.** 15.01 − 4.4

3. 8,001 + 2,890 **4.** 25,003 − 12,900

Set D, pages 34–36

Find 6,259 − 2,488.

Estimate: 6,000 − 2,000 = 4,000.

Subtract each place, starting from the right.

$$
\begin{array}{r}
\scriptstyle 5\ \ 11\ 15 \\
\not{6},\not{2}\not{5}9 \\
-\ 2,488 \\
\hline
3,771
\end{array}
\qquad \text{Check:} \qquad
\begin{array}{r}
\scriptstyle 1\ 1\ \ \ \\
3,771 \\
+\ 2,488 \\
\hline
6,259
\end{array}
$$

The answer 3,771 is reasonable because it is close to the estimate.

Remember to first estimate and then check that your answer is reasonable.

1. $\begin{array}{r} 9,371 \\ +\ 6,059 \\ \hline \end{array}$ **2.** $\begin{array}{r} 14,506 \\ -\ 8,759 \\ \hline \end{array}$

3. $\begin{array}{r} 41,974 \\ +\ 32,821 \\ \hline \end{array}$ **4.** $\begin{array}{r} 178,312 \\ -\ 140,987 \\ \hline \end{array}$

5. 72,555 + 38,055

Reteaching

Set E, pages 38–41

Find 7.83 − 3.147.

Estimate: 8 − 3 = 5.

Step 1

Write the numbers. Line up the decimal points. Annex zeros to show place value.

$$\begin{array}{r} 7.830 \\ -\ 3.147 \\ \hline \end{array}$$

Step 2

Subtract as you would whole numbers. Bring the decimal point straight down in the answer.

$$\begin{array}{r} \scriptstyle 7\ 12\ 10 \\ 7.83\not{0} \\ -\ 3.147 \\ \hline 4.683 \end{array}$$

Step 3

Check your answer by adding. The answer checks.

$$\begin{array}{r} \scriptstyle 1\ \ 1\ \ \\ 4.683 \\ +\ 3.147 \\ \hline 7.830 \end{array}$$

The difference is reasonable because 4.683 is close to the estimate of 5.

Remember to line up the decimal points before you add or subtract.

1. 3.77 + 4.66
2. 12.68 + 31.919
3. 6.142 + 1.322
4. 67.8 + 14.755
5. 7.029 + 48.7
6. 10.93 + 0.967
7. 9.21 − 1.72
8. 15.51 − 11.302
9. 5.7 – 0.623
10. 16.209 – 14.5
11. 17.099 – 9.7
12. 81.12 – 37.202

Set F, pages 42–44

Steve exercises 910 minutes a week in the summer. This is 190 minutes more than he exercises each week during the school year. How many minutes a week does he exercise during the school year?

Draw a bar diagram to show the main idea.

910 minutes	
m	190 min

Let *m* = minutes per week of exercise during the school year.

910 − 190 = *m*
m = 720

$$\begin{array}{r} 910 \\ -\ 190 \\ \hline 720 \end{array}$$

Martin exercises 720 minutes a week during the school year.

Remember that drawing a picture can help you before writing an equation to solve a problem.

Draw a picture and write an equation. Solve.

1. Jay's parents celebrated their 25th wedding anniversary in 2005. In what year did they get married?
2. One football stadium, built in 1982, has 64,035 seats. Another stadium, built in 1987, has 74,916 seats. How many more seats does the newer stadium have?
3. The two fifth-grade classes at school are having a fundraiser. The first class raised $2,187. Both classes raised $4,136 together. How much did the second class raise?

Topic 3

Reviewing Multiplication of Whole Numbers

1

This black-chinned hummingbird is eating nectar from a redbud. How can you make food for a hummingbird? You will find out in Lesson 3-3.

2

Kilauea is the most active volcano in the world. About how many cubic meters of lava does it discharge every minute? You will find out in Lesson 3-2.

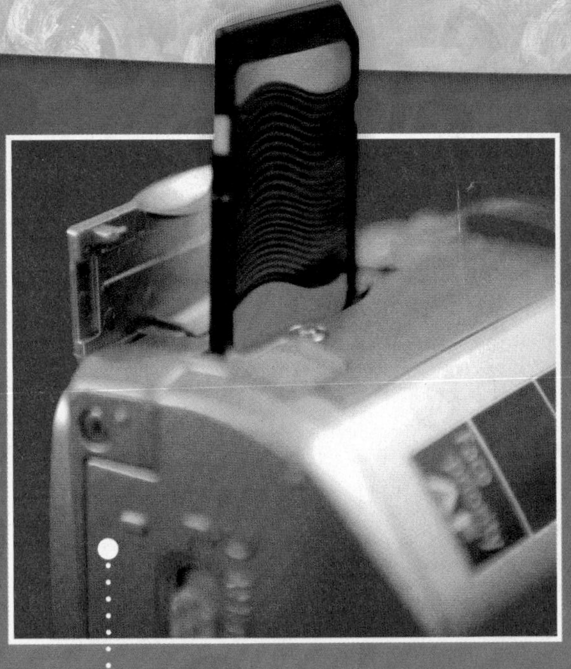

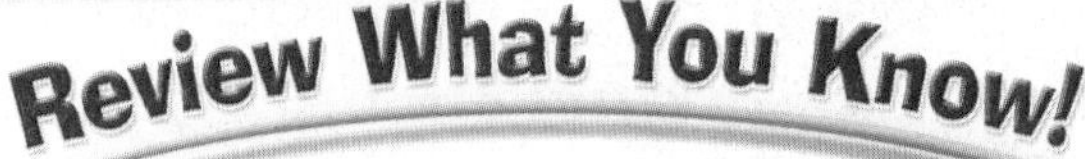

Review What You Know!

Vocabulary

Choose the best term from the box.

- equation
- factors
- product
- round

1. A(n) __?__ is another word for a number sentence.

2. One way to estimate a number is to __?__ the number.

3. A(n) __?__ is the answer you get when you multiply.

4. In the equation $9 \times 5 = 45$, 9 and 5 are both __?__.

Multiplication Facts

Find each product.

5. 3×9	**6.** 5×6	**7.** 4×8
8. 6×9	**9.** 7×4	**10.** 9×8
11. 7×6	**12.** 8×8	**13.** 7×9

Rounding

Round each number to the nearest hundred.

14. 864	**15.** 651	**16.** 348
17. 985	**18.** 451	**19.** 749

Multiplication Properties

Writing to Explain Write an answer to the question.

20. How do you know that $(3 \times 6) \times 4 = 3 \times (6 \times 4)$?

3

Technology companies, like those located in California's Silicon Valley, design and build digital products. How many images can a 32 MB memory stick for a digital camera hold? You will find out in Lesson 3-3.

4

One man balanced 75 drinking glasses on his chin. What was the capacity of the drinking glasses he balanced? You will find out in Lesson 3-4.

Lesson

3-1

AF 1.3, Grade 6 Apply algebraic order of operations and the commutative, associative, and distributive properties to evaluate expressions; and justify each step in the process.

Multiplication Properties

What are the properties of multiplication?

Do 2 groups of 5 beach balls equal 5 groups of 2 beach balls?

Factors are numbers that are multiplied to get a product.

Commutative Property of Multiplication

The order of factors can be changed.

The product stays the same.

$2 \times 5 = 5 \times 2$

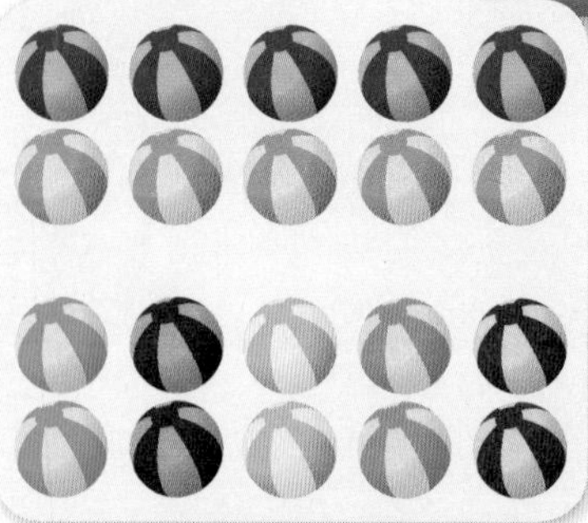

Guided Practice*

Do you know HOW?

In **1** through **5**, write the multiplication property used in each equation.

1. $65 \times 1 = 65$

2. $45 \times 6 = 6 \times 45$

3. $33 \times 0 = 0$

4. $11 \times 9 = 9 \times 11$

5. $(6 \times 20) \times 5 = 6 \times (20 \times 5)$

Do you UNDERSTAND?

6. Using equations, give an example for each property of multiplication.

7. In the following equations, what number should replace each ▢? Which property of multiplication is used?

a $40 \times 8 = ▢ \times 40$

b $1{,}037 \times ▢ = 1{,}037$

Independent Practice

In **8** through **19**, write the multiplication property used in each equation.

8. $537 \times 1 = 537$

9. $24 \times 32 = 32 \times 24$

10. $400 \times 0 = 0$

11. $73 \times 14 = 14 \times 73$

12. $5 \times (40 \times 9) = (5 \times 40) \times 9$

13. $1 \times 111 = 111$

14. $0 \times 1{,}247 = 0$

15. $8 \times (4 \times 3) = (8 \times 4) \times 3$

16. $(9 \times 3) \times 5 = 9 \times (3 \times 5)$

17. $1 \times 90 = 90 \times 1$

18. $76 \times 1 = 76$

19. $0 \times 563 = 0$

*For another example, see Set A on page 74.

Associative Property of Multiplication

You can change the grouping of the factors. The product stays the same.

$(2 \times 5) \times 3 = 2 \times (5 \times 3)$

Identity Property of Multiplication

When you multiply any number by 1, the product is that number.

$5 \times 1 = 5$

Zero Property of Multiplication

When you multiply any number by 0, the product is 0.

$5 \times 0 = 0$

Reasoning In **20** through **25**, use the multiplication properties to determine the number that belongs in each box.

20. $1{,}037 \times \square = 1{,}037$

21. $5 \times (20 \times 9) = (5 \times 20) \times \square$

22. $(635 \times 47) \times \square = 0$

23. $8 \times (\square \times 4) = (8 \times 5) \times 4$

24. $75 \times \square = 42 \times 75$

25. $(9 \times 6) \times 4 = 9 \times (\square \times 4)$

Problem Solving

26. Writing to Explain Haley said that she would always know her 0 and 1 multiplication facts. Explain why Haley would say this.

27. Writing to Explain How can one of the multiplication properties help you evaluate $(77 \times 25) \times 4$?

28. Last month 48,097 people visited the zoo. The number 48,097 is how many more than 25,000?

A 2,079 **C** 23,097

B 12,097 **D** 320,079

29. Think About the Process Naomi ordered 2 bottles of water for $1.00 each and 1 turkey sandwich for $3.00. Which expression would you use to find how much Naomi paid?

A (2 × $1) × $3

B 2 × (1 × $3)

C (2 + $1) + $2

D (2 × $1) + (1 × $3)

30. Compare. Write >, <, or = for each ◯.

a 34,304 ◯ 43,403

b 5.70 ◯ 5.7

c 21,978 ◯ 21,789

31. Three hundred fifty 10-year olds registered for a city-wide bowling tournament. If 205 participants are boys, how many are girls?

32. Critical Thinking Think of two numbers that will round to 14,000.

Lesson

3-2

NS 1.1 Estimate, round, and manipulate very large (e.g., millions) and very small (e.g., thousandths) numbers.

Estimating Products

How can you estimate products?

A store needs to take in at least $15,000 in sales per month to make a profit. If the store is open every day in March and takes in an average of $525 per day, will the store make a profit in March?

Another Example What is another way to estimate products?

Estimate 24×39.

You can also use compatible numbers to estimate products.

It is easy to find 25×40, since 25 and 40 are compatible numbers. Remember that $25 \times 4 = 100$. So, $25 \times 40 = 1{,}000$, and 1,000 is a good estimate for 24×39.

Both numbers used to estimate were greater than the actual numbers. So, 1,000 is an overestimate.

Guided Practice*

Do you know HOW?

In **1** and **2**, estimate by using rounding. Tell if your estimate is an overestimate or underestimate.

1. 58×6

2. 733×21

In **3** and **4**, estimate by using compatible numbers. Tell if your estimate is an overestimate or underestimate.

3. $43 \times 27 \times 4$

4. 38×69

Do you UNDERSTAND?

5. Writing to Explain Susan used rounding to estimate 243×4 and found 200×4. Jeremy used compatible numbers and found 250×4. The actual product is 972. Whose method gives an estimate closer to the actual product?

6. Reasonableness In the example above, why is it better to adjust $525 to $500 rather than leave the number at $525?

*For another example, see Set B on page 74.

You can use rounding to estimate products.

$525 rounds to $500.

31 rounds to 30.

Find 30 × 500.

30 × 500 = 15,000

Think I know that 3 × 5 = 15.

Both numbers used to estimate were less than the actual numbers, so 15,000 is an underestimate. The store will actually take in more than $15,000.

So, the store will make a profit in March.

Independent Practice

In **7** through **18**, estimate each product.

7. 75 × 28

8. 3 × 118

9. 39 × 58

10. 97 × 15

11. 513 × 19

12. 64 × 55

13. 286 × 9

14. 11 × 83

15. 10 × 66

16. 26 × 29 × 41

17. 18 × 999,999

18. 3 × 1,029,000

Problem Solving

19. **Reasoning** Estimate 53 × 375. Is the estimated product closer to 15,000 or 20,000?

20. Kilauea has been active since 1983. About how many cubic meters of lava is discharged in one minute?

21. **Writing to Explain** Samuel needs to estimate the product of 95 × 23 × 4. Explain two different methods Samuel could use to estimate.

22. Give two factors whose estimated product is about 800.

23. Jacque uses 11 sheets of notebook paper each day at school. If he has a package of 150 sheets, will that be enough paper for him to use for 3 weeks at school? Use an estimate to find out.

Lava is discharged from the volcano at about 7 cubic meters per second.

Lesson
3-3

NS 1.0 Students compute with very large and very small numbers, positive integers, decimals, and fractions and understand the relationship between decimals, fractions, and percents. They understand the relative magnitude of numbers.

Multiplying by 1-Digit Numbers

How do you multiply by 1-digit numbers?

How many beads are in 7 containers?

Choose an Operation
Multiply to join equal groups.

Another Example **How do you multiply a 1-digit number by a 4-digit number?**

A sports arena has 9 sections with 1,237 seats in each section. What is the total number of seats in the arena?

A 11,034 **B** 11,100 **C** 11,121 **D** 11,133

Choose an Operation Multiply to join equal groups.

Find 1,237 × 9.

Step 1

Multiply the ones, and regroup if necessary.

$$\begin{array}{r} {}^{6} \\ 1{,}237 \\ \times \quad 9 \\ \hline 3 \end{array}$$

9 × 7 ones = 63 ones
Regroup 63 ones as 6 tens 3 ones.

Step 2

Multiply the tens. Add any extra tens. Regroup if necessary.

$$\begin{array}{r} {}^{36} \\ 1{,}237 \\ \times \quad 9 \\ \hline 33 \end{array}$$

9 × 3 = 27 tens
27 tens + 6 tens = 33 tens
Regroup as 3 hundreds 3 tens

Step 3

Multiply the hundreds and thousands.
Add any extra hundreds and thousands.
Regroup if necessary.

$$\begin{array}{r} {}^{2\,36} \\ 1{,}237 \\ \times \quad 9 \\ \hline 11{,}133 \end{array}$$

9 × 2 = 18 hundreds
18 hundreds + 3 hundreds = 21 hundreds
Regroup as 2 thousands 1 hundred.
9 × 1 = 9 thousands
9 thousands + 2 thousands = 11 thousands

The arena can hold 11,133 people. The correct choice is D.

One Way

Remember how to multiply using partial products.

$$\begin{array}{r} 36 \\ \times \quad 7 \\ \hline 42 \\ +\ 210 \\ \hline 252 \end{array}$$

42 ← 7 × 6

210 ← 7 × 30

The partial products are 42 and 210. You add them to find the product.

Another Way

Step 1 Multiply the ones. Regroup if necessary.

$$\begin{array}{r} {\scriptstyle 4} \\ 36 \\ \times \quad 7 \\ \hline 2 \end{array}$$

7 × 6 ones = 42 ones
Regroup 42 ones as 4 tens 2 ones.

Step 2 Multiply the tens. Add any extra tens. Regroup if necessary.

$$\begin{array}{r} {\scriptstyle 4} \\ 36 \\ \times \quad 7 \\ \hline 252 \end{array}$$

7 × 3 tens = 21 tens
21 tens + 4 tens = 25 tens
Regroup 25 tens as 2 hundreds 5 tens.

There are 252 beads in 7 containers.

Guided Practice*

Do you know HOW?

In **1** and **2**, follow the steps from above to multiply.

1. 63 × 8

2. 274 × 3

Do you UNDERSTAND?

3. Writing to Explain In step 2 of Another Example, why is it necessary to regroup the 33 tens?

4. In the example at the top, how many beads would be in 9 containers?

Independent Practice

In **7** through **29**, find each product. Estimate to check that your answer is reasonable.

5. 62 × 7

6. 1,247 × 2

7. 921 × 8

8. 438 × 3

9. 2,979 × 6

10. 73 × 9

11. 18 × 5

12. 38 × 8

13. 1,218 × 7

14. 55 × 4

15. 264 × 4

16. 873 × 6

17. 237 × 6

18. 9,843 × 4

19. 627 × 3

For another example, see Set C on page 74.

Independent Practice

20. 795×5

21. 227×3

22. $4{,}596 \times 4$

23. 25×9

24. $6{,}330 \times 9$

25. 41×8

26. $5{,}532 \times 6$

27. 69×7

Problem Solving

For **28** and **29**, use the table below.

Paper towels needed to be collected for a school science project.

Data

Mr. Green's Class

Day	Number of Paper Towel Rolls
Monday	8
Tuesday	6
Wednesday	5
Thursday	3
Friday	4

28. Ms. Martinez's class collected three times as many paper towel rolls as Mr. Green's class. What is the total number of paper towel rolls collected by the two classes?

29. Order the days of the week from least paper towel rolls collected to greatest paper towels collected.

30. Use partial products to solve: 89×6.

31. **Writing to Explain** Why is it important to regroup correctly?

32. **Think About the Process** A popular Mexican restaurant has 48 tables. Each table has 3 different types of salsa. In one day, all of the tables are used for 9 different sets of customers. Which of the following would be best to estimate how many containers of salsa will be needed for all the tables in one day?

A 50×9

B $48 \times 3 \times 9$

C $50 \times 3 \times 10$

D $40 \times 5 \times 5$

33. A group of 24 students and 2 teachers went to a school fair. Each student spent \$8 on tickets and \$3 on snacks. What information is not needed to find out how much the 24 students and 2 teachers spent for tickets?

A The number of teachers

B The price of snacks

C The price of tickets

D The number of students

34. Hummingbirds eat simple syrup, which is a sugar and water solution. To make simple syrup, you need 4 parts sugar and 1 part water. If you have 12 cups of water, how many cups of sugar do you need?

35. A memory stick can be used to store images from a digital camera. The first memory stick was available in 1998. A 32 MB memory stick can hold up to 491 images. How many images can 7 memory sticks hold?

36. **Writing to Explain** Paul needs to estimate the product of $87 \times 23 \times 4$. Explain two different estimation strategies he can use.

Mixed Problem Solving

Newbery Medal Winners for Children's Literature

Author	Title of Book	Year	Pages
Jerry Spinelli (1941–Present)	*Maniac Magee*	1991	184
Beverly Cleary (1916–Present)	*Dear Mr. Henshaw*	1984	160
Nancy Willard (1936–Present)	*A Visit to William Blake's Inn*	1982	48
E.L. Konigsburg (1930–Present)	*From the Mixed-Up Files of Mrs. Basil E. Frankweiler*	1968	176

For **1** through **6**, use the table above.

1. Which writer has lived the longest?

2. The first Newbery Medal was awarded in 1923. How many years after this first award did Jerry Spinelli receive his award?

3. How old was E.L. Konigsburg when she published *From the Mixed-Up Files of Mrs. Basil E. Frankweiler*?

4. What is the difference in the number of pages between the shortest and longest books in the table?

5. How much older is the author of *Dear Mr. Henshaw* than the author of *A Visit to William Blake's Inn*?

6. **Strategy Focus** Solve using the strategy Draw a Picture and Write an Equation.

In the first quarter of the year, Paul has to write two book reports. He chose to read *Maniac Magee* and *Dear Mr. Henshaw*. How many pages will Paul have to read in all for his book reports? Let p = the number of pages Paul has to read.

p pages in all

184	160

Lesson
3-4

NS 1.0 Students compute with very large and very small numbers, positive integers, decimals, and fractions and understand the relationship between decimals, fractions, and percents. They understand the relative magnitude of numbers. Also **NS 3.3**, **Grade 4**

Multiplying by 2-Digit Numbers

How do you multiply by 2-digit numbers?

Sammy's Car Wash had 38 full-service car washes in one day. How much money did Sammy's Car Wash make in one day from full-service car washes?

Choose an Operation
Multiply to join equal groups.

CAR WASH
SERVICE
COST
EXTERIOR ONLY
$8.00
FULL SERVICE
$12.00
VACUUM
$5.00

Other Examples

In Lesson 3-3. you learned how to multiply by 1-digit numbers. In this lesson you multiply by 2-digit numbers and have partial products to add.

2-digit by 2-digit

$$\begin{array}{r} 57 \\ \times\ 43 \\ \hline 171 \\ 2280 \\ \hline 2{,}451 \end{array}$$

3-digit by 2-digit

$$\begin{array}{r} 982 \\ \times\ 37 \\ \hline 6874 \\ 29460 \\ \hline 36{,}334 \end{array}$$

4-digit by 2-digit

Step 1

Multiply the ones. Regroup.

$$\begin{array}{r} 2538 \\ \times\ 31 \\ \hline 2538 \end{array}$$

Step 2

Multiply the tens. Use one zero as a placeholder in your second partial product. Regroup.

$$\begin{array}{r} ^{1\,1\,2}\\ 2538 \\ \times\ 31 \\ \hline 2538 \\ 76140 \end{array}$$

Step 3

Add the partial products.

$$\begin{array}{r} 2538 \\ \times\ 31 \\ \hline 2538 \\ 76140 \\ \hline 78{,}678 \end{array}$$

Explain It

1. Explain why the second partial product always has a zero in the ones place.
2. **Reasonableness** How can you use compatible numbers to determine if 78,678 is reasonable?

Step 1

Multiply the ones. Regroup.

$$\begin{array}{r} {}^{1}\\ 38 \\ \times 12 \\ \hline 76 \end{array}$$

2 × 8 ones = 16 ones
Regroup 16 ones as 1 ten and 6 ones.

2 × 3 tens = 6 tens
6 tens + 1 ten = 7 tens

Step 2

Multiply the tens. Regroup.

$$\begin{array}{r} {}^{1}\\ 38 \\ \times 12 \\ \hline 76 \\ 380 \end{array}$$

10 × 8 ones = 80 ones or 8 tens

10 × 3 tens = 30 tens or 3 hundreds

Step 3

Add the partial products.

$$\begin{array}{r} {}^{1}\\ 38 \\ \times 12 \\ \hline 76 \\ +\ 380 \\ \hline 456 \end{array}$$

76 ← partial product
380 ← partial product

Sammy's Car Wash made $456.

Guided Practice*

Do you know HOW?

In **1** through **6**, find each product. Find each product. Estimate to check that your answer is reasonable.

1. 72 × 16 = ▒
2. 843 × 21 = ▒
3. 253 × 13 = ▒
4. 3,419 × 62 = ▒
5. 38 × 95 = ▒
6. 75 × 5,614 = ▒

Do you UNDERSTAND?

7. **Reasonableness** How can you use estimation to decide if the $456 Sammy's Car Wash made is reasonable?

8. In the example at the top, what would the car wash make if it charged $15 for each full-service car wash?

Independent Practice

In **9** through **28**, find the product. Estimate to check that your answer is reasonable.

9. $\begin{array}{r} 44 \\ \times\ 23 \\ \hline \end{array}$

10. $\begin{array}{r} 115 \\ \times\ \ 89 \\ \hline \end{array}$

11. $\begin{array}{r} 67 \\ \times\ 57 \\ \hline \end{array}$

12. $\begin{array}{r} 984 \\ \times\ \ 45 \\ \hline \end{array}$

13. $\begin{array}{r} 56 \\ \times\ 37 \\ \hline \end{array}$

14. $\begin{array}{r} 23 \\ \times\ 76 \\ \hline \end{array}$

15. $\begin{array}{r} 127 \\ \times\ \ 45 \\ \hline \end{array}$

16. $\begin{array}{r} 679 \\ \times\ \ 21 \\ \hline \end{array}$

17. 17 × 12
18. 263 × 18
19. 3,519 × 29
20. 7,227 × 51
21. 19 × 15
22. 838 × 47
23. 5,215 × 36
24. 77 × 18
25. 23 × 16
26. 442 × 11
27. 33 × 42
28. 1,236 × 12

*For another example, see Set D on page 75.

Problem Solving

29. The principal of your school is buying 3 computers at $900 each. She can pay $98 per month instead of paying the full price. Will she have paid for them by the end of 12 months?

30. The 2001 record for balancing drinking glasses on one's chin was 75 glasses. If the capacity of each glass was 20 fluid ounces, how many total fluid ounces could all the glasses contain?

31. How much would 85 barrels of oil have cost in 1984?

32. How much more would 65 barrels of oil have cost in 2004 than in 1974?

33. **Writing to Explain** How can finding the answer to 5×700 help you find the answer to 5×789?

Data

World Oil Prices

Year	Price per Barrel
1974	$9
1984	$29
1994	$16
2004	$38

34. The label on Bonnie's jigsaw puzzle states that the puzzle had more than 1,000 pieces. After Bonnie and her friend put the puzzle together, they counted 44 pieces across the top and 28 pieces down the side. Estimate to determine if the label was correct.

35. There are 21 classrooms at Pine Elementary School. The classes range between 27 and 33 students. Which is the best estimate of the total number of students in the school?

A 300 **C** 500

B 400 **D** 600

36. Which of the following is 8,004,231,900?

A eight billion, four hundred twenty three million, nine hundred

B eight billion, four million, two hundred thirty-one thousand, nine hundred

C eight million, two hundred thirty-one thousand, nine hundred four

D eight million, four thousand, two hundred thirty-one

37. A teacher asks 11 students to help set up chairs for an assembly. Each student can set up 3 chairs per minute. If the students work for 15 minutes, will there be enough chairs to seat 500 people at the assembly? Explain.

38. The Explorer Hiking Club has 64 members. How much will it cost for all members to buy new Terrain backpacks?

39. The club also needs to buy 16 dome tents and 16 propane stoves. Will they spend more or less on these items than on the backpacks? How much more or less?

Data

Camping Gear Prices

Gear	Price
Dome Tent	$99
Propane Stove	$28
Terrain Backpack	$87

Find the product. Estimate to check if the answer is reasonable.

1. 58 × 4

2. 355 × 7

3. 6,044 × 6

4. 5,137 × 3

5. 236 × 17

6. 23 × 25

7. 117 × 33

8. 65 × 29

9. 45 × 12

10. 1,001 × 25

11. 8 × 3,030

12. 6 × 3,373

Find the sum. Estimate to check if the answer is reasonable.

13. 76,095 + 3,950

14. 9,713 + 9,328

15. 888 + 726

16. 7,566 + 8,092

17. 27,444 + 9,507

Error Search Find each answer that is not correct. Write it correctly and explain the error.

18. 703 × 88 = 11,248

19. 348 × 17 = 5,916

20. 202 × 15 = 1,010

21. 19 × 18 = 344

22. 2,456 × 73 = 179,288

Number Sense

Estimating and Reasoning Write whether each statement is true or false. Explain your reasoning.

23. The product of 7 and 6,943 is closer to 42,000 than 49,000.

24. The difference of 15.9 and 4.2 is closer to 11 than 12.

25. The sum of 33,345 and 60,172 is less than 93,000.

26. The product of 43 and 5,116 is greater than 200,000.

27. The sum of 3.98 + 4.62 is 0.02 less than 8.62.

28. The product of 9 and 48 is 18 less than 450.

Lesson

3-5

NS 1.0 Students compute with very large and very small numbers, positive integers, decimals, and fractions and understand the relationship between decimals, fractions, and percents. They understand the relative magnitudes of numbers. Also **MR 2.1**

Estimating and Multiplying with Greater Numbers

How do you estimate the product of greater numbers and then find the actual product?

A team played 145 home games. They sold about the same number of tickets for each game. How many tickets did they sell in all?

Choose the Operation Find 9,212 × 145.

Estimate: 9,000 × 100 = 900,000

9,212 tickets sold last night

Guided Practice*

Do you know HOW?

In **1** and **2**, estimate each product.

1. 7,893 × 456 **2.** 5,083 × 923

In **3** and **4**, multiply to find the product. Check for reasonableness.

3. 4,816 × 253

4. 2,152 × 148

Do you UNDERSTAND?

5. In the example above, to what place were the factors rounded?

6. **Writing to Explain** In the example above, would using the compatible numbers 10,000 and 100 give a closer estimate to the product? Explain.

Independent Practice

In **7** through **10** estimate each product.

7. 5,691 × 451

8. 155 × 989

9. 4,449 × 723

10. 2,505 × 118

In **11** through **19**, multiply to find the product. Check for reasonableness.

11. 1,862 × 561

12. 4,726 × 907

13. 7,152 × 283

14. 9,814 × 509

15. 6,479 × 362

16. 1,279 × 445

17. 8,922 × 290

18. 2,311 × 875

19. 3,271 × 231

*For another example, see Set D on page 75.

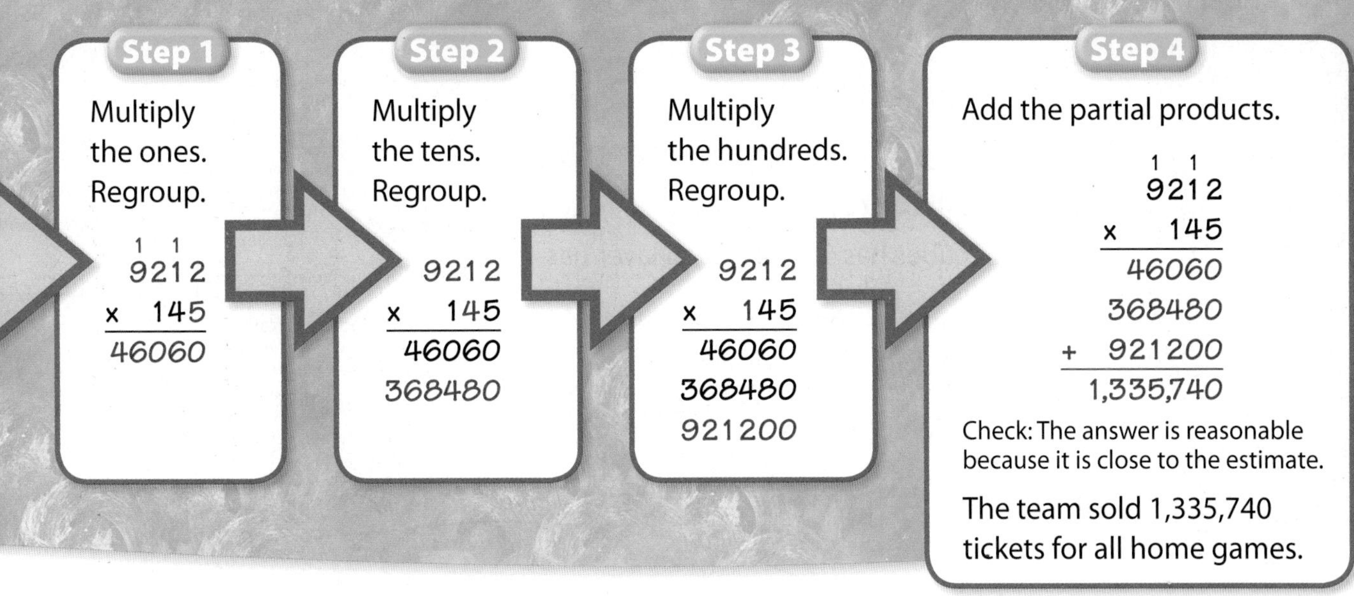
Step 1
Multiply the ones. Regroup.
1 1
9212
x 145
46060
Step 2
Multiply the tens. Regroup.
9212
x 145
46060
368480
Step 3
Multiply the hundreds. Regroup.
9212
x 145
46060
368480
921200
Step 4
Add the partial products.
1 1
9212
x 145
46060
368480
+ 921200
1,335,740
Check: The answer is reasonable because it is close to the estimate.
The team sold 1,335,740 tickets for all home games.

Problem Solving

20. An electronics store pays $2,876 for each 42-inch LCD TV they sell. If the store sells 32 of these TVs, how much will the store have made? Use the chart at the right.

Data

Sale	
36 inch LCD TV	$2,299
42 inch LCD TV	$3,256
Stereo System	$869

21. Geometry If each side of a hexagon is 32 cm, what is the perimeter of the hexagon?

A 128 cm

B 160 cm

C 192 cm

D 1,024 cm

22. Estimation The fifth-grade class at Monticello Elementary School sold more bags of popcorn than any other class. They ordered 17 cases of popcorn. Each case had 242 bags. About how many bags of popcorn did the class sell?

A 3,000 **C** 5,500

B 4,000 **D** 6,000

23. Think About the Process A dog's heart rate is about 100 beats per minute. A rabbit's is about 212 beats per minute. Which expression shows how to find the total number of heartbeats in about 1 hour for a dog and a rabbit?

A $(100 \times 1) = (212 \times 1)$

B $60 \times 100 \times 212$

C $(60 \times 100) + (60 \times 212)$

D $(212 \times 100) + 60$

24. Estimation The length of the Nile River in Africa is about 14 times the length of Lake Michigan. About how many miles long is the Nile River?

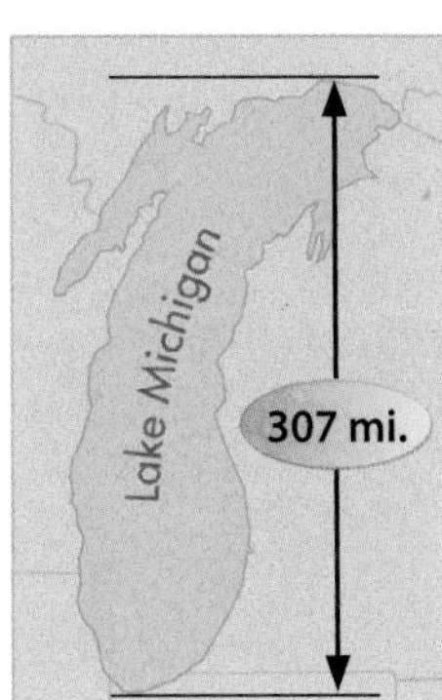
Lake Michigan
307 mi.

Lesson

3-6

NS 1.3 Understand and compute positive integer powers of non-negative integers; compute examples as repeated multiplication.

Exponents

How can you use exponents to write large numbers?

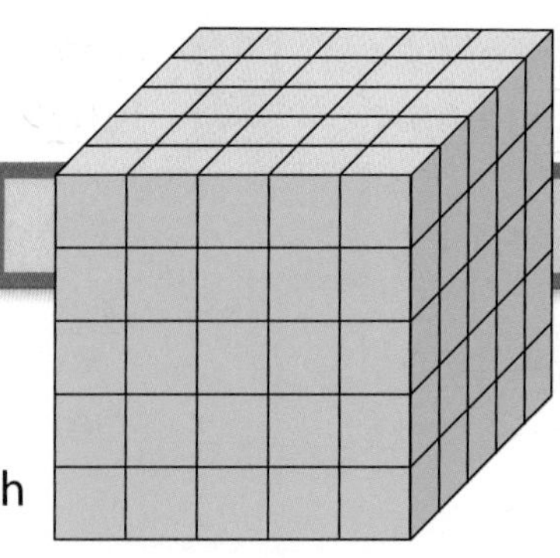

A box of cubes has 5 layers. Each layer has 5 rows, with 5 cubes in each row.

There are $5 \times 5 \times 5$ cubes in the box.

You can use exponential notation to represent repeated multiplication of the *same* number such as $5 \times 5 \times 5$.

Other Examples

Standard form
Write 2^5 in standard form.

$2^5 = 2 \times 2 \times 2 \times 2 \times 2$
$= 32$

Expanded form
Write 10^4 in expanded form.

$10^4 = 10 \times 10 \times 10 \times 10$

Exponential notation
Write $4 \times 4 \times 4$ in exponential notation.

$4 \times 4 \times 4 = 4^3$

An exponent is also called a power. You can read 4^6 as "4 to the sixth power". The second and third powers have special names. Read 3^2 as "3 to the second power," or 3 squared. Read 6^3 as "6 to the third power," or 6 cubed.

Guided Practice*

Do you know HOW?

1. Write 3^5 in expanded form.
2. Write 2^4 in standard form.
3. Write $7 \times 7 \times 7 \times 7 \times 7$ using exponential notation.
4. Write 5^4 in expanded form and standard form.

Do you UNDERSTAND?

5. In 3^5, what is the base? The exponent?
6. In the example at the top, how is 125 written in expanded form?
7. What is the standard form of 3 squared? For 6 cubed?

*For another example, see Set E on page 75.

The base is the number to be multiplied.

The exponent is the number that tells how many times the base is used as a factor.

factors exponent

$5 \times 5 \times 5 = 5^3$

base

Numbers involving exponents can be written in three different forms.

Exponential notation	5^3
Standard form	125
Expanded form	$5 \times 5 \times 5$

Independent Practice

In **8** through **14**, write in exponential notation.

8. $10 \times 10 \times 10 \times 10 \times 10$ **9.** $9 \times 9 \times 9$ **10.** 81×81 **11.** $5 \times 5 \times 5 \times 5$

12. $7 \times 7 \times 7$ **13.** $13 \times 13 \times 13 \times 13 \times 13 \times 13$ **14.** $6 \times 6 \times 6 \times 6$

In **15** through **22**, write in expanded form.

15. 17^5 **16.** 35 squared **17.** 4^3 **18.** 7^6

19. 55^4 **20.** 11^6 **21.** 8 cubed **22.** 1^9

In **23** through **30** write in standard form.

23. 5^4 **24.** 10^3 **25.** $4 \times 4 \times 4$ **26.** 12 squared

27. 1^{10} **28.** 2^6 **29.** 3 cubed **30.** 9^4

Problem Solving

31. Writing to Explain Why is the standard form of 8^2 NOT equal to 16?

32. Number Sense Find the number that equals 81 when it is squared.

33. Darnell earned $10 each week for 10 weeks walking a neighbor's dog.

a How much did he earn?

b Write the amount Darnell earned using exponential notation.

34. Which of the following, when written in standard form, is equal to the standard form of 2^6?

A 6^2 **C** 8^2

B 3^4 **D** 4^4

Lesson
3-7

MR 1.1 Analyze problems by identifying relationships, distinguishing relevant from irrelevant information, sequencing and prioritizing information, and observing patterns. Also **MR 1.2, NS 2.0**

Problem Solving

Multiple-Step Problems

Monica wants to buy all of the fruit shown on this sign. She has coupons for $0.45 off the cost of one pint of blueberries, and $0.35 off one watermelon. What will Monica's total cost be after the discounts?

FRESH FRUIT TODAY
(3 lb) $1.29
(1 pt) $3.29
(2 lb) $0.92
(each) $5.65

Another Example

A children's news and talk show is broadcast for 2 hours each weekday. On Saturday and Sunday, the show is an hour longer than during the week. How many hours is this show broadcast each week?

What is one hidden question?

How many hours of the show are broadcast during weekdays?

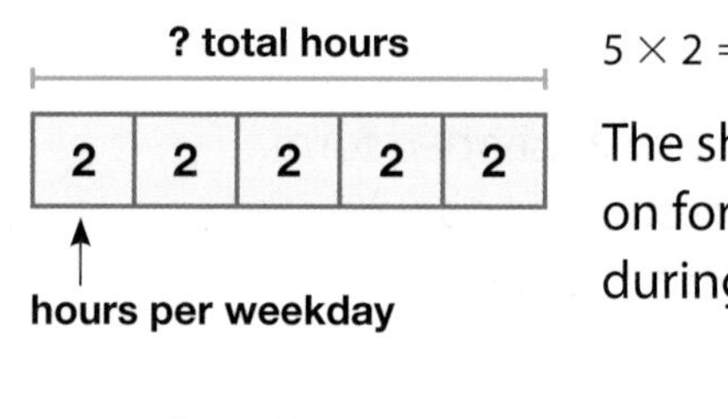

$5 \times 2 = 10$

The show is on for 10 hours during weekdays.

What is another hidden question?

How many hours of the show are broadcast during the weekend?

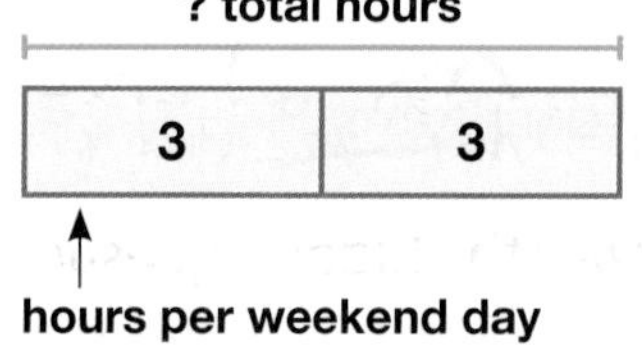

$2 \times 3 = 6$

The show is on for 6 hours during the weekend.

Add the number of weekday and weekend hours.

10 weekday hours + 6 weekend hours = 16 hours
The show is on for 16 hours each week.

Check for reasonableness: I can estimate 2 hrs × 7 days = 14 hrs. This is close to 16 hrs.

Explain It

1. Why do you find and answer the hidden questions before solving the problem?

Read and Understand

What do I know?

Monica wants to buy the fruit with prices shown on a store sign. She has coupons for $0.45 and $0.35 off the price of one pint of blueberries and one watermelon.

What am I asked to find?

The cost of all the fruit after the discount

Plan and Solve

Find and answer the hidden question or questions.

1. How much does the fruit cost?

? total cost

$1.29	$3.29	$0.92	$5.65

$1.29 + $3.29 + $0.92 + $5.65 = $11.15

2. How much are the coupons worth?

? total saved

$0.45	$0.35

$$\begin{array}{r} \$0.45 \\ +\ \$0.35 \\ \hline \$0.80 \end{array}$$

Subtract the total saved from the cost of the fruit.
$11.15 − $0.80 = $10.35

Monica will pay $10.35 for the fruit after the discount.

Guided Practice*

Do you know HOW?

Solve.

1. Nate has a $5 bill and a $10 bill. He spends $2.50 for a smoothie and $2 for a muffin. How much money does he have left?

Do you UNDERSTAND?

2. What are the hidden questions and answers for Problem 1?

3. **Write a Problem** Write a real-world multiple-step problem that can be solved using addition and subtraction.

Independent Practice

In **4** through **6**, write and answer the hidden question or questions. Then solve.

4. Elias saved $30 in July, $21 in August, and $50 in September. He spent $18 on movies and $26 on gas. How much money does Elias have left?

5. Paige takes riding lessons 5 days per week for 2 hours each day. Maggie takes guitar lessons twice a week for $2\frac{1}{2}$ hours each day, and piano lessons three days per week for 1 hour each day. Which girl spends more hours on lessons? How many more hours?

6. Lonny planted 15 roses, 12 geraniums, and 6 daisies. His dog digs up 4 roses and 2 daisies. How many flowers are left planted?

Stuck? Try this....

- What do I know?
- What am I asked to find?
- What diagram can I use to help understand the problem?
- Can I use addition, subtraction, multiplication, or division?
- Is all of my work correct?
- Did I answer the right question?
- Is my answer reasonable?

*For another example, see Set F on page 75.

Independent Practice

For **7** and **8**, write and answer the hidden question or questions. Then solve.

7. At the right is a driving log that Mr. Smith kept for the last three days of his trip. How many more miles did he drive for business than for personal use?

Driving Log

	Business	Personal Use
Monday	48 mi	11 mi
Tuesday	59 mi	8 mi
Wednesday	78 mi	28 mi

8. The table at the right shows the amount of salad a deli had on Monday morning. During the morning, the deli served 5 lb of macaroni salad, 16 lb of pasta salad, and 14 lb of potato salad. How many total pounds of salad did the deli have left Monday afternoon?

Salad Inventory

Macaroni Salad	11 lb
Pasta Salad	22 lb
Potato Salad	15 lb

9. At the craft festival, Tuan spent $12 for food, $19.50 for a small painting, and $6 for a straw hat. Tuan had $4 left. How much did Tuan spend on the small painting and the hat together? Draw a picture and write an equation to solve.

10. Look for a pattern, and then describe it. What are the missing numbers?

0.39, 0.45, 0.51, ▢, ▢, ▢

11. Writing to Explain Pull-over shirts cost $24.95 each. Describe how to estimate the cost of 4 shirts. What is the estimate?

Think About the Process

12. A men's store has 63 blue oxford shirts and 44 tan oxford shirts. The same store has 39 red rugby shirts. Which hidden question needs to be answered to find the difference between the number of oxford shirts and rugby shirts?

A How many oxford shirts does the store have?

B How many blue and red shirts does the store have?

C How many total shirts does the store have?

D Why does the store sell oxford shirts?

13. Rita budgeted $250 to refurnish her home. She spent $156 on two rugs and $205 on a new lamp. Rita wants to know how much more money she'll need. Which expression can be evaluated to answer this hidden question: How much has Rita spent on the rugs and the lamps?

A $156 + $205

B $250 − $156

C $156 + $250

D $250 + $205

Algebra Connections

Changing Words to Expressions

Remember that words can be translated to numerical expressions. Sometimes there is more than one word phrase for a numerical expression.

Example:

Word Phrase	Numerical Expression
• twenty minus five • five less than twenty • the difference of twenty and five	20 − 5

For **1** through **16**, write a numerical expression for each word phrase.

1. ten more than thirty

2. twelve fewer than fifty

3. twice as many as ten

4. one less than thirty

5. three times twelve

6. four minus three

7. the product of two and four

8. the sum of one and two

9. thirty more than ten

10. fifty divided by ten

11. three times fifty

12. six groups of three

13. the quotient of four and two

14. fifty less twelve

15. the total of ten and twenty

16. six more than a hundred

17. A person's height is x feet. Which expression represents the height in yards?

$3x$ $x \div 3$ $x + 3$

18. A yard has 36 inches. Which expression represents the number of inches in y yards?

$36y$ $y \div 36$ $y + 36$

19. A room is f feet long. Which expression represents the length of the room in inches?

$12f$ $f + 12$ $f \div 12$

Test Prep

1. Dr. Peterson works about 11 hours each day. Which of the following can be used to find the best estimate of the number of hours he works in 48 days? (3-2)

A 10×40

B 9×50

C 10×50

D 15×45

2. What number makes the number sentence true? (3-1)

$(4 \times 8) \times 7 = 4 \times (8 \times \square)$

A 3

B 7

C 28

D 56

3. At a garage sale, Josefina bought a TV for $34 and a couch for $79. If she used three $50 bills to pay for the items, how many dollars in change did she receive? (3-7)

A $113

B $37

C $16

D $13

4. A small town newspaper prints 8,250 copies each day. How many copies will the newspaper print in 365 days? (3-5)

A 115,500

B 301,250

C 2,565,750

D 3,011,250

5. A CD costs $9. The table shows the sales of that CD by a store. What was the total value of the sales in September? (3-3)

Data

Month	Number of CDs Sold
August	1,104
September	1,521
October	1,003
November	1,253
December	1,642

A $9,589

B $9,689

C $13,589

D $13,689

6. Jason drives 21 miles to work and 21 miles back home each day. Which of the following is the best estimate of how many miles he drives in 28 days? (3-2)

A 1,200

B 900

C 400

D 300

7. Rosemary reads 295 words per minute. If she reads 3.5 hours a day for 5 days, she will read 1,050 minutes. Which of the following is the best estimate of the number of words she can read in 1,050 minutes? (3-5)

A 300,000

B 200,000

C 30,000

D 20,000

Test Prep

8. Mt. Waialeale in Hawaii has an average rainfall of 460 inches per year. How much rain would this location expect to receive in 5 years? (3-3)

A 2,000

B 2,030

C 2,300

D 2,305

9. A banana contains 105 calories. Last week, Brendan ate 14 bananas. How many calories were in the bananas that Brendan ate last week? (3-4)

A 525

B 1,450

C 1,470

D 4,305

10. Which of the following is the best estimate of $4 \times 26 \times 7$ using compatible numbers? (3-2)

A 800

B 700

C 650

D 400

11. Monica bought a skirt for \$15 and a hat for \$12. Which of the following is a way to find how much change she would get from \$40? (3-7)

A Add 40 to the difference of 15 and 12

B Add 12 to the difference of 40 and 15

C Subtract the sum of 15 and 12 from 40

D Subtract 15 from the sum of 12 and 40

12. What is $48 \times 2,375$? (3-4)

A 114,000

B 113,920

C 109,500

D 28,500

13. Which of the following is equal to 4^5? (3-6)

A 4×5

B $5 \times 5 \times 5 \times 5$

C $4 \times 4 \times 4 \times 4$

D $4 \times 4 \times 4 \times 4 \times 4$

14. Four bags with 7 apples in each bag is the same amount as 7 bags with 4 apples in each bag. Which property of multiplication does this represent? (3-1)

A Commutative

B Associative

C Identity

D Zero

15. A cube with sides 2 inches long has a volume of 2^3 cubic inches. Which of the following is equal to 2^3? (3-6)

A 6

B 8

C 9

D 36

Reteaching

Set A, pages 52–53

Recall the multiplication properties.

Data

Property of Multiplication	Example
Commutative	$4 \times 8 = 8 \times 4$ $32 = 32$
Associative	$(4 \times 5) \times 6 = 4 \times (5 \times 6)$ $120 = 120$
Zero	$12 \times 0 = 0$
Identity	$9 \times 1 = 9$

Remember that properties of multiplication can help you find products more easily.

Identify the multiplication property.

1. $625 \times 1 = 625$

2. $9 \times 2 = 2 \times 9$

3. $2 \times (3 \times 4) = (2 \times 3) \times 4$

4. $0 \times 451 = 0$

Complete the following equations.

5. $1 \times 6{,}984 = \square$

6. $78 \times 4 = 4 \times \square$

7. $\square \times (75 \times 62) = (81 \times 75) \times 62$

Set B, pages 54–55

Estimate 37×88.

Round both factors. 37 is about 40 and 88 is about 90.

Step 2 Multiply the rounded factors. $40 \times 90 = 3{,}600$

Remember to either round the factors or use compatible numbers when estimating.

1. 7×396 **2.** 17×63

3. 91×51 **4.** 70×523

5. 32×400 **6.** 116×787

7. $4 \times 24 \times 91$ **8.** $29 \times 51 \times 67$

Set C, pages 56–58

Find 193×5. Estimate: $200 \times 5 = 1{,}000$

Step 1 Multiply ones. Regroup if needed.

```
   1
  193
×   5
-----
    5
```

Step 2 Multiply tens. Add extra tens. Regroup if necessary.

```
  41
  193
×   5
-----
   65
```

Step 3 Multiply hundreds. Add extra hundreds. Regroup if necessary.

```
  41
  193
×   5
-----
  965
```

Remember that you can round to estimate first.

Multiply. Check for reasonableness.

1. 672×6 **2.** 99×4

3. $1{,}074 \times 9$ **4.** 26×5

5. $1{,}306 \times 9$ **6.** $5{,}984 \times 2$

7. $9{,}511 \times 6$ **8.** 998×9

Set D, pages 60–62, 64–65

Find 425 × 38. Estimate: 400 × 40 = 16,000

Step 1

Multiply the ones.

```
   24
  425
×  38
 3400
```

Step 3

Multiply the tens.

```
    1
  425
×  38
 3400
12750
```

Step 3

Add the partial products.

```
   425
×   38
  3400
+12750
16,150
```

Remember to regroup if necessary. Estimate to check that your answer is reasonable.

1. 67 × 48
2. 81 × 19
3. 51 × 605
4. 32 × 871
5. 3,345 × 472
6. 192 × 2,497
7. 9,413 × 162
8. 4,706 × 980

Set E, pages 66–67

Write 7^3 in expanded form and standard form.

The base is 7.
The exponent is 3.

Expanded form: 7 × 7 × 7
Exponential notation: 7^3
Standard form: 343

Remember that the exponent tells how many times the base is used as a factor.

Write each in expanded form and standard form.

1. 17^2 2. 10^5 3. 2^6 4. 5^4

Set F, pages 68–70

Gene wants to buy a catcher's mitt for $52.00 and a pair of baseball shoes for $95.75. He has a coupon for $8.50 off the price of the mitt. How much will Gene owe for his purchase?

What is the hidden question or questions?

What will Gene pay for the mitt after the coupon?

$52.00	
$8.50	**? Cost after Coupon**

$52.00 – $8.50 = $43.50

Now, add the discounted price of the mitt to the price of the shoes to find Gene's total.

$43.50 + $95.75 = $139.25

Remember to look for the hidden question or questions before solving.

Write and answer the hidden question or questions. Then solve.

1. Pedro earned $13.50 for mowing lawns, $11 for raking leaves, and $14.75 for walking dogs. If Pedro bought a magazine subscription for $16.95 from his earnings, how much money did he have left?

Topic 4

Division of Whole Numbers

1 During the Gold Rush, cattle herding was an important part of California's economy. How many cattle could each cowboy have been responsible for? You will find out in Lesson 4-4.

2 Scientists have been tagging turtles at Turtle Island for years in order to study turtle behavior. How many turtles have the scientists tagged? You will find out in Lesson 4-4.

3 How fast can the Thorny Devil lizard eat ants, which are its favorite food? You will find out in Lesson 4-7.

Review What You Know!

4

Some comets can be seen from Earth fairly often. About how many of these comets are seen each year? You will find out in Lesson 4-2.

Vocabulary

Choose the best term from the box.

- dividend
- divisor
- quotient
- remainder

1. In the number sentence 180 ÷ 45 = 4, 180 is the $\underline{?}$ and 4 is the $\underline{?}$.

2. The number used to divide another number is the $\underline{?}$.

3. 15 ÷ 6 = 2 with a $\underline{?}$ of 3.

Place Value

Copy and complete.

4. 7,896 is the same as 7 $\underline{?}$ + 8 $\underline{?}$ + 9 $\underline{?}$ + 6 $\underline{?}$.

5. 36,000 is the same as 36 $\underline{?}$.

6. 75,800 is the same as 75 $\underline{?}$ + 8 $\underline{?}$.

Rounding

Round each number to the place of the underlined digit.

7. 6$\underline{7}$9 **8.** $\underline{3}$,769 **9.** 90,$\underline{3}$24

10. $\underline{8}$77 **11.** $\underline{6}$,542 **12.** 4$\underline{2}$,376

Writing to Explain Write an answer to the question.

13. Explain one way to estimate 738 ÷ 84.

Lesson
4-1

NS 2.2 Demonstrate proficiency with division, including division with positive decimals and long division with multidigit divisors.

Using Patterns to Divide

How can patterns help you divide large multiples of 10?

A jet carries 18,000 passengers in 90 trips. The plane is full for each trip. How many passengers does the plane hold?

Choose an Operation Divide to find how many people were on each trip.

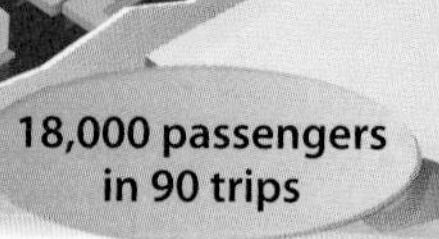

18,000 passengers in 90 trips

Guided Practice*

Do you know HOW?

In **1** through **4**, find each quotient. Use mental math.

1. 210 ÷ 30 = 21 tens ÷ 3 tens = ☐

2. 480 ÷ 60 = 48 tens ÷ 6 tens = ☐

3. 8,100 ÷ 90 = ☐

4. 2,800 ÷ 70 = ☐

Do you UNDERSTAND?

5. In Exercise 1, why is 210 ÷ 30 the same as 21 tens ÷ 3 tens?

6. In the example at the top, if the jet carried 10,000 people in 40 trips, how many people did it carry for each trip?

Independent Practice

In **7** through **22**, find each quotient. Use mental math.

7. 560 ÷ 70 = 56 tens ÷ 7 tens = ☐

8. 360 ÷ 60 = 36 tens ÷ 6 tens = ☐

9. 6,000 ÷ 50 = 600 tens ÷ 5 tens = ☐

10. 24,000 ÷ 60 = 2,400 tens ÷ 6 tens = ☐

11. 2,000 ÷ 20 = ☐

12. 6,300 ÷ 90 = ☐

13. 240 ÷ 10 = ☐

14. 21,000 ÷ ☐ = 700

15. 9,000 ÷ 90 = ☐

16. 72,000 ÷ ☐ = 200

17. 30,000 ÷ ☐ = 600

18. 7,200 ÷ ☐ = 80

19. 56,000 ÷ ☐ = 800

20. 10,000 ÷ 100 = ☐

21. 25,000 ÷ 50 = ☐

22. 45,000 ÷ 90 = ☐

*For another example, see Set A on page 108.

Think of a basic fact to help you solve.

$18 \div 9 = 2$

Think about multiples of 10:

$180 \div 90 = 18$ tens $\div$ 9 tens $= 2$

$1{,}800 \div 90 = 180$ tens $\div$ 9 tens $= 20$

$18{,}000 \div 90 = 1{,}800$ tens $\div$ 9 tens $= 200$

The pattern shows us that $18{,}000 \div 90 = 200$.

So, the jet can hold 200 people during each trip.

You can multiply to check your answer.

$200 \times 90 = 18{,}000$

Problem Solving

For **23** and **24**, use the information at the right.

23. If all the flights were full and all planes carried the same number of passengers, how many people were on each flight?

Data

Total passengers	3,000
Flights per day	20
Bottles of water	6,000

24. If each flight was stocked with the same number of bottles of water, how many bottles were on each flight?

25. There are 12 school campuses in the community. Each campus has a 14-member volleyball team. How many students play volleyball?

26. Helen bowled 5 games. Her scores were 97, 108, 114, 99, and 100. What was the total of her scores?

27. **Think About the Process** Dividing 420 by 60 is the same as

A dividing 42 ones by 6 ones.

B dividing 42 tens by 6 ones.

C dividing 42 tens by 6 tens.

D dividing 42 hundreds by 6 tens.

28. Suppose there are 1,500 pencils in 20 bins. You want to put the same number of pencils in each bin. Which expression shows how to find the number of pencils in each bin?

A $1{,}500 + 20$ **C** $1{,}500 \times 20$

B $1{,}500 - 20$ **D** $1{,}500 \div 20$

29. One dozen eggs is 12 eggs. A farmer harvested 1,260 eggs from the hen-house. Which expression shows how to find how many dozen eggs the farmer harvested?

A $1260 + 12$ **C** $1260 \div 12$

B $1260 - 12$ **D** 1260×12

30. It takes 18,000 kg of sand to fill 600 school sandboxes. How much sand will a construction company need to put in each of the 600 sandboxes to get ready for the new school year?

Lesson

4-2

NS **1.0** Students compute with very large and very small numbers, positive and negative numbers, decimals, and fractions and understand the relationship between decimals, fractions, and percents. They understand the relative magnitudes of numbers.
Also **NS 1.1, MR 3.0**

Estimating Quotients

How can you use compatible numbers to estimate quotients?

Betty made $159 by selling 75 bracelets. Each bracelet costs the same. About how much did each bracelet cost?

Choose an Operation We know the total amount made and the number of bracelets. Divide to find the estimated price of each bracelet.

Guided Practice*

Do you know HOW?

In **1** through **6**, estimate using compatible numbers.

1. 287 ÷ 42
2. 320 ÷ 11
3. 208 ÷ 72
4. 554 ÷ 62
5. 1,220 ÷ 59
6. 3,390 ÷ 42

Do you UNDERSTAND?

7. Writing to Explain If you use rounding to estimate in the example above, can you divide easily? Explain.

8. Reasonableness Betty has 425 more bracelets to sell. She wants to store these in plastic bags that hold 20 bracelets each. She estimates she will need about 25 bags. Is she right? Why or why not?

Independent Practice

In **9** through **26**, estimate using compatible numbers.

9. 412 ÷ 84
10. 288 ÷ 37
11. 2,964 ÷ 73
12. 228 ÷ 19
13. 1,784 ÷ 64
14. 7,620 ÷ 53
15. 2,280 ÷ 12
16. 485 ÷ 92
17. 540 ÷ 61
18. 1,710 ÷ 32
19. 2,740 ÷ 67
20. 4,322 ÷ 81
21. 5,700 ÷ 58
22. 7,810 ÷ 44
23. 6,395 ÷ 78
24. 4,877 ÷ 74
25. 2,495 ÷ 48
26. 6,284 ÷ 93

*For another example, see Set B on page 108.

The question asks, "About how much?" So, an estimate is enough.

Use compatible numbers to estimate $159 \div 75$.

Find compatible numbers for 159 and 75.

Think 16 can be divided evenly by 8.

160 and 80 are close to 159 and 75.

So, 160 and 80 are compatible numbers.

Divide.

$160 \div 80 = 2$.

So, Betty charged *about* $2 for each bracelet.

Check for reasonableness:

$2 \times 80 = 160$

Problem Solving

27. A high school volleyball team has made it to the state tournament. There are 586 students that want to go, and 32 students can fit on each bus. About how many buses are needed?

28. Each player contributed $3 for a gift for the head coach. The two assistant coaches each donated $10. If there were 22 players on the team, how much money did the team raise in all?

29. There are 135 comets that are visible from Earth every 20 years or less. What is an estimate of how many of these comets are seen each year?

30. Leon bought 8 CDs on sale for $88. The regular price for 8 CDs is $112. How much did Leon save per CD by buying them on sale?

31. Estimate the product for the following expression.

805×62

A 4,800

B 48,000

C 54,000

D 64,000

32. Which property does the following equation illustrate?

$2 + (11 + 19) = (2 + 11) + 19$

A Commutative Property of Addition

B Associative Property of Addition

C Identity Property of Addition

D Commutative Property of Multiplication

33. Donald bought a clock radio. The radio weighs 18 ounces. Donald paid $12 less than the normal sales price. If the normal sales price was $38, how much did Donald spend on the radio?

34. **Writing to Explain** Autumn needs to estimate the quotient $817 \div 91$. Explain how Autumn can use compatible numbers to make a reasonable estimate.

Lesson

4-3

NS 1.0 Students compute with very large and very small numbers, positive integers, decimals, and fractions, and understand the relationship between decimals, fractions, and percents. They understand the relative magnitudes of numbers. Also **MR 2.3**

Connecting Models and Symbols

play money

How can you model division?

Abbott Middle School raised $148 selling spaghetti at the school's fund-raiser dinner. How can the principal divide the money equally among 4 school projects?

Choose an Operation Divide since you are sharing.

Another Example How can you record division?

Suppose 4 people needed to share $148.

What You Think	What You Write
The $100 bill needs to be shared. Exchange the $100 bill for ten $10 bills. There are now 14 $10 bills. Each person gets three $10 bills. ($4 \times 3 = 12$).	$\begin{array}{r} 3 \\ 4\overline{)148} \\ -12 \\ \hline 2 \end{array}$
Two $10 bills are left to share. Exchange the $10 bills for 20 $1 bills. That gives 28 $1 bills to be divided into four groups. Each person gets seven $1 bills. ($4 \times 7 = 28$).	$\begin{array}{r} 37 \\ 4\overline{)148} \\ -12 \\ \hline 28 \\ -28 \\ \hline 0 \end{array}$
After each person gets seven $1 bills, there is no money left to share.	Each person gets $37.

Explain It

1. Explain how you can exchange bills to divide four $10 bills equally among 5 people.
2. Suppose Abbott Middle School raised $75 more. In all, how much would each of the four projects receive?

Exchange the $100 bill for ten $10 bills. There are now 14 $10 bills. Share the $10 bills. Each project gets three $10 bills. Two $10 bills are left.

Exchange the two remaining $10 bills for 20 $1 bills. This gives 28 $1 bills.

Each project gets a total of $37.

Guided Practice*

Do you know HOW?

In **1** through **4**, use models to help you divide.

1. $3\overline{)69}$

2. $7\overline{)490}$

3. $9\overline{)225}$

4. $3\overline{)186}$

Do you UNDERSTAND?

5. Writing to Explain In the example above, why do you have to exchange the two remaining $10 bills?

6. If 4 people divide $244 equally, how much will each person get?

Independent Practice

Leveled Practice In **7**, use play money or draw diagrams of the bills shown at the right to symbolize division. Copy and complete the calculation as you answer the questions below.

7. Six people need to share $576 equally.

a All $100 bills are replaced with $10 bills. How many $10 bills are there altogether?

b How many $10 bills will each person get?

c How many $10 bills are left?

d Replace the remaining $10 bills with $1 bills. How many $1 bills are left in all to divide among 6 people?

e What is the total amount each person gets?

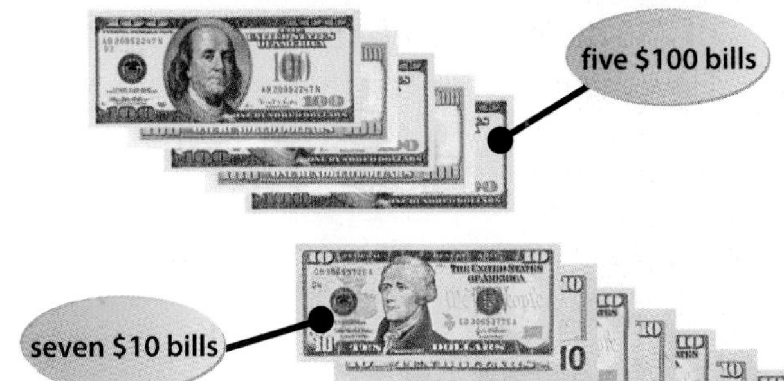

$6\overline{)576}$
−
6
−

*For another example, see Set C on page 108.

Independent Practice

In **8** through **17**, copy and complete. You may use play money to help you divide.

8. $5\overline{)355}$ **9.** $7\overline{)693}$ **10.** $4\overline{)364}$ **11.** $6\overline{)492}$

12. 484 divided by 4

13. 672 divided by 6

14. 312 divided by 2

15. 765 divided by 5

16. 385 divided by 7

17. 759 divided by 3

Problem Solving

18. Twenty bags of dog food were donated to the animal shelter. The total cost of the dog food, including $5.95 tax, was $145.95. How much did one bag of dog food cost before taxes?

19. Paulo helped his grandmother with her garden for five days after school. He worked for two hours each day. Paulo's grandmother gave him $75. How much money did Paulo earn each day?

20. **Number Sense** Nick and 3 friends unloaded 224 folding chairs for the community theater. Each person unloaded the same number of chairs. How many chairs did Nick unload?

21. **Writing to Explain** Explain how division facts and patterns can help you find 20,000 ÷ 5.

22. The Stanton Ferry transports a maximum of 756 people to Green Island in 4 trips. How many people can the ferry transport in 1 trip?

A 151 **C** 189

B 164 **D** 199

23. The Napoleon Bonaparte Broward Bridge is 10,646 feet long. The Sunshine Sky Bridge is 29,040 feet long. Which bridge is shorter and by how much?

24. **Writing to Explain** Why is 3.892 greater than 3.289?

25. **Think About the Process** The art museum sold 1,770 tickets to the modern art exhibit on Sunday. Each ticket cost $12. The ticket holders were divided into five groups to organize the viewing for that day. Which expression tells how to find the number of people in each group?

A 1,770 ÷ $12 + 5

B 1,770 ÷ 5 + $12

C 1,770 ÷ $12

D 1,770 ÷ 5

26. Kirstin is starting a swimming club. She is the only member the first month. She plans to have each member find 2 new members each month. How many members will the club have at the end of 4 months?

Find the product. Estimate to check if the answer is reasonable.

1. 692×414

2. 365×212

3. 405×326

4. 444×222

5. 732×551

6. 605×706

7. 117×515

8. 275×625

Find the quotient.

9. 720 ÷ 9

10. 3,200 ÷ 8

11. 30,000 ÷ 50

12. 48,000 ÷ 6

13. 54,000 ÷ 90

14. 21,000 ÷ 70

15. 30,000 ÷ 5

16. 2,700 ÷ 30

Error Search Find each answer that is not correct. Write it correctly and explain the error.

17. 42,000 ÷ 70 = 6,000

18. $398 \times 602 = 24{,}676$

19. 180 ÷ 6 = 20

20. $883 \times 445 = 392{,}935$

Number Sense

Estimating and Reasoning Write whether each statement is true or false. Explain your reasoning.

21. The quotient of 388 ÷ 8 is closer to 50 than 40.

22. The sum of 4.95 + 3.68 is 0.05 more than 8.68.

23. The product of 5 and 3,003 is 15 more than 15,000.

24. The product of 28 and 485 is greater than 15,000.

25. The quotient of 4,479 ÷ 61 is closer to 80 than 70.

26. The product of 7 and 409 is greater than the product of 4 and 709.

27. The quotient of 42,000 ÷ 6 is greater than 700 and less than 70,000.

Lesson

4-4

NS 2.2 Demonstrate proficiency with division, including division with positive decimals and long division with multidigit divisors.

Dividing by 1-Digit Divisors

Why use division?

Students are selling candles to raise money. A shipment arrived yesterday. The candles will be sold in boxes of 6 each. How many boxes can be filled? A diagram can help you decide what operation to use.

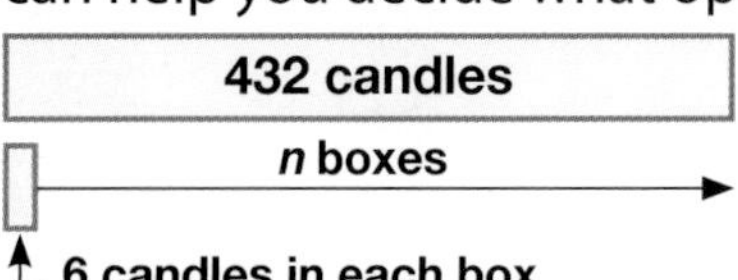

432 candles

6 candles per box

Other Examples

2-digit quotient with remainder

Find 380 ÷ 6.

```
   6
6)380
 - 36
    2
```

```
   63 R2
6)380
 - 36↓
    20
  - 18
     2
```

380 is the dividend,
6 is the divisor,
63 is the quotient, and
2 is the remainder.

3-digit quotient with remainder

Find 547 ÷ 4.

```
   1
4)547
 - 4
   1
```

```
   13
4)547
 - 4↓
   14
 - 12
    2
```

```
   136 R3
4)547
 - 4 |
   14
 - 12↓
    27
  - 24
     3
```

Explain It

1. Name the quotient, divisor, remainder, and dividend in these two examples.
2. Why did the second example have a 3-digit quotient?

Step 1

Find 432 ÷ 6.

Estimate. Decide where to place the first digit in the quotient.

Use compatible numbers.
420 ÷ 6 = 70
The first digit is in the tens place.

Step 2

Divide the tens.
Multiply and subtract.

$$\begin{array}{r} 7 \\ 6\overline{)432} \\ -42 \\ \hline 1 \end{array}$$

Divide. 43 ÷ 6 = 7
Multiply. 7 × 6 = 42
Subtract. 43 − 42 = 1
Compare. 1 < 6

Step 3

Bring down the ones.
Divide the ones. Multiply and subtract.

$$\begin{array}{r} 72 \\ 6\overline{)432} \\ -42\downarrow \\ \hline 12 \\ -12 \\ \hline 0 \end{array}$$

Divide. 12 ÷ 6 = 2
Multiply. 2 × 6 = 12
Subtract. 12 − 12 = 0
Compare. 0 < 6

There can be 72 boxes filled with candles.

Guided Practice*

Do you know HOW?

In **1** through **6**, find each quotient.

1. $9\overline{)270}$ **2.** $6\overline{)684}$

3. $3\overline{)65}$ **4.** $5\overline{)339}$

5. $5\overline{)564}$ **6.** $4\overline{)724}$

Do you UNDERSTAND?

7. Writing to Explain How can estimating with compatible numbers help you find the quotient?

8. In the first example, find the quotient if the total number of candles is 561.

Independent Practice

In **9** through **12**, use compatible numbers to decide where to place the first digit of the quotient.

9. $5\overline{)762}$ **10.** $3\overline{)289}$ **11.** $8\overline{)637}$ **12.** $3\overline{)567}$

In **13** through **32**, copy and complete the calculation.

13. $8\overline{)616}$ **14.** $6\overline{)486}$ **15.** $4\overline{)448}$ **16.** $9\overline{)828}$

17. $7\overline{)644}$ **18.** $2\overline{)131}$ **19.** $9\overline{)836}$ **20.** $5\overline{)413}$

21. $5\overline{)4,673}$ **22.** $2\overline{)3,182}$ **23.** $5\overline{)469}$ **24.** $6\overline{)3,105}$

25. $2\overline{)995}$ **26.** $9\overline{)73}$ **27.** $5\overline{)4,626}$ **28.** $6\overline{)1,884}$

29. $3\overline{)86}$ **30.** $2\overline{)345}$ **31.** $9\overline{)7,645}$ **32.** $5\overline{)942}$

*For another example, see Set Set D on page 109.

Problem Solving

33. **Writing to Explain** How can you tell, before you divide 387 by 4, that the first digit of the quotient is in the tens place?

34. **Writing to Explain** Why is the following incorrect? $296 \div 6 = 48$ R8. Write your answer before you complete the calculation.

35. **Think About the Process** A team of 10 people in the Netherlands rolled a 140-lb barrel a distance of 164 miles in 24 hours. Each person rolled the same distance. Which of the following shows how to determine how many miles each person rolled the barrel?

 A $164 \div 24$ **C** $140 \div 24$

 B $164 \div 10$ **D** $140 \div 10$

36. Ray walked for 9 hours to raise money for his favorite charity. He raised $225. How much money did he raise for each hour he walked?

37. For 9 years, scientists tagged 450 turtles at Turtle Island. How many turtles did they tag each year?

450 turtles

?	?	?	?	?	?	?	?	?

38. The High Sierra Trail at Mt. Whitney is 49 miles long each way. Park rangers report that to walk the trail one way takes hikers 6 days. About how many miles must the hikers walk each day to finish all 49 miles in 6 days?

 A 6 miles **C** 10 miles

 B 8 miles **D** 12 miles

39. **Algebra** What is the value of c in the equation $c \times 3 = 324$?

 A 18 **C** 180

 B 108 **D** 1,080

40. **Algebra** Find the value of n.

 $3 \times 7 = n \times 3$

41. **Geometry** What is the perimeter of the rectangle in inches? (Hint: 1 ft = 12 in.)

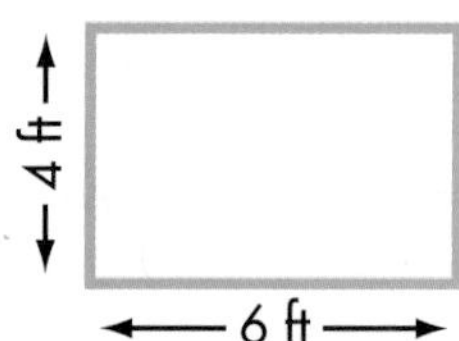

42. **Estimation** There are 7 days in a week. About how many weeks are there for the amounts of time below?

 a 621 days

 b 2,423 days

43. **Strategy Focus** Suppose 8 cowboys drove a herd of 104 cattle along the Warner Mountains near Cedarville, California. How many animals was each cowboy responsible for? Write an equation, then solve. Let a = the number of animals for each cowboy.

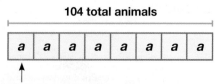

104 total animals

a	a	a	a	a	a	a	a

Animals for each cowboy

Algebra Connections

Simplifying Numerical Expressions

In order to simplify numerical expressions, you must follow the order of operations.

- Complete the operations inside the parentheses.
- Multiply and/or divide in order from left to right.
- Add and/or subtract in order from left to right.

Example:

Simplify $50 - (9 \times 3)$.

Start with the operation inside the parentheses. What is 9×3?

$9 \times 3 = 27$

Then subtract.

$50 - 27 = 23$

So, $50 - (9 \times 3) = 23$.

Simplify. Follow the order of operations.

1. $4 + 2 \times 9$

2. $16 + 8 \div 2$

3. $25 + (3 \times 6) - 5$

4. $8 \times 6 + 9$

5. $10 + 27 \div 3$

6. $(6 + 3) \times 5$

7. $(5 \times 2) + (10 \div 2)$

8. $5 \times 7 \times (6 - 3)$

9. $(12 - 3) \times (3 + 4)$

10. $35 + 5 \div 5 - 2$

11. $20 \times 2 + 3 \times (8 + 2)$

12. $(10 + 7) \times 3 - 4 \times (2 + 5)$

13. $3 \times 3 \div 3 + 6 - 3$

14. $(5 + 63) - 4 \times (12 \div 4)$

Insert parentheses to make each statement true.

15. $11 - 6 - 1 = 6$

16. $10 + 2 \times 4 + 1 = 60$

17. $30 - 4 \times 2 + 5 = 2$

18. $64 \div 2 \times 4 \div 2 = 4$

19. **Write a Problem** Write a real-world problem that you could solve by simplifying the expression $50 - (2 \times 9)$.

Lesson

4-5

NS 2.2 Demonstrate proficiency with division, including division with positive decimals and long division with multidigit divisors.

Zeros in the Quotient

When do you write a zero in the quotient?

On vacation the McQueen family drove a total of 830 miles in four days. What is the average number of miles they drove each day?

Choose an Operation Divide to find how many miles per day.

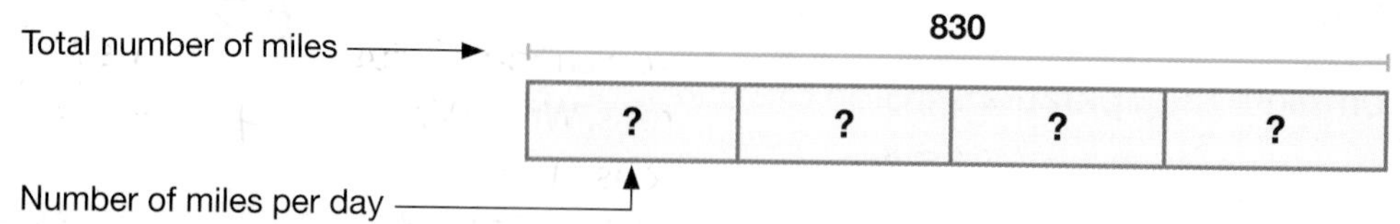

Other Examples

Find 2,240 ÷ 4.

Step 1

Estimate. Use compatible numbers. Decide where to place the first digit in the quotient.

2,000 ÷ 4 = 500

The first digit in the quotient is in the hundreds place.

Step 2

Divide the hundreds.

$$\begin{array}{r} 5 \\ 4\overline{)2{,}240} \\ -\,20 \\ \hline 2 \end{array}$$

22 ÷ 4 = 5
5 × 4 = 20
22 − 20 = 2
2 < 4

Step 3

Bring down the tens. Divide the tens. Multiply and subtract.

$$\begin{array}{r} 56 \\ 4\overline{)2{,}240} \\ -\,20\downarrow \\ \hline 24 \\ -\,24 \\ \hline 0 \end{array}$$

24 ÷ 4 = 6
6 × 4 = 24
24 − 24 = 0
0 < 4

Step 4

Bring down the ones. Divide the ones. Multiply and subtract.

$$\begin{array}{r} 560 \\ 4\overline{)2{,}240} \\ -\,20\downarrow \\ \hline 24 \\ -\,24\downarrow \\ \hline 00 \\ 0 \\ \hline 0 \end{array}$$

There are 0 ones and 0 < 4. Put a 0 in the quotient in the ones place. 2,240 ÷ 4 = 560.

Guided Practice*

Do you know HOW?

For **1** through **4**, find each quotient. Check your answers by multiplying.

1. $9\overline{)972}$

2. $7\overline{)714}$

3. $5\overline{)453}$

4. $2\overline{)1{,}941}$

Do you UNDERSTAND?

5. Why is the zero placed in the tens place of the quotient in the example at the top, but in the ones place in Another Example?

*For another example, see Set D on page 109.

Step 1

Find 830 ÷ 4.

Estimate first. Use compatible numbers. 800 ÷ 4 = 200
So, the first digit in the quotient is in the hundreds place. Divide the hundreds.

$$\begin{array}{r} 2 \\ 4\overline{)830} \\ -8 \\ \hline 0 \end{array}$$

Divide. 8 ÷ 4 = 2
Multiply. 2 × 4 = 8
Subtract. 8 − 8 = 0
Compare. 0 < 4

Step 2

$$\begin{array}{r} 20 \\ 4\overline{)830} \\ -8\downarrow \\ \hline 03 \end{array}$$

You cannot divide tens. Write 0 in the tens place.

Step 3

$$\begin{array}{r} 207 \text{ R2} \\ 4\overline{)830} \\ -8\downarrow \\ \hline 030 \\ -28 \\ \hline 2 \end{array}$$

30 ÷ 4 ≈ 7
7 × 4 = 28
30 − 28 = 2
2 < 4

The McQueens drove about 207 miles each day.

Independent Practice

For **6** through **17**, find each quotient. Check your answers by multiplying.

6. $2\overline{)880}$ **7.** $5\overline{)540}$ **8.** $6\overline{)8,340}$ **9.** $3\overline{)3,230}$

10. $7\overline{)707}$ **11.** $4\overline{)829}$ **12.** $2\overline{)6,080}$ **13.** $9\overline{)2,781}$

14. $3\overline{)620}$ **15.** $5\overline{)1,535}$ **16.** $7\overline{)14,206}$ **17.** $4\overline{)20,024}$

Problem Solving

18. **Writing to Explain** Is 513 ÷ 5 a little less than 10, a little more than 10, a little less than 100, or a little more than 100? How do you know?

19. Miguel earned $505 doing chores for $5 per hour. How many hours did Miguel work?

A 11 **B** 101 **C** 110 **D** 111

20. **Reasoning** Which compatible numbers would you use for 327 ÷ 6? Explain your reasoning.

21. David runs 9 miles per day. Last year, he ran 972 miles. How many days did it take him to run 972 miles?

22. **Writing to Explain** Javier said 1,621 ÷ 4 is 405 R1. Josiah disagreed. Who is correct? Explain Javier's mistake, if any.

23. **Reasoning** Why is it helpful in using estimation to solve a division problem at the beginning?

24. **Think About the Process** Is the process of solving 1,760,008 ÷ 8 the same as the process in the example? Explain.

25. The world's longest cartoon strip has 242 panels. It was drawn by 35 artists in about 8 hours. About how many panels were drawn in one hour?

A 15 **B** 20 **C** 30 **D** 45

Lesson

4-6

NS 2.2 Demonstrate proficiency with division, including division with positive decimals and long division with multidigit divisors.

Dividing by 2-Digit Divisors

What are the steps for dividing by 2-digit numbers?

A theater sold 428 tickets for a show. A section in this theater has 64 seats. How many sections must there be to seat all the ticket holders?

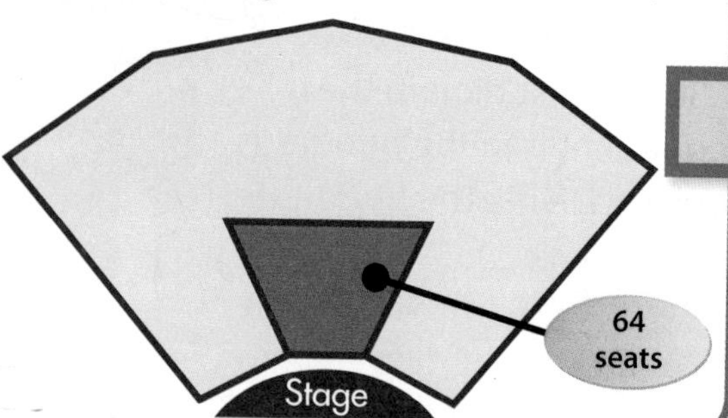

Choose an Operation Divide to find the total number of sections.

Another Example How can estimation help you find $330 \div 42$?

Step 1

Estimate first.

$330 \div 42$ is about $320 \div 40$, or 8.

Tip *Think of 32 tens ÷ 4 tens = 8.*

Step 2

Divide the ones. Multiply and subtract.

8 groups of 42 or $8 \times 42 = 336$.

Since $336 > 330$, my estimate is too high.

$$\begin{array}{r} 8 \\ 42\overline{)330} \\ -\ 336 \\ \hline \end{array}$$

Oops!

Step 3

Revise your estimate. Since 8 was too high, try 7 and divide.

7 groups of 42 or $7 \times 42 = 294$

$330 - 294 = 36$

$36 < 42$, so I do not have to divide again.

$$\begin{array}{r} 7 \\ 42\overline{)330} \\ -\ 294 \\ \hline 36 \end{array}$$

Answer: 7 R36

Step 4

Check your work.

$7 \times 42 = 294$

$294 + 36 = 330$

Explain It

1. In Step 1, how did the estimate tell you to start dividing ones?
2. In Step 2, how did you know that your first estimate of 8 was too high?

Step 1

Estimate to help decide where to place the first digit in the quotient.

428 ÷ 64 is about 420 ÷ 70, or 6.

Start dividing ones.

Step 2

Divide the ones. Multiply and subtract.

```
     6 R44
64)428
 - 384
    44
```

428 ÷ 64 = 6 R44

Step 3

Check:

```
   64
×   6
  384
+  44
  428
```

So, the theater must have 7 sections.

Guided Practice*

Do you know HOW?

Copy and complete.

1. 12)115 = ▯ R ▯; − ▯▯▯; ▯

2. 31)243 = ▯ R ▯▯; − ▯▯▯; ▯▯

Do you UNDERSTAND?

3. Can the remainder in either example be greater than the divisor? Why or why not?

4. In the example above, if the theater had sold 612 tickets, how many sections must it have?

Independent Practice

Leveled Practice Copy and complete.

5. 38)325 = ▯ R2▯; − 3▯▯; 2▯

6. 52)403 = 7 R ▯9; − ▯▯4; ▯9

7. 74)693 = ▯ R ▯7; − 66▯; ▯7

8. 33)301 = ▯ R ▯; − ▯▯▯; ▯

In **9** through **24**, divide.

9. 57)550	**10.** 29)254	**11.** 46)260	**12.** 56)528
13. 51)293	**14.** 19)119	**15.** 91)628	**16.** 40)180
17. 396 ÷ 42	**18.** 275 ÷ 38	**19.** 179 ÷ 22	**20.** 345 ÷ 85
21. 48)4,407	**22.** 91)5,543	**23.** 75)2,969	**24.** 82)3,616

*For another example, see Set E on page 109.

Problem Solving

25. Use the table at the right to answer the following questions.

    a What is the total capacity for all four exhibits at the History Museum?

    b How many class groups of 24 could view the showing at the Interactive Exhibit at the same time?

Data

History Museum Capacity	
Governor Exhibit	68
Landmark Exhibit	95
Early 1900s Exhibit	85
Interactive Exhibit	260

26. Chen's band put on a concert at school. There were 702 people in the audience. Each ticket cost $8. The audience was seated in 13 sections. If each section had the same number of people, how many people were in each section?

27. Mrs. Dugan collects antiques. She bought 7 antique chairs for which she paid a total of $1,050. Each chair was made with a different type of wood. If each chair cost the same amount, how much did each chair cost?

28. Mr. Nolan changes the oil in his car every 4,000 miles. He uses 3 quarts of oil each time. How many quarts of oil will he have used after 12,000 miles?

29. If you estimate 125×22 by rounding to the nearest ten, will you get an overestimate or an underestimate?

30. Twenty members of the photography club took 559 pictures. If they use memory cards that hold 85 pictures per card, how many cards will they use?

31. The annual music festival featured different posters for sale. The sale of jazz band posters brought in $1,312. If each poster was $16, how many were sold?

32. **Writing to Explain** Explain how you know the answer to the problem shown below has an error.

```
     8 R24
16)152
  - 128
     24
```

33. Rachel wanted to get 8 hours of sleep before a test. She went to bed at 9:00 P.M. and woke up at 6:00 A.M. How many more hours of sleep did Rachel get than the 8 hours she wanted?

    A 3 more hours **C** 1 more hour

    B 9 more hours **D** No more hours

34. **Writing to Explain** Explain why 0.2 and 0.02 are NOT equivalent.

35. In a large restaurant, there are 9 times as many chairs as tables. The restaurant is famous for its very spicy chili. If the restaurant has 342 chairs, how many tables are in the restaurant?

Mixed Problem Solving

Math and Social Studies

1. Before the Gold Rush of 1849, most people traveling to the west were headed to California, Oregon, or Utah. Between 1841 and 1848, about 11,000 people had migrated to Oregon. This was about four times as many people as had migrated to California in the same period. About how many people had migrated to California during that time?

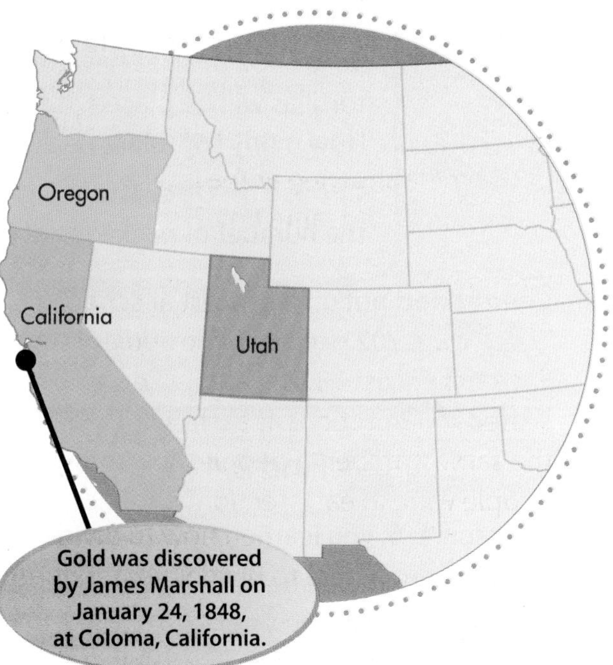
Oregon
California
Utah
Gold was discovered by James Marshall on January 24, 1848, at Coloma, California.

2. During the peak Gold Rush Years of 1849–1854, about six times as many people traveled to California as traveled to Oregon. If about 35,000 traveled to Oregon in that time, about how many people traveled to California?

3. Before the discovery of gold in California in 1848, California had a population of about 150,000 Native Americans plus about 13,000 people other than Native Americans. By 1860, California's population had grown to about 380,000. How much did the population increase from 1848 to 1860?

4. Even though James Marshall discovered gold, he never "struck it rich" and spent his last years in poverty. He died in 1885. How many years passed after he discovered gold until he died?

5. From April 1849 to April 1850, about 62,000 gold seekers arrived on ships at the port in San Francisco. From January, 1849, through December, 1849, 20,000 had migrated overland on various southern routes. About how many gold seekers traveled to California by ship or overland by southern routes from January, 1849, through April, 1850?

6. **Strategy Focus** Solve using the strategy Act it Out.

   How many different teams of 3 can be chosen from 4 people?

Lesson

4-7

NS 2.2 Demonstrate proficiency with division, including division with positive decimals and long division with multidigit divisors.

More Dividing by 2-Digit Divisors

How can you divide larger numbers?

So far, 467 tortillas have been made. These tortillas will be placed in packages of 15. How many complete packages will be filled?

Choose an Operation Divide to find the number of packages of tortillas.

15 per package

Another Example **Find 2,413 ÷ 21.**

In Lesson 4–6, you learned how to divide by 2-digit divisors. You will use the same procedure to divide greater numbers by 2-digit divisors.

Step 1

Estimate. Decide where to place the first digit.

Use compatible numbers.

2,400 ÷ 24 = 100

Start dividing hundreds.

Step 2

Divide the hundreds. Multiply and subtract. Continue the process.

```
     114 R19
21)2,413
  - 21
     31
   - 21
     103
   - 84
     19
```

Step 3

Check.

```
   114
 ×  21
   114
  2280
 2,394
 +  19
 2,413
```

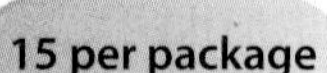

Explain It

1. How do you know that the first digit goes in the hundreds place?
2. Complete the problem above if you substitute 2,155 for 2,413.
3. If you are asked to find 6,319 ÷ 59, how do you know the quotient is greater than 100 before you actually divide?

Step 1

Estimate to help decide where to place the first digit in the quotient.

Use compatible numbers.

450 ÷ 15 = 30

Start dividing tens.

Step 2

Divide the tens. Multiply and subtract. Continue the process.

```
   31 R2
15)467
 - 45
    17
  - 15
     2
```

Step 3

Check:

```
   31
 × 15
  465
 +  2
  467
```

So far, 31 packages of tortillas will be filled.

Guided Practice*

Do you know HOW?

Copy and complete.

1. 47)985 (R)
2. 33)678 (R)

For **3** and **4**, divide.

3. 16)298
4. 23)292

Do you UNDERSTAND?

5. **Writing to Explain** In the problem above, why will 31 packages be filled instead of 32?
6. How many packages will 627 tortillas fill?
7. How do you decide where to place the first digit in the quotient for Exercises 1–4?

Independent Practice

Leveled Practice Copy and complete.

8. 36)584 (R), − ▢▢, ▢▢▢, − ▢1▢, 8
9. 45)981 (R), − ▢0, ▢1, − ▢▢, ▢▢
10. 56)674 (R), − ▢▢, ▢▢▢, − ▢▢▢, ▢

In **11** through **22**, divide.

11. 76)864
12. 23)279
13. 63)710
14. 18)638
15. 48)582
16. 26)784
17. 13)989
18. 72)2,532
19. 76)8,641
20. 23)2,799
21. 63)7,109
22. 38)5,821

For another example, see Set E on page 109.

Problem Solving

23. Writing to Explain If you are asked to find 621 ÷ 59, how do you know the quotient will be greater than 10 before you actually divide?

24. Julita bought a sandwich for $3.50 and a glass of juice for $1.75. The tax was $0.42. She paid with a $10 bill. How much change did she get?

25. An outdoor concert company is putting on 12 concerts this summer. Each concert is sold out. The company sold a total of 972 seats. How many people will attend each performance?

A 8 **B** 79 **C** 80 **D** 81

26. Julio spends about $\frac{1}{2}$ hour reading every night. Julio owns 8 science fiction books, 12 mystery books, and 7 history books. He wants to add enough books to his collection to have 40 books. How many more books does he need?

27. There are 120 minutes in 2 hours. How many minutes are there in 15 hours?

28. What compatible numbers can you use to estimate 803 ÷ 86?

29. One of the Thorny Devil lizard's favorite foods is ants. It can eat up to 45 ants per minute. How long would it take it to eat 540 ants?

A 9 minutes

B 10 minutes

C 12 minutes

D 15 minutes

30. Number Sense Decide if each statement is true or false. Explain.

a 710 ÷ 20 is greater than 30.

b 821 ÷ 40 is less than 20.

c 300 ÷ 15 is exactly 20.

31. Braedy had $5 when she left the county fair. She spent $11 on her ticket, and she bought lunch for $6. After lunch, she spent $17 on games and rides. How much money did Braedy bring to the county fair?

Stop and Practice

Find the quotient. Estimate to check if the answer is reasonable.

1. 96 ÷ 4 **2.** 77 ÷ 8 **3.** $9\overline{)475}$ **4.** 805 ÷ 2

5. $3\overline{)1{,}804}$ **6.** $6\overline{)87}$ **7.** 95 ÷ 32 **8.** $17\overline{)35}$

9. 299 ÷ 74 **10.** $74\overline{)614}$ **11.** 608 ÷ 67 **12.** $23\overline{)281}$

13. $24\overline{)984}$ **14.** 847 ÷ 84 **15.** $56\overline{)702}$ **16.** 600 ÷ 51 **17.** 728 ÷ 51

Find the difference. Estimate to check if the answer is reasonable.

18. 9,000 − 486 **19.** 8,030 − 6,090 **20.** 436 − 85 **21.** 6,821 − 5,932 **22.** 8,005 − 3,213

Error Search Find each quotient that is not correct. Write it correctly and explain the error.

23. 47 ÷ 3 = 15 R2 **24.** $6\overline{)606}$ = 11 **25.** 629 ÷ 2 = 314 R1

26. 89 ÷ 31 = 2 R27 **27.** $51\overline{)154}$ = 3 **28.** 879 ÷ 27 = 31 R42

Number Sense

Estimating and Reasoning Write whether each statement is true or false. Explain your reasoning.

29. The quotient of 7,528 ÷ 9 is greater than 800.

30. The product of 19 and 487 is closer to 10,000 than 8,000.

31. The sum of 73,342 and 27,120 is less than 100,000.

32. The quotient of 759 ÷ 25 has a remainder that is less than 25.

33. The difference of 57.6 − 12.3 is 0.3 greater than 45.6.

34. The sum of 4.143 and 5.709 is between 9 and 11.

Lesson

4-8

NS 2.2 Demonstrate proficiency with division, including division with positive decimals and long division with multidigit divisors.
Also **NS 1.1**

Estimating and Dividing with Greater Numbers

How do you divide greater numbers?

Maria purchased 43 computers for her business. Because she bought so many, the final cost was $11,094. What was the cost of one computer?

Choose an Operation Divide to find how many times 43 will go into $11,094.

Guided Practice*

Do you know HOW?

For **1** and **2**, estimate each quotient.

1. 22,649 ÷ 29

2. 34,143 ÷ 62

For **3** and **4**, divide. Check by multiplying.

3. $12\overline{)14{,}555}$

4. $23\overline{)31{,}897}$

Do you UNDERSTAND?

5. Writing to Explain How can you use multiplication to check if the quotient in the problem above is correct?

6. For Exercises 3 and 4, how do you know the first digit of each quotient is in the thousands place?

Independent Practice

For **7** through **10**, estimate each quotient.

7. 5,185 ÷ 17

8. 18,852 ÷ 38

9. 13,014 ÷ 56

10. 52,846 ÷ 93

Leveled Practice Copy and complete.

11.
```
     3▢
97)3,298
  ▢▢1
   38
 - ▢8
    0
```

12.
```
       ▢2▢ R62
72)23,390
   2▢
    17▢
    1▢4
     3▢▢
     28▢
      6▢
```

13.
```
      ▢,4▢▢ R▢▢
31)44,573
   ▢▢
    135
    ▢▢▢
     11▢
     ▢▢
     24▢
     2▢▢
      ▢6
```

14.
```
      ▢,▢▢▢ R▢▢
45)99,740
   ▢▢
    ▢▢
    ▢▢
     ▢▢
     ▢▢
     ▢▢▢
     ▢▢▢
      ▢▢
```

15. $51\overline{)57{,}928}$

16. $68\overline{)72{,}743}$

17. $83\overline{)87{,}282}$

18. $76\overline{)18{,}240}$

*For another example, see Set B on page 108.

Step 1

Estimate. Decide where to place the first digit.

$12{,}000 \div 40 = 300$

The first digit in the quotient is in the hundreds place.

Start dividing hundreds.

Step 2

$$\begin{array}{r} 3 \\ 43\overline{)11{,}094} \\ -129 \\ \hline \end{array}$$

Oops!

$3 \times 43 = 129$

The estimate is too high. Try 2.

$$\begin{array}{r} 2 \\ 43\overline{)11{,}094} \\ -86 \\ \hline 24 \end{array}$$

$2 \times 43 = 86$

Step 3

Bring down the tens. Continue dividing.

$$\begin{array}{r} 25 \\ 43\overline{)11{,}094} \\ -86 \\ \hline 249 \\ -215 \\ \hline 34 \end{array}$$

$5 \times 43 = 215$

Step 4

Bring down the ones.

$$\begin{array}{r} 258 \\ 43\overline{)11{,}094} \\ -86 \\ \hline 249 \\ -215 \\ \hline 344 \\ -344 \\ \hline 0 \end{array}$$

$8 \times 43 = 344$

Each computer costs $258.

Problem Solving

19. The city of Santa Barbara held a chess tournament. Shown are the fees charged for the tournament.

Data

Chess Tournament	
Student entry fee	$15
Adult entry fee	$18
Reserve a chess board	$12

a The total student entry fees paid were $3,105. How many students participated?

b There are about ten times as many students as adults registered for the tournament. About how many adults are registered?

20. The Arches National Park in Utah covers over 73,000 acres and has 2,000 stone arches. A 40-mile round-trip paved road in the park takes visitors past most of the arches. If a visitor drove the entire paved road, about how many arches would he or she see per mile?

A 20 **C** 50

B 26 **D** 75

21. **Number Sense** Give three factors whose product is about 10,000.

22. There are 12 inches in 1 foot. How many inches are there in 120 feet?

23. There are 1,185 possible words that can be used for a spelling bee. This number is 15 times more than would be used in the contest. How many words will be used in the contest?

A 7.9 **C** 709

B 79 **D** 790

24. Tabitha's class is making flash cards to study the 1,185 words for the spelling bee. There are 5 teams in her class. How many flash cards will each team need to make?

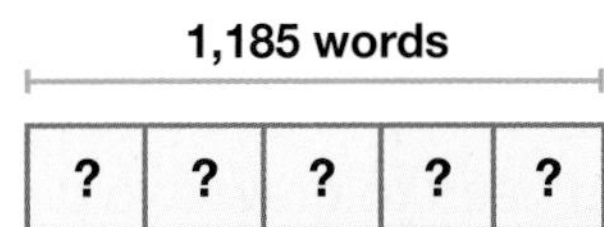

Lesson

4-9

AF 1.1 Grade 6 Write and solve one-Step linear equations in one variable.
Also **MR 2.3**

Problem Solving

Draw a Picture and Write an Equation

The students in Bryan's class sold tickets to the annual school band concert. How many tickets did the class sell?

Total ticket sales
$568

Another Example

Marcella bought a new computer for $449 and a printer for $79. The store allows her to pay the total cost in 24 equal monthly installments. How much will her monthly payments be?

The total cost of the computer and printer is unknown.
Marcella will pay the total cost in 24 equal monthly installments.

Draw a Picture

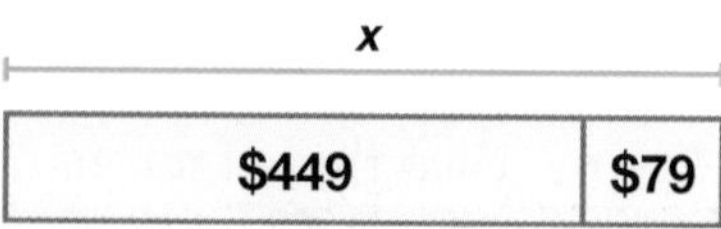

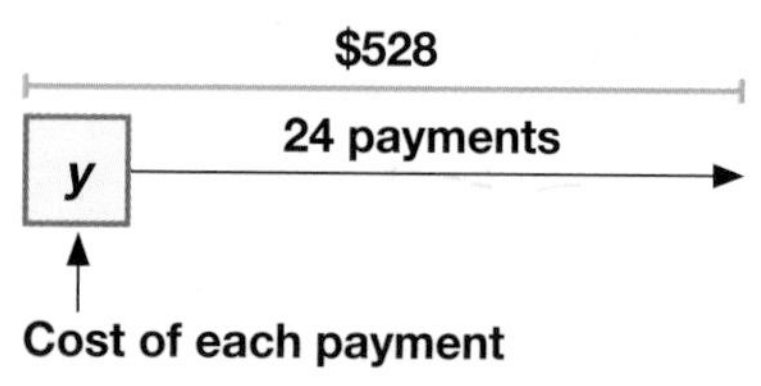

Write an Equation

Let x = the total cost of the computer and printer.

$\$449 + \$79 = x$
$x = \$528$

$$\begin{array}{r} \overset{1\,1}{449} \\ +\ \ 79 \\ \hline 528 \end{array}$$

Now, divide the total cost by the number of monthly payments.

Let y = the monthly payment.

$\$528 \div 24 = y$
$y = \$22$

$$\begin{array}{r} 22 \\ 24\overline{)528} \\ -\ 48 \\ \hline 48 \\ 48 \\ \hline 0 \end{array}$$

The monthly payments will be $22.

Explain It

1. Why did you need to draw two pictures?
2. How can you check your answer?

Read and Understand

What do I know?

Each ticket cost $8. Total ticket sales were $568.

What am I asked to find?

The number of tickets sold by the class.

Plan and Solve

Draw a Picture

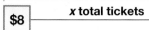

$568

$8 | ***x* total tickets** →

Cost per ticket

Write an Equation

Let x = the number of tickets the class sold.

Divide: $\$568 \div \$8 = x$

$\$568 \div \$8 = 71$

$$\begin{array}{r} 71 \\ 8\overline{)568} \\ -\ 56 \\ \hline 8 \\ 8 \\ \hline 0 \end{array}$$

The class sold 71 tickets.

Look Back and Check

Check the solution by multiplying.

Each ticket cost $8. There were 71 tickets sold.

$$\begin{array}{r} 71 \\ \times\ 8 \\ \hline 568 \end{array}$$

Guided Practice*

Do you know HOW?

Write an equation and solve.

1. A state in the U.S. has 990 acres set aside for 11 parks. If each park has the same number of acres, how many acres does each park have?

Total area: 990 acres

n	*n*	*n*	*n*	*n*	*n*	*n*	*n*	*n*	*n*	*n*

Acres for each park

Do you UNDERSTAND?

2. How can you check your answer for Problem 1? Show your work.

3. Write a Problem Write a real-world problem that uses division and can be solved by drawing a picture and writing an equation.

Independent Practice

In **4**, copy and complete the picture. Then write an equation and solve.

4. An auditorium has 230 seats with 46 seats in each section. How many sections does the auditorium have?

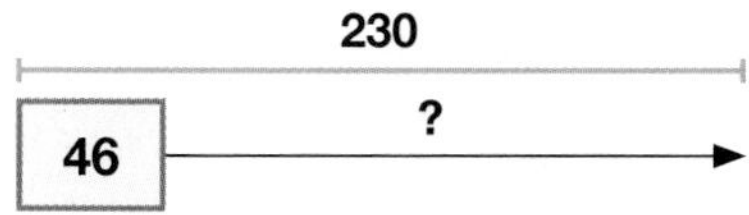

In **5**, draw a picture and write an equation. Solve.

5. Peter can put 20 cans in one box. How many boxes will he need for 489 cans?

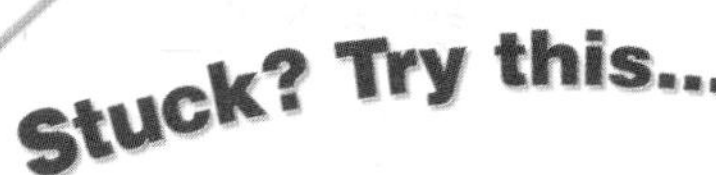

- What do I know?
- What am I asked to find?
- What diagram can I use to help understand the problem?
- Can I use addition, subtraction, multiplication, or division?
- Is all of my work correct?
- Did I answer the right question?
- Is my answer reasonable?

*For another example, see Set F on page 109.

Independent Practice

For **6** through **8**, use the table at the right.

Maple Tree Price List	
Name of Tree	**Box of 25**
Japanese Maple	$450
Bigleaf Maple	$200
Silver Maple	$725
Norway Maple	$550

6. Schock's Tree Farm has a large variety of young deciduous trees. Trees can be bought individually or in boxes of 25. What is the cost for 1 Silver Maple tree? Write an equation and solve.

7. What is the difference between the cost of one Japanese Maple tree and one Norway Maple tree?

8. Mr. Belding is purchasing trees for landscaping a house. What will be his total cost for 1 box of Bigleaf Maple trees, and 5 separate Norway Maple trees?

9. Brad has saved $1,095 for a 15-day vacation. If he spends the same amount each day, how much money can Brad spend each day?

10. Mrs. Beckman's class has a 15-minute break in the morning and a 10-minute break in the afternoon. How many minutes of break do the students have in two weeks?

11. Mindy's family planted a tree when it was 10 ft tall. It has grown about the same amount each year for the last 10 years. It was 12 ft tall after one year, 14 ft tall after two years, 16 ft tall after three years. How tall was the tree after six years? 10 years?

12. At the fifth-grade play, student tickets were $4, and adult tickets were $6. A total of $312 dollars was collected for all the tickets. If 54 students came to the play, how much money was collected for adult tickets?

Think About the Process

13. A total of 476 books were donated to a school. Out of those books, 56 were damaged and could not be used. The remaining books were packed into boxes holding 20 books apiece. Which expression could you use to find the number of books for each box?

A 476 + 56 + 20 **C** (476 − 56) ÷ 20

B (476 − 56) + 20 **D** (476 + 56) ÷ 20

14. Zoe bought 1.6 pounds of slaw and 2.8 pounds of macaroni. For lunch she served 0.9 pound of slaw. Which expression could you use to find the amount of the food she has left?

A 1.6 + 2.8 + 0.9 **C** 2.8 − 1.6 − 0.9

B 1.6 + 2.8 − 0.9 **D** 2.8 − 0.9

Mixed Problem Solving

1. A Pony Express rider named Tom traveled his route 15 times in one month. Approximately how many miles did Tom travel?

2. A letter sent from St. Joseph, Missouri was carried by 27 riders as it traveled to Sacramento, California. Approximately how many miles did the letter travel?

3. How many Pony Express riders would be needed to travel the 375 miles between Los Angeles and San Francisco?

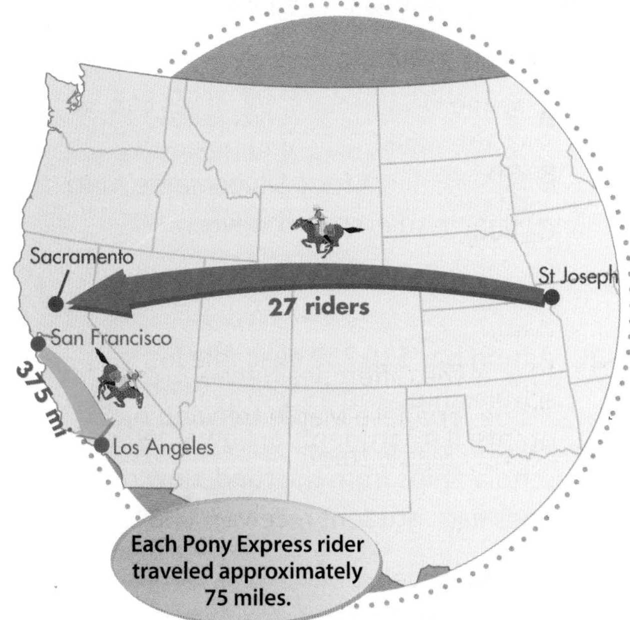

4. Marco Polo's journey through Asia lasted 24 years. If he traveled 72 miles per year, how many miles did he travel?

5. In 1542, the first European explorer landed in California. Gold was discovered in 1848. How many years passed after the first explorer landed until gold was discovered?

6. San Bernardino County, California, is about 33 times larger than Sutter County. Sutter County covers 609 square miles. About how many square miles is San Bernardino County?

7. At the "Boston Tea Party," there were 3 groups of colonists who boarded ships and dumped 342 crates of tea into the water. About how much tea was destroyed by each group of colonists?

8. One of Ferdinand Magellan's ships sailed around the Earth. If the trip took 16 months and there are about 30 days in each month, about how many days did the voyage take?

9. **Strategy Focus** Solve using the strategy Draw a Picture and Write an Equation.

   John bought 6 chairs that cost $49 each. How much did John pay for all of the chairs?

Test Prep

1. What is 2,400 ÷ 80? (4-1)

   A 3

   B 30

   C 300

   D 3,000

2. A fund has $10,752 available for scholarships and $5,250 available for grants. If 42 students are awarded equal scholarships from the fund, how much does each student receive? (4-8)

   A $125

   B $255

   C $256

   D $264

3. If the money shown is to be divided among 3 people, what should be the first step? (4-3)

   A Exchange the $100 bill for eight $10 bills and twenty $1 bills.

   B Exchange the two $10 bills for twenty $1 bills.

   C Exchange the $100 dollar bill for a hundred $1 bills.

   D Exchange the $100 dollar bill for ten $10 bills.

4. If 283 is divided by 4, where should the first digit of the quotient be placed? (4-4)

   A Because 4 is greater than 2, it should be in the tens place.

   B Because 4 is less than 2, it should be in the tens place.

   C Because 4 is greater than 2, it should be in the hundreds place.

   D Because 4 is less than 2, it should be in the hundreds place.

5. There are 12,156 special agents who work for the FBI. If the special agents are to be divided into groups of 32, about how many agents would be in each group? (4-8)

   A 4,000

   B 3,000

   C 400

   D 300

6. A company ordered 384 note pads. If there are 48 note pads in each box, how many boxes were ordered? (4-6)

   A 7

   B 8

   C 9

   D 12

7. Which of the following is another way to think of 27,000 ÷ 30? (4-1)

   A 27 tens ÷ 30 tens

   B 27 tens ÷ 3 tens

   C 270 tens ÷ 3 tens

   D 2,700 tens ÷ 3 tens

Test Prep

8. What is 818 ÷ 4? (4-5)

A 24 R2

B 25 R3

C 204 R2

D 205 R3

9. Shady Rivers summer camp has 188 campers this week. If there are 22 campers to each cabin, what is the least number of cabins needed? (4-6)

A 10

B 9

C 8

D 7

10. The lengths of two canals are given in the table. About how many times longer is the Erie Canal than the Chesapeake and Delaware? (4-2)

Data

Ship Canal	Length (in miles)
Chesapeake and Delaware Canal	14
Erie Canal	363

A 20

B 25

C 40

D 180

11. What is 384 ÷ 30? (4-7)

A 12

B 12 R14

C 12 R24

D 13

12. What is 186 ÷ 8? (4-4)

A 23 R2

B 23 R6

C 24 R2

D 24 R6

13. For a class project, Mr. Ray purchased 400 inches of ribbon. If the ribbon is to be divided evenly among 16 students, which of the following can be used to find p, the number of inches each piece will be? (4-9)

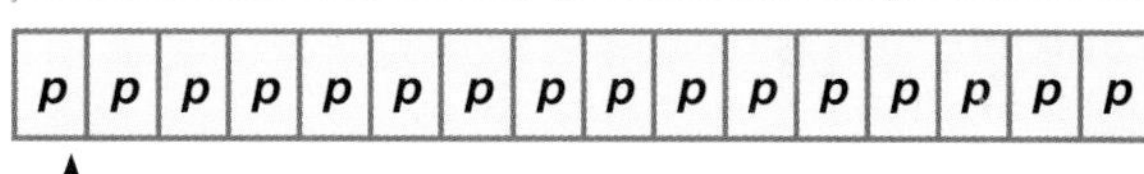

A $400 - 16 = p$

B $400 + 16 = p$

C $400 \times 16 = p$

D $400 \div 16 = p$

14. The Eades family is renting a lodge for a family reunion. The cost to rent the lodge is $975. If 65 people attend the reunion and each person pays the same price, how many dollars will each person pay? (4-7)

A $16

B $15

C $14

D $13

Reteaching

Set A, pages 78–79

Find 32,000 ÷ 80 using mental math. Use basic facts and patterns to help.

32 ÷ 8 = 4
320 ÷ 80 = 4
3,200 ÷ 80 = 40
32,000 ÷ 80 = 400

Think 32,000 ÷ 80 is the same as 3,200 tens ÷ 8 tens.

Remember that if the basic fact has a zero in the dividend, it should NOT be used to find the number of zeros in the quotient.

1. 360 ÷ 40 =
2. 270 ÷ 90 =
3. 180 ÷ 20 =
4. 750 ÷ 50 =
5. 2,100 ÷ 30 =
6. 4,800 ÷ 80 =
7. 5,400 ÷ 60 =
8. 6,300 ÷ 90 =

Set B, pages 80–81, 100–101

Estimate 364 ÷ 57.

Use compatible numbers and patterns.

364 ÷ 57
↓ ↓
360 ÷ 60 = 6

So, 364 ÷ 57 is about 6.

Remember that compatible numbers are numbers that are easy to compute in your head.

Estimate each quotient.

1. 168 ÷ 45
2. 525 ÷ 96
3. 379 ÷ 63
4. 234 ÷ 72
5. \$6,513 ÷ 73
6. \$7,489 ÷ 92
7. $47\overline{)51{,}908}$
8. $58\overline{)72{,}124}$

Set C, pages 82–84

Tell how much each person will get if 5 people share \$375 equally.

Use play money to help you divide. You can record your work as shown below.

$$\begin{array}{r} 75 \\ 5\overline{)375} \\ -35 \\ \hline 25 \\ 25 \\ \hline \end{array}$$

Each person gets \$75.

So, \$375 ÷ 5 = \$75.

Remember to regroup when necessary. Use play money to divide. Tell how much each person will get.

1. 4 people share \$284 equally
2. 6 people share \$546 equally
3. 9 people share \$675 equally
4. 7 people share \$728 equally
5. 8 people share \$872 equally
6. 2 people share \$184 equally
7. 3 people share \$627 equally

Set D, pages 86–88, 90–91

Find 549 ÷ 6.

Estimate first. 540 ÷ 6 = 90.

```
   91 R3
6)549
- 54
    9
  - 6
    3
```

Check: 91 × 6 = 546; 546 + 3 = 549.
The quotient is close to the estimate too.

So, 549 ÷ 6 = 91 R3.

Remember to multiply the quotient and the divisor, and then add the remainder, to check your problem.

1. 89 ÷ 9
2. 87 ÷ 3
3. 138 ÷ 8
4. 755 ÷ 5
5. 816 ÷ 4
6. 484 ÷ 6
7. 91 ÷ 3
8. 846 ÷ 7

Set E, pages 92–94, 96–98

Find 789 ÷ 19.

Estimate first. 800 ÷ 20 = 40.

```
    41 R10
19)789
 - 76
    29
  - 19
    10
```

Divide the tens. Multiply, subtract, and compare. Bring down the ones.

Divide the ones. Multiply, subtract, and compare. Check the quotient with your estimate.

Remember to check the quotient with your estimate.

1. 16)348
2. 24)819
3. 38)792
4. 42)523
5. 68)9,323
6. 77)9,664
7. 65)8,245
8. 46)7,956

Set F, pages 102–104

Draw a picture and write an equation. Solve.

A grocery store has 12 crates of apples. If each crate contains the same amount and there is a total of 696 apples, how many apples are in each crate?

696 apples											
a	*a*	*a*	*a*	*a*	*a*	*a*	*a*	*a*	*a*	*a*	*a*

Let *a* = apples in each crate.
696 ÷ 12 = *a*; *a* = 58

There are 58 apples in each crate.

Remember that drawing a picture can help you before writing an equation.

1. If marbles are packaged in bags of 50, how many bags are needed to package 1,750 marbles?
2. Bill has $1,045 to spend on his 11-day vacation. If Bill spends the same amount each day, how much will he spend?

Topic 5 Variables and Expressions

1 Passengers on a cruise ship can go ashore when the ship stops at ports of call like those in San Diego. How can order of operations be used to find the number of passengers left on the ship when other passengers get off the ship? You will find out in Lesson 5-5.

2 How can an algebraic expression be used to show the number of minutes you spend exercising each day? You will find out in Lesson 5-3.

3 If a hermit crab grows 1 inch per year, how long will it be in 5 years? 10 years? *x* years? You will find out in Lesson 5-2.

4 What is the total height of this giant ball of jeans sculpture, including the base? You will find out in Lesson 5-1.

Review What You Know!

Vocabulary

Choose the best term from the box.

- difference
- quotient
- product
- sum

1. The answer to a division problem is the _?_.
2. The _?_ of 5 and 7 is 12.
3. To find the _?_ between 16 and 4 you subtract.
4. Multiplying is the same as finding the _?_.

Mixed Practice

Find each answer.

5. $32 \div 4$
6. 35×100
7. $47 + 92$
8. $\frac{1}{4} + \frac{2}{4}$
9. $3.4 - 2.7$
10. $1.9 + 7$
11. $3 + \frac{1}{2}$
12. $75 \div 5$
13. $\$3.75 + \$2.49$
14. $8\frac{5}{8} - 1\frac{2}{8}$

Patterns

Writing to Explain Write an answer for the question.

15. What comes next in the pattern below? Explain how you know.

$$7 \times 10 = 70$$
$$7 \times 100 = 700$$
$$7 \times 1{,}000 = 7{,}000$$

Lesson

5-1

AF 1.2 Use a letter to represent an unknown number; write and evaluate simple algebraic expressions in one variable by substitution. Also AF 1.0

Variables and Expressions

How can you translate words into expressions?

What expression shows the weight of the mixed nuts after the weight of the jar is subtracted?

A variable is a letter or symbol that represents an unknown amount that can vary, or change.

Guided Practice*

Do you know HOW?

In **1** through **4**, use a variable to write an algebraic expression that represents the word phrase.

1. twice the number of people

2. $7 less than the current price

3. 8 more gumballs than Javier has

4. a number of students divided into 2 teams

Do you UNDERSTAND?

5. What would the expression for the weight of the mixed nuts be if the weight of the jar was 8 oz?

6. **Writing to Explain** Why is a variable used in the example at the top?

7. Write two word phrases that could be translated as $25 \times p$.

Independent Practice

For **8** through **11**, translate each algebraic expression into words.

8. $n + 9$ **9.** $x \div 12$ **10.** $y - 4$ **11.** $8m$

For **12** through **20**, write each word phrase as an algebraic expression.

12. subtract a number from 10 **13.** the product of 9 and a number **14.** add 6 to a number

15. 6 divided by a number **16.** a number decreased by 12 **17.** 9 plus a number

18. a number added to 4 **19.** the quotient of a number and 8 **20.** 4 less a number

*For another example, see Set A on page 132.

An algebraic expression is a mathematical phrase involving variables, numbers, and operations.

Operation	Word Phrase	Algebraic Expression
Addition	a number *plus* 4 a number *added* to 4	$w + 4$
Subtraction	a number *minus* 4 a number *less* 4	$w - 4$
Multiplication	4 *times* a number	$4 \times w$ or $4w$
Division	a number *divided* by 4	$w \div 4$ or $\frac{w}{4}$

Since the weight of the mixed nuts varies, let w represent the total weight of the jar and the mixed nuts.

So, $w - 4$ is the weight of the mixed nuts after the weight of the jar is subtracted.

Problem Solving

21. You and three of your friends are going to share a package of granola bars equally. Write an algebraic expression to show this situation.

22. In January, Winifred had $1,369.57 in her savings account. In December, she had $2,513.34 in her account. How much more money did she have in December than in January?

23. Jeff added $\frac{4}{5}$ cup of water to $\frac{2}{3}$ cup of lemonade concentrate. Is there more water or concentrate?

24. **Writing to Explain** How are the expressions $7 - g$ and $g - 7$ different?

25. **Think About the Process** Nao has 6 fewer CDs than Emily. If c represents the number of CDs Emily has, which expression tells how many CDs Nao has?

A $c + 6$ **C** $6 - c$

B $c - 6$ **D** $6 + c$

26. A person has to be at least 48 inches tall to ride a roller coaster. Jill, who is 12 years old, is taller than 48 inches. Which expression shows Jill's height?

A $(12 + t) - 48$ **C** $(48 - 12) + t$

B $48t$ **D** $48 + t$

27. This drawing of the sculpture of a ball of jeans shows a stand beneath it. If the stand and sculpture measure 18 feet, which equation shows how to find the height of the sculpture?

x

2 ft

A $18 + x = 2$ **C** $x - 18 = 2$

B $x + 2 = 18$ **D** $2 - 18 = x$

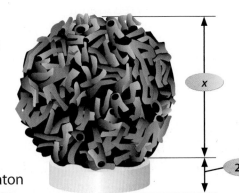

28. The largest capitol building in the U.S. is located in Baton Rouge, Louisiana. It is 164 feet taller than the United States Capitol in Washington, D.C. which is x feet tall. Write an expression for the height of the capitol in Baton Rouge.

Lesson

5-2

AF 1.2 Use a letter to represent an unknown number; write and evaluate simple algebraic expressions in one variable by substitution. Also **AF 1.0**

Patterns and Expressions

How can you use patterns to show relationships?

Shawna wanted to buy tickets to the concert for herself and some friends. What is the total cost of all of the tickets?

Let t = the number of tickets purchased.

Other Examples

How can you evaluate an algebraic expression?

In Lesson 5-1 you learned how to write an algebraic expression. Now you will write and evaluate an expression to solve a problem.

Evaluating an Addition Expression

Evaluate $x + 7$ for $x = 6$.
Replace x with 6 in the expression.

$x + 7$

↓

$6 + 7 = 13$

Evaluating a Division Expression

Evaluate $z \div 3$ for $z = 9$.
Replace z with 9 in the expression.

$z \div 3$

↓

$9 \div 3 = 3$

Writing and Evaluating an Expression

After 5 weeks, Sean's plant was h inches tall and Fred's plant was 3 inches taller.

Write an algebraic expression for the height of Fred's plant.

$h + 3$

Evaluate the expression for $h = 3$ and $h = 5$.

h	3	5
$h + 3$	$3 + 3 = 6$	$5 + 3 = 8$

Explain It

1. Explain how you could figure out the height of Fred's plant if you knew the height of Sean's plant.
2. What is the shortest possible height of Fred's plant after 5 weeks?

Shawna made a table.

Number of Tickets	Total Cost (in dollars)
2	8
3	12
4	16
5	20
t	$4 \times t$

+4 +4 +4

Shawna saw a pattern: For each ticket, the total cost increased by $4.

She wrote an algebraic expression to show the relationship between the number of tickets and the total cost.

The total cost of tickets for any number of friends can be represented by the algebraic expression $4 \times t$.

Guided Practice*

Do you know HOW?

1. Megan and Travis have the same birthday, but Travis is 6 years older. In the table, m is Megan's age and $m + 6$ is Travis's age. Complete the table.

m	3	5	
$m + 6$			14

Do you UNDERSTAND?

2. When Megan was 5 years old, how old was Travis?

3. What was Megan's age when Travis was 14?

4. **Writing to Explain** If you know Travis's age, how can you find Megan's age?

Independent Practice

In **5** through **19**, evaluate each expression for $n = 5$ and $n = 2$.

5. $\frac{40}{n}$ **6.** $4.5 + n$ **7.** $n \times 16$ **8.** $50 - n$ **9.** $12n$

10. $\frac{30}{n}$ **11.** $8.6 + n$ **12.** $9n$ **13.** $36 - n$ **14.** $8 \times n$

15. $\frac{10}{n}$ **16.** $3n$ **17.** $n + 5$ **18.** $7 - n$ **19.** $\frac{70}{n}$

In **20** through **31**, evaluate each expression for $n = 10$ and $n = 12$.

20. $\frac{n}{2}$ **21.** $n + 4.9$ **22.** $18n$ **23.** $44.7 - n$

24. $n - 5$ **25.** $n + 6.2$ **26.** $10n$ **27.** $33.6 - n$

28. $\frac{60}{n}$ **29.** $3n$ **30.** $n - 8$ **31.** $n + 3.17$

*For another example, see Set B on page 132.

Problem Solving

32. **Strategy Focus** Use the strategy Make a Table to solve the following problem.

There are 3 classrooms in the second grade. There are 24 students in Mrs. Smithfield's room, 27 students in Mr. Rodgers's room, and 21 students in Miss Jones's room. Each student gets 2 tangerines for a snack. How many tangerines does each teacher need?

33. Henry has 7 quarters, 4 dimes, 17 nickels, and 26 pennies in his bank. If he doesn't count the pennies, what is the value of his other coins?

A \$2.15

B \$2.60

C \$3.00

D \$3.26

34. A plane can travel 400 miles for each hour it flies. How long will it take you to travel approximately 1,600 miles from Oakland, California, to Beaumont, Texas?

35. Joseph is 50 inches tall. Paul is y inches taller than Joseph, and 3 inches taller than Dan. Write an expression for how much taller Paul is than Joseph.

36. Which number is less than 0.09?

F 0.9 **H** 0.11

G 0.1 **J** 0.01

37. Write an algebraic expression to represent the cost of a CD for m dollars with a \$2 off coupon.

38. What is another way to write the expression $\frac{56}{n}$?

39. **Writing to Explain** Why can a variable be used to represent a number?

40. For a science experiment, you need to mix 4 grams of baking soda for every 25 milliliters of vinegar. How many grams of baking soda do you need to do an experiment with 75 milliliters of vinegar? How did you find the answer?

41. **Think About the Process** A century is a period of time that is 100 years long. Which expression can be used to find the number of years in x centuries?

A $100 + x$ **C** $\frac{100}{x}$

B $100 - x$ **D** $100x$

42. **Writing to Explain** The size of the hermit crab's shell depends on the size of the crab. Look at the table below. If a 2-inch hermit crab grows 1 inch per year, use words to describe a rule that will show how long a 2-inch crab will grow in x years. Write an expression to find how large this crab will grow in x years.

Length	2	3	4	5	6	7	8	9	10	11	12	
Number of Years	0	1	2	3	4	5	6	7	8	9	10	x

Stop and Practice

Find the value of each expression for $w = 8$.

1. $w + 8$ **2.** $12 - w$ **3.** $8w$ **4.** $\frac{72}{w}$

5. $6w$ **6.** $\frac{w}{2}$ **7.** $4.98 + w$ **8.** $w - 2.4$

Find the value of each expression for $p = 3.8$.

9. $7.25 - p$ **10.** $4.08 + p$ **11.** $p + 1.2$ **12.** $p - 2.75$

13. $p + p$ **14.** $6 - p$ **15.** $7 + p$ **16.** $p - 3.75$

Find the product. Estimate to check if the answer is reasonable.

17. 587×340 **18.** $5{,}950 \times 45$ **19.** 238×479 **20.** 74×60 **21.** $8{,}007 \times 6$

22. $8{,}118 \times 27$ **23.** 94×62 **24.** $5{,}750 \times 3$ **25.** $1{,}234 \times 15$ **26.** 590×64

Error Search Find each expression that is not correct when $a = 5$. Write it correctly and explain the error.

27. $a + 9 = 14$ **28.** $a - a = 10$ **29.** $6.95 + a = 7$ **30.** $a - 3.7 = 1.3$

Number Sense

Estimating and Reasoning Write whether each statement is true or false. Explain your reasoning.

31. $6 - p$ has a value less than 5, when $p = 1.5$.

32. The sum of 15.26 and 60.56 is greater than 75 but less than 77.

33. The product of 30 and 420 is 600 less than 12,000.

34. The difference of 2,624 – 1,307 is 7 less than 1,324.

35. The sum of 16.3 and 11.9 is less than 27.

36. The product of 3 and 6,495 is closer to 21,000 than 18,000.

Lesson

5-3

AF 1.2 Use a letter to represent an unknown number; write and evaluate simple algebraic expressions in one variable by substitution.

More Patterns and Expressions

How can you write and evaluate expressions with variables?

Write an expression for finding the total cost of a service call from Matteo's Electrical Repair. Evaluate the expression for service calls that last 2 hours, 4 hours, and 5 hours.

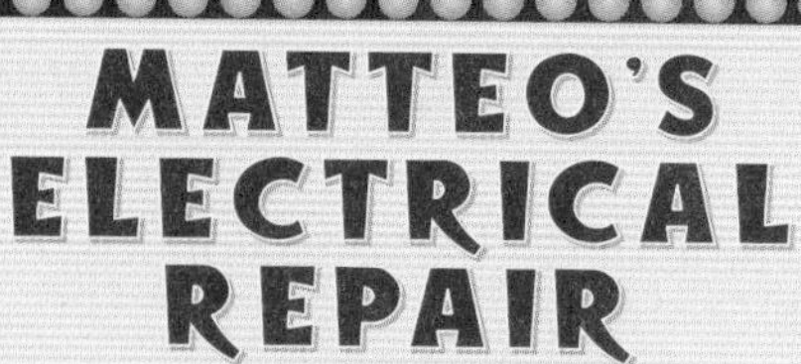

Another Example How can you write a word phrase as an algebraic expression?

Let n stand for the number.

Word Phrase	Algebraic Expression
Five times a number, plus two	$5n + 2$
Two less than five times a number	$5n - 2$
Two more than five times a number	$5n + 2$
Two minus five times a number	$2 - 5n$

Sometimes a word phrase can be interpreted in different ways. The word phrase below can be interpreted in two different ways. Parentheses are used to make the algebraic expression clear.

Word Phrase: Five times a number plus 2

Algebraic Expressions: $(5 \times n) + 2$, or $5 \times (n + 2)$

Remember that operations inside parentheses are completed first.

Explain It

1. Why is the comma in the first word phrase above important?

2. How do the parentheses make the expressions $(5 \times n) + 2$ and $5 \times (n + 2)$ different?

Step 1

The total cost is the fee plus the charge per hour times the number of hours.

Write an expression for the total cost. Use h for the number of hours.

The expression for the total cost in dollars is $55 + 65h$.

Step 2

Evaluate the expression for various numbers of hours. Substitute each value for h in the expression $55 + 65h$.

For 2 hours: $55 + (65 \times 2) = 55 + 130 = 185$

For 4 hours: $55 + (65 \times 4) = 55 + 260 = 315$

For 5 hours: $55 + (65 \times 5) = 55 + 325 = 380$

The total cost for a 2 hour service call is $185, for a 4 hour service call is $315, and for a 5 hour service call is $380.

Guided Practice*

Do you know HOW?

Write an algebraic expression for each word phrase. Let x stand for the number.

1. Three times a number, plus 10
2. Four less than a number times 2
3. Eight plus a number times 5
4. Forty minus two times a number

Do you UNDERSTAND?

5. How much does Matteo Electrical Repair charge for 3 hours of work?
6. Evaluate $3n + 18$ for $n = 2$.
7. Evaluate $3n + 18$ for $n = 3$.
8. Does $3n + 18$ have the same meaning as $3 \times n + 18$? Explain.

Independent Practice

For **9** through **12**, write an algebraic expression for each phrase. Let n stand for the number.

9. Nine times a number, minus six
10. Seven less than a number times three
11. Four more than a number, times twelve
12. Eight plus a number times sixteen

For **13** through **16**, evaluate the expressions for $p = 21$ and $k = 64$.

13. $3p + 52$
14. $10k - 249$
15. $432 - 2p$
16. $3p + 4k$

For **17** through **20**, evaluate the expressions for $r = 13$ and $h = 52$

17. $(8 + r) \times 3$
18. $352 - 4h$
19. $5r + 97$
20. $9r - 2h$

*For another example, see Set C on page 132.

Problem Solving

You walk for 30 minutes each day on a treadmill. You also do a number of weight-lifting exercises. You do each weight-lifting exercise for 5 minutes.

21. Write an expression for the number of minutes you spend exercising each day. Let *e* represent the number of weight-lifting exercises.

22. How many minutes do you exercise on a day when you do 3 weight-lifting exercises? 6 weight-lifting exercises?

Sasha works in a clothing store. She earns $20 per day, plus a $2 commission for each sale.

23. Write an expression for the amount of money Sasha earns each day. Let *s* represent the number of sales she makes.

24. How much does Sasha earn per day if she has 12 sales?
19 sales?
32 sales?

For **25** through **27**, use the table at right.

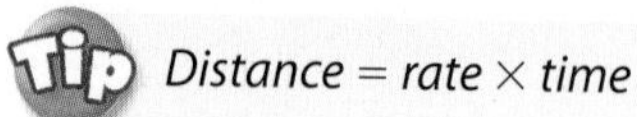
Distance = rate × time

Data

Travel Times	
From Los Angeles, CA	**Time**
To Dallas, TX	3 hrs
To Tampa, FL	5 hrs

25. A plane travels 425 miles per hour. Write an expression to show the distance it travels, if *t* represents hours.

26. How far is it from Los Angeles to Tampa?

27. How far is it from Los Angeles to Dallas?

28. A plane traveled 200 miles before arriving in Los Angeles. It then departed Los Angeles and traveled at a speed of 395 miles per hour. Write an expression for the total distance it will have traveled when it reaches the next stop.

29. Josephine fixes cars at the rate of $50 an hour. She also charges a cleanup fee of $30. Write an expression for her total charges.

30. A human infant can weigh about 8 pounds. A baby humpback whale can weigh over 500 times as much. About how much can a baby humpback whale weigh?

31. All DVDs at the See These video store cost $12. You have a coupon for $2 off the total purchase. Which expression represents the total cost of *d* videos?

A $2 - 12d$ **B** $12d - 2d$ **C** $12d - 2$ **D** $12 - 2d$

Algebra Connections

Completing Number Sentences

Remember that a number sentence has two numbers or expressions that are connected by the symbols $>$, $<$, or $=$.

Estimation can be used to see if the left or right side is greater.

Copy and complete the comparisons using estimation. Check your answers.

Remember:
$>$ means "is greater than."
$<$ means "is less than."
$=$ means "is equal to."

Example: $6 \times 80 \bigcirc 6 \times 77$

Think Is 6 groups of 80 more than 6 groups of 77?

Since 80 is more than 77, 6 groups of 80 is more than 6 groups of 77. Complete the comparison with "$>$."

$$6 \times 80 > 6 \times 77$$

This means 6 groups of 80 is greater than 6 groups of 77.

Copy and complete. Write $<$, $>$, or $=$ in the circle.

1. $6 \times 50 \bigcirc 51 \times 6$

2. $40 \times 5 \bigcirc 45 \times 5$

3. $56 + 56 \bigcirc 55 \times 2$

4. $7 \times 67 \bigcirc 67 \times 7$

5. $320 \bigcirc 8 \times 43$

6. $8 \times 72 \bigcirc 560$

7. $20 \times 20 \bigcirc 17 \times 18$

8. $5 \times 20 \bigcirc 100$

9. $3 + 48 \bigcirc 3 \times 48$

10. $3 \times 19 \bigcirc 60$

11. $5 \times 20 \bigcirc 19 \times 4$

12. $6 + 18 \bigcirc 6 \times 18$

For **13** through **14**, write a number sentence to help solve each problem.

13. Marina bought a lavender backpack for herself and a green backpack for her brother. Charley bought an orange backpack. Who spent more money?

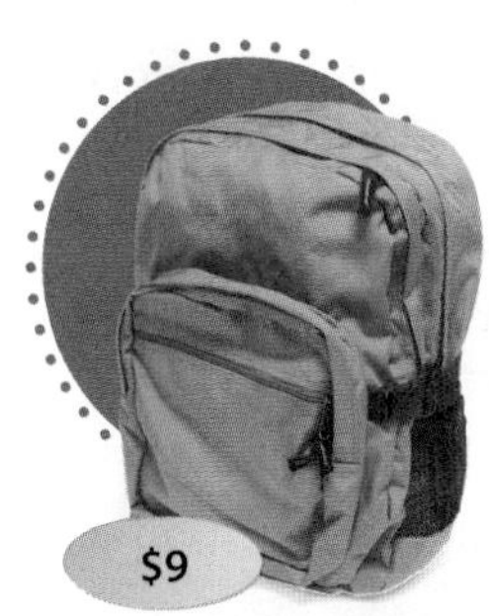

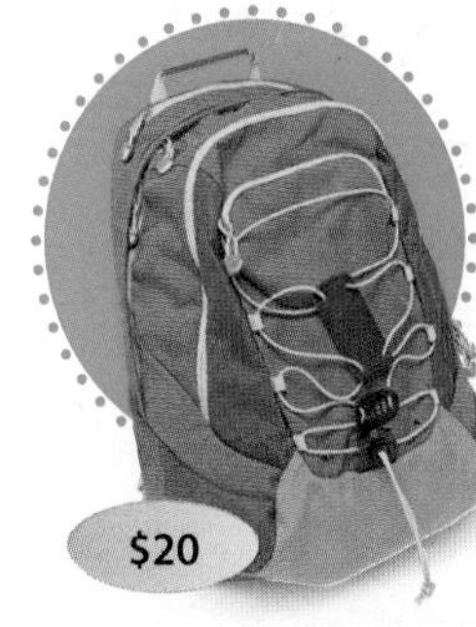

14. Mr. Wozniak purchased a green backpack. Ms. Chivas purchased 4 lavender backpacks. Who paid more?

15. Write a Problem Write a word problem using the prices of the backpacks.

Lesson

5-4

AF 1.3 Know and use the distributive property in equations and expressions with variables.

Distributive Property

How can you use the distributive property to write expressions and solve equations?

What expressions can you write to represent the number of square units inside the rectangle?

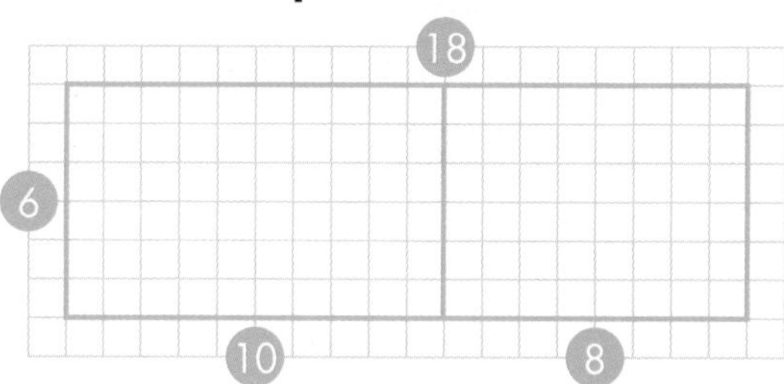

Guided Practice*

Do you know HOW?

1. Use the distributive property to complete the equation.

$12 \times 308 = 12 \times (\ \ + 8)$

$= (12 \times \ \ ) + (\ \ \times 8)$

$= \ \ + \ \ $

$= \ \ $

2. Show how can you use the distributive property to find the product of 4×105.

3. Show how can you use the distributive property to find the product of 20×32.

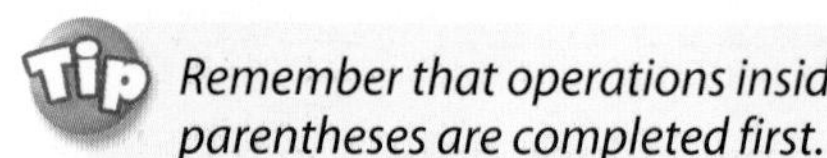
Remember that operations inside parentheses are completed first.

Do you UNDERSTAND?

4. Do these expressions name the same number of square units in the shaded area?

$4 \times (13 - 5)$ and $(4 \times 13) - (4 \times 5)$

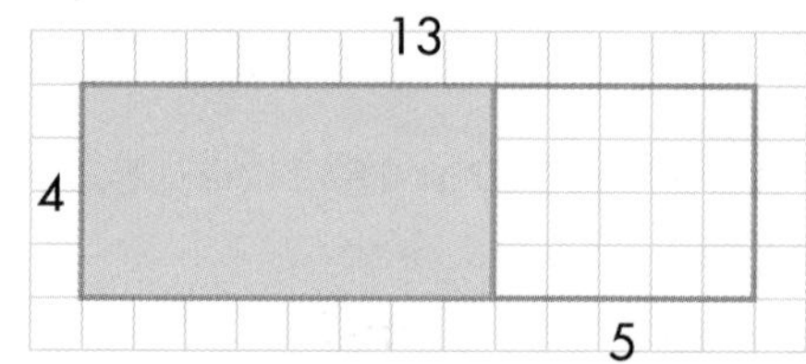

5. Write the distributive property to state that multiplication distributes over subtraction.

6. **Writing to Explain** Is $20 - (4 \times 2) = (20 - 4) \times (20 - 2)$? Explain your answer.

Independent Practice

Use the distributive property to complete each equation.

7. $509 \times 11 = (500 + 9) \times 11$

$= (500 \times \ \ ) + (9 \times \ \ )$

$= \ \ + 99$

$= \ \ $

8. $12 \times 47 = 12 \times (50 - \ \ )$

$= (12 \times \ \ ) - (12 \times 3)$

$= 600 - \ \ $

$= \ \ $

*For another example, see Set D on page 133.

Three ways to find the number of square units:

1) Think of 6 rows with 18 in each row. **6 × 18**

2) Think of 18 as 10 + 8. **6 × (10 + 8)**

3) Think of the figure in two parts.
The orange part has 6 × 10 square units.
The green part has 6 × 8 square units.

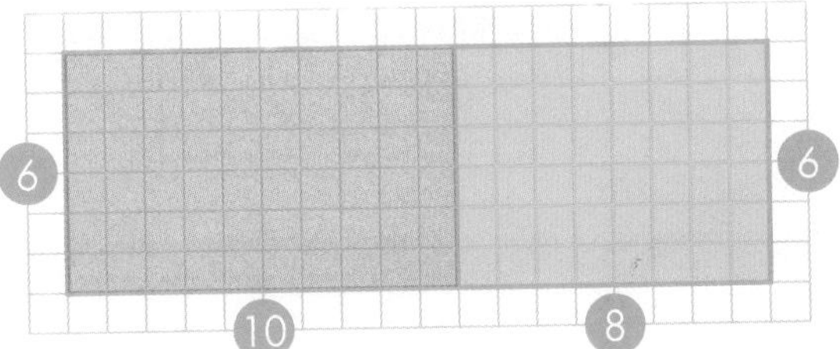

The total is the sum of the two parts.
(6 × 10) + (6 × 8)

Since the expressions name the same number of square units, you can write an equation.

6 × (10 + 8) = (6 × 10) + (6 × 8)

The distributive property states: Multiplying a sum (or difference) by a number is the same as multiplying each number in the sum (or difference) by that number and adding (or subtracting) the products.

For **9** through **16**, rewrite each expression using the distributive property. Then find each product.

9. 7 × 86 **10.** 7 × 420 **11.** 220 × 8 **12.** 45 × 60

13. 80 × 64 **14.** 16 × 102 **15.** 101 × 23 **16.** 390 × 40

Problem Solving

For **17** through **19**, use the table at the right and the following information.

Wendy brought the lemonade and iced tea for the school picnic. Since more people like lemonade than iced tea, she brought 2 gallons of lemonade for every 10 people. She also brought 5 gallons of iced tea for people who don't like lemonade.

Data

Number of People	Gallons of Lemonade	Total Gallons
10	2	
20		
30		
40		

17. Write an algebraic expression to show how many gallons Wendy would need to bring. Let *n* represent the number of groups of ten people.

18. How many gallons does she need for 10 people?

19. Fill in the rest of the table.

20. Use the distributive property to find another expression for 3(2*x* + 7).

A 6*x* + 7 **C** (2*x* + 7) × 3

B 3(14*x*) **D** 6*x* + 21

21. Estimation The highest point in California is Mount Whitney, at 14,505 feet. About how many miles is that?

Tip *1 mile = 5,280 feet*

Lesson

5-5

AF 1.3 Grade 6
Apply algebraic order of operations and the commutative, associative, and distributive properties to evaluate expressions; and justify each step in the process.

Order of Operations

How can you evaluate a numerical expression with more than one operation?

Two students evaluated the same expression, but got different answers.

To avoid getting more than one answer, use the order of operations. Rebecca used the correct order.

Find the value of $12 \div 4 + (9 - 2) \times (3 + 5)$.

Rebecca's Way	Juan's Way
$36 + 9 \div 3 \times 5$	$36 + 9 \div 3 \times 5$
$36 + 3 \times 5$	$45 \div 3 \times 5$
$36 + 15$	15×5
51	75

Another Example How can you evaluate an algebraic expression with more than one operation?

You can use order of operations when evaluating algebraic expressions.

What is the value of $4v + 2w - 3$, if $v = 5$ and $w = 3$?

Step 1 Replace all of the variables with given values. Remember that $4v$ means $4 \times v$.

Step 2 Using the order of operations, multiply or divide in order from left to right.

Step 3 Add or subtract in order from left to right.

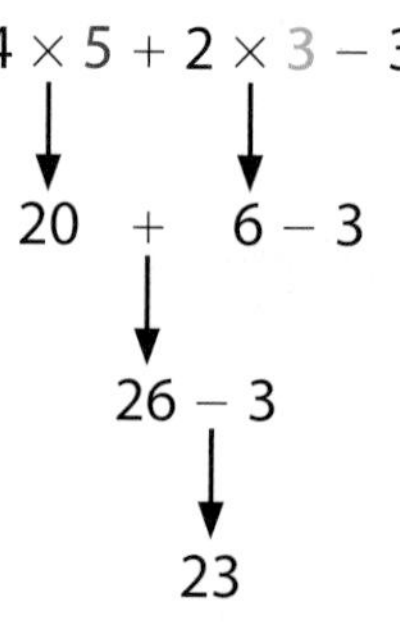

The value of the expression is 23.

Explain It

1. How could the value of a numerical expression such as $4 \times 5 + 2 \times 3 - 3$ be changed?

Guided Practice*

Do you know HOW?

For **1** through **4**, name the operation you should do first.

1. $6 + 27 \div 3$

2. $5 \times 2 + 12 \div 6$

3. $17 - (4 + 3)$

4. $(14 - 7) + (3 + 5)$

Do you UNDERSTAND?

5. In the first example, why was Juan's answer incorrect?

6. Insert parentheses to make the following statement true.
$3 + 5 \times 2 - 10 = 6$

Step 1

In using order of operations, do the operations inside parentheses first.

$12 \div 4 + (9 - 2) \times (3 + 5)$

$12 \div 4 + 7 \times 8$

Remember to rewrite the operations not yet performed.

Step 2

Then, multiply and divide in order from left to right.

$12 \div 4 + 7 \times 8$

$3 + 56$

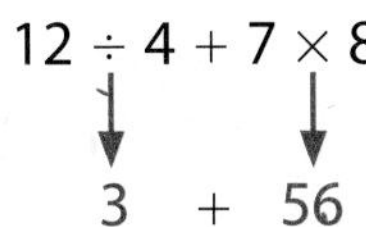

Step 3

Finally, add and subtract in order from left to right.

$3 + 56$

59

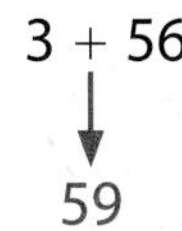

Independent Practice

For **7** through **18**, find the value of each expression using order of operations.

7. $3 + 7 \times 6 \div 3 - 4$

8. $(29 - 18) + 14 \div 2 + 6$

9. $64 \div 8 \times 2$

10. $(19 - 5) \times 3 + 4$

11. $3(6 + 2) - 12 \times 2$

12. $36 - 5(16 - 11)$

13. $8 \times (3 + 2) - 6$

14. $3 \div (9 - 6) + 4 \times 2$

15. $(3 + 4) \times (3 + 5)$

16. $3 + (2 \times 4 + 6) - 2$

17. $4 \times (3 - 2) + 18$

18. $8 \times 6 - 4 \times 3$

For **19** through **24**, insert parentheses to make each statement true.

19. $30 - 4 \times 2 + 5 = 2$

20. $17 - 8 - 5 = 14$

21. $10 \div 2 - 3 + 1 = 3$

22. $30 - 4 \times 2 + 5 = 57$

23. $17 - 8 - 5 = 4$

24. $10 \div 2 - 3 + 1 = 1$

25. Writing to Explain Would the value of the expression in Exercise 21 be different if no parentheses were used?

For **26** through **34**, evaluate each expression for $x = 16$ and $y = 4$.

26. $3x - 3y$

27. $x \div (2y - 4)$

28. $5y + x \div 8$

29. $4x - 2y$

30. $y \div (x \div y)$

31. $3y + 2x - 7$

32. $5x - 4y$

33. $x \div y$

34. $2x + 4y - 10$

DIGITAL Animated Glossary www.pearsonsuccessnet.com

*For another example, see Set E on page 133.

Problem Solving

35. Draw the next figure in the following pattern.

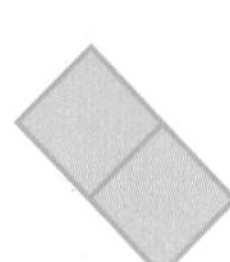
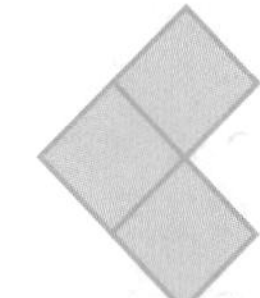
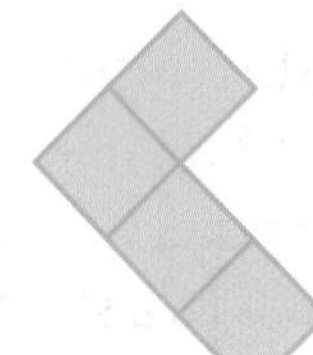

For **36** through **38**, use the table at the right.

36. The girls' gym teacher needs to purchase 15 softballs, 5 packages of tennis balls, and 2 soccer balls. She plans to collect \$1 from each of her 15 students to help pay for the balls. Write and evaluate an expression to show how much more the teacher will have to pay.

Data

Baseballs	\$20 per dozen
Softballs	\$3 each
Basketballs	\$15 each
Soccer balls	\$17 each
Tennis balls	\$4 per package of 3

37. The boys' gym teacher needs to buy 2 dozen baseballs, 4 basketballs, and 24 tennis balls. Write and evaluate an expression to show how much the balls will cost.

38. Writing to Explain Did you use parentheses in the expression you wrote for Exercise 36? Why or why not?

39. A small cruise ship has 220 passengers. At the San Diego port, 2 groups of 12 passengers go ashore to shop and 5 groups of 6 passengers go sightseeing. Evaluate $220 - (2 \times 12) - (5 \times 6)$ to find the number of passengers that are left on the ship.

40. Geometry California is about 770 miles long and about 250 miles wide. What is its approximate area?

Tip *Area = length × width.*

41. At a ski lift, 41 people are waiting to board cars that hold 6 people each. How many cars will be completely filled? How many people are left to board the last car?

A 6; 6 **C** 5; 6

B 6; 5 **D** 5; 5

42. Mark bought 3 boxes of pencils that contained 20 pencils each and 4 boxes of pens that contained 10 pens each. Which expression represents the total number of pencils and pens Mark bought?

A $(3 \times 10) + (4 \times 20)$

B $(3 \times 4) + (10 \times 20)$

C $(3 \times 20) + (4 \times 10)$

D $(3 + 20) + (4 + 10)$

43. Number Sense True or false? Explain.
$4(3 + 5) - 10 = 4 \times 3 + 5 - 10$

Mixed Problem Solving

A state song is an official symbol of the state it represents. Each of the 50 states, with the exception of New Jersey, has at least one state song. Some of the states chose songs that are famous on their own, while other states chose a song that is known only as a state song. Here are a few examples of some of the state songs:

Data

United States State Songs

State	Song Title	Year Written	Year Adopted
California	*"I Love You, California"*	1913	1988
Kentucky	*"My Old Kentucky Home"*	1853	1928
Oklahoma	*"Oklahoma"*	1943	1953
Maryland	*"Maryland, My Maryland"*	1861	1939

For **1** through **5**, use the table above.

1. How many years passed between the time Kentucky's state song was written before it was adopted?

2. About how many decades passed between the writing of *"I Love You, California"* and its adoption?

3. How many years earlier was *"Maryland, My Maryland"* written than *"Oklahoma"*?

4. Put the years each song was adopted in order from least to greatest.

5. **Writing to Explain** A lustrum is a period of 5 years. Richard said that 15 lustrums occurred between California's state song being written and then adopted by the state. Is he correct? Explain.

6. **Strategy Focus** Solve using the strategy Draw a Picture and Write an Equation.

Tricia ran 5 times as far as Ali. Ali ran 375 meters. How did Tricia run?

Lesson

5-6

MR 2.3 Use a variety of methods, such as words, numbers, symbols, charts, graphs, tables, diagrams, and models to explain mathematical reasoning. Also **NS 2.0, MR 2.0**

Problem Solving

Act It Out and Use Reasoning

Hands-On
unit cubes

A children's zoo displays birds in 3 different cages. The zoo has three kinds of birds. There are 36 birds in all. How many of each type of bird are in the zoo?

Use objects to show the birds and then use reasoning to solve the problem.

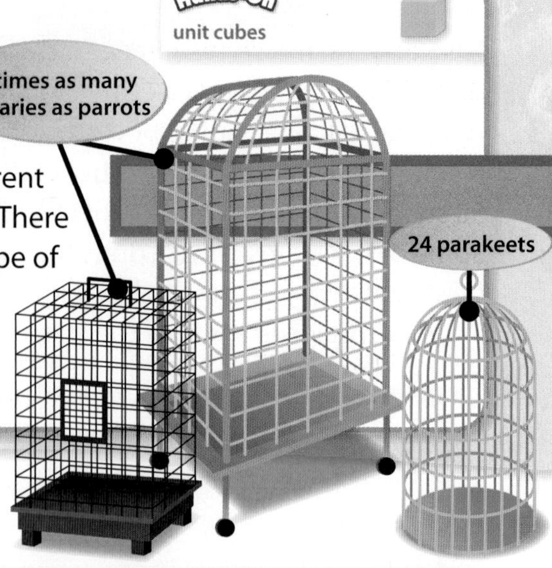

Guided Practice*

Do you know HOW?

Solve. You can use cubes to act out the problem.

1. The Rodriquez family is donating 25 baseball caps to a charity auction. There are 11 blue caps. There are 2 more white caps than green caps. How many of each color caps are they donating?

Do you UNDERSTAND?

2. If you use 25 cubes to represent all the caps and 11 are used to show the blue caps, how many cubes are left for the white and green caps?

3. **Write a Problem** Write a real-world problem that can be solved by acting it out and using reasoning.

Independent Practice

Solve. Use cubes to act out the problems.

4. Mr. Niles has a box of accessories for clarinets. He has a total of 42 objects. He has 12 mouthpieces. He has four times as many reeds as neck straps. How many of each object does he have?

5. Sylvia has a jewelry collection of bracelets, necklaces, and earrings. She has 16 bracelets. The number of earrings is 2 times the number of necklaces. She has 43 pieces of jewelry in all. How many of each piece of jewelry does she have?

- What do I know?
- What am I asked to find?
- What diagram can I use to help understand the problem?
- Can I use addition, subtraction, multiplication, or division?
- Is all of my work correct?
- Did I answer the right question?
- Is my answer reasonable?

*For another example, see Set F on page 133.

Read and Understand

Use objects and show what you know.
Let 36 cubes represent all the birds.
Use reasoning to make conclusions.

24 parakeets

12 canaries and parrots

There are 24 parakeets and 36 birds in all. That leaves a total of 12 canaries and parrots.

Plan and Solve

Use 12 cubes. There are 3 times as many canaries as parrots.

There are 24 parakeets, 9 canaries, and 3 parrots.
$24 + 9 + 3 = 36$, so the answer is correct.

For **6** through **8**, use and complete the table at the right.

Data

Instrument	Number of Students
Group 1	44
Oboe	8
Clarinet	
Flute	
Group 2	41
Saxophone	8
Trumpet	
Trombone	

6. Brady joined the band. In Group 1, there are a total of 44 students. There are 8 students who play the oboe. There are $\frac{1}{2}$ as many students playing the clarinet as the flute. How many students from Group 1 play each instrument?

7. There are 41 students in Group 2. Twice as many students play the trumpet as play the trombone, but 8 students play the saxophone. How many students in Group 2 play each instrument?

8. Later, 7 students joined Group 2 and 1 student left to join Group 1. Some students decided to play a different instrument. Now 20 students play trombone and 7 more students play trumpet as play saxophone. How many students play each instrument?

9. Jane worked 1.5 hours on Monday, 3 hours on Tuesday, and 4.5 hours on Wednesday. If the pattern continues, how many hours will she work on Friday?

10. Reggie earned \$360 in the summer. If he earned \$40 per week, how many weeks did he work?

total earned: \$360

\$40 | ? number of weeks

amount earned per week

11. The Garden Theater presented a play. A total of 179 people attended in 3 days. The first day, 58 people attended. On the second day, 47 people attended. How many attended on the third day?

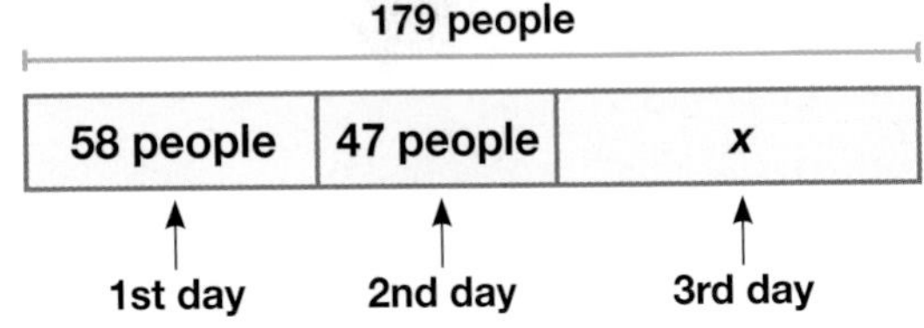

Test Prep

1. Which expression can be used to represent the phrase "three times the amount of money"? (5-1)

A $3 + m$

B $3 - m$

C $3 \times m$

D $3 \div m$

2. If Lisa travels an average of 65 miles per hour for 8 hours, she will travel 8×65 miles. Which of the following is equal to 8×65. (5-4)

A $(8 + 60) \times (8 + 5)$

B $(8 + 60) - (8 + 5)$

C $(8 \times 60) + (8 \times 5)$

D $(8 \times 60) - (8 \times 5)$

3. Ryan had 18 more shots on goal during the soccer season than Peyton, who had 36. Evaluate the expression $x + 18$ for $x = 36$. (5-2)

A 2

B 18

C 52

D 54

4. Jerry has a coupon for $3 off. If p stands for the original price of a shirt, which expression tells Jerry's cost, before tax, when he uses the coupon? (5-1)

A $p \div 3$

B $3 - p$

C $p - 3$

D $p + 3$

5. The expression $f - 3$ represents the number of years Mark has taken piano lessons when Fatima has taken lessons for f years. How many years of lessons will Mark have when Fatima has 9 years? (5-2)

A 27

B 12

C 6

D 3

6. What is the first step in evaluating the expression shown below? (5-5)

$8 - 7 + 12 \div (3 + 1)$

A Add 3 and 1.

B Divide 12 by 3.

C Add 7 and 12.

D Subtract 7 from 8.

7. What value of n makes the equation true? (5-4)

$15 \times 110 = (15 \times 100) + (15 \times n)$

A 10

B 15

C 90

D 110

8. The cost for n students to attend a workshop is $7n + 12$ dollars. What is the cost for 6 students to attend? (5-3)

A $25

B $54

C $126

D $156

Test Prep

9. Tennessee, New Mexico, and Michigan have a total of 27 representatives in the U.S. House of Representatives. Michigan has 15 representatives and Tennessee has 3 times as many as New Mexico. How many representatives does the state of Tennessee have? (5-6)

A 12

B 9

C 6

D 3

10. The expression $n \div 6$ can represent which of the following phrases? (5-1)

A *n* students divided into groups of 6

B 6 times *n* students

C 6 students divided into *n* groups

D 6 less than *n* students

11. What is the value of the expression $6 + (13 - 1) \div 4 + 2$? (5-5)

A 20

B 11

C 8

D 3

12. Which expression can be used to represent the phrase "3 more than 7 times the number of pages, *p*"? (5-3)

A $7p + 3$

B $p + 3 \times 7$

C $3p + 7$

D $7p - 3$

13. The expression $8 - 2x$ can be used to represent which phrase? (5-3)

A Eight less than two times a number

B Two less than eight times a number

C Eight more than two times a number

D Eight minus two times a number

14. What is the value of $7 + 3m - 2$ when $m = 4$? (5-5)

A 11

B 17

C 20

D 38

15. Which of the following expressions has a value equal to 3? (5-5)

A $8 + (4 \div 2) - 1 \times 3$

B $8 + 4 \div (2 - 1) \times 3$

C $(8 + 4 \div 2) - 1 \times 3$

D $(8 + 4) \div 2 - 1 \times 3$

16. The table shows the cost to board Lucy's dog at a kennel. Which expression shows the cost to board the dog for *d* days? (5-2)

Data

Number of Days	Total Cost
3	$36
4	$48
5	$60

A $d + 36$

B $d + 12$

C $36d$

D $12d$

Reteaching

Set A, pages 112–113

Translate a word phrase into an algebraic expression.

Five more cards than Steve owns

		Step 3
Decide what the variable will represent.	**What operation should be used? The word *more* is a clue.**	**Write an algebraic expression.**
Let s = cards Steve owns	Addition	$s + 5$

Remember to look for words that give you clues as to what operation to use.

Write an algebraic expression for each.

1. A puzzle costs p less than a magazine. The magazine costs \$1.99. How much is the puzzle?
2. The evergreen is twice as tall as a hosta. The hosta is h inches tall. How tall is the evergreen?

Set B, pages 114–116

When you evaluate an algebraic expression, you replace the variable with a given number value.

Evaluating a Division Expression

Evaluate $\frac{t}{6}$ for $t = 18$.

Replace t with 18 in the expression.

$\frac{18}{6}$

Divide.

$\frac{18}{6} = 3$

Remember to replace the variable with the given values and perform the operation.

Evaluate each expression for $d = 2$ and $d = 3$.

1. $\frac{30}{d}$
2. $3.6 + d$
3. $d \times 20$
4. $57 - d$
5. $11d$

Set C, pages 118–120

Write an algebraic expression for the following word phrase. Let n represent the number.

Word Phrase
five less than a number times 3

Algebraic Expression
$3n - 5$

Remember that placing a number next to a variable means multiplication.

Write an algebraic expression for each. Let n represent the number.

1. Four times a number, plus 8
2. Six less than a number times 3
3. Ten more than a number times 4
4. Fifty minus five divided by a number.

Set D, pages 122–123

The Distributive Property states that multiplying a sum by a number is the same as multiplying each number in the sum by the number, and then adding the products.

Use the Distributive Property to find 5×23.

Think of 23 as $20 + 3$.

$$\begin{aligned} 5 \times 23 &= 5 \times (20 + 3) \\ &= (5 \times 20) + (5 \times 3) \\ &= 100 + 15 \\ &= 115 \end{aligned}$$

Remember that you write one of the numbers as a sum, multiply each of those numbers by the other number, and then add the products.

Use the Distributive Property to find each product.

1. 7×45 **2.** 29×9

3. 72×6 **4.** 3×46

5. 5×78 **6.** 29×5

Set E, pages 124–126

When evaluating an expression, you need to use the order of operations. Otherwise, more than one answer is possible.

Evaluate $(8 + 2) \times (3 + 7) + 50$.

Step 1

Do the operations inside the parentheses.

$(8 + 2) \times (3 + 7) + 50$
$= 10 \times 10 + 50$

Step 2

Multiply and divide in order from left to right.

$10 \times 10 + 50$
$= 100 + 50$

Step 3

Add and subtract in order from left to right.

$100 + 50$
$= 150$

Remember that there is an order of operations that you must use when you evaluate an expression with more than one operation. Otherwise, more than one answer is sometimes possible.

Find the value of each expression using the order of operations.

1. $4 + 8 \times 6 \div 2 + 3$

2. $(18 - 3) \div 5 + 4$

3. $8 \times 5 + 7 \times 3 - (10 - 5)$

4. $10 \times 10 + 5 \times 2 - 3 \times 5$

Set F, pages 128–129

Use objects to show what you know and then use reasoning to solve the problem.

A pet shop has a total of 19 dogs, cats, and ferrets. There are 4 ferrets, and twice as many cats as dogs. How many of each kind of pet are in the shop?

Use 19 cubes and let 4 of them represent the ferrets. That leaves 15 cubes to represent the cats and dogs. There must be 10 cats and 5 dogs.

Remember that objects can help you reason through a problem.

1. Kerry has 12 paperweights in her collection. She has twice as many glass paperweights as metal, and 3 are wood. How many of each type of paperweight does she have?

Topic 6

Multiplying Decimals

1

The fastest growing flowering plant is the *Hesperoyucca Whipplei.* How many centimeters did one of these plants grow in 7 days? You will find out in Lesson 6-2.

2

An astronaut's spacesuit weighs much less on the Moon than on Earth. If you know the weight of the spacesuit on the Moon, how can you find its weight on Earth? You will find out in Lesson 6-4.

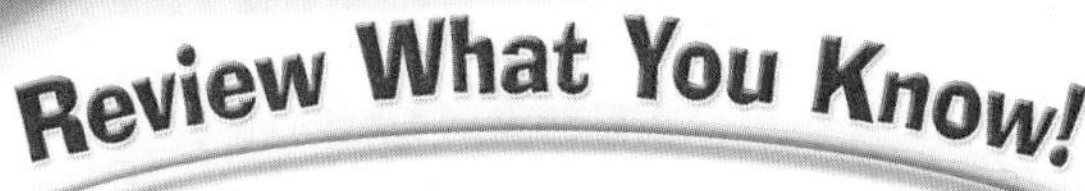

Review What You Know!

Vocabulary

Choose the best term from the box.

- equivalent fractions
- mixed numbers
- factors
- product

1. In the equation $5 \times 5 = 25$, the number 25 is the __?__ and the digits 5 and 5 are __?__.

2. __?__ have a whole number and a fraction.

3. Fractions that name the same part of a whole are __?__.

Number Theory

Write whether each number is prime or composite.

4. 32 **5.** 7 **6.** 45

List all the factors for each number.

7. 10 **8.** 18 **9.** 50

Fractions

Write each quotient as a fraction.

10. $5 \div 18$ **11.** $5 \div 6$ **12.** $9 \div 12$

Using Number Lines

Writing to Explain Write an answer for the question.

340 350

13. How can you use this number line to round 347 to the nearest ten?

3 During early California history, some Native American tribes used disc-shaped shells called dentalia as valuable trading shells. The shells were also used to make jewelry, like this necklace. What is the estimated length of one of these necklaces? You will find out in Lesson 6-3.

4 Numismatics is the study and collection of coins, money, and related objects. What is the value of different collections of coins? You will find out in Lesson 6-1.

Lesson
6-1

NS 2.1 Add, subtract, multiply, and divide with decimals; add with negative integers; subtract positive integers from negative integers; and verify the reasonableness of the results.

Multiplying Decimals by 10, 100, or 1,000

What is the rule for multiplying decimals by 10, 100, or 1,000?

A baker buys some of the ingredients he uses in bulk. He needs to purchase 10 lb of pecans and 100 lb of flour. How much will the baker spend for each amount?

Choose an Operation Multiply to join equal groups.

Guided Practice*

Do you know HOW?

In **1** through **8**, use mental math to find each product.

1. 0.009 × 10

2. 0.45 × 100

3. 3.1 × 1,000

4. 7.4 × 10

5. 0.062 × 100

6. 1.24 × 1,000

Do you UNDERSTAND?

7. To find the product of 5.8 × 1,000, move the decimal point ▢ places to the right and annex ▢ zeros.

8. How much will the baker spend if he buys 10 lb of flour? 1,000 lb of flour?

Independent Practice

In **9** through **36**, use mental math to find each product.

9. 4.23 × 1	**10.** 4.23 × 10	**11.** 4.23 × 100	**12.** 4.23 × 1,000
13. 0.0867 × 10	**14.** 0.0867 × 100	**15.** 0.0867 × 1	**16.** 0.0867 × 1,000
17. 63.7 × 10	**18.** 56.37 × 1,000	**19.** 0.365 × 100	**20.** 5.02 × 1,000
21. 94.6 × 1,000	**22.** 0.9463 × 100	**23.** 0.678 × 10	**24.** 681.7 × 100
25. 4.3 × 10	**26.** 0.32 × 100	**27.** 5.1 × 100	**28.** 1.02 × 1,000
29. 0.004 × 1,000	**30.** 0.001 × 10	**31.** 6.02 × 100	**32.** 5.07 × 10
33. 0.063 × 100	**34.** 7.25 × 1,000	**35.** 19.212 × 100	**36.** 0.62 × 10

For another example, see Set A on page 150.

Use the patterns in this table to find 0.45×100 and 2.89×10.

Multiply by	Move the decimal point to the right
1	0 places
10	1 place
100	2 places
1,000	3 places

When you need to move the decimal point beyond the number of digits in the number you are multiplying, *annex* 1 or more zeros.

Cost of flour:

$0.45 \times 100 = 0.45 = 45$

Cost of pecans:

$2.89 \times 10 = 2.89 = 28.9$

The flour will cost $45.00, and the pecans will cost $28.90.

If 100 lb or 1,000 lb of pecans needed to be purchased, the pattern can be continued to find the cost.

$2.89 \times 100 = 2.89 = 289$

$2.89 \times 1{,}000 = 2.890 = 2{,}890$

Problem Solving

The table at the right shows the coins saved by Tina and her sister for one year.

Type of Coin	Number Saved
 (penny)	1,000
 (nickel)	100
 (dime)	1,000
 (quarter)	10

37. **Number Sense** Find the total value of each type of coin the girls have saved.

38. **Number Sense** Find the total value for the coins saved by the sisters.

39. The principal of Mountain Middle School has a big glass jar of marbles. The empty jar weighs 40.5 ounces, and each of the 1,000 marbles weighs 1.25 ounces. Find the total weight in ounces of the marbles.

40. **Writing to Explain** Marcia and David each multiplied 5.6×10 and 0.721×100. Marcia got 0.56 and 7.21 for her products. David got 56 and 72.1 for his products. Which student multiplied correctly? How do you know?

41. The Parents' Club is trying to decide on favors for International Night. They will need 100 items, and they have a budget of $250. They can choose from 100 baseball hats at $2.45 each, 100 sports bottles at $2.50 each, or 100 flags at $2.75 each. Which item(s) can they afford to buy?

42. **Algebra** In which of the following equations does $n = 1{,}000$?

A $n \times 0.426 = 42.6$

B $7.078 \times n = 7{,}078$

C $n \times 100 = 630$

D $5.9 \times n = 0.59$

Lesson

6-2

NS 2.1 Add, subtract, multiply, and divide with decimals; add with negative integers; subtract positive integers from negative integers; and verify the reasonableness of the results.

Multiplying a Whole Number and a Decimal

How do you multiply a whole number by a decimal?

The price of admission to a minor league baseball game increased by 0.17 times the amount of last year's admission. If last year's admission was $26, how much is the increase?

Choose an Operation Multiply to find 26 × 0.17.

Guided Practice*

Do you know HOW?

Find each product.

1. 9.8 × 2

2. 0.67 × 8

3. 0.457 × 3

4. 34 × 5.3

5. 45 × 0.003

6. 34.6 × 21

Do you UNDERSTAND?

7. **Writing to Explain** What is the difference between multiplying a whole number by a decimal and multiplying two whole numbers?

8. Use the information from the example above. How much will admission cost to a minor league game this year?

Independent Practice

Find each product.

9. 34.6 × 9

10. 56.3 × 22

11. 405 × 0.47

12. 9.32 × 16

13. 12.9 × 8

14. 27.4 × 7

15. 336 × 0.4

16. 88 × 1.8

17. 84 × 0.005

18. 34,000 × 2.65

19. 64.2 × 20

20. 38.6 × 19

21. 40 × 0.22

22. 57 × 2.3

23. 5.8 × 11

24. 56 × 0.4

25. 0.1 × 22

26. 170 × 0.003

27. 4.02 × 9

28. 514 × 0.4

29. 0.3 × 99

30. 52 × 3.6

31. 105 × 0.4

32. 92 × 0.9

For another example, see Set B on page 150.

Step 1

Multiply as you would with whole numbers.

```
  1 4
 0.1 7
×   2 6
 1 0 2
 3 4 0
 4 4 2
```

Step 2

Count the decimal places in both factors, and then place the decimal point in the product the same number of places from the right.

```
  1 4
 0.1 7    2 decimal places
×   2 6   0 decimal places
  1 0 2
  3 4 0
 4.4 2    2 decimal places
```

The increase from last year's admission is $4.42.

Problem Solving

For **33**, refer to the prices at the right.

33. Mia is shopping and finds a sale. She has $25 in her wallet and a coupon worth $4 off the cost of a dress.

a How much money will the dress cost if she uses the coupon?

b Find the total cost of 3 T-shirts.

c How much change will Mia get back from $25 after she buys the 3 T-shirts?

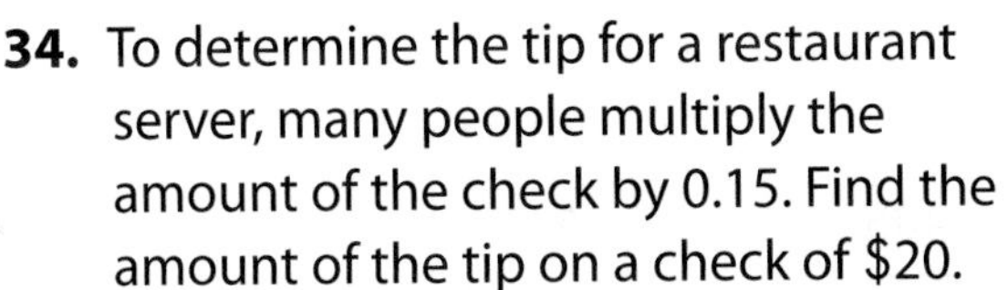

34. To determine the tip for a restaurant server, many people multiply the amount of the check by 0.15. Find the amount of the tip on a check of $20.

35. Gary had 10 rosebushes to plant. On Friday, he planted 4 of the bushes. In simplest form, what fraction of the bushes did he plant?

36. The fastest growing flowering plant is the *Hesperoyucca Whipplei*. It was recorded that one of these plants grew at a rate of 25.4 cm per day. How many centimeters did this plant grow in 7 days?

37. The airline that Vince is using has a baggage weight limit of 41 pounds. He has two green bags, each weighing 18.4 pounds, and one blue bag weighing 3.7 pounds. What is the combined weight of his baggage?

A 22.1 lbs

B 38.7 lbs

C 40.5 lbs

D 41 lbs

38. Raul, Tim, Yuko, and Joe have to line up according to height from tallest to shortest. Raul is 145.52 cm tall; Tim is 151 cm tall; Yuko is 159.5 cm tall; and Joe is 145.25 cm tall. Who is first in line?

Lesson

6-3

NS 2.1 Add, subtract, multiply, and divide with decimals; add with negative integers; subtract positive integers from negative integers; and verify the reasonableness of the results.
Also **NS 1.1**

Estimating the Product of a Whole Number and a Decimal

What are some ways to estimate products with decimals?

A planner for a wedding needs to buy 16 pounds of sliced cheddar cheese. About how much will the cheese cost?

Estimate $2.15 × 16.

$2.15 per pound

Another Example How can you estimate products of decimals that are less than 1?

You already know how to estimate products of whole numbers using rounding and compatible numbers. You can use the same methods to estimate products with decimals.

Manuel found the total distance he walks to and from school is equal to 0.75 mile. If Manuel walks to and from school 184 days in one year, about how many total miles will he walk?

Using rounding

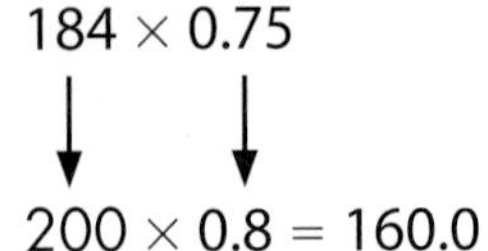

184×0.75

$200 \times 0.8 = 160.0$

Tip *Be sure to place the decimal point correctly.*

Using compatible numbers

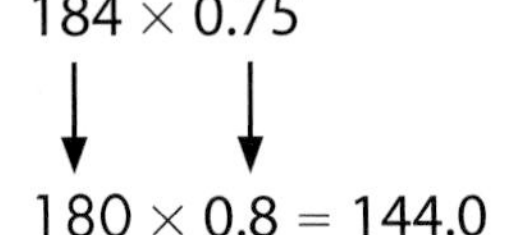

184×0.75

$180 \times 0.8 = 144.0$

Compatible numbers are close to the actual numbers and are easy to multiply.

Since the compatible numbers are closer to the actual numbers than the rounded numbers, that estimate is closer to the actual product.

Manuel will walk about 144 miles to and from school in one year.

Guided Practice*

Do you know HOW?

In **1** through **6**, estimate each product using rounding or compatible numbers.

1. 0.87×412

2. 104×0.33

3. 9.02×80

4. 0.54×24

5. 33.05×200

6. 0.79×51

Do you UNDERSTAND?

7. **Writing to Explain** How can estimating be helpful before finding an actual product?

8. About how much money would have to be spent on 16 pounds of cheese if the price is $3.95 per pound?

For another example, see Set C on page 150.

One Way

Round each number to the greatest place that has a non-zero digit.

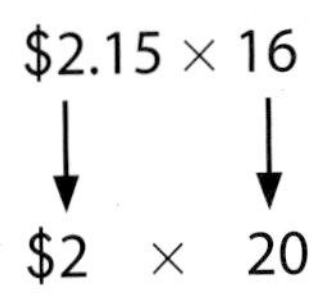

$\$2 \times 20 = \$40$.

The cheese will cost about $40.

Another Way

Use compatible numbers that you can multiply with mentally.

$\$2.15 \times 16$

$\downarrow \quad \downarrow$

$\$2 \times 15$

$\$2 \times 15 = \$30$.

The cheese will cost about $30.

Independent Practice

Estimate each product.

9. 0.12×5

10. 45.3×4

11. 99.2×82

12. 37×0.93

13. 0.667×4

14. 0.6×184

15. 25×0.37

16. 0.904×75

Problem Solving

For **17** and **18**, use the chart.

17. **Number Sense** About how much money does Stan need to buy 5 T-shirts and 10 buttons?

18. **Number Sense** Pat has $55. Does she have enough money to buy 4 T-shirts?

Data

Souvenir	Cost
Button	$1.95
T-Shirt	$12.50

19. **Think About the Process** You want to estimate 0.67×85. Which way will give you an estimate that is closest to the actual product?

A Round 0.67 to 1.0 and 85 to 90, multiply.

B Round 0.67 to 0.7 and 85 to 90, multiply.

C Round 0.67 to 70 and 85 to 80, multiply.

D Round 0.67 to 1.0 and 85 to 80, multiply.

20. Dentalia shells were used by some Native American tribes in California to make jewelry. Each dentalia shell is 1.25 inches long. If a necklace had been made with 18 dentalia shells, about how long was this necklace? Explain your estimate.

21. **Reasoning** Will the actual product of 7.69×5 be greater than or less than its estimate of 8×5? Why?

22. **Algebra** If $n \times 4.16$ is about 200, what is a reasonable estimate for n?

Lesson

6-4

NS 2.1 Add, subtract, multiply, and divide with decimals; add with negative integers; subtract positive integers from negative integers; and verify the reasonableness of the results.
Also **MR 2.1**

Multiplying Two Decimals

How can you multiply two decimals?

Nancy walked 1.7 miles in 1 hour. If she walks at the same rate, how far will she walk in 1.5 hours?

Choose an Operation
Multiply to find 1.7×1.5.

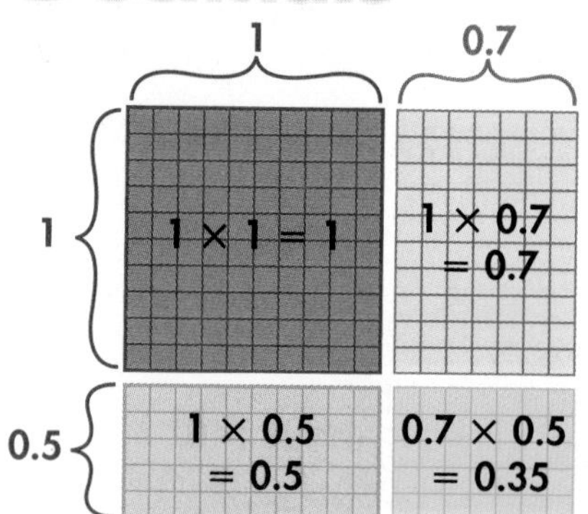

Guided Practice*

Do you know HOW?

For **1** through **6**, estimate first. Then find each product. Check that your answer is reasonable.

1. 9.3×4.1

2. 3.02×0.6

3. 0.7×1.9

4. 12.6×0.2

5. 8.3×10.7

6. 2.04×1.8

Do you UNDERSTAND?

7. Writing to Explain How is multiplying two decimals different from multiplying one decimal by a whole number?

8. Using the example above, how many miles will Nancy walk in 2.8 hours? Show an estimate first.

Independent Practice

For **9** through **28**, estimate first. Then find each product. Check that your answer is reasonable.

9. 5.2×4.6

10. 0.05×4.5

11. 19.1×8.5

12. 8.6×0.08

13. 0.6×0.49

14. 32.3×0.7

15. 3.42×4.7

16. 8.11×0.05

17. 3.5×0.4

18. 28.6×0.17

19. 0.21×1.5

20. 1.11×6.1

21. 6.8×7.2

22. 8.3×6.4

23. 9.1×11.6

24. 0.04×15.6

25. 18.1×3.7

26. 0.06×15

27. 0.28×3.7

28. 3.14×6.2

For another example, see Set D on page 151.

Step 1

Estimate 1.7 × 1.5

$2 \times 2 = 4$

Step 2

Multiply as you would with whole numbers.

```
   1.7
 × 1.5
    85
   170
   255
```

Step 3

Count decimal places in *both* factors.

Write the decimal point in the product.

```
   1.7  ←— 1 decimal place
 × 1.5  ←— 1 decimal place
    85
   170
  2.55  ←— 2 places
```

Step 4

Check your answer.

Since 2.55 is close to your estimate of 4, the answer is reasonable.

In 1.5 hours, Nancy will walk 2.55 miles.

Problem Solving

29. The fifth-grade planning committee needs to buy items for sandwiches for its annual lunch. Fill in the chart and determine the amount of money they'll need to buy the items for sandwiches.

Item	Amount	Price	Total
	15.5 pounds	$3.50 per pound	
	10.5 pounds	$2.90 per pound	
	12 packages	$2.50 per package	

30. Geometry Karly's bedroom measures 13.2 feet long by 10.3 feet wide. Use the formula Area = length × width to determine the number of square feet for the floor of Karly's bedroom.

31. A bag of grass seed weighs 5.8 pounds. How many pounds would 2.5 bags weigh?

A 14.5

B 13.8

C 8.3

D 3.3

32. Joy drinks 4 bottles of water per day. Each bottle contains 16.5 fluid ounces. She wants to find the total number of fluid ounces she drinks per day. How many decimal places will be in the product?

A One

B Two

C Three

D Four

33. Mary Ann ordered 3 pens and a box of paper on the Internet. Each pen cost $1.65 and the paper cost $3.95 per box. How much did she spend?

34. An astronaut's Apollo space suit weighs 29.8 pounds on the moon. It weighs approximately 6.02 times as much on Earth. About how much does an Apollo space suit weigh on Earth?

35. Writing to Explain How does estimation help you place the decimal point in a product correctly?

Lesson

6-5

NS 2.1 Add, subtract, multiply, and divide with decimals; add with negative integers; subtract positive integers from negative integers; and verify the reasonableness of the results.

Multiplying with Zeros in the Product

When do you insert zeros in the product?

The smallest mammal in the world is the bumblebee bat.

The weight of the bumblebee bat is equal to 0.05 times the weight of a mouse. How much does the bumblebee bat weigh?

Choose an Operation Multiply to find 1.5×0.05.

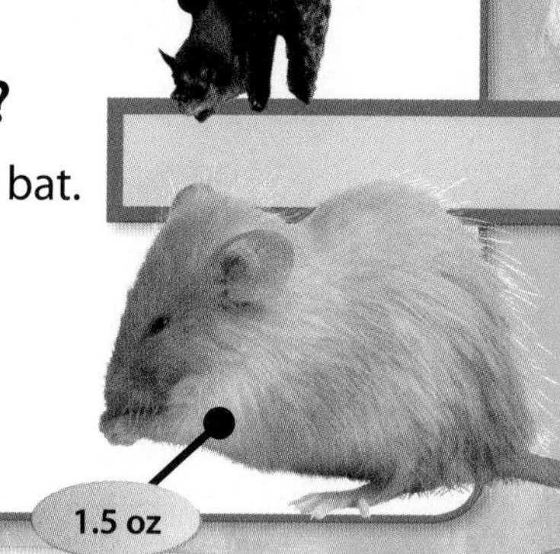

Guided Practice*

Do you know HOW?

Find each product.

1. 1.4×0.06

2. 0.4×0.12

3. 0.002×9

4. 0.97×0.04

5. 2.5×0.023

6. 0.5×0.009

Do you UNDERSTAND?

7. In the example above, why do you need to move the decimal point 3 places to place it in the product?

8. **Writing to Explain** Is the product of 0.03×0.03 the same as the product of 0.3×0.003? Explain.

Independent Practice

Find each product.

9. 0.3×0.2

10. 0.02×0.17

11. 6.04×0.01

12. 0.12×0.05

13. 0.4×0.5

14. 0.03×0.16

15. 3.1×0.06

16. 0.92×0.03

17. 0.87×0.04

18. 0.002×6.01

19. 0.6×0.08

20. 0.005×9

21. 0.09×0.01

22. 0.18×0.07

23. 0.4×0.06

24. 0.71×0.09

25. 1.07×0.08

26. 5.02×0.002

27. 3.74×0.003

28. 0.09×0.7

29. 3.04×0.009

30. 6.03×0.04

31. 8.68×0.5

32. 0.08×0.3

 For another example, see Set E on page 151.

Step 1

Multiply as you would with whole numbers.

$$\begin{array}{r} \overset{2}{1.5} \\ \times\ 0.05 \\ \hline 75 \end{array}$$

Step 2

Count the decimal places in *both* factors. Sometimes you have to insert one or more zeros into the product to place the decimal point.

$$\begin{array}{r} 1.5 \\ \times\ 0.05 \\ \hline 0.075 \end{array}$$

1.5 ← 1 decimal place
0.05 ← 2 decimal places
0.075 ← 3 decimal places

Since 3 decimal places are needed, insert a zero for the extra place.

The bumblebee bat weighs 0.075 of an ounce.

Problem Solving

33. In a phone survey, people were asked to name their favorite type of television show. The results are shown at the right.

a How many people named comedy as their favorite type of show?

b How many people were surveyed in all?

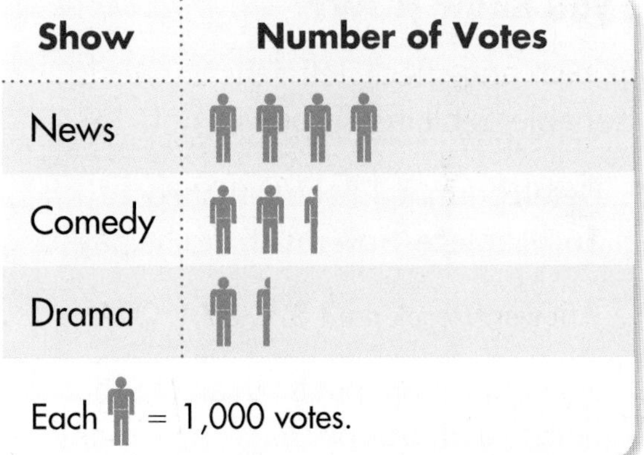

34. To promote a sale, a local supermarket is mailing postcards. Each postcard costs \$0.08 to print and \$0.29 to mail. How much will it cost to print and mail the postcards to 10,000 people?

35. Algebra The numbers below follow a pattern and are arranged from greatest to least. What number does *x* represent?

678,944 678,942 678,940 *x*

36. Erik spends 2.5 hours each day using his home computer. If the computer uses 0.8 kilowatt of electricity per hour, how many kilowatts of electricity does Erik use each day?

A 0.02 kilowatts

B 0.2 kilowatts

C 2 kilowatts

D 20 kilowatts

37. Find the missing factor represented by the diagram below. Then write the equation.

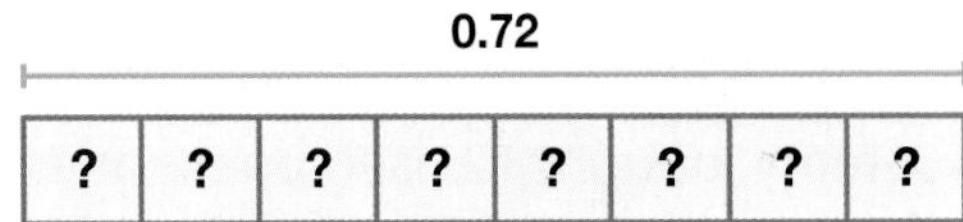

38. A Baltimore oriole weighs about 1.2 ounces. Is the weight of 10 orioles greater than or less than one pound?

Lesson 6-6

MR 2.5 Indicate the relative advantages of exact and approximate solutions to problems and give answers to a specified degree of accuracy.
Also **MR 2.0, 2.6, NS 2.1**

Problem Solving

Reasonableness

Julia bought 4 new hubcaps for her car. What was the total cost?

Is the following cost reasonable?

Answer: $\$75.80 \times 4 = \$30.320$
So, the total cost was $30.32.

After you solve a problem, check to see if your answer is reasonable.

Guided Practice*

Do you know HOW?

Look back and check. Tell if the answer is reasonable. Explain why or why not.

1. Derek bought 3 T-shirts that cost $6.79 apiece. How much did he pay?

   Answer: Derek paid $20.37.

2. If 54 photos are put in an album that holds 10 photos per page, how many pages are needed in all?

   Answer: 5 pages with 4 photos left

Do you UNDERSTAND?

3. If an estimate is close to the calculated answer, does that always mean that the calculated answer is correct? Explain.

4. **Write a Problem** Write a real-world problem that you can solve by multiplying. Give an answer to be checked for reasonableness.

Independent Practice

In **5** through **7**, look back and check. Tell if the answer is reasonable. Explain why or why not.

5. Nicole bought 1.8 pounds of cashews for $3.80 a pound. How pay did she pay?

   Answer: Nicole paid $68.40.

6. Jeremy bought 12 used books at a book fair. He paid $1.25 for each book. How much did he pay?

   Answer: Jeremy paid $18.

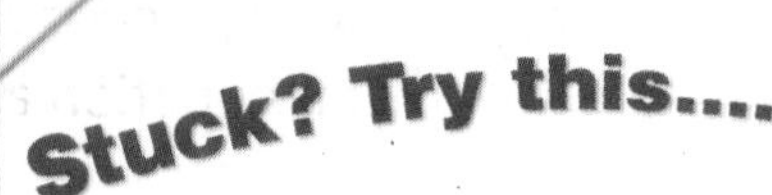

- What do I know?
- What am I asked to find?
- What diagram can I use to help understand the problem?
- Can I use addition, subtraction, multiplication, or division?
- Is all of my work correct?
- Did I answer the right question?
- Is my answer reasonable?

*For another example, see Set F on page 151.

Look Back and Check

Is my calculation reasonable?

Think *I can use estimation.*

\$75.80 is about 80.

\$80 × 4 = \$320.

My answer was \$30.32, but my estimate was \$320. My answer is not reasonable. I put the decimal point in the wrong place.

Did I answer the right question?

Think *The question asked for the total cost. I answered the right question, but my calculation was incorrect.*

The correct answer is \$303.20.

7. Mrs. Goia has 49 students in her art classes. She is ordering art supplies. Use the table at the right.

a How many cases of pastels does she need to order?

Answer: 17 cases

b How many cases of charcoals does she need to order?

Answer: 8 cases with 1 student left

Data

Art Supplies

Item	Number of Students
Case of pastels	3
Case of paints	4
Case of charcoals	6

8. Lionel is buying ice chests to hold 144 bottles of lemonade for a picnic. Each ice chest holds 20 bottles and some ice. How many ice chests should he buy? Explain.

9. Estimation Bridget sold 62 tickets to a school concert at \$3.95 each. About how much money did she collect for all 62 tickets?

10. Marcia has 27 red beads and 42 blue beads. How many beads does she have in all? Write an equation and solve.

b	
27	42

11. Pia needs 100 red beads to make a necklace. She already has 38 red beads. How many more red beads does she need? Write an equation and solve.

100	
38	*r*

12. Will earned \$1,800 in 12 months for delivering newspapers. He earned the same amount each month. How much did he earn each month?

13. Joyce bought a sweater for \$25.79 and a skirt for \$19.95. She paid with a \$50 bill. How much change did she receive?

Test Prep

1. April rode 12.3 miles on her bicycle on Monday. Which is the best estimate of the total distance April will ride if she rides the same distance each day for 7 days? (6-3)

A 84

B 91

C 105

D 120

2. A farmer plants 0.4 of a field with wheat. The field is 3.45 acres in size. How many acres are planted with wheat? (6-4)

A 0.126

B 0.138

C 1.26

D 1.38

3. If the product of 1,251 and 30 is 37,530, what is the product of 12.51 and 30? (6-2)

A 3.753

B 37.53

C 375.3

D 3,753

4. LaDonna bought 6 DVDs for presents. Each DVD was $24.57, including tax. Which is the best estimate of the amount of money LaDonna spent on the DVDs? (6-3)

A $100

B $120

C $130

D $150

5. A marathon race has 522 runners divided into 6 groups. What is a reasonable number of runners in each group? (6-6)

A 112, because 522 ÷ 6 is about 550 ÷ 5 = 110

B 98, because 522 ÷ 6 is about 500 ÷ 5 = 100

C 87, because 522 ÷ 6 is about 540 ÷ 6 = 90

D 82, because 522 ÷ 6 is about 480 ÷ 6 = 80

6. The table shows the average travel time to work for some cities. How many minutes would a resident of Philadelphia spend traveling to work and back home in a month with 22 work days? (6-2)

Data

City	Minutes Traveled to Work
New York	39.0
Los Angeles	28.1
Philadelphia	29.2

A 123.64

B 128.48

C 1,236.4

D 1,284.8

7. If the product of 475 and 2 is 950, what is the product of 4.75 and 0.002? (6-5)

A 0.00095

B 0.0095

C 0.095

D 0.95

Test Prep

8. Lucia scored an 8.65 on her first gymnastics event at a meet. If she scores the same score on each of four events, what will be her total score at the meet? (6-2)

A 32.48

B 34.6

C 34.8

D 346

9. Ahmad is downloading 10 files onto his computer. Each file is 4.82 MB in size. How many megabytes are used by all the files combined? (6-1)

A 482

B 48.2

C 0.482

D 0.0482

10. What is 3.57×4.6? (6-4)

A 3.570

B 13.882

C 16.422

D 164.22

11. What steps can be taken to find the product of 7.1 and 1,000? (6-1)

A Move the decimal point 4 places to the right and annex 3 zeros.

B Move the decimal point 4 places to the right and annex 2 zeros.

C Move the decimal point 3 places to the right and annex 3 zeros.

D Move the decimal point 3 places to the right and annex 2 zeros.

12.

Data

Notebook Prices

Quantity	Cost
1	$1.29
2	$2.32
5	$4.80
10	$9.00

How much would 10 students save if they bought 10 notebooks as a group rather than individually. (6-3)

A $3.90

B $4.20

C $5.51

D $7.71

13. Which of the following provides the best estimate of the product of 204 and 0.46? (6-3)

A $200 \times 0.5 = 100$

B $250 \times 0.5 = 125$

C $200 \times 1 = 200$

D $250 \times 1 = 250$

14. What is 2.1×0.005? (6-5)

A 0.0105

B 0.0150

C 0.1005

D 0.1050

15. What is 0.42×100? (6-1)

A 0.042

B 4.2

C 42

D 420

Reteaching

Set A, pages 136–137

Use the patterns in this table to find \$8.56 × 10 and \$0.36 × 100.

Multiply by	Move the decimal point to the right
1	0 places
10	1 place
100	2 places
1,000	3 places

\$8.56 × 10 = \$85.6 = \$85.60

\$0.36 × 100 = \$36 = \$36.00

Remember when you need to move the decimal point beyond the number of digits in the number you are multiplying, annex 1 or more zeros.

Use mental math to solve each problem.

1. 10 × 4.5
2. 100 × 4.5
3. 1,000 × 4.5
4. 10 × 0.89
5. 1,000 × 0.98
6. 10 × 0.0089

Set B, pages 138–139

Find 12 × 0.15.

Multiply as you would with whole numbers.

```
   12
 ×0.15
   60
 +120
  180
```

Count the decimal places in both factors. Then place the decimal point in the product the same number of places from the right.

12 × 0.15 = 1.80

Remember to count the decimal places in both factors before you place the decimal point in the product.

Find each product.

1. 100 × 3.67
2. 5.86 × 5
3. 14 × 9.67
4. 8 × 56.7
5. 11 × 0.006
6. 2.03 × 6

Set C, pages 140–141

Estimate \$4.78 × 18.

Round each number to the greatest place that has a non-zero digit.

```
$4.78 × 18
  ↓      ↓
 $5   × 20
```

\$5 × 20 = \$100.

Remember that compatible numbers can also be used to estimate products.

Estimate each product.

1. 24 × 3.67
2. 5.86 × 52
3. 14 × 9.67
4. 11 × 59.7
5. \$1.52 × 71
6. 34 × 41.5

Reteaching

Set D, pages 142–143

Find 3.6 × 2.15.
Estimate first: 4 × 2 = 8

Multiply as you would with whole numbers.

```
   2.1 5
×    3.6
  1290
+6450
  7740
```

Count the decimal places in both factors.
Place the decimal point in the product.

3.6 × 2.15 = 7.74.

Remember to count the decimal places in both factors before placing the decimal point in the product.

Find each product.

1. 2.4 × 3.67
2. 5.86 × 5.2
3. 8.3 × 10.7
4. 3.42 × 4.7
5. 1.4 × 9.67
6. 11.2 × 9.7
7. 3.4 × 8.42
8. 3.9 × 10.6

Set E, pages 144–145

Find 1.07 × 0.08.

Multiply as you would with whole numbers.

```
   1.07
× 0.08
    856
```

Count the decimal places in both factors. You may need to insert one or more zeros in the product to place the decimal point.

1.07 × 0.08 = 0.0856

Remember that zeros may have to be inserted at the beginning of the product before you place the decimal in the product.

Find each product.

1. 0.12 × 0.05
2. 0.08 × 0.6
3. 6.01 × 0.002
4. 0.01 × 6.04

Set F, pages 146–147

An album holds 4 photos per page. How many pages are needed for 30 photos?

30 ÷ 4 = 7 R2

Possible answer: 7 pages

Ask: *Is my calculation reasonable?*
Did I answer the right question?

In this case, the calculation is reasonable, but the question asked for the number of pages needed. Since there is a remainder of 2, one more page is needed. The correct answer is 8 pages.

Remember to check the reasonableness of a solution.

Tell if the answer is reasonable. Explain why or why not.

1. Sarah's DVD collection is stored in a cabinet that holds 6 DVDs on each shelf. She has 89 DVDs in her collection. How many shelves will she need to hold her collection?

Possible answer: 15 shelves

Topic 7

Dividing Decimals

1 About how many hours does it take to drive from Cheyenne, Wyoming, to the Devil's Tower National Monument in Wyoming? You will find out in Lesson 7-3.

2 How many times as fast does a quarter horse run than a garden snail moves per hour? You will find out in Lesson 7-4.

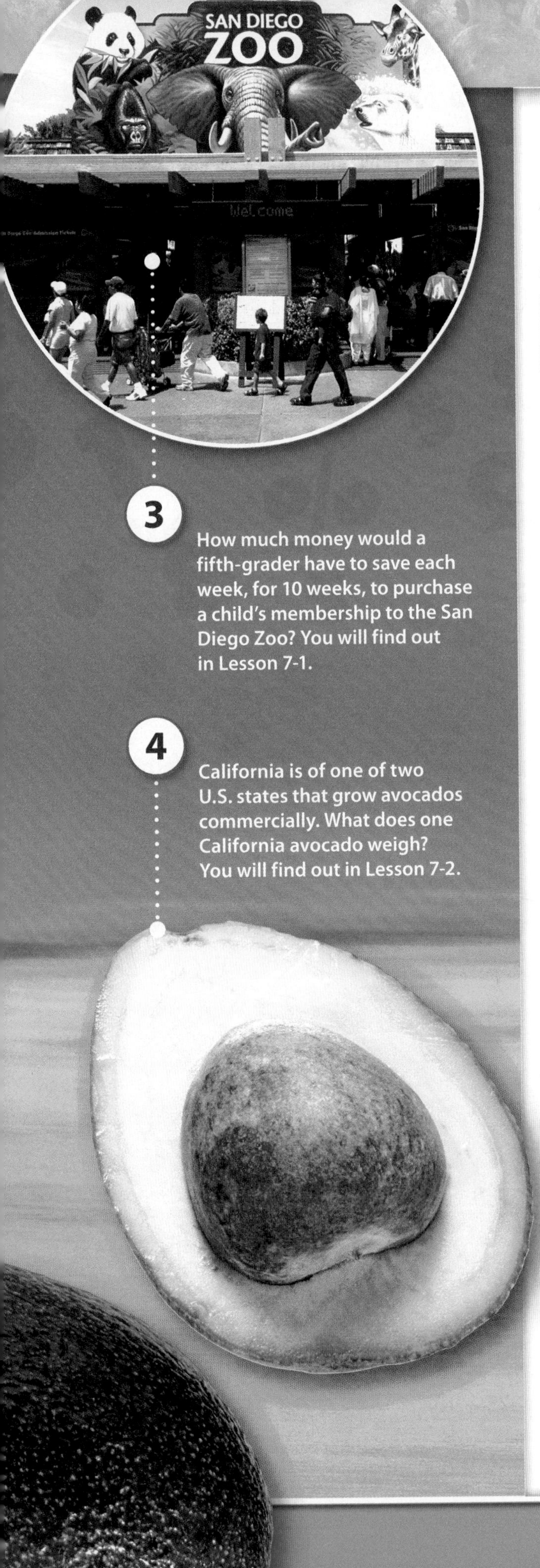

3

How much money would a fifth-grader have to save each week, for 10 weeks, to purchase a child's membership to the San Diego Zoo? You will find out in Lesson 7-1.

4

California is of one of two U.S. states that grow avocados commercially. What does one California avocado weigh? You will find out in Lesson 7-2.

Review What You Know!

Vocabulary

Choose the best term from the box.

- divisor
- remainder
- thousandths
- quotient
- tenths

1. The __?__ is the number that is left over after the division is complete.

2. In 450 ÷ 5 = 90, 90 is the __?__ and 5 is the __?__.

3. In 45.927, the 9 is in the __?__ place and the 7 is in the __?__ place.

Division Facts

4. 12 ÷ 3 **5.** 45 ÷ 9 **6.** 72 ÷ 9

7. 54 ÷ 6 **8.** 63 ÷ 7 **9.** 18 ÷ 6

Division Patterns

Use basic facts and patterns to divide mentally.

10. 36 ÷ 6
360 ÷ 6
3,600 ÷ 6

11. 49 ÷ 7
490 ÷ 7
4,900 ÷ 7

Division

Writing to Explain Write an answer for each question.

12. How is the number of zeros in the quotient of 5,600 ÷ 8 related to the number of zeros in the dividend?

13. How is dividing 240 by 80 similar to dividing 24 by 8?

Lesson

7-1

NS 2.1 Add, subtract, multiply, and divide with decimals; add with negative integers; subtract positive integers from negative integers; and verify the reasonableness of the results.
Also NS 2.2

Dividing Decimals by 10, 100, or 1,000

How can you divide decimals by 10, 100, and 1,000?

Shondra wants to cut a cloth into 10 strips. All the strips should be exactly the same size. How wide will each strip be?

Choose an Operation Divide to find equal parts of a whole.

89.5 cm

Guided Practice*

Do you know HOW?

In **1** through **6**, use mental math to find each quotient.

1. 370.2 ÷ 10

2. 126.4 ÷ 100

3. 684.5 ÷ 1,000

4. 72.5 ÷ 10

5. 28.14 ÷ 100

6. 42.5 ÷ 1,000

Do you UNDERSTAND?

7. Look at the table above. When dividing by 1,000, why was it necessary to place a zero in the tenths place?

8. If Shondra wanted to cut the cloth into 100 strips, how wide would each strip be?

Independent Practice

In **9** through **31**, find each quotient. Use mental math.

9. 23.75 ÷ 1
23.75 ÷ 10
23.75 ÷ 100
23.75 ÷ 1,000

10. 509.3 ÷ 1,000
509.3 ÷ 100
509.3 ÷ 10
509.3 ÷ 1

11. 98.2 ÷ 100
98.2 ÷ 1
98.2 ÷ 1,000
98.2 ÷ 10

12. 13.65 ÷ 10

13. 75.3 ÷ 100

14. 890.1 ÷ 1,000

15. 5.67 ÷ 100

16. 8.74 ÷ 100

17. 32.40 ÷ 1,000

18. 12.33 ÷ 10

19. 0.5 ÷ 10

20. 4.5 ÷ 10

21. 9.78 ÷ 100

22. 7,446.5 ÷ 1,000

23. 234.5 ÷ 10

24. 0.27 ÷ 100

25. 121.6 ÷ 1,000

26. 8.373 ÷ 10

27. 6.9 ÷ 1,000

28. 8.25 ÷ 10

29. 31.8 ÷ 100

30. 0.36 ÷ 1,000

31. 9.47 ÷ 100

For another example, see Set A on page 170.

Find 89.5 ÷ 10.

The quotient of a number divided by 10, 100, or 1,000 is less than the number.

Moving the decimal point in a number to the left decreases the number's value.

Since place-value is based on 10, dividing by 10, 100, or 1,000 gives the same result as moving the decimal point 1, 2, or 3 places.

Notice the patterns in the table.

Data

Divide by	Examples	Move decimal point to the left
1	12.5 ÷ 1 = 12.5	0 places
10	12.5 ÷ 10 = 1.25	1 place
100	12.5 ÷ 100 = 0.125	2 places
1,000	12.5 ÷ 1,000 = 0.0125	3 places

So, 89.5 ÷ 10 = 8.9.5 = 8.95

Each cloth strip will be 8.95 centimeters wide.

Problem Solving

For **32** through **34**, use the chart.

Pacific Middle School posted the winning times at the swim meet.

50-yard freestyle	22.17 seconds
100-yard backstroke	53.83 seconds
100-yard butterfly	58.49 seconds

32. What was the time per yard of the swimmer who swam the butterfly?

33. If the 50-yard freestyle swimmer could swim the 100-yard freestyle in exactly double his 50-yard time, what would his time per yard be?

34. What was the time per yard of the swimmer who swam the backstroke?

35. Rodella has a jar full of dimes. The total amount of money in her jar is $45.60. How many dimes does she have?

36. **Writing to Explain** How is dividing 360 by 10 similar to dividing 3,600 by 100? Explain.

37. Helen is saving to buy a Koala Club child's membership to the San Diego Zoo as a present for her brother. The membership fee is $21.50. Helen has 10 weeks in which to save for it. How much money should she save each week?

38. **Algebra** In which of the following equations does $n = 100$?

A $1946.8 \div n = 1.9468$

B $61.5 \div n = 0.615$

C $11.73 \div n = 0.01173$

D $4.12 \div n = 0.412$

39. The dimensions of a room are shown on a blueprint by the measures of 12 inches long and 10 inches wide. The actual room is 12 times as big. How many feet long and wide is the actual room?

Lesson
7-2

NS 2.1 Add, subtract, multiply, and divide with decimals; add with negative integers; subtract positive integers from negative integers; and verify the reasonableness of the results.
Also NS 2.2

Dividing a Decimal by a Whole Number

How do you divide a decimal by a whole number?

The three children in the Diego family are equally sharing the cost of an anniversary gift for their parents. How much will each child pay?

Choose an Operation Divide to find equal shares of the whole price.

Other Examples

When do you write more zeros to the right of the decimal point in the dividend?

You know how to divide decimals by 10, 100, or 1,000. Now you will learn to divide decimals by other whole numbers.

Ann hiked for 6 hours on the river trail. She hiked a total of 19.5 miles. How many miles did she hike each hour?

Find 19.5 ÷ 6.

```
   3.25
6)19.50
  18
   15
   12
    30
    30
     0
```

You can annex a 0 at the end of 19.5 in order to continue dividing.

Ann hiked 3.25 miles each hour.

Ann bought hiking and camping gear for a total of $239.49. She paid for the gear in 5 equal installments. How much was each installment?

Find 239.49 ÷ 5.

```
   $ 47.898
5)$239.490
   20
    39
    35
     44
     40
      49
      45
       40
       40
        0
```

Sometimes when you divide with money, there is a remainder after you divide the hundredths.

Annex a zero after the hundredths place of the dividend and continue dividing to determine the thousandths place of the quotient.

Then round the quotient to the nearest hundredth. So, $239.49 ÷ 5 is about $47.90.

Ann paid in installments of $47.90.

Explain It

1. Why must a zero be annexed to the right of the decimal point in the dividend?
2. Why is a quotient that represents money rounded to the nearest hundredth?

Step 1

Find 42.45 ÷ 3.

Write the decimal point in the quotient directly above the decimal point in the dividend.

$3\overline{)\$42.45}$

Step 2

Divide the same way you would divide whole numbers.

$$\begin{array}{r} \$14.15 \\ 3\overline{)\$42.45} \\ -3 \\ \hline 12 \\ 12 \\ \hline 4 \\ 3 \\ \hline 15 \\ 15 \\ \hline 0 \end{array}$$

Step 3

Use multiplication to check.

$$\begin{array}{r} \$14.15 \\ \times \quad 3 \\ \hline \$42.45 \end{array}$$

Each child will pay $14.15.

Guided Practice*

Do you know HOW?

In **1** through **10**, find each quotient.

1. $4\overline{)\$6.48}$

2. $3\overline{)\$7.32}$

3. $5\overline{)4.50}$

4. $50\overline{)5.5}$

5. 1.90 ÷ 19

6. 13.2 ÷ 11

7. 5.6 ÷ 8

8. 12.5 ÷ 25

9. 22.1 ÷ 17

10. 26.52 ÷ 13

Do you UNDERSTAND?

11. For 3.6 ÷ 60, why do you need to write a zero to the right of the decimal point in the quotient?

12. How is dividing decimals unlike dividing whole numbers?

13. **Reasonableness** All 5 members of the Diego family went to dinner and shared the bill, which was $78.49, equally. Was each person's share less than $16.50?

Independent Practice

In **14** through **28**, find each quotient.

14. $2\overline{)\$56.84}$

15. $6\overline{)\$120.72}$

16. $7\overline{)\$35.14}$

17. $9\overline{)36.27}$

18. $16\overline{)39.68}$

19. $18\overline{)324.18}$

20. 64.33 ÷ 5

21. 406.2 ÷ 30

22. 489.6 ÷ 32

23. 297.81 ÷ 9

24. 175.75 ÷ 25

25. 35.902 ÷ 58

26. 432.88 ÷ 8

27. 28.4 ÷ 40

28. 1.5 ÷ 20

*For another example, see Set B on page 170.

Problem Solving

29. If one dozen of the same size California avocados weighs 7.2 lb, what does one avocado weigh?

30. **Number Sense** Without doing the division, how do you know that 84 ÷ 17 could not be 14?

31. While traveling in the car, Juanita counted 27 out-of-state license plates, Carol counted 19, and Ramon counted 22. How many more out-of-state license plates did Juanita count than Carol?

32. Cora is saving for a vacation. The total cost of the vacation is $1,800.36, and she has a year to save the money. How much should she save per month so she can meet her goal?

33. Joe took out a $7,200 loan to buy a used car. He will make monthly payments for 4 years. How much will Joe pay each month on his loan?

34. **Algebra** A college baseball stadium holds 6,000 people. At a recent game only 5,145 seats were filled. Tickets to the game cost $12 each. Write and solve an equation to find how many seats were empty.

35. **Think About the Process** Tina bought 3 plants at $2.50 each and 3 clay pots at $4.25 each. Which expression shows how to find how much Tina spent on the plants and pots?

A ($2.50 + $4.25) + 3

B (3 + $4.25) × (3 + $2.50)

C (3 × $4.25) + (3 × $2.50)

D 3 × ($4.25 × $2.50)

36. **Think About the Process** Jill is 4 years older than Keiko. Robert is 2 years older than Keiko. If you know that Keiko is 12 years old, which number sentence can you use to find the sum, *s*, of the three ages?

A $s = 2 + 4 + 12$

B $s = (12 - 4) + (12 - 2) + 12$

C $s = (12 + 4) + (12 - 2) + 12$

D $s = (12 + 4) + (12 + 2) + 12$

37. Four college friends decided to share an apartment and some expenses equally.

a They plan to paint the apartment before they move in. The cost of paint and supplies is $76.80. What is each person's share?

b They plan to budget $225 for food each month. What is each person's share?

c The telephone service will cost $36.95 per month. What is each person's share?

38. Alyson works as a waitress. Last week she earned a total of $128.60 in tips in 5 days. How much did she earn in tips each day, if she earned the same amount each day?

39. **Writing to Explain** Why don't the expressions 4 × 6 + 9 and 4 × (6 + 9) have the same value?

Algebra Connections

Completing Tables

Remember that multiplication and division have an inverse relationship.

Since $9 \times 7 = 63$, you also know:

$$63 \div 9 = 7$$

$$63 \div 7 = 9$$

You can use inverse relationships to help complete tables.

Example:

There are 4 quarts in a gallon. Complete the table.

gallons	1	3	8	
quarts	4	12		40

You can multiply the number of gallons by 4 to find the number of quarts.

$8 \times 4 = 32$. So, 8 gallons = 32 quarts.

You can divide the number of quarts by 4 to find the number of gallons.

$40 \div 4 = 10$. So, 40 quarts = 10 gallons.

Copy and complete each table below.

1. Each box holds 5 pencils.

Pencils	15	30	35	40	45
Boxes	3				9

2. Each shelf has 10 books.

Shelves	2	3	4		
Books	20			50	90

3. A frame holds 4 photos.

Frames	2	3		5	
Photos			16		36

4. Each package has 8 markers.

Packages	2	4	5		
Markers				72	80

5. Mallory swims 2 miles per day.

Days	1	3		10	
Miles			16		60

6. Each week has 7 days.

Weeks	2	4			12
Days			35	63	

Lesson

7-3

NS 2.1 Add, subtract, multiply, and divide with decimals; add with negative integers; subtract positive integers from negative integers; and verify the reasonableness of the results.
Also NS 2.2, NS 1.1

Estimation: Decimals Divided by Whole Numbers

How can you estimate quotients with decimals?

Cheryl is saving $23 every week to buy a digital camera. About how many weeks will it take her to save enough money to buy the digital camera?

Choose an Operation Divide to find equal parts of the price. Estimate $269.95 ÷ $23.

$269.95

Guided Practice*

Do you know HOW?

In **1** through **8**, estimate each quotient.

1. 63.5 ÷ 8

2. 72.8 ÷ 10

3. 19.45 ÷ 4

4. 34.25 ÷ 7

5. 105.8 ÷ 11

6. 245.74 ÷ 83

7. 290.6 ÷ 31

8. 564.9 ÷ 90

Do you UNDERSTAND?

9. When would you estimate a quotient instead of finding a more accurate answer?

10. In the example above, if Cheryl could save $32 every week, about how many weeks would it take her to save enough money to buy the camera?

Independent Practice

In **11** through **13**, choose the best estimate for each quotient.

11. 47.52 ÷ 83

A 60 **C** 0.6

B 6 **D** 0.06

12. 18.9 ÷ 21

A 1 **C** 0.01

B 0.1 **D** 0.001

13. 36.6 ÷ 40

A 0.009 **C** 0.9

B 0.09 **D** 9

In **14** through **28**, estimate each quotient.

14. 270.9 ÷ 3

15. 87.3 ÷ 11

16. 7.75 ÷ 4

17. 556.3 ÷ 61

18. 31.77 ÷ 8

19. 56.4 ÷ 19

20. 976.4 ÷ 47

21. 869.77 ÷ 27

22. 195.6 ÷ 12

23. 91.26 ÷ 2

24. 44.8 ÷ 5

25. 88.34 ÷ 4

26. $15.75 ÷ 9

27. $274.89 ÷ 26

28. $346.95 ÷ 52

*For another example, see Set C on page 170.

One Way

Round each number to the greatest place that has a nonzero digit.

$$\$269.95 \div 23$$
$$\downarrow \quad \downarrow$$
$$300 \div 20$$

$300 \div 20 = 15$

Cheryl will take about 15 weeks to save enough money to buy the digital camera.

Another Way

Use compatible numbers that you can divide mentally.

$$\$269.95 \div 23$$
$$\downarrow \quad \downarrow$$
$$275 \div 25 = 11$$

Cheryl will take about 11 weeks to save enough money to buy the digital camera.

Problem Solving

29. There are 40 mg of caffeine in a 3-cup teapot of green tea. About how many milligrams of caffeine would be in one cup?

30. Jeremy paid \$575 for a plane ticket, including tax of \$21 and an airport fee of \$12. What was the cost of the ticket before tax and the airport fee?

31. A three-pound package of ground beef costs \$11.78. About how much does one pound cost?

32. Kira cycles about 10 miles every day. About how many miles does she cycle in 4 weeks?

33. **Writing to Explain** Rosa babysits from 10 A.M. until 3 P.M. five days per week during the summer. She watches four children, makes lunch, and drives them to swim practice. Her pay is \$380.25 per week. How would you estimate the amount she is paid per hour?

34. **Algebra** Tickets to a movie cost \$9 for an adult. Student tickets cost \$5. Which expression shows the cost of tickets for a group, g, of students?

A $5 + g$ **C** $5 \times g$

B $9 + g$ **D** $9 \times g$

35. In science class, a student weighed three samples and found the weights to be 0.098 gram, 0.58 gram, and 0.005 gram. Which sample weighed the most?

36. One route from Cheyenne, Wyoming, to Devil's Tower National Monument is approximately 305.4 miles. If a car is driven between 55 and 60 miles per hour, about how many hours will the trip take?

37. A 300-foot fence has a flag on each post. There are posts at each end and every 6 feet along the fence. How many flags are on the fence?

38. **Reasoning** Find the pattern in the numbers below, and then write the next three numbers.

32, 16, 8, 4, 2, 1, 0.5, . . .

Lesson
7-4

NS 2.1 Add, subtract, multiply, and divide with decimals; add with negative integers; subtract positive integers from negative integers; and verify the reasonableness of the results.
Also **NS 2.2**

Dividing a Decimal by a Decimal

How can you divide a decimal by a decimal?

Ms. Hendricks bought 0.84 pound of almonds. What is the price per pound of almonds?

Choose an Operation Divide the amount paid by the number of pounds bought to find the price per pound.

Guided Practice*

Do you know HOW?

In **1** through **6**, find each quotient. Write more zeros in the dividends when needed.

1. 4.2 ÷ 0.7

2. 4.52 ÷ 0.2

3. 0.081 ÷ 0.9

4. 23.28 ÷ 9.7

5. 37.2 ÷ 2.4

6. 25.2 ÷ 0.5

Do you UNDERSTAND?

7. For the example above, how would you check the answer?

8. Mary paid $3.60 for pecans that cost $3.75 per pound. How many pounds of pecans did she buy?

Independent Practice

Leveled Practice In **9** through **12**, find each quotient.

9. $0.6\overline{)43.2}$ = 7▢.
42
1 2
▢▢
0

10. $0.7\overline{)1.61}$ = 2.▢
14
▢▢
▢▢
0

11. $3.9\overline{)7.02}$ = 1.▢
3 9
▢▢▢
▢▢▢
0

12. $1.5\overline{)4.8}$ = 3.▢
45
30
▢▢
0

In **13** through **24**, find each quotient.

13. $0.08\overline{)0.104}$

14. $1.3\overline{)6.89}$

15. $0.9\overline{)5.49}$

16. $5.8\overline{)3.48}$

17. 69.09 ÷ 0.7

18. 0.410 ÷ 0.2

19. 91.53 ÷ 0.3

20. 0.804 ÷ 0.4

21. 9.483 ÷ 8.7

22. 0.427 ÷ 6.1

23. 28.14 ÷ 1.2

24. 36.8 ÷ 0.25

*For another example, see Set D on page 171.

Step 1

Find 3.99 ÷ 0.84.

Multiply the divisor by a power of 10 to make it a whole number.

$0.84 \times 100 = 84$

$0.84.\overline{)3.99}$

Step 2

Multiply the dividend by the same power of 10.

$3.99 \times 100 = 399$

$0.84.\overline{)3.99.}$

Step 3

Place the decimal point in the quotient. Divide as you would with whole numbers.

$$\begin{array}{r} 4.75 \\ 84\overline{)399.00} \\ -\,336 \\ \hline 630 \\ 588 \\ \hline 420 \\ 420 \\ \hline 0 \end{array}$$

Since the quotient represents money, annex two more zeros in the dividend to show cents.

The almonds cost $4.75 per pound.

Problem Solving

For **25** through **27**, use the chart at the right.

The chart below shows a few recent prices at The Farm Stand.

Fruit	Price per Pound
Pears	$1.38
Apples	$1.25
Cherries	$1.17
Bananas	$0.39

25. How many pounds of apples could you buy for $8.00?

26. How much would a half pound of pears cost?

27. The price of a pound of cherries is how many times the price of a pound of bananas?

28. An overseas phone call costs $57.66 for 31 minutes. How much does the call cost per minute?

29. Jean paid $21.42 for the 6.8 gallons of gasoline that she put in her car's tank. What was the price per gallon?

30. Tom arranged tiles in the pattern below.

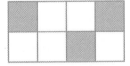

In which pair do both fractions describe the floor tiles that are shaded?

A $\frac{1}{2}, \frac{4}{8}$

B $\frac{3}{8}, \frac{6}{8}$

C $\frac{3}{8}, \frac{6}{16}$

D $\frac{3}{8}, \frac{3}{16}$

31. A quarter horse can run 53.16 miles per hour, and a garden snail can move 0.02 of a mile per hour. How many times as fast does the quarter horse run than the garden snail moves?

32. Writing to Explain How could you use estimation to check the reasonableness of the quotient for 3.99 ÷ 0.84?

Lesson

7-5

MR 1.2 Determine when and how to break a problem into simpler parts.
Also NS 2.1 and MR 2.3

Problem Solving

Multiple-Step Problems

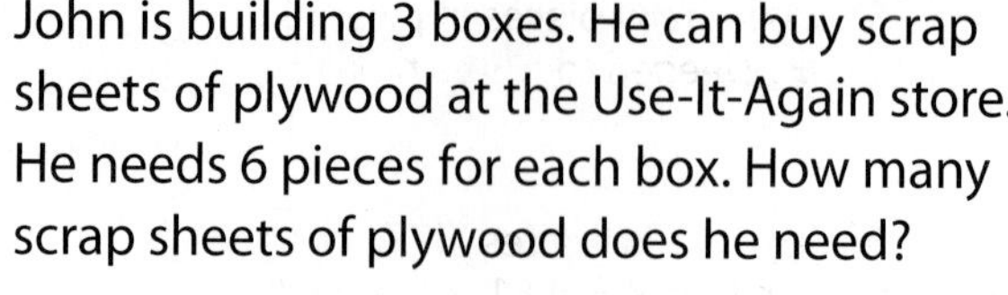

John is building 3 boxes. He can buy scrap sheets of plywood at the Use-It-Again store. He needs 6 pieces for each box. How many scrap sheets of plywood does he need?

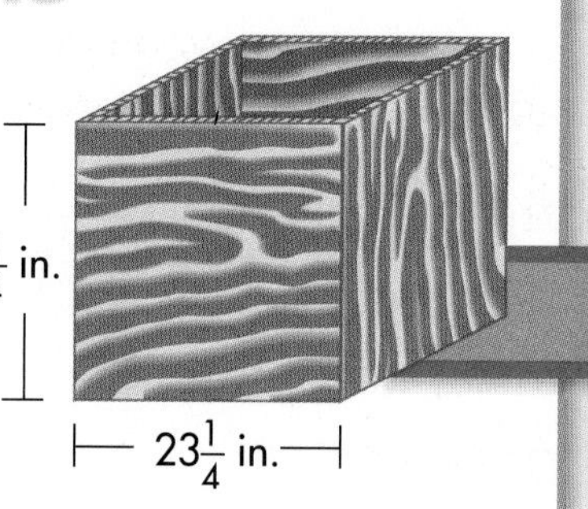

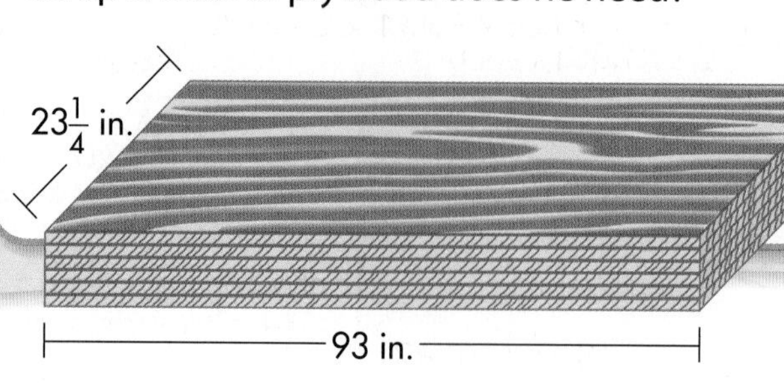

Another Example

The Marcos family went on a 2-week trip to San Diego. They drove 575 miles to get there and 627 miles to return home. In San Diego, they drove 121 miles while sightseeing. Their car can travel an average of 31.5 miles on 1 gallon of gas. If the car's gas tank can hold 14 gallons of gas, how many tanks of gas did they use on vacation?

What is one hidden question?

How many miles did the Marcos family drive?

575 miles + 627 miles + 121 miles = 1,323 miles

The Marcos family drove 1,323 miles on their trip.

What is another hidden question?

How many gallons of gas did they use on their trip?

1,323 miles ÷ 31.5 miles per gallon = 42 gallons

The Marcos family used 42 gallons of gas on their trip.

Divide the number of gallons used by the number of gallons in a full tank of gas.

42 gallons used ÷ 14 gallons in a full tank = 3 full tanks

The Marcos family used 3 tanks of gas on their trip to San Diego.

Explain It

1. Why do you need to find the hidden questions in order to solve the problem?

Read and Understand

What do I know?

Six pieces of plywood for each of 3 boxes are needed.

Boxes are $23\frac{1}{4}$ inch cubes.

Each sheet of plywood is $23\frac{1}{4}$ inches wide and 93 inches long

What am I asked to find?

The number of sheets of plywood needed to buy

Plan and Solve

Find the hidden question or questions.

1. How many pieces of plywood are needed for three boxes?

3	×	6	=	18
boxes		pieces in each		pieces in all

2. How many pieces of plywood can be cut from 1 scrap sheet of plywood?

$93 \div 23.25 = 4$

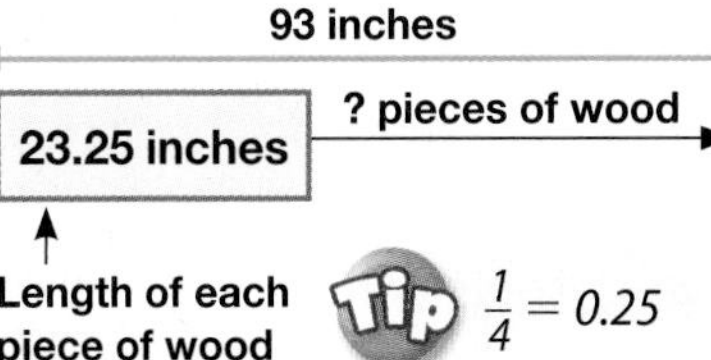

Tip $\frac{1}{4} = 0.25$

3. How many sheets of plywood are needed for three boxes?

$18 \div 4 = 4 \text{ R2}$

John needs to buy 5 sheets of plywood.

Guided Practice*

Do you know HOW?

Solve the problem.

1. Tom bought 8 chicken breasts and 5 steaks. Each chicken breast weighed 0.35 pound and each steak weighed 1.25 pound. How many pounds of meat did Tom buy?

Do you UNDERSTAND?

2. What are the hidden questions and answers in Problem 1?

3. **Write a Problem** Write a real-world multiple-step problem that can be solved using multiplication and division.

Independent Practice

In **4** through **7**, write the hidden question or questions. Then solve.

4. Alyssa has a CD that holds 700 megabytes of information. She has saved 53 pictures, each using 2.24 megabytes, to the CD. How much space is left on the CD?

5. Lori bought some plums and 4 peaches. The peaches cost $1.88 in all and the plums cost $0.33 each. She paid $3.86 in all, not including tax. How many plums did she buy?

Stuck? Try this....

- What do I know?
- What am I asked to find?
- What diagram can I use to help understand the problem?
- Can I use addition, subtraction, multiplication, or division?
- Is all of my work correct?
- Did I answer the right question?
- Is my answer reasonable?

For another example, see Set E on page 171.

Independent Practice

For **6**, use the chart at the right.

6. The school cafeteria manager needs to know how many food trays are needed during a week. All of the students eat lunch each school day, and half of all the students eat breakfast. How many trays will be needed in one week?

Data

Grade	Number of Students	Grade	Number of Students
K	95	3	107
1	112	4	100
2	104	5	114

7. Juan used first-class mail to send two baseballs to his grandson. Each baseball weighed 5 ounces. The postage was \$0.39 for the first ounce and \$0.24 for each additional ounce. How much was the postage?

8. The Meadows Farm has 160 acres. Three times as many acres are used to plant crops as are used for pasture. Draw a picture and write an equation to find how many acres are used for pasture.

9. A youth group charged \$6 per car at their car wash to raise money. They raised \$858. Of that amount, \$175 was given as donations and the rest of the money came from washing cars. Stella estimated that they washed more than 100 cars. Is her estimate reasonable? Explain your reasoning.

10. A hardware store has 5 employees. Each employee works the same number of hours every week, and each one earns \$10.50 per hour. Last week they worked a total of 167.5 hours. Draw a picture and write an equation to find how many hours each employee worked.

Think About the Process

11. Matt is saving to buy a skateboard and a helmet. The skateboard costs \$57 and the helmet costs \$45. Matt has saved \$19 so far. Which hidden question needs to be answered before you can find how much more he needs to save?

A Is the skateboard on sale?

B How much more does the skateboard cost than the helmet?

C What is the price of the skateboard minus the price of the helmet?

D What is the total price of the helmet and the skateboard?

12. Two restaurant waiters share $\frac{1}{4}$ of their tips with the dishwasher. On Saturday, one waiter earned \$122 in tips, and the other waiter earned \$136 in tips. Which expression shows how to find the solution to the hidden question?

A $122 + 136$

B $\frac{1}{4} \times 136$

C $\frac{1}{4} \times 122$

D $136 - 122$

Stop and Practice

Find the quotient. Estimate to check if the answer is reasonable.

1. 14.5 ÷ 2.5 **2.** 2.28 ÷ 0.6 **3.** 69.02 ÷ 0.7 **4.** 88.5 ÷ 0.03

5. 0.08 ÷ 0.025 **6.** 3.2 ÷ 0.004 **7.** 15.5 ÷ 6.2 **8.** 2.35 ÷ 4.7

Find the product. Estimate to check if the answer is reasonable.

9. 0.07×0.09 **10.** 5.6×0.08 **11.** 6.98×3.8 **12.** 1.3×0.04

13. 0.67×3.6 **14.** 6.8×9.4 **15.** 8.88×0.08 **16.** 0.03×0.3

Evaluate each expression. Use order of operations.

17. $2 \times 7 + 25 \div 5$ **18.** $(17 - 8) \times 5 + 1$ **19.** $47 - (3 + 6) \times 5 + 1$

Error Search Find each answer that is not correct. Write it correctly and explain the error.

20. 2.748 ÷ 0.6 = 0.0458 **21.** 7.86 ÷ 6 = 1.31 **22.** $26.82 \times 3 = 80.45$ **23.** $5.87 \times 4.9 = 287.63$

Number Sense

Estimating and Reasoning Write whether each statement is true or false. Explain your reasoning.

24. The quotient of 4.35 ÷ 6 is closer to 0.7 than 0.8.

25. The expression $8e + 6$ equals 30 when $e = 3$.

26. The product of 5.7 and 8.63 is less than 54.

27. The quotient of 3,467 ÷ 5 is closer to 700 than the quotient of 5,598 ÷ 8.

28. The sum of 99,999 and 3,879 is 1 more than 103,879.

29. The product of 6 and 808 is greater than the product of 8 and 606.

Test Prep

1. Mr. Dodd filled the gas tank on his lawn mower with 3.8 gallons of gas. If he mowed his yard 10 times on the same tank of gas, how much gas did he use each time the lawn was mowed? (7-1)

A 0.038 gallons

B 0.38 gallons

C 38 gallons

D 380 gallons

2. Gilbert bought a package of 48 golf balls for $13.44. What is the price of each golf ball? (7-2)

A $0.28

B $0.30

C $2.80

D $2.81

3. The table shows the amount of different types of produce Mrs. Cuzalina bought, and the total price she paid for each. What is the price per pound she paid for the apples? (7-4)

Data

Produce	Pounds	Total Price
Apples	3.4	$2.89
Bananas	2.6	$1.27
Grapes	3.7	$2.85

A $0.09

B $0.80

C $0.84

D $0.85

4. The chef at a restaurant in San Francisco bought 37 pounds of salad for $46.25. How much did she pay for 1 pound of salad? (7-2)

A $0.125

B $1.25

C $1.30

D $12.50

5. What is 171.84 ÷ 0.8? (7-4)

A 214.8

B 201.48

C 21.48

D 20.48

6. Trevor grew 3.28 inches over a 16 week period. What is the average number of inches he grew each week? (7-2)

A 0.025

B 0.205

C 0.3

D 2.05

7. If 249 ÷ 6 = 41.5, what is 2.49 ÷ 6? (7-2)

A 41.5

B 4.15

C 0.415

D 0.0415

8. What is 32.62 ÷ 100? (7-1)

A 0.3262

B 3.262

C 326.2

D 3,262

Test Prep

9. Mrs. Delgato needs to buy 50 begonias for her flowerbed. According to the prices shown, how much would she save if she bought them by the flat instead of separately? (7-5)

Begonias
$1.75 each
$35.50 per flat (25 plants per flat)

A $8.25

B $16.50

C $33.00

D $52.00

10. Which of the following is the best estimate of 78.4 ÷ 18? (7-3)

A 740

B 50

C 5

D 4

11. What is 2.48 ÷ 1,000? (7-1)

A 0.248

B 0.0248

C 0.00248

D 0.000248

12. Which of the following uses show the best way to estimate 62.45 ÷ 9? (7-3)

A 64 ÷ 10 = 6.4

B 60 ÷ 10 = 6

C 62 ÷ 10 = 6.2

D 63 ÷ 9 = 7

13. Which step should be taken to find the quotient of 56.8 ÷ 100? (7-1)

A Move the decimal point in 56.8 two places to the left.

B Move the decimal point in 56.8 one place to the left.

C Move the decimal point in 56.8 two places to the right.

D Move the decimal point in 56.8 one place to the right.

14. A developer owns 24 acres of land. If he plans to use 1.2 acres of the land for an entrance into a housing development and divide the remaining land into 0.6 acre lots, how many lots will he have? (7-5)

A 42

B 40

C 38

D 2

15. What is 43.68 ÷ 5.2? (7-4)

A 0.84

B 7.99

C 8.04

D 8.4

16. Mrs. Frohock bought a watermelon that weighed 10.25 pounds. If she cut it into 5 pieces of equal weight, how many pounds did each piece weigh? (7-2)

A 2.5

B 2.15

C 2.05

D 0.25

Reteaching

Set A, pages 154–155

Find 34.05 ÷ 100.

Dividing by 100 means moving the decimal point two places to the left.

34.05 ÷ 100 = 0.3405

Dividing by 10 means moving the decimal point one place to the left.

Dividing by 1,000 means moving the decimal point three places to the left.

Remember that when dividing decimals by 10, 100, or 1,000, you may need to use one or more zeros as placeholders:
24.3 ÷ 1,000 = 0.**0**243.

Use mental math to find each quotient.

1. 34.6 ÷ 10 **2.** 64.83 ÷ 100

3. 148.3 ÷ 1,000 **4.** 2.99 ÷ 100

5. 7.07 ÷ 10 **6.** 59.13 ÷ 1,000

7. 8.94 ÷ 100 **8.** 6.34 ÷ 10

Set B, pages 156–158

Find 3.60 ÷ 15.

$$\begin{array}{r} 0.24 \\ 15\overline{)3.60} \\ \underline{3\,0} \\ 60 \\ \underline{60} \\ 0 \end{array}$$

Place the decimal point in the quotient directly above the decimal point in the dividend. Then divide.

So, 3.60 ÷ 15 = 0.24.

Multiply to check.

0.24 × 15 = 3.60

Remember to write a zero placeholder in the quotient when you cannot divide a place in the dividend.

Find each quotient.

1. $7\overline{)12.6}$ **2.** $31\overline{)17.05}$

3. $8\overline{)51.2}$ **4.** $12\overline{)60.12}$

5. 199.68 ÷ 64 **6.** 152.5 ÷ 5

7. 47.61 ÷ 23 **8.** 51.6 ÷ 43

Set C, pages 160–161

Estimate: 25.1 ÷ 11.

Use compatible numbers.

25.1 ÷ 11
↓ ↓
24 ÷ 12 = 2

So, 25.1 ÷ 11 is about 2.

Remember that compatible numbers are numbers that are easy to compute in your head.

Estimate each quotient.

1. 26.2 ÷ 5 **2.** 31.9 ÷ 3

3. 49.6 ÷ 6 **4.** 163.5 ÷ 80

5. 4,352.9 ÷ 74 **6.** 538.6 ÷ 64

7. 251.6 ÷ 38 **8.** 819.7 ÷ 21

9. 83.62 ÷ 7 **10.** 571.3 ÷ 79

Set D, pages 162–163

Find 57.9 ÷ 0.6.

Since 0.6 has one decimal place, move the decimal point one place to the right in both numbers. Then divide.

```
       96.5
0.6)57.90
     54
     39
     36
      30
      30
       0
```

Annex more zeros in the dividend if needed.

57.9 ÷ 0.6 = 96.5

Remember to place the decimal point in the quotient above the decimal point in the dividend before dividing.

1. 79.36 ÷ 3.2
2. 73.44 ÷ 3.6
3. 78.6 ÷ 0.03
4. 9.315 ÷ 0.81
5. 0.903 ÷ 2.1
6. 4.56 ÷ 0.5
7. 16.4 ÷ 0.8
8. 136.5 ÷ 4.2
9. 22.22 ÷ 2.2
10. 54.78 ÷ 6.6
11. 71.04 ÷ 7.4
12. 40.02 ÷ 8.7
13. 9.6 ÷ 0.03
14. 74.48 ÷ 9.8

Set E, pages 164–166

A football coach spent a total of $890.40, including $50.40 tax, for 35 shirts for the team. Each shirt was the same price. What was the price of one shirt?

What is the hidden question or questions?

How much did all of the shirts cost without tax?

$890.40

$50.40	?

$890.40 – $50.40 = $840.00

What is the price of one shirt?

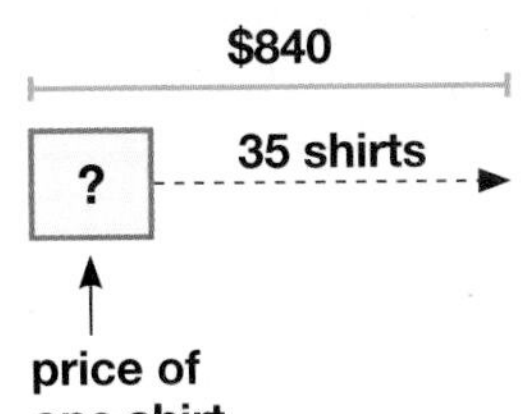

$840 ÷ 35 = $24

The price of one shirt was $24.00.

Remember to answer the hidden question or questions first to solve the problem.

Write and answer the hidden question or questions. Then solve.

1. Royce bought a book for $12.49 and 2 DVDs. Both DVDs were the same price. The tax on all the items is $1.76. He paid a total of $46.23. What was the price of each DVD?

2. Kim bought sandwiches for the football team. Each sandwich cost $3.49. She paid $142.39, including $2.79 tax. How many sandwiches did she buy?

Topic 8

Shapes

1 The Louvre Pyramid serves as the main entrance to the Louvre Museum in Paris, France. How can you classify one of the triangular faces of the pyramid? You will find out in Lesson 8-4.

2 What polygons can be found in the architecture of the Palace of Fine Arts in San Francisco, California? You will find out in Lesson 8-3.

3

What shape do these wasps create when they build their hive? You will find out in Lesson 8-3.

4

What kinds of angles are formed by the handles of the world's largest basket? You will find out in Lesson 8-2.

Review What You Know!

Vocabulary

Choose the best term from the box.

- algebraic expression
- equation
- variable

1. $3x = 15$ is a(n) __?__.

2. $3x$ is a(n) __?__.

3. In $3x$, x is the __?__.

Rules and Tables

Write the rule using words, and then with a variable.

4.

in	*out*
36	6
42	7
48	8

5.

in	*out*
5	12
10	17
15	22

Fractions

Write the fraction. Simplify if necessary.

6. If 2 out of 4 bananas are green, what fraction names the green bananas?

7. If $\frac{5}{6}$ of a loaf of bread is eaten, what part of the loaf is NOT eaten?

Multiplying Factors

Writing to Explain Write an answer to the question.

8. Clint bought 3 T-shirts at \$9 each and 2 pairs of shorts at \$12 each. Explain how to find the total Clint spent.

Lesson
8-1

MG 2.1 Measure, identify, and draw angles, perpendicular and parallel lines, rectangles, and triangles by using appropriate tools (e.g., straightedge, ruler, compass, protractor, drawing software).

Basic Geometric Ideas

How can you describe locations and parts of space?

Points, lines, and planes are basic geometric concepts. Engineers and architects use these concepts in designing streets, buildings, and structures.

Other Examples

	What You Draw	What You Say	What You Write
A line segment is part of a line and has 2 endpoints.	R ● —— ● S	Line segment *RS*	$\overline{RS}$
A ray is part of a line. It has only one endpoint and extends forever in one direction.	J ● ——→ K	Ray *JK*	$\overrightarrow{JK}$
Parallel lines never cross and stay the same distance apart.	A, D; V, W	Line *AD* is parallel to line *VW*.	$\overleftrightarrow{AD} \parallel \overleftrightarrow{VW}$
Intersecting lines pass through the same point.	P, C; Q, E	Line *PE* intersects line *QC*.	$\overleftrightarrow{PE}$ intersects $\overleftrightarrow{QC}$
Perpendicular lines are intersecting lines that form square corners.	F, R, H, S This symbol means square corner or right angle.	Line *RS* is perpendicular to line *FH*.	$\overleftrightarrow{RS} \perp \overleftrightarrow{FH}$

Explain It

1. Are $\overleftrightarrow{XB}$ and $\overleftrightarrow{YU}$ parallel or intersecting? Explain how you know.
2. Are all perpendicular lines intersecting? Are all intersecting lines perpendicular?

A point is an exact location in space.

What you draw: • C

What you say: Point C

What you write: C

A line is a straight path of points that goes on forever in two directions.

What you draw:

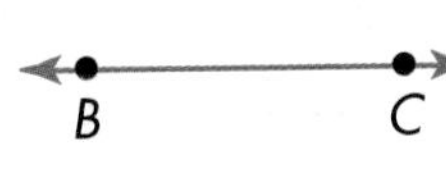

What you say: Line BC

What you write: $\overleftrightarrow{BC}$

A plane is an endless flat surface.

What you draw:

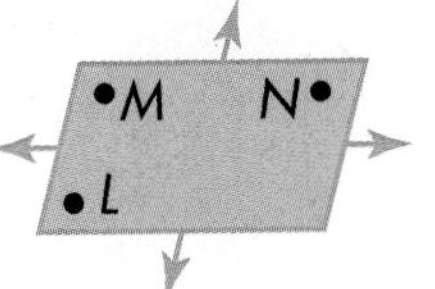

What you say: Plane LMN

What you write: ▱ LMN

Guided Practice*

Do you know HOW?

In **1** through **4**, use the diagram at the right.

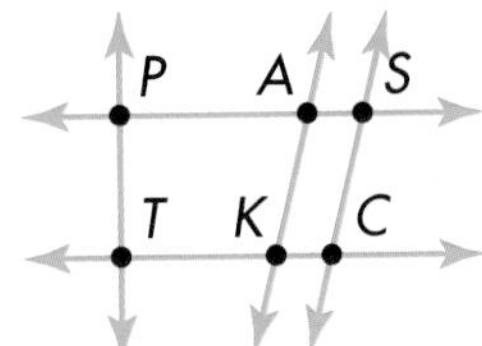

1. Name 4 points.

2. Name 3 line segments.

3. Name 2 intersecting lines

4. Name 2 parallel lines.

Do you UNDERSTAND?

In **5** through **7** use the diagram at the left.

5. If $\overleftrightarrow{PS}$ and $\overleftrightarrow{TC}$ are parallel and $\overleftrightarrow{PS}$ is perpendicular to $\overleftrightarrow{PT}$, is $\overleftrightarrow{TC}$ also perpendicular to $\overleftrightarrow{PT}$?

6. Do $\overleftrightarrow{PS}$ and $\overleftrightarrow{SP}$ name the same line?

7. Do $\overrightarrow{PS}$ and $\overrightarrow{SP}$ name the same ray? Explain.

Independent Practice

In **8** through **13**, use the diagram at the right.

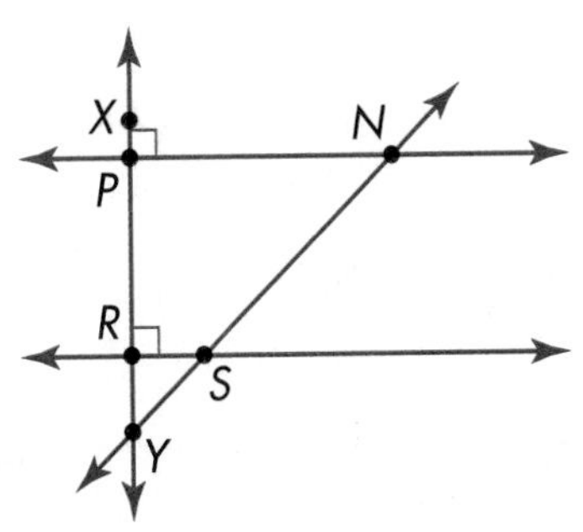

8. Name two parallel lines.

9. Name two perpendicular lines.

10. Name two intersecting but not perpendicular lines.

11. Name three line segments.

12. Name a plane.

13. Name three rays.

DIGITAL
Animated Glossary
www.pearsonsuccessnet.com

For another example, see Set A on page 190.

Problem Solving

14. Use the diagram below to name each of the following.

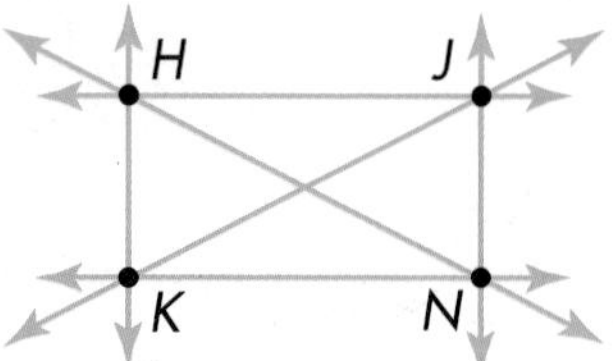

a 2 sets of parallel lines

b 2 sets of perpendicular lines

15. Think About the Process Minh bought 2 pounds of apples for $0.50 a pound, and a gallon of milk for $2. Which operations would you use to find Minh's total cost for the apples and milk?

A Multiply and divide

B Add and add

C Multiply and subtract

D Multiply and add

16. Reasoning Points *D*, *E*, and *F* lie in plane *DEF*. How many lines in plane *DEF* can you draw that contain both points *D* and *E*?

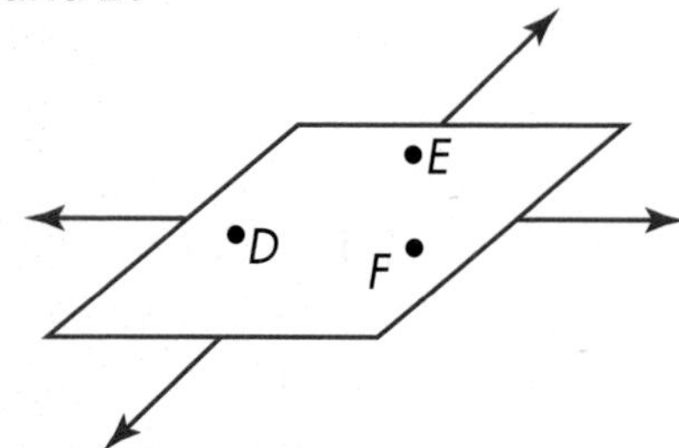

17. Think About the Process Joshua bought a basketball for $22 and 3 T-shirts for $9 each. Which expression shows how to find how much Joshua spent?

A $22 + (3 × $9)

B 3 × ($22 + $9)

C (3 × $22) + (3 × $9)

D (3 + $22) × (3 + $9)

18. Rover weighs 5 pounds more than the neighbor's dog. Rover is 7 years old, and the neighbor's dog is 9 years old. Together they weigh 75 pounds. How much does Rover weigh?

19. An airplane is carrying 148 passengers. There are 110 adults and 38 children. If half of the passengers get off the plane at Houston, how many passengers are left on the plane?

20. Writing to Explain How are perpendicular lines like intersecting lines? What is the difference between perpendicular and intersecting lines?

For **21**, use the diagram below.

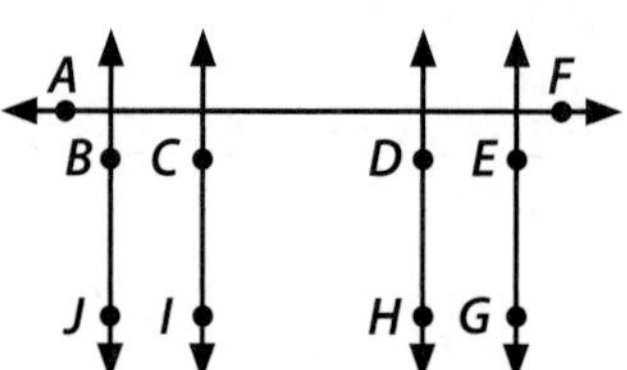

21. a Name a pair of parallel lines.

b What kind of lines are $\overleftrightarrow{AF}$ and $\overleftrightarrow{DH}$?

22. In how many different ways can you arrange the books shown at the right on a shelf? Make a list of the possible ways.

Find the product. Estimate to check if the answer is reasonable.

1. 19.38×7
2. 4.25×9
3. 9.345×12
4. 7.43×10
5. 0.076×9
6. 0.0089×100
7. 23.89×6
8. $12.0005 \times 1{,}000$

Find the quotient. Estimate to check if the answer is reasonable.

9. $5\overline{)7.75}$
10. $4.35 \div 5$
11. $3\overline{)10.53}$
12. $9.24 \div 6$
13. $8\overline{)8.24}$
14. $0.08 \div 4$
15. $3\overline{)12.48}$
16. $28.56 \div 2$
17. $1.28 \div 8$
18. $2\overline{)15.42}$
19. $60.06 \div 6$
20. $9\overline{)28.8}$

Error Search Find each answer that is not correct. Write it correctly and explain the error.

21. $\begin{array}{r} 182 \\ 3\overline{)547} \end{array}$
22. $\begin{array}{r} 4{,}879 \\ +\ \ 236 \\ \hline 4{,}643 \end{array}$
23. $\begin{array}{r} 3{,}193 \\ -\ 3{,}094 \\ \hline 101 \end{array}$
24. $\begin{array}{r} 52.03 \\ +\ 21.67 \\ \hline 73.70 \end{array}$
25. $\begin{array}{r} 56.7 \\ \times\ \ 2.1 \\ \hline 11.907 \end{array}$

Number Sense

Estimating and Reasoning Write whether each statement is true or false. Explain your reasoning.

26. The product of 50×8.58 is between 400 and 450.
27. The sum of 45.69 and 10.92 is 0.08 less than 56.69.
28. The expression $18 - 6 + 5 \times 2$ equals 34.
29. The quotient of $3{,}216 \div 8$ is 2 more than 400.
30. The expression $\frac{10k}{5}$ equals 12 when $k = 6$.
31. The quotient $15.89 \div 2$ is greater than 8.

Lesson

8-2

MG 2.1 Measure, identify, and draw angles, perpendicular and parallel lines, rectangles, and triangles by using appropriate tools (e.g., straightedge, ruler, compass, protractor, drawing software).

Measuring and Classifying Angles

Hands-On
protractor

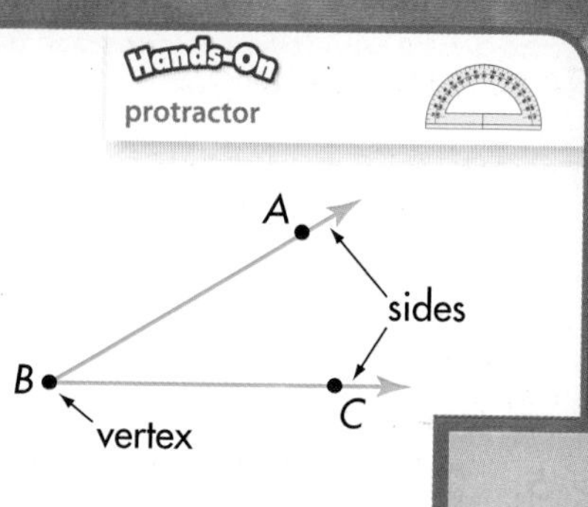

How can you measure an angle?

An angle is formed by two rays that have the same endpoint. The common endpoint is called the vertex (plural: vertices.)

Angle *ABC* is shown above to the right. We write this as $\angle ABC$. It can also be named $\angle CBA$ or just $\angle B$.

Another Example How can you classify angles?

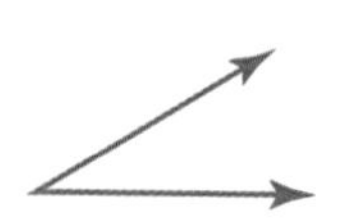

An acute angle has a measure between 0° and 90°.

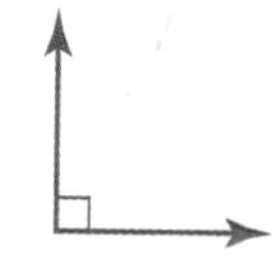

A right angle has a measure of 90°.

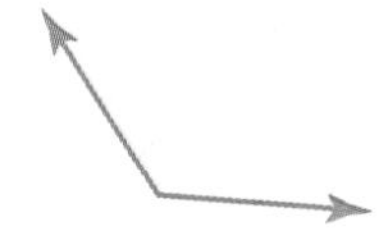

An obtuse angle has a measure between 90° and 180°.

A straight angle has a measure of 180°.

Guided Practice*

Do you know HOW?

In **1** and **2**, measure and classify each angle.

1.

2.

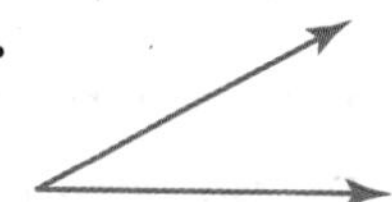

3. **Reasoning** Give three different names for this angle. Identify the vertex and sides.

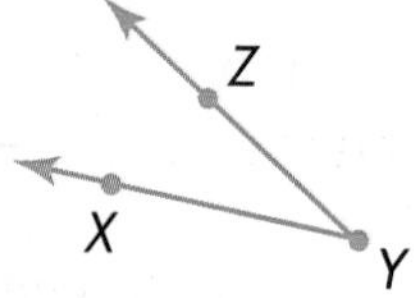

Do you UNDERSTAND?

4. In the figure below, how many angles are formed? What are their measures? Are the angles acute, right, or obtuse?

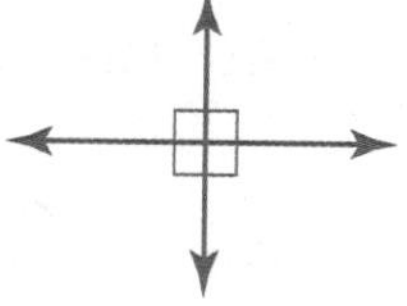

5. Draw an obtuse angle. Label it with 3 points and the angle measure.

*For another example, see Set B on page 190.

To measure an angle

You use a protractor to measure and draw angles. Angles are measured in degrees. It takes 90° to fill a square corner.

Place the protractor's center on the angle's vertex. Place the 0° mark on one side of the angle. Read the measure where the other side of the angle crosses the protractor.

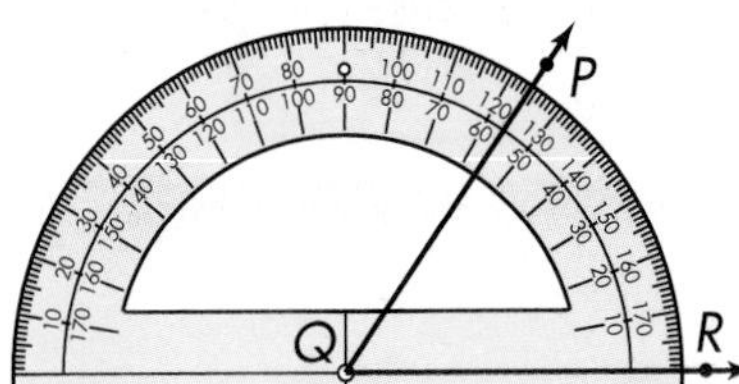

The measure of $\angle PQR$ is 56°.

To draw an angle of 140°

Draw $\overrightarrow{TU}$. Be sure to label the endpoint T. Place the protractor's center on T. Line up $\overrightarrow{TU}$ with the 0° mark. Place a point at 140°. Label it W. Draw $\overrightarrow{TW}$.

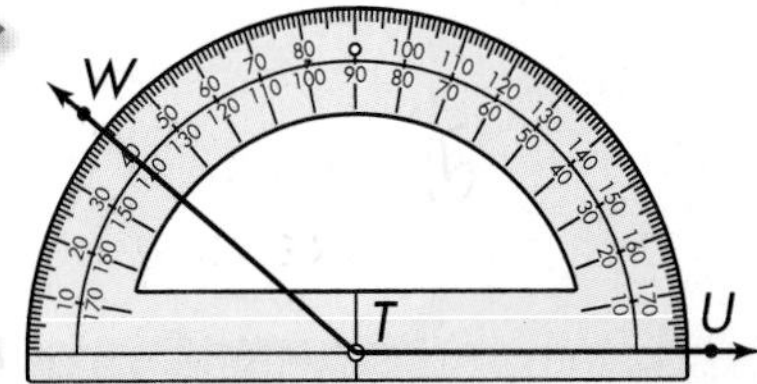

The measure of $\angle WTU$ is 140°.

Independent Practice

In **6** through **8**, classify each angle as acute, right, obtuse, or straight. Then measure each angle.

6. 

7. 

8. 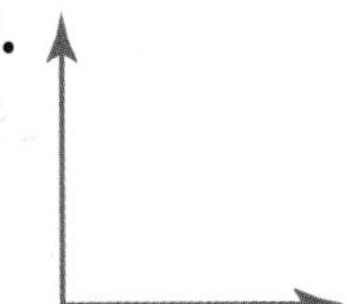

In **9** through **12**, draw the angles with a protractor. Classify the angles as acute, right, or obtuse.

9. 35° **10.** 110° **11.** 90° **12.** 76°

Problem Solving

13. Reasoning If $\overrightarrow{CB}$ is perpendicular to $\overrightarrow{CD}$, then $\angle BCD$ is

A an acute angle. **C** an obtuse angle.

B a right angle. **D** a straight angle.

14. For his birthday, John received the same amount of money from each of his 10 friends, plus $20 from his brother. If John received a total of $120, how much did each friend give him?

15. Angles can be found on the world's largest basket. What kind of angle is $\angle ADC$? $\angle CBD$? $\angle ADB$?

16. Writing to Explain Carlos says that two times the measure of an acute angle will always equal the measure of an obtuse angle. Is he right? Give examples to explain your answer.

Lesson
8-3

MG 2.0 Identify, describe, and classify the properties of, and the relationships between, plane and solid geometric figures.

Polygons

How do you name a polygon?

A polygon is a closed plane figure made up of line segments.

A regular polygon has sides of equal length and angles of equal measure.

Guided Practice*

Do you know HOW?

Name the polygon and classify it as regular or irregular.

1. 

2. 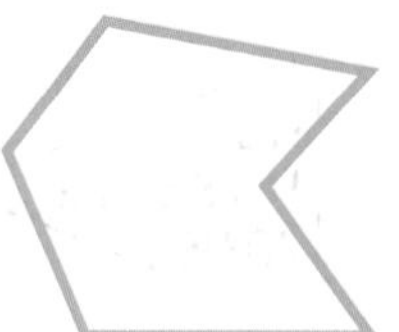

Do you UNDERSTAND?

3. How many sides and how many vertices does a pentagon have? A hexagon?

4. What type of polygon does each road sign in the example at the top appear to be? Which one is a regular polygon?

Independent Practice

In **5** through **8**, name each polygon. Then write yes or no to tell if it is regular.

5. 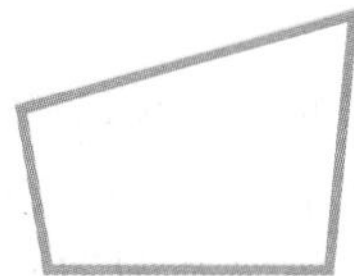

6. 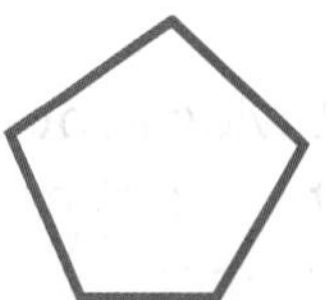

7. 

8. 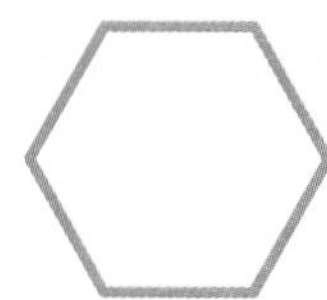

Which figures are polygons? If not, explain why.

9. 

10. 

11. 

12. 

DIGITAL Animated Glossary
www.pearsonsuccessnet.com

**For another example, see Set C on page 190.*

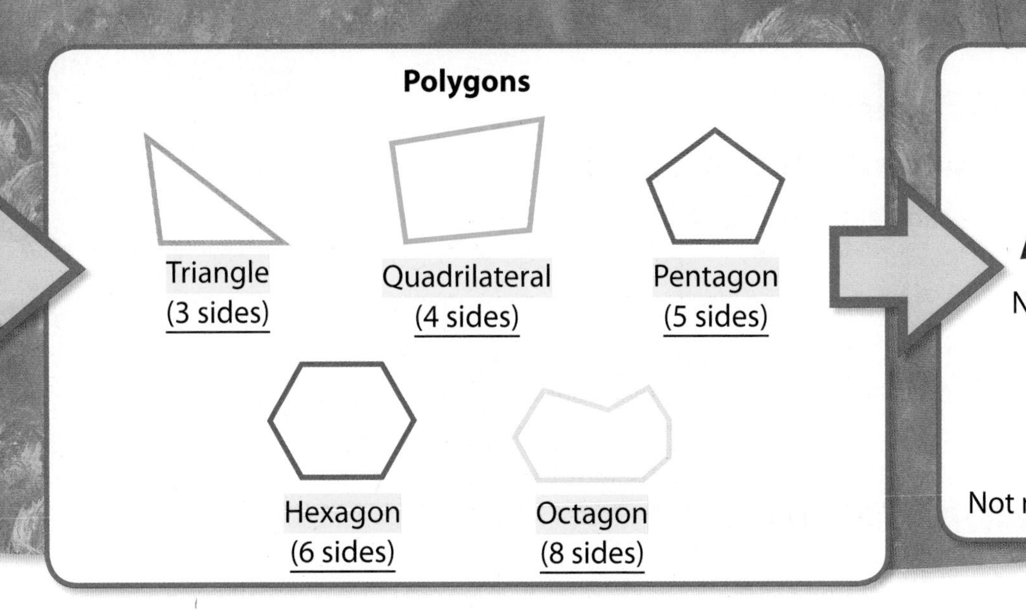

Not Polygons

Not a closed figure

Not made of line segments

Problem Solving

For **13**, use the picture below.

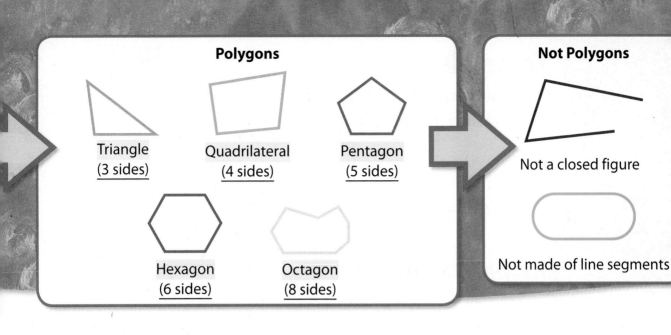

13. What kinds of polygons can you find in the architecture of the Palace of Fine Arts in San Francisco, California?

14. While driving, Shania saw a No Passing Zone sign and an Interstate Highway sign. Are these polygons? If so, are they regular?

15. After a party, there was one pizza left. It was divided into 8 pieces. Kip shared it equally among 4 friends. Which shows how many pieces each friend got?

A 8 **C** 4

B 6 **D** 2

16. If each side of a regular pentagon equals 4 feet, what is its perimeter?

17. Divide a square in half by connecting two vertices. What type polygons are formed? Are they regular or irregular?

18. Think About the Process Juanita's car gets 28 miles per gallon. Which expression shows how many gallons it will take to drive 720 miles?

A 720×28 **C** $720 + 28$

B $720 \div 28$ **D** $720 - 28$

19. Each cell from a wasps' hive has 6 sides. What is the name of this polygon?

Lesson

8-4

MG 2.0 Identify, describe, and classify the properties of, and the relationships between, plane and solid geometric figures.
Also MG 2.2

Triangles

How can you classify triangles?

Triangles can be classifed by the length of their sides.

Equilateral triangle
All sides are the same length.

Isosceles triangle
Two sides are the same length.

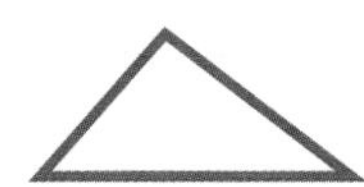

Scalene triangle
No sides are the same length.

Another Example How can you find a missing angle measure in a triangle?

The sum of the measures of the angles of a triangle is 180°. What is the measure of the third angle?

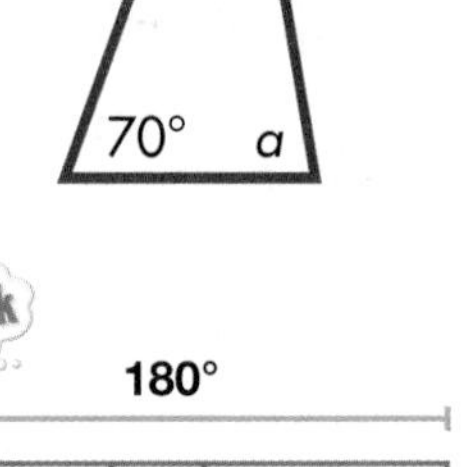

Step 1 Add the two measures you know. $70° + 30° = 100°$

Step 2 Subtract the sum from 180° to find the measure of the third angle. $180° - 100° = 80°$

Think

180°		
70°	30°	*a*

So, the third angle measures 80°.

Explain It

1. If two angles of a triangle measure 35° and 45°, how would you find the measure of the third angle?

Guided Practice*

Do you know HOW?

Classify each triangle by its sides and then by its angles.

1. 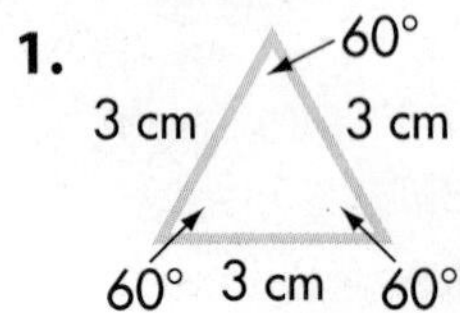

2.
9.9 in.
7 in.
7 in.

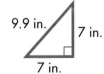

Do you UNDERSTAND?

3. Can a right triangle have an obtuse angle in it? Why or why not?

4. Can an equilateral triangle have only two sides of equal length? Why or why not?

*For another example, see Set D on page 191.

Triangles can also be classified by the measures of their angles.

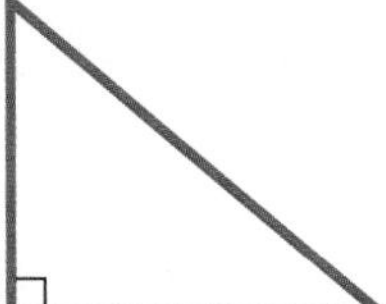

Right triangle
One angle is a right angle.

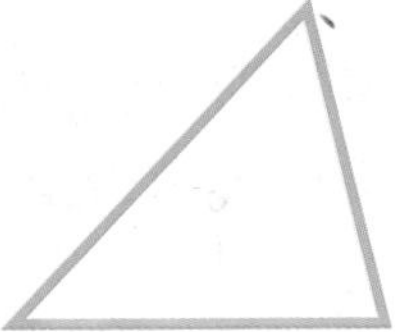

Acute triangle
All three angles are acute angles.

Obtuse triangle
One angle is an obtuse angle.

Independent Practice

Classify each triangle by its sides and then by its angles.

5. 30°, 6 in., 6 in., 75°, 75°, 3.1 in.

6. 9 yd, 12 yd, 15 yd

7. 11 cm, 11 cm, 11 cm, 60°, 60°, 60°

8. 9.2 m, 15.1 m, 110°, 9.2 m

Two angle measures of a triangle are given. Find the measure of the third angle.

9. 48°, 63°

10. 90°, 40°

11. 65°, 50°

12. 130°, 24°

Problem Solving

For **13**, use the picture at the right.

13. The Louvre Museum is located in Paris, France. The Louvre Pyramid serves as an entrance to the museum. Classify the green triangle on the picture by the lengths of its sides and the measures of its angles.

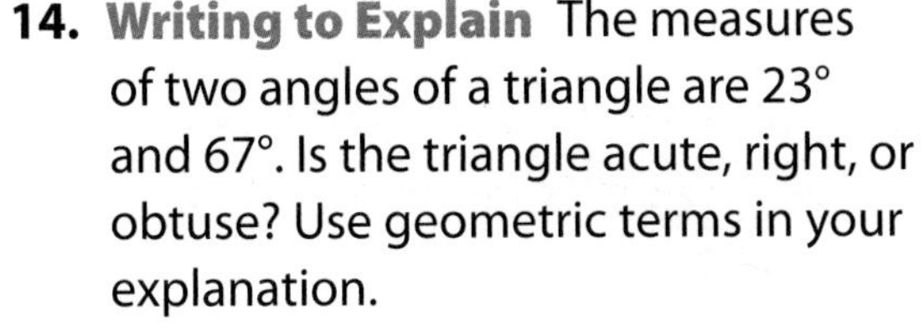

14. Writing to Explain The measures of two angles of a triangle are 23° and 67°. Is the triangle acute, right, or obtuse? Use geometric terms in your explanation.

15. Strategy Focus During a sale at the bookstore, books sold for $3 and magazines sold for $2.50. Jan spent $16 and bought a total of 6 books and magazines. How many of each did she buy? Use Try, Check, and Revise.

Lesson

8-5

MG 2.0 Identify, describe, and classify the properties of, and the relationships between, plane and solid geometric figures.
Also **MG 2.2**

Quadrilaterals

How can you classify quadrilaterals?

A quadrilateral is any polygon with 4 sides. Quadrilaterals can be classified by their angles or pairs of sides.

Parallelogram
both pairs of opposite sides parallel and equal in length

Trapezoid
only one pair of parallel sides

Another Example **How can you find a missing angle measure in a quadrilateral?**

The sum of the measures of the angles of a quadrilateral is 360°. What is the measure of the fourth angle?

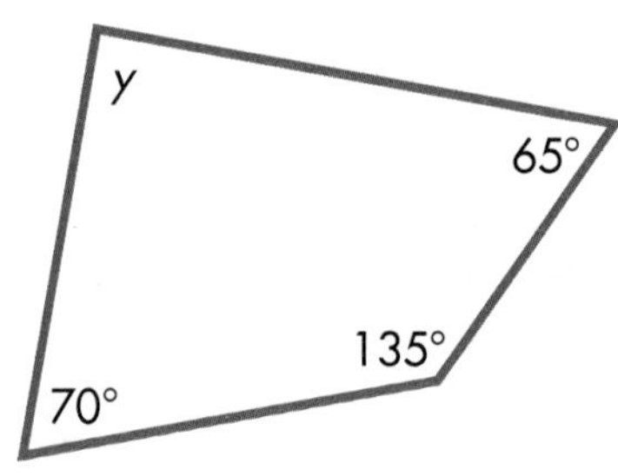

Step 1 Add the known measures. $65° + 135° + 70° = 270°$

Step 2 Subtract 270° from 360° to find the measure of the fourth angle. $360° - 270° = 90°$

So, the fourth angle measures 90°.

Guided Practice*

Do you know HOW?

In **1** through **4**, classify each quadrilateral.

1. 

2. 

3. 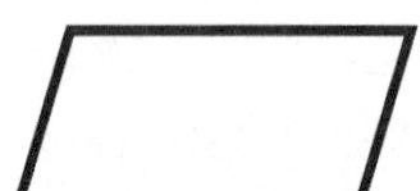

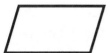

4. 

Do you UNDERSTAND?

5. A square and a rhombus both have four sides that are equal in length. How can you tell the difference between the two quadrilaterals?

6. **Writing to Explain** Why can a rectangle also be called a parallelogram?

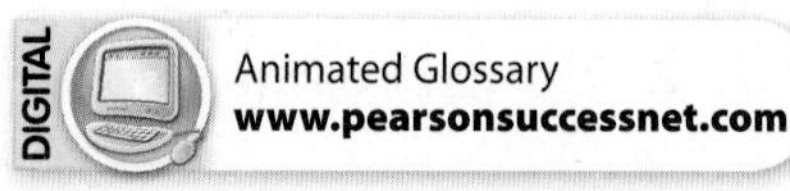

*For another example, see Set E on page 191.

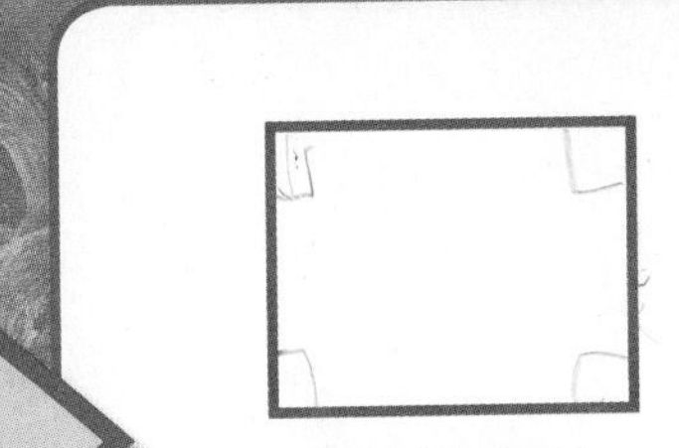

Rectangle
a parallelogram with four right angles

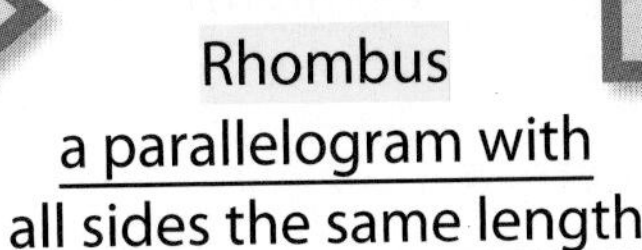

Rhombus
a parallelogram with all sides the same length

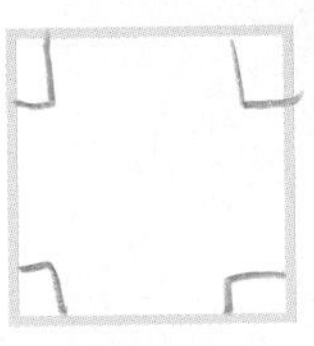

Square
a rectangle with all sides the same length

A square can also be called a rhombus.

Independent Practice

Classify each quadrilateral.

7. 

8. 9 ft, 9 ft, 9 ft, 9 ft

9. 6 m, 9 m, 9 m, 6 m

10. 3 ft, 3 ft, 3 ft, 3 ft

Three angle measures of a quadrilateral are given. Find the measure of the fourth angle.

11. 54°, 100°, 120°

12. 150°, 30°, 30°

13. 90°, 106°, 117°

Problem Solving

14. Which quadrilateral never has 4 equal sides?

A Square

B Trapezoid

C Rectangle

D Rhombus

15. Draw a quadrilateral that is not a parallelogram.

16. Draw rectangle *ABCD*. Then draw a diagonal line connecting points *B* and *D*. If triangle *BCD* is a right isosceles triangle, what do you know about rectangle *ABCD*?

17. Think About the Process Hot dog buns come in packages of 12. Which of the following is NOT needed to find out how much you will spend on hot dog buns?

A The cost of one pack of buns

B The cost of the hot dogs

C The number of buns you need

D All of the information is necessary.

Lesson

8-6

MR 3.3 Develop generalizations of the results obtained and apply them in other circumstances. Also **MR 2.4, 3.2, MG 2.0**

Problem Solving

Make and Test Generalizations

A generalization or general statement can be made about a rectangle.

Make a Generalization

All rectangles can be cut in half diagonally to make two congruent triangles.

Guided Practice*

Do you know HOW?

Test the generalization and state whether it appears to be correct or incorrect. If incorrect, give an example to support why.

1. All even numbers have more than 2 factors.
2. Two congruent equilateral triangles can be joined to make a rhombus.

Do you UNDERSTAND?

3. In the exercise above, how was the conclusion reached?
4. What is another generalization you can make and test about rectangles?
5. **Write a Problem** Write a real-world problem that can be solved by making and testing a generalization.

Independent Practice

In **6** through **10**, test the generalization and state whether it appears to be correct or incorrect. If incorrect, give an example to support why.

6. The sum of the angles of any triangle is 180°.
7. Parallel lines never intersect.
8. Trapezoids are parallelograms.
9. All even numbers are composite.
10. All cubes are three-dimensional.

Stuck? Try this....

- What do I know?
- What am I asked to find?
- What diagram can I use to help understand the problem?
- Can I use addition, subtraction, multiplication, or division?
- Is all of my work correct?
- Did I answer the right question?
- Is my answer reasonable?

*For another example, see Set F on page 191.

Test Your Generalization

Draw a rectangle with the length at the base.

I can cut this rectangle diagonally to make two congruent triangles.

Test Again if Possible

Draw a different rectangle.

I can also cut this rectangle diagonally to make two congruent triangles.

Conclusion

To prove a generalization incorrect, you need an example of when the test shows the generalization being incorrect.

Based on the results of the tests, this generalization appears to be correct.

11. What is the same about all of these polygons?

12. One pint of blueberries contains about 80 berries. You have a fruit salad recipe that calls for 20 blueberries per serving. You have all of the other fruit necessary for the salad, but only 1 quart of blueberries. How many servings of the fruit salad can you prepare?

13. What is the best estimate of the shaded portion of the picture shown below?

14. Draw the next figure in the pattern shown below.

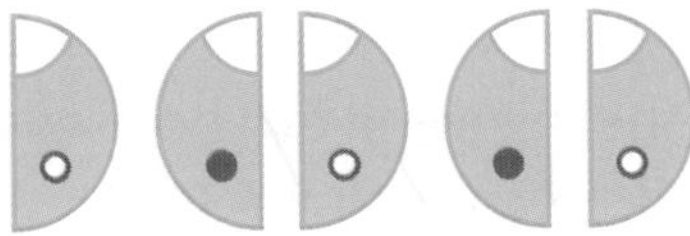

15. Mike weighs 24 more pounds than Marcus. Together, they weigh 250 pounds. How much do they each weigh?

16. Find the missing numbers in each table. Then, write the rule.

a

Days	1	2	4	7
Dollars	$8		$32	

b

Team	1	2	4	9
Players		10	20	

17. Marcia and Tim played Ping-Pong. Marcia won the game with a score of 21. She won by 7 points. Draw a picture and write an equation to find Tim's score.

18. How many whole numbers have exactly two digits? Hint: 99 is the greatest two-digit whole number.

DIGITAL Animated Glossary **www.pearsonsuccessnet.com**

Test Prep

1. Which of the following correctly describes the triangles shown? (8-4)

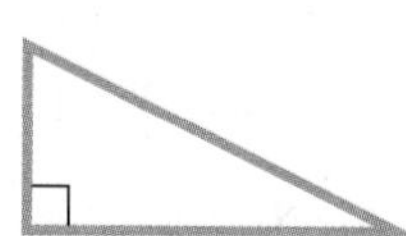

A Both triangles have a right angle.

B Only one triangle has an acute angle.

C Both triangles have at least two obtuse angles.

D Both triangles have at least two acute angles.

2. A right triangle has an angle whose measure is 35°. What is the measure of the other angle in the triangle? (8-4)

A 35°

B 55°

C 72.5°

D 145°

3. Which of the following can be used to describe the shape below? (8-5)

A Opposite sides are perpendicular.

B All angles are obtuse.

C Adjacent sides are parallel.

D All sides are congruent.

4. What is the relationship between segments *AD* and *BC*? (8-1)

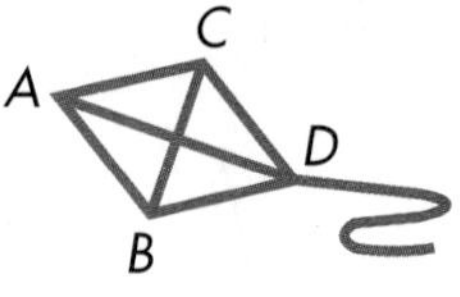

A They are congruent.

B They are adjacent.

C They are perpendicular.

D They are parallel.

5. Sabra's glasses have lenses that are the shape shown in the picture below. Which of the following could NOT be used to describe the lenses? (8-3)

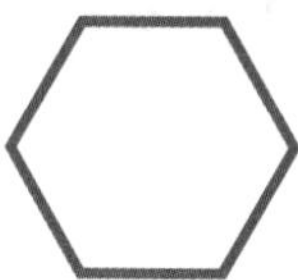

A Quadrilateral

B Regular polygon

C Hexagon

D Opposite sides parallel

6. Which of the following appear to be parallel lines in the diagram shown? (8-1)

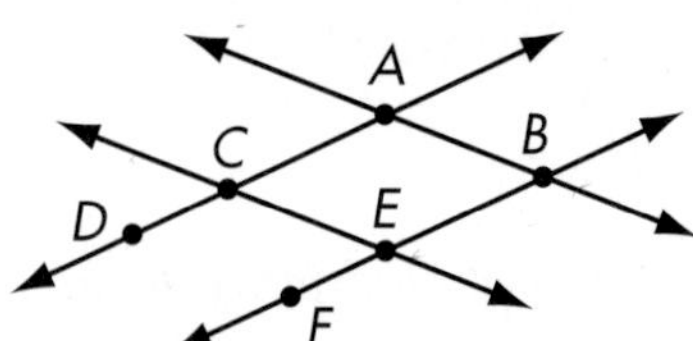

A $\overleftrightarrow{AB}$ and $\overleftrightarrow{CE}$

B $\overleftrightarrow{AB}$ and $\overleftrightarrow{FB}$

C $\overleftrightarrow{CE}$ and $\overleftrightarrow{DA}$

D $\overleftrightarrow{FB}$ and $\overleftrightarrow{CE}$

7. The figures below are rhombuses. Which generalization is incorrect, based on these figures? (8-6)

A A square can be a rhombus.

B A rhombus can be a square.

C All rhombuses are squares.

D All squares are rhombuses.

8. A sail on a sailboat is a triangle with two sides perpendicular and no two sides congruent. What two terms could be used to describe the sail? (8-4)

A Equilateral and right

B Right and isosceles

C Scalene and right

D Isosceles and acute

9. How many degrees is the measure of the fourth angle in the necklace charm shown? (8-5)

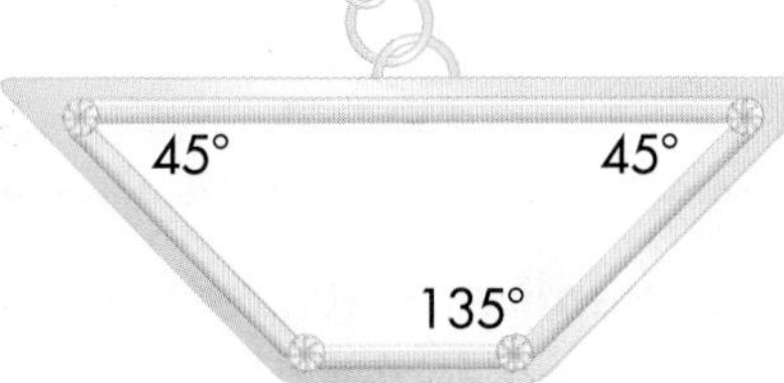

A 45°

B 135°

C 180°

D 360°

10. Which of the following is closest to the measure of the angle shown? (8-2)

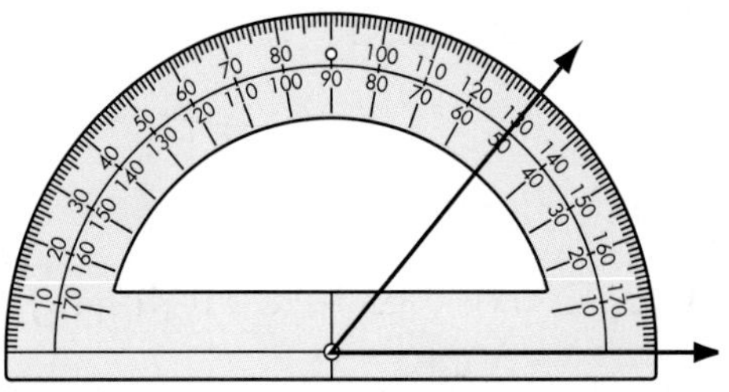

A 40°

B 50°

C 130°

D 140°

11. Triangle *HJK* is an isosceles triangle. The measures of angles *J* and *K* are equal. The measure of angle *H* is 100°. What is the measure of angle *J*? (8-4)

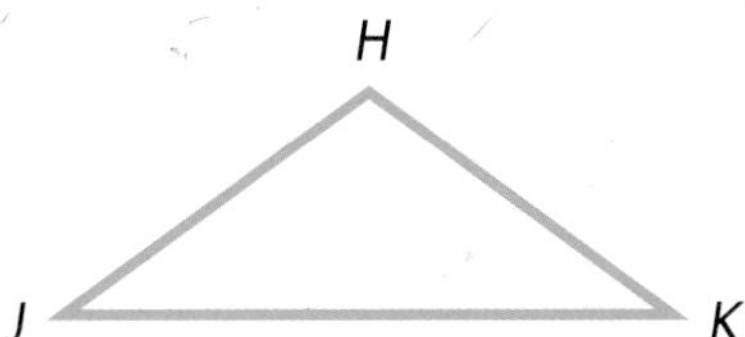

A 40°

B 45°

C 50°

D 80°

12. Which of the following quadrilaterals must have all four sides of equal length? (8-5)

A Rhombus

B Rectangle

C Trapezoid

D Parallelogram

Reteaching

Set A, pages 174–176

Geometric ideas are shown in the diagram below.

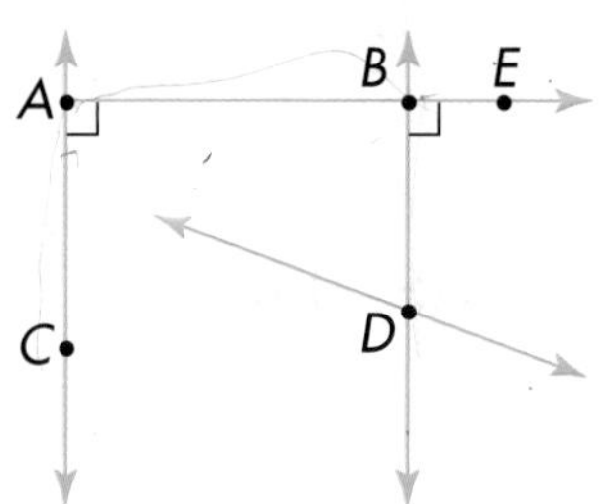

Name a line segment on $\overrightarrow{AE}$. $\overline{AB}$

Name two perpendicular rays. $\overrightarrow{AE}$ and $\overrightarrow{BD}$

Name two parallel lines. $\overleftrightarrow{AC}$ and $\overleftrightarrow{BD}$

Name three points. *C*, *B*, *A*

Remember that intersecting lines pass through the same point. If they form a right angle, they are perpendicular lines.

Use the figure at the left to name each of the following.

1. A ray that intersects two parallel line segments.
2. A vertical ray.
3. A horizontal ray.
4. A line segment that is perpendicular to two rays.

Set B, pages 178–179

Measure the angle below with a protractor and classify it as acute, right, or obtuse.

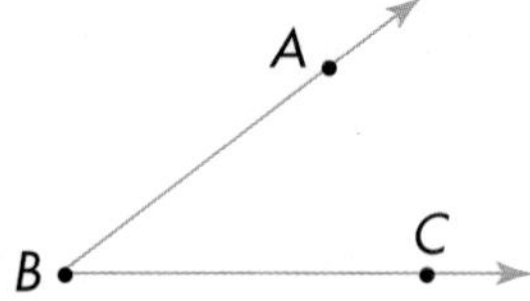

An acute angle measures less than 90°. This angle measures 38°. So, this angle is acute.

Remember that you can compare most angles to a right angle and know whether it is greater or less than 90°, or you can measure it with a protractor.

Measure each angle with a protractor and classify it as acute, right, or obtuse.

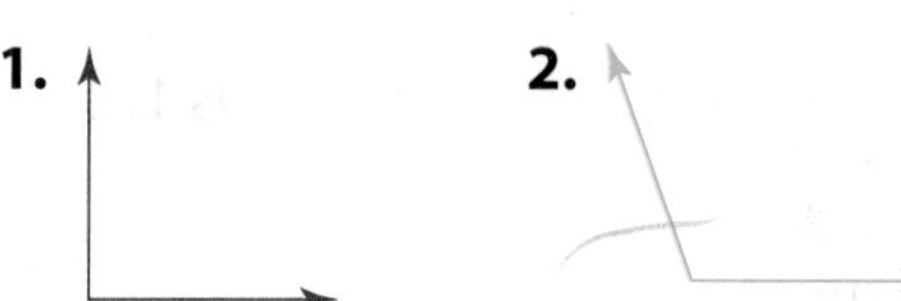

Set C, pages 180–181

Name the polygon and state whether it is regular or irregular.

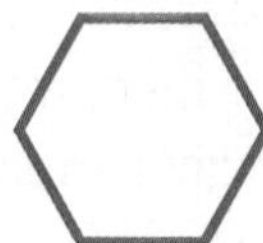

The polygon has six sides that are all equal in length and angles that are equal in measure. It is a regular hexagon.

Remember that a regular polygon has sides and angles of equal length and measure.

1.

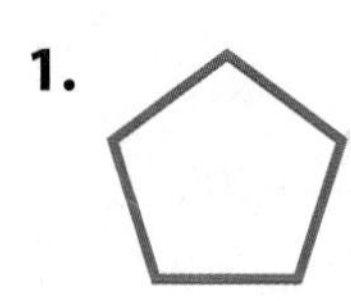

2.

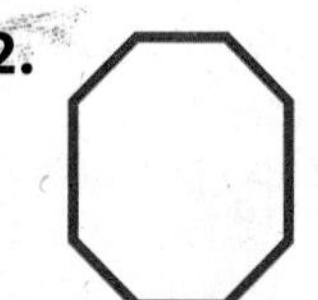

Reteaching

Set D, pages 182–183

Classify the triangle by the measure of its angles and the length of its sides.

Since one of the angles is right, this is a right triangle. Since two of the sides are the same length, this is an isosceles triangle.

4 m

4 m

Using both terms, this is a right, isosceles triangle.

Remember that right, obtuse, and acute describe the angles of a triangle. Equilateral, scalene, and isosceles describe the sides of a triangle.

Classify each triangle by the size of its angles and the length of its sides.

1.

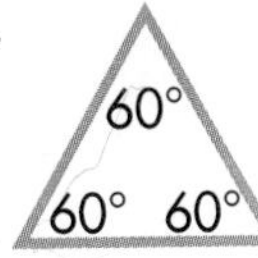

2.

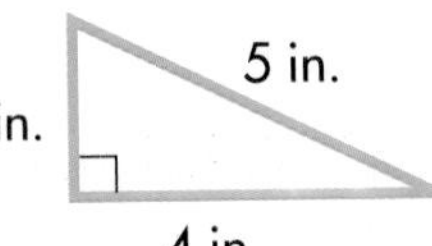

Set E, pages 184–185

Classify the quadrilateral. Then find the missing angle measure.

The quadrilateral has two sets of parallel lines with all sides the same length. It is a rhombus.

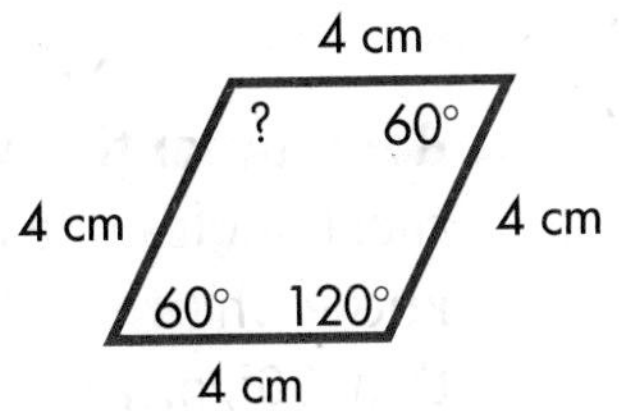

The sum of the measures of the angles in a quadrilateral is 360°.

$360° - (60° + 60° + 120°) = 120°$

So, the missing angle measure is 120°.

Remember that the sum of the angles of a quadrilateral is 360°.

1.

110° ?
3 cm
70° 110°
6 cm

2.

4 ft
?
5.7 ft
4 ft
45°
8 ft

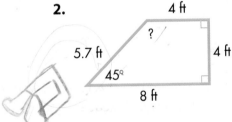

Set F, pages 186–187

Test the following generalization and state whether it appears to be correct or incorrect. If incorrect, give an example to support why.

Generalization
The sum of the angles in any rectangle is 180°.

Test Your Generalization
Draw a rectangle.
Notice that each of the four angles is 90°.
Add to find the sum of the angles.
$90° + 90° + 90° + 90° = 360°$

Conclusion
The generalization is incorrect.

Remember to test a generalization more than once before drawing a conclusion that the generalization is true.

Test the generalization. State if it appears to be correct or not. If incorrect, give an example to support why.

1. Triangular prisms always have two bases that are equilateral triangles.

Topic 9

Factors and Multiples

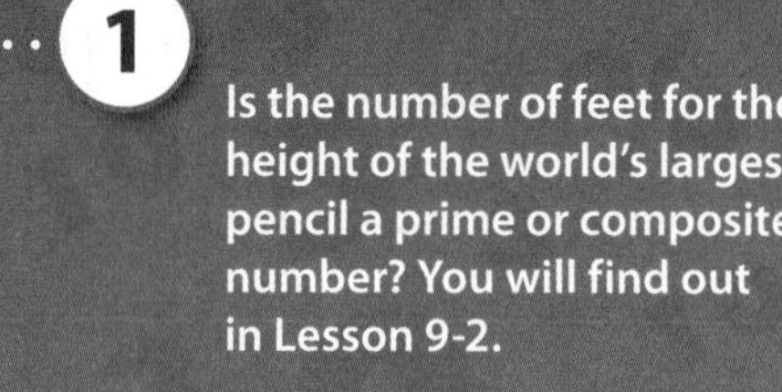

1 Is the number of feet for the height of the world's largest pencil a prime or composite number? You will find out in Lesson 9-2.

2 Roadrunners live year-round in California and prefer to run, rather than fly. How can you tell whether or not the top speed of a roadrunner is an example of a composite number? You will find out in Lesson 19-2.

3

Rick Hansen wheeled his chair across more miles than anyone else. What is the Greatest Common Factor of the number of continents and countries that Rick traveled through? You will find out in Lesson 9-4.

4

As of 2006, the Kingda Ka is the fastest roller coaster in the world. How can you find the prime factorization of its top speed? You will find out in Lesson 9-3.

Review What You Know!

Vocabulary

Choose the best term from the box.

- equivalent
- factor
- product
- quotient

1. Two fractions which have the same value are __?__.
2. In the equation $6 \times 3 = 18$, the number 3 is a __?__ and 18 is the __?__.
3. In the equation $56 \div 8 = 7$, the number 7 is the __?__.

Fractions and the Number Line

Find the point on the number line that represents each fraction.

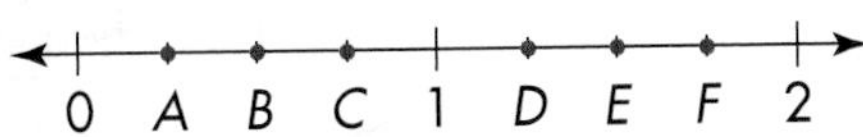

4. $\frac{1}{4}$
5. $1\frac{1}{2}$
6. $\frac{1}{2}$
7. $1\frac{3}{4}$
8. $1\frac{1}{4}$
9. $\frac{3}{4}$

Arrays

Writing to Explain Write an answer for the question.

10. Draw an array to show 3 rows of 8 objects. Then circle groups of 4. How many groups of 4 are in the array? What division equation is shown?

Lesson

9-1

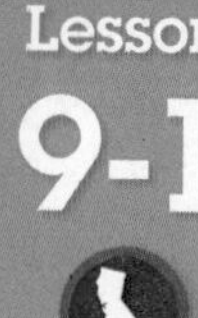

NS 4.1 Grade 4
Understand that many whole numbers break down in different ways.

Understanding Factors

How can you find all the factors of a number?

Three possible arrays of 12 buttons are shown. The arrays can help find all the factors of 12. The factors of 12 are 1, 2, 3, 4, 6, and 12.

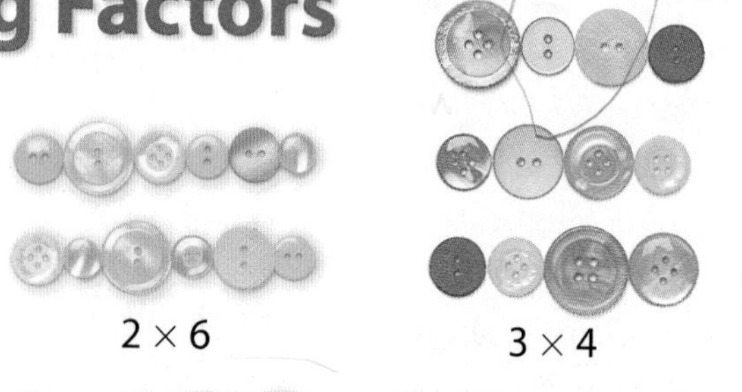

Another Example **How can you use divisibility rules to find factors?**

A factor pair is a pair of whole numbers whose product equals a given whole number. A factor pair for 12 is 3 and 4.

Find all the factor pairs of 32. Then list all the factors of 32.

Try	Is It a Factor?	Factor Pair
1	Yes, 1 is a factor of every whole number.	1 and 32
2	Yes, because 32 is even.	2 and 16
3	No. Since 3 + 2 = 5, it is not divisible by 3.	
4	Yes; 32 is divisible by 4.	4 and 8
5	No, because 32 does not end in 0 or 5.	
6	No, because 32 is not divisible by both 2 and 3.	
7	No.	
8	Yes; 32 is divisible by 8.	4 and 8

Numbers greater than 8 do not need to be tested because after 8 the factor pairs repeat. The factors of 32 are 1, 2, 4, 8, 16, and 32.

Explain It

1. Why is it helpful to know the divisibility rules?
2. If 15 and 14 are factors of a number, what other numbers will be factors of the same number? Explain.

Algebra Connections

Properties and Equations

Number properties help you solve equations. Examples of each property are shown.

Commutative Properties

Addition $3 + 7 = 7 + 3$

Multiplication $7 \times 9 = 9 \times 7$

Associative Properties

Addition $3 + (7 + 5) = (3 + 7) + 5$

Multiplication $2 \times (4 \times 3) = (2 \times 4) \times 3$

Identity Properties

Addition $10 + 0 = 10$

Multiplication $13 \times 1 = 13$

Zero Property of Multiplication

$9 \times 0 = 0$

Distributive Property

$3 \times (10 + 4) = (3 \times 10) + (3 \times 4)$

Example:

Solve the following equation.

$8 \times (10 + 2) = (8 \times 10) + (y \times 2)$

Think The Distributive Property means that $8 \times (10 + 2) = (8 \times 10) + (8 \times 2)$

So, $y = 8$

Tip *Remember that $3 \times m$ can be written as $3m$.*

Solve each equation.

1. $z + 37 = 37 + 4$

2. $38y = 38$

3. $8 + (3 + 9) = (8 + 3) + x$

4. $8y = 0$

5. $21 + z = 21$

6. $17 \times 25 = 25 \times t$

7. $10 \times (3 \times 9) = (10 \times 3) \times z$

8. $16 + (y + 4) = (16 + 3) + 4$

9. $8 \times (10 + 3) = (8 \times 10) + (8 \times y)$

10. $346y = 346$

11. One display in a store has 12 rows of 4 photos. Another display has same number of photos arranged in 4 rows. How many photos are in each row of the second display?

12. **Write a Problem** Write a real-world problem that can be solved by writing and solving the equation $3 + 10 = x + 3$.

Lesson

9-2

NS 4.2 Grade 4 Know that numbers such as 2, 3, 5, 7, and 11 do not have any factors except 1 and themselves and that such numbers are called prime numbers.

Prime and Composite Numbers

What are prime and composite numbers?

Every whole number greater than 1 is either a prime number or a composite number. A prime number has exactly two factors, 1 and itself. A composite number has more than two factors.

$1 \times 3 = 3$

$1 \times 8 = 8$

$2 \times 4 = 8$

Another Example What is another way to find out if a number is prime or composite?

Eratosthenes was born in Cyrene (now Libya) about 230 B.C. He developed a method for deciding if a number is prime. It is called the Sieve of Eratosthenes because it "strains out" prime numbers from other numbers.

Use a number chart to find all the prime numbers between 1 and 60.

Cross out 1. It is neither prime nor composite.

Circle 2, the least prime number. Cross out every second number after 2.

Circle 3, the next prime number. Cross out every third number after 3 (even if it has already been crossed out).

Circle 5, and repeat the process.

Circle 7, and repeat the process.

Continue the process for 11, 13, and so on.

The numbers left are prime.

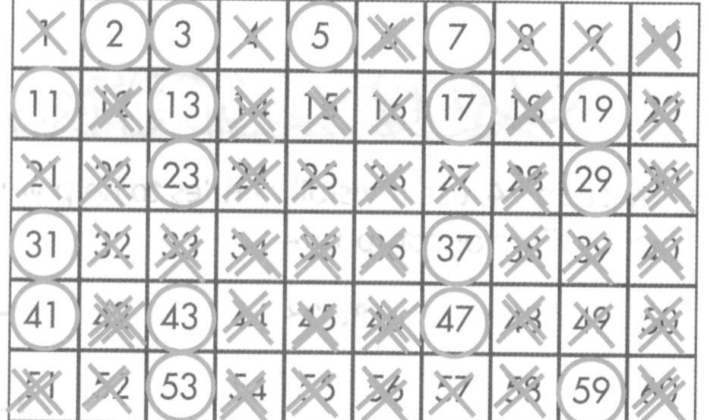

Explain It

1. What are the first 10 prime numbers? How do you know?
2. Why is 1 not a prime number?

Prime or Composite?

Is 27 a prime number or a composite number?

You can use divisibility rules to help you decide.

Since 27 is an odd number it is not divisible by 2.

Since the sum of the digits is $2 + 7 = 9$, then 27 is divisible by 3. So, 27 also has factors of 3 and 9.

So, 27 is composite.

Is 11 prime or composite?

Since 11 is an odd number, it is NOT divisible by 2.

It is also NOT divisible by 3, 4, 5, 6, 7, 8, 9, or 10.

So, 11 is prime.

Guided Practice*

Do you know HOW?

For **1** through **4**, use divisibility rules to help you decide whether the number is prime or composite.

1. 71 **2.** 63

3. 86 **4.** 97

Do you UNDERSTAND?

5. Is every even number greater than 2 a composite number? Explain.

6. Which of the first ten prime numbers are even numbers?

Independent Practice

For **7** through **14**, use divisibility rules to help you decide whether the number is prime or composite.

7. 106 **8.** 93 **9.** 87 **10.** 103

11. 83 **12.** 77 **13.** 89 **14.** 287

For **15** through **17**, list all of the factors for each number. Then tell if the number is prime or composite. Circle the factors that are prime.

	Number	Factors	Prime or Composite
15.	24		
16.	43		
17.	65		

**For another example, see Set B on page 210.*

Problem Solving

18. Name two decimals shown by the model below.

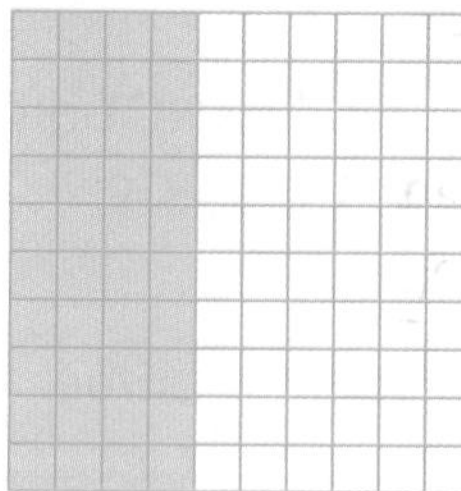

19. Which number has the digit 6 in the ten-thousands place?

A 6,147,218 **C** 1,562,803

B 642,180 **D** 16,095

20. An emperor penguin can grow to be about 45 inches tall. A king penguin can grow to be about 3 feet tall. Which penguin grows to be taller? About how much taller?

21. Twin primes are two prime numbers with a difference of 2. The prime numbers 5 and 3 are twin primes because $5 - 3 = 2$. Which of the following pairs of numbers are NOT twin primes?

A 41 and 43

B 59 and 61

C 71 and 73

D 109 and 111

22. **Think About the Process** Every Sunday Jay walks 6 blocks one way to his grandmother's house for lunch. After lunch, he walks 2 blocks farther to the park. He then walks home on the same exact route. Which shows how to find the number of blocks Jay walks in 4 weeks?

A $(6 + 2) \times (4 + 6)$

B $6 \times (2 \times 4)$

C $6 \times 2 \times 2$

D $(6 + 2) \times 2 \times 4$

23. **Algebra** If *n* is a prime factor of both 15 and 50, what is the value of *n*?

24. The world's largest pencil is 65 feet tall. Is 65 a prime number or a composite number?

25. **Reasonableness** Shirley multiplied 379×8 and got 3,032. Use estimation to check the reasonableness of her answer.

26. **Writing to Explain** Roadrunners live year-round in some parts of California and can get to a top speed of 15 miles per hour. Explain how you know that 15 is a composite number.

27. Which pair of compatible numbers would be best to estimate the sum of 249 and 752?

A 200 and 700 **C** 300 and 800

B 250 and 750 **D** 400 and 700

28. Jonah said that 143 is prime because it is not divisible by any numbers from 2 through 10. Is he right? Explain.

29. Which of the following is a composite number?

A 13 **C** 91

B 37 **D** 101

Find the sum. Estimate to check if the answer is reasonable.

1. $1{,}247 + 997$
2. $9{,}012 + 3{,}993$
3. $55{,}391 + 73{,}428$
4. $19{,}601 + 993$
5. $14{,}823 + 16{,}762$
6. $36{,}228 + 44{,}634$
7. $88{,}692 + 608$
8. $19{,}832 + 16{,}588$

Find the product. Estimate to check if the answer is reasonable.

9. $6{,}078 \times 91$
10. 516×545
11. $7{,}938 \times 68$
12. 515×5
13. 123×123
14. $5{,}004 \times 28$
15. $3{,}333 \times 44$
16. $8{,}332 \times 8$
17. 605×706
18. 422×381

Error Search Find each answer that is not correct. Write it correctly and explain the error.

19. $4{,}000 - 2{,}745 = 2{,}255$
20. $13.05 \times 5 = 65.05$
21. $8{,}605 + 2{,}503 = 6{,}102$
22. $9.1 \div 2 = 4.55$
23. $18{,}502 \div 36 = 513$ R34

Number Sense

Estimating and Reasoning Write whether each statement is true or false. Explain your reasoning.

24. The expression $12 \div 3 + 8 \div 2$ equals 6.
25. The product of 4.8 and 3 is between 12 and 15.
26. The sum of 4,863 and 3,990 is 10 less than 8,863.
27. The quotient of $6{,}598 \div 9$ is greater than 700.
28. The expression $20 - 8m$ equals 24 when $m = 2$.
29. The sum of 74,132 and 26,873 is greater than 90,000.

Lesson

9-3

NS.1.4 Determine the prime factors of all numbers through 50 and write the numbers as the product of their prime factors by using exponents to show multiples of a factor. (e.g., $24 = 2 \times 2 \times 2 \times 3 = 2^3 \times 3$).

Finding Prime Factors

How can you write a number as a product of prime factors?

Every composite number can be written as a product of prime numbers. This product is the prime factorization of the number.

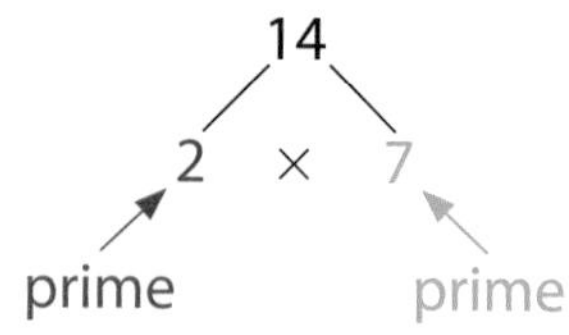

A **factor tree** is a diagram that shows the prime factorization of a composite number.

Guided Practice*

Do you know HOW?

In **1** through **4**, use exponents to write each product.

1. 3×3

2. $5 \times 5 \times 5$

3. $2 \times 3 \times 5 \times 7 \times 7$

4. $2 \times 3 \times 3$

Do you UNDERSTAND?

5. Which property of multiplication tells you that $2 \times 3 \times 2 = 2 \times 2 \times 3$?

6. In the example above, if you selected 6 and 8 for the first factors, would the prime factors in the last row be different?

Independent Practice

In **7** through **9**, complete each factor tree.

7.

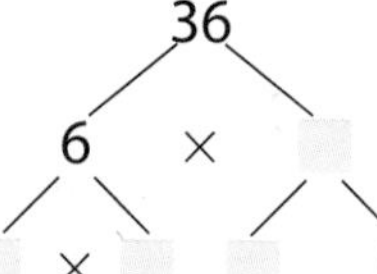

8.

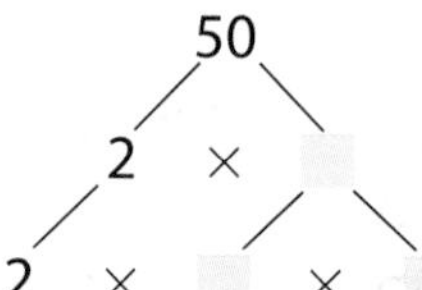

9.

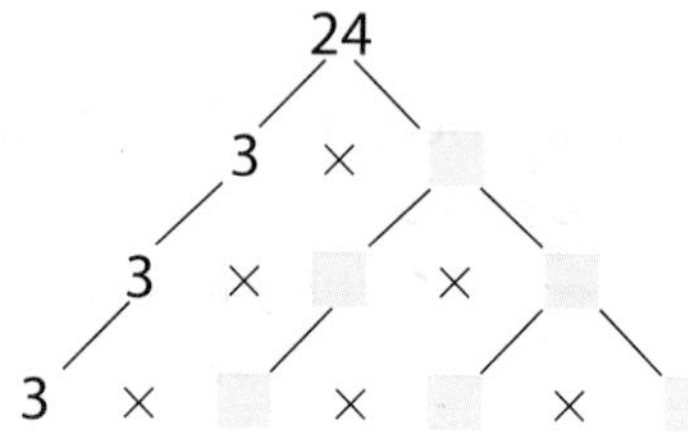

In **10** through **21**, find the prime factorization of each composite number, using exponents when possible. If the number is prime, write prime.

10. 20

11. 14

12. 22

13. 26

14. 30

15. 54

16. 48

17. 37

18. 93

19. 84

20. 75

21. 304

*For another example, see Set C on page 210.

Use a factor tree to write 48 as the product of two factors.

$$48 = 4 \times 12$$

4 and 12 are not prime.

Any factor which is not a prime is broken down further.

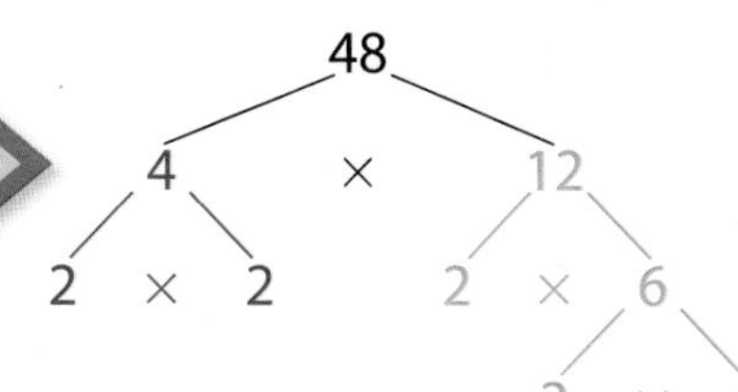

The process continues until each "branch" ends at a prime number.

So, $48 = 2 \times 2 \times 2 \times 2 \times 3$.

Using exponents, you can write $2 \times 2 \times 2 \times 2$ as 2^4.

So, $48 = 2^4 \times 3$.

Problem Solving

22. Reasoning What is the smallest whole number that has 2 different prime factors?

23. How do you know immediately that 2,056 is not a prime number?

24. Writing to Explain How do you know when a factor tree is finished?

25. Evaluate $11.4n$ when $n = 5$, $n = 6.5$, and $n = 10$.

26. Geometry How many edges does the cube have?

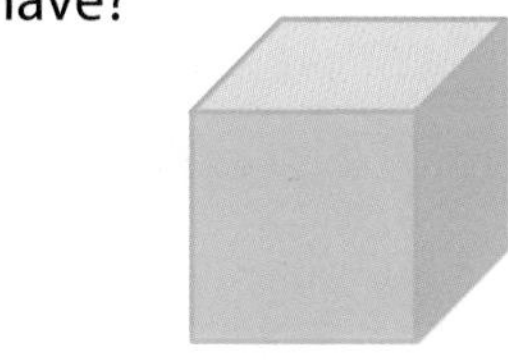

27. Tanya is packing her collection of snow globes in a crate with sections. The case is 2 sections high, 4 sections long, and 2 sections wide. How many globes can fit in the crate?

28. As of 2006, the Kingda Ka is the fastest and tallest roller coaster in the world. Its maximum height is 456 feet, and its top speed is 128 miles per hour. What is the prime factorization of 128?

A $2^2 \times 4^4$

B 2^6

C 2^7

D $2 \times 2 \times 4 \times 8$

29. Marcia's birthday is in December on a day that is a prime number. Which date could it be?

A December 4

B December 20

C December 27

D December 31

30. From a catalog, Stephen ordered 3 pounds of oranges at \$3.25 per pound, and 4 pounds of pears at \$3.50 per pound. He had to pay \$6.25 for shipping. What was his total cost?

31. There are 63 couples lined up for an egg-tossing contest. Each couple will get one egg. There are 12 eggs in a dozen, and eggs come in one dozen cartons. How many cartons of eggs are needed for the contest?

Lesson

9-4

NS 2.4 Grade 6 Determine the least common multiple and the greatest common divisor of whole numbers; use them to solve problems with fractions (e.g., to find a common denominator to add two fractions or to find the reduced form for a fraction).

Common Factors and Greatest Common Factor

How can you find the greatest common factor?

A pet store has goldfish and angelfish that have to be put into the fewest number of glass containers. Each container must contain the same number of fish, and each must contain all goldfish or all angelfish.

Another Example How can you use prime factorization to find the GCF of two numbers?

Step 1 Find the prime factors of each number.

Step 2 List the prime factors of each number.

$24 = 2 \times 2 \times 2 \times 3$

$18 = 2 \times 3 \times 3$

24: 4 × 6; 2 × 2 × 2 × 3

18: 2 × 9; 2 × 3 × 3

Step 3 Circle the prime factors that both numbers share. Here they share the numbers 2 and 3.

$24 = 2 \times 2 \times 2 \times 3$

$18 = 2 \times 3 \times 3$

Step 4 Multiply the common factors. $2 \times 3 = 6$

So, the GCF of 18 and 24 is 6.

Guided Practice*

Do you know HOW?

For **1** through **4**, find the GCF of each pair of numbers.

1. 9 and 12

2. 20 and 45

3. 7 and 28

4. 18 and 32

Do you UNDERSTAND?

5. If two numbers are prime, what is their GCF?

6. **Writing to Explain** In the example above, how would the GCF change if there were 40 goldfish?

*For another example, see Set D on page 211.

Find the Greatest Common Factor (GCF) of 20 and 30 to find the greatest number of fish that could be put into each container.

If a number is a factor of two numbers, it is called a common factor.

The greatest common factor (GCF) of two numbers is the greatest number that is a factor of both numbers.

One Way

To find the greatest common factor of 20 and 30, you can list all the factors of each number and circle all the common factors.

20: 1, 2, 4, 5, 10, 20

30: 1, 2, 3, 5, 6, 10, 15, 30

The GCF of 20 and 30 is 10.

So, the store can put 10 fish in each container.

Independent Practice

In **7** through **18**, find the greatest common factor (GCF) of each number using prime factorization or a list of factors.

7. 20 and 35 **8.** 16 and 18 **9.** 15 and 6 **10.** 24 and 36

11. 48 and 30 **12.** 22 and 77 **13.** 100 and 96 **14.** 60 and 32

15. 90 and 81 **16.** 72 and 27 **17.** 11 and 15 **18.** 14 and 21

Problem Solving

19. Henry wrote an example of the Associative Property as $31 - (9 - 2) = (31 - 9) - 2$. What is Henry's mistake?

20. The GCF of an odd number and an even number is 19. The greater number is 57. What is the other number?

21. Rick Hansen holds the record for the longest journey by wheelchair. He wheeled his wheelchair across 4 continents and 34 countries. What is the GCF of 4 and 34?

A 1 **C** 4

B 2 **D** 17

22. Which list shows all the common factors of 36 and 54?

A 1, 2, 3, 6

B 1, 2, 3, 6, 9

C 1, 2, 3, 6, 9, 18

D 1, 2, 3, 6, 9, 12, 18

23. If you buy a television for $486, including tax, and are allowed to pay for it in 6 equal payments, how much will each payment be?

24. How many pairs of factors does 40 have? List them.

Lesson
9-5

MR 1.1 Analyze problems by identifying relationships, distinguishing relevant from irrelevant information, sequencing and prioritizing information, and observing patterns. Also **MR 2.6, 3.1, MG 1.0**

Problem Solving

Try, Check, and Revise

Which of these square tiles can be used to completely cover the area of this floor without cutting tiles, or combining tiles of different sizes?

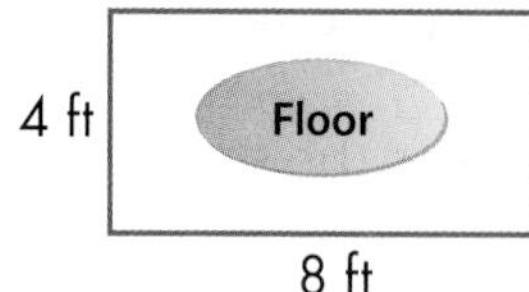

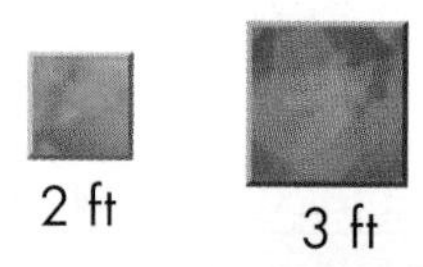

Guided Practice*

Do you know HOW?

1. Which of these tiles can be used to cover a 10 ft × 10 ft floor: 2 × 2 ft, 3 × 3 ft, 4 × 4 ft or 5 × 5 ft tile?

2. What size rectangular tile floor can be completely covered by using only 2 × 2 ft tiles OR 3 × 3 ft tiles? Remember, you can't cut tiles or combine the two tile sizes.

Do you UNDERSTAND?

3. How do you use Try, Check, and Revise to help you find the solution to a problem?

4. **Write a Problem** Write a real-world problem that involves common factors and can be solved using the Try, Check, and Revise strategy.

Independent Practice

For **5** through **9**, use try, check, and revise to solve.

5. Bert is planning to tile a floor that measures 9 ft × 11 ft. What size square tile can he use to completely cover it?

6. Mrs. Gonzales wants to tile her floor with a pattern that repeats every 3 feet. Can she cover the floor without cutting off part of the pattern? Explain.

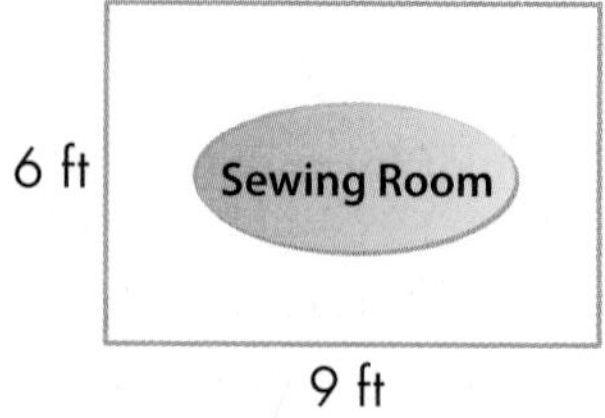

Stuck? Try this....

- What do I know?
- What am I asked to find?
- What diagram can I use to help understand the problem?
- Can I use addition, subtraction, multiplication, or division?
- Is all of my work correct?
- Did I answer the right question?
- Is my answer reasonable?

*For another example, see Set E on page 211.

Use reasoning to make good tries. Then check.

One side of the floor is 4 feet so I think the 4 × 4 ft tile is the only one that works.

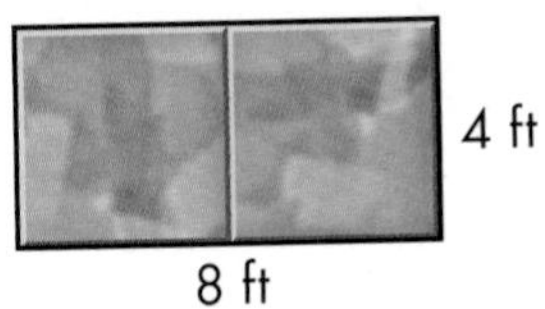

It works!

Next I'll try the 3 × 3 ft tile.

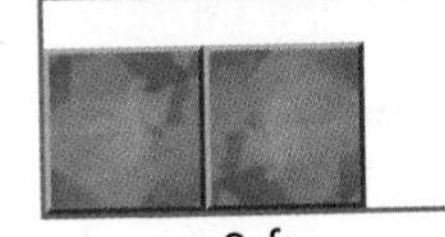

3 does not work for the 4 ft width and 8 ft length because 3 is not a factor of 4 or 8.

Revise what you know.

4 works for the 4 ft width.

4 works for the 8 ft length.

5 is not a factor of 4 or 8, so the 5 × 5 ft tile won't work.

2 is a factor of 4 and 8, so the 2 × 2 ft tile will work too.

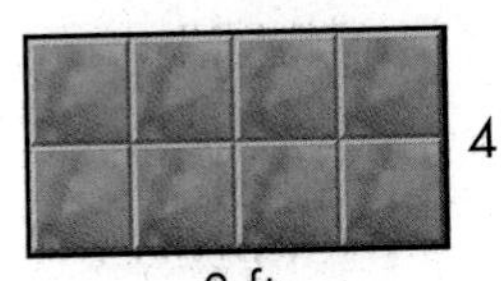

7. You buy a baseball and a bat and spend $31. The bat costs $19 more than the baseball. What is the price of the baseball? What is the price of the bat?

8. The difference between the prices of two bikes is $22. The sum of the prices is $328. How much does each bike cost?

For **9**, use the picture at the right.

9. Kyle's mother spent $115 on shirts and pairs of socks for him. If she bought at least 3 shirts, how many pairs of socks and how many shirts did she buy?

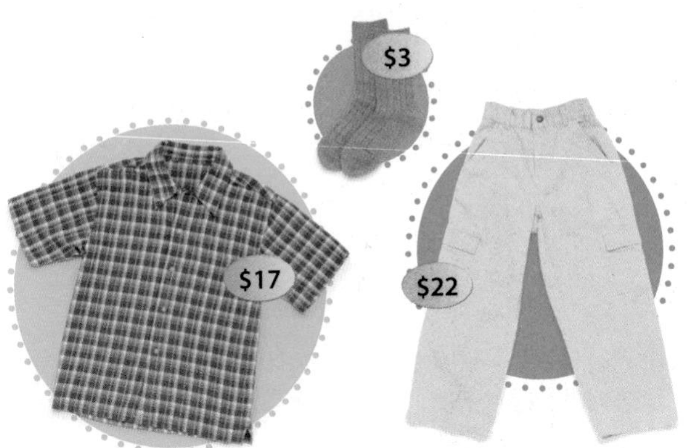

For **10**, draw a picture, write an equation, and solve.

10. Each of the 13 members of a basketball team bought a team emblem. The emblems cost the team $78. How much did it cost each member of the team for an emblem?

11. A group of 168 students are going to a ball game. They will travel on buses that hold 36 students. How many buses could be completely filled? How many buses will be needed? How many seats are left on the bus that is not filled?

12. It costs $2 for each person to ride the bus in the city. A transfer costs $0.50. If 10 people get on the bus, and 5 of those people want a transfer, what is the total amount the bus driver collects?

13. A farmer has 9 cows, 10 pigs, and 25 sheep on his farm. Special food for all the animals costs $3 a pound. If the farmer needs to buy 100 pounds of food for each animal, what will his total cost be?

Test Prep

1. A leap year occurs during years that are divisible by 4. Which of the following will help determine if the year 2078 will be a leap year? (9-1)

A Because 8 is divisible by 4, 2078 is divisible by 4.

B Because 2078 is even, it is divisible by 4.

C Because $2 + 7 + 8 = 17$ and 17 is not divisible by 4, 2078 is not divisible by 4.

D Because 78 is not divisible by 4, 2078 is not divisible by 4.

2. Which of the following lists all the common factors of 45 and 60? (9-4)

A 1, 3, 5

B 1, 3, 5, 15

C 1, 2, 3, 5

D 1, 15

3. What is the prime factorization of 84? (9-3)

A $2^2 \times 3 \times 7$

B $3 \times 4 \times 7$

C $2^2 \times 21$

D $2^3 \times 7$

4. In 1999, there were 64 teams chosen to play in the NCAA basketball tournament. Which list includes all the factors of 64? (9-1)

A 1 and 64

B 1, 2, 32, and 64

C 1, 2, 4, 8, 16, 32, and 64

D 1, 2, 3, 4, 8, 16, 32, and 64

5. Mr. Santorico likes to have a composite number of students enrolled in his class so that he can divide them into groups. Which of the following numbers is composite? (9-2)

A 17

B 19

C 21

D 23

6. The I-95 interstate highway crosses 16 states, the most of any interstate. What is the prime factorization of 16? (9-3)

A $8 \times 8 = 8^2$

B $4 \times 4 = 4^2$

C $2 \times 2 \times 2 = 2^3$

D $2 \times 2 \times 2 \times 2 = 2^4$

7. The table shows the scores of several games played by a football team. During one game, the home team scored only field goals, which are 3 points each. For which game does the score shown make that possible? (9-1)

Data

Game	Home	Visitor
1	13	6
2	16	10
3	20	22
4	21	7

A Game 1

B Game 2

C Game 3

D Game 4

Test Prep

8. Casey has $56 to spend on juice and crackers for a party. Juice costs $2 per bottle, and crackers cost $3 per box. If Casey would like to buy 2 more boxes of crackers than bottles of juice, how many of each should Casey buy to spend exactly $56? (9-5)

A 12 bottles of juice and 10 boxes of crackers

B 8 bottles of juice and 10 boxes of crackers

C 10 bottles of juice and 12 boxes of crackers

D 7 bottles of juice and 14 boxes of crackers

9. What is the missing exponent in the equation showing the prime factorization of 50? (9-3)

$50 = 5^{\square} \times 2$

A 2

B 3

C 5

D 10

10. There are 32 boys and 28 girls in the fifth grade. If they are to be divided into groups of equal size with each group having only boys or only girls, what is the largest number that can be in each group? (9-4)

A 16

B 14

C 4

D 2

11. Which number of apple pieces can not be divided equally except by giving one piece to each person? (9-2)

A 14

B 19

C 27

D 39

12. What is the prime factorization of 90? (9-3)

A $2 \times 3^2 \times 5$

B $2^2 \times 3 \times 5$

C $2 \times 3 \times 5^2$

D $4 \times 3 \times 5$

13. Which number is prime? (9-2)

A 21

B 14

C 12

D 11

14. The table shows the number of items received by a charity for back to school packets. If each packet contains only one type of item with the same number of items in each packet, what is the greatest number of items that can be in each packet? (9-4)

Data

Item	Number
Notebook	30
Markers	36

A 15

B 6

C 3

D 2

Reteaching

Set A, pages 194–196

Determine the factor pairs for 12.

Factors are numbers you multiply to give a particular product. Two factors form a factor pair.

$1 \times 12 = 12$, $2 \times 6 = 12$, $3 \times 4 = 12$

1 and 12, 2 and 6, and 3 and 4 form factor pairs.

Each of these factor pairs gives the product 12.

Remember to use divisibility rules to help you find factors of a number.

Determine the factor pairs for each number.

1. 15 **2.** 20

3. 24 **4.** 36

5. 70 **6.** 80

Set B, pages 198–200

Is 6 a prime or composite number?

A prime number is a whole number with no other factors besides 1 and itself. A composite number is a number that is not prime; it has factors other than 1 and itself.

Factors of 6: 1 and 6, and 2 and 3

6 is a composite number.

Remember that a prime number is a whole number greater than 1 that has exactly two factors, 1 and itself.

Classify each as prime or composite.

1. 11 **2.** 15

3. 18 **4.** 19

5. 27 **6.** 33

Set C, pages 202–203

Find the prime factorization of 56.

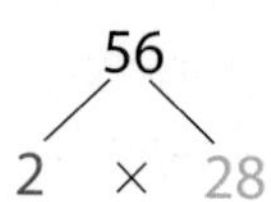

Use a factor tree to write 56 as the product of two factors.

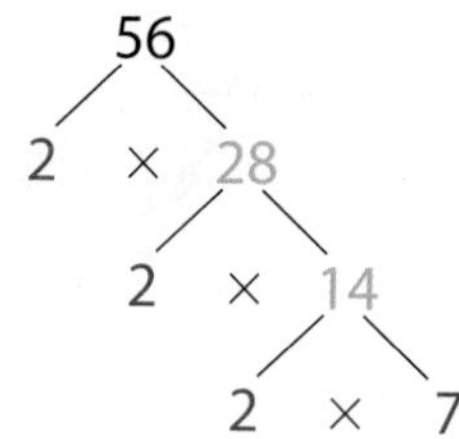

Continue to write factors until all the factors are prime.

So, $56 = 2 \times 2 \times 2 \times 7$. Using exponents, you can write 56 as $2^3 \times 7$.

Remember that you can use exponents when you write the prime factorization of a number.

Find the prime factorization of each number. If the number is prime, write prime.

1. 40 **2.** 32

3. 18 **4.** 17

5. 100 **6.** 60

Set D, pages 204–205

What is the greatest common factor of 10 and 35?

Common factors are factors shared by a group of numbers. The **GCF** is the largest factor shared by a group of numbers.

List factors for 10 and 35.

10: 1, 2, 5, 10

35: 1, 5, 7, 35

Circle common factors. The greatest common factor is the GCF.

10: (1), 2, (5), 10

35: (1), (5), 7, 35

Common factors of 10 and 35 are 1 and 5.
The GCF of 10 and 35 is 5.

Remember that the GCF is the greatest common factor of the numbers.

Find the GCF for each pair of numbers.

1. 15, 45
2. 60, 80
3. 12, 14
4. 24, 56
5. 24, 36
6. 21, 30
7. 27, 45
8. 12, 18
9. 16, 32
10. 18, 27

Set E, pages 206–207

When you use *Try*, *Check*, and *Revise* to solve a problem, follow these steps:

Step 1

Think to make a reasonable first try.

Step 2

Check by using information given in the problem.

Step 3

Revise by using your first try to make a reasonable second try. Check.

Step 4

Use previous tries to continue trying and checking until you find the answer.

Remember that *Try*, *Check*, and *Revise* can help when there is no clear way to solve a problem.

Solve each problem.

1. Mr. Herrera wants to tile his living room floor with a square pattern that repeats every 3 feet. Could he cover the floor without cutting off part of the pattern? Explain.

Living Room

8 ft

20 ft

2. Hector is planning to cover a floor that measures 6 ft $\times$ 15 ft. What size of square tile could he use to cover it exactly?

Topic 10

Fractions, Mixed Numbers, and Decimals

1

The Great Owlet Moth of Brazil has one of the largest wingspans of all insects. Just how large is it? You will find out in Lesson 10-7.

2

How many miles per hour do San Francisco's cable cars travel? You will find out in Lesson 10-3.

3

What fraction is equivalent to the weight of this goliath spider? You will find out in Lesson 10-4.

4

How can you write the height of the Long Term Parking Sculpture in France as a mixed number and an improper fraction? You will find out in Lesson 10-3.

Review What You Know!

Vocabulary

Choose the best term from the box.

- difference
- product
- quotient
- thousandths

1. In $55 \div 5 = 11$, 11 is the __?__.
2. In 0.456, the 6 is in the __?__ place.
3. To find the __?__ between 16 and 4 you subtract.
4. Multiplying is the same as finding the __?__.

Division

Find each answer.

5. $32 \div 4$
6. $97 \div 8$
7. $69 \div 16$
8. $95 \div 10$
9. $163 \div 31$
10. $725 \div 25$

Multiplication

Find each answer.

11. 40×8
12. 30×500
13. 31×46
14. 92×18
15. 319×4
16. $2 \times 25 \times 30$

Properties of Multiplication

Writing to Explain Write an answer for each question.

17. Explain how you can use the Associative Property to multiply $(7 \times 50) \times 4$.
18. Can you use the Associative Property for $3 \times (4 + 5)$?

Lesson

10-1

NS 1.5 Grade 4 Explain different interpretations of fractions, for example, parts of a whole, parts of a set, and division of whole numbers by whole numbers; explain equivalence of fractions (see Standard 4.0). Also **NS 1.0**

Meanings of Fractions

What is the meaning of a fraction?

A fraction describes one or more parts of a whole that is divided into equal parts. The whole can be a region, a set, or a segment.

numerator $\frac{3}{5}$ ← number of equal parts that are red
denominator ← total number of equal parts

In the flag shown at the right, $\frac{3}{5}$ of the flag is red.

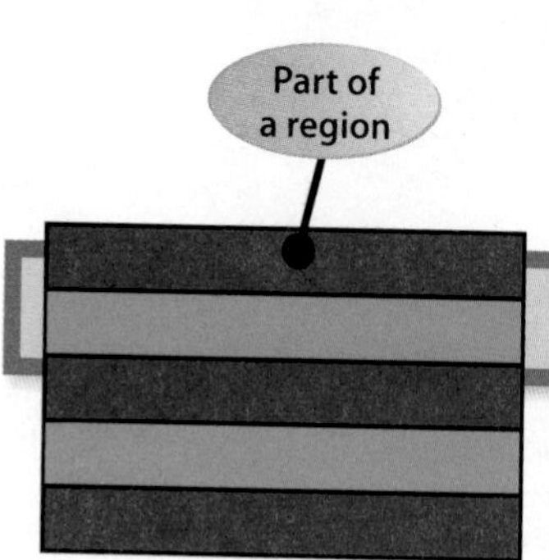

Another Example Does a fraction such as $\frac{1}{2}$ always represent the same amount?

In each figure below, $\frac{1}{2}$ of the figure is shaded. Does $\frac{1}{2}$ represent the same amount for both figures? Explain.

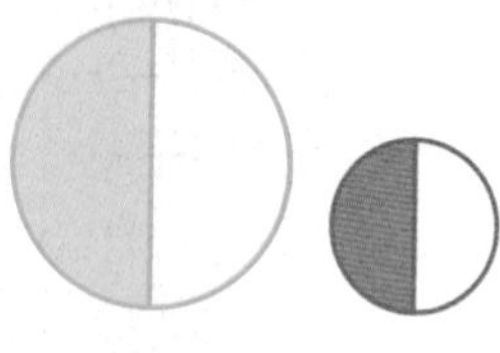

No. Even though $\frac{1}{2}$ of each figure is shaded, the whole in the first figure is much larger than the whole in the second figure. The amount of the whole determines what the fraction represents.

Explain It

1. In each segment, $\frac{3}{4}$ of the segment is shaded. Does $\frac{3}{4}$ of the first segment represent the same amount as $\frac{3}{4}$ of the second? Explain.

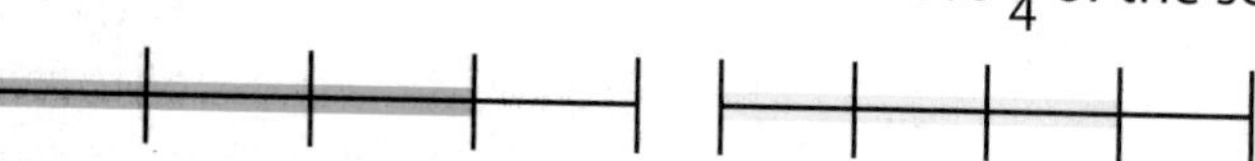

Guided Practice*

Do you know HOW?

In **1** and **2**, write the fraction that names the shaded part.

1. 

2. 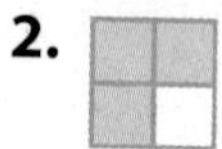

Do you UNDERSTAND?

3. What fraction names the blue part of the flag in the example at the top?

4. What fraction names the part of the animals that are dogs in the example at the top?

5. If a quilt has 16 equal parts and 4 of the parts are yellow, what fraction names the part that is yellow? What fraction names the part that is not yellow?

*For another example, see Set A on page 242.

There are 8 animals.

3 out of 8 are cats.

$\frac{3}{8}$ of the animals are cats.

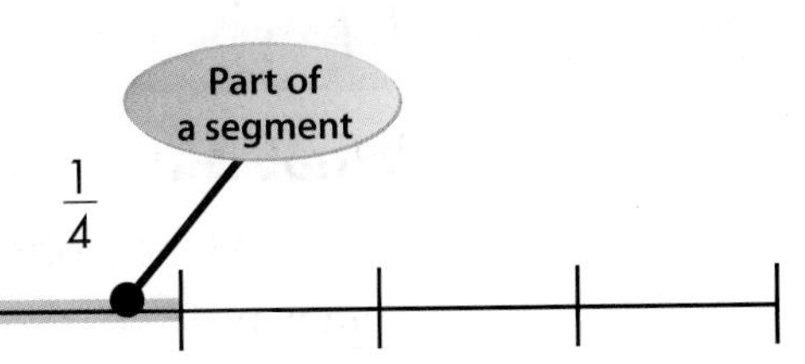

There are 4 parts to the segment.

1 of the parts is shaded.

$\frac{1}{4}$ of the segment is shaded.

Independent Practice

In **6** through **10**, write the fraction that names the shaded part.

You can count the number of shaded parts to find the numerator.

6. 

7. 

8. 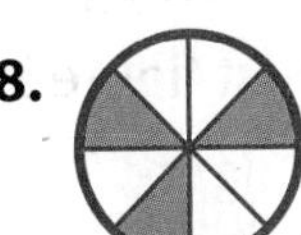

9.

10.

In **11** through **14**, write the fraction that names the unshaded part.

11.

12.

13.

14.

In **15** through **17**, draw a model to show each fraction.

15. 8 out of 9 as part of a region

16. 6 out of 7 as part of a set

17. 3 out of 5 as part of a segment

Problem Solving

18. Ladybugs are easy to identify because they are red with black spots. What fraction of the insects shown below are ladybugs?

19. What fraction of the fruit are pineapples?

20. Write a numerical expression for each word expression:

   a fifty-two divided by 2

   b the product of twenty-two and two

   c five dollars less than eighteen dollars

   d eighty increased by 5

21. What fraction of the parking spaces are in use?

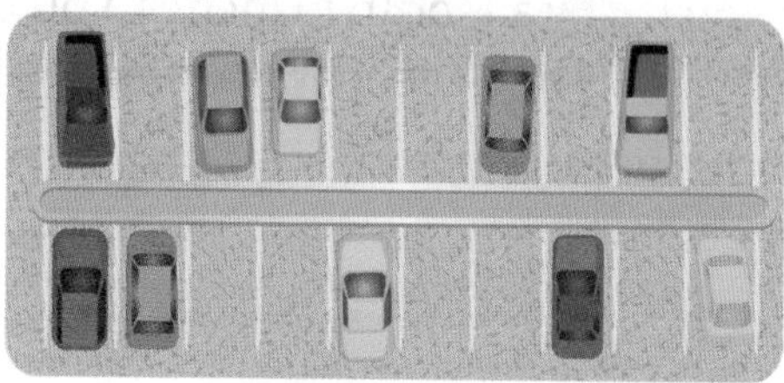

22. John bought a shirt and a CD. The CD cost $13 and the shirt cost $17 more than the CD. How much did John spend in all?

23. **Writing to Explain** Explain how to round 456 to the hundreds place.

24. If you throw a bowling ball and knock down four pins, what fraction of the total number of pins are still standing?

   A $\frac{4}{10}$

   B $\frac{6}{10}$

   C $\frac{4}{6}$

   D $\frac{4}{5}$

25. **Think About the Process** How could you find the numerator of the fraction that represents the shaded part of the square that is divided into 4 equal parts?

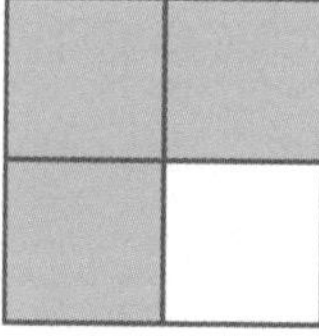

   A Count the total parts that are shaded.

   B Count the total parts that are unshaded.

   C Count the total number of shaded and unshaded parts.

   D Subtract the number of unshaded parts from the shaded parts.

26. About 4 square feet out of every 5 square feet of exhibit space at a state fair is used by the Auto Show. What fraction of the exhibit space represents this estimated space used by the Auto Show?

Algebra Connections

What's a Rule?

Remember that tables can be used to show relationships between pairs of numbers.

Number of Feet	1	2	3	4
Number of Inches	12	24	36	48

If you know a length in feet, you can multiply by 12 to find the length in inches. When you know a length in inches, you can divide by 12 to find the length in feet.

Example:
What rule connects the number of hours to the number of days? Find the missing numbers.

Number of Days	1	2	3	4		
Number of Hours	24	48	72	96	120	240

Rule:
Divide the number of hours by 24 to find the number of days.

120 ÷ 24 = 5. So, 120 hours = 5 days.
240 ÷ 24 = 10. So, 240 hours = 10 days.

For **1** through **7**, find a rule. Then find the missing numbers in the chart.

1.

Quarters	4	8	12	16	20	60
Dollars	1	2	3	4		

2.

Apples	30	35	40	45	50	75
Baskets	6	7	8	9		

3.

Loaves	1	2	3	4	5	9
Slices	20	40	60	80		

4.

Cups	3	4	5	6	7	10
Fluid Ounces	24	32	40	48		

5.

Marbles	*Bags*
50	1
100	2
150	3
200	
450	

6.

Tomatoes	*Containers*
30	2
45	3
60	4
75	5
120	

7.

Yards	*Inches*
1	36
2	72
3	108
4	144
10	

Lesson

10-2

NS 1.5 Identify and represent on a number line decimals, fractions, mixed numbers, and positive and negative integers.

Fractions and Division

How can fractions be used to show division?

Al, Lisa, Franco, and Laura are making a collage. They will share 3 rectangular strips of colored paper. What fraction represents the part of a whole strip of paper each will get?

1 whole   1 whole   1 whole

Find 3 ÷ 4.

Another Example How can you use a number line to represent fractions?

One way to find a point on a number line that represents a fraction is to divide a unit segment (0 to 1) into equal parts. To find $\frac{4}{5}$, divide the segment into 5 equal parts.

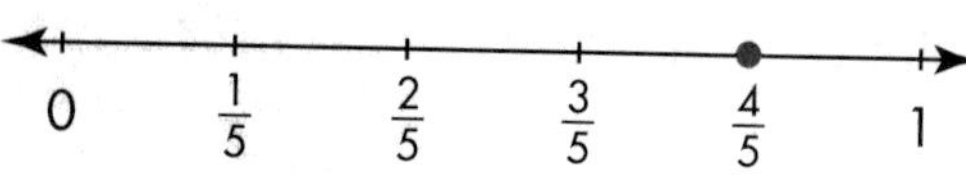

Then find the point $\frac{4}{5}$ of the way from 0 to 1.

Explain It

1. Explain how you would find the fraction $\frac{2}{5}$ on the number line above.
2. What fraction is shown by Point *A* below? Point *B*?

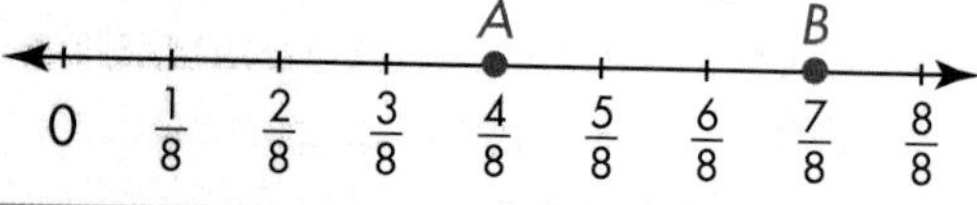

Guided Practice*

Do you know HOW?

Give each answer as a fraction.

1. 1 ÷ 2
2. 1 ÷ 4
3. 9 ÷ 10
4. 5 ÷ 8
5. 3 ÷ 4
6. 7 ÷ 9
7. 7 ÷ 11
8. 3 ÷ 6

Do you UNDERSTAND?

9. **Writing to Explain** How can you represent $\frac{3}{4}$ on a number line?
10. Four friends want to share three loaves of bread. One student suggests that each of the three loaves be divided into 4 equal parts. If each person gets 3 of the parts, how much of a whole loaf does each person get in all?

*For another example, see Set B on page 242.

One way to divide 3 wholes into 4 equal parts is to first divide each whole into 4 equal parts. Each part is $\frac{1}{4}$ of a whole.

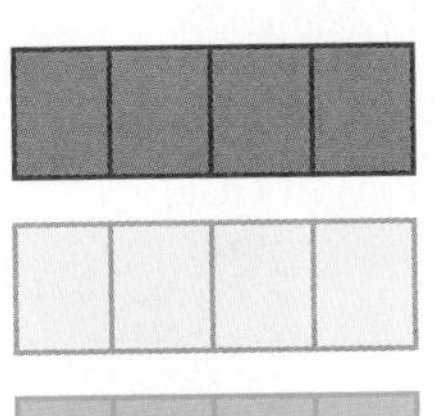

Rearrange the $\frac{1}{4}$ pieces. Each person gets 3 of the $\frac{1}{4}$ pieces. Each gets $\frac{3}{4}$. So $3 \div 4 = \frac{3}{4}$.

Al

Franco 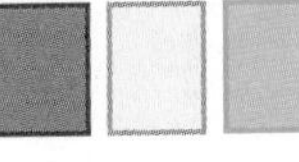

Lisa 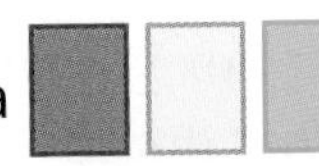

Laura 

Independent Practice

In **11** through **14**, write each as a fraction. Then show each on a number line.

11. $1 \div 3$ **12.** $2 \div 3$ **13.** $3 \div 4$ **14.** $1 \div 2$

In **15** through **18**, use the number line to name each point with a fraction.

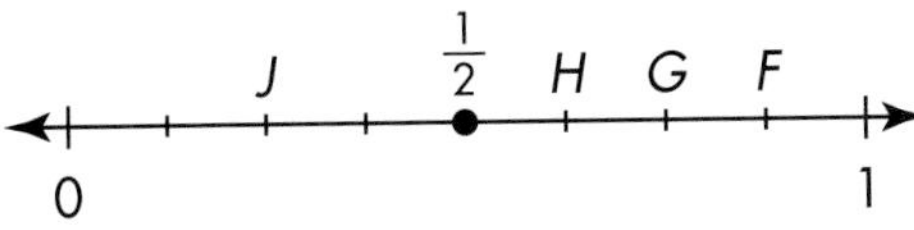

15. *F* **16.** *G* **17.** *H* **18.** *J*

Problem Solving

19. Algebra Which expression represents "30 subtracted from a number"?

A $30n$

B $30 - n$

C $30 + n$

D $n - 30$

21. Which fraction is closer to 1: $\frac{3}{4}$ or $\frac{5}{12}$? Use the number lines below to justify your answer.

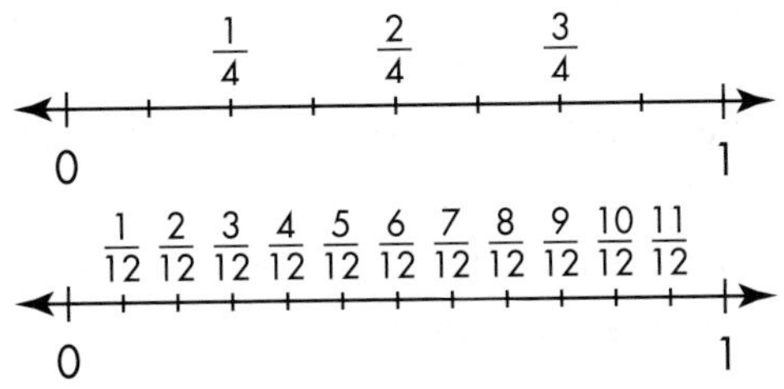

20. Think About the Process There are 6 pieces of construction paper for 7 people. Each person needs an equal amount. What is the first step to divide the construction paper?

A Cut each piece of construction paper into 6 equal parts.

B Cut each piece of construction paper into 7 equal parts.

C Cut each piece of construction paper into 13 equal parts.

D Cut each piece of construction paper into 42 equal parts.

Lesson

10-3

NS 1.0 Students compute with very large and very small numbers, positive integers, decimals, and fractions and understand the relationship between decimals, fractions, and percents. They understand the relative magnitudes of numbers.

Mixed Numbers and Improper Fractions

How are mixed numbers and improper fractions related?

Jack has 20 square tiles. He uses them to cover box lids with 3 rows of 3 square tiles. What number can name the total region covered by the tiles?

Guided Practice*

Do you know HOW?

Write each improper fraction as a mixed number or each mixed number as an improper fraction.

1. $\frac{3}{2}$

2. $2\frac{3}{4}$

3. $3\frac{1}{4}$

4. $\frac{7}{6}$

5. $9\frac{1}{10}$

6. $\frac{21}{2}$

Do you UNDERSTAND?

7. What is a general rule for writing a mixed number as an improper fraction?

8. **Writing to Explain** Simone thinks that $\frac{8}{4}$ is not an improper fraction because $8 \div 4 = 2$. Is she correct? Explain.

Independent Practice

In **9** and **10**, write an improper fraction and a mixed number for the model.

9.

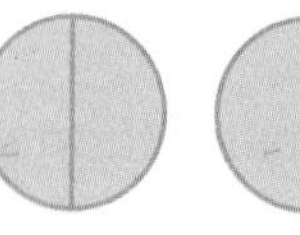
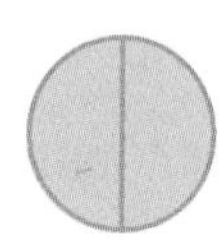
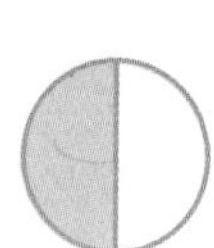

10.

In **11** through **18**, write each improper fraction as a mixed number or each mixed number as an improper fraction.

11. $4\frac{1}{2}$

12. $\frac{3}{2}$

13. $4\frac{9}{10}$

14. $5\frac{3}{4}$

15. $\frac{22}{3}$

16. $\frac{5}{4}$

17. $8\frac{2}{3}$

18. $6\frac{1}{3}$

*For another example, see Set C on page 242.

A mixed number is a whole number and a fraction. You can write $20 \div 9$ as a mixed number. You know that $20 \div 9 = \frac{20}{9}$.

Divide the numerator by the denominator.

$$\begin{array}{r} 2 \\ 9\overline{)20} \\ \underline{18} \\ 2 \end{array}$$

Write the remainder as a fraction. Put the remainder over the divisor.

So, $20 \div 9 = \frac{20}{9}$ or $2\frac{2}{9}$.

An improper fraction is a fraction whose numerator is greater than or equal to its denominator.

Write $2\frac{2}{9}$ as an improper fraction.

Multiply the denominator of the fraction by the whole number. $9 \times 2 = 18$.

Add the numerator of the fraction. $18 + 2 = 20$

$2 \frac{2}{9}$ (+, ×)

Write using the same denominator.

So, $2\frac{2}{9} = \frac{20}{9}$

Problem Solving

19. The Long Term Parking sculpture in France contains 60 cars embedded in concrete. It is 65.6 feet high. How tall is the Long Term Parking sculpture as a mixed number and an improper fraction?

20. **Reasoning** Is $\frac{5}{5}$ an improper fraction? Explain your reasoning.

21. When transporting passengers, cable cars in San Francisco travel at a steady rate of $9\frac{5}{10}$ miles per hour. Write $9\frac{5}{10}$ as an improper fraction.

22. The weights in pounds of 4 packages are given below. Order the weights from least to greatest.

0.9 0.03 1.8 0.14

23. Write an improper fraction and mixed number for the shaded portion of the model.

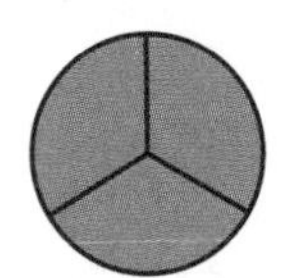 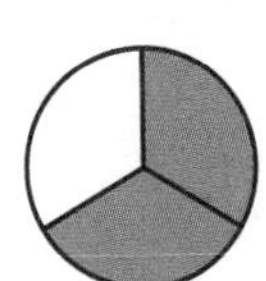

24. A board is $4\frac{2}{3}$ feet long. How could you change $4\frac{2}{3}$ into an improper fraction?

A Add 4 and $\frac{2}{3}$.

B Divide 4 by $\frac{2}{3}$.

C Multiply 4 by 3. Then, add 2. Write that number as a numerator over a denominator of 3.

D Multiply 4 by 2 and then add 3. Write as a numerator over a denominator of 3.

Lesson

10-4

NS 1.5 Grade 4 Explain different interpretations of fractions, for example, parts of a whole, parts of a set, and division of whole numbers by whole numbers; explain equivalence of fractions (see Standard 4.0).

Equivalent Fractions

How do you find equivalent fractions?

Out of 12 apples, 8 are red. So, $\frac{8}{12}$ of the apples are red. Hannah says that $\frac{4}{6}$ of the apples are red, and Sam says that $\frac{2}{3}$ are red. Who is correct?

Guided Practice*

Do you know HOW?

In **1** through **6**, find two equivalent fractions for each fraction.

1. $\frac{1}{3}$

2. $\frac{5}{6}$

3. $\frac{2}{5}$

4. $\frac{3}{8}$

5. $\frac{9}{18}$

6. $\frac{8}{10}$

Do you UNDERSTAND?

7. Sam said that $\frac{4}{12}$ of the apples are green. Name two equivalent fractions for $\frac{4}{12}$.

8. **Writing to Explain** Jon said that it would be impossible to write all fractions equivalent to $\frac{1}{2}$. Is he right?

Independent Practice

In **9** through **12**, find the missing nonzero number to make the fractions equivalent.

9. $\frac{1 \times \square = 6}{3 \times \square = 18}$

10. $\frac{17 \div \square = 1}{34 \div \square = 2}$

11. $\frac{30 \div \square = 6}{35 \div \square = 7}$

12. $\frac{9 \times \square = 36}{12 \times \square = 48}$

In **13** through **16**, find the missing numerator to make the fractions equivalent.

13. $\frac{1}{3} = \frac{\square}{9}$

14. $\frac{7}{9} = \frac{\square}{63}$

15. $\frac{30}{40} = \frac{\square}{8}$

16. $\frac{15}{35} = \frac{\square}{7}$

In **17** through **24**, find the missing denominator to make the fractions equivalent.

17. $\frac{5}{12} = \frac{10}{\square}$

18. $\frac{2}{7} = \frac{10}{\square}$

19. $\frac{14}{80} = \frac{7}{\square}$

20. $\frac{6}{18} = \frac{3}{\square}$

21. $\frac{80}{100} = \frac{20}{\square}$

22. $\frac{12}{\square} = \frac{3}{16}$

23. $\frac{10}{\square} = \frac{2}{5}$

24. $\frac{7}{\square} = \frac{21}{36}$

*For another example, see Set D on page 243.

You can multiply or divide the numerator and denominator by the same nonzero number to get equivalent fractions.

One Way

Use multiplication.

Multiply 4 and 6 by 2.

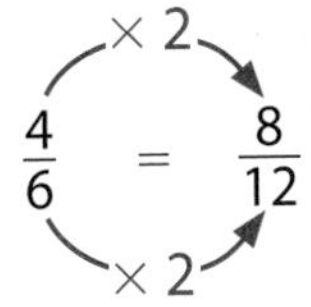

The fractions $\frac{4}{6}$ and $\frac{8}{12}$ are equivalent fractions.

Another Way

Use division.

Divide 4 and 6 by 2.

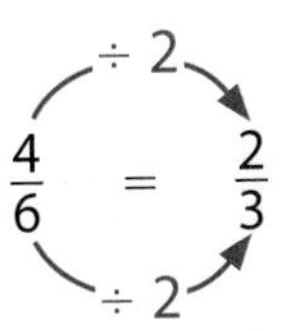

The fractions $\frac{4}{6}$ and $\frac{2}{3}$ are equivalent fractions.

So, Hannah and Sam were both correct since $\frac{8}{12}$ is equivalent to $\frac{4}{6}$, and $\frac{2}{3}$ is equivalent to $\frac{4}{6}$.

Problem Solving

25. Ming dropped a package of 8 light bulbs and 2 of the bulbs broke. Write two equivalent fractions to represent the fraction of the bulbs that broke.

26. Marcus spelled 20 out of 25 words correctly. What fraction of the words did he spell correctly? What fraction of the words did he spell incorrectly? Write two equivalent fractions for each.

27. What is the least amount you can spend to buy 7 books?

28. **Writing to Explain** Explain why $\frac{6}{15}$ and $\frac{3}{5}$ are NOT equivalent fractions.

29. It rained 0.45 inch on Friday, 2.2 inches on Saturday, and 1.02 inches on Sunday. How much more did it rain on Saturday than on Friday and Sunday combined?

30. It takes about 12 minutes to hard boil an egg. What fraction of an hour is 12 minutes?

A $\frac{1}{4}$ **C** $\frac{2}{5}$

B $\frac{1}{5}$ **D** $\frac{2}{3}$

31. A 2-year old goliath bird-eating spider weighs 6 ounces, or $\frac{6}{16}$ of a pound. Which fraction is equivalent to $\frac{6}{16}$?

A $\frac{1}{4}$

B $\frac{1}{3}$

C $\frac{1}{8}$

D $\frac{3}{8}$

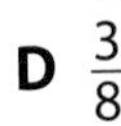

32. Maurice ran $\frac{1}{2}$ of a mile, or 2,640 feet in 3 minutes 30 seconds. Which of the following is NOT an equivalent fraction for $\frac{1}{2}$?

A $\frac{2}{4}$ **C** $\frac{17}{34}$

B $\frac{10}{20}$ **D** $\frac{16}{30}$

Lesson
10-5

NS 1.1 Grade 6 Compare and order positive and negative fractions, decimals, and mixed numbers and place them on a number line.

Comparing and Ordering Fractions and Mixed Numbers

How can you compare fractions?

Shawna and Tom walked two different paths in Trout park. Shawna walked $\frac{5}{6}$ mile. Tom walked $\frac{3}{4}$ mile. Which is greater, $\frac{5}{6}$ or $\frac{3}{4}$?

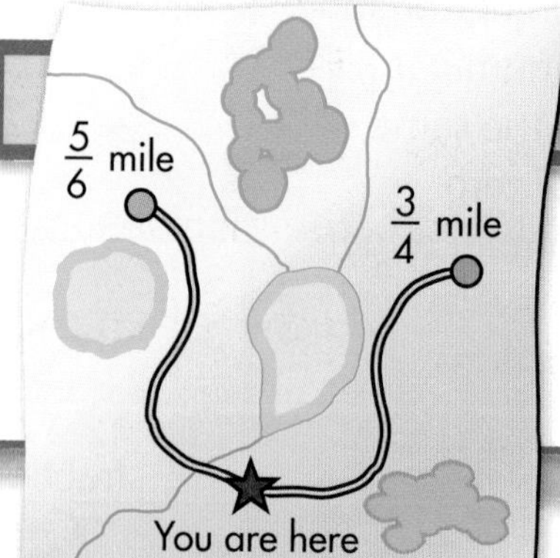

Another Example How can you order fractions and mixed numbers?

Write $2\frac{5}{12}$, $\frac{11}{12}$, $3\frac{1}{6}$, and $2\frac{1}{3}$ in order from greatest to least.

You know that $\frac{11}{12} < 1$ and all the mixed numbers are greater than 1. So, $\frac{11}{12}$ is the least number.

When comparing mixed numbers, look at the whole number parts. Since $3 > 2$, you know that $3\frac{1}{6}$ is greater than both $2\frac{1}{3}$ and $2\frac{5}{12}$.

Next, compare $2\frac{1}{3}$ and $2\frac{5}{12}$.
Since the whole numbers are the same, compare the fractions.

Compare $\frac{1}{3}$ and $\frac{5}{12}$. Change $\frac{1}{3}$ to $\frac{4}{12}$. $\frac{4}{12} < \frac{5}{12}$.

So, $2\frac{1}{3} < 2\frac{5}{12}$.

From greatest to least, the numbers are $3\frac{1}{6}$, $2\frac{5}{12}$, $2\frac{1}{3}$, $\frac{11}{12}$.

Guided Practice*

Do you know HOW?

Compare. Write >, < or = for each ◯.

1. $\frac{3}{5}$ ◯ $\frac{4}{5}$

2. $\frac{1}{4}$ ◯ $\frac{2}{3}$

Order the numbers from least to greatest.

3. $\frac{2}{3}$, $\frac{1}{4}$, $\frac{9}{10}$

4. $1\frac{2}{3}$, $2\frac{1}{4}$, $1\frac{9}{10}$

Do you UNDERSTAND?

5. How do you know that $\frac{5}{12}$ is less than $\frac{1}{2}$?

6. How do you know that $5\frac{1}{12} > 4\frac{1}{2}$ without finding a common denominator for both fraction parts?

*For another example, see Set E on page 243.

One Way

To compare fractions, find a common denominator by writing the multiples of each denominator.

4: 4, 8, (12), 16, 20, . . .

6: 6, (12), 18, 24, . . .

Use 12 as the common denominator.

$\frac{5}{6} \times \frac{2}{2} = \frac{10}{12}$ $\frac{3}{4} \times \frac{3}{3} = \frac{9}{12}$

$\frac{10}{12} > \frac{9}{12}$, so, $\frac{5}{6} > \frac{3}{4}$.

Another Way

You can multiply the denominators to find a common denominator.

Compare $\frac{3}{4}$ and $\frac{5}{6}$.

Multiply denominators: $4 \times 6 = 24$.

Use 24 as the common denominator.

$\frac{5}{6} \times \frac{4}{4} = \frac{20}{24}$ $\frac{3}{4} \times \frac{6}{6} = \frac{18}{24}$

$\frac{20}{24} > \frac{18}{24}$, so, $\frac{5}{6} > \frac{3}{4}$.

Independent Practice

In **7** through **10**, compare the numbers. Write >, < or = for each ◯.

You can always multiply the denominators to find a common denominator.

7. $\frac{3}{4}$ ◯ $\frac{4}{5}$ **8.** $\frac{9}{10}$ ◯ $\frac{18}{20}$ **9.** $3\frac{6}{7}$ ◯ $3\frac{13}{14}$ **10.** $1\frac{7}{8}$ ◯ $1\frac{2}{3}$

In **11** and **12**, order the numbers from least to greatest.

11. $\frac{1}{2}, \frac{1}{4}, \frac{5}{6}, \frac{3}{4}$ **12.** $2\frac{1}{2}, 1\frac{7}{8}, 2\frac{3}{4}, 2\frac{3}{5}$

Problem Solving

13. Birdhouses can provide homes for many different kinds of birds. The size of the opening will determine the kind of bird that can use it. Order the data in the table from least to greatest.

Type of Bird	Size of Birdhouse Opening (in inches)
Screech owl	3
Chickadee	$1\frac{1}{8}$
House wren	1
Tree swallow	$1\frac{1}{2}$

14. Sarah rode her bike $2\frac{1}{2}$ miles on Thursday, $2\frac{7}{10}$ miles on Friday, and $2\frac{5}{8}$ miles on Saturday. Which day did she ride farthest?

15. At the school fair, 157 tickets were sold. The tickets cost $3 apiece. The goal was to make $300 in ticket sales. By how much was the goal exceeded?

A $71 **C** $371

B $171 **D** $471

Lesson

10-6

NS 2.4 Grade 6 Determine the least common multiple and the greatest common divisor of whole numbers; use them to solve problems with fractions (e.g., to find a common denominator to add two fractions or to find the reduced form for a fraction).

Fractions in Simplest Form

How can you write a fraction in simplest form?

A stained glass window has 20 panes. Out of 20 sections, 12 are yellow. So $\frac{12}{20}$ of the panes are yellow. Notice how the picture also shows that $\frac{3}{5}$ are yellow.

Another Example **How can you use the GCF to find the simplest form of a fraction?**

There are 36 students in the fifth-grade class. Twenty-seven will go to the mathematics competition. What is the simplest form of the fraction of the class going to competition?

A $\frac{1}{9}$ **B** $\frac{2}{5}$ **C** $\frac{3}{4}$ **D** $\frac{7}{8}$

Factors of 27: 1, 3, 9, 27

Factors of 36: 1, 2, 3, 4, 6, 9, 18, 36.

The GCF of 27 and 36 is 9.

Then, divide the numerator and denominator by the GCF.

$$\frac{27 \div 9}{36 \div 9} = \frac{3}{4}$$

The simplest form of $\frac{27}{36}$ is $\frac{3}{4}$.

The correct choice is **C**.

Explain It

1. In finding the simplest form in the Another Example, do you get the same answer if you list factor pairs? Explain.
2. John said that he divided the numerator and denominator of $\frac{18}{54}$ by 2, so $\frac{9}{27}$ is the simplest form of the fraction. Do you agree? Explain.

A fraction is in simplest form when its numerator and denominator have no common factor other than 1.

To write $\frac{12}{20}$ in simplest form, find a common factor of the numerator and the denominator. Since 12 and 20 are even numbers, they have 2 as a factor.

Divide both 12 and 20 by 2.

$$\frac{12 \div 2}{20 \div 2} = \frac{6}{10}$$

Both 6 and 10 are even. Divide both by 2.

$$\frac{6 \div 2}{10 \div 2} = \frac{3}{5}$$

Since 3 and 5 have no common factor other than 1, $\frac{3}{5}$ is in simplest form.

Guided Practice*

Do you know HOW?

In **1** through **6**, write each fraction in simplest form.

1. $\frac{16}{32}$ **2.** $\frac{10}{14}$

3. $\frac{33}{77}$ **4.** $\frac{16}{20}$

5. $\frac{30}{40}$ **6.** $\frac{10}{15}$

Do you UNDERSTAND?

7. In the stained glass window pattern above, what fraction in simplest form names the green tiles?

8. **Writing to Explain** Why is it easier to divide the numerator and denominator by the GCF rather than any other factor?

Independent Practice

For **9** through **32**, write each fraction in simplest form.

9. $\frac{300}{400}$ **10.** $\frac{55}{60}$ **11.** $\frac{3}{6}$ **12.** $\frac{75}{100}$

13. $\frac{14}{21}$ **14.** $\frac{4}{12}$ **15.** $\frac{42}{48}$ **16.** $\frac{63}{70}$

17. $\frac{18}{21}$ **18.** $\frac{22}{44}$ **19.** $\frac{6}{42}$ **20.** $\frac{15}{25}$

21. $\frac{9}{81}$ **22.** $\frac{12}{100}$ **23.** $\frac{7}{21}$ **24.** $\frac{16}{30}$

25. $\frac{99}{121}$ **26.** $\frac{122}{144}$ **27.** $\frac{28}{42}$ **28.** $\frac{32}{80}$

29. $\frac{40}{80}$ **30.** $\frac{11}{22}$ **31.** $\frac{60}{80}$ **32.** $\frac{8}{100}$

DIGITAL  Animated Glossary
www.pearsonsuccessnet.com

For another example, see Set F on page 244.

Problem Solving

33. Write a fraction in simplest form that shows the shaded part of the figure.

34. Mrs. Lok is planning a 600-mile trip. Her car has an 18-gallon gas tank and gets 29 miles per gallon. Will 1 tank full of gas be enough for the trip?

35. Writing to Explain Explain how you know that $\frac{55}{80}$ is not in simplest form.

36. If 5 packages of hot dogs cost \$10.25, what is the cost of 1 package?

37. Writing to Explain Can you assume that any fraction is in simplest form if either the numerator or denominator is a prime number?

38. A store manager wants to give away the last 84 samples of hand cream. She counts 26 customers in the store. She will give each customer the same number of free samples. How many free samples will each customer get?

39. Mayflies can live at the bottom of lakes for 2 to 3 years before they become winged adults. Mayflies are between $\frac{4}{10}$ inches and 1.6 inches long. If this mayfly is $\frac{4}{10}$ of an inch long, how can you write $\frac{4}{10}$ in simplest form?

A $\frac{1}{6}$

B $\frac{1}{4}$

C $\frac{2}{5}$

D $\frac{8}{20}$

40. Reasoning Use divisibility rules to find a number that satisfies the given conditions.

a a number greater than 75 that is divisible by 2 and 5.

b a three-digit number divisible by 3, 5 and 6.

41. Think About the Process Rita sells birdhouses for \$10 each. She uses $3\frac{1}{2}$ ft of wood for each birdhouse. Which operation would she use to find how much money she will receive if she sells 14 birdhouses?

A Multiplication

B Division

C Addition

D Subtraction

42. Think About the Process A parking garage has 4 levels with 28 spaces on each level. If 52 spaces are occupied, which of the following shows a way to find the number of spaces that are unoccupied?

A Add 28 to the product of 52 and 4.

B Add 52 to the product of 28 and 4.

C Subtract 28 from the product of 52 and 4.

D Subtract 52 from the product of 4 and 28.

Find the difference. Estimate to check if the answer is reasonable.

1. $19{,}450 - 8{,}275$
2. $81{,}025 - 4{,}827$
3. $75{,}075 - 6{,}038$
4. $67{,}890 - 23{,}458$
5. $96{,}375 - 5{,}240$
6. $6{,}363 - 5{,}454$
7. $51{,}515 - 17{,}171$
8. $8{,}898 - 7{,}361$

Find the sum. Estimate to check if the answer is reasonable.

9. $45.98 + 3.4$
10. $17.9 + 0.87$
11. $35.89 + 3.4$
12. $41.28 + 7.9$
13. $650.05 + 25.2$
14. $9.4 + 0.186$
15. $0.345 + 2.34 + 14.7$
16. $6.87 + 4.512 + 18.4$
17. $37.02 + 0.98$

Error Search Find each answer that is not correct. Write it correctly and explain the error.

18. $6.78 \times 5 = 33.9$
19. $0.27 + 0.85 = 1.11$
20. $3.5 - 0.29 = 0.6$
21. $7.60 \div 2 = 0.38$ (2)7.60 with quotient 0.38)

Number Sense

Estimating and Reasoning Write whether each statement is true or false. Explain your reasoning.

22. The value of $n \div n \times n$ will always equal n, as long as n is not zero.

23. The difference of 6.8 and 1.02 is closer to 5 than 6.

24. The expression $(8 + 8) \div 8 \times 8$ equals 16.

25. The quotient of $45{,}894 \div 2$ will have a remainder of 1.

26. The product of 400×750 is 20,000 less than 280,000.

27. The expression $3.56d$ equals 12.816 when $d = 3.6$.

Lesson

10-7

NS 1.0 Compute with very large and very small numbers, positive integers, decimals, and fractions and understand the relationship between decimals, fractions, and percents. They understand the relative magnitudes of numbers.

Tenths and Hundredths

How can you write a fraction as a decimal?

A fraction such as $\frac{3}{10}$ or $\frac{9}{100}$ can be shown by a model.

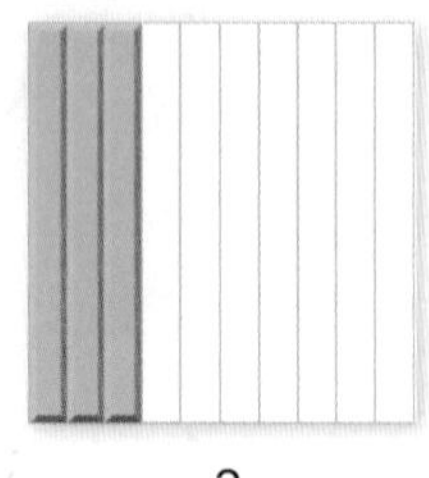

$\frac{3}{10}$

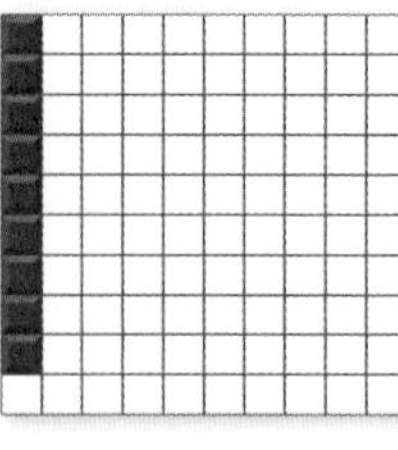

$\frac{9}{100}$

Other Examples

How can you use division to write a fraction as a decimal?

Write $\frac{3}{5}$ as a decimal.

$\frac{3}{5} = 3 \div 5$

Divide the numerator by the denominator.

$$\begin{array}{r} 0.6 \\ 5\overline{)3.0} \\ -\ 3\,0 \\ \hline 0 \end{array}$$

Insert a decimal point after 3 and annex zeros as needed.

So, $\frac{3}{5} = 0.6$.

Write $\frac{1}{4}$ as a decimal.

$\frac{1}{4} = 1 \div 4$

$$\begin{array}{r} 0.25 \\ 4\overline{)1.00} \\ -\ 8\downarrow \\ \hline 20 \\ -\ 20 \\ \hline 0 \end{array}$$

Insert a decimal point after 1 and annex zeros as needed.

So, $\frac{1}{4} = 0.25$.

Explain It

1. How can you write $\frac{9}{100}$ as a division problem?
2. In the second example, how many zeros did you need to annex after 1 when you divided 1 by 4?

Guided Practice*

Do you know HOW?

Write each decimal as a fraction and each fraction as a decimal.

1. 0.1
2. 0.02
3. $\frac{9}{10}$
4. $\frac{7}{100}$
5. Use division to change $\frac{11}{20}$ to a decimal.

Do you UNDERSTAND?

6. Describe two ways to write a decimal as a fraction.
7. **Writing to Explain** How is $\frac{3}{10}$ equal to 0.3?

*For another example, see Set G on page 244.

The word name for $\frac{3}{10}$ is three tenths. Three tenths can be shown on a place-value chart,

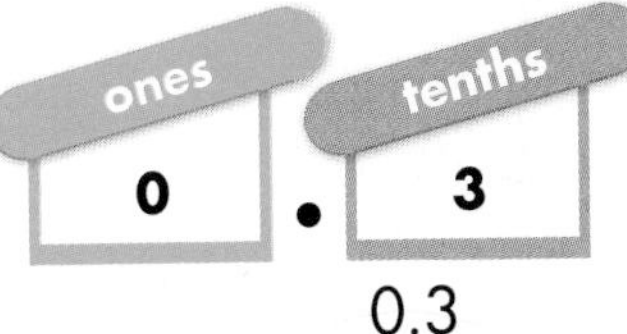

0.3

So, $\frac{3}{10} = 0.3$.

The word name for $\frac{9}{100}$ is nine hundredths. Nine hundredths can be shown on a place-value chart,

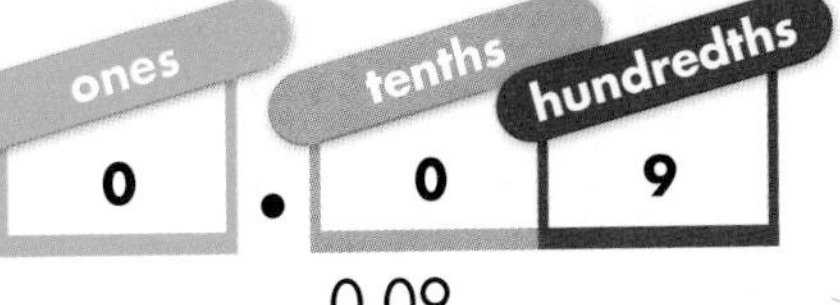

0.09

So, $\frac{9}{100} = 0.09$.

Independent Practice

In **8** through **11**, write a decimal and fraction for the shaded portion of each model.

8. 

9. 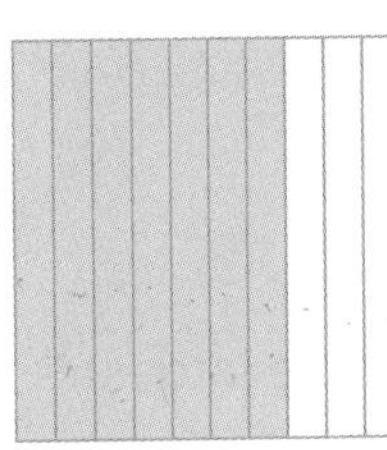

10. 

11. 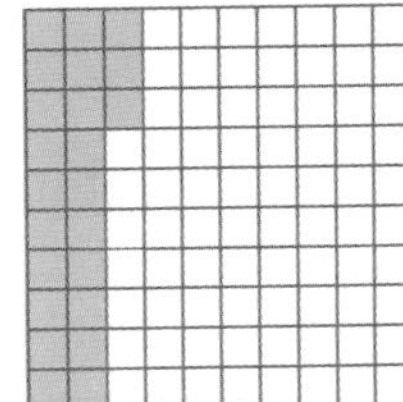

In **12** through **19**, write each decimal as either a fraction or a mixed number.

12. 3.2 **13.** 0.7 **14.** 0.23 **15.** 9.75

16. 7.7 **17.** 0.4 **18.** 0.81 **19.** 2.43

In **20** through **27**, write each fraction or mixed number as a decimal.

20. $2\frac{1}{100}$ **21.** $9\frac{3}{10}$ **22.** $\frac{9}{10}$ **23.** $1\frac{18}{100}$

24. $6\frac{31}{100}$ **25.** $4\frac{1}{10}$ **26.** $\frac{4}{10}$ **27.** $6\frac{6}{100}$

Use division to change each fraction to a decimal.

28. $\frac{2}{5}$ **29.** $\frac{3}{25}$ **30.** $\frac{7}{50}$ **31.** $\frac{9}{20}$

Problem Solving

32. What is $\frac{97}{100}$ as a decimal?

A 97.0
B 9.7
C 0.97
D 0.097

33. Kate drives 234 miles in 5 hours. Felix only has to drive one half the distance that Kate does. How many miles does Felix have to drive?

34. What is the value of the underlined digit? 45$\underline{7}$,140,167

35. What is the best estimate for this product? 81×409

36. Jorge is packing books into boxes. Each box can hold 16 books. Which expression can be used to find the total number of boxes that he needs in order to pack 96 books?

A $96 \div 16$
B $96 - 16$
C $96 + 16$
D 96×16

37. At a high-school graduation, there were 200 students in the class. They were seated in 5 different sections of the auditorium. How many graduates were seated in each section?

A 40
B 195
C 400
D 1,000

38. *Titanus giganteus* is one of the largest known beetles on Earth.

a How long is *Titanus giganteus* written as a mixed number?

b How long is *Titanus giganteus* written as an improper fraction?

39. The Great Owlet Moth has a wingspan of 12.13 inches. Write this number as a mixed number.

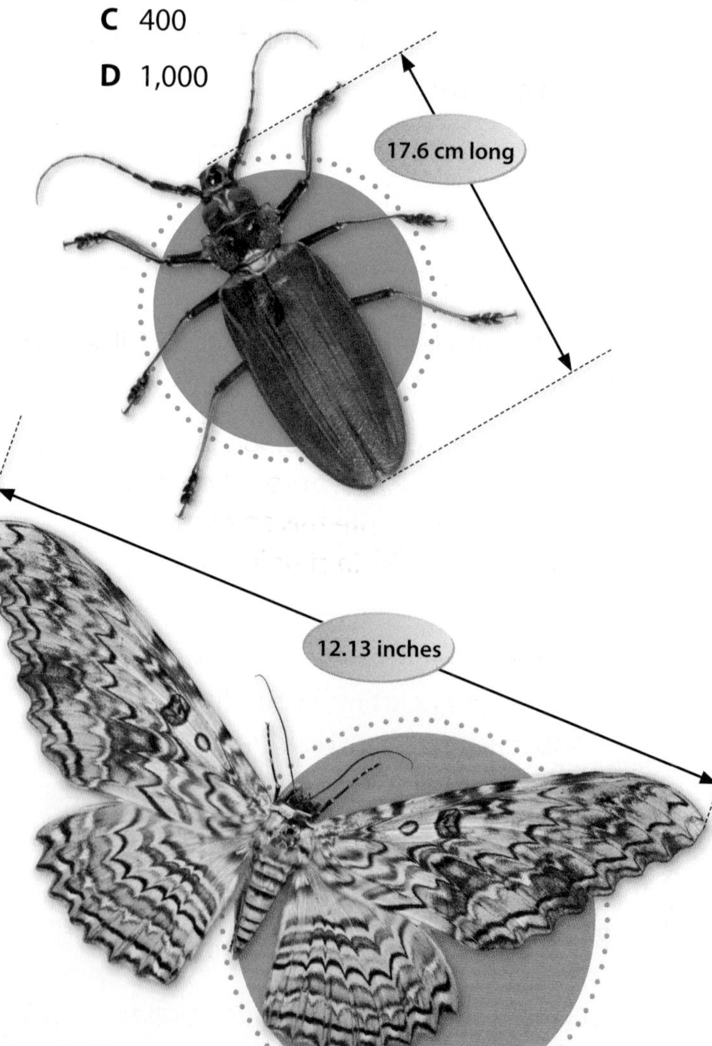

40. **Think About the Process** A design is divided into 5 equal parts and $\frac{2}{5}$ are shaded. How would you change $\frac{2}{5}$ to a decimal?

A Divide 2 by 5.
B Divide 5 by 2.
C Multiply 2 by 5.
D Add 2 and 5.

Mixed Problem Solving

The human body is very complex. It is made up of systems of organs. These organs consist of tissues, which are made of many cells.

1. Muscles make up about $\frac{4}{10}$ of the average person's body mass. Write $\frac{4}{10}$ in decimal form.

2. An average ten-year-old weighs about $86\frac{1}{2}$ pounds and has muscles that weigh about $34\frac{1}{5}$ pounds. Write these weights in decimal form.

3. A person is born with about $\frac{25}{100}$ liters of blood. Write $\frac{25}{100}$ in decimal form.

4. About how much do the muscles of two average ten-year-olds weigh? Write this weight in decimal form.

5. A cell is comprised of mostly water. About $\frac{70}{100}$ of the material in a typical cell is water. What is this fraction written in decimal form?

6. The part of the brain called the gray matter is a layer about $2\frac{5}{10}$ millimeters thick. Write the thickness of the gray matter in decimals.

In **7** and **8**, use the following information.

The left ventricle of an average person can pump about 5.25 liters of blood per minute.

7. The total volume of blood in the body is the same as the amount pumped per minute. Write this amount as a mixed number in simplest form.

8. The left ventricle pumps blood away from the heart into your body's largest artery, the aorta. How much blood is pumped into the aorta in 10 minutes?

A 0.525 liters

B 5.25 liters

C 52.5 liters

D 525 liters

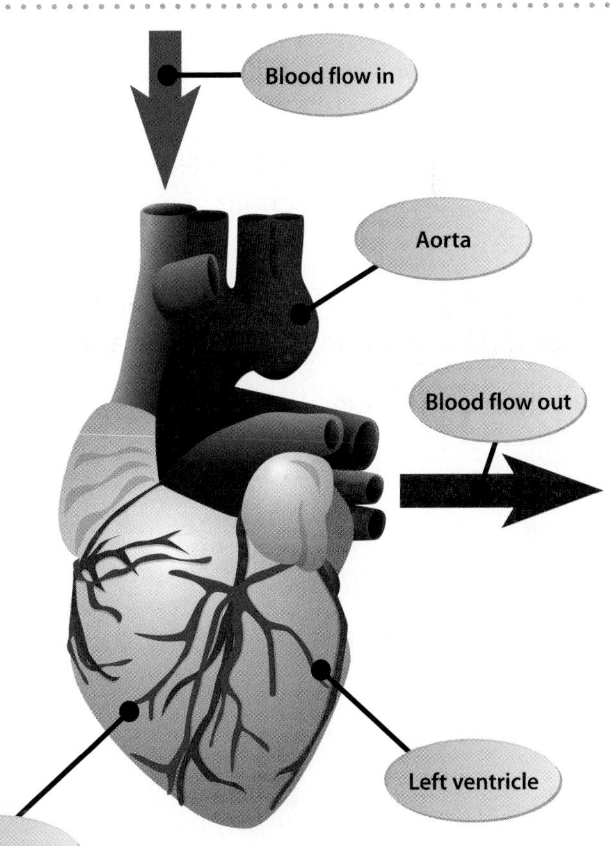

Lesson

10-8

NS 1.0 Compute with very large and very small numbers, positive integers, decimals, and fractions and understand the relationship between decimals, fractions, and percents. They understand the relative magnitudes of numbers.

Thousandths

How are fractions related to decimals?

A large box is filled with cubes. There are 1,000 cubes in all. Each cube can be thought of as $\frac{1}{1,000}$ of the whole box.

Think about pulling 3 cubes from the box. Since one cube can be shown as $\frac{1}{1,000}$, this means that 3 cubes could be shown by $\frac{3}{1,000}$. How can you use a decimal to represent this fraction?

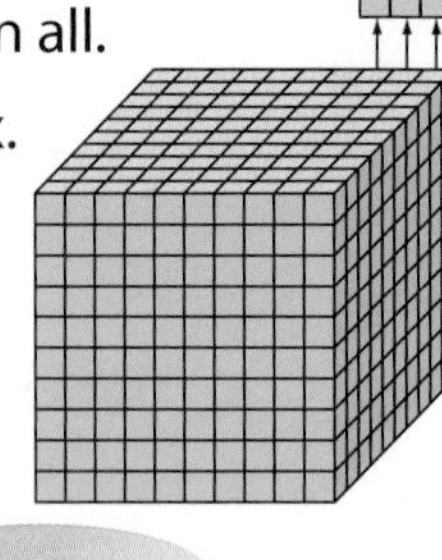

Guided Practice*

Do you know HOW?

In **1** through **4**, write each decimal as a fraction or mixed number.

1. 0.003

2. 0.050

3. 7.001

4. 0.393

In **5** through **8**, write each fraction a decimal.

5. $\frac{389}{1,000}$

6. $3\frac{673}{1,000}$

7. $\frac{211}{1,000}$

8. $\frac{90}{1,000}$

Do you UNDERSTAND?

9. Writing to Explain How is $\frac{3}{10}$ different from $\frac{3}{1000}$ in place value?

10. How would you write the fraction of cubes that are left when 3 cubes are pulled from the box in the model above?

Independent Practice

In **11** through **18**, write each decimal as a fraction or mixed number.

11. 0.007

12. 0.008

13. 0.065

14. 0.900

15. 0.832

16. 0.023

17. 3.078

18. 5.001

In **19** through **26**, write each fraction or mixed number as a decimal.

19. $\frac{434}{1,000}$

20. $3\frac{499}{1,000}$

21. $\frac{873}{1,000}$

22. $\frac{309}{1,000}$

23. $1\frac{17}{1,000}$

24. $\frac{9}{1,000}$

25. $\frac{990}{1,000}$

26. $5\frac{707}{1,000}$

For another example, see Set H on page 244.

The word name for $\frac{3}{1,000}$ is three thousandths. A decimal place-value chart can help you determine the decimal.

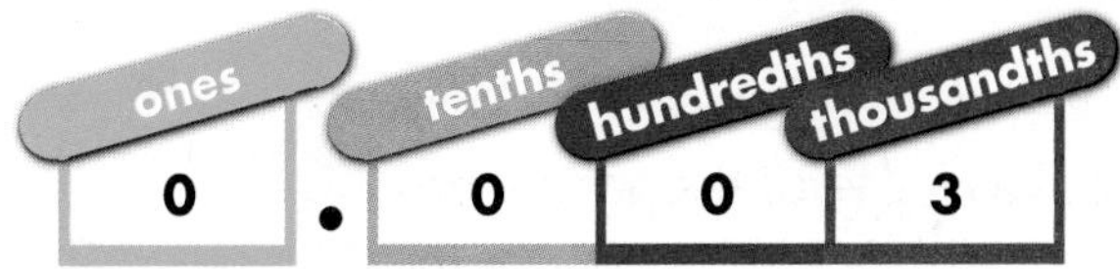

So, $\frac{3}{1,000}$ can be represented by the decimal 0.003.

Problem Solving

27. A bagel costs \$1.25, the cream cheese costs \$0.30, and a glass of juice costs \$2.25. How much change would you get from \$10.00 if you buy all three items?

28. The largest egg on record was laid by an ostrich. The weight was 5.476 pounds. Which digit is in the tenths place?

A 4 **C** 6

B 5 **D** 7

29. Write the fractions $\frac{9}{10}$, $\frac{9}{100}$, and $\frac{9}{1,000}$ as decimals.

30. Frank reasoned that $\frac{97}{1,000}$ can be written as 0.97. Is this correct? If not, justify your reasoning.

31. **Writing to Explain** How many cubes are in the box? What fraction of the entire box do the 7 cubes represent? Explain your answer.

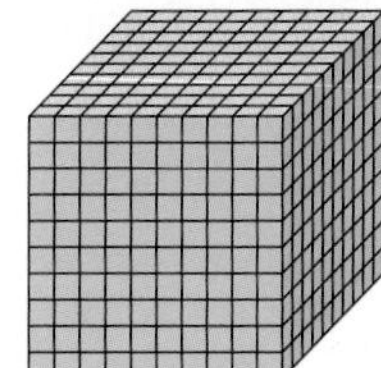

$10 \times 10 \times 10$

32. What part of the entire square is shaded?

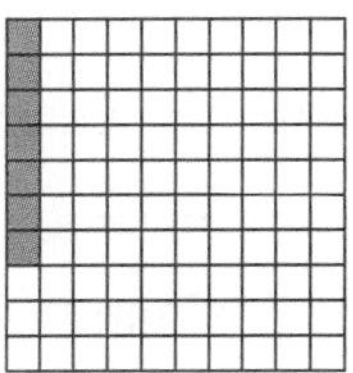

A 0.007 **C** 0.7

B 0.07 **D** 7.0

33. Which illustrates the Associative Property of Multiplication?

A $5 \times 7 = 7 \times 5$

B $0 \times 8 = 0$

C $6 \times 1 = 6$

D $1 \times (2 \times 3) = (1 \times 2) \times 3$

Lesson

10-9

NS 1.5 Identify and represent on a number line decimals, fractions, mixed numbers, and positive and negative integers.

Fractions and Decimals on the Number Line

How can you locate fractions and decimals on the same number line?

Jules is playing a game in which she chooses 3 cards. Each is labeled with a fraction or a decimal. Then she must locate a point for each number on a number line that is divided into 10 segments between 0 and 1.

Another Example How can you name points on a number line?

What fraction or mixed number can name Point *A*? Point *B*?
What decimal can name Point *A*? Point *B*?

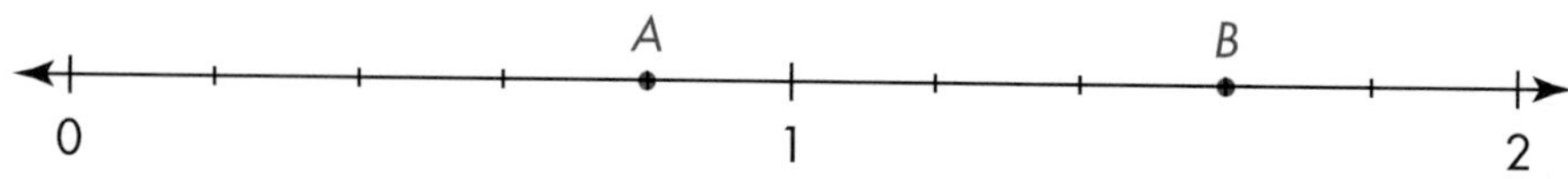

The segment between 0 and 1 is divided into 5 equal parts. So, Point *A* is named by $\frac{4}{5}$. You could use division to change $\frac{4}{5}$ to 0.8. Point *B* is named by $1\frac{3}{5}$. Since $3 \div 5 = 0.6$, another name for Point *B* is 1.6.

$$\begin{array}{r} 0.8 \\ 5\overline{)4.0} \\ -\ 4\,0 \\ \hline 0 \end{array} \qquad \begin{array}{r} 0.6 \\ 5\overline{)3.0} \\ -\ 3\,0 \\ \hline 0 \end{array}$$

Explain It

1. Which is farther to the right on the number line, $\frac{1}{4}$ or 0.2? Why?

Guided Practice*

Do you know HOW?

Show each set of numbers on the same number line.

1. $\frac{8}{10}$, 0.2, 0.7
2. $\frac{18}{20}$, 0.1, $\frac{6}{10}$
3. $\frac{11}{10}$, 0.65, 0.311

Do you UNDERSTAND?

4. Is $\frac{9}{10}$ to the left or right of 1 on the number line? Explain.
5. Will 0.617 be to the left or right of $\frac{6}{10}$ on a number line?
6. **Writing to Explain** Explain how you can find 0.311 on the number line.

*For another example, see Set I on page 245.

What You Think

- I know that 0.9 also means $\frac{9}{10}$. I can easily locate $\frac{9}{10}$.
- I know that $\frac{3}{20}$ means $3 \div 20$. I can divide to find $3 \div 20 = 0.15$.

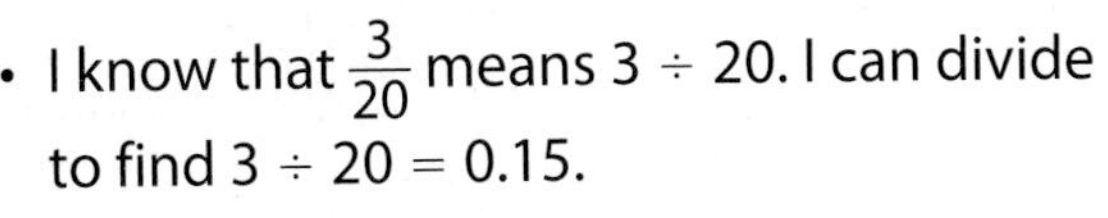

  0.1 = 0.10 and 0.2 = 0.20. So, 0.15 is halfway between 0.1 and 0.2.
- 0.6 = 0.600 and 0.7 = 0.700. So 0.617 is between 0.6 and 0.7. It is closer to 0.6 than 0.7.

What You Show

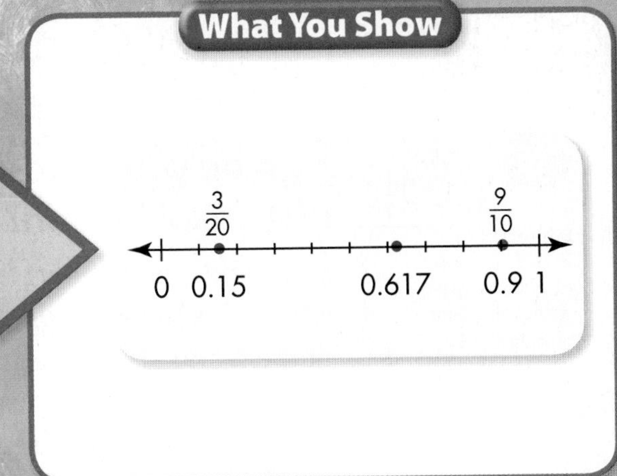

Independent Practice

In **7** through **10**, name the fraction or mixed number and decimal that identifies each point.

Remember to count over from 0 on the number line to find the number of parts of the whole.

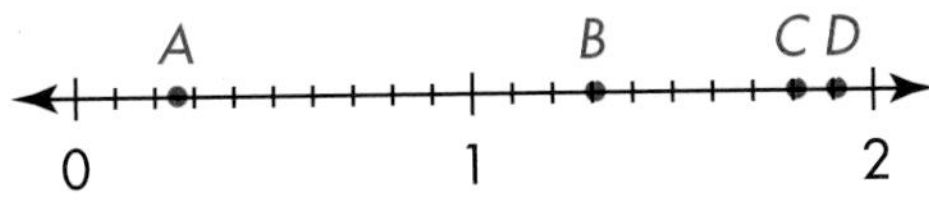

7. Point *A*

8. Point *B*

9. Point *C*

10. Point *D*

Draw a number line to show each set of numbers. Then order the numbers from least to greatest.

11. $\frac{2}{5}$, 0.35, 0.7

12. $\frac{7}{20}$, 0.15, $\frac{12}{25}$

13. $\frac{3}{4}$, 0.1, 0.22

Problem Solving

14. **Number Sense** Nadia has $2\frac{1}{2}$ pounds of tomatoes, 2.7 pounds of chicken, 2.1 pounds of celery, and $2\frac{2}{5}$ pounds of tomatillos. Which food weighs the most?

15. The top three scores in an ice-dancing competition were 60.53, 59.29, and 61.07. Order the scores from least to greatest.

16. If you located the following numbers on a number line, which would be closest to 0?

0.2, $\frac{2}{100}$, $\frac{3}{5}$, $\frac{2}{20}$

A 0.2

B $\frac{2}{100}$

C $\frac{3}{5}$

D $\frac{2}{20}$

17. Chris bought an apple for $0.58 with a $1 bill and received $0.42 in change. What is the least number of coins he could have received?

A 4

B 5

C 6

D 7

Lesson
10-10

MR 2.3 Use a variety of methods, such as words, numbers, symbols, charts, graphs, tables, diagrams, and models, to explain mathematical reasoning. Also **NS 1.1, 1.7** **Grade 4**

Problem Solving

Writing to Explain

How do you write a math explanation?

The circle graph shows the continents where the 20 most populated countries of the world are located. Estimate the fractional part for each continent. Explain how you decided.

Locations of the 20 Most Populated Countries in the World

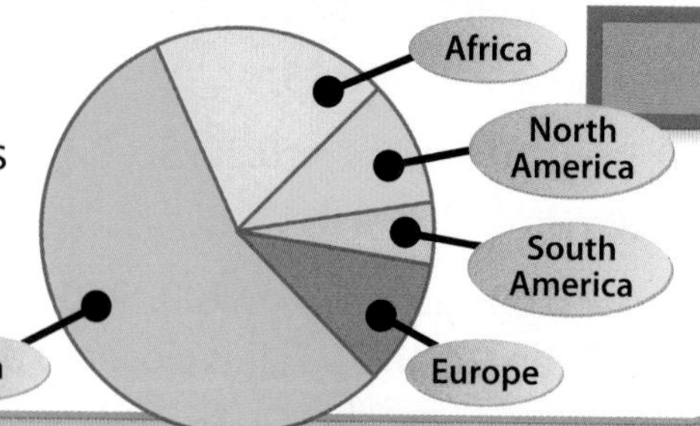

Guided Practice*

Do you know HOW?

1. Estimate the fractional part of the square that is shaded. Explain how you decided.

Do you UNDERSTAND?

2. Draw a picture to show $\frac{2}{3}$ as a benchmark fraction.

3. **Write a Problem** Write a real-world problem that involves a benchmark fraction. Your problem should ask for an explanation as part of the solution.

Independent Practice

For **4** and **5**, use the picture below.

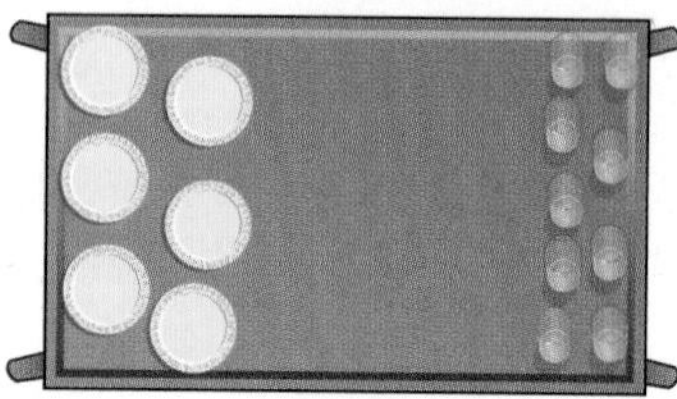

4. Estimate the part of the table that is covered with plates. Explain how you decided.

5. Estimate the part of the table that is covered with glasses. Explain how you decided.

6. Draw a kitchen table. Using plates, show the benchmark fraction, $\frac{3}{4}$. Explain how you decided the number of many plates to draw.

Stuck? Try this....

- What do I know?
- What am I asked to find?
- What diagram can I use to help understand the problem?
- Can I use addition, subtraction, multiplication, or division?
- Is all of my work correct?
- Did I answer the right question?
- Is my answer reasonable?

*For another example, see Set J on page 245.

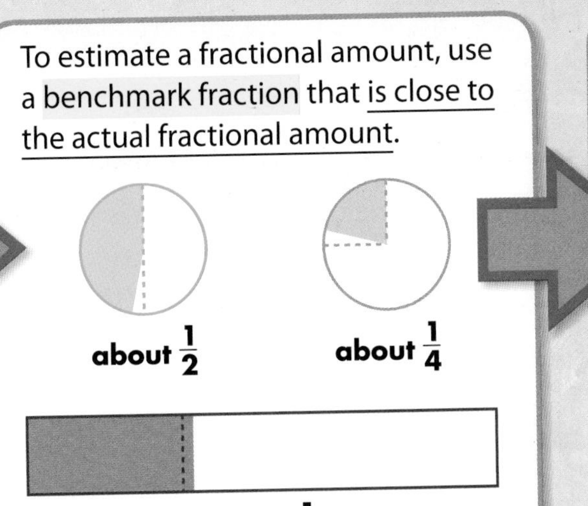

To estimate a fractional amount, use a benchmark fraction that is close to the actual fractional amount.
about $\frac{1}{2}$
about $\frac{1}{4}$
about $\frac{1}{3}$

Writing a Math Explanation

Use *words*, *pictures*, *numbers*, or *symbols* to write a good math explanation.

Asia: *If you draw a line from the top of the graph to the bottom, you can see this continent is a little more than* $\frac{1}{2}$.

Africa: *This part is a little less than* $\frac{1}{4}$.

Europe and North America: *About 10 of each of these can fill the circle, so this is about* $\frac{1}{10}$.

South America: *This part is less than the part for Europe, so I'll say about* $\frac{1}{20}$.

7. Estimate the fractional part of the square that is shaded. Explain how you decided.

8. Estimate the part of the square that is NOT shaded. Explain how you decided.

9. Draw a rectangle and shade about $\frac{1}{3}$ of it. Explain how you decided how much to shade.

10. Draw two circles that are different sizes. Shade about $\frac{1}{8}$ of each. Are the shaded parts the same amount? Explain.

11. The Mayfield Little League baseball diamond is being covered with a tarp because of rain. About how much of the diamond is NOT covered with the tarp?

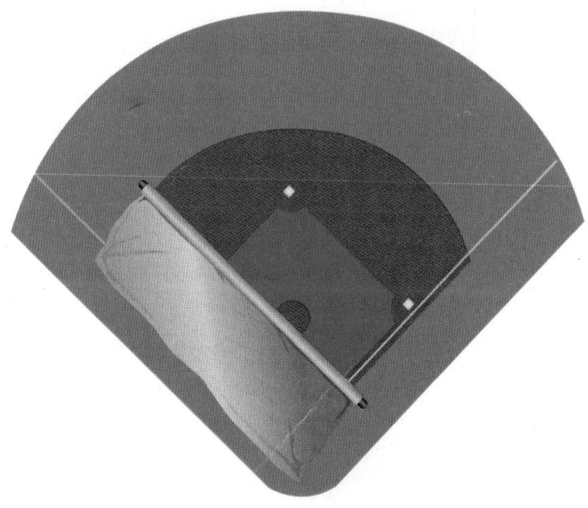

12. Cereal is a good source of protein. How many quarter cups of cereal are there in $6\frac{1}{4}$ cups?

13. A refreshment stand at the fair was open for 3 hours. Four people each took turns working at the stand for the same amount of time. How many minutes did each person work?

For **14**, decide if there is extra or missing information. Solve if possible.

14. Gene's new car gets 35 miles per gallon. Matt's car gets 32 miles per gallon. How many more gallons of gas will Matt's car use than Gene's car to go to the beach?

Test Prep

1. To make a stained glass window, Robert used 16 pieces of glass. Seven of the pieces were red. What fraction of the pieces were red? (10-1)

A $\frac{7}{16}$

B $\frac{9}{16}$

C $\frac{7}{9}$

D $\frac{16}{7}$

2. How can $\frac{12}{18}$ be written in simplest form? (10-6)

A Multiply 12 and 18 by their GCF, 3.

B Multiply 12 and 18 by their GCF, 6.

C Divide 12 and 18 by their GCF, 3.

D Divide 12 and 18 by their GCF, 6.

3. Which point on the number line represents 1.2 or $1\frac{1}{5}$? (10-9)

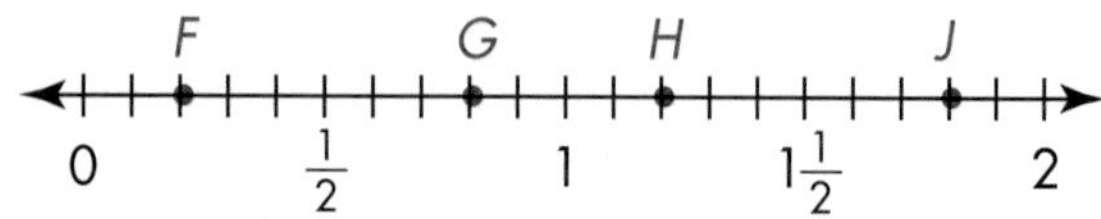

A Point *F*

B Point *G*

C Point *H*

D Point *J*

4. Jason ran $2\frac{9}{10}$ miles on Monday, $1\frac{4}{5}$ miles on Tuesday, and $1\frac{7}{10}$ miles on Thursday. Which list has the miles Jason ran from least to greatest? (10-5)

A $1\frac{4}{5}, 2\frac{9}{10}, 1\frac{7}{10}$

B $1\frac{4}{5}, 1\frac{7}{10}, 2\frac{9}{10}$

C $1\frac{7}{10}, 2\frac{9}{10}, 1\frac{4}{5}$

D $1\frac{7}{10}, 1\frac{4}{5}, 2\frac{9}{10}$

5. The atomic weight of hydrogen is 1.008. Which of the following mixed numbers is the same as 1.008? (10-8)

A $1\frac{8}{1000}$

B $1\frac{8}{100}$

C $1\frac{8}{10}$

D $1\frac{10}{8}$

6. A store has the floor plan shown. The area of the women's department is 600 ft^2. Find the best estimate of the total area of the store. (10-10)

A Women's is about $\frac{1}{3}$ of the total area, so the store is about 600×3 or 200 ft^2.

B Women's is about $\frac{1}{3}$ of the total area, so the store is about 3×600 or 1,800 ft^2.

C Women's is about $\frac{1}{4}$ of the total area, so the store is about $600 \div 4$ or 150 ft^2.

D Women's is about $\frac{1}{4}$ of the total area, so the store is about 4×600 or 2,400 ft^2.

Test Prep

7. To amend the Constitution of the United States, $\frac{2}{3}$ of each house of Congress must approve the amendment. Is $\frac{7}{12}$ of a house's approval enough? (10-5)

A No, because $\frac{7}{12} < \frac{2}{3}$

B No, because $\frac{7}{12} > \frac{2}{3}$

C Yes, because $\frac{7}{12} < \frac{2}{3}$

D Yes, because $\frac{7}{12} > \frac{2}{3}$

8. Which is equal to $5\frac{3}{10}$? (10-3)

A $\frac{53}{50}$

B $\frac{25}{10}$

C $\frac{53}{10}$

D $\frac{15}{10}$

9. About $\frac{2}{5}$ of U.S. households own at least one dog. Which is equal to $\frac{2}{5}$? (10-7)

A 0.6

B 0.4

C 0.2

D 0.04

10. What is the value of Point *A* on the number line? (10-9)

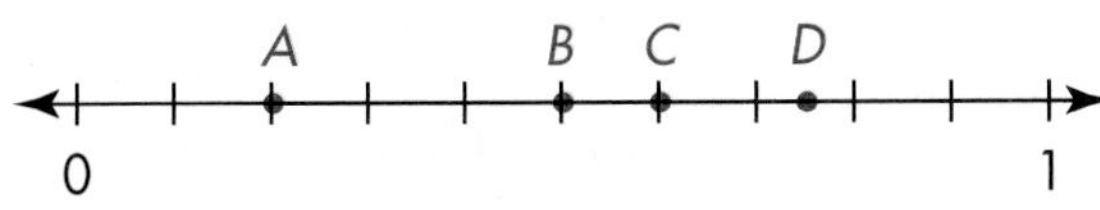

A $\frac{2}{5}$

B $\frac{1}{5}$

C 0.5

D 0.4

11. The table shows water fowl that Hong counted at the lake. What fraction of the water fowl listed are Mallards? (10-6)

Data

Water Fowl Type	Number
Canadian geese	5
Crane	3
Mallards	12

A $\frac{3}{5}$

B $\frac{8}{12}$

C $\frac{3}{2}$

D $\frac{5}{3}$

12. Which of the following fractions is equivalent to $\frac{3}{8}$? (10-4)

A $\frac{13}{18}$

B $\frac{9}{14}$

C $\frac{9}{24}$

D $\frac{1}{6}$

13. Which of the following equals $\frac{15}{8}$? (10-8)

A 1.875

B 1.625

C 1.58

D 1.375

14. Which represents $3 \div 5$ written as a fraction? (10-2)

A $\frac{5}{3}$

B $1\frac{2}{3}$

C $\frac{3}{5}$

D 0.6

Topic 10

Reteaching

Set A, pages 214–216

You can find the part of the whole, part of the set, or part of a segment using a model.

Write the fraction that names the shaded part.

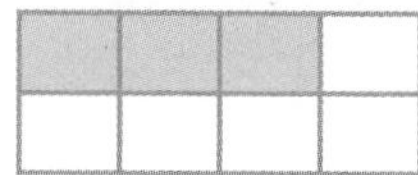

The model shows $\frac{3}{8}$ shaded.

Remember that the numerator tells you how many equal-sized parts are shaded. The denominator tells you the total number of equal-sized parts.

Write fractions for the shaded and unshaded portions of each model.

1. 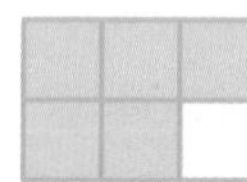

2. 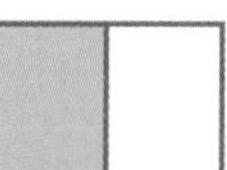

Set B, pages 218–219

José and three friends want to create chalkboard art in three equal-sized spaces on the playground. How much of each space will each student get?

To show $3 \div 4$, you can use a fraction.

$3 \div 4 = \frac{3}{4}$

Each student will get $\frac{3}{4}$ of one space.

Remember that to show a fraction on the number line, you need to divide the number line into equal parts.

Give each answer as a fraction. Then show each on a number line.

1. $1 \div 4$

2. $2 \div 5$

Set C, pages 220–221

Write the improper fraction and mixed number.

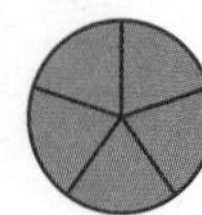 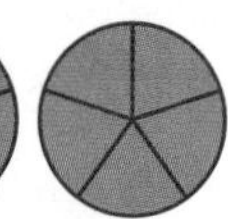 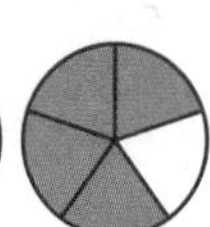

There are 2 wholes shaded and $\frac{4}{5}$ of 1 whole shaded. You can see that this is $2\frac{4}{5}$ or $\frac{14}{5}$. You can also follow the steps below to write $2\frac{4}{5}$ as an improper fraction.

Step 1

Multiply the denominator of the fraction by the whole number.
$2 \times 5 = 10$

Step 2

Add the numerator of the fraction to the product of the denominator and the whole number.
$10 + 4 = 14$

Step 3

Write the fraction using the same denominator. $\frac{14}{5}$

Remember that an improper fraction and a mixed number can represent the same value.

Write each mixed number as an improper fraction.

1. $3\frac{1}{2}$

2. $2\frac{2}{3}$

3. $5\frac{1}{6}$

4. $3\frac{4}{5}$

5. $1\frac{1}{5}$

6. $9\frac{7}{8}$

Write each improper fraction as a mixed number.

7. $\frac{4}{3}$

8. $\frac{3}{2}$

9. $\frac{6}{4}$

10. $\frac{12}{9}$

11. $\frac{31}{7}$

12. $\frac{46}{5}$

Reteaching

Set D, pages 222–223

Write two fractions equivalent to $\frac{3}{7}$.

To form equivalent fractions, multiply both the numerator and denominator of the given fraction by the same number.

$\frac{3 \times 4}{7 \times 4} = \frac{12}{28}; \frac{3 \times 5}{7 \times 5} = \frac{15}{35}$

So, $\frac{12}{28}$ and $\frac{15}{35}$ are equivalent to $\frac{3}{7}$.

Remember that you multiply or divide both the numerator and denominator to find equivalent fractions.

Write two fractions that are equivalent to each of the following.

1. $\frac{1}{2}$ **2.** $\frac{3}{4}$

3. $\frac{2}{3}$ **4.** $\frac{5}{7}$

Set E, pages 224–225

Compare $\frac{4}{16}$ and $\frac{3}{8}$.

To compare numbers, you can find a common denominator. Write multiples of each number.

Circle the common multiple.

16: 16, 32, 48, . . .

8: 8, 16, 24, . . .

Use 16 as the common denominator.

$\frac{4}{16} = \frac{4}{16}$ $\frac{3 \times 2}{8 \times 2} = \frac{6}{16}$

$\frac{4}{16} < \frac{6}{16}$, and so $\frac{4}{16} < \frac{3}{8}$.

Write $\frac{1}{5}, \frac{1}{8}, \frac{3}{10}$, and $1\frac{1}{2}$ in order from least to greatest.

$\frac{1}{8} < \frac{1}{5}$ because both numerators are 1, and $8 > 5$.

$\frac{1}{5} < \frac{3}{10}$ because $\frac{1}{5} = \frac{2}{10}$ and $\frac{2}{10} < \frac{3}{10}$.

$1\frac{1}{2}$ is greater than any of the values because it is greater than 1.

So, the order is $\frac{1}{8}, \frac{1}{5}, \frac{3}{10}, 1\frac{1}{2}$.

Remember that you can always find a common denominator by multiplying the denominators together.

Compare. Write >, <, or = for each ◯.

1. $\frac{2}{5}$ ◯ $\frac{3}{10}$ **2.** $\frac{9}{12}$ ◯ $\frac{1}{5}$

3. $\frac{7}{12}$ ◯ $\frac{1}{3}$ **4.** $\frac{8}{15}$ ◯ $\frac{20}{45}$

5. $\frac{3}{6}$ ◯ $\frac{4}{7}$ **6.** $\frac{9}{10}$ ◯ $\frac{18}{19}$

Order the numbers from the least to greatest.

7. $\frac{2}{3}, \frac{1}{4}, \frac{2}{5}, \frac{1}{3}$

8. $\frac{2}{7}, \frac{1}{10}, \frac{1}{3}, \frac{5}{6}$

9. $\frac{9}{10}, 1\frac{3}{5}, \frac{4}{7}, \frac{11}{12}$

10. $3\frac{1}{2}, 3\frac{1}{8}, 3\frac{2}{5}, 3\frac{7}{8}$

Reteaching

Set F, pages 226–228

Write $\frac{21}{36}$ in simplest form.

To express a fraction in simplest form, divide the numerator and denominator by the greatest common factor.

The GCF of 21 and 36 is 3.

$\frac{21 \div 3}{36 \div 3} = \frac{7}{12}$

Remember that the simplest form can also be found by dividing by common factors until the common factor is 1.

Write each fraction in simplest form.

1. $\frac{45}{60}$
2. $\frac{32}{96}$
3. $\frac{24}{30}$
4. $\frac{42}{49}$

Set G, pages 230–232

You can write fractions as decimals using a place-value chart. You read $\frac{60}{100}$ as 60 hundredths. The decimal for $\frac{60}{100}$ is shown below.

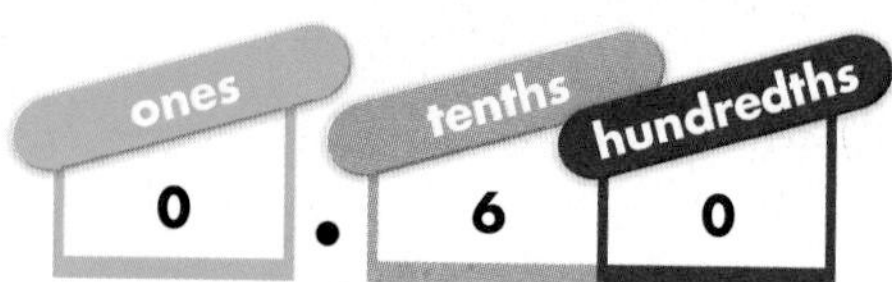

You can see that $\frac{60}{100} = 0.60$.

Remember that to write a decimal, you need to pay particular attention to the denominator of the fraction.

For **1** and **2**, write each decimal as a fraction.

1. 0.3
2. 0.42

For **3** and **4**, write each fraction or mixed number as a decimal.

3. $1\frac{2}{10}$
4. $\frac{9}{100}$

Set H, pages 234–235

You can write fractions as decimals using a place value chart. You read $\frac{7}{1,000}$ as seven thousandths. The decimal for $\frac{7}{1,000}$ is shown below.

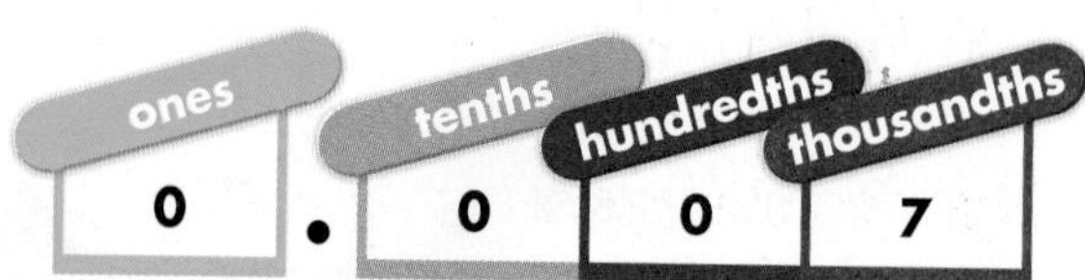

You can see that $\frac{7}{1,000} = 0.007$.

Remember that to write a decimal with thousandths place, you need to use three decimal places after the decimal.

For **1** and **2**, write each decimal as a fraction.

1. 0.192
2. 0.042

For **3** and **4**, write each fraction as a decimal.

3. $\frac{189}{1,000}$
4. $\frac{3}{1,000}$

Reteaching

Set I, pages 236–237

You can use a number line to locate fractions and decimals, and compare values.

Locate 0.2, $\frac{18}{20}$, and 0.75 on a number line.

You know that 0.2 also means $\frac{2}{10}$.

You know that $\frac{18}{20}$ also means $18 \div 20$.
Use division to find $18 \div 20 = 0.90$.

$0.7 = 0.70$ and $0.8 = 0.80$. So, 0.75 is halfway between 0.7 and 0.8.

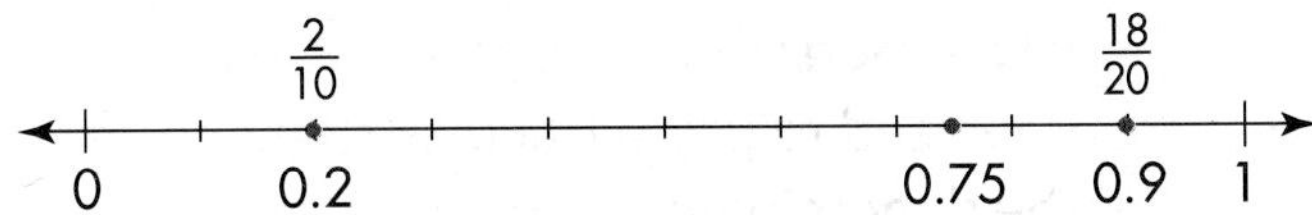

So the order from least to greatest is 0.2, 0.75, and $\frac{18}{20}$.

Remember to divide the number line into equal sized segments to find the correct location for each fraction or decimal.

In **1** through **4**, name the fraction that identifies each point on the number line.

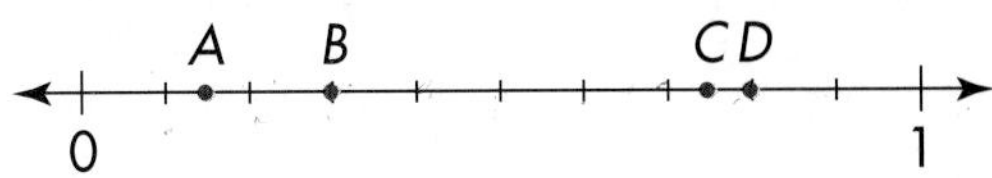

1. Point *A**

2. Point *B*

3. Point *C*

4. Point *D*

Set J, pages 238–239

When you are asked to explain how you found your answer, follow these steps:

Step 1

Break the process into steps.

Step 2

Use pictures and words to explain.

Step 3

Tell about things to watch out for and be careful about.

Step 4

Write your steps in order using words like *find* and *put*.

Remember to show your work clearly so that others can understand it.

1. Sara's paper airplane flew 8.5 yards. Jason's flew $8\frac{2}{3}$ yards. Michael's flew $8\frac{1}{4}$ yards and Denise's flew $8\frac{1}{6}$ yards. Whose airplane flew the farthest? Explain how you found your answer.

2. The school play lasted 1 hour 45 minutes. It ended at 9:15 P.M. What time did the play start? Explain how you found your answer.

Topic 11

Adding and Subtracting Fractions and Mixed Numbers

1

This Parsons chameleon can extend its tongue up to $1\frac{1}{2}$ times the length of its body. What is the total length of the chameleon when its tongue is fully extended? You will find out in Lesson 11-5.

2

How much smaller is the bumblebee bat than the Estruscan pygmy shrew? You will find out in Lesson 11-6.

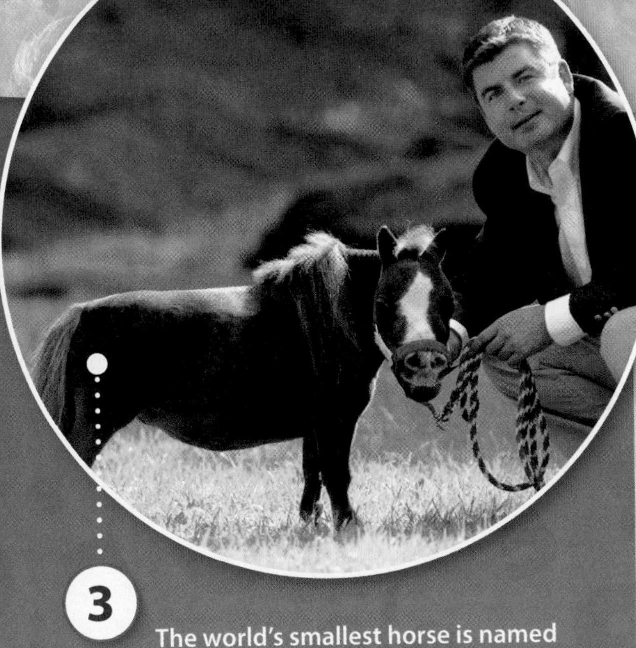

3 The world's smallest horse is named Thumbelina. How much shorter is Thumbelina than the next shortest horse? You will find out in Lesson 11-6.

4 The Hupa Tribe, in northwestern California, made baskets like this one in the early 1900s. How can you find the perimeter of one of the triangles shown on the basket? You will find out in Lesson 11-3.

Review What You Know!

Vocabulary

Choose the best term from the box.

- common denominator
- denominator
- numerator

1. In the fraction $\frac{7}{15}$, the number 15 is the __?__.
2. In the fraction $\frac{11}{21}$, the number 11 is the __?__.
3. Fractions with the same denominator have a __?__.

Fractions in Simplest Form

Write each fraction in simplest form.

4. $\frac{6}{18}$
5. $\frac{12}{22}$
6. $\frac{15}{25}$
7. $\frac{8}{26}$
8. $\frac{14}{35}$
9. $\frac{4}{18}$

Common Denominators

Compare. Write >, <, or = for each ◯.

10. $\frac{5}{25}$ ◯ $\frac{2}{5}$
11. $\frac{12}{27}$ ◯ $\frac{6}{9}$
12. $\frac{11}{16}$ ◯ $\frac{2}{8}$
13. $\frac{2}{7}$ ◯ $\frac{1}{5}$

Fractions

Writing to Explain Write an answer for each question.

14. How do you know when a fraction is in simplest form?
15. How can the greatest common factor help you write a fraction in simplest form?

Lesson
11-1

NS 2.3 Key Solve simple problems, including ones arising in concrete situations, involving the addition and subtraction of fractions and mixed numbers (like and unlike denominators of 20 or less) and express answers in the simplest form.

Adding and Subtracting Fractions with Like Denominators

How do you add or subtract fractions with like denominators?

If Miguel and Alma ride 2 roller coasters in the morning and 5 in the afternoon, on what fraction of the park's roller coasters will they ride?

Choose an Operation Add to find the total.

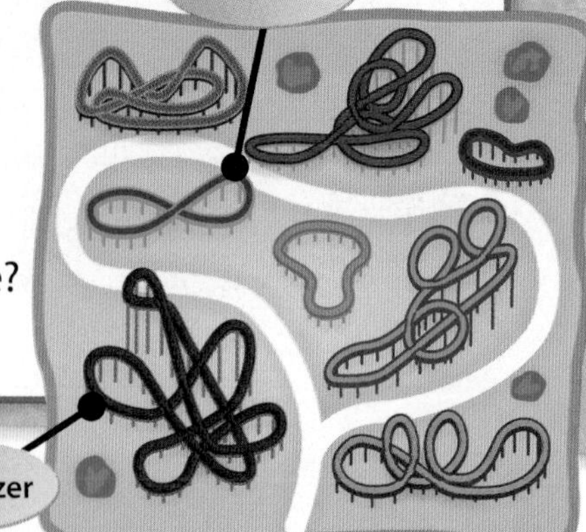

Another Example

How do you subtract fractions with like denominators?

The Trailblazer has the longest track. It is $\frac{9}{10}$ of a mile. The Gold Rush has only $\frac{3}{10}$ mile of track. How much longer is the Trailblazer's track?

Choose an Operation Subtract to compare two lengths.

What You Show

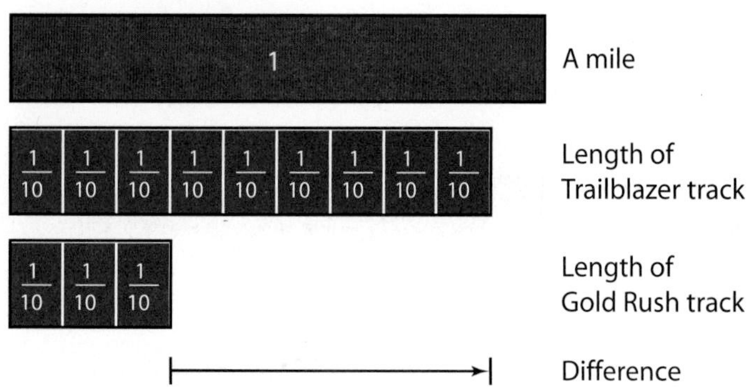

What You Write

$\frac{9}{10}$ The fractions have like denominators.

$-\frac{3}{10}$ Subtract the numerators.

$\frac{6}{10}$ Write the difference over the common denominator.

Tip *Fractions have a common denominator when their denominators are the same.*

The Trailblazer's track is $\frac{6}{10}$, or $\frac{3}{5}$, of a mile longer than the Gold Rush's track.

Explain It

1. How do you simplify $\frac{6}{10}$ to $\frac{3}{5}$?

What You Show

Since there are 8 roller coasters, use 2 eighths to show the morning rides and 5 eighths to show the afternoon rides.

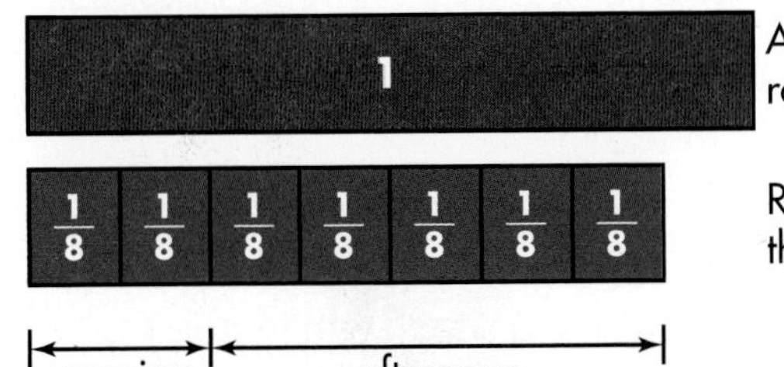

What You Write

$$\begin{array}{r} \frac{2}{8} \\ + \frac{5}{8} \\ \hline \frac{7}{8} \end{array}$$

The fractions have like denominators. Add the numerators.

Write the sum over the common denominator.

Miguel and Alma will ride on $\frac{7}{8}$ of the roller coasters that day.

Guided Practice*

Do you know HOW?

In **1** through **6**, find each sum or difference. Simplify your answers.

1. $\frac{1}{4} + \frac{1}{4}$

2. $\frac{5}{6} - \frac{3}{6}$

3. $\frac{6}{9} + \frac{2}{9}$

4. $\frac{6}{7} + \frac{5}{7}$

5. $\frac{7}{12} - \frac{5}{12}$

6. $\frac{4}{5} - \frac{2}{5}$

Do you UNDERSTAND?

7. In the example above, why is the sum of $\frac{2}{8}$ and $\frac{5}{8}$ not equal to $\frac{7}{16}$?

8. In the example above, if Miguel and Alma were able to ride only on 3 coasters in the afternoon, on what fraction of the roller coasters will they ride?

Independent Practice

In **9** through **25**, find each sum or difference. Simplify your answers.

9. $\frac{1}{2} + \frac{1}{2}$

10. $\frac{3}{4} - \frac{1}{4}$

11. $\frac{4}{6} - \frac{1}{6}$

12. $\frac{3}{10} + \frac{5}{10}$

13. $\frac{3}{8} + \frac{1}{8}$

14. $\frac{6}{7} - \frac{3}{7}$

15. $\frac{5}{18} + \frac{1}{18}$

16. $\frac{8}{11} - \frac{2}{11}$

17. $\frac{1}{3} + \frac{1}{3} + \frac{1}{3}$

18. $\frac{11}{12} - \frac{2}{12} - \frac{1}{12}$

19. $\frac{1}{2} + \frac{1}{2} + \frac{1}{2}$

20. $\frac{12}{20} + \frac{5}{20} + \frac{2}{20}$

21. $\frac{1}{12} + \frac{3}{12} + \frac{5}{12}$

22. $\frac{13}{16} - \left(\frac{4}{16} + \frac{3}{16}\right)$

23. $\frac{5}{9} - \left(\frac{1}{9} + \frac{1}{9}\right)$

24. $\frac{1}{8} + \left(\frac{5}{8} - \frac{3}{8}\right)$

25. $\left(\frac{7}{10} - \frac{3}{10}\right) + \frac{1}{10}$

*For another example, see Set A on page 266.

Problem Solving

26. On a Greatest Rock Bands CD, all-men groups sing $\frac{5}{13}$ of the songs and all-women groups sing $\frac{3}{13}$ of the songs. What fraction of the songs are sung by those two groups combined?

27. Jolene paid $10.50 to bowl 3 games. She also paid $2.50 to rent bowling shoes. How much did Jolene pay per game she bowled?

28. A painter mixes $\frac{1}{4}$ gallon of red paint with $\frac{1}{4}$ gallon of yellow paint. How much paint is in the bucket?

29. Nadia made a snack with $\frac{3}{4}$ cup of raisins and $\frac{1}{4}$ cup of peanuts. How many cups of snack did she make?

For **30**, use the data in the table at the right.

30. a How many students are in the class?

b What fraction of the class selected surfing or softball?

c What fraction of the class did not select soccer or football?

Data

Results of Mr. Willis's Class Survey Favorite Sport

Sport	Number of Students
Soccer	7
Basketball	2
Football	3
Softball	2
Surfing	6

31. Writing to Explain Mr. Hughes made 33 birdhouses that he will sell for $28.95 each. If he sells all the birdhouses, will he earn more than $1,000? Explain how to use estimation to find the answer.

32. Tanya has 8 bird posters and 12 reptile posters to display in groups. She wants each group to have the same number of posters and to have one type of animal. What is the greatest number of posters she can put in each group?

33. Brenda spent 0.6 hour practicing the drums. How many minutes did she practice?

34. Reasoning Suppose two fractions are both less than 1. Can their sum be greater than 1? greater than 2?

35. Algebra Which operation should be done first in $(14 - 5) \times 5 + 1$?

36. Think About the Process Mrs. Morales's flowers are starting to bloom. Last week, $\frac{1}{11}$ of the buds bloomed and $\frac{4}{11}$ bloomed this week. Which expression shows how to find the fraction of the buds that have not yet bloomed?

A $\frac{1}{11} + \frac{11}{11} - \frac{4}{11}$

B $\frac{1}{11} - \frac{4}{11} - \frac{11}{11}$

C $\frac{1}{11} + \left(\frac{11}{11} - \frac{4}{11}\right)$

D $\frac{11}{11} - \left(\frac{1}{11} + \frac{4}{11}\right)$

37. Ms. Hall's company pays her $0.32 for each mile she drives for work. How much did she receive for a 621-mile trip?

Algebra Connections

Fractions and Equations

Remember that an equation uses an equal sign to show that two expressions have the same value.

$\frac{1}{3} + \frac{1}{3} = \frac{2}{3}$

Example

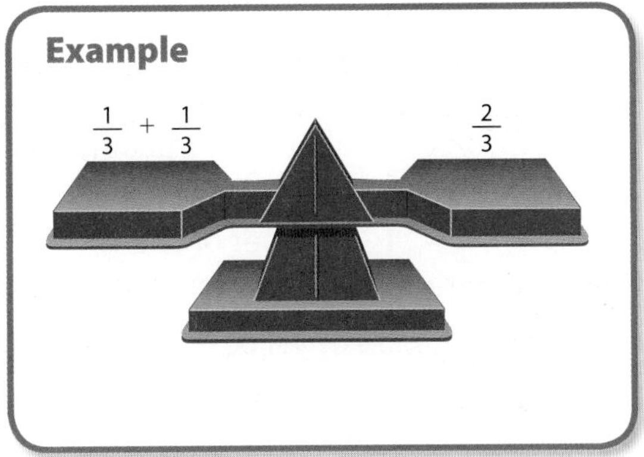

In **1** through **12**, complete each equation by filling in the missing value(s). Check your answers by making sure the expressions in the equations are equal to each other.

1. $\frac{3}{8} + \frac{\square}{\square} = \frac{5}{8}$

2. $\frac{\square}{\square} - \frac{1}{15} = \frac{1}{15}$

3. $\frac{9}{\square} + \frac{4}{\square} = \frac{13}{18}$

4. $\frac{8}{10} - \frac{3}{\square} = \frac{5}{\square}$

5. $\frac{\square}{4} + \frac{\square}{4} = \frac{3}{4}$

6. $\frac{5}{6} - \frac{\square}{\square} = \frac{2}{6}$

7. $\frac{\square}{\square} - \frac{7}{12} = \frac{3}{12}$

8. $\frac{5}{16} + \frac{\square}{\square} = \frac{11}{16}$

9. $\frac{1}{2} - \frac{\square}{\square} = 0$

10. $\frac{4}{9} + \frac{\square}{\square} = \frac{7}{9}$

11. $\frac{1}{4} + \frac{\square}{\square} + \frac{1}{4} = \frac{3}{4}$

12. $\frac{8}{10} - \frac{\square}{\square} - \frac{1}{10} = \frac{6}{10}$

For **13** through **24**, use the number line below to write and solve each equation. Simplify, if possible. The distance between each consecutive pair of numbers is the same.

0 A B C D E F G H I J K **1**

13. A + A = $\square$

14. K − A = $\square$

15. B + D = $\square$

16. F − B = $\square$

17. H + A = $\square$

18. I − C = $\square$

19. J − $\square$ = E

20. G + $\square$ = K

21. C − $\square$ = 0

22. B + B + B = $\square$

23. K − A − $\square$ = $\frac{3}{4}$

24. G + $\square$ + B = $\frac{5}{6}$

25. Write a word problem using one of the equations in **13** through **24**.

Lesson

11-2

NS 2.4, Grade 6 Determine the least common multiple and the greatest common divisor of whole numbers; use them to solve problems with fractions (e.g., to find a common denominator to add two fractions or to find the reduced form for a fraction).

Common Multiples and LCM

How do you find the least common multiple of two numbers?

Loren is buying fish fillets and buns for the soccer team dinner. What is the smallest number of fish fillets and buns she can buy to have the same number of each?

Guided Practice*

Do you know HOW?

In **1** through **6**, find the LCM for each pair of numbers.

1. 2 and 4
2: 2, 4, 6, 8
4: 4, 8, 12, 16

2. 3 and 4
3: 3, 6, 9, 12, 15
4: 4, 8, 12, 16

3. 3 and 7

4. 8 and 15

5. 12 and 9

6. 6 and 18

Do you UNDERSTAND?

7. In the example above, why is 24 the LCM of 6 and 8?

8. How many packages of each does Loren need to buy to have 24 fish fillets and 24 buns?

Independent Practice

Leveled Practice In **9** through **27**, find the LCM of each pair of numbers.

9. 2 and 4
2: 2, 4, . . .
4: 4, 8, . . .

10. 2 and 3
2: 2, 4, 6, 8, . . .
3: 3, 6, 9, 12, . . .

11. 5 and 6
5: 5, 10, 15, 20, 25, 30, 35, 40, . . .
6: 6, 12, 18, 24, 30, 36, 42, . . .

12. 3 and 5 **13.** 6 and 8 **14.** 4 and 5 **15.** 3 and 10

16. 4 and 9 **17.** 8 and 20 **18.** 6 and 9 **19.** 10 and 12

20. 8 and 12 **21.** 4 and 6 **22.** 8 and 16 **23.** 12 and 16

24. 8 and 9 **25.** 4 and 12 **26.** 5 and 10 **27.** 14 and 21

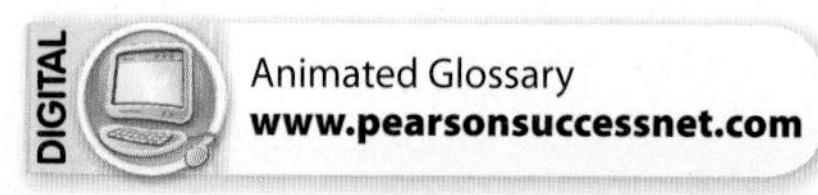

*For another example, see Set B on page 266.

Step 1

Find the common multiples of 6 and 8.

A multiple of a number is a product of a given whole number and another whole number.

A common multiple is a number that is a multiple of two or more numbers.

List the multiples of 6 and 8.

6: 6, 12, 18, 24, 30, 36, 42, 48, 54, ...

8: 8, 16, 24, 32, 40, 48, 56, ...

Two common multiples of 6 and 8 are 24 and 48.

Step 2

Find the least common multiple of 6 and 8.

A least common multiple (LCM) is the least number that is a multiple of both numbers.

Both 24 and 48 are common multiples of 6 and 8. So, the LCM of 6 and 8 is 24.

Loren will need to buy 24 fish fillets and 24 buns.

Problem Solving

28. Pecans are sold in 6-oz cans, almonds in 9-oz cans, and peanuts in 12-oz cans. What is the least number of ounces you can buy to have equal amounts of pecans, almonds, and peanuts?

29. Writing to Explain Can you always find the LCM for two numbers by multiplying them together? Why or why not?

30. Number Sense The batting averages of three players are 0.261, 0.267, 0.264. Write the averages in order from least to greatest. Use $<$.

31. A cell phone call costs \$0.07 per minute for the first 25 minutes and \$0.10 per minute for each additional minute. How much would a 47-minute call cost?

32. a Peter is distributing pamphlets about dog care and samples of dog biscuits. The dog biscuits come in packages of 12 and the pamphlets are in packages of 20. What is the smallest number of samples and pamphlets he needs to distribute without having any left over?

b How many packages of dog biscuits and pamphlets will Peter need?

33. Katie bought dinner at 5 different restaurants. Each dinner cost between \$12 and \$24. What is a reasonable total cost for all 5 dinners?

A less than \$60

B more than \$150

C between \$24 and \$60

D between \$60 and \$120

34. Julie drank $1\frac{2}{3}$ cups of cranberry juice. Her brother said she drank $\frac{5}{3}$ cups of juice. Is her brother correct? Explain your answer.

35. A factory whistle blows every 30 minutes. The clock tower chimes every 15 minutes. If they both sounded at 1:00 P.M., at what time will you hear them both at the same time again?

Lesson

11-3

NS 2.3 Solve simple problems, including ones arising in concrete situations, involving the addition and subtraction of fractions and mixed numbers (like and unlike denominators of 20 or less) and express answers in the simplest form.

Adding Fractions with Unlike Denominators

How can you add fractions with unlike denominators?

Alex rode his scooter from his house to the park. Later, he rode from the park to baseball practice. How far did Alex ride?

Choose an Operation Add to find the total distance Alex rode his scooter.

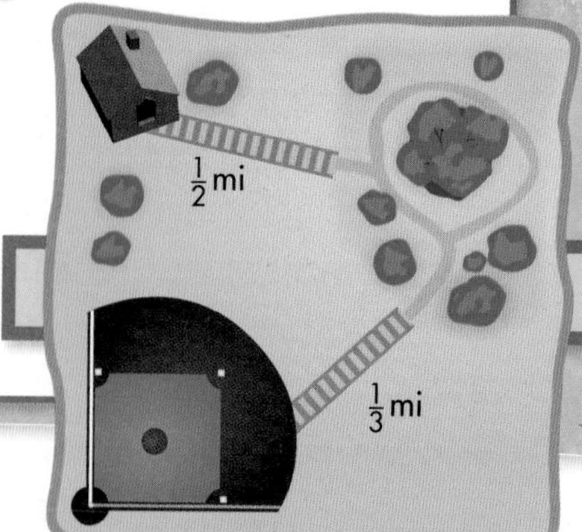

Guided Practice*

Do you know HOW?

In **1** through **4**, find each sum. Simplify, if necessary.

1. $\frac{1}{2} = \frac{9}{18}$
$+ \frac{2}{9} = \frac{4}{18}$

2. $\frac{2}{6} = \frac{8}{24}$
$+ \frac{3}{8} = \frac{9}{24}$

3. $\frac{3}{4} + \frac{7}{10}$

4. $\frac{5}{12} + \frac{1}{8}$

Do you UNDERSTAND?

5. Writing to Explain In the example above, would you get the same sum if you used 12 as the common denominator?

6. In the example above, if the park was $\frac{4}{5}$ mile from baseball practice, how far would Alex ride his scooter?

Independent Practice

Leveled Practice In **7** through **22**, find each sum. Simplify, if necessary.

7. $\frac{1}{9} = \frac{\square}{18}$
$+ \frac{5}{6} = \frac{\square}{18}$

8. $\frac{1}{12} = \frac{\square}{12}$
$+ \frac{2}{3} = \frac{\square}{12}$

9. $\frac{1}{3} = \frac{\square}{15}$
$+ \frac{1}{5} = \frac{\square}{15}$

10. $\frac{1}{8} = \frac{\square}{56}$
$+ \frac{3}{7} = \frac{\square}{56}$

11. $\frac{2}{9} + \frac{2}{3}$

12. $\frac{5}{8} + \frac{1}{6}$

13. $\frac{3}{4} + \frac{2}{5}$

14. $\frac{1}{6} + \frac{3}{10}$

15. $\frac{7}{8} + \frac{1}{12}$

16. $\frac{11}{16} + \frac{1}{2}$

17. $\frac{5}{6} + \frac{3}{4}$

18. $\frac{7}{12} + \frac{9}{16}$

19. $\frac{1}{2} + \frac{1}{8} + \frac{1}{4}$

20. $\frac{1}{3} + \frac{5}{6} + \frac{4}{9}$

21. $\frac{1}{2} + \frac{1}{3} + \frac{1}{4}$

22. $\frac{1}{2} + \frac{3}{4} + \frac{3}{5}$

DIGITAL Animated Glossary **www.pearsonsuccessnet.com**

*For another example, see Set C on page 266.

Step 1

Change the fractions to equivalent fractions with a common, or like, denominator.

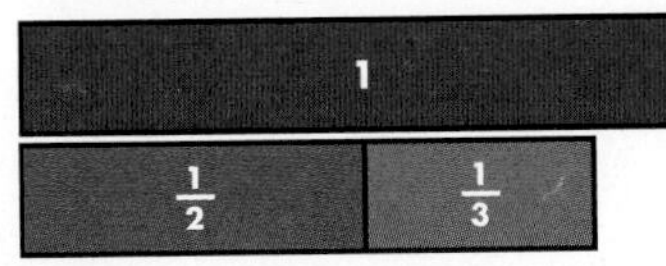

The least common denominator (LCD) of two fractions is the least common multiple of the denominators.

Multiples of 2: 2, 4, 6, 8, 10, 12, . . .

Multiples of 3: 3, 6, 9, 12, . . .

The LCM is 6, so the LCD is 6.

Step 2

Write the equivalent fractions.

1

$\frac{1}{2}$ $\frac{1}{3}$

$\frac{1}{6}$ $\frac{1}{6}$ $\frac{1}{6}$ $\frac{1}{6}$ $\frac{1}{6}$

$\frac{1}{2} \overset{\times 3}{=} \frac{3}{6}$ $\quad$ $\frac{1}{3} \overset{\times 2}{=} \frac{2}{6}$

Step 3

Add. Simplify if necessary.

$$\begin{array}{r} \frac{1}{2} = \frac{3}{6} \\ + \frac{1}{3} = + \frac{2}{6} \\ \hline \frac{5}{6} \end{array}$$

Alex rode his scooter $\frac{5}{6}$ mile.

Problem Solving

23. Cindy added $\frac{7}{8}$ cup of water to $\frac{1}{4}$ cup of juice concentrate. How much juice did Cindy make?

24. Abdul bought 10 packages of string cheese. If each package costs $1.59, how much did Abdul spend?

25. Mr. Perez is building a fence. He wants to bolt together 2 boards. One is $\frac{3}{4}$ inches thick and the other is $\frac{7}{8}$ inches thick. What will be the total thickness of the 2 boards?

26. About $\frac{1}{10}$ of the bones in your body are in your skull. Your hands have about $\frac{1}{4}$ of the bones in your body. What fraction of the bones in your body are in your hands and skull?

27. **Number Sense** At an auction, the bid for a painting starts at $150,000. The next bid is $170,000. The next 2 bids are $190,000 and $210,000. If the pattern continues, what is the next bid?

28. Dennis spent $\frac{1}{4}$ hour walking his dog. He spent another $\frac{1}{3}$ hour giving it food and water. What fraction of an hour did Dennis spend with the dog?

29. The Hupa Tribe in California made baskets like this one in the early 1900s. If two sides of the triangle shown on the basket measure $\frac{1}{4}$ in., and the third side measures $\frac{3}{8}$ in., what is the perimeter of the triangle?

30. A girls' club is selling hats to raise money. They ordered 500 hats that cost $5.15 each. They will sell the hats for $18.50 each. All the hats were sold. Which expression shows how to find the amount of money the club made after expenses?

A $500 \times (18.50 + 5.15)$

B $(500 \times 18.50) + (500 \times 5.15)$

C $(500 \times 5.15) - (500 \times 18.50)$

D $500 \times (18.50 - 5.15)$

Lesson

11-4

NS 2.3 Solve simple problems, including ones arising in concrete situations, involving the addition and subtraction of fractions and mixed numbers (like and unlike denominators of 20 or less) and express answers in the simplest form.

Subtracting Fractions with Unlike Denominators

How can you subtract fractions with unlike denominators?

Linda used $\frac{1}{4}$ yard of the fabric she bought for a sewing project. How much fabric did she have left?

Choose an Operation Subtract to find how much fabric was left.

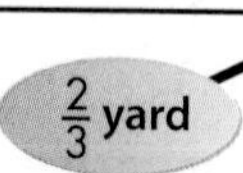

Guided Practice*

Do you know HOW?

In **1** through **4**, find each difference. Simplify, if necessary.

1. $\frac{5}{6} = \frac{5}{6}$
$- \frac{1}{2} = \frac{3}{6}$

2. $\frac{4}{7} = \frac{12}{21}$
$- \frac{1}{3} = \frac{7}{21}$

3. $\frac{1}{2} - \frac{3}{10}$

4. $\frac{7}{8} - \frac{1}{3}$

Do you UNDERSTAND?

5. In the example above, is it possible to use a common denominator greater than 12 and get the correct answer? Why or why not?

6. In the example above, if Linda had started with one yard of fabric and used $\frac{5}{8}$ of a yard, how much fabric would be left?

Independent Practice

Leveled Practice In **7** through **24**, find each difference. Simplify, if necessary.

7. $\frac{1}{3} = \frac{\square}{6}$
$- \frac{1}{6} = \frac{\square}{6}$

8. $\frac{2}{3} = \frac{\square}{12}$
$- \frac{5}{12} = \frac{\square}{12}$

9. $\frac{3}{5} = \frac{\square}{15}$
$- \frac{1}{3} = \frac{\square}{15}$

10. $\frac{2}{9} = \frac{\square}{72}$
$- \frac{1}{8} = \frac{\square}{72}$

11. $\frac{1}{4} = \frac{\square}{8}$
$- \frac{1}{8} = \frac{\square}{8}$

12. $\frac{2}{3} = \frac{\square}{6}$
$- \frac{1}{2} = \frac{\square}{6}$

13. $\frac{3}{4} = \frac{\square}{8}$
$- \frac{3}{8} = \frac{\square}{8}$

14. $\frac{5}{6} = \frac{\square}{6}$
$- \frac{1}{3} = \frac{\square}{6}$

15. $\frac{5}{8} - \frac{1}{4}$ **16.** $\frac{9}{16} - \frac{3}{8}$ **17.** $\frac{1}{5} - \frac{1}{7}$ **18.** $\frac{7}{10} - \frac{2}{4}$ **19.** $\frac{5}{6} - \frac{3}{4}$

20. $\frac{2}{3} - \frac{5}{9}$ **21.** $\frac{4}{5} - \frac{1}{4}$ **22.** $\frac{5}{8} - \frac{7}{12}$ **23.** $\frac{6}{7} - \frac{1}{2}$ **24.** $\frac{5}{12} - \frac{4}{16}$

*For another example, see Set C on page 266.

Step 1

Change the fractions to equivalent fractions with a common denominator.

Find the LCM of the denominators

Multiples of 3:
3, 6, 9, 12, . . .

Multiples of 4:
4, 8, 12, . . .

The LCM is 12, so the LCD is 12.

Step 2

Write the equivalent fractions.

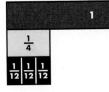

$\frac{2}{3} \overset{\times 4}{=} \frac{8}{12}$

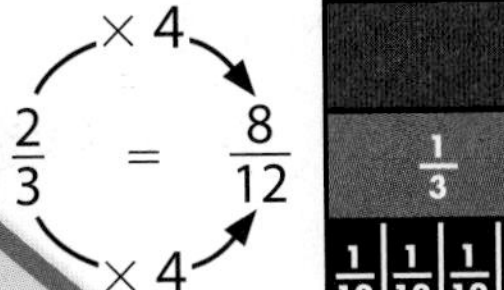

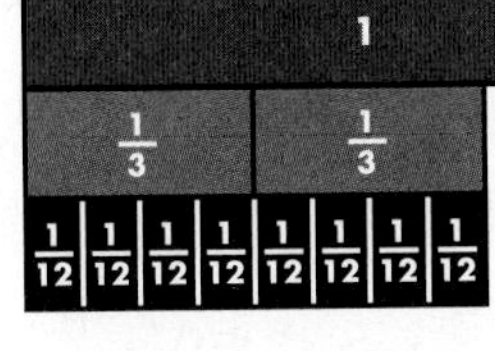

$\frac{1}{4} \overset{\times 3}{=} \frac{3}{12}$

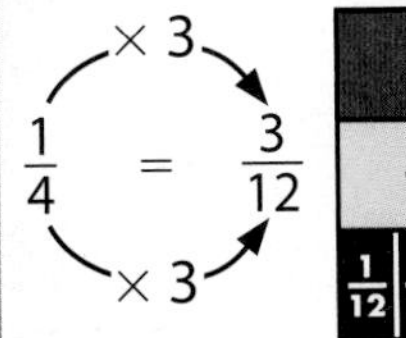

Step 3

Subtract. Simplify if necessary.

$$\begin{array}{r} \frac{2}{3} = \frac{8}{12} \\ -\frac{1}{4} = -\frac{3}{12} \\ \hline \frac{5}{12} \end{array}$$

Linda has $\frac{5}{12}$ yard of fabric left.

Problem Solving

25. Write a number sentence to name the difference between Point *A* and Point *B*.

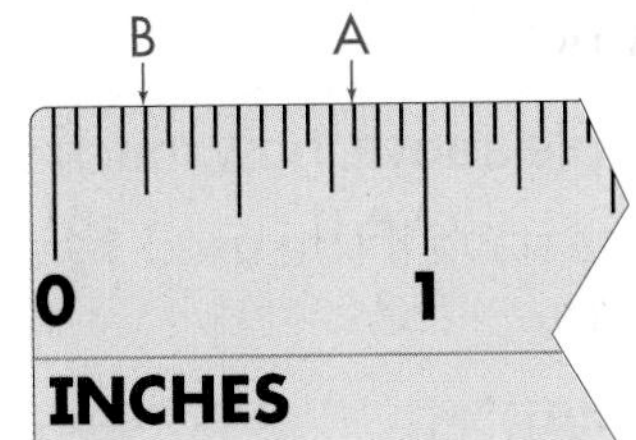

26. Geometry Find the perimeter of the figure below.

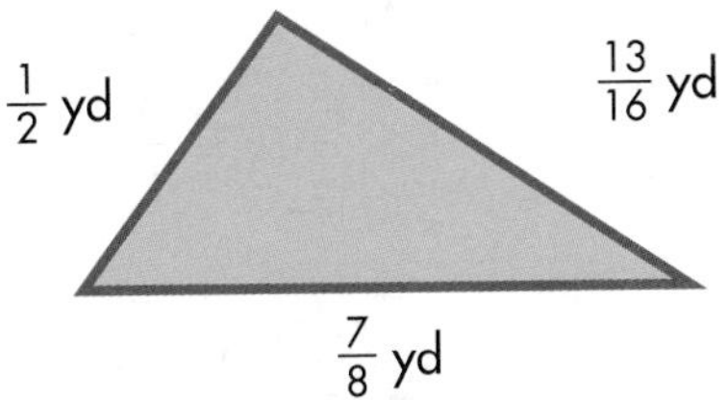

27. When Mr. Goldman left on a business trip, his car had $\frac{3}{4}$ of a tank of gas. At the first rest stop, there was only $\frac{1}{2}$ tank left. How much gas had the car used?

28. Mariko's social studies class lasts $\frac{5}{6}$ of an hour. Only $\frac{3}{12}$ of an hour has gone by. What fraction of an hour remains of Mariko's social studies class?

29. Estimation Roy earned \$72.50, \$59, and \$41.75 in tips when waiting tables last weekend. About how much did Roy earn in tips?

30. Nate exercises $\frac{1}{2}$ hour every day. LaDonna exercises $4\frac{1}{4}$ hours each week. Who exercises more in one week? How much more?

31. Writing to Explain Why do fractions need to have a common denominator before you add or subtract them?

32. Algebra Jay saved \$300 to buy a new laptop computer. The computer costs \$800. Which equation shows how to find the amount Jay still needs to save?

A $300 - n = 800$ **C** $n - 300 = 800$

B $800 + 300 = n$ **D** $n + 300 = 800$

33. Number Sense What is the greatest common multiple of 3 and 4?

Lesson

11-5

NS 2.3 Solve simple problems, including ones arising in concrete situations, involving the addition and subtraction of fractions and mixed numbers (like and unlike denominators of 20 or less) and express answers in the simplest form.

Adding Mixed Numbers

How can you add mixed numbers?

Rhoda mixes sand with $2\frac{2}{3}$ cups of potting mixture to prepare soil for her cactus plants. After mixing them together, how many cups of soil does Rhoda have?

Choose an Operation Add to find the total amount of soil.

$1\frac{1}{2}$ cups

Guided Practice*

Do you know HOW?

Find each sum. Simplify, if necessary.

1. $1\frac{7}{8} = 1\frac{\square}{8}$; $+\ 1\frac{1}{4} = +\ 1\frac{\square}{8}$

2. $2\frac{2}{5} = 2\frac{\square}{30}$; $+\ 5\frac{5}{6} = +\ 5\frac{\square}{30}$

3. $4\frac{1}{9} + 1\frac{1}{3}$

4. $6\frac{5}{12} + 4\frac{5}{8}$

Do you UNDERSTAND?

5. **Reasoning** How is adding mixed numbers like adding fractions and whole numbers?

6. In the example above, how much soil would Rhoda have if she used $1\frac{3}{4}$ cups of sand?

Independent Practice

Leveled Practice Find each sum. Simplify, if necessary.

7. $3\frac{1}{6} = 3\frac{\square}{6}$; $+\ 5\frac{2}{3} = +\ 5\frac{\square}{6}$

8. $11\frac{1}{2} = 11\frac{\square}{10}$; $+\ 10\frac{3}{5} = +\ 10\frac{\square}{10}$

9. $9\frac{3}{16} + 7\frac{5}{8}$

10. $5\frac{6}{7} + 8\frac{1}{7}$

11. $3\frac{5}{8} + 2\frac{2}{3}$

12. $2\frac{2}{3} + 3\frac{1}{2}$

13. $6\frac{5}{8} + 4\frac{3}{4}$

14. $1\frac{3}{8} + 3\frac{5}{6}$

15. $4\frac{1}{10} + 6\frac{1}{2}$

16. $9\frac{7}{12} + 4\frac{3}{4}$

17. $5 + 3\frac{1}{8}$

18. $8\frac{3}{4} + 7\frac{3}{4}$

19. $2\frac{3}{4} + 7\frac{3}{5}$

20. $3\frac{8}{9} + 8\frac{1}{2}$

21. $1\frac{7}{12} + 2\frac{3}{8}$

22. $3\frac{11}{12} + 9\frac{1}{16}$

*For another example, see Set D on page 267.

Step 1

Find $2\frac{2}{3} + 1\frac{1}{2}$.
Write equivalent fractions with the least common denominator.

$$\begin{array}{rl} 2\frac{2}{3} = & 2\frac{4}{6} \\ +\ 1\frac{1}{2} = & +\ 1\frac{3}{6} \\ \hline \end{array}$$

Step 2

Add the fractions.

$$\begin{array}{rl} 2\frac{2}{3} = & 2\frac{4}{6} \\ +\ 1\frac{1}{2} = & +\ 1\frac{3}{6} \\ \hline & 3\frac{7}{6} \end{array}$$

Step 3

Add the whole numbers. Simplify the sum if necessary.

$$\begin{array}{rl} 2\frac{2}{3} = & 2\frac{4}{6} \\ +\ 1\frac{1}{2} = & +\ 1\frac{3}{6} \\ \hline & 3\frac{7}{6} \end{array}$$

$3\frac{7}{6} = 4\frac{1}{6}$

Rhoda prepared $4\frac{1}{6}$ cups of soil.

Problem Solving

23. Arnie rollerblades $1\frac{3}{4}$ miles from home to the lake, then goes $1\frac{1}{3}$ miles around the lake, and then back home. How many miles did he skate?

A $2\frac{1}{12}$ miles

B $3\frac{1}{12}$ miles

C $4\frac{5}{6}$ miles

D $4\frac{5}{12}$ miles

24. a Use the map below to find the distance from the start of the trail to the end.

START

BIRD LOOKOUT

END

$3\frac{7}{8}$ MILE

$2\frac{5}{6}$ MILE

b Louise walked from the start of the trail to the bird lookout and back. Did the she walk more or less than if she had walked from the start of the trail to the end?

25. Geometry Find the perimeter of the parallelogram below.

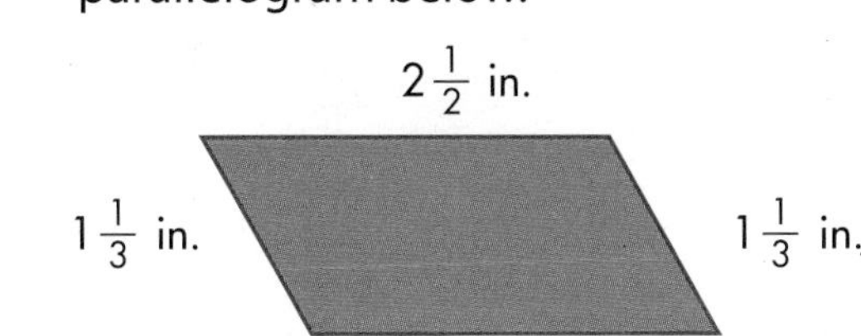

26. The length of a male Parsons chameleon can be up to $23\frac{1}{2}$ inches. It can extend its tongue up to $35\frac{1}{4}$ inches to catch its food. What is the total length of a male Parsons chameleon when its tongue is fully extended?

27. Number Sense Can the sum of two mixed numbers be less than 1? Why or why not?

28. Pedro wants to put 122 baseball cards into his album. Each page holds 8 cards. How many pages does Pedro need?

29. Amy's pop-up tent weighs $3\frac{7}{8}$ pounds and her sleeping bag weighs $1\frac{1}{2}$ pounds. What is the total weight of both items?

30. Writing to Explain Kris says that the sum of two mixed numbers is always a mixed number? Do you agree? Explain.

Lesson

11-6

NS 2.3 Solve simple problems, including ones arising in concrete situations, involving the addition and subtraction of fractions and mixed numbers (like and unlike denominators of 20 or less) and express answers in the simplest form.

Subtracting Mixed Numbers

How can you subtract mixed numbers?

A golf ball measures about $1\frac{2}{3}$ inches in diameter. What is the difference between the diameter of the hole and the golf ball?

Choose an Operation Subtract to find the difference in diameters.

Guided Practice*

Do you know HOW?

Find each difference. Simplify, if necessary.

1. $7\frac{2}{3} = 7\frac{\square}{6} = 6\frac{\square}{6}$
   $-\ 3\frac{5}{6} = -\ 3\frac{\square}{6} = 3\frac{\square}{6}$

2. $5 = \square\frac{\square}{4}$
   $-\ 2\frac{3}{4} = -\ 2\frac{3}{4}$

3. $6\frac{3}{10} - 1\frac{4}{5}$

4. $9\frac{1}{3} - 4\frac{3}{4}$

Do you UNDERSTAND?

5. In **2**, why do you need to rename 5?

6. **Reasonableness** Could two golf balls fall into the hole at the same time? Explain your reasoning.

Independent Practice

Leveled Practice Find each difference. Simplify, if necessary.

7. $8\frac{1}{4} = 8\frac{\square}{8} = 7\frac{\square}{8}$
   $-\ 2\frac{7}{8} = -\ 2\frac{\square}{8} = 2\frac{\square}{8}$

8. $3\frac{1}{2} = 3\frac{\square}{6}$
   $-\ 1\frac{1}{3} = 1\frac{\square}{6}$

9. $4\frac{1}{8}$
   $-\ 1\frac{1}{2}$

10. 6
    $-\ 2\frac{4}{5}$

11. $5\frac{1}{2}$
    $-\ 2\frac{2}{5}$

12. $4\frac{1}{6}$
    $-\ 2\frac{3}{4}$

13. 9
    $-\ 4\frac{5}{8}$

14. $6\frac{4}{9}$
    $-\ 3\frac{2}{3}$

15. $6\frac{1}{3} - 5\frac{2}{3}$

16. $9\frac{1}{2} - 6\frac{3}{4}$

17. $8\frac{3}{16} - 3\frac{5}{8}$

18. $7\frac{1}{2} - \frac{7}{10}$

19. $15\frac{1}{6} - 4\frac{3}{8}$

20. $13\frac{1}{12} - 8\frac{1}{4}$

21. $6\frac{1}{3} - 2\frac{3}{5}$

22. $10\frac{5}{12} - 4\frac{7}{8}$

*For another example, see Set E on page 267.

Step 1

Write equivalent fractions with the least common denominator.

$$\begin{array}{r} 4\frac{1}{4} = \ \ 4\frac{3}{12} \\ -\ 1\frac{2}{3} = -\ 1\frac{8}{12} \\ \hline \end{array}$$

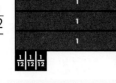

Tip *You cannot subtract* $\frac{8}{12}$ *from* $\frac{3}{12}$.

Step 2

Rename $4\frac{3}{12}$ to show more twelfths.

$$\begin{array}{r} 4\frac{3}{12} = \ \ 3\frac{15}{12} \\ -\ 1\frac{8}{12} = -\ 1\frac{8}{12} \\ \hline \end{array}$$

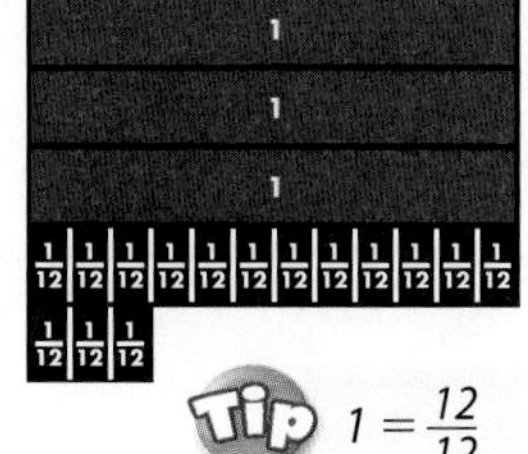

Tip $1 = \frac{12}{12}$

Step 3

Subtract the fractions. Then subtract the whole numbers. Simplify, if necessary.

$$\begin{array}{r} 4\frac{1}{4} = \ \ 4\frac{3}{12} = \ \ 3\frac{15}{12} \\ -\ 1\frac{2}{3} = -\ 1\frac{8}{12} = -1\frac{8}{12} \\ \hline 2\frac{7}{12} \end{array}$$

The hole is $2\frac{7}{12}$ inches wider.

Problem Solving

23. A kit contained $3\frac{1}{8}$ meters of wire. Carol used $1\frac{1}{3}$ meters to hang pictures in her living room. How much wire does Carol have left?

24. The average weight of a basketball is $21\frac{1}{10}$ ounces. The average weight of a baseball is $5\frac{1}{4}$ ounces. How many more ounces does the basketball weigh?

25. **Algebra** What is the missing number in the equation? Name the property that can help you.

$4(5 + 12) = (4 \times n) + (4 \times 12)$

26. As of 2006, the world's shortest horse is Thumbelina. She is $17\frac{1}{4}$ inches tall. The second shortest horse, Black Beauty, is $18\frac{1}{2}$ inches tall. How much shorter is Thumbelina than Black Beauty?

27. The smallest mammals on Earth are the bumblebee bat and the Etruscan pygmy shrew. A length of a bumblebee bat is $1\frac{9}{50}$ inches. A length of an Etruscan pygmy shrew is $1\frac{21}{50}$ inches. How much smaller is the bat than the shrew?

28. **Geometry** How are the parallelogram and the rectangle alike? How are they different?

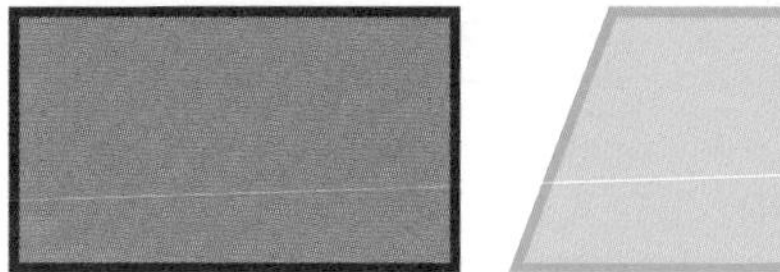

29. **Writing to Explain** Could the difference of two mixed numbers be less than 1? Use an example to explain why or why not.

30. **Reasoning** Rose, Vanya, Emile and Jerry ran a race. Rose was not first. Jerry finished before Rose. Emile did not finish before Vanya or Jerry. Jerry was not first. Which of the following choices is possible for the order in which the racers finished the race?

A Rose, Vanya, Emile, Jerry
B Vanya, Jerry, Emile, Rose
C Emile, Jerry, Vanya, Rose
D Vanya, Emile, Jerry, Rose

Lesson

11-7

MR 1.1 Analyze problems by identifying relationships, distinguishing relevant from irrelevant information, sequencing and prioritizing information, and observing patterns. Also NS 2.3

Problem Solving

Look for a Pattern

A 12-mile walk/run has distance signs posted along the race using a pattern shown below. Look for a pattern to find the missing distances in miles.

Guided Practice*

Do you know HOW?

Look for a pattern. Write the missing fractions or draw the missing figures.

1. $\frac{1}{4}$, $\frac{2}{4}$, $\frac{3}{4}$, ▢, ▢, ▢, ▢, $\frac{8}{4}$

2.

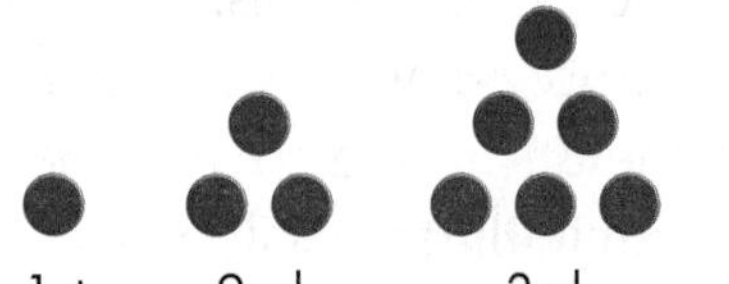

1st 2nd 3rd 4th

Do you UNDERSTAND?

3. Describe the rule you used after you identified the pattern in Problem 2.

4. **Write a Problem** Write a problem that you can solve by using a fraction or picture pattern.

Independent Practice

Look for a pattern. Write the missing numbers or draw the missing figures.

5. $\frac{24}{4}$, $\frac{21}{4}$, $\frac{18}{4}$, $\frac{15}{4}$, ▢, ▢, ▢, ▢, $\frac{0}{4}$

6. 5, 20, 80, ▢, ▢, ▢, ▢

7.

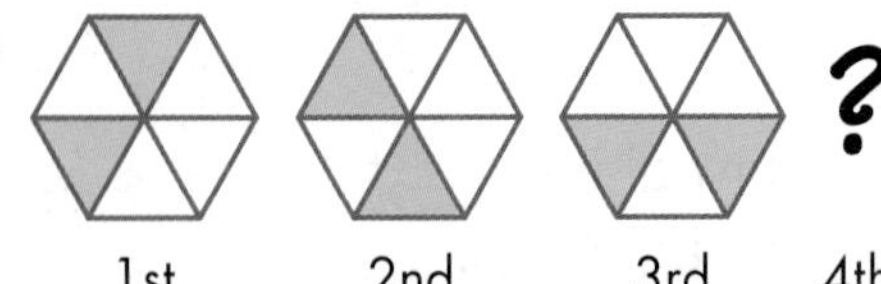

1st 2nd 3rd 4th

8.

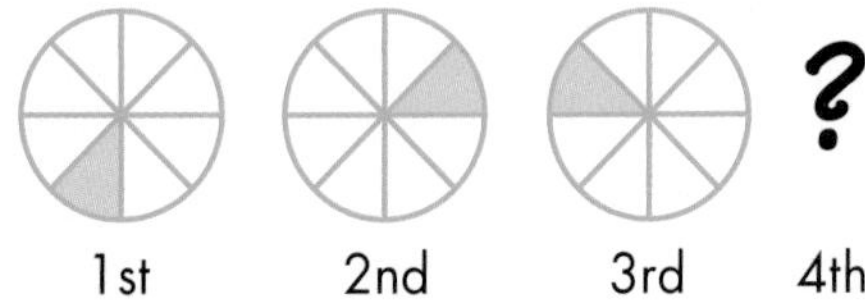

1st 2nd 3rd 4th

Stuck? Try this....

- What do I know?
- What am I asked to find?
- What diagram can I use to help understand the problem?
- Can I use addition, subtraction, multiplication, or division?
- Is all of my work correct?
- Did I answer the right question?
- Is my answer reasonable?

*For another example, see Set F on page 267.

Step 1

Try to identify a pattern and write a rule.

12 | $10\frac{1}{2}$

START

$12 - 10\frac{1}{2} = 1\frac{1}{2}$

So far, the rule is subtract $1\frac{1}{2}$.

Step 2

Check your rule.
Compare the next term.

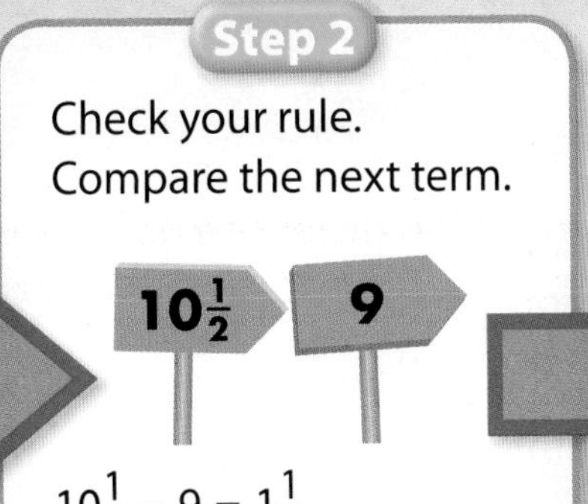

$10\frac{1}{2} - 9 = 1\frac{1}{2}$.

The rule works.

Step 3

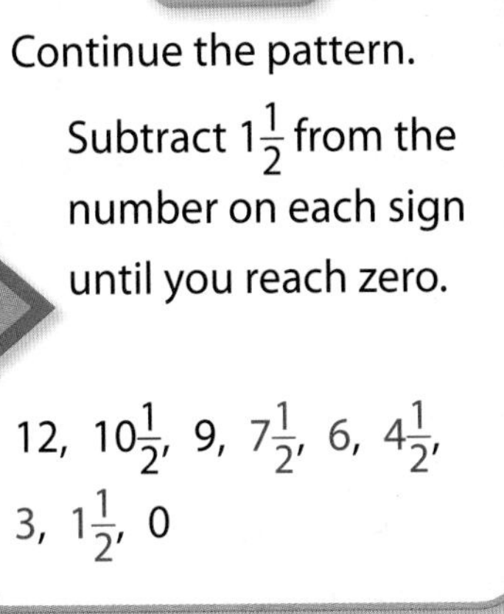

Continue the pattern.

Subtract $1\frac{1}{2}$ from the number on each sign until you reach zero.

12, $10\frac{1}{2}$, 9, $7\frac{1}{2}$, 6, $4\frac{1}{2}$, 3, $1\frac{1}{2}$, 0

9. Madeline made up a fraction pattern problem. Find the missing fractions in the pattern. Is the last number in her problem correct? Explain.

$\frac{1}{3}, \frac{2}{3}, 1, 1\frac{1}{3}, 1\frac{2}{3}$, ___, ___, ___, 3

10. The numbers below are called Fibonacci numbers.

1, 1, 2, 3, 5, 8, 13, 21, 34, 55, . . .

Write a rule for the pattern. What are the next three numbers?

11. How do you know the fractions shown in the pattern below get smaller as you continue? What are the next three fractions in the pattern?

$\frac{4}{2}, \frac{2}{2}, \frac{1}{2}, \frac{1}{4}, \ldots$

12. A box of 20 colored pencils contains red, blue, and yellow pencils. There are the same number of yellow and blue pencils in the box. There are two more red pencils than blue pencils. How many red pencils are in the box?

13. Derek makes \$90 a week mowing 6 lawns. If he charges the same amount for each job, how much money does he make mowing each lawn?

14. Look for a pattern in the chart. Find the missing quotient.

Data
$5 \div 5 = 1$
$55 \div 5 = 11$
$555 \div 5 = 111$
⋮
$55{,}555 \div 5 =$ ___

a What would the next three quotients in the pattern be?

b Explain the pattern.

15. Paco and his friend have been collecting baseball cards for 2 years. Paco has 632 cards and his friend has 259 cards. If the friends continue to collect their cards at the same rate for two more years, about how many cards will each of them have?

Test Prep

1. Manny used the computer for $\frac{2}{10}$ of his allotted time before school and $\frac{3}{10}$ after school. Which of the following can be used to find how much of his allotted time he used the computer? (11-1)

A Write $\frac{2+3}{10+10}$ to get $\frac{5}{20}$. Simplify to $\frac{1}{4}$.

B Write $\frac{2+3}{10+10}$ to get $\frac{5}{20}$. Simplify to $\frac{1}{5}$.

C Write $\frac{2+3}{10}$ to get $\frac{5}{10}$. Simplify to $\frac{1}{2}$.

D Write $\frac{2+3}{10+10}$ to get $\frac{5}{0}$.

2. Rick made a paper football that was $1\frac{1}{6}$ inches long. Carly made one $\frac{5}{6}$ of an inch long. How much longer was Rick's paper football than Carly's? (11-6)

A $1\frac{4}{6}$ inches

B $1\frac{2}{3}$ inches

C $\frac{2}{3}$ inch

D $\frac{1}{3}$ inch

3. What is $4\frac{1}{6} + 3\frac{1}{5}$? (11-5)

A $7\frac{1}{15}$

B $7\frac{2}{11}$

C $7\frac{11}{60}$

D $7\frac{11}{30}$

4. Which of the following pairs of numbers has a least common multiple of 24? (11-2)

A 4 and 6

B 3 and 8

C 2 and 12

D 3 and 6

5. In music, a sixteenth note often receives $\frac{1}{4}$ of a beat and an eighth note often receives $\frac{1}{2}$ of a beat. How much of a beat would a sixteenth note and an eighth note receive together? (11-3)

A $\frac{3}{4}$

B $\frac{3}{8}$

C $\frac{3}{16}$

D $\frac{1}{4}$

6. The table lists sizes of packages of school supplies. What is the smallest number of pencils and erasers that Mrs. Deng can buy so that she will have the same number of each? (11-2)

Data

Item	Number in Package
Paper	50
Pencils	12
Erasers	10

A 24

B 30

C 60

D 120

7. Mrs. Jin said that $\frac{4}{12}$ of the test items are multiple choice, $\frac{5}{12}$ are short answer, and the rest are matching. What fraction of the items are either multiple choice or short answer? (11-1)

A $\frac{1}{12}$

B $\frac{1}{4}$

C $\frac{3}{8}$

D $\frac{3}{4}$

Test Prep

8. Teri and her friends bought a submarine sandwich that was 28 inches or $\frac{7}{9}$ yards long. They ate 24 inches or $\frac{2}{3}$ of a yard. What part of a yard was left? (11-4)

A $\frac{5}{6}$

B $\frac{5}{9}$

C $\frac{1}{9}$

D $\frac{1}{18}$

9. The table shows how long Frank practiced piano over a period of days. If the pattern continues, how long will he practice on the 4th day? (11-7)

Data

Number of Days after His Lesson	Practice Time in Hours
1	$\frac{3}{10}$
2	$\frac{6}{10}$
3	$\frac{9}{10}$

A $\frac{3}{10}$ hour

B $1\frac{1}{10}$ hour

C $1\frac{2}{10}$ hours

D $1\frac{3}{10}$ hours

10. A green snake is about $\frac{8}{9}$ of a yard long. A garter snake is about $\frac{13}{18}$ of a yard. About how much longer is the green snake than the garter? (11-4)

A $\frac{1}{6}$ yard

B $\frac{4}{18}$ yard

C $\frac{5}{18}$ yard

D $\frac{5}{9}$ yard

11. Of the balls shown, $\frac{1}{3}$ are basketballs and $\frac{1}{15}$ are soccer balls. What fraction of the balls are either basketballs or soccer balls? (11-3)

A $\frac{1}{9}$

B $\frac{2}{15}$

C $\frac{1}{5}$

D $\frac{2}{5}$

12. The Jacobys went on a 600 mile trip. On the first day they drove $5\frac{2}{3}$ hours and on the second day they drove $4\frac{3}{5}$ hours. How long did they drive during the first two days? (11-5)

A $10\frac{4}{15}$ hours

B 10 hours

C $9\frac{19}{30}$ hours

D $9\frac{4}{15}$ hours

13. Marie needs $2\frac{1}{4}$ yards of fabric. She already has $1\frac{3}{8}$ yards. How many yards of fabric does she need? (11-6)

A $\frac{3}{4}$ yard

B $\frac{7}{8}$ yard

C $1\frac{1}{4}$ yard

D $1\frac{7}{8}$ yard

14. Which equals $\frac{5}{12} - \frac{3}{12}$? (11-1)

A $\frac{1}{12}$

B $\frac{1}{6}$

C $\frac{8}{12}$

D $\frac{2}{3}$

Reteaching

Set A, pages 248–250

Find $\frac{3}{8} + \frac{7}{8}$.

$\frac{3}{8} + \frac{7}{8} = \frac{10}{8}$ Add the numerators. Write the sum over the common denominator.

$= 1\frac{2}{8}$ Simplify the sum.

$= 1\frac{1}{4}$

Remember when adding or subtracting fractions with like denominators, the common denominator does not change.

1. $\frac{2}{7} + \frac{4}{7}$
2. $\frac{8}{12} - \frac{3}{12}$
3. $\frac{7}{9} - \frac{4}{9}$
4. $\frac{7}{10} + \frac{7}{10}$
5. $\frac{3}{6} + \frac{5}{6}$
6. $\frac{3}{4} - \frac{1}{4}$

Set B, pages 252–253

Find the least common multiple (LCM) of 9 and 12.

Make a list of the common multiples of each number.

Multiples of 9: 9, 18, 27, 36, 45, …

Multiple of 12: 12, 24, 36, 48, …

Identify the least number that is a multiple of both 9 and 12.

The least common multiple of 9 and 12 is 36.

Remember that the least common multiple of two numbers is the least number that is a multiple of both of the numbers. Multiples do not involve fractions.

1. 3 and 5
2. 4 and 6
3. 5 and 9
4. 6 and 10
5. 8 and 12
6. 8 and 3
7. 10 and 4
8. 6 and 9

Set C, pages 254–257

Find $\frac{5}{6} + \frac{3}{4}$.

Find the least common multiple (LCM) of 6 and 4.
The LCM is 12, so, the least common denominator (LCD) is 12.

Use the LCD to write equivalent fractions.

$\frac{5}{6} = \frac{5 \times 2}{6 \times 2} = \frac{10}{12}$ $\frac{3}{4} = \frac{3 \times 3}{4 \times 3} = \frac{9}{12}$

Step 3 Add the equivalent fractions. Simplify, if possible.

$\frac{10}{12} + \frac{9}{12} = \frac{19}{12} = 1\frac{7}{12}$

Remember to multiply the numerator and denominator by the same number when writing equivalent fractions.

1. $\frac{2}{5} + \frac{3}{10}$
2. $\frac{7}{9} + \frac{5}{6}$
3. $\frac{3}{4} - \frac{5}{12}$
4. $\frac{7}{8} - \frac{2}{3}$
5. $\frac{5}{16} - \frac{1}{8}$
6. $\frac{7}{10} - \frac{1}{6}$
7. $\frac{2}{3} + \frac{3}{4}$
8. $\frac{1}{4} + \frac{3}{8}$
9. $\frac{4}{5} - \frac{1}{3}$
10. $\frac{5}{8} - \frac{1}{2}$
11. $\frac{2}{3} + \frac{1}{2} + \frac{3}{4}$
12. $\frac{7}{10} + \frac{4}{5} + \frac{3}{4}$

Topic 11

Reteaching

Set D, pages 258–259

Find $1\frac{5}{6} + 2\frac{3}{8}$.

$$\begin{array}{rcr} 1\frac{5}{6} & = & 1\frac{20}{24} \\ +\ 2\frac{3}{8} & = & +\ 2\frac{9}{24} \\ \hline & & 3\frac{29}{24} = 4\frac{5}{24} \end{array}$$

Step 1 Write equivalent fractions with the LCD.

Step 2 Add the fractions.

Step 3 Add the whole numbers. Simplify the sum, if necessary.

Remember that mixed numbers are added the same way whole numbers and fractions are added.

1. $5\frac{1}{2} + 2\frac{1}{8}$
2. $3\frac{1}{4} + 1\frac{5}{6}$
3. $5\frac{7}{10} + 4\frac{2}{5}$
4. $7\frac{3}{5} + 6\frac{2}{3}$
5. $8\frac{5}{9} + 9\frac{1}{3}$
6. $2\frac{5}{12} + 3\frac{3}{4}$

Set E, pages 260–261

Find $5\frac{1}{5} - 3\frac{1}{2}$.

$$\begin{array}{rcrcr} 5\frac{1}{5} & = & 5\frac{2}{10} & = & 4\frac{12}{10} \\ -\ 3\frac{1}{2} & = & -\ 3\frac{5}{10} & = & -\ 3\frac{5}{10} \\ \hline & & & & 1\frac{7}{10} \end{array}$$

Step 1 Write equivalent fractions with the LCD.

Step 2 Rename $5\frac{2}{10}$ to show more tenths.

Step 3 Subtract the fractions. Subtract the whole numbers. Simplify the difference.

Remember that subtracting mixed fractions may require renaming.

1. $7\frac{5}{6} - 3\frac{2}{3}$
2. $2\frac{3}{5} - 1\frac{1}{2}$
3. $5\frac{2}{3} - 4\frac{5}{6}$
4. $9 - 3\frac{3}{8}$
5. $3\frac{1}{9} - 1\frac{1}{3}$
6. $6\frac{1}{4} - 3\frac{2}{5}$
7. $9\frac{1}{4} - 2\frac{5}{8}$
8. $4 - 1\frac{2}{5}$

Set F, pages 262–263

Find the next three numbers in the pattern.

$1\frac{1}{2}, 3, 4\frac{1}{2},$ ▭, ▭, ▭

Step 1 Figure out how to get the second number from the first number.

$3 - 1\frac{1}{2} = 1\frac{1}{2}$

Write the rule. Add $1\frac{1}{2}$.

Step 2 Check your rule by using it to see if you get the third number from the second number.

$3 + 1\frac{1}{2} = 4\frac{1}{2}$ The rule works.

Step 3 Continue the pattern.

$1\frac{1}{2}, 3, 4\frac{1}{2}, 6, 7\frac{1}{2}, 9$

Step 4 Make sure all numbers agree with the rule.

Remember that you need to look at the relationship between several items in the pattern in order to write the rule.

1. Marie cut equal pieces (in yards) from a bolt of fabric. Continue the pattern to find the amount remaining after each cut.

   $22\frac{1}{4}, 20, 17\frac{3}{4},$ ▭, ▭, ▭

2. Dan put equal amounts (in cups) of 6 ingredients in his trail mix. Continue the pattern to find how much trail mix he had after adding each ingredient.

   $\frac{2}{3}, 1\frac{1}{3}, 2,$ ▭, ▭, ▭

Topic 12

Multiplying and Dividing Fractions and Mixed Numbers

1 What would a fifth- grader who weighs 96 pounds on Earth weigh on Mars? You will find out in Lesson 12-1.

2 How much silver does this half-dollar contain? You will find out in Lesson 12-1.

3 The world's largest leather work boot is taller than a regular work boot. How many times taller? You will find out in Lesson 12-3.

4

The Akashi Kaikyo Bridge in Japan (top) is the longest suspension bridge in the world. How does the length of this bridge compare to the length of the Golden Gate Bridge in San Francisco? You will find out in Lesson 12-6.

Review What You Know!

Vocabulary

Choose the best term from the box.

- denominator
- least common multiple
- numerator
- least common denominator

1. The number above the fraction bar is the __?__.

2. The smallest common multiple of two numbers is called the __?__.

3. The number below the fraction bar is the __?__.

4. The smallest common multiple of two denominators is called the __?__.

Least Common Denominator

Write each pair of fractions with their LCD.

5. $\frac{5}{12}$ and $\frac{1}{4}$

6. $\frac{3}{4}$ and $\frac{1}{6}$

7. $\frac{5}{6}$ and $\frac{3}{8}$

8. $\frac{7}{9}$ and $\frac{1}{2}$

Adding and Subtracting

Find each sum or difference. Simplify, if possible.

9. $\frac{5}{8} + \frac{1}{4}$

10. $\frac{11}{12} - \frac{1}{4}$

11. $\frac{4}{5} + \frac{1}{2}$

12. $\frac{6}{15} - \frac{1}{3}$

Adding Mixed Numbers

13. Writing to Explain Write an answer to the question.

How would you find $2\frac{1}{3} + 1\frac{2}{3}$?

Lesson

12-1

NS 2.4 Understand the concept of multiplication and division of fractions. Also **NS 2.5**.

Multiplying Fractions and Whole Numbers

What are some ways to think about multiplying fractions and whole numbers?

How many cups of orange juice are needed to make 8 batches of fruit drink?

One way to find $8 \times \frac{3}{4}$ is to use repeated addition.

$$8 \times \frac{3}{4} = \frac{3}{4} + \frac{3}{4} + \frac{3}{4} + \frac{3}{4} + \frac{3}{4} + \frac{3}{4} + \frac{3}{4} + \frac{3}{4} = \frac{8 \times 3}{4} = \frac{24}{4} = 6$$

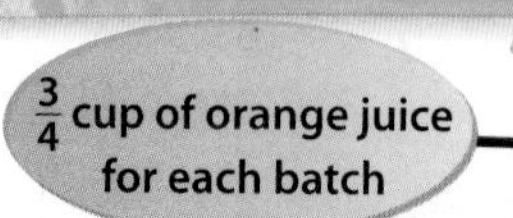

$\frac{3}{4}$ cup of orange juice for each batch

Guided Practice*

Do you know HOW?

In **1** through **4**, find each product.

1. $\frac{1}{7}$ of 14

2. $\frac{3}{7}$ of 14

3. $25 \times \frac{1}{5}$

4. $25 \times \frac{4}{5}$

Do you UNDERSTAND?

5. How is finding $8 \times \frac{3}{4}$ similar to finding $\frac{3}{4}$ of 8?

6. If you wanted to make 4 batches using the recipe above, how many cups of orange juice would you need?

Independent Practice

In **7** through **38**, find each product.

7. $\frac{1}{4}$ of 40

8. $\frac{1}{3}$ of 15

9. $\frac{1}{5}$ of 40

10. $\frac{1}{7}$ of 28

11. $\frac{2}{9}$ of 90

12. $\frac{2}{5}$ of 40

13. $\frac{1}{2}$ of 50

14. $\frac{5}{8}$ of 32

15. $\frac{3}{4}$ of 12

16. $\frac{6}{7}$ of 49

17. $\frac{3}{5}$ of 25

18. $\frac{2}{7}$ of 35

19. $\frac{5}{8}$ of 24

20. $\frac{3}{7}$ of 21

21. $\frac{8}{9}$ of 81

22. $\frac{7}{8}$ of 56

23. $\frac{2}{3} \times 27$

24. $\frac{3}{8} \times 16$

25. $\frac{5}{6} \times 18$

26. $50 \times \frac{7}{10}$

27. $25 \times \frac{4}{5}$

28. $12 \times \frac{2}{3}$

29. $32 \times \frac{1}{4}$

30. $18 \times \frac{2}{9}$

31. $\frac{2}{5} \times 35$

32. $\frac{8}{9} \times 18$

33. $\frac{4}{7} \times 35$

34. $\frac{5}{8} \times 16$

35. $\frac{3}{8} \times 24$

36. $\frac{7}{9} \times 36$

37. $\left(\frac{3}{4} - \frac{1}{4}\right) \times 24$

38. $\left(\frac{3}{5} - \frac{3}{10}\right) \times 30$

*For another example, see Set A on page 292.

To find $8 \times \frac{3}{4}$, you can multiply first and then divide.

$8 \times \frac{3}{4} = \frac{24}{4} = 6$

Another way to think about multiplication of a whole number and a fraction is to find a part of a whole group.

Martin has 8 oranges to make juice. If he uses $\frac{3}{4}$ of the oranges, how many will he use? To find $\frac{3}{4}$ of 8, you can draw a picture.

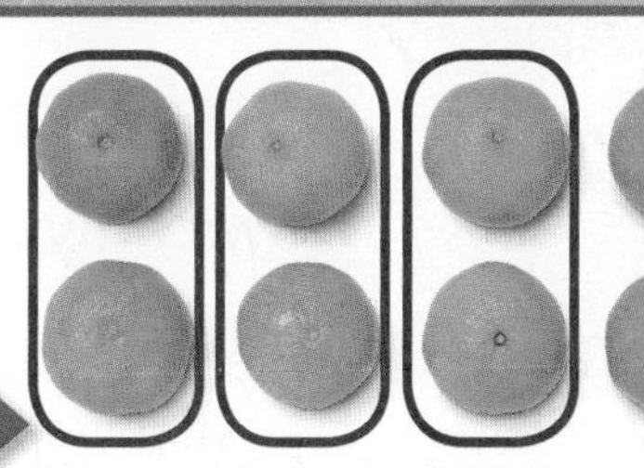

To find $\frac{3}{4}$ of 8, you can divide first and then multiply.

Think $\frac{1}{4}$ of $8 = 2$.

So, $\frac{3}{4}$ of $8 = 3 \times 2$ or 6.

Remember that $\frac{3}{4}$ of 8 means $\frac{3}{4} \times 8$.

So, $\frac{3}{4} \times 8 = 6$.

Problem Solving

39. **Number Sense** Explain how you would find $36 \times \frac{3}{4}$ mentally.

40. Lions spend about $\frac{5}{6}$ of their days sleeping. How many hours a day does a lion sleep?

41. **Writing to Explain** Jo said that when you multiply a nonzero whole number by a fraction less than 1, the product is always less than the whole number. Do you agree?

42. Who ran the most miles by the end of the week? Use the table below.

	Monday	Wednesday	Saturday
Pat	2.75 mi	3 mi	2.5 mi
Toby	2 mi	2.25 mi	3.5 mi

43. On Mars, your weight is about $\frac{1}{3}$ of your weight on Earth. If a fifth grader weighs 96 pounds on Earth, about how much would be his or her weight on Mars?

44. How much change will Stacy get if she buys two CDs and two books and gives the clerk two $20 bills?

Sale: CDs for $8.25 each

Sale: 2 books for $10.00

45. A recipe calls for $\frac{1}{2}$ cup of walnuts and $\frac{3}{16}$ cup of dates. Which of the following shows the correct relationship?

A $\frac{1}{2} > \frac{3}{16}$

B $\frac{1}{2} = \frac{3}{16}$

C $\frac{3}{8} < \frac{1}{4}$

D $\frac{1}{2} < \frac{3}{16}$

46. A 1965 U.S. half dollar contains $\frac{2}{5}$ ounce of silver. How many ounces of silver do 100 of those coins contain?

Lesson

12-2

NS 2.4 Understand the concept of multiplication and division of fractions. Also **NS 2.5.**

Multiplying Two Fractions

How can you multiply fractions?

Tom has $\frac{3}{4}$ of a pan of lasagna. His friends ate $\frac{2}{3}$ of this amount of lasagna. What fraction of a whole pan of lasagna did his friends eat?

Find $\frac{2}{3}$ of $\frac{3}{4}$.

Another Example How can you simplify before you multiply?

A fraction times a fraction

Find $\frac{3}{4} \times \frac{5}{6}$.

Find the GCF of any numerator and any denominator.

The GCF of 3 and 6 is 3.

Divide 3 and 6 by 3.

$$\frac{\overset{1}{\cancel{3}}}{4} \times \frac{5}{\underset{2}{\cancel{6}}} = \frac{1 \times 5}{4 \times 2} = \frac{5}{8}$$

So, $\frac{3}{4} \times \frac{5}{6} = \frac{5}{8}$.

A fraction times a whole number

Find $\frac{2}{3} \times 18$.

Write 18 as an improper fraction.

$\frac{2}{3} \times 18 = \frac{2}{3} \times \frac{18}{1}$

The GCF of 3 and 18 is 3.

Divide 3 and 18 by 3.

$$\frac{2}{3} \times 18 = \frac{2}{\underset{1}{\cancel{3}}} \times \frac{\overset{6}{\cancel{18}}}{1} = \frac{12}{1} = 12$$

Explain It

1. To find $\frac{3}{4} \times \frac{5}{6}$ in the first example above, why is the 3 crossed out with a 1 written above it, and why is the 6 crossed out with a 2 written below it?
2. To find $\frac{2}{3} \times 18$ in the second example above, how is the problem changed so that you could multiply a fraction by a fraction?

One Way

Draw a picture to represent $\frac{3}{4}$. Shade 3 of the 4 parts red. Then draw two horizontal lines to show thirds. Use yellow to shade $\frac{2}{3}$ of the whole rectangle. Where the two shadings overlap is orange.

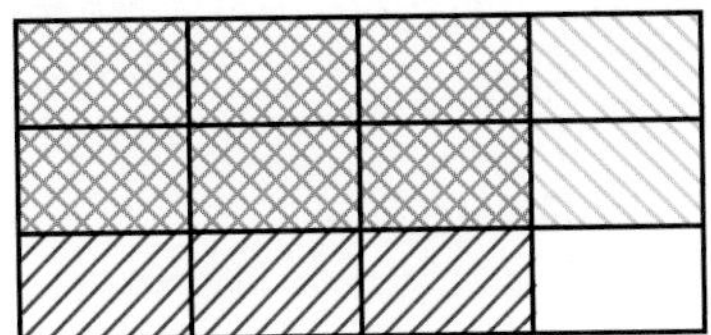

2×3 out of 3×4 parts are shaded orange.

They ate $\frac{6}{12}$ or $\frac{1}{2}$ of the pan of lasagna.

Another Way

Multiply the numerators and denominators. Simplify if possible.

$$\frac{2}{3} \times \frac{3}{4} = \frac{2 \times 3}{3 \times 4} = \frac{6}{12} = \frac{1}{2}$$

Guided Practice*

Do you know HOW?

In **1** through **4**, find each product. Simplify, if necessary.

1. $\frac{3}{4} \times \frac{7}{8}$

2. $15 \times \frac{3}{4}$

3. $\frac{3}{4} \times \frac{1}{4} \times 2$

4. $\frac{2}{3} \times \frac{1}{2} \times \frac{5}{8}$

Do you UNDERSTAND?

5. How can you find the product of $\frac{6}{6} \times \frac{3}{8}$ mentally?

6. In the problem above, find the fraction of a whole pan of lasagna that Tom's friends ate if he started with $\frac{7}{8}$ of a pan.

Independent Practice

In **7** through **31**, find each product. Simplify, if necessary.

7. $\frac{3}{5} \times \frac{5}{9}$

8. $13 \times \frac{1}{5}$

9. $\frac{3}{4} \times \frac{1}{3} \times 2$

10. $\frac{2}{3} \times \frac{5}{8} \times 4$

11. $\frac{1}{6} \times \frac{5}{6}$

12. $\frac{1}{3} \times \frac{1}{4} \times \frac{2}{3}$

13. $\frac{1}{7} \times \frac{2}{3} \times 6$

14. $\frac{1}{2} \times \frac{3}{8} \times \frac{3}{4}$

15. $\frac{1}{3} \times \frac{2}{5}$

16. $\frac{7}{8} \times \frac{2}{3}$

17. $\frac{2}{5} \times \frac{3}{4} \times 10$

18. $\frac{1}{8} \times \frac{1}{3} \times 24$

19. $\frac{2}{9} \times \frac{3}{10}$

20. $\frac{3}{7} \times \frac{1}{3}$

21. $\frac{1}{6} \times \frac{3}{5} \times 20$

22. $\frac{1}{2} \times \frac{2}{5} \times 5$

23. $\left(\frac{3}{4} - \frac{1}{4}\right) \times \frac{7}{8}$

24. $\left(\frac{2}{3} - \frac{1}{3}\right) \times \frac{4}{9}$

25. $\left(\frac{5}{8} - \frac{1}{8}\right) \times \frac{2}{5}$

26. $\left(\frac{2}{3} - \frac{1}{4}\right) \times \frac{5}{6}$

27. $\left(\frac{3}{4} - \frac{1}{2}\right) \times \frac{5}{9}$

28. $\left(\frac{3}{4} - \frac{1}{3}\right) \times \frac{3}{5}$

29. $\left(\frac{5}{8} - \frac{1}{4}\right) \times \frac{1}{2}$

30. $\left(\frac{4}{5} - \frac{1}{2}\right) \times \frac{3}{8}$

31. $\left(\frac{1}{2} - \frac{4}{8}\right) \times \frac{3}{7}$

*For another example, see Set B on page 292.

32. In the voting for City Council Precinct 5, only $\frac{1}{2}$ of all eligible voters cast votes. What fraction of all eligible voters voted for Shelley? Daley? Who received the most votes?

Data

Candidate	Fraction of Votes Received
Shelley	$\frac{1}{10}$
Daley	$\frac{2}{8}$

33. **Geometry** The stained glass shown here is a regular hexagon. How can you use multiplication to find its perimeter?

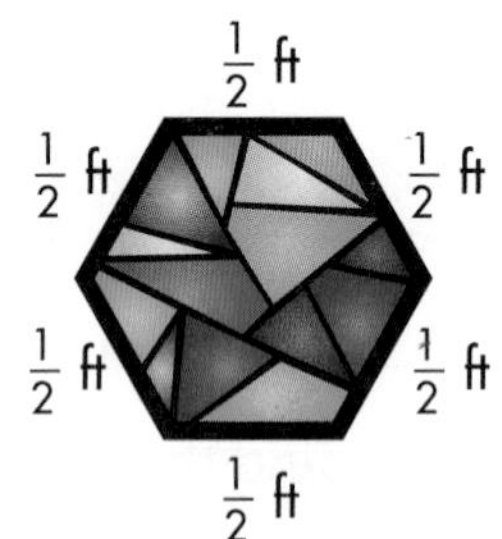

34. **Writing to Explain** Will \$50 be enough to buy 6 cans of paint?

35. **Algebra** What is the value of n in the equation $\frac{2}{3} \times n = \frac{4}{9}$?

36. **Number Sense** $\frac{4}{9} \times \frac{7}{8} = \frac{7}{18}$. What is $\frac{7}{8} \times \frac{4}{9}$? How do you know without multiplying?

37. **Writing to Explain** To amend the U.S. Constitution, $\frac{3}{4}$ of the states must approve the amendment. If 35 of the states approve an amendment, will the constitution be amended?

38. A plumber charges \$45 for the first hour and \$30 for each additional hour. How much does he charge if it takes him 4 hours to make a repair?

A \$165 **C** \$120
B \$135 **D** \$75

39. Naomi has 3 pounds of apples and $2\frac{1}{2}$ pounds of grapes. If she gives $\frac{1}{3}$ of her apples to Christine, how many pounds of apples does she have left?

A $\frac{1}{6}$ pound **C** 1 pound
B $\frac{1}{2}$ pound **D** 2 pounds

40. A video rental store has 6,000 movies. One Friday, $\frac{3}{5}$ of the movies were rented. How many movies were rented that Friday night?

41. One lap around the Lincoln School track is $\frac{1}{4}$ mile. If Eddie runs 6 laps around the track and then runs $2\frac{1}{2}$ miles to get home, how far will he run in all?

42. Ben found a recipe that calls for $\frac{3}{4}$ cup of chopped apples. If he wants to make half the recipe, how many cups of chopped apples should he use?

Find each product. Simplify if possible.

1. $\frac{1}{8} \times 6$ **2.** $7 \times \frac{1}{2}$ **3.** $\frac{4}{5} \times 3$ **4.** $5 \times \frac{7}{10}$

5. $8 \times \frac{5}{6}$ **6.** $\frac{2}{3} \times 9$ **7.** $4 \times \frac{5}{12}$ **8.** $\frac{1}{6} \times 12$

Find each product. Simplify if possible.

9. $\frac{2}{3} \times \frac{1}{4}$ **10.** $\frac{3}{5} \times \frac{3}{10}$ **11.** $\frac{1}{2} \times \frac{5}{12}$ **12.** $\frac{1}{4} \times \frac{1}{8}$ **13.** $\frac{2}{3} \times \frac{4}{5}$

14. $\frac{3}{4} \times \frac{1}{3}$ **15.** $\frac{8}{9} \times \frac{1}{2}$ **16.** $\frac{1}{5} \times \frac{1}{5}$ **17.** $\frac{3}{8} \times \frac{5}{6}$ **18.** $\frac{1}{2} \times \frac{1}{2}$

Find each sum. Simplify if possible.

19. $\frac{5}{6} + \frac{1}{12}$ **20.** $\frac{1}{2} + \frac{3}{8}$ **21.** $\frac{1}{3} + \frac{5}{12}$ **22.** $\frac{2}{3} + \frac{1}{9}$ **23.** $\frac{1}{5} + \frac{3}{10}$

Error Search Find each product that is not correct. Write it correctly and explain the error.

24. $\frac{2}{3} \times 3 = 2$ **25.** $\frac{3}{4} \times \frac{2}{5} = \frac{3}{20}$ **26.** $\frac{2}{10} \times \frac{3}{10} = \frac{6}{10}$

Number Sense

Estimating and Reasoning Write whether each statement is true or false. Explain your reasoning.

27. The product of 7 and 4.83 is greater than 35.

28. The sum of 45,752 and 36,687 is greater than 70,000 but less than 90,000.

29. The difference of $\frac{1}{2}$ and $\frac{1}{3}$ equals their product.

30. The product of $\frac{3}{4}$ and 5 is less than 5.

31. The quotient of 534 ÷ 9 greater than 60.

32. The sum of 21.45 and 4.2 is less than 25.

Lesson
12-3

NS 2.4 Understand the concept of multiplication and division of fractions. Also NS 2.5.

Dividing a Whole Number by a Fraction

How can you divide by a fraction?

Joyce is making sushi rolls. She needs $\frac{1}{4}$ cup of rice for each sushi roll. How many sushi rolls can she make if she has 3 cups of rice?

Guided Practice*

Do you know HOW?

In **1** and **2**, use the picture below to find each quotient. Simplify, if necessary.

1. How many $\frac{1}{3}$s are in 3?

$3 \div \frac{1}{3} = \square$

2. How many $\frac{2}{3}$s are in 6?

$6 \div \frac{2}{3} = \square$

Do you UNDERSTAND?

3. Reasoning Explain how you could draw a picture to find $4 \div \frac{2}{3}$.

4. In the example above, if Joyce had 4 cups of rice, how many rolls could she make?

5. Writing to Explain In the example above, why is 3 written as a fraction with the same denominator as $\frac{1}{4}$?

Independent Practice

In **6** through **7**, use the picture to find each quotient.

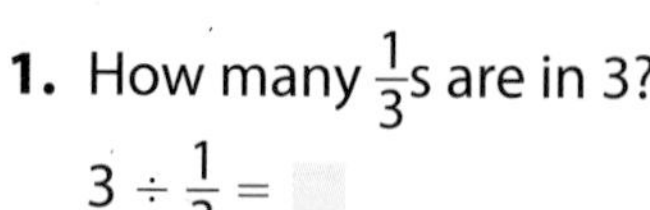

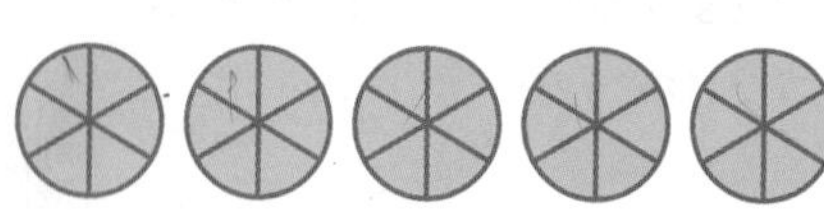

6. How many $\frac{1}{6}$s are in 1? $1 \div \frac{1}{6} = \square$

7. How many $\frac{1}{6}$s are in 5? $5 \div \frac{1}{6} = \square$

In **8** through **17**, find each quotient. You can draw pictures to help.

8. $4 \div \frac{1}{2}$ **9.** $8 \div \frac{1}{4}$ **10.** $3 \div \frac{1}{5}$ **11.** $2 \div \frac{1}{8}$ **12.** $3 \div \frac{1}{10}$

13. $8 \div \frac{1}{3}$ **14.** $9 \div \frac{3}{8}$ **15.** $6 \div \frac{3}{4}$ **16.** $15 \div \frac{3}{5}$ **17.** $10 \div \frac{5}{8}$

*For another example, see Set C on page 292.

One Way

Draw a diagram.

How many $\frac{1}{4}$s are in 3?

This is the same as finding $3 \div \frac{1}{4}$.

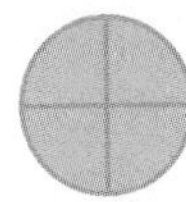 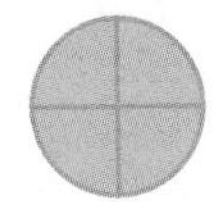 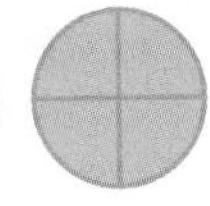

There are twelve $\frac{1}{4}$s in three whole cups.

So, Joyce can make 12 sushi rolls.

Another Way

Write 3 as an equivalent fraction with the same denominator as $\frac{1}{4}$.

$3 \div \frac{1}{4} = \frac{12}{4} \div \frac{1}{4}$

Divide the numerators and the denominators.

$\frac{12}{4} \div \frac{1}{4} = \frac{12}{1} = 12$

So, Joyce can make 12 sushi rolls.

Problem Solving

For **18** and **19**, use the following information.

Bijan is making a banner for his school. Along the bottom edge of the banner is a row of smaller squares. Each square is 6 inches by 6 inches.

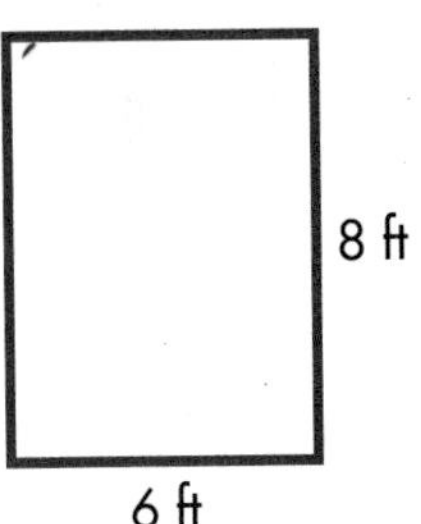

18. How many small squares did Bijan put along the bottom (width) of the banner?

19. If every fourth square is colored blue, how many blue squares are along the bottom?

20. **Reasoning** When you divide a whole number by a fraction with a numerator of 1, explain how you can find the quotient.

21. **Writing to Explain** Write a word problem that can be solved by dividing 10 by $\frac{2}{3}$. Include the answer to the problem.

22. As of 2006, the world's largest leather work boot is 16 feet tall. A typical men's work boot is $\frac{1}{2}$ foot tall. How many times as tall is the largest boot as the height of a typical work boot?

23. **Estimation** The Nile River is 4,160 miles long. You want to spend three weeks traveling the entire length of the river. Estimate the number of miles you must travel each day.

24. Maria used one bag of flour. She baked two loaves of bread. Each loaf required $2\frac{1}{4}$ cups of flour. Then she used $1\frac{3}{4}$ cups of flour to make muffins. She used the remaining $4\frac{1}{3}$ cups of flour to bake cookies. How much flour was in the bag when she started?

25. Rudy has 8 yards of twine. If he cuts the twine into equal pieces of $\frac{3}{4}$ feet each, how many pieces can he cut?

A $10\frac{1}{2}$

B 24

C 32

D $96\frac{1}{2}$

Lesson

12-4

NS **2.4** Understand the concept of multiplication and division of fractions. Also **NS 2.5**.

Dividing Two Fractions

How do you divide with fractions?

Max is slicing a wooden dowel into thin circular slices to make wooden chips for a game. How many chips will he have after slicing the dowel?

Choose an Operation Divide to find how many groups of $\frac{1}{8}$ are in $\frac{3}{4}$.

Find $\frac{3}{4} \div \frac{1}{8}$.

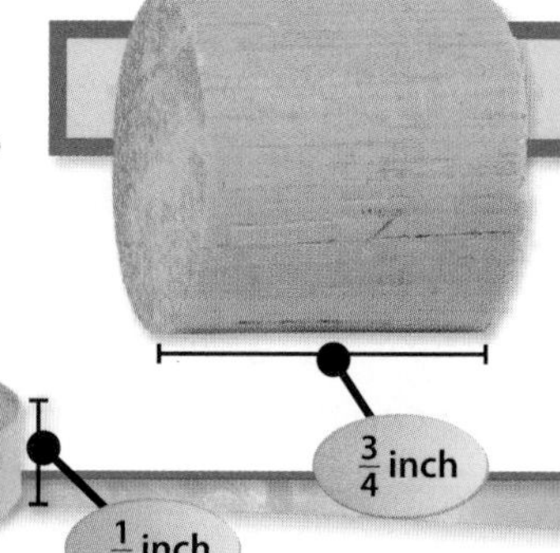

Other Examples

Simplifying before you divide two fractions

Find $\frac{3}{8} \div \frac{1}{4}$.

$\frac{3}{8} \div \frac{1}{4} = \frac{3}{8} \times \frac{4}{1}$ Rewrite the problem as a multiplication problem with the reciprocal of the divisor. The reciprocal of $\frac{1}{4}$ is $\frac{4}{1}$.

$= \frac{3}{\cancel{8}_2} \times \frac{\cancel{4}^1}{1}$ Look for common factors in the numerators and denominators.

$= \frac{3 \times 1}{2 \times 1}$ Multiply.

$= \frac{3}{2} = 1\frac{1}{2}$ Convert to a mixed number, if possible.

Dividing a fraction by a whole number

Find $\frac{5}{6} \div 2$.

Write 2 as an improper fraction.

$\frac{5}{6} \div 2 = \frac{5}{6} \div \frac{2}{1}$

Then multiply by the reciprocal of $\frac{2}{1}$.

$\frac{5}{6} \div \frac{2}{1} = \frac{5}{6} \times \frac{1}{2} = \frac{5 \times 1}{6 \times 2} = \frac{5}{12}$

Explain It

1. How is dividing 7 by $\frac{1}{2}$ different from multiplying 7 by 2?

2. Write and solve $42 \div 7$ as a multiplication problem.

One Way

Draw a picture.

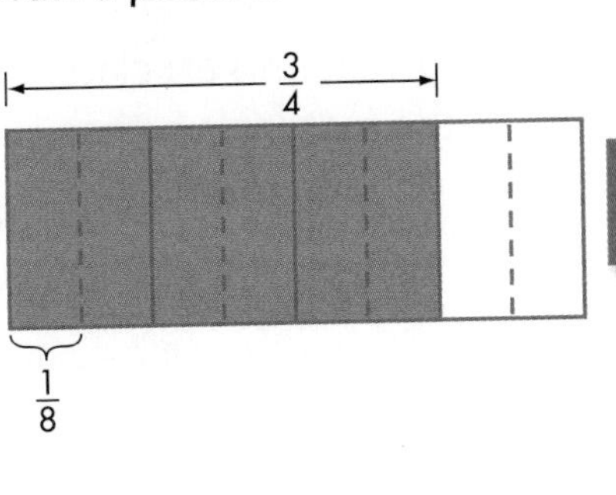

$\frac{3}{4} \div \frac{1}{8} = 6$

Another Way

Dividing by a fraction is the same as multiplying by its reciprocal.

Two fractions whose product is 1 are **reciprocals**. For example, $\frac{1}{8} \times \frac{8}{1} = 1$, so $\frac{1}{8}$ and $\frac{8}{1}$ are reciprocals. Reciprocals are also called **multiplicative inverses**.

To divide by a fraction, multiply by the reciprocal of the divisor.

$\frac{3}{4} \div \frac{1}{8} = \frac{3}{4} \times \frac{8}{1} = \frac{24}{4} = 6.$

Max can make 6 chips from the dowel.

Guided Practice*

Do you know HOW?

In **1** and **2**, write the reciprocal of each fraction or number.

1. $\frac{4}{7}$

2. 15

In **3** and **4**, find each quotient. Simplify if possible.

3. $7 \div \frac{2}{3}$

4. $\frac{2}{3} \div \frac{3}{4}$

Do you UNDERSTAND?

5. How can you write $5 \div \frac{1}{4}$ as a product? How can you write $\frac{1}{4} \div 5$ as a product?

6. How did you find the answer to Exercise 3?

7. If Max started with a dowel $\frac{1}{2}$ inch in length, how many chips could he make?

Independent Practice

In **8** through **11**, write the reciprocal of each fraction or whole number.

8. $\frac{3}{14}$

9. 6

10. $\frac{1}{18}$

11. $\frac{7}{3}$

In **12** through **23**, find each quotient. Simplify, if possible.

12. $9 \div \frac{3}{5}$

13. $\frac{3}{8} \div \frac{1}{4}$

14. $\frac{4}{5} \div 6$

15. $\frac{6}{7} \div \frac{1}{3}$

16. $24 \div \frac{2}{3}$

17. $\frac{5}{6} \div \frac{2}{11}$

18. $\left(\frac{1}{6} + \frac{1}{3}\right) \div \frac{3}{4}$

19. $\left(\frac{1}{9} + \frac{2}{3}\right) \div \frac{2}{5}$

20. $8 \div \frac{3}{4}$

21. $\frac{7}{9} \div \frac{5}{6}$

22. $\left(\frac{1}{4} + \frac{1}{3}\right) \div \frac{1}{2}$

23. $\left(\frac{1}{8} + \frac{1}{4}\right) \div \frac{1}{3}$

*For another example, see Set D on page 292.

For **24** through **26**, use the information in the chart at the right.

24. How many pieces can Carl make from the dowel rods?

25. How many shorter pieces of copper wire can Carl get from his original length?

26. If Carl has 2 lengths of plastic tubing, how many pieces can he make?

Carl is creating a sculpture for his art class. Here is a summary of the materials he has and what he needs to do with them:

Total Materials	Final Artwork
18 in. dowel rods	$\frac{2}{3}$ in. pieces
28 in. copper wire	$\frac{7}{8}$ in. pieces
10 in. plastic tubing	$\frac{1}{2}$ in. pieces

27. Number Sense Explain how to use decimals to find $6 \div \frac{3}{4}$.

28. Reasoning Will $5 \div \frac{2}{5}$ have a whole-number answer? Explain.

29. Writing to Explain Is the following explanation correct? If not, tell why and write a correct response.

Find $6 \div \frac{2}{3}$.

I can rewrite this problem as $\frac{1}{6} \times \frac{3}{2}$, because dividing fractions is the same as multiplying their reciprocals.

$\frac{1}{6} \times \frac{3}{2} = \frac{3}{12} = \frac{1}{4}$.

30. Think About the Process Ms. Troy wants to save her students' computer projects on CDs. Each CD holds 750 MB. Each project is 2 MB, and Ms. Troy has four CDs. Which shows how she can determine how many projects she can save?

A $(750 + 2) \div 4$

B $(750 \times 2) \div 4$

C $(750 \times 4) \div 2$

D $(750 \div 4) \times 2$

For **31** and **32**, use the information at the right.

31. The Bayou Theater is raising its ticket prices. The new price of each ticket will be the original price plus half the original price. How much will each type of ticket cost after the price increase takes effect?

Original Ticket Prices	
Student	\$2.50
Adult	\$4.50
Senior	\$3.50

32. If Tracy's family buys 2 student tickets, 1 adult ticket, and 1 senior ticket at the new prices, how much will they pay to go to the theater?

A \$5.50 **C** \$13.75

B \$6.75 **D** \$19.50

33. There are 32 students in Mr. Smith's class. Three-eighths of them are in the math club. How many of Mr. Smith's students are in the math club?

Mixed Problem Solving

Data

New England Colonies			Middle Colonies			Southern Colonies		
Colony	**Year**	**Reason**	**Colony**	**Year**	**Reason**	**Colony**	**Year**	**Reason**
Mass. Bay	1630	Escape religious persecution	New York	1664	Build colony on Dutch land	Virginia	1607	Search for gold
Conn.	1639	Farming, trade, political freedom	New Jersey	1664	Build colony on Dutch land	Maryland	1634	Refuge for Catholics
Rhode Island	1636	Colony for all religions	Penna.	1682	Establish religious colony	North Carolina	1729	Farming
New Hampshire	1679	Trade, fishing	Delaware	1704	Trade, farming	South Carolina	1670	Farming
						Georgia	1733	Military defense, religious refuge, farming

1. What fraction of the colonies were founded for farming?

2. What fraction of the colonies are the Southern Colonies?

3. What fraction of the colonies were founded in 1729?

4. What fraction of the New England Colonies were founded in 1636?

5. James stated that $\frac{1}{3}$ of the colonies were the Middle Colonies. Is he correct? Why or why not?

6. Write a problem using the fraction $\frac{1}{5}$. Use the chart to help you.

7. What fraction tells you how many colonies were founded because of trade?

   A $\frac{1}{13}$ **C** $\frac{1}{2}$
   B $\frac{3}{13}$ **D** $\frac{3}{4}$

8. What fraction of the colonies are the Middle Colonies and the Southern Colonies together?

   F $\frac{1}{2}$ **H** $\frac{8}{13}$
   G $\frac{9}{13}$ **J** $\frac{4}{13}$

9. **Strategy Focus** Solve using the strategy, Draw a Picture and Write an Equation.

   How many years passed from the time the first colony was founded until the last one was founded?

Lesson
12-5

MR 1.1 Analyze problems by identifying relationships, distinguishing relevant from irrelevant information, sequencing and prioritizing information, and observing patterns.
Also NS 2.4

Problem Solving

Missing or Extra Information

How do I identify missing or extra information in a word problem?

Sela has a large vase that cost $19. She used a watering can to fill the vase with water. If she filled the watering can 3 times to fill the vase, how many quarts of water did she put in the vase?

Guided Practice*

Do you know HOW?

Decide if each problem has extra or missing information. Solve if you have enough information.

1. Allie feeds her dog $\frac{1}{2}$ can of food each day. Each can costs $0.49. How much food does she feed her dog in 7 days?

2. Lacey is buying dried fruit to feed her pet bird. How much will it cost to feed the bird for one month?

Do you UNDERSTAND?

3. Draw a diagram to show what you know and want to find in Exercise 1.

4. **Write a Problem** Write a real-world problem that does not include all of the information needed to solve it. Under the problem, write what the missing information is.

Independent Practice

In **5** through **7**, decide if each problem has extra or missing information. Solve if you have enough information.

5. Eli is cutting a length of wire into pieces that are $\frac{1}{2}$ foot long. How many pieces can he cut from the length of wire?

6. Sonja posted 45 band concert flyers in 2 days. Over the next 2 days, Elsie posted 60 flyers, and Frank posted 30 flyers. How many flyers did the 3 students post altogether?

Stuck? Try this....

- What do I know?
- What am I asked to find?
- What diagram can I use to help understand the problem?
- Can I use addition, subtraction, multiplication, or division?
- Is all of my work correct?
- Did I answer the right question?
- Is my answer reasonable?

*For another example, see Set E on page 293.

Read and Understand

Draw a diagram to show what you know and what you want to find.

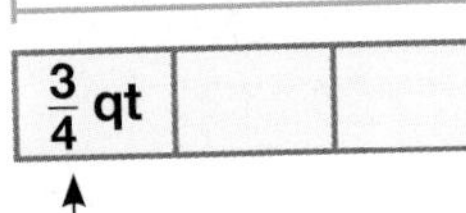

Capacity of watering can

Plan

Is there extra information not needed to solve the problem?

Yes. The cost of the vase is not needed.

Is there missing information needed to solve the problem?

No. All the information I need is given.

Solve

Let n = number of quarts to fill the vase.

$3 \times \frac{3}{4} = n$

$3 \times \frac{3}{4} = \frac{9}{4} = 2\frac{1}{4}$

Sela put $2\frac{1}{4}$ quarts of water into the vase.

7. Mrs. Torance has invited 16 people to a party. What information is missing if Mrs. Torance wants to serve submarine sandwiches at the party?

8. Kara and her 4 friends went camping. Each day they hiked $2\frac{1}{2}$ miles before lunch and $3\frac{1}{2}$ miles after lunch. How many total miles did all the girls hike on their camping trip?

Provide possible information needed to solve the problem, then solve it.

9. A package of printing paper contains 500 sheets. If a printer uses 4,000 sheets of paper per week, how many packages are used?

10. Juan and his sister visited an aquarium. While there, they learned that 1 catfish produces 40 eggs. How many eggs will 60 catfish produce?

11. Sylvia had $20 to spend at the circus. She spent $5.00 on admission. During lunch Sylvia bought a hot dog and drink for $6.50. How much money did Sylvia have left to spend after lunch?

12. A carpenter cut $\frac{1}{2}$ foot from a board that was $3\frac{1}{4}$ feet long. How long was the board after the cut?

13. Greg bought a sandwich and a drink. He paid $4.50. Which sandwich and drink did he buy?

Dunstan's Sandwiches	
Chicken	$4.25
Roast Beef	$3.75
Tuna	$3.50
Milk	$0.60
Juice	$0.75

14. Ken is making a salad using a recipe that calls for pasta, 3 cherry tomatoes, and 6 sliced carrots. Ken only needs enough salad for two people, so he will make $\frac{2}{3}$ of the recipe. How many people does the whole recipe serve?

Lesson

12-6

NS 2.4 Understand the concept of multiplication and division of fractions. Also NS 2.5.

Multiplying Mixed Numbers

How do you find the product of mixed numbers?

A clothing factory has machines that make jackets. The machines operate for $7\frac{1}{2}$ hours each day. How many jackets can each machine make in one day?

Data

Jackets Per Hour	
Machine A	Machine B
$2\frac{3}{4}$	$3\frac{1}{3}$

Choose an Operation Use multiplication to find how many jackets each machine can make in a day.

Guided Practice*

Do you know HOW?

In **1** and **2**, estimate the product. Then copy and complete the multiplication.

1. $2\frac{3}{4} \times 8 = \frac{\square}{4} \times \frac{8}{1}$

2. $4\frac{1}{2} \times 1\frac{1}{4} = \frac{\square}{2} \times \frac{\square}{4}$

Do you UNDERSTAND?

3. Explain how you would use improper fractions to multiply $5 \times 2\frac{1}{2}$.

4. How many jackets a day can Machine A make if it can make $4\frac{1}{4}$ jackets an hour?

Independent Practice

In **5** through **10**, estimate the product. Then copy and complete the multiplication.

5. $3\frac{4}{5} \times 5 = \frac{\square}{5} \times \frac{5}{1}$

6. $1\frac{3}{5} \times 2\frac{1}{4} = \frac{\square}{5} \times \frac{\square}{4}$

7. $1\frac{1}{2} \times 3\frac{5}{6} = \frac{\square}{2} \times \frac{\square}{6}$

8. $4\frac{2}{3} \times 4 = \frac{\square}{3} \times \frac{4}{1}$

9. $3\frac{1}{7} \times 1\frac{1}{4} = \frac{\square}{7} \times \frac{\square}{4}$

10. $1\frac{1}{3} \times 2\frac{1}{6} = \frac{\square}{3} \times \frac{\square}{6}$

In **11** through **22**, estimate the product. Then find each product. Simplify if possible.

11. $2\frac{1}{6} \times 4\frac{1}{2}$

12. $\frac{3}{4} \times 8\frac{1}{2}$

13. $1\frac{1}{8} \times 3\frac{1}{3}$

14. $3\frac{1}{4} \times 6$

15. $5\frac{1}{3} \times 3$

16. $2\frac{3}{8} \times 4$

17. $\left(\frac{1}{3} + 1\frac{4}{9}\right) \times \left(2\frac{3}{4} - 1\frac{1}{2}\right)$

18. $\left(1\frac{2}{9} + 2\frac{1}{3}\right) \times \left(2\frac{3}{4} - 1\frac{1}{8}\right)$

19. $\left(1\frac{1}{8} + 1\frac{1}{2}\right) \times \left(2\frac{2}{5} - 1\frac{1}{10}\right)$

20. $\left(\frac{1}{6} + 2\frac{2}{3}\right) \times \left(1\frac{1}{4} - \frac{1}{2}\right)$

21. $\left(2\frac{4}{9} + \frac{1}{3}\right) \times \left(1\frac{1}{4} - \frac{1}{8}\right)$

22. $\left(1\frac{7}{8} + 2\frac{1}{2}\right) \times \left(1\frac{1}{5} - \frac{1}{10}\right)$

*For another example, see Set F on page 293.

Machine A

Estimate $7\frac{1}{2} \times 2\frac{3}{4}$ is about the same as 8×3, so the answer should be about 24 jackets a day.

Change the mixed numbers to improper fractions.

$$7\frac{1}{2} \times 2\frac{3}{4} = \frac{15}{2} \times \frac{11}{4} = \frac{165}{8} = 20\frac{5}{8}$$

Machine A makes $20\frac{5}{8}$ jackets each day.

Machine B

Estimate $7\frac{1}{2} \times 3\frac{1}{3}$ is about the same as 8×3, so the answer should be about 24 jackets per day.

$$7\frac{1}{2} \times 3\frac{1}{3} = \frac{\overset{5}{\cancel{15}}}{\underset{1}{\cancel{2}}} \times \frac{\overset{5}{\cancel{10}}}{\underset{1}{\cancel{3}}} = \frac{25}{1} = 25$$

Machine B makes 25 jackets each day.

Problem Solving

For **23** through **25**, use the diagram at the right.

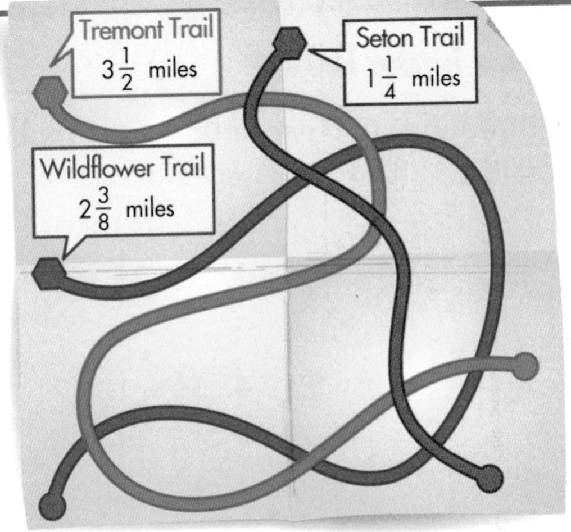

23. Bernie and Chloe hiked the Tremont Trail to the end and back. Then they hiked the Wildflower Trail to the end before stopping to eat lunch. How far did they hike before they ate lunch?

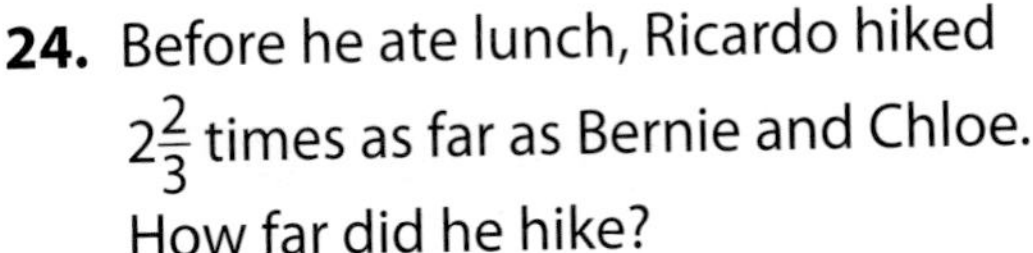

24. Before he ate lunch, Ricardo hiked $2\frac{2}{3}$ times as far as Bernie and Chloe. How far did he hike?

25. The city plans to extend the Wildflower Trail $2\frac{1}{2}$ times its current length in the next 5 years. How long will the Wildflower Trail be at the end of 5 years?

26. Writing to Explain How can you use multiplication to find $3\frac{3}{5} + 3\frac{3}{5} + 3\frac{3}{5}$?

27. The tail of an alligator is $\frac{1}{2}$ of its total length. The longest recorded length for an alligator is $19\frac{1}{6}$ feet. How long was the tail of this alligator?

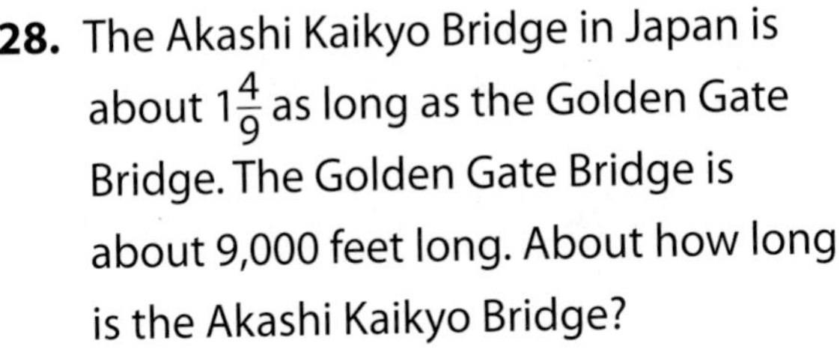

28. The Akashi Kaikyo Bridge in Japan is about $1\frac{4}{9}$ as long as the Golden Gate Bridge. The Golden Gate Bridge is about 9,000 feet long. About how long is the Akashi Kaikyo Bridge?

29. Patty spent $3\frac{1}{2}$ times as much as Sandy on their shopping trip. If Sandy spent \$20.50, how much did Patty spend?

A \$71.75
B \$92.20
C \$100.25
D \$143.50

Lesson

12-7

NS 2.4 Understand the concept of multiplication and division of fractions. Also **NS 2.5**.

Dividing Mixed Numbers

How do you find the quotient of two mixed numbers?

Henry has $12\frac{1}{2}$ feet of lumber. How many birdhouses can he build?

Choose an Operation Use division to find how many groups of $3\frac{3}{4}$ are in $12\frac{1}{2}$.

Estimate: $12\frac{1}{2} \div 3\frac{3}{4}$ is about $12 \div 4$ or 3.

$3\frac{3}{4}$ feet of lumber for each birdhouse

Guided Practice*

Do you know HOW?

In **1** through **6**, find each quotient. Simplify, if possible.

1. $1\frac{3}{4} \div 4\frac{2}{3}$

2. $3 \div 2\frac{1}{4}$

3. $3\frac{3}{4} \div 1\frac{1}{2}$

4. $5\frac{1}{6} \div 1\frac{2}{3}$

5. $2\frac{1}{5} \div 1\frac{1}{4}$

6. $4 \div 1\frac{1}{4}$

Do you UNDERSTAND?

7. Explain how to estimate and then find $7\frac{4}{5} \div 4$.

8. Why do you change mixed numbers to improper fractions before you divide?

9. How many birdhouses can Henry build if he starts with 15 feet of lumber?

Independent Practice

In **10** through **28**, find each quotient. Simplify, if possible.

10. $6\frac{1}{2} \div 1\frac{4}{9}$

11. $3\frac{1}{3} \div 1\frac{1}{6}$

12. $3 \div 5\frac{1}{5}$

13. $2\frac{5}{8} \div 3$

14. $5\frac{1}{2} \div 4\frac{2}{3}$

15. $5\frac{1}{4} \div 1\frac{5}{8}$

16. $4\frac{4}{5} \div 1\frac{7}{8}$

17. $3\frac{2}{3} \div 1\frac{5}{6}$

18. $4\frac{1}{2} \div 1\frac{1}{3}$

19. $8 \div 1\frac{2}{5}$

20. $3\frac{1}{5} \div 1\frac{2}{5}$

21. $2\frac{1}{6} \div 1\frac{5}{8}$

22. $2\frac{1}{3} \div 1\frac{1}{8}$

23. $5\frac{1}{4} \div 1\frac{3}{4}$

24. $7\frac{1}{5} \div 4\frac{1}{2}$

25. $8\frac{1}{4} \div 3\frac{2}{3}$

26. $\left(6\frac{2}{3} - 3\frac{1}{2}\right) \div 1\frac{1}{2}$

27. $\left(3\frac{3}{4} - \frac{1}{2}\right) \div 2\frac{1}{2}$

28. $\left(3\frac{3}{4} - 2\frac{1}{2}\right) \div 5$

*For another example, see Set G on page 293.

Step 1

Write each mixed number as an improper fraction.

$12\frac{1}{2} \div 3\frac{3}{4} = \frac{25}{2} \div \frac{15}{4}$

Step 2

Find the reciprocal of the divisor.

Rewrite as a multiplication problem.

$\frac{25}{2} \times \frac{4}{15}$

Step 3

Look for common factors.

Simplify and then multiply.

Convert the improper fraction to a mixed number, if necessary.

$\frac{\overset{5}{\cancel{25}}}{\underset{1}{\cancel{2}}} \times \frac{\overset{2}{\cancel{4}}}{\underset{3}{\cancel{15}}} = \frac{5 \times 2}{1 \times 3} = \frac{10}{3} = 3\frac{1}{3}$

Henry can make 3 birdhouses.

Problem Solving

For **29** through **31**, use the table at the right.

29. How many coffee tables can Brian make from an 8-foot board? Explain.

30. How many lamp bases can Brian build with the lumber needed for a coffee table? Explain.

31. If Brian makes 4 magazine holders from one 8-foot board, will he have enough lumber left to make any of the items shown? Explain.

The chart below identifies the amount of lumber needed for each item.

Data

Item	Lumber
Lamp base	$1\frac{1}{4}$ ft
Patio table	$3\frac{3}{8}$ ft
Coffee table	$4\frac{2}{3}$ ft
Magazine holder	$1\frac{7}{8}$ ft

32. Geometry What kind of angle is shown below?

A Acute
B Right
C Obtuse
D Straight

33. The bird-watching club is going to a national park this weekend. How many people are going on the trip?

A 5
B 8
C 10
D 12

34. Writing to Explain Marcy and her friends are making ponchos for the band. Explain how to find the number of ponchos they could make from 26 yards of fabric if each poncho takes $1\frac{1}{2}$ yards of fabric.

35. Write a Problem Write your own word problem that involves dividing with mixed numbers.

Lesson

12-8

AF 1.1, Grade 6 Write and solve one-step linear equations in one variable. Also MR 2.3.

Problem Solving

Draw a Picture and Write an Equation

The string on Josie's kite is $12\frac{1}{2}$ feet long. Marcus's kite string is 5 times as long as Josie's kite string. How long is the string on Marcus's kite?

Marcus ?

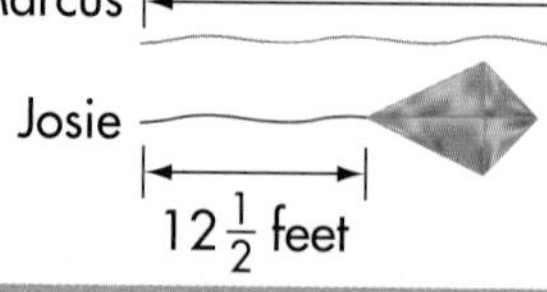

Guided Practice*

Do you know HOW?

Solve. Draw a picture and write an equation.

1. If one bottle of yogurt contains $6\frac{1}{4}$ ounces, how much yogurt is in a 4-pack of yogurt?

Do you UNDERSTAND?

2. How do you know your answer for Exercise 1 is reasonable?

3. **Write a Problem** Write a real-world problem that you can solve by using multiplication of fractions.

Independent Practice

4. Danielle has a board that is $41\frac{2}{3}$ inches long. It is 5 times as long as the board Gina has. How long is Gina's board? Write an equation, then solve.

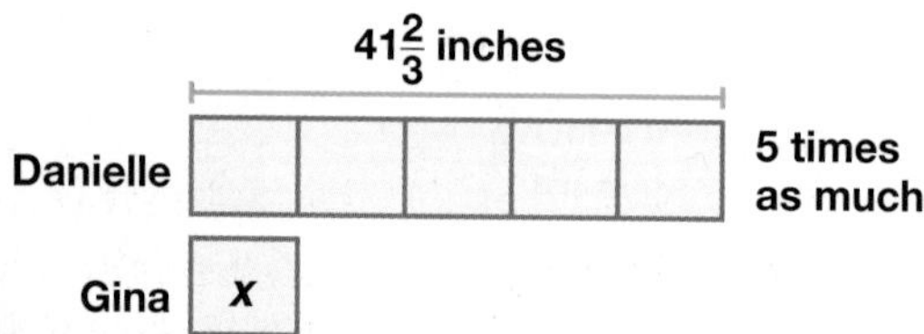

For **5** through **7**, draw a picture, write an equation, then solve.

5. Phil collected $3\frac{1}{2}$ buckets of shells at the beach. Caleb collected three times as many buckets. How many buckets of shells did Caleb collect?

- What do I know?
- What am I asked to find?
- What diagram can I use to help understand the problem?
- Can I use addition, subtraction, multiplication, or division?
- Is all of my work correct?
- Did I answer the right question?
- Is my answer reasonable?

*For another example, see Set H on page 293.

Read and Understand

What do I know?

Josie's kite string is $12\frac{1}{2}$ feet long. Marcus's kite string is 5 times as long.

What am I asked to find?

The length of the string on Marcus's kite

Plan and Solve

Draw a Picture

	n feet					
Marcus	$12\frac{1}{2}$	$12\frac{1}{2}$	$12\frac{1}{2}$	$12\frac{1}{2}$	$12\frac{1}{2}$	**5 times as long**
Josie	$12\frac{1}{2}$					

Write an Equation

Let n = the length of Marcus's kite.

$12\frac{1}{2} \times 5 = n$

$62\frac{1}{2} = n$

Marcus's kite string is $62\frac{1}{2}$ feet long.

6. Josh volunteered at the zoo for 14 hours in one month. This was $3\frac{1}{2}$ times as many hours as Gina volunteered. How many hours did Gina volunteer?

7. Tina is making a sign to advertise the school play. The width of the sign is $2\frac{2}{3}$ feet. If the length is $4\frac{1}{2}$ times as much, then what is the length of the sign?

8. Brown bats sleep for 20 hours each day. How many hours per week are they awake? How many hours per year are they awake?

9. Brenda says a good estimate for $50 \times 31\frac{3}{4}$ is 800. Is she correct? Explain.

10. Wanda needs to buy at least 50 stickers. Will 1 sheet of stickers be enough? How do you know?

11. Jin's friends collected 149 bottles of water for riders going on a bike trip. If each rider needs 4 bottles, how many riders can they supply with water?

12. **Think About the Process** A ticket to Los Angeles costs \$390, and a ticket to Hong Kong costs $2\frac{1}{2}$ times as much. Which equation can you solve to show how much the ticket to Hong Kong costs?

A $\$390 + \$390 = c$

B $\$390 \times 2\frac{1}{2} = c$

C $\$390 \div 2\frac{1}{2} = c$

D $(2 \times \$390) + (2 \times \$390) = c$

13. **Think About the Process** Each shelf holds 24 books. There are 8 shelves. Which equation could you solve to find how many books there are in all?

A $24 + 8 = b$

B $24 - 8 = b$

C $24 \times 8 = b$

D $24 \div 8 = b$

Test Prep

1. How many $\frac{3}{4}$s are in 6? (12-3)

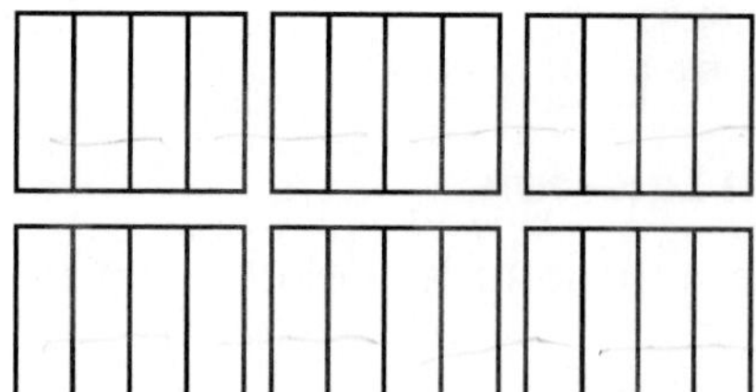

A $4\frac{1}{2}$

B $6\frac{3}{4}$

C 8

D 24

2. Alberto runs $3\frac{1}{4}$ miles each day. Which of the following can be used to find n, the number of miles he will run in a week? (12-8)

***n* total miles**

$3\frac{1}{4}$	$3\frac{1}{4}$	$3\frac{1}{4}$	$3\frac{1}{4}$	$3\frac{1}{4}$	$3\frac{1}{4}$	$3\frac{1}{4}$

A $3\frac{1}{4} \times n = 7$

B $7 \times n = 3\frac{1}{4}$

C $7 \times 3\frac{1}{4} = n$

D $3\frac{1}{4} \div 7 = n$

3. If the diameter of a tree trunk is growing $\frac{1}{4}$ inch each year, how many years will it take for the diameter to grow 8 inches? (12-3)

A 2 years

B 8 years

C 24 years

D 32 years

4. Monica lives $\frac{8}{10}$ of a mile from Wally and $\frac{3}{4}$ of this distance from Adam. How far does Monica live from Adam? (12-2)

A $\frac{1}{2}$ mile

B $\frac{3}{5}$ mile

C $\frac{15}{16}$ mile

D $1\frac{11}{20}$ miles

5. Mrs. Webster wants to divide the milk shown into 6 equal servings. What will be the size, in gallons, of each serving? (12-4)

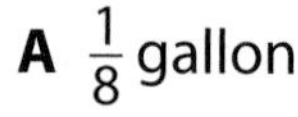

A $\frac{1}{8}$ gallon

B $\frac{2}{9}$ gallon

C $\frac{1}{4}$ gallon

D $4\frac{1}{2}$ gallons

6. Mary is making a window covering that is $6\frac{1}{2}$ feet wide, divided into 5 equal sections. What is the width of each section? (12-7)

A $1\frac{3}{10}$ feet

B $1\frac{1}{2}$ feet

C $6\frac{1}{10}$ feet

D $32\frac{1}{2}$ inches

7. What is $\frac{5}{6} \div \frac{5}{11}$? (12-4)

A $\frac{1}{66}$

B $\frac{25}{66}$

C $\frac{6}{11}$

D $1\frac{5}{6}$

8. Tracy took a quiz containing 12 items. If she got $\frac{5}{6}$ of the items correct, how many did she get correct? (12-1)

A 5

B 6

C 9

D 10

9. A retaining wall on the playground is shown below. If $\frac{2}{3}$ of the wall is made from brick, what is the height of the brick portion of the wall? (12-6)

A $2\frac{1}{2}$ feet

B $1\frac{5}{6}$ feet

C $\frac{7}{12}$ foot

D $\frac{2}{9}$ foot

10. Which of the following is equal to $\frac{2}{9} \div \frac{4}{7}$? (12-4)

A $\frac{9}{2} \div \frac{4}{7}$

B $\frac{2}{9} \times \frac{7}{4}$

C $\frac{2}{9} \div \frac{7}{4}$

D $\frac{9}{2} \times \frac{4}{7}$

11. What is $\frac{1}{4} \times \frac{1}{6}$? (12-2)

A $\frac{1}{5}$

B $\frac{1}{10}$

C $\frac{1}{12}$

D $\frac{1}{24}$

12. What product does the diagram show? (12-2)

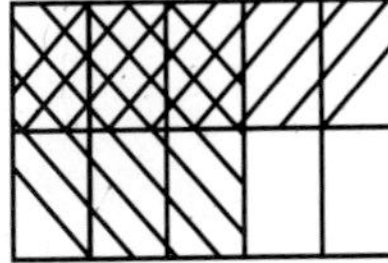

A $\frac{1}{2} \times \frac{3}{5} = \frac{3}{10}$

B $\frac{1}{2} \times \frac{3}{4} = \frac{3}{8}$

C $\frac{1}{3} \times \frac{1}{2} = \frac{1}{6}$

D $\frac{1}{3} \times \frac{3}{5} = \frac{1}{5}$

13. Which equals $5\frac{4}{5} \div 3\frac{2}{3}$? (12-7)

A $\frac{29}{5} \times \frac{11}{3}$

B $\frac{29}{5} \times \frac{3}{11}$

C $5\frac{4}{5} \times 3\frac{3}{2}$

D $\frac{5}{29} \times \frac{3}{11}$

14. What is $2\frac{2}{5} \times 3\frac{1}{4}$? (12-6)

A $7\frac{4}{5}$

B $7\frac{7}{10}$

C $6\frac{1}{10}$

D $3\frac{1}{5}$

15. Two-fifths of the students in Mrs. Navares' fifth grade class ride the bus to school. What other information is needed to find the number of students in her class that ride the bus? (12-5)

A The number of students who walk to school.

B The number of students in the fifth grade.

C The number of students in Mrs. Navares' class.

D The number of different buses the students ride.

Reteaching

Set A, pages 270–271

Find $\frac{2}{3}$ of 6.

One Way

$\frac{1}{3}$ of 6 is 2.

$\frac{2}{3}$ is twice as much as $\frac{1}{3}$.

So, $\frac{2}{3}$ of 6 is 4.

Another Way

Multiply first, and then divide.

$\frac{2}{3} \times 6 = \frac{12}{3} = 4$

Remember that the fraction bar means to divide.

Find each product. Simplify if possible.

1. $4 \times \frac{1}{2}$
2. $\frac{3}{4}$ of 16
3. $24 \times \frac{1}{8}$
4. $\frac{4}{7}$ of 28
5. $10 \times \frac{1}{5}$
6. $\frac{5}{6}$ of 24
7. $16 \times \frac{1}{4}$
8. $\frac{7}{8}$ of 32

Set B, pages 272–274

Find $\frac{5}{6} \times \frac{2}{3}$.

Multiply.

$\frac{5}{6} \times \frac{2}{3} = \frac{5 \times 2}{6 \times 3} = \frac{10}{18}$

Simplify, if possible. $\frac{10}{18} = \frac{5}{9}$

Remember to multiply both the numerators and denominators.

Find each product. Simplify, if possible.

1. $\frac{3}{5} \times \frac{1}{4}$
2. $\frac{6}{7} \times \frac{1}{2}$
3. $\frac{4}{9} \times \frac{2}{3}$
4. $\frac{3}{8} \times \frac{1}{3}$

Set C, pages 276–277

Find $6 \div \frac{2}{3}$.

What fraction in thirds is equivalent to 6? $\frac{18}{3}$

Or, what number divided by 3 = 6? $\frac{18}{3}$

$\frac{18}{3} \div \frac{2}{3} = \frac{18 \div 2}{3 \div 3} = \frac{9}{1} = 9$

Remember to change the whole number to its equivalent fraction.

Find each quotient. Simplify, if possible.

1. $3 \div \frac{3}{8}$
2. $6 \div \frac{1}{6}$
3. $8 \div \frac{1}{2}$
4. $9 \div \frac{3}{4}$
5. $4 \div \frac{4}{5}$
6. $3 \div \frac{2}{3}$

Set D, pages 278–280

Find $\frac{2}{3} \div \frac{1}{8}$.

Rewrite the division problem as a multiplication problem. Multiply by the reciprocal of the divisor.

$\frac{2}{3} \div \frac{1}{8} = \frac{2}{3} \times \frac{8}{1} = \frac{16}{3} = 5\frac{1}{3}$

($\frac{1}{8}$: divisor; $\frac{8}{1}$: reciprocal)

Remember to multiply by the reciprocal of the divisor.

Find each quotient. Simplify, if possible.

1. $\frac{1}{2} \div \frac{2}{7}$
2. $\frac{1}{3} \div \frac{1}{2}$
3. $\frac{2}{3} \div \frac{1}{8}$
4. $\frac{1}{4} \div \frac{1}{5}$
5. $\frac{3}{4} \div \frac{2}{9}$
6. $\frac{1}{6} \div \frac{8}{9}$
7. $\frac{7}{8} \div \frac{3}{4}$
8. $\frac{3}{4} \div \frac{5}{6}$

Set E, pages 282–283

Decide if the problem has extra or missing information. Then solve if you can.

Chris has 7 bowls. Each bowl has 4 types of fruit. How many apples does Chris have?

Identify what you know: 7 bowls, 4 types of fruit.
Identify the question: How many apples does Chris have?

Can you solve? No, it does not tell how many apples are in each bowl.

Remember that some problems have too much information.

1. Anna has $35.65. She went to the store and bought 3 items. How much change did she get back?
2. Donna bought one pair of shoes for $29.50 and another for half that price. She paid with a $50 bill. How much did the other pair of shoes cost?

Set F, pages 284–285

Find $3\frac{1}{2} \times 2\frac{7}{8}$.

Estimate. $3\frac{1}{2} \times 2\frac{7}{8}$ is about 4×3 or 12.

Change mixed numbers to improper fractions and multiply.

$\frac{7}{2} \times \frac{23}{8} = \frac{161}{16} = 10\frac{1}{16}$

Remember to check your answer against your original estimate to be sure your answer is reasonable.

1. $2\frac{1}{3} \times 4\frac{1}{5}$
2. $4\frac{1}{2} \times 6\frac{2}{3}$
3. $5\frac{1}{2} \times 3\frac{1}{3}$
4. $2\frac{1}{8} \times 2\frac{2}{7}$

Set G, pages 286–287

Find $9\frac{1}{2} \div 2\frac{2}{3}$.

Change mixed numbers to improper fractions. Then multiply by the reciprocal of the divisor.

$\frac{19}{2} \div \frac{8}{3} = \frac{19}{2} \times \frac{3}{8} = \frac{57}{16} = 3\frac{9}{16}$.

Remember to change your divisor to an improper fraction **before** finding its reciprocal.

1. $3\frac{2}{3} \div 1\frac{1}{2}$
2. $6\frac{1}{2} \div 2\frac{3}{4}$
3. $1\frac{3}{16} \div 1\frac{3}{8}$
4. $8\frac{1}{4} \div 3\frac{1}{3}$

Set H, pages 288–289

A $4\frac{1}{2}$-foot board is cut into 3 equal pieces. How long is each piece?

$4\frac{1}{2}$ feet

x	x	x

Length of each piece

$x = 4\frac{1}{2} \div 3$

$= \frac{9}{2} \times \frac{1}{3} = 1\frac{1}{2}$

Each piece is $1\frac{1}{2}$ feet.

Remember to draw a picture to help write an equation.

1. A total of 60 students are being separated into 5 equal teams. How many students are on each team?

Topic 13

Length, Perimeter, and Area

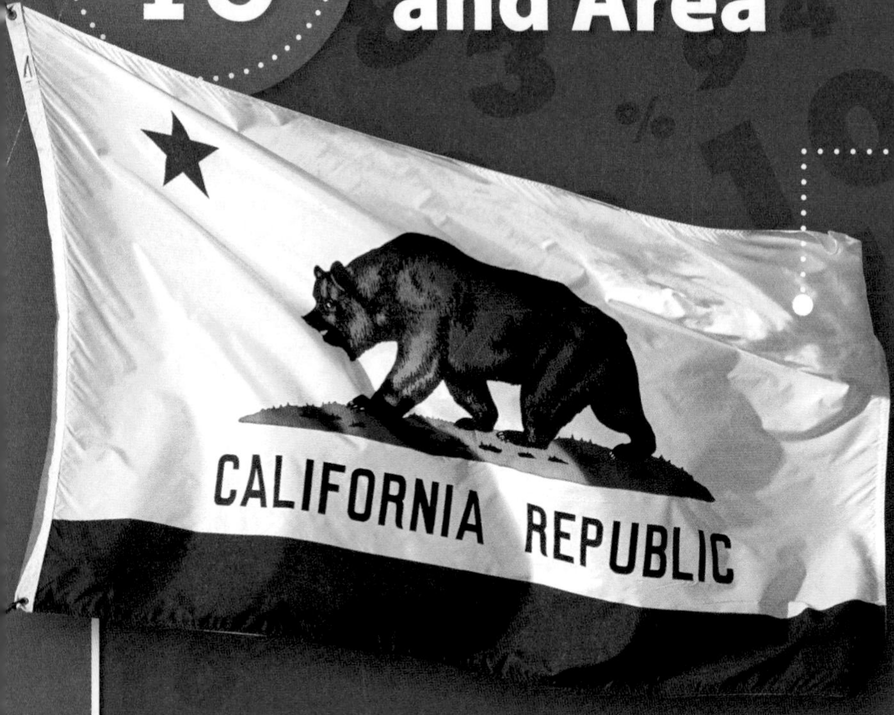

1 What is the perimeter of this California State Flag? You will find out in Lesson 13-3.

2 Mechanics put buses on parallelogram lifts in order to work on the bottom of the bus. What is the area of the parallelogram that is used to hold up a bus? You will find out in Lesson 13-5.

3

The East Room is the largest room in the White House. What is its area? You will find out in Lesson 13-4.

4

Cowboys on cattle drives were called to dinner by the ringing of a triangular bell. What is the area of a triangular dinner bell? You will find out in Lesson 13-6.

Review What You Know!

Vocabulary

Choose the best term from the box.

- divisor
- quotient
- hundredths
- tenths

1. The number 2.45 has a four in the __?__ place and a five in the __?__ place.

2. In 36 ÷ 9 = 4, the 4 is called the __?__, and the 9 is called the __?__.

Division Facts

3. 24 ÷ 6	**4.** 81 ÷ 9	**5.** 49 ÷ 7
6. 36 ÷ 6	**7.** 40 ÷ 8	**8.** 63 ÷ 9
9. 42 ÷ 7	**10.** 64 ÷ 8	**11.** 48 ÷ 8
12. 25 ÷ 5	**13.** 36 ÷ 9	**14.** 35 ÷ 7
15. 48 ÷ 6	**16.** 56 ÷ 8	**17.** 54 ÷ 9

Multiplication Facts

18. 8 × 8	**19.** 9 × 4	**20.** 7 × 4
21. 10 × 10	**22.** 11 × 11	**23.** 12 × 12
24. 8 × 4	**25.** 7 × 8	**26.** 10 × 8
27. 7 × 6	**28.** 8 × 5	**29.** 9 × 6
30. 9 × 9	**31.** 8 × 6	**32.** 7 × 9

Properties of Multiplication

Writing to Explain Write an answer to the question.

33. How can the Associative Property of Multiplication be used to compute 14 × 2 × 50 mentally?

Lesson

13-1

MG 1.4 Differentiate between, and use appropriate units of measures for, two- and three-dimensional objects (i.e., find the perimeter, area, volume). Also NS 1.9 (Grade 4)

Using Customary Units of Length

Hands-On
inch ruler

How can you use fractions to measure more precisely?

Since an inch is divided into equal parts, you can use fractions to measure lengths. You can estimate the length of this DVD case first. What is the length of the DVD case to the nearest $\frac{1}{8}$ inch?

Guided Practice*

Do you know HOW?

For **1** and **2**, measure each segment to the nearest inch, $\frac{1}{2}$ inch, $\frac{1}{4}$ inch, and $\frac{1}{8}$ inch.

1.

2.

Do you UNDERSTAND?

3. In the example above, why isn't the length of the DVD case 8 inches to the nearest inch?

4. **Writing to Explain** Would it be reasonable to measure pieces of lumber needed to build a house only to the nearest inch?

Independent Practice

In **5** through **7**, use a ruler to measure each object to the nearest inch, $\frac{1}{2}$ inch, $\frac{1}{4}$ inch, and $\frac{1}{8}$ inch.

5. 

6. 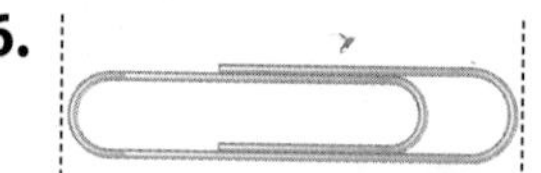

7. 

In **8** through **13**, estimate each measure first. Then use a ruler to measure each to the nearest $\frac{1}{4}$ inch and $\frac{1}{8}$ inch.

8. The length of a pencil

9. The width of your foot

10. The length of a piece of chalk

11. The length of your index finger

12. The length of your math book

13. The width of your hand

*For another example, see Set A on page 314.

Your estimate for the length of the DVD case should be about 7 inches. You can use a ruler to find the length to the nearest 1 in., $\frac{1}{2}$ in., $\frac{1}{4}$ in., and $\frac{1}{8}$ in.

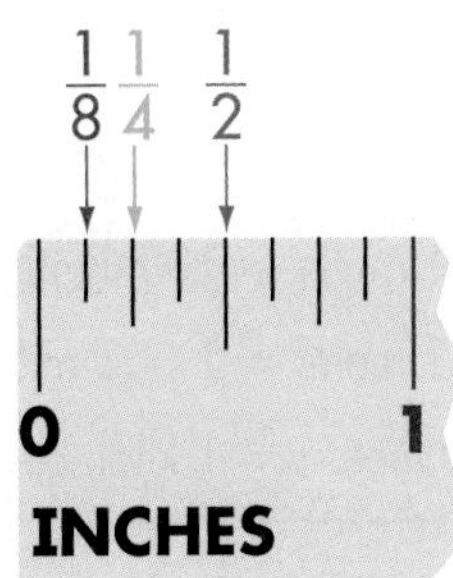

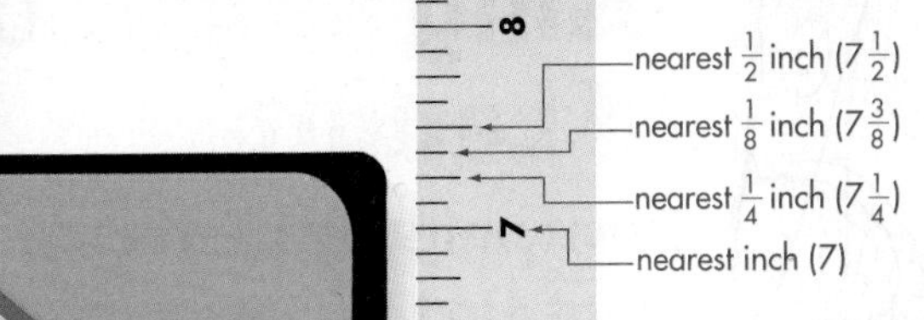

Since the length of the DVD case ends at $7\frac{3}{8}$ in., this is its length to the nearest $\frac{1}{8}$ inch.

Problem Solving

14. Which line segment measures about $2\frac{1}{2}$ inches long?

A ├────────┤

B ├──────┤

C ├────────────┤

D ├──────────┤

15. **Think About the Process** Mae spent \$12 on a new purse, \$6 on lunch, and \$14 for a book. She had \$12 when she got home. Which expression shows much money Mae started with?

A $12 - 12 + 6 + 14$

B $(2 \times 12) + 14 + 6$

C $12 - 6 - (14 + 12)$

D $2 \times (12 + 12) - 14$

16. **Writing to Explain** When you measure the length of an object, will your measure ever be exact? Explain.

17. Jan has \$49 to spend on poster board. If each poster board costs \$3, how many poster boards can she buy?

18. **Estimation** Sheri played 4 computer games in 48 minutes. She scored about 825 points per game. About how many points did she score per minute?

19. **Number Sense** To find $8.3 \times 1{,}000$, how many places will you move the decimal point to the right? How many zeros will you need to annex? What is the product?

20. The measure of the length of a paper clip to the nearest inch, $\frac{1}{2}$ inch, and $\frac{1}{4}$ inch is 2 inches. How is this possible?

21. **Writing to Explain** Fifteen pounds of meat cost \$26.85. Is it reasonable to say that the price per pound is \$11? Explain.

Lesson
13-2

MG 1.4 Differentiate between, and use appropriate units of measures for, two- and three-dimensional objects (i.e., find the perimeter, area, volume).

Using Metric Units of Length

What units are used to measure length in the metric system?

Measurements in the metric system are based on the meter. The chart at the right lists other commonly used metric units and their equivalents.

Data

Metric Equivalents
1 centimeter = 10 millimeters (mm)
1 meter = 100 centimeters (cm)
1 meter = 1,000 millimeters (mm)
1,000 meters = 1 kilometer (km)

Another Example How do you measure length using metric units?

CM 1 2 3 4 5 6 7 8 9 10 11 12 13 14 15

To the nearest centimeter: 12 cm   To the nearest millimeter: 118 mm

Guided Practice*

Do you know HOW?

1. Which unit would be most appropriate to measure the length of a kitchen?
2. Measure this segment to the nearest centimeter and nearest millimeter.

Do you UNDERSTAND?

3. What two units can be used to measure the thickness of a stack of 10 dimes?
4. **Writing to Explain** Why is the millimeter not an appropriate unit to measure the distance across a town?

Independent Practice

For **5** through **7**, write mm, cm, m, or km as the most appropriate unit.

5. Thickness of a fingernail
6. Length of a picnic table
7. Length of a road

In **8** through **13**, measure each segment to the nearest centimeter and to the nearest millimeter.

8.
9.
10.
11.
12.
13.

*For another example, see Set B on page 314.

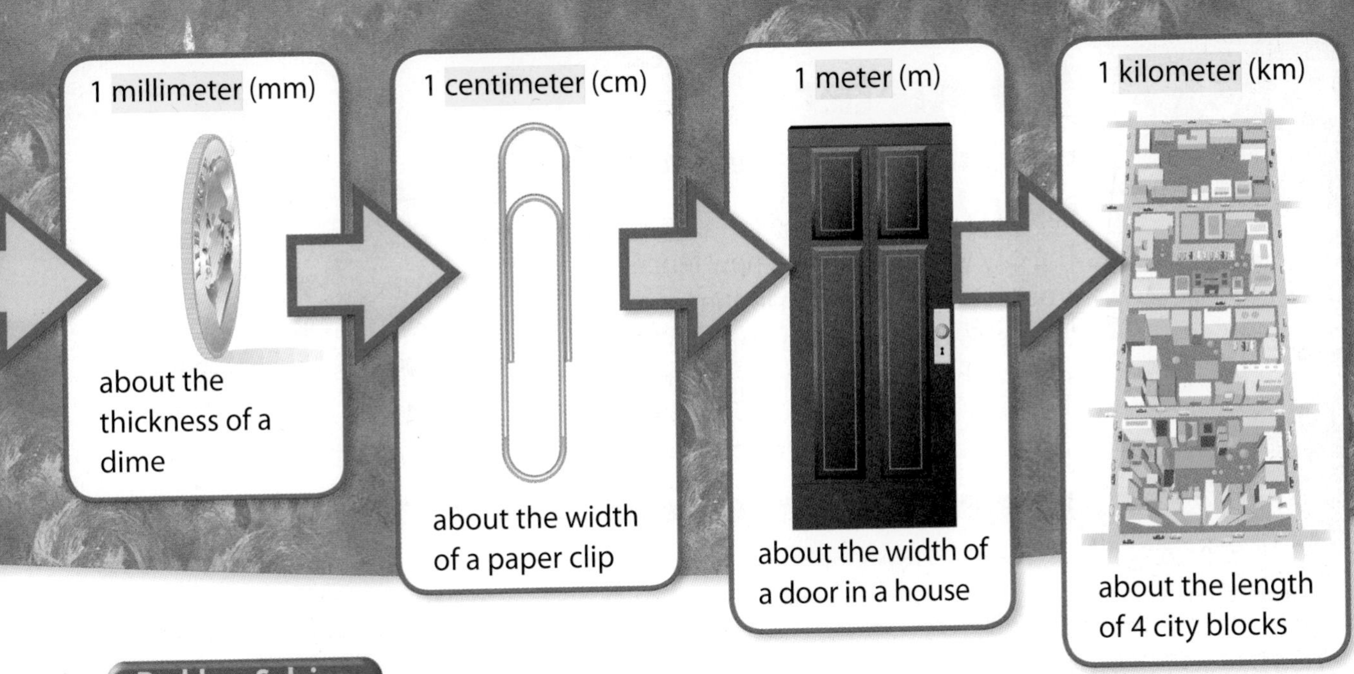

Problem Solving

14. Which object is 65 millimeters wide?

A

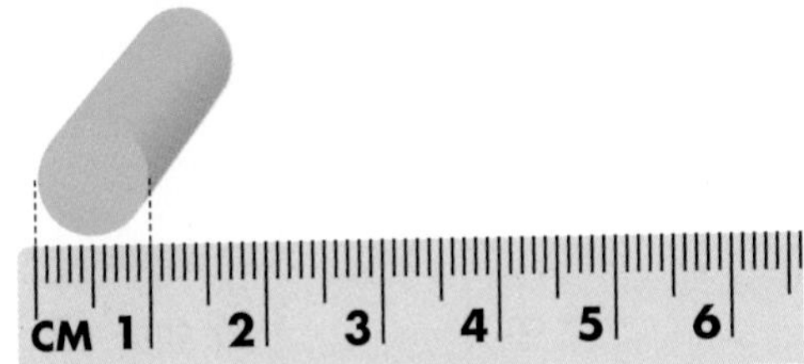

B

C

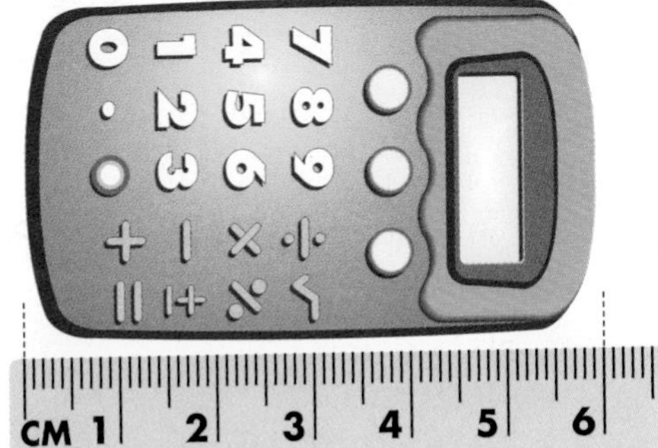

D

CM 1 2 3 4 5 6

15. **Writing to Explain** Darcy is estimating how much fabric she will need to make a new jacket. Is estimating reasonable in this situation? Why or why not?

16. Dana ordered 1 medium cheese pizza with 8 slices. She ate 2 pieces. Write 2 equivalent fractions to show the part of the pizza Dana did NOT eat.

17. Choose from the measures listed below to determine the most appropriate lengths.

40 mm	**2 m**
18 cm	**200 km**

a The distance between two cities

b The length of a bicycle

c The length of a drinking straw

d The length of a caterpillar

18. **Reasoning** If a measuring cup has $\frac{1}{4}$ cup milk in it, what fraction represents the amount of milk needed to finish filling the cup?

Lesson

13-3

MG 1.4 Grade 4 Understand and use formulas to solve problems involving perimeters and areas of rectangles and squares. Use those formulas to find the areas of more complex figures by dividing the figures into basic shapes.
Also **MG 1.4**

Perimeter

How can you find the distance around a polygon?

The city wants to build a new fence around the rose garden in the town square. Perimeter is the distance around the outside of any polygon.

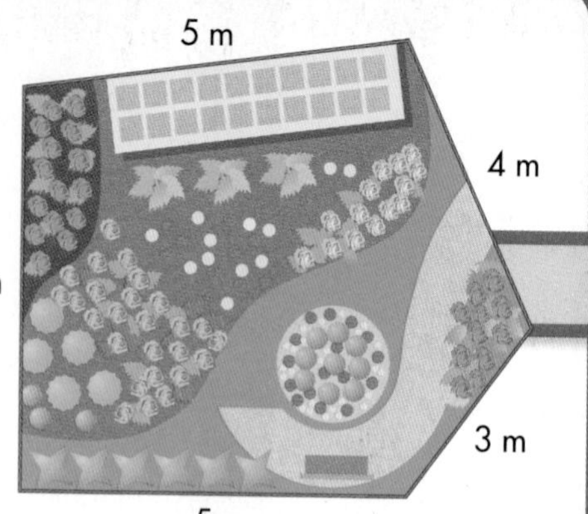

Another Example **How can you use a formula to find the perimeter of a square and a rectangle?**

A formula is a rule that uses symbols.

Use a formula to find the perimeter of the square.

Perimeter = 4 × side

$P = 4 \times s$

$P = 4 \times 29 = 116$ cm

Tip s = side

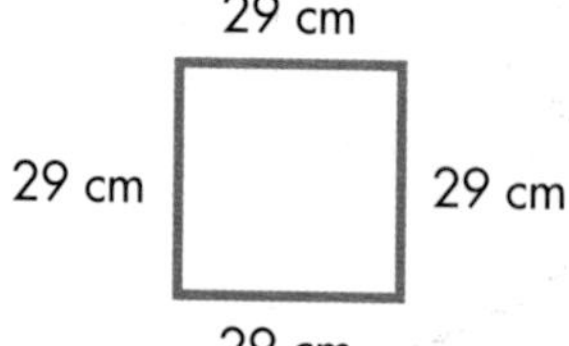

Use either of these formulas to find the perimeter of the rectangle.

8 m

5 m

One Way

Perimeter = (2 × length) + (2 × width)

$P = (2 \times \ell) + (2 \times w)$

$P = (2 \times 8) + (2 \times 5)$

$P = 16 + 10 = 26$ m

Tip ℓ = length
w = width

Another Way

Perimeter = 2 × (length + width)

$P = 2 \times (\ell + w)$

$P = 2 \times (8 + 5)$

$P = 2 \times 13 = 26$ m

Explain It

1. Will the formula for finding the perimeter of a square work for finding the perimeter of a rectangle?

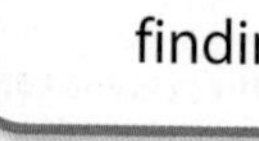

Find the perimeter of the rose garden to find the total length of the new fence needed.

Perimeter is equal to the sum of the side lengths of a polygon.

One Way

Add the lengths of the sides.

$P = 5 + 5 + 4 + 3 + 5$
$P = 22$ m

The perimeter of the rose garden is 22 m.

Another Way

Since the longest side lengths are the same, multiplication can be used in the equation.

$P = 5 + 5 + 4 + 3 + 5$
$P = (3 \times 5) + 4 + 3$
$P = \quad 15 \quad + \quad 7$
$P = 22$ m

The perimeter of the rose garden is 22 m.

Guided Practice*

Do you know HOW?

In **1** and **2**, find the perimeter of each figure.

1. 6 cm, 6 cm, 2 cm, 2 cm, 8 cm

2. 12 in., 12 in., 10 in.

Do you UNDERSTAND?

3. Look at the dimensions of the garden above. If the longest sides of the garden were 9 m, how long would the fence need to be?

4. **Writing to Explain** In the above example, why can you add the lengths of the sides of the garden in any order to find its perimeter?

Independent Practice

For **5** through **10**, find the perimeter of each figure.

5.

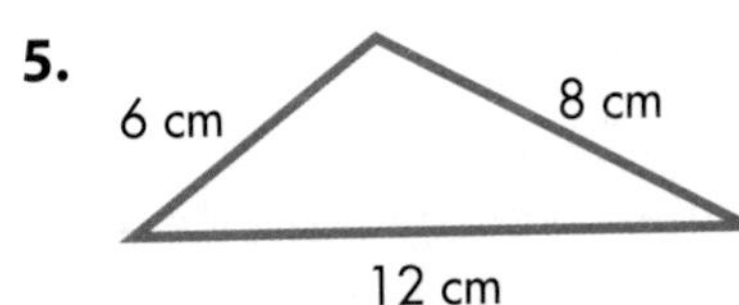

6. 12 m, 12 m, 12 m, 12 m

7.

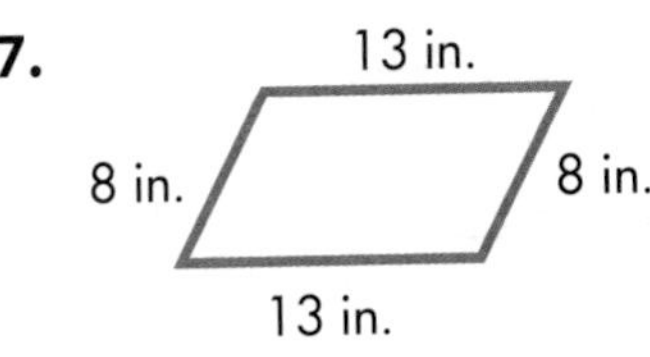

8.

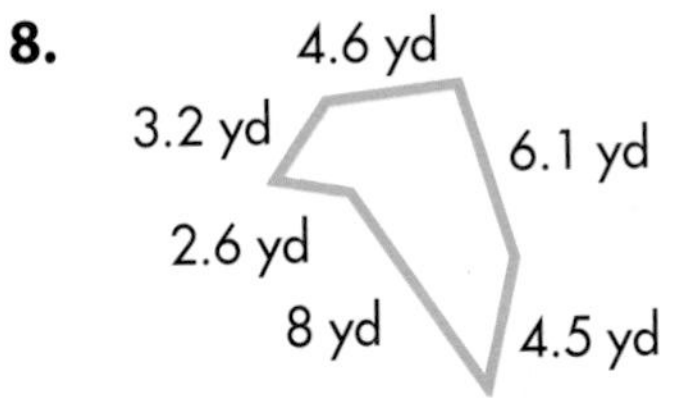

9.

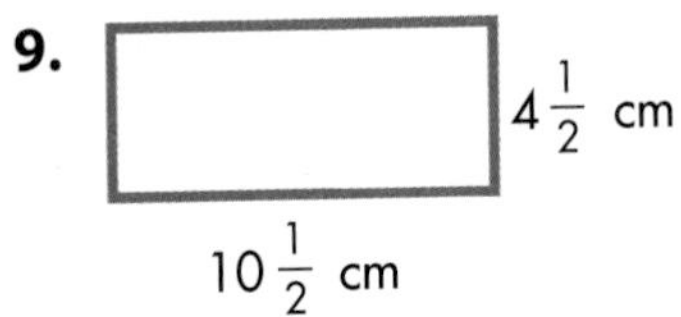

10.

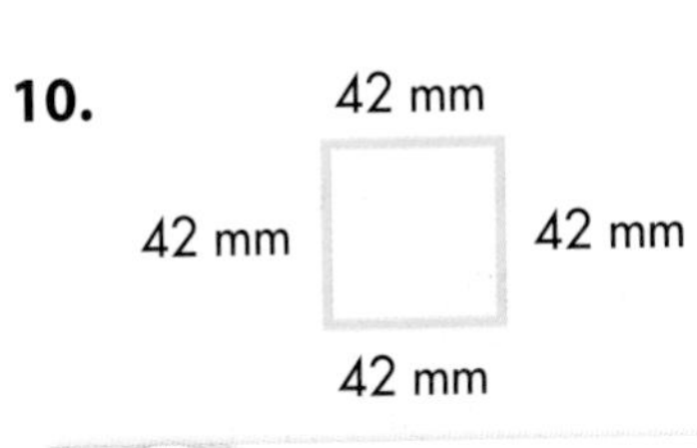

DIGITAL Animated Glossary **www.pearsonsuccessnet.com**

For another example, see Set C on page 314.

Problem Solving

11. **Number Sense** The perimeter of an equilateral triangle is 51 feet. What is the length of each of its sides?

A 13 ft **C** 17 ft

B 15 ft **D** 21 ft

12. Find the perimeter of a parallelogram with sides measuring $3\frac{3}{10}$ m, $8\frac{5}{10}$ m, $3\frac{3}{10}$ m, and $8\frac{5}{10}$ m.

A $23\frac{8}{10}$ m **C** $24\frac{6}{10}$ m

B $23\frac{3}{5}$ m **D** 24 m

13. What is the perimeter of the Pentagon near Washington, D.C.?

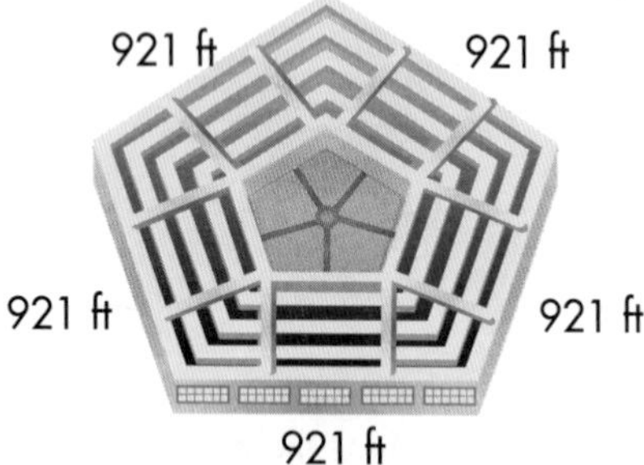

14. What is the perimeter of the California State flag?

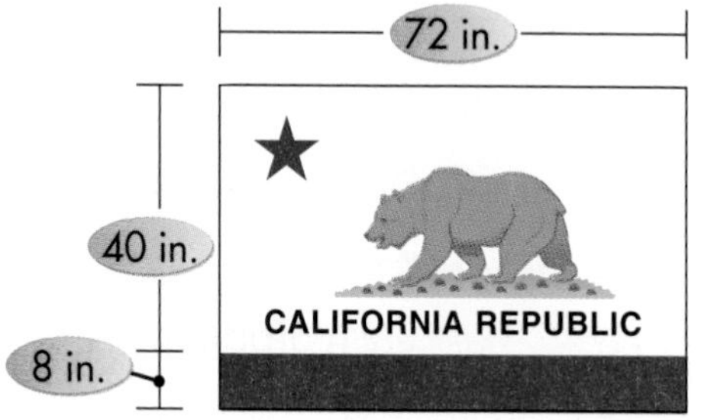

15. **Writing to Explain** Alfonso said that the perimeter of this triangle is 66 cm. What was his error? What should the perimeter be? Explain.

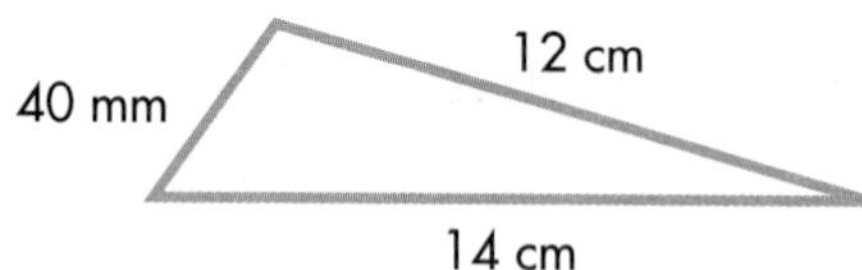

16. Which unit (mm, cm, m, or km) would be the most appropriate for each measurement?

a Distance across Lake Michigan

b Length of a spoon

c Thickness of an envelope

d Height of a building

17. Which is the least common denominator of $\frac{1}{12}$ and $\frac{4}{5}$?

A 5 **C** 30

B 12 **D** 60

18. **Reasoning** Maria says her pencil is 1.7 meters long. Is this measurement reasonable? Explain.

19. It takes Neptune about 165 Earth years to complete one orbit around the Sun. How many Earth months does it take Neptune to orbit the Sun once?

20. The planet Neptune was discovered in 1846. Neptune's average distance from the Sun is four billion, four hundred ninety-eight million, two hundred fifty-two thousand, nine hundred kilometers. Write this number in standard form.

21. Stan has $2\frac{3}{4}$ pounds of oranges, $1\frac{1}{4}$ pounds of lemons, and $1\frac{3}{4}$ pounds of limes. How many pounds of fruit does Stan have altogether?

Find each quotient. Simplify if possible.

1. $5 \div \frac{9}{10}$ **2.** $10 \div \frac{1}{2}$ **3.** $4 \div \frac{3}{8}$ **4.** $6 \div \frac{3}{4}$

5. $8 \div \frac{7}{8}$ **6.** $2 \div \frac{3}{4}$ **7.** $12 \div \frac{1}{12}$ **8.** $3 \div \frac{1}{4}$

Find each quotient. Simplify if possible.

9. $\frac{1}{3} \div \frac{2}{5}$ **10.** $\frac{1}{2} \div \frac{1}{4}$ **11.** $\frac{5}{6} \div \frac{2}{3}$ **12.** $\frac{3}{8} \div \frac{3}{4}$ **13.** $\frac{7}{12} \div \frac{1}{2}$

14. $\frac{3}{10} \div \frac{2}{5}$ **15.** $\frac{2}{3} \div \frac{1}{6}$ **16.** $\frac{2}{9} \div \frac{2}{3}$ **17.** $\frac{3}{5} \div \frac{3}{5}$ **18.** $\frac{7}{8} \div \frac{5}{8}$

Find each product. Simplify if possible.

19. $2\frac{1}{2} \times 3\frac{1}{4}$ **20.** $1\frac{3}{8} \times 4\frac{2}{3}$ **21.** $3\frac{1}{2} \times 3\frac{1}{2}$ **22.** $1\frac{2}{5} \times 1\frac{3}{5}$

Error Search Find each product or quotient that is not correct. Write it correctly and explain the error.

23. $6 \div \frac{1}{6} = \frac{1}{36}$ **24.** $\frac{5}{6} \div \frac{1}{2} = 1\frac{2}{3}$ **25.** $2\frac{1}{2} \times 3\frac{1}{2} = 6\frac{1}{4}$

Number Sense

Estimating and Reasoning Write whether each statement is true or false. Explain your reasoning.

26. The expression $(21 \div 3) + (5 - 4) \times 2$ equals 9.

27. The product of 9 and 6.65 is closer to 54 than 63.

28. The sum of $\frac{2}{3}$ and $\frac{7}{10}$ is less than 1.

29. The quotient of $5\frac{4}{5}$ divided by 1 is 1.

30. The product of 385 and 286 is less than 120,000.

31. The difference of $4\frac{4}{5}$ and $4\frac{1}{3}$ is less than 1.

Lesson

13-4

MG 1.1 Derive and use the formula for the area of a triangle and of a parallelogram by comparing each with the formula for the area of a rectangle (i.e., two of the same triangles make a parallelogram with twice the area; a parallelogram is compared with a rectangle of the same area by pasting and cutting a right triangle on the parallelogram).
Also **MG 1.0.**

Area of Squares and Rectangles

How can a formula be used to find area?

The area of a figure is the amount of surface it covers. What are the areas of the baseball infield and the tennis court?

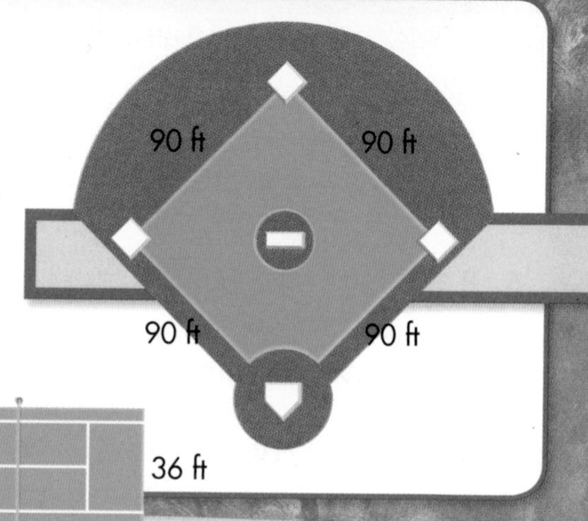

Guided Practice*

Do you know HOW?

In **1** and **2**, find the area of each figure.

1. Find the area of a square with a side that measures 34 cm.

2. Find the area of a rectangle with length 21 m and width 9 m.

Do you UNDERSTAND?

3. Which two dimensions are multiplied when finding the area of a rectangle?

4. **Writing to Explain** In the example above, how can you decide which figure has the greater area, without using the formula?

Independent Practice

For **5** through **10**, find the area of each figure.

5.

6.

7.

8.

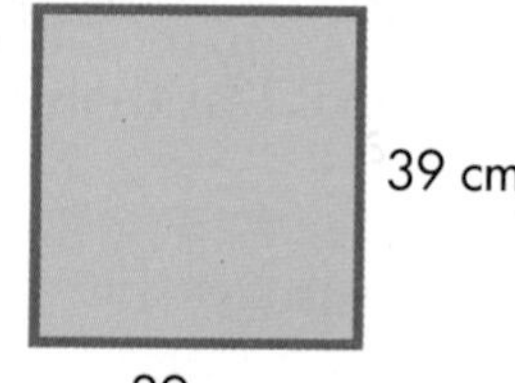

9. A rectangle with length 245 in. and width 167 in.

10. A square with a side that measures 31 yd

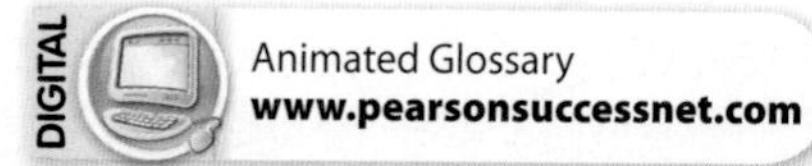

*For another example, see Set D on page 315.

The infield is a square, so all of its sides are equal.

Use the formula below to find the area of a square. Area is measured in square units.

Area = side × side

$A = s \times s = s^2$

$A = 90 \text{ feet} \times 90 \text{ feet}$

$A = 8{,}100 \text{ square feet (ft}^2\text{)}$

s
s

The area of the infield is 8,100 ft^2.

The tennis court is a rectangle, so its opposite sides are equal.

Use the formula below to find the area of a rectangle.

Area = length × width

$A = \ell \times w$

$A = 78 \text{ feet} \times 36 \text{ feet}$

$A = 2{,}808 \text{ square feet (ft}^2\text{)}$

w
ℓ

The area of the tennis court is 2,808 ft^2.

Problem Solving

11. The East Room of the White House is 79 feet long by 36 feet wide. What is the area of the room?

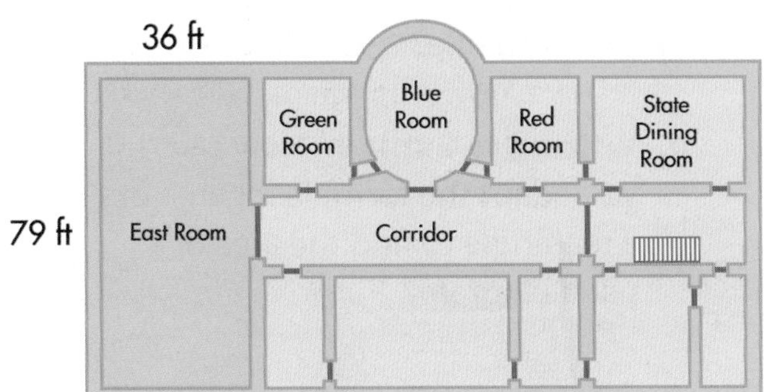

12. Ben's mom wants to buy new carpet for the family room that measures 12 feet by 11 feet. She can purchase the carpet on sale for $6 per square foot including installation. How much will Ben's mom spend to carpet the family room?

A $132

B $791

C $792

D $794

13. **Number Sense** A set of four postcards cost $1.00. Single postcards cost $0.50. What is the least amount of money you can spend to buy exactly 15 postcards?

14. Which has the greater area: a square with a side that measures 7 meters, or a 6-by-8-meter rectangle? What is the area?

For **15** through **17**, use the drawing at the right.

15. What is the perimeter of an Olympic-size swimming pool?

16. What is the area of the swimming pool?

17. What is the perimeter of each lane?

18. What is the perimeter and area of a square with a side that measures 15 m?

Olympic-Size Pool

25 m

1 2 3 4 5 6 7 8

2.5 m
2.5 m
2.5 m
2.5 m
2.5 m
2.5 m
2.5 m
2.5 m
2.5 m
2.5 m

50 m

Lesson

13-5

MG 1.1 🔑 Derive and use the formula for the area of a triangle and of a parallelogram by comparing each with the formula for the area of a rectangle (i.e., two of the same triangles make a parallelogram with twice the area; a parallelogram is compared with a rectangle of the same area by pasting and cutting a right triangle on the parallelogram).
Also **MG 1.0.**

Area of Parallelograms

How can finding the area of a rectangle help you find the area of a parallelogram?

Southwestern rugs often have parallelograms as part of the design. The base of this parallelogram is 8 cm. The height is 4 cm. What is its area?

Guided Practice*

Do you know HOW?

in **1** and **2**, find the area of each parallelogram.

1.

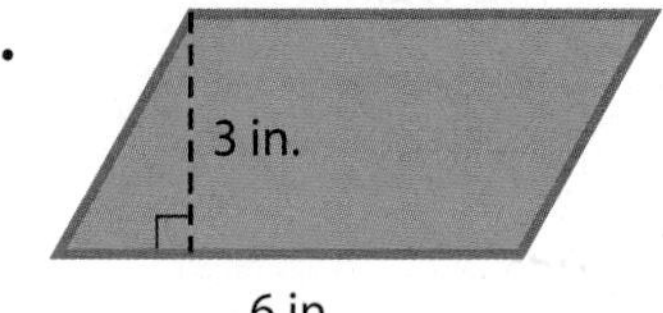

2.

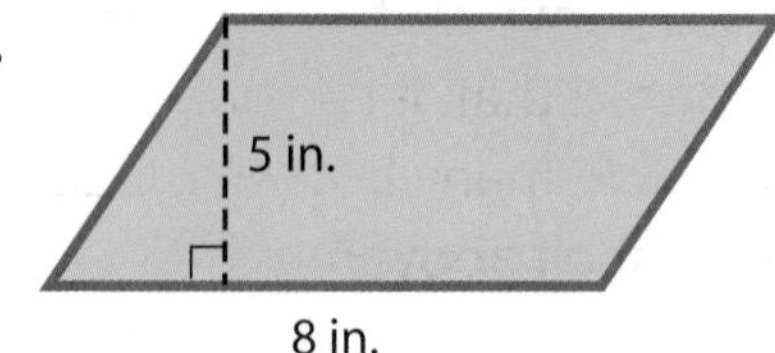

Do you UNDERSTAND?

3. In the example above, which dimensions of the parallelogram correspond to the dimensions of the rectangle?

4. **Writing to Explain** How can you adapt the formula for area of a rectangle to find the area of a parallelogram?

Independent Practice

For **5** through **11**, find the area of each parallelogram.

5.

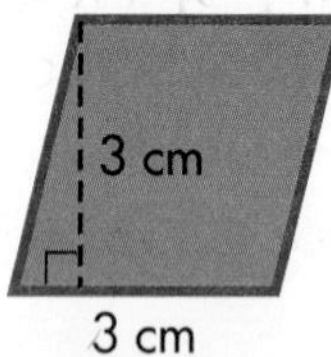

6.

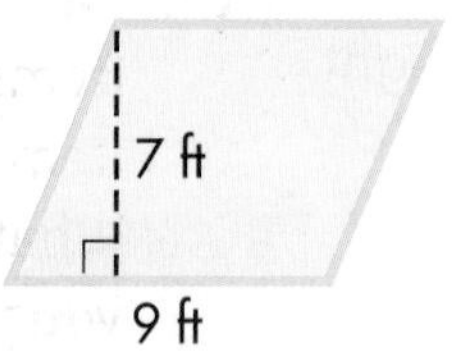

7.

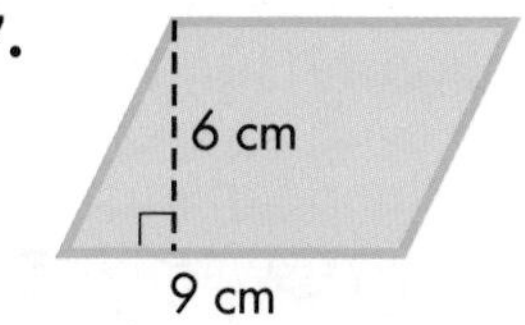

8.

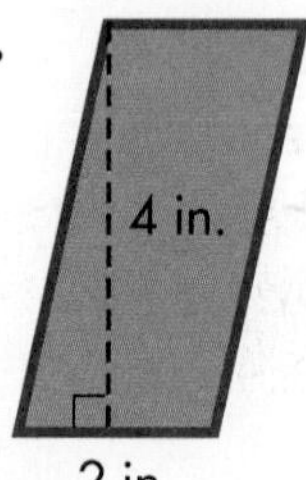

9.

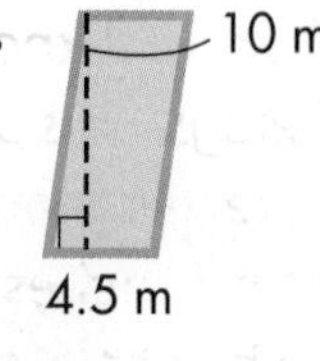

10.

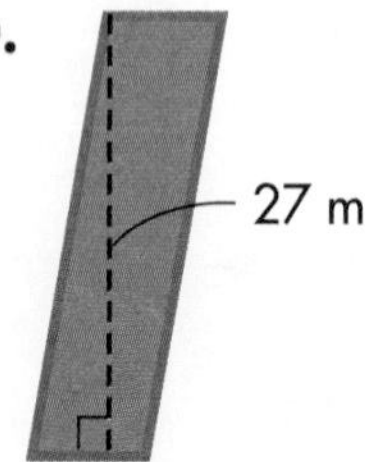

11.

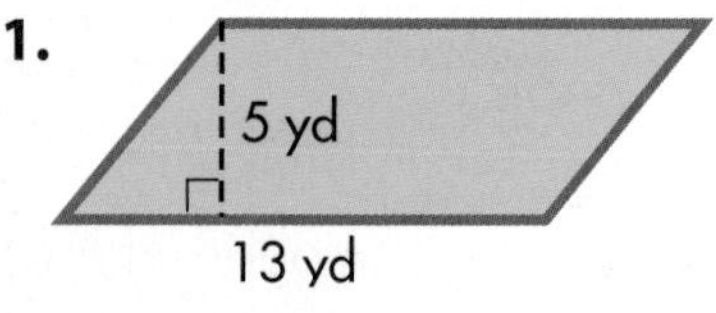

Animated Glossary
www.pearsonsuccessnet.com

**For another example, see Set D on page 315.*

Step 1

The shaded triangle of the parallelogram can be cut off.

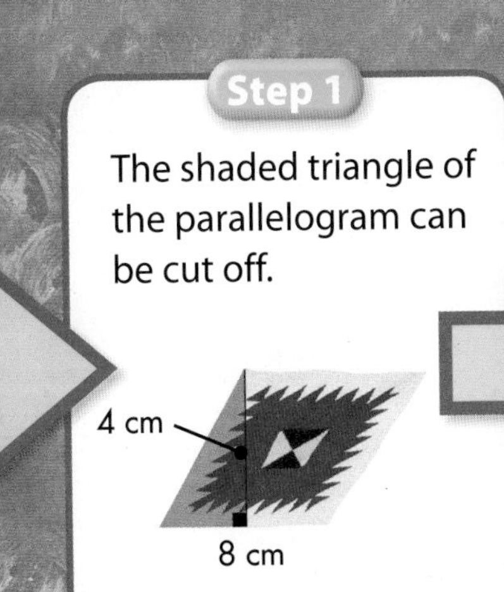

Step 2

The triangle can be placed along the other side to form a rectangle.

Think length = base (b)
width = height (h)

Use the formula to find the area of a parallelogram.

Area = base $\times$ height

$A = b \times h$

$A = 8 \text{ cm} \times 4 \text{ cm}$

$A = 32 \text{ cm}^2$

The area of the parallelogram is 32 cm^2.

Problem Solving

12. Parallelogram A has a base of 12 ft and a height of 11 ft. Parallelogram B has a base of 13 ft and a height of 10 ft. Which parallelogram has the greater area? How much greater is the area?

13. Each morning, Kathie rides the train 9 km to work. The train takes 10 minutes to travel $4\frac{1}{2}$ km. How much time does Kathie spend on the train each day going to and from work?

14. Which of these figures has the greatest area?

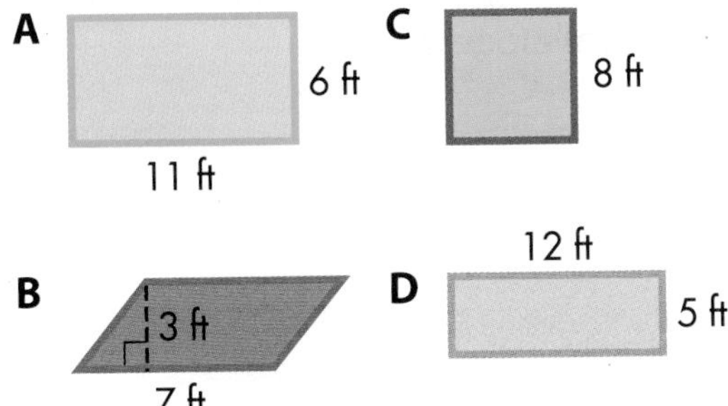

15. A store display has 36 bottles of perfume on the bottom shelf, 30 bottles on the shelf above that, and 24 on the shelf above that. If this pattern continues, how many bottles will be on the next shelf above?

16. What is the area of the parallelogram lift shown below?

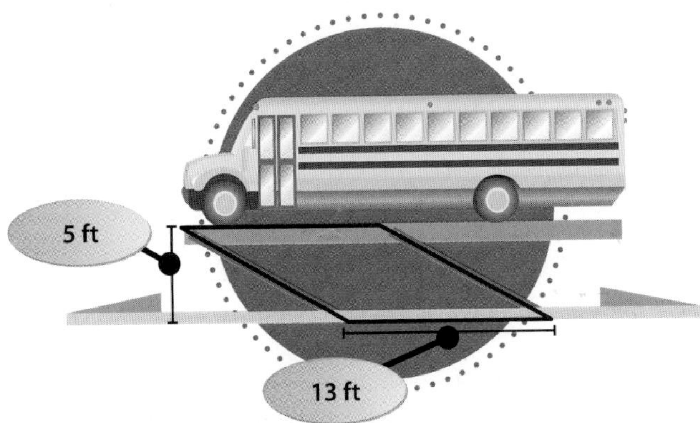

17. Writing to Explain Kurt bought two items that cost a total of \$100. One item cost \$10 more than the other. What was the cost of each item? Explain your reasoning.

18. Algebra Karl knows the area of a parallelogram is 54 in^2. The base of this parallelogram is 9 inches, and the height is h inches. What is the measure for the height of this parallelogram?

Lesson 13-6

MG 1.1 Derive and use the formula for the area of a triangle and of a parallelogram by comparing each with the formula for the area of a rectangle (i.e., two of the same triangles make a parallelogram with twice the area; a parallelogram is compared with a rectangle of the same area by pasting and cutting a right triangle on the parallelogram). Also MG 1.0.

Area of Triangles

How can you use a parallelogram to find the area of a triangle?

This parallelogram is divided into two congruent triangles. The area of each triangle is equal to half the area of the parallelogram.

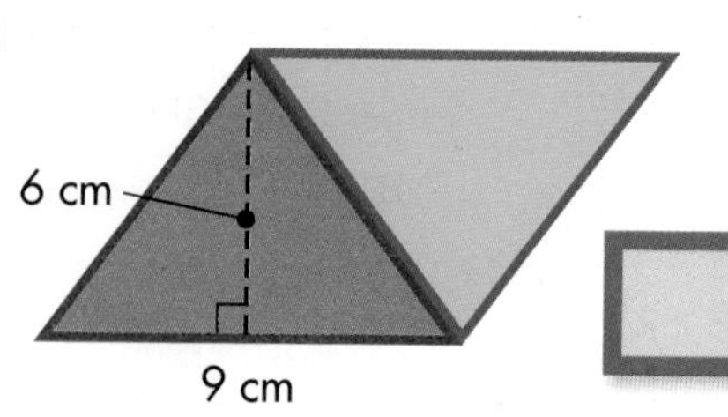

Guided Practice*

Do you know HOW?

In **1** and **2**, find the area of each triangle.

1.

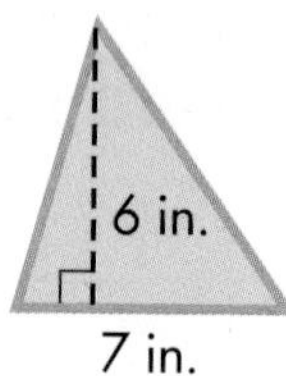

2.

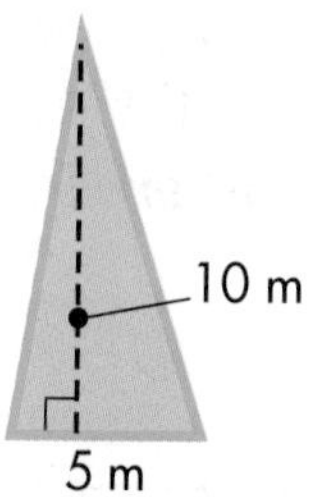

Do you UNDERSTAND?

3. **Writing to Explain** In the example above, how do you know the area of the triangle is equal to half the area of the parallelogram?

4. In the example above, find the area of the red triangle if the base measures 12 cm and the height remains the same.

Independent Practice

In **5** through **10**, find the area of each triangle.

5.

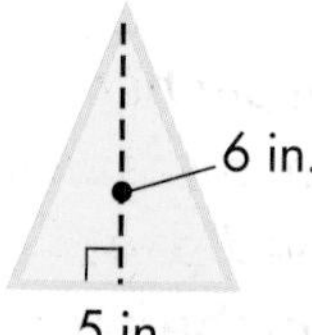

6.

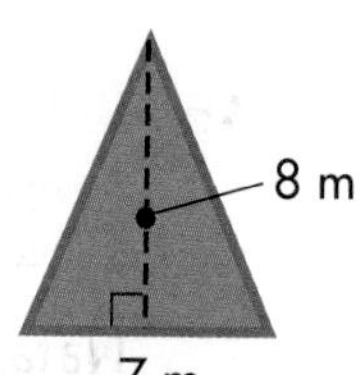

7.

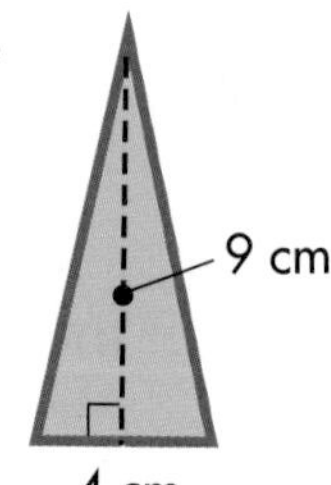

8.

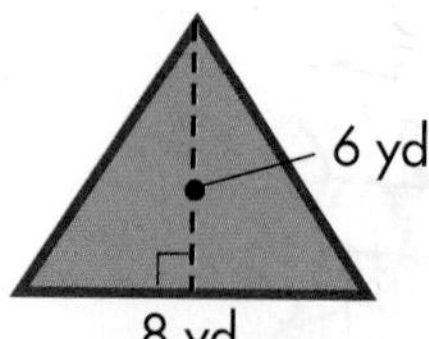

9.

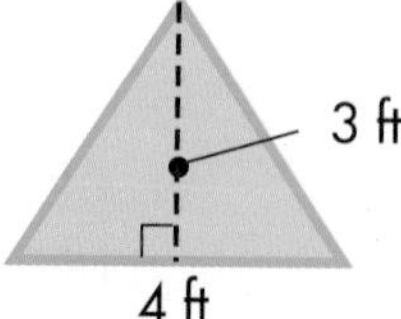

10.

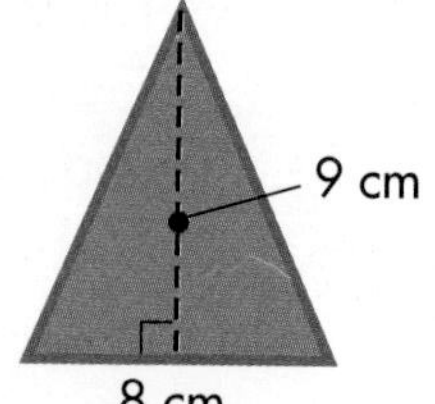

*For another example, see Set D on page 315.

Step 1

Find the area of the red triangle.

Identify the measures of the base and height of the triangle.

base (b) = 9 cm
height (h) = 6 cm

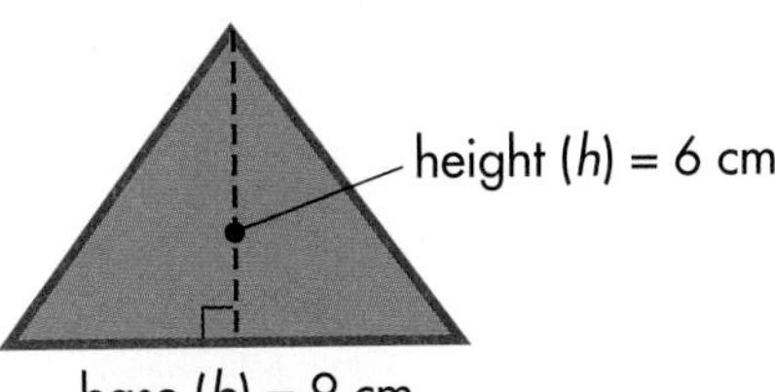

Step 2

To find the area of a triangle, adapt the formula for the area of a parallelogram—just multiply by $\frac{1}{2}$.

Substitute the values into the formula.

Area $= \frac{1}{2} \times$ base $\times$ height

$A = \frac{1}{2} \times b \times h$

$A = \frac{1}{2} \times 9 \times 6$

$A = 27 \text{ cm}^2$

The area of the red triangle is 27 cm^2.

Problem Solving

11. Writing to Explain Jay says that this triangle has an area of 3,000 square inches. Is Jay correct? Explain.

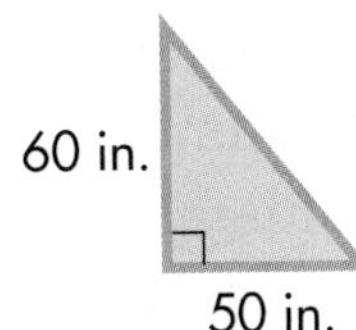

12. Terry wants to buy one pair of moccasins. She can choose from some that cost \$22.50, \$27.00, \$20.95, and \$24.75. How much will Terry save if she buys the least expensive instead of the most expensive pair?

13. Reasoning The difference between the prices of two bikes is \$18. The sum of the prices is \$258. How much does each bike cost?

14. What is the area of a triangle with a base of 7 inches and a height of 8 inches?

A 15 in^2 **C** 56 in^2

B 28 in^2 **D** 64 in^2

15. Which of the following numbers is a composite number?

A 2 **C** 7

B 5 **D** 9

16. Natalie is going to wallpaper her room. Each wall in her bedroom measures 10 ft by 8 ft. How much wallpaper will Natalie need to cover 3 of the bedroom walls?

17. Algebra A lunar module has triangular-shaped windows. The base of each window is 60 cm. The height is h cm. The area of each window is 1,200 square centimeters. Find the height of each window.

18. What is the area of the dinner bell shown at the right?

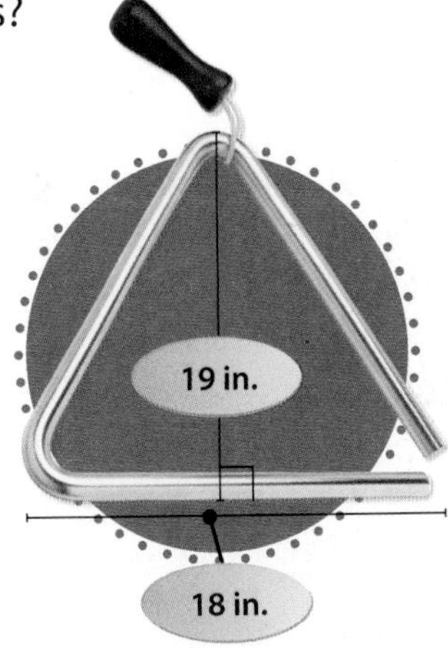

MR 2.3 Use a variety of methods such as words, numbers, symbols, charts, graphs, tables, diagrams, and models, to explain mathematical reasoning. Also MR 2.0, MG 1.4.

Problem Solving

Draw a Picture and Make an Organized List

Hands-On
grid paper

The Diaz family has 12 one-foot sections of fence to build a rectangular kennel for their dog. They want the kennel to have a perimeter of 12 ft, and have the greatest possible area. What should the dimensions of the kennel be?

Guided Practice*

Do you know HOW?

Draw a picture and make a list to solve.

1. Ali has 18 meters of fence to enclose her garden. She wants this garden to have the greatest possible area. What should the dimensions of Ali's garden be?

2. Eric painted a square picture that has an area of 400 sq cm. He wants to frame it, but needs to know the perimeter. What is the perimeter of Eric's picture?

Do you UNDERSTAND?

3. How does drawing a picture and making a list help you solve these problems?

4. **Write a Problem** Write a real-world problem that can be solved by drawing a picture and making a list.

Independent Practice

In **5** through **9**, draw a picture and make a list to solve.

5. Julie will be making a quilt. If she wants the quilt to have a perimeter of 30 ft, and cover the greatest area possible, what should its dimensions be?

6. A kitchen is 8 feet long and 6 feet wide. If the dimensions of the kitchen are doubled, how will the area change? How will the perimeter change?

Stuck? Try this....

- What do I know?
- What am I asked to find?
- What diagram can I use to help understand the problem?
- Can I use addition, subtraction, multiplication, or division?
- Is all of my work correct?
- Did I answer the right question?
- Is my answer reasonable?

*For another example, see Set E on page 315.

Read and Understand

The length of the kennel cannot be longer than 5 ft because the perimeter needs to be 12 ft.

I can draw a picture on grid paper to show this.

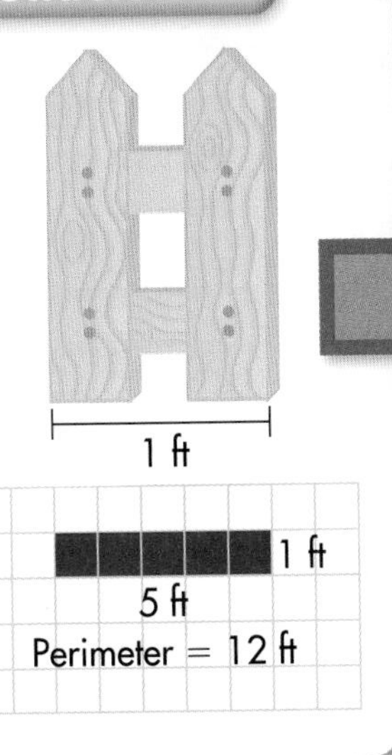

The area is $5 \times 1 = 5 \text{ ft}^2$

Plan and Solve

I can draw more pictures and make a list of all possible dimensions and areas.

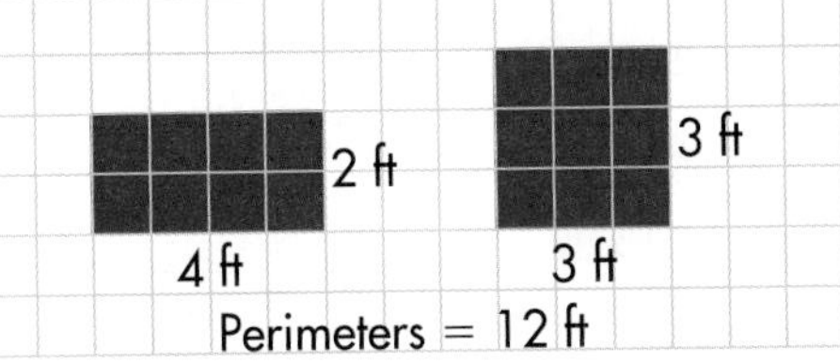

$5 \times 1 = 5 \text{ ft}^2$ $\quad 4 \times 2 = 8 \text{ ft}^2$

$3 \times 3 = 9 \text{ ft}^2$

The dimensions of the kennel should be 3 ft wide by 3 ft long.

7. Mary is designing a geometric picture that will be put on a banner. The parallelogram in the picture has an area of 625 in^2. The square in the picture has the same area as the parallelogram. What are the dimensions of the square?

8. Beth's garden is 6 ft by 3 ft. She wants to plant 6 flowers per square foot.

a How many flowers will she plant?

b How can you check your answer?

9. The length of a rectangular sandbox is 8 ft. The area of the sandbox is 40 ft^2. If the length of the box is extended 2 more feet, how many feet does the width of the box need to be to have a final area of 60 ft^2?

10. Rocio finished 21 pages in a scrapbook. On Monday, she finished half as many pages as on Tuesday. On Wednesday, Rocio finished twice as many pages as on Tuesday. How many pages did Rocio complete each day?

11. Robert has \$107.56 in his savings account. He withdraws \$30.60. Draw a picture and write an equation that can be solved to find Robert's new balance. Let b = Robert's new balance.

12. **Writing to Explain** Maria says that rectangles with the same perimeter can have different areas. Is Maria correct? Use a drawing to support your explanation.

13. You want to buy 12 comic books. The store sells small and large comics and is having a special. You have \$24. Do you have enough money to buy 12 small books? Twelve large books?

DIGITAL eTools www.pearsonsuccessnet.com

Test Prep

1. Use a ruler to measure. Which book on the bookcase has a width of $\frac{7}{8}$ inch? (13-1)

A Book A

B Book B

C Book C

D Book D

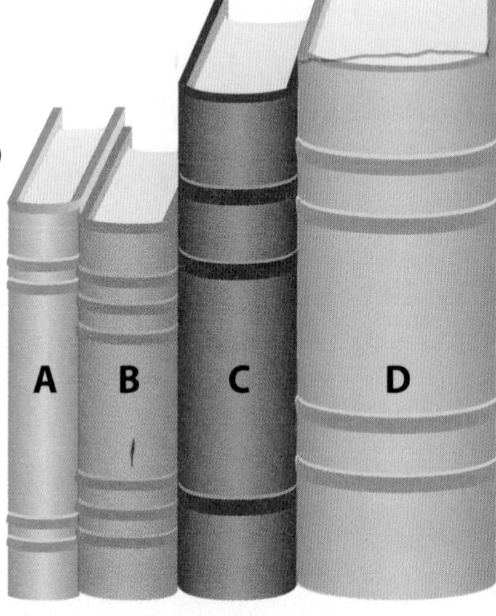

2. Jenny made a scarf with the dimensions shown. What is the area of the scarf? (13-5)

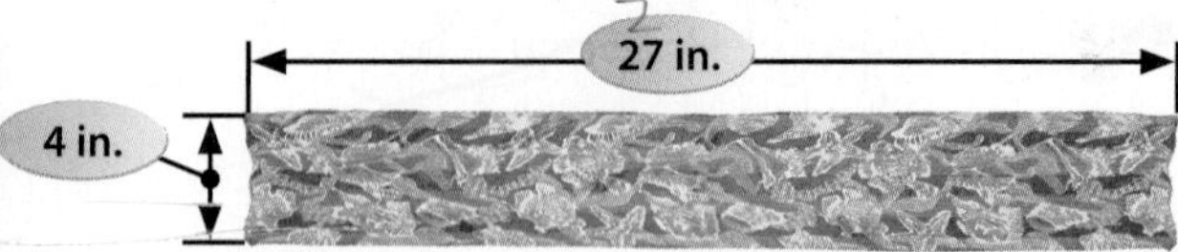

A 108 in^2

B 78 in^2

C 54 in^2

D 39 in^2

3. Yvonne glued sequins around the outside of each of her party invitations. If the invitations are 5 inches wide and 2.5 inches tall, what is the perimeter of the invitations? (13-3)

A 7.5 inches

B 7.5 in^2

C 15 inches

D 15 in^2

4. Mr. Santiago wants to build a horse corral with the greatest area possible, using exactly 40 yards of fencing. Which dimensions should he use? (13-7)

A 12 yards by 12 yards

B 15 yards by 5 yards

C 12 yards by 8 yards

D 10 yards by 10 yards

5. The area of rectangle *ABCD* is 24 square centimeters. What is the area of parallelogram *EFCD*? (13-5)

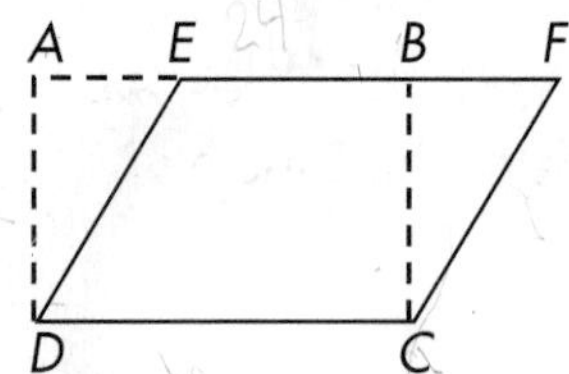

A 48 cm^2

B 24 cm^2

C 12 cm^2

D 6 cm^2

6. Use a ruler to measure. Which is closest to the height of the treble clef shown? (13-1)

A $\frac{1}{4}$ inch

B $\frac{3}{4}$ inch

C $\frac{5}{6}$ inch

D $\frac{7}{8}$ inch

7. Use a ruler to measure. Which is closest to the length of the drill bit shown? (13-2)

A 4 cm

B 5 cm

C 6 cm

D 7 cm

Topic 13
Test Prep

8. The area of the rectangle is 120 yd^2. What is the area of the shaded triangle? (13-6)

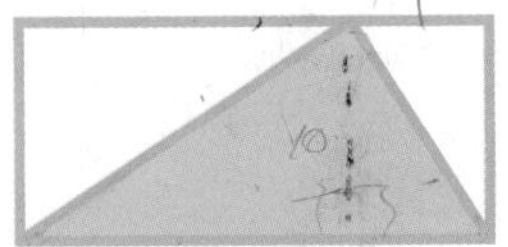

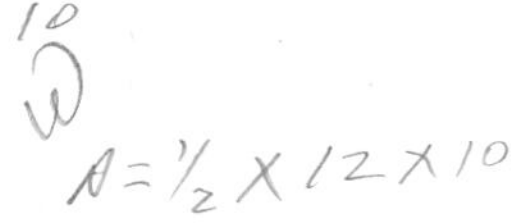

A 40 yd^2

B 60 yd^2

C 120 yd^2

D 240 yd^2

9. A rectangular window measures 36 inches wide and 48 inches tall. What is the area of the window? (13-4)

A 1,728 in^2

B 1,728 inches

C 1,488 in^2

D 1,488 inches

10. What is the area of the parking lot shown shaded in the diagram? (13-6)

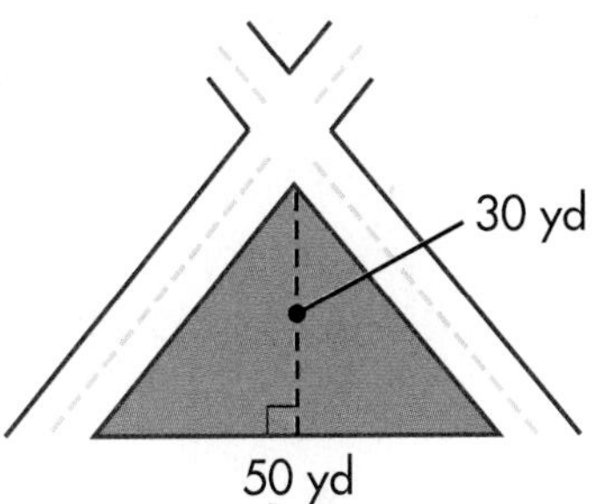

A 110 yd^2

B 375 yd^2

C 750 yd^2

D 1,500 yd^2

11. Figure *MNPQ* is a square. Which of the following can be used to find the area of triangle *MNP*? (13-6)

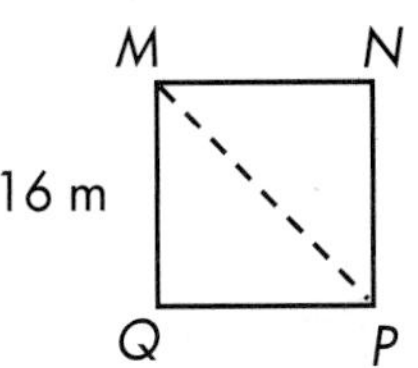

A $A = \frac{1}{2}(16 \times 16)$

B $A = \frac{1}{2}(4 \times 4)$

C $A = \frac{1}{2}(4 \times 16)$

D $A = 16 \times 16$

12. Chelsey is going to line the perimeter of the table shown with flowers for her wedding. What is the perimeter of the table top? (13-3)

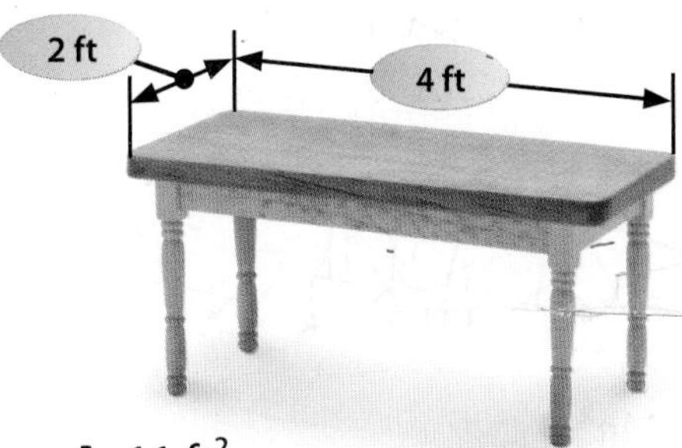

A 11 ft^2

B 11 feet

C 12 ft^2

D 12 feet

13. Which of the following can be used to find the area in square meters of a parallelogram whose base measures 20 m and height measures 12 m? (13-5)

A $A = (2 \times 20) + (2 \times 12)$

B $A = \frac{1}{2} \times 20 \times 2$

C $A = 20 \times 12$

D $A = 20 + 12$

Topic 13
Reteaching

Set A, pages 296–297

Find the length to the nearest inch, $\frac{1}{2}$ inch, $\frac{1}{4}$ inch, and $\frac{1}{8}$ inch.

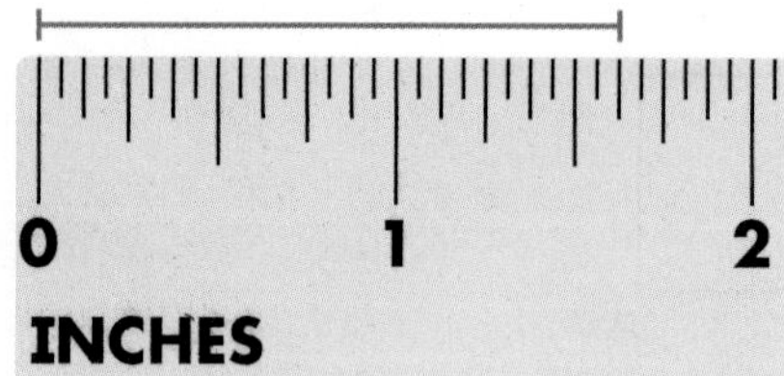

To the nearest:

inch: 2 in.

$\frac{1}{2}$ inch: $1\frac{1}{2}$ in.

$\frac{1}{4}$ inch: $1\frac{3}{4}$ in.

$\frac{1}{8}$ inch: $1\frac{5}{8}$ in.

Remember to write your measurements in fractions using simplest form. Use a ruler.

1. Find the length to the nearest $\frac{1}{4}$ inch and $\frac{1}{2}$ inch.

2. Find the length to the nearest inch and $\frac{1}{8}$ inch.

Set B, pages 298–299

Choose a reasonable metric unit for the length of a driveway.

The meter is the most reasonable unit.

The millimeter and centimeter are too small and the kilometer is too large.

Remember the shortest to longest measures are: millimeter (mm), centimeter (cm), meter (m), and kilometer (km).

1. length of a calculator
2. distance from Chicago to Denver
3. thickness of a thumbtack

Set C, pages 300–302

Find the perimeter.

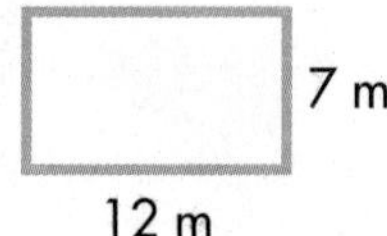

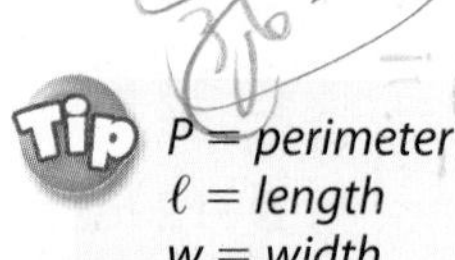

Use a formula:

Perimeter = (2 × length) + (2 × width)

$P = (2 \times \ell) + (2 \times w)$

$P = (2 \times 12) + (2 \times 7)$

$P = 24 + 14 = 38$ m

Add the side lengths:

$P = 12 + 7 + 12 + 7 = 38$ m

Remember that perimeter is the distance around the outside of any polygon.

Find the perimeter.

1.

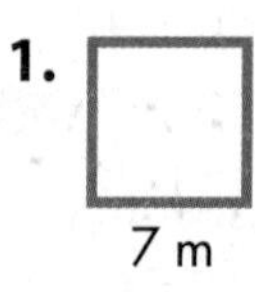

2.

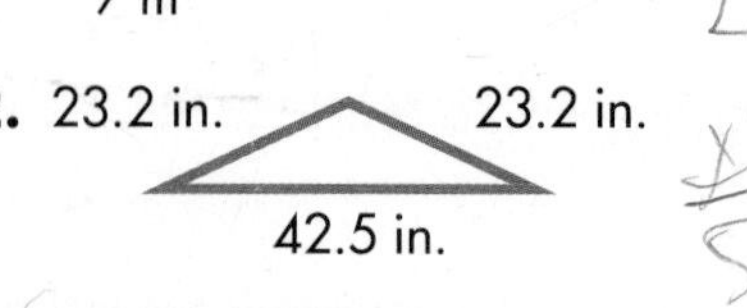

3.

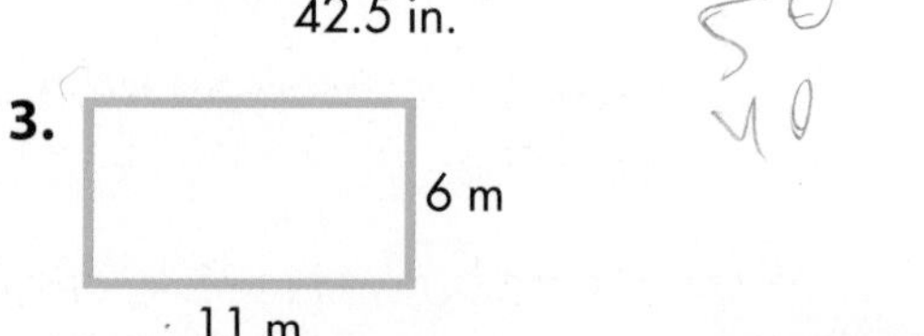

Set D, pages 304–309

Find the area of the square.

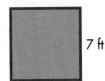

Use the formula: $A = s \times s$.

$A = 7 \times 7 = 49\ \text{ft}^2$

Find the area of the parallelogram.

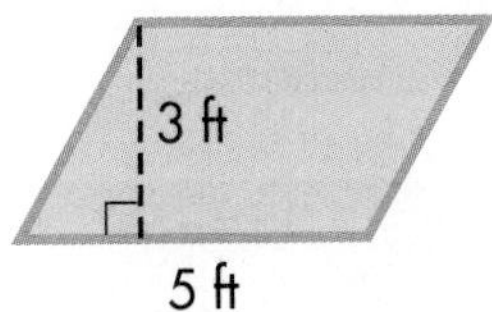

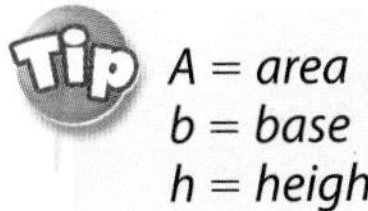

Use the formula: $A = b \times h$.

$A = 5 \times 3 = 15\ \text{ft}^2$

Find the area of the triangle.

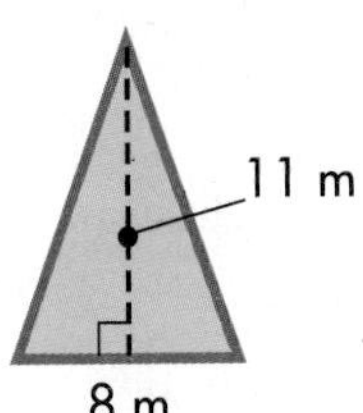

Tip
A = *area*
b = *base*
h = *height*

Use the formula: $A = \frac{1}{2} \times b \times h$.

$A = \frac{1}{2} \times 11 \times 8 = 44\ \text{m}^2$

Remember to use the appropriate area formula for each polygon.

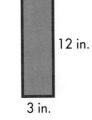

Find the area of each figure.

1. 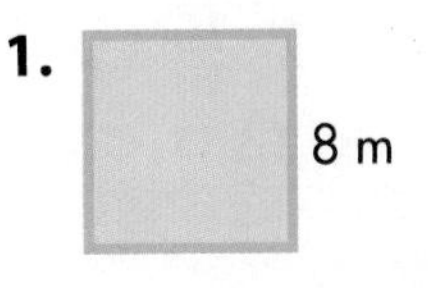

2. 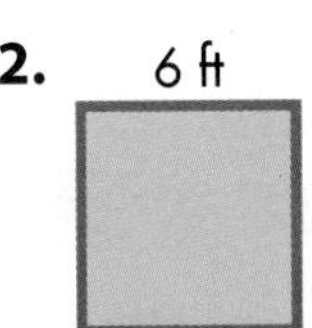

3. 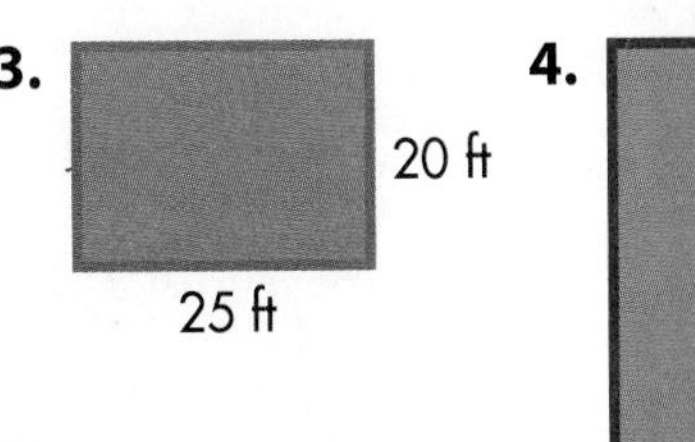

4. 12 in. 3 in.

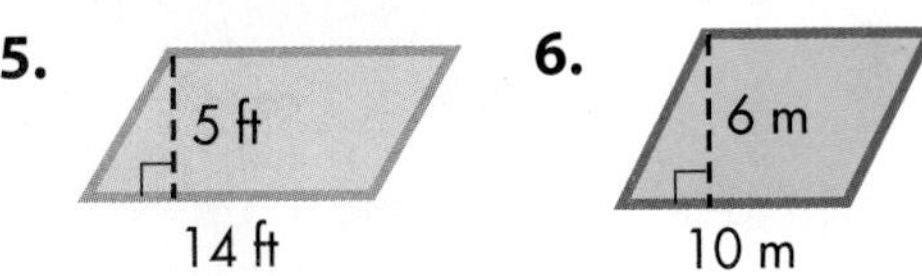

5.

6.

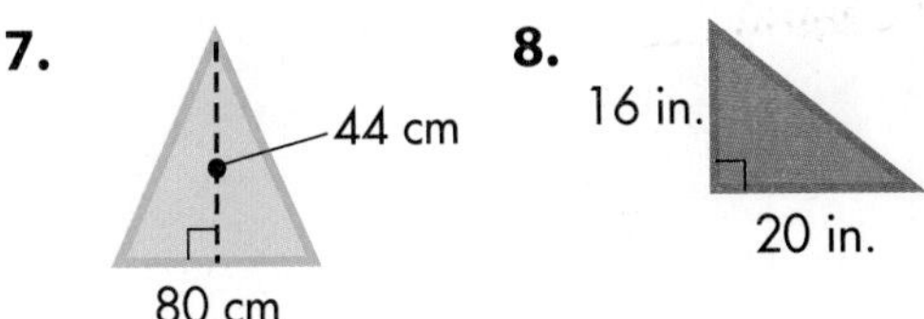

7.

8.

Set E, pages 310–311

When you are asked to draw a picture and make a list to solve a problem, follow these steps:

Read and understand the problem.

Make a plan by creating a list of different possible solutions.

Test each of the items in your list to find a solution.

Look back and check to see that your work is correct.

Remember that drawing a picture can help you make a list.

1. Cristina has 16 square feet of material to make a rectangular quilt. She wants the quilt to have the least possible (minimum) perimeter. If Cristina uses all 16 square feet, what dimensions should she use for the quilt?

Topic 14 Solids

1 How can you find the surface area of the outer walls and roof of one of these pueblo houses? You will find out in Lesson 14-3.

2 What kinds of solid figures can you find in this Tori gate? You will find out in Lesson 14-1.

3

Over 1.6 million one-inch-square glass tiles cover the walls of the Outer Bay exhibit in Monterey, California. What is an estimate for the volume of the main viewing window of this exhibit? You will find out in Lesson 14-6.

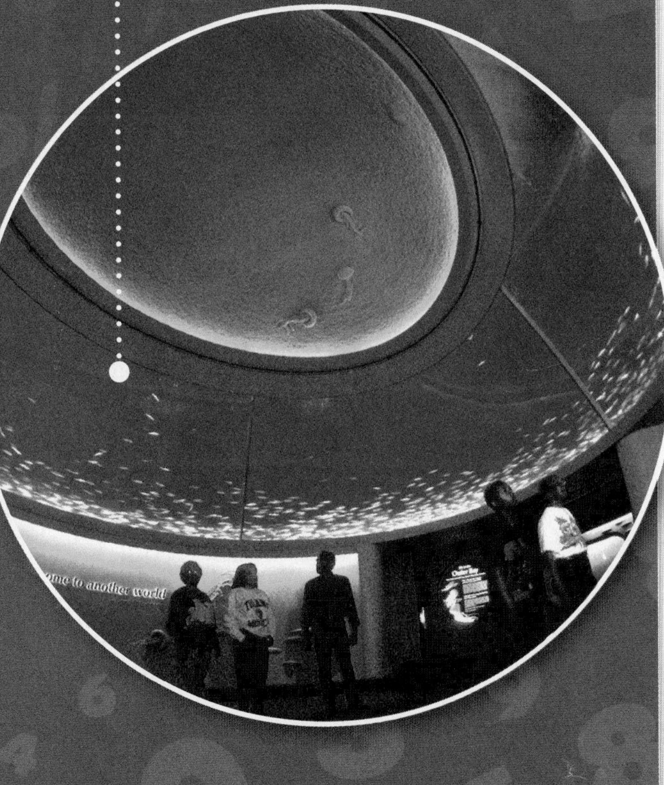

Review What You Know!

Vocabulary

Choose the best term from the box.

- quadrilateral
- square
- triangle

1. A polygon with only 3 sides is a __?__.
2. Every rectangle is a __?__.
3. A rectangle with all sides the same length is a __?__.

Area

Find the area of each figure.

4. Rectangle: 10 ft by 6 ft

5. Triangle: 8 cm, 12 cm

Multiplication

Find each product.

6. $10 \times 8 \times 5$
7. $20 \times 40 \times 5$
8. $15 \times 15 \times 15$
9. $\frac{1}{2} \times 10 \times 8$

Geometry

10. **Writing to Explain** How are parallel lines different from intersecting lines?

Lesson
14-1

MG 3.6, Grade 4 Visualize, describe, and make models of geometric solids (e.g., prisms, pyramids) in terms of the number and shape of faces, edges, and vertices; interpret two-dimensional representations of three-dimensional objects; and draw patterns (of faces) for a solid that, when cut and folded, will make a model of the solid.

Solids

What is a solid figure?

A solid figure has 3 dimensions and takes up space. One solid is the cube. It has 6 flat surfaces or faces. All the faces are squares. Each pair of faces intersects in a segment called an edge, and each pair of edges intersects at a point called the vertex. The plural of vertex is vertices.

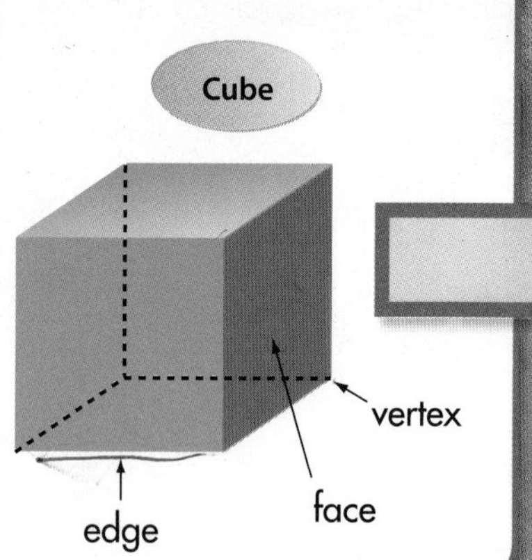

Other Examples

Some solid figures have curved surfaces, while others have all flat surfaces.

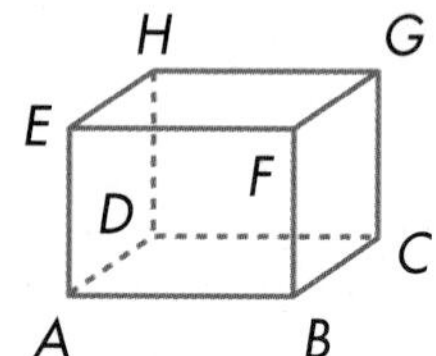

Prism
Solid with two congruent parallel bases and faces that are parallelograms.

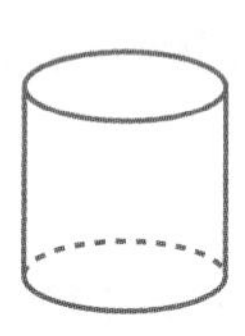

Cylinder
Solid with two circular bases that are congruent and parallel.

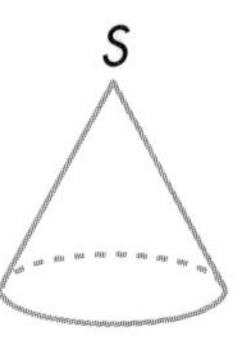

Cone
Solid with one circular base. The points on this circle are joined to one point outside the base.

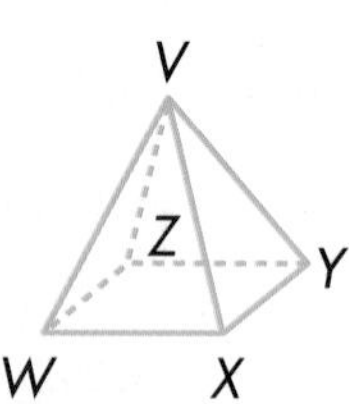

Pyramid
Solid with a base that is a polygon. The edges of the base are joined to a point outside the base.

Naming the parts of a solid

Name the vertices, edges, and faces of the triangular prism.

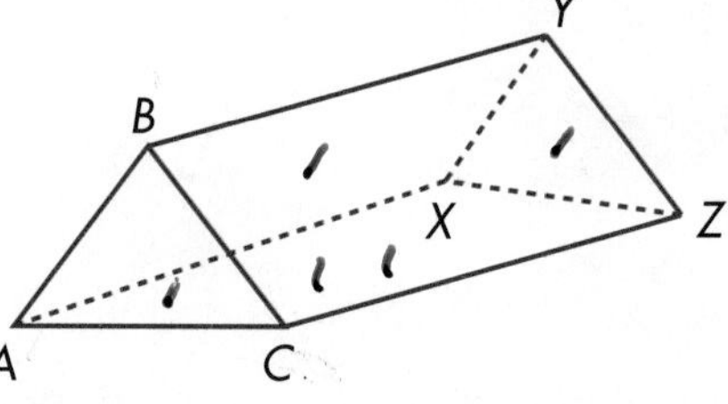

Vertices: *A*, *B*, *C*, *X*, *Y*, and *Z*

Edges: $\overline{AB}$, $\overline{AC}$, $\overline{BC}$, $\overline{XY}$, $\overline{XZ}$, $\overline{YZ}$, $\overline{AX}$, $\overline{BY}$, and $\overline{CZ}$

Faces: triangles *ABC* and *XYZ*, quadrilaterals *ABYX*, *CBYZ*, and *AXZC*

Explain It

1. How many faces, vertices, and edges are there in the triangular prism above?
2. Name other objects in the real world that have similar shapes to the solids described above.

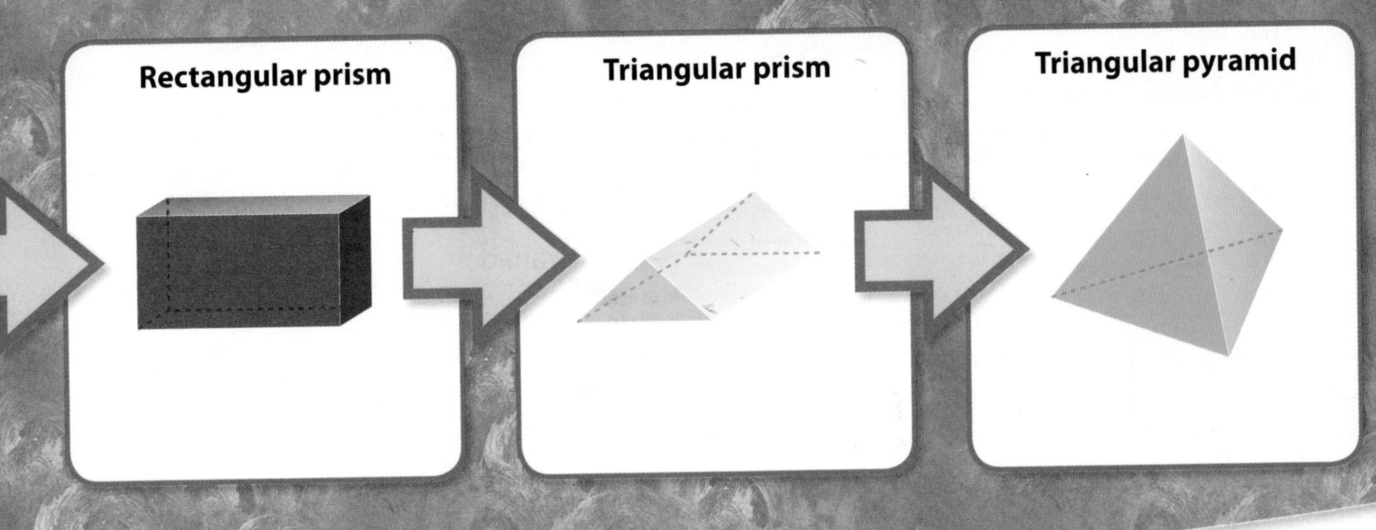

Guided Practice*

Do you know HOW?

For **1** through **3**, use the solid at the right.

1. Name the vertices.

2. Name the faces.

3. Name the edges.

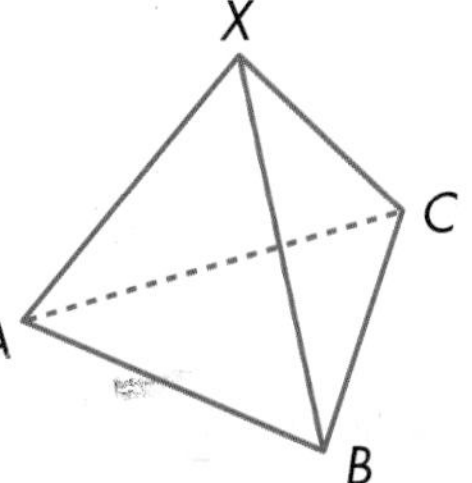

Do you UNDERSTAND?

4. What is the name of the solid figure at the left?

5. Which of the solid figures in Other Examples have curved surfaces?

6. How many faces does a triangular prism have?

Independent Practice

For **7** through **9**, tell which solid figure each object resembles.

7. 

8. 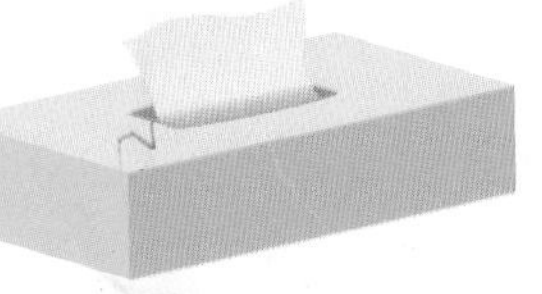

9. 

For **10** through **12**, use the drawing to the right.

10. Name the faces.

11. Name the vertices.

12. Name the edges.

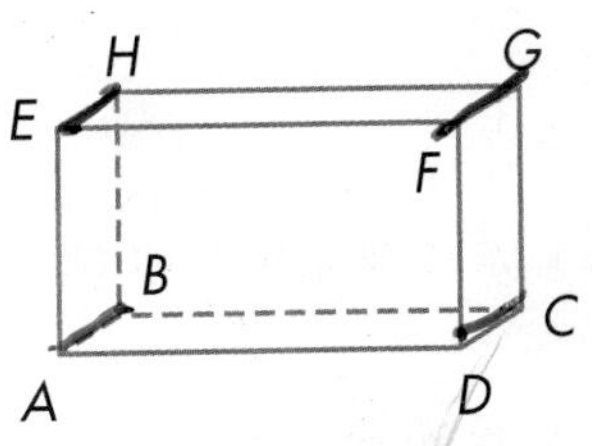

Animated Glossary
www.pearsonsuccessnet.com

For another example, see Set A on page 338.

Problem Solving

13. Which of the following decimals is equivalent to 12.45?

A 12.0045

B 12.0450

C 12.4500

D 124.5000

14. Which of the following solids has a curved surface?

A Pyramid

B Cube

C Prism

D Cone

15. Luke's tent weighs $6\frac{1}{2}$ pounds. His fishing tackle weighs $5\frac{1}{2}$ pounds. What is the total weight of both items?

16. **Reasoning** A certain kind of prism has 9 edges and 5 faces. What kind of prism is it?

17. One week, Mary worked for 29 hours. She earned $6 per hour. How much did Mary earn for the time she worked?

18. Wei made two square pyramids and glued the congruent bases together. How many faces does her figure have?

19. Before Andy went shopping, he added $5 he had earned to the money that was already in his wallet. He bought a backpack for $19 and a headset for $12. After he paid for the items, Andy had $8.25 left. How much money did Andy have to begin with?

20. Which of the following is NOT a rectangular prism?

A 

C 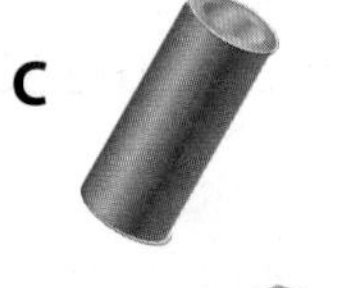

B 

D 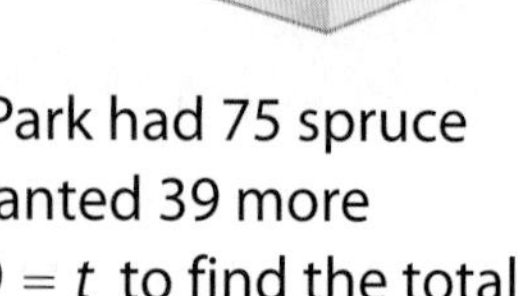

21. Tori gates are often found in Japan. where they originate. What kinds of solids can you find in a Tori gate?

22. **Algebra** Fillmore Park had 75 spruce trees. Volunteers planted 39 more trees. Solve $75 + 39 = t$ to find the total number of spruce trees there are in the park now.

23. Draw a picture of a pyramid that has a pentagon as its base.

24. An airplane has 37 rows of seats, and there are 3 seats on each side of the center aisle. How many passengers can this plane hold if all the seats are occupied?

Algebra Connections

Shape Patterns

Look at the shapes below. Can you identify a pattern?

The pattern is 1 rectangle, 1 circle, 1 square, and 1 circle.

In **1** through **6**, name the shape asked for in each pattern.

Example:

Name the 10th shape in the pattern at left.

Think How many shapes before the pattern repeats itself?

The pattern of 1 rectangle, 1 circle, 1 square, 1 circle repeats after 4 shapes.

$$4 + 4 + 2 = 10$$

The 2nd shape in the pattern is a circle, so the 10th shape is also a circle.

1. What is the 13th shape?

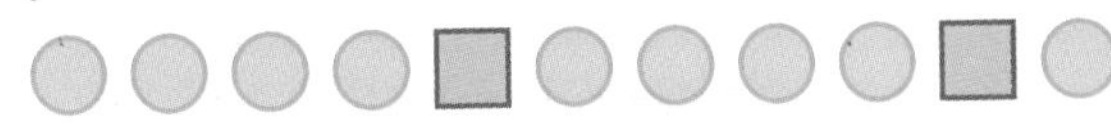

2. What is the 20th shape?

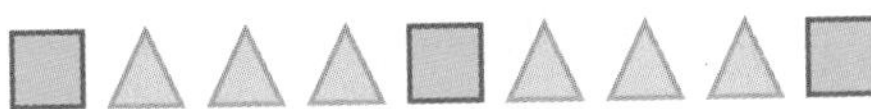

3. What is the 50th shape?

4. What is the 28th shape?

5. What is 11th shape?

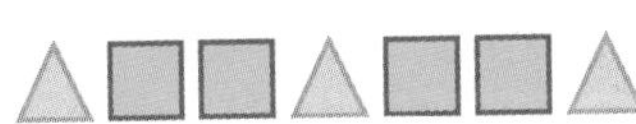

6. What is the 50th shape?

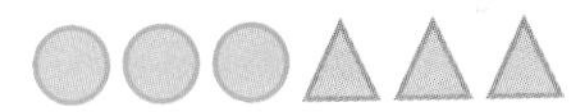

In **7** through **12**, continue each pattern for two more figures.

7. 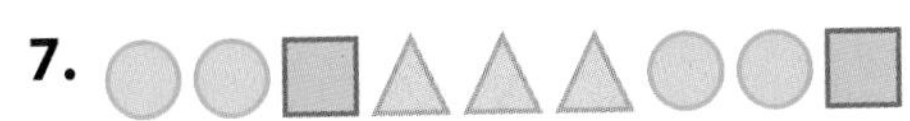

8. 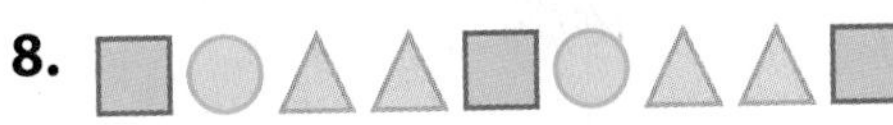

9. 

10. 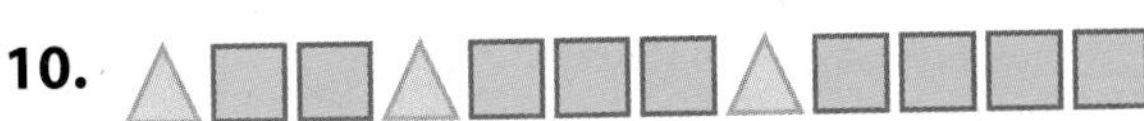

11. 

12.

Lesson

14-2

MG 3.6, Grade 4 Visualize, describe, and make models of geometric solids (e.g., prisms, pyramids) in terms of the number and shape of faces, edges, and vertices; interpret two-dimensional representations of three-dimensional objects; and draw patterns (of faces) for a solid that, when cut and folded, will make a model of the solid.

Relating Shapes and Solids

How can you use a two-dimensional shape to represent a three-dimensional solid?

A net is a plane figure which, when folded, gives a solid figure.

How can you draw a net for this solid figure?

Guided Practice*

Do you know HOW?

Predict what solid each net will make.

1. 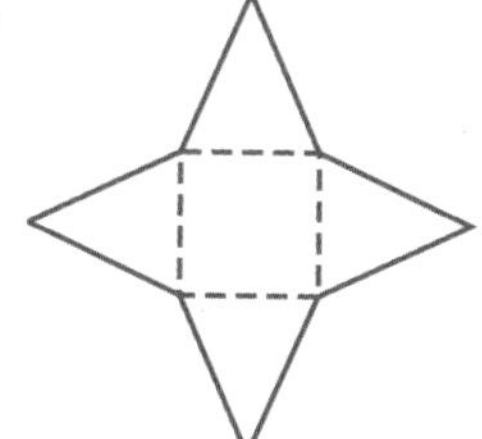

2. 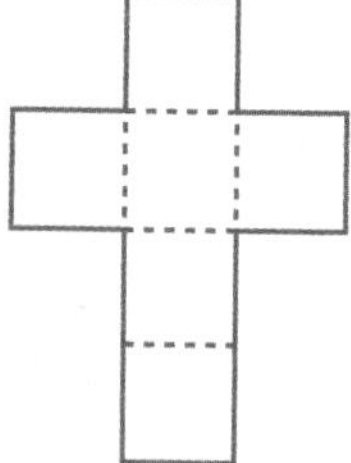

Do you UNDERSTAND?

3. **Writing to Explain** How did you make your predictions in Exercises 1 and 2?

4. A solid may have different nets. Draw a different net for the solid you identified in Exercise 2.

Independent Practice

For **5** through **7**, predict what solid each net will make.

5. 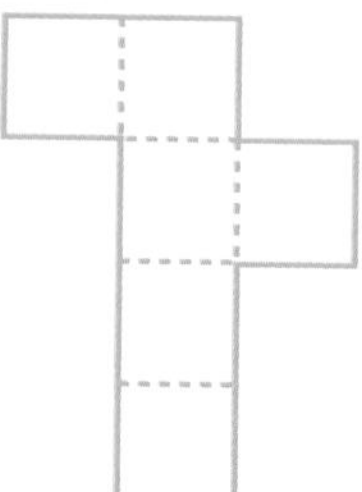

6. 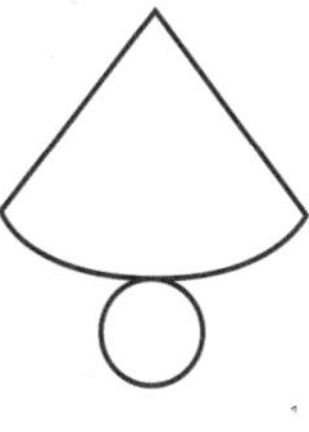

7. 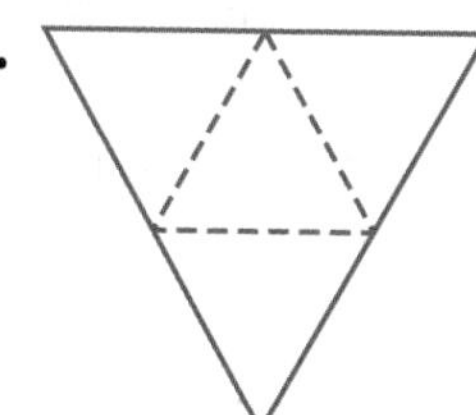

In **8** and **9**, draw a net for each solid.

8. 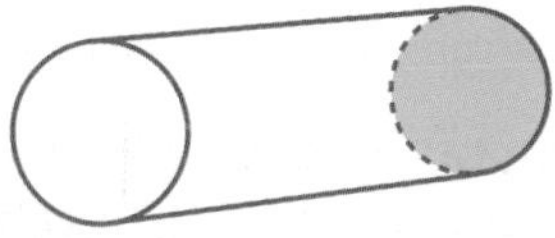

9. 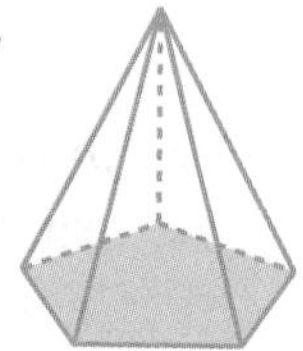

*For another example, see Set B on page 338.

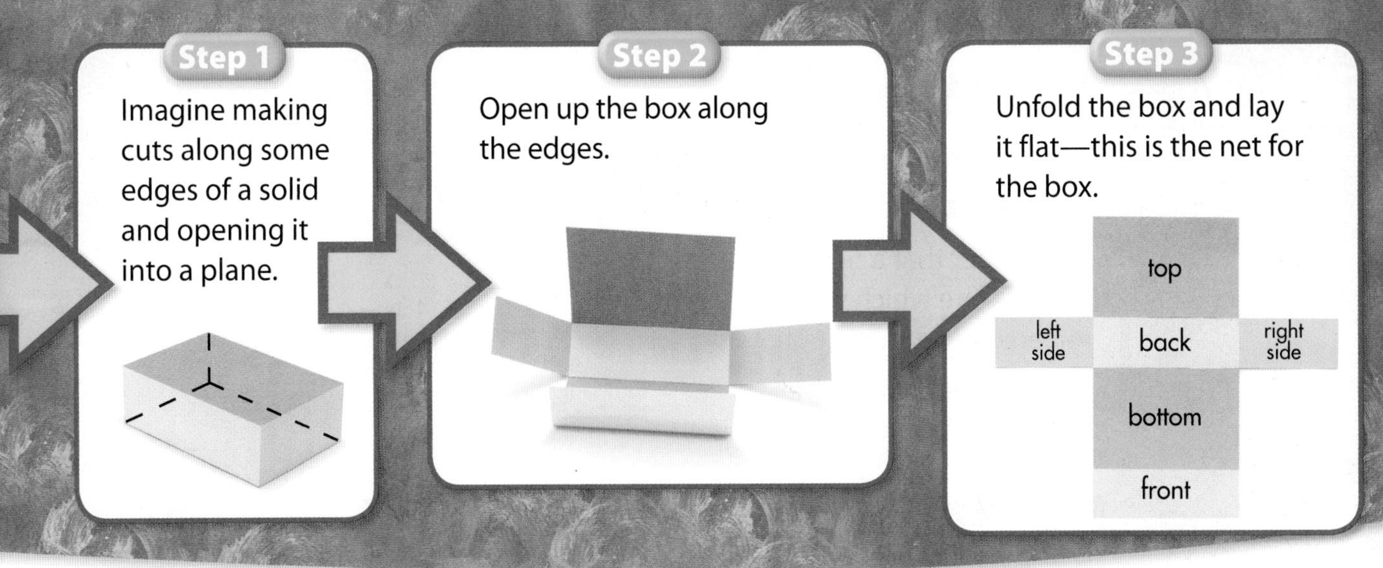

Step 1
Imagine making cuts along some edges of a solid and opening it into a plane.
Step 2
Open up the box along the edges.
Step 3
Unfold the box and lay it flat—this is the net for the box.
top
left side
back
right side
bottom
front

Problem Solving

10. A net has 4 large rectangles and 2 small rectangles. What solid figure might it make?

A Rectangular prism

B Square pyramid

C Triangular prism

D Rectangular pyramid

11. Molly spent $120 on two items. One cost $10 more than the other. Which shows the correct cost for each?

A $60, $50

B $50, $60

C $60, $70

D $55, $65

12. Strategy Focus When some rock music is played unamplified its sound has been measured at 62 decibels. Sound for amplified music can be measured at 124 decibels. Draw a picture and write an equation to find the difference between the number of decibels measured.

13. One company offers customers an Internet coupon to get a $2 discount on their Web site. If the value of the coupons downloaded so far is $6,000, how many coupons have been downloaded?

14. Algebra Diane is thinking of a number. She doubles it and adds 10. Her result is 50. Which equation could you use to find Diane's number?

A $(2 \times n) - 10 = 50$

B $2 \times 10n = 50$

C $2 \times n = 50$

D $(2 \times n) + 10 = 50$

For **15**, use the table below.

Temperature

Day	1	2	3	4	5	6	7
Temperature °F	34°	45°	37°	39°	48°	29°	36°

15. In what fraction of the days was the temperature between 30°F and 40°F? In what fraction was the temperature greater than 40°F?

Lesson

14-3

MG 1.2 Construct a cube and rectangular box from two-dimensional patterns and use these patterns to compute the surface area for these objects. Also **MG 1.0**

Surface Area

Hands-On
grid paper

How can you find the surface area of a rectangular prism?

Remember that a net is a plane figure which when folded gives a solid figure. The surface area (SA) of a rectangular prism is the sum of the area of all its faces.

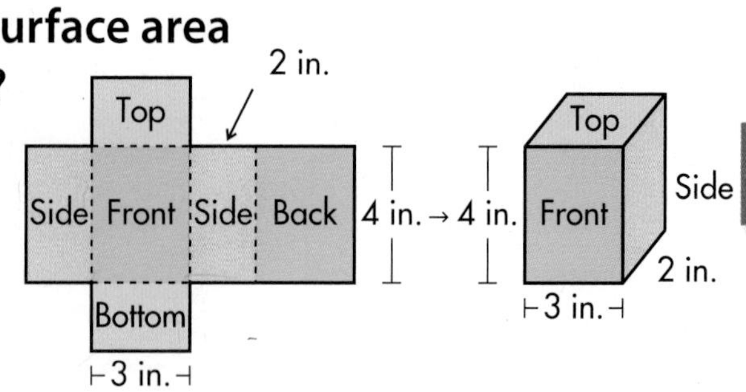

Guided Practice*

Do you know HOW?

Copy the following net on grid paper. Make each rectangle the size shown by the labels. Then cut out the net and fold it to make a rectangular prism.

1.

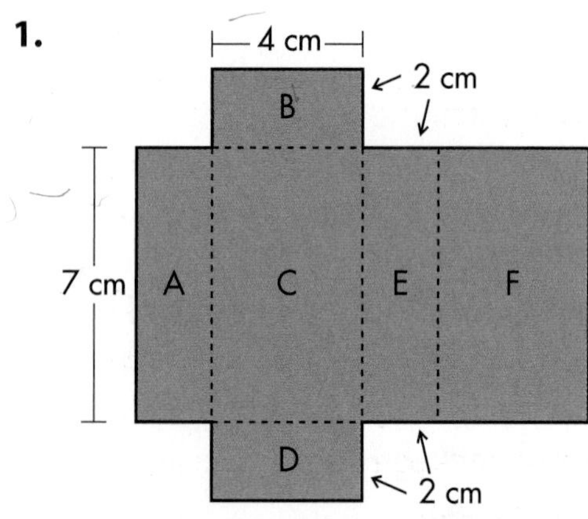

Do you UNDERSTAND?

2. List the congruent faces in the net in Exercise 1.

3. Find the surface area of the solid you built in Exercise 1.

4. For which type of rectangular prism could you find the surface area by finding the area of 1 face and multiplying by 6?

5. What is the surface area of a cube with an edge that measures 3 cm?

Independent Practice

In **6** through **8**, find the surface area of each solid.

6.

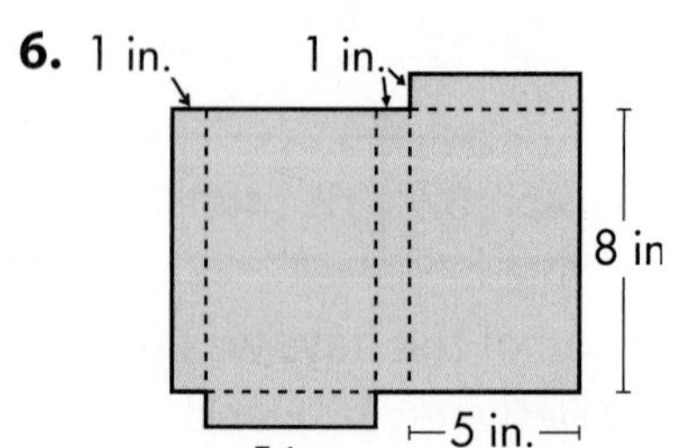

7.

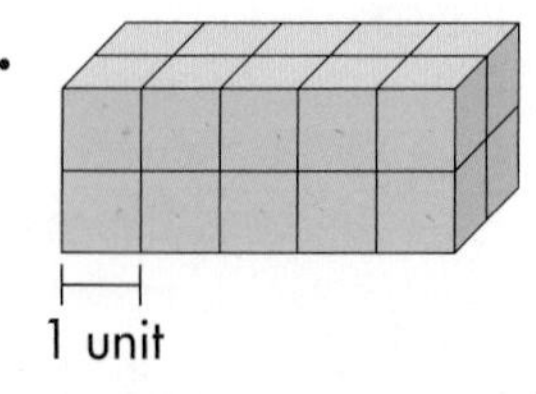

8.

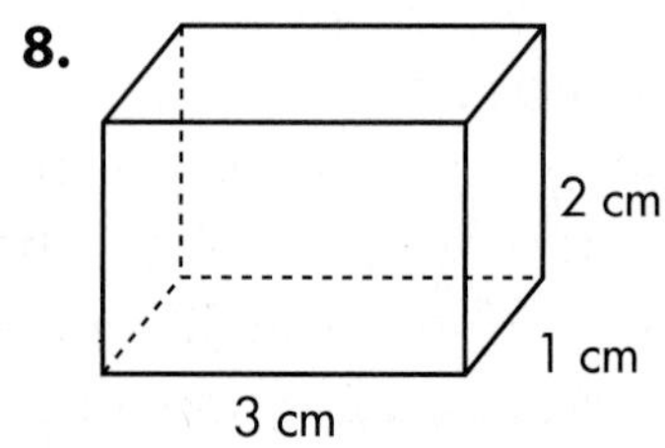

*For another example, see Set B on page 338.

Notice that the solid figure has 6 faces that are rectangles.

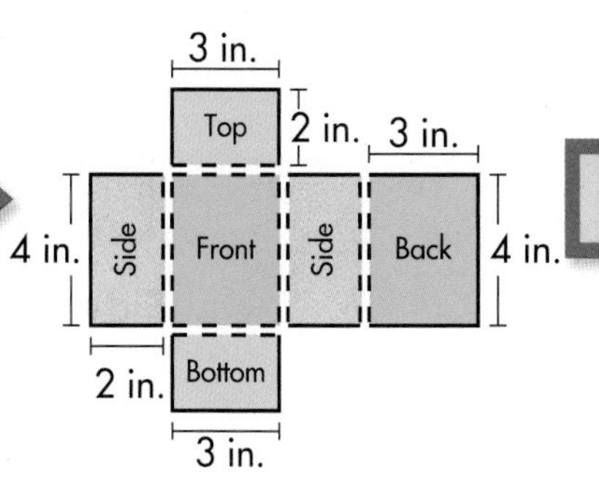

Add the areas of all the faces to find the surface area (SA).

side, side, front, back, top, bottom

$SA = (4 \times 2) + (4 \times 2) + (4 \times 3) + (4 \times 3) + (3 \times 2) + (3 \times 2)$

$= 8 + 8 + 12 + 12 + 6 + 6$

$= 52$ square inches (in^2)

The surface area of the rectangular prism is 52 in^2.

Problem Solving

Use the drawing at the right to answer **9** through **11**.

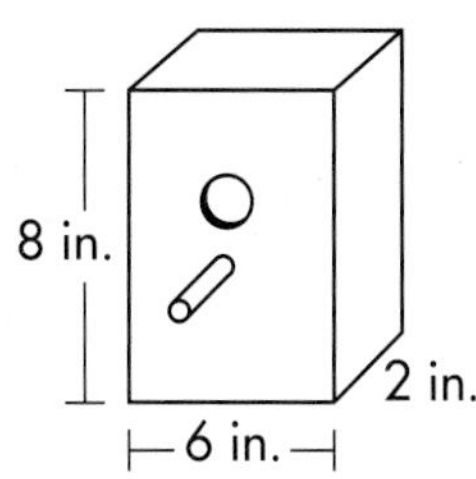

9. Draw a net to represent Mylah's birdhouse. Find the surface area.

10. If Mylah buys paint to cover 76 square inches, will she have enough paint to cover the surface area of the bird house? Explain.

11. **Writing to Explain** If Mylah puts a ribbon around the base of the birdhouse, would she need to find the perimeter or the area of the base?

12. What transformation is shown below?

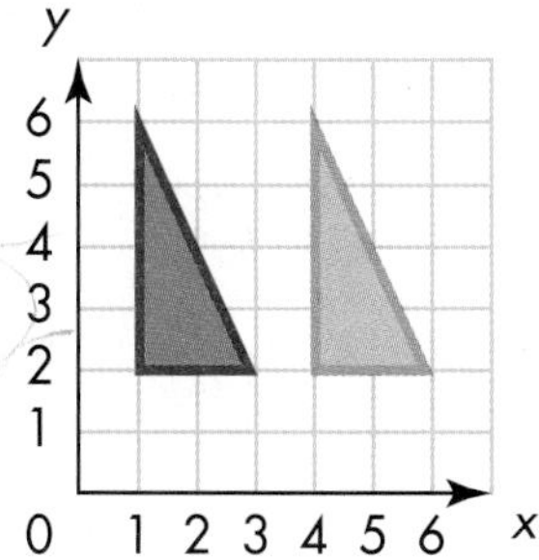

13. Morgan received a parcel that was 4 ft by 2 ft by 3 ft. Kenley received a parcel that was 3 ft by 1 ft by 5 ft. Whose package had the greater surface area? Explain.

14. The Pueblo tribe of New Mexico lived in houses that looked like boxes stacked on top of one another. What would the surface area of the outer walls and roof of a pueblo house be if it had the dimensions shown at the right?

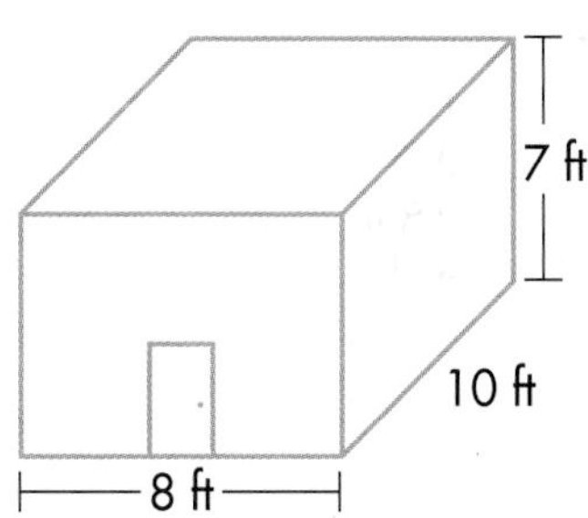

Lesson

14-4

MG 2.3 Visualize and draw two-dimensional views of three-dimensional objects made from rectangular solids.

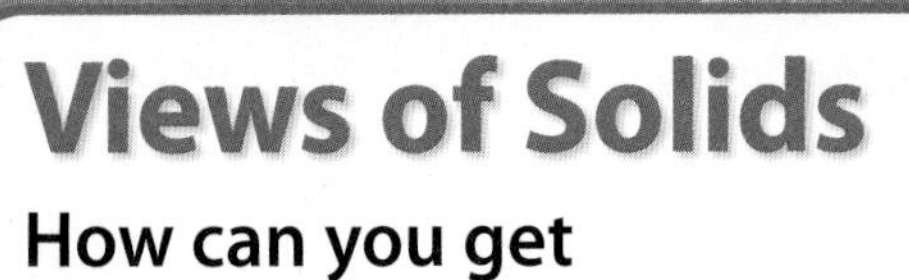

Views of Solids

How can you get information about a solid by viewing it from different perspectives?

What do the different views of this stack of cubes look like?

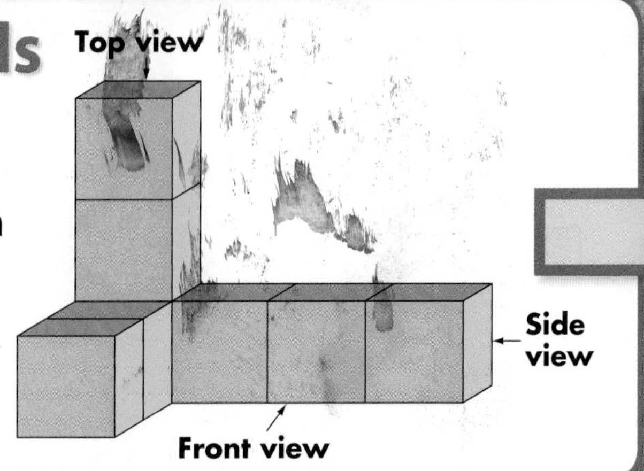

Guided Practice*

Do you know HOW?

1. Sketch the front, top and side views of the solid figure below.

Do you UNDERSTAND?

2. How many blocks are not visible in the diagram at the left?

3. Draw what the bottom view looks like.

Independent Practice

In **4** through **9**, draw front, side, and top views of each stack of unit blocks.

4.
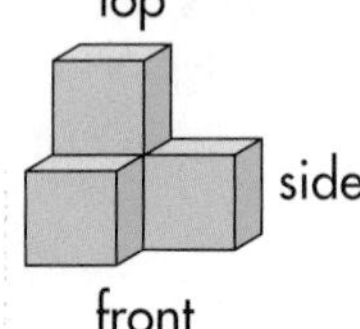

5.
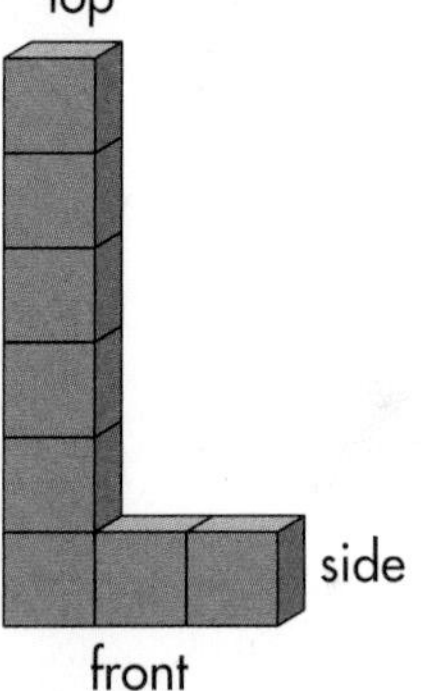

6.
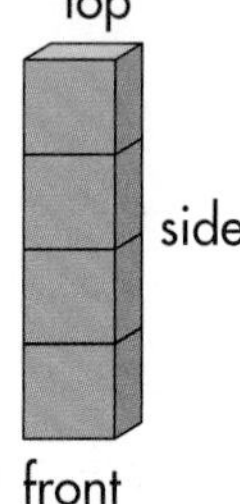

7.
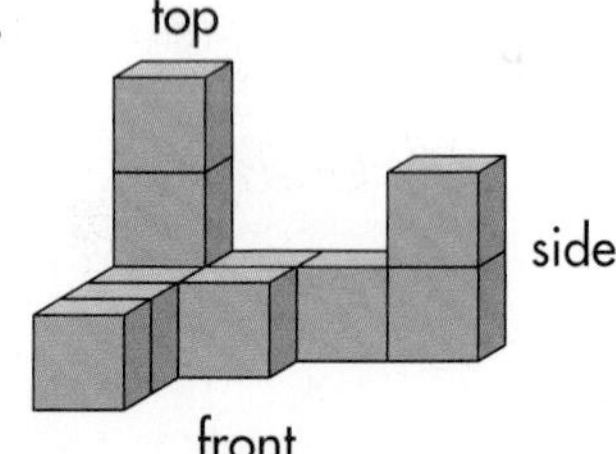

8.
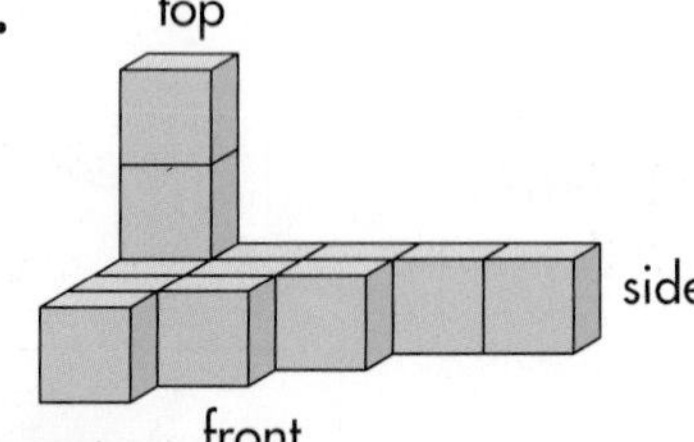

9.
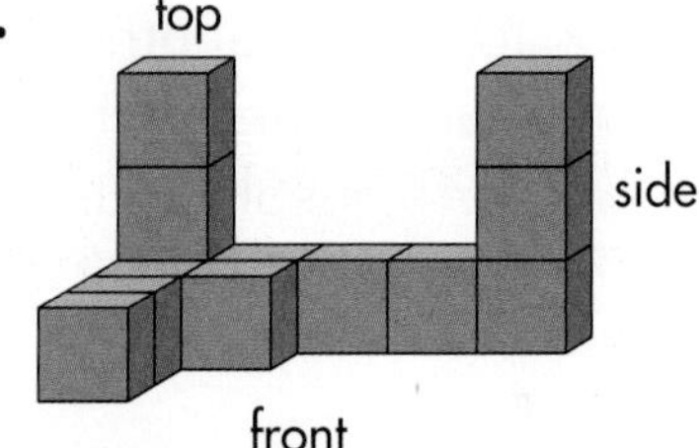

*For another example, see Set C on page 338.

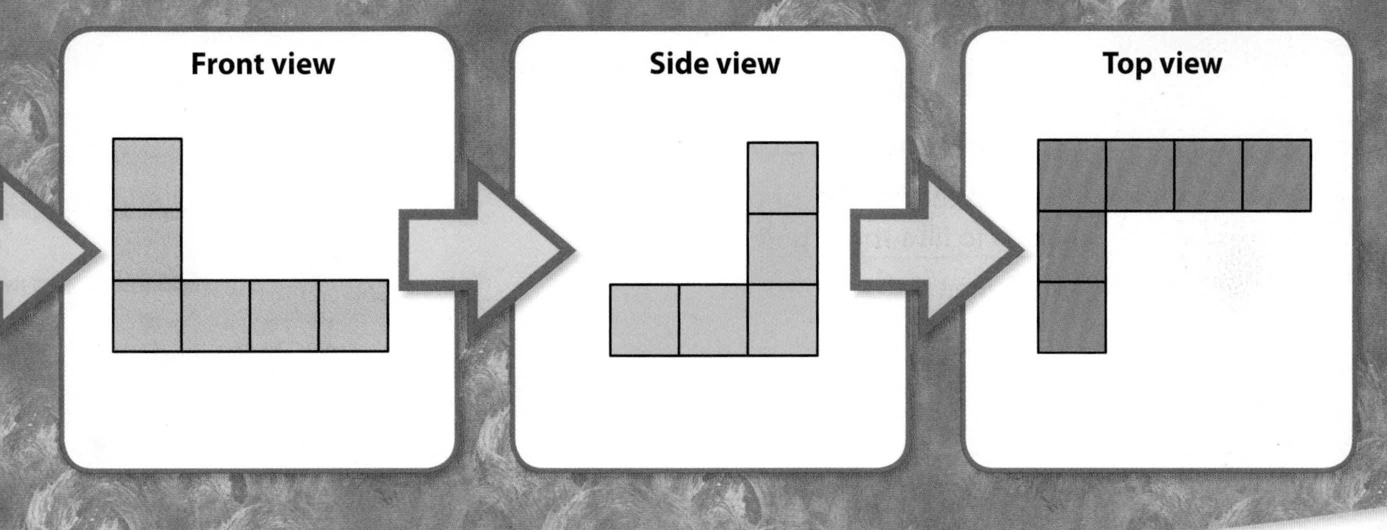

Problem Solving

10. Beth, Toby, Juan, and Patricia walked 6 miles to raise money. Beth and Patricia each raised $3.50 for each mile walked. Toby raised $3 for each mile walked, and Juan raised $22 in all. Who raised the most money?

A Beth **C** Juan

B Toby **D** Patricia

11. Hina bought 21 stickers and 7 rope bracelets. She wants to make small gift packs for her friends. Each gift pack has 3 stickers and 1 rope bracelet. Stickers cost $1.50 each, and bracelets cost $2 each. How much does it cost Hina to make each gift pack?

A $45.50 **C** $3.50

B $6.50 **D** None of the above

12. Draw the front, side, and top view of this stack of cubes and cylinders.

13. A bag contains 5 red marbles, 1 green marble, and 1 yellow marble. If you choose one marble, describe the chance of drawing a red marble.

A Certain **C** Likely

B Impossible **D** Unlikely

14. How many blocks are not visible from the top view?

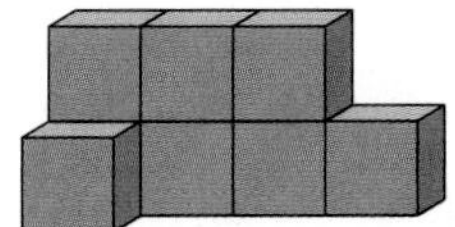

15. In the figure below, which face is parallel to Face *ABCD*?

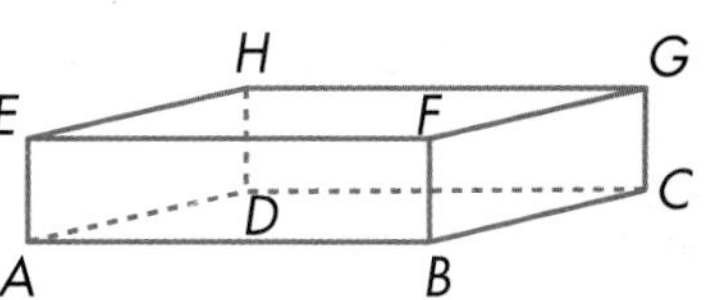

A *BCGF* **C** *EFGH*

B *ADHE* **D** *DCGH*

16. If 10 cubes are stacked vertically, how many cubes are not visible from the top view?

Lesson

14-5

MG 1.3 Understand the concept of volume and use the appropriate units in common measuring systems (i.e., cubic centimeter [cm^3], cubic meter [m^3], cubic inch [in^3], cubic yard [yd^3]) to compute the volume of rectangular solids. Also **MG 1.0, 1.4.**

Models and Volume

unit cubes

How can you measure space inside a solid figure?

Volume is the number of cubic units needed to fill a solid figure.

A cubic unit is the volume of a cube 1 unit on each edge. What is the volume of this solid?

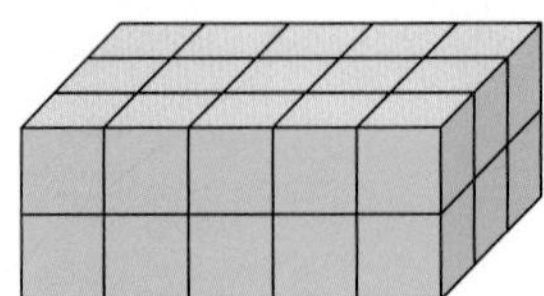

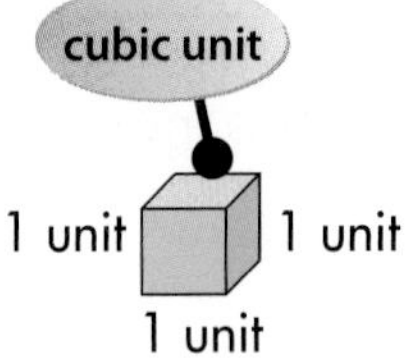

Guided Practice*

Do you know HOW?

Use cubes to make a model of each rectangular prism. Find the volume by counting the number of cubes needed to make the model.

1. 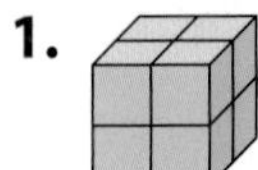

2. 

Do you UNDERSTAND?

3. Make a model of a rectangular prism with a base that is 3 cubes long by 3 cubes wide. The height of the prism is 2 cubes. Then draw a picture of your model.

4. If you add another layer to the top of the prism in Exercise 1, what is the new volume?

Independent Practice

In **5** through **8**, find the number of cubes needed to make each rectangular prism. You can use unit cubes or you can count the cubes by looking at the drawing.

5. 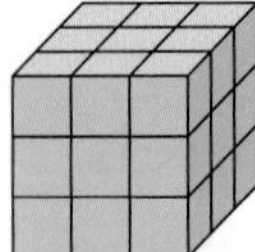

6. 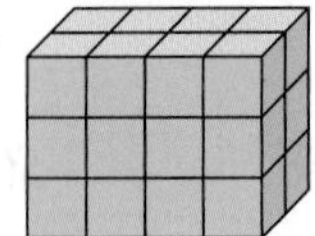

7. 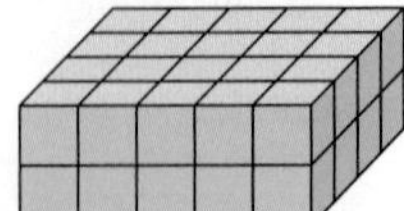

8. 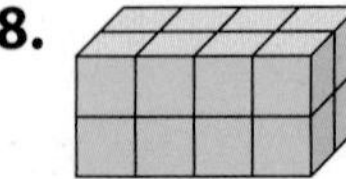

9. How many cubes would it take to make a model of a rectangular prism that is 4 units long by 3 units wide by 3 units high?

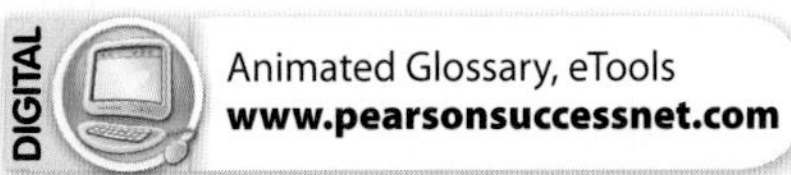

*For another example, see Set D on page 339.

Use cubic units to make a model.

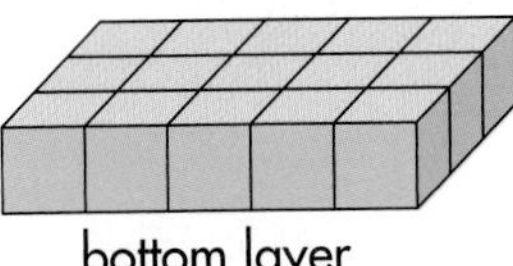

Count the number of cubes.

There are 15 cubes in the bottom layer

There are two layers.

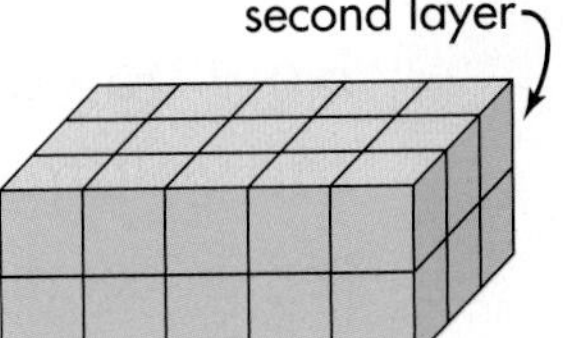

Multiply the volume of the bottom layer by 2.

The volume of the prism is 2×15 or 30 cubic units.

Problem Solving

For **10** through **13**, use the table at the right.

Prism	Model
A	
B	
C	

Compare the volumes of the prisms. Write $<$, $>$, or $=$ for each ◯.

10. Prism A ◯ Prism B

11. Prism B ◯ Prism C

12. If you added another layer of unit cubes on top of Prism A, what would its volume be?

13. If you put Prism C on top of Prism A, what would the volume of the new solid be?

14. **Number Sense** A jaguar is 80 inches long. A school's jaguar mascot is 7 feet tall. Is the mascot longer or shorter than a real jaguar?

15. **Reasoning** Ms. Kellson's storage closet is 3 feet long, 3 feet wide, and 7 feet high. Can she fit 67 boxes that are 1-foot cubes in her closet? Explain your answer.

16. **Think About the Process** One carton of books weighs 8.4 kg. Ramon put a book weighing 1.2 kg into the carton and removed 2 books weighing 1.1 kg each. Which number sentence could be used to find the final weight of the carton?

A $8.4 + 1.2 + 2.2$

B $8.4 + 1.2 - (2 \times 1.1)$

C $(8.4 + 1.2) \times 2 - 1.1$

D $8.4 + 1.2 + 2(1.1)$

Lesson

14-6

MG 1.3 Understand the concept of volume and use the appropriate units in common measuring systems (i.e., cubic centimeter [cm^3], cubic meter [m^3], cubic inch [$in.^3$], cubic yard [yd^3]) to compute the volume of rectangular solids.
Also **MG 1.4**

Volume

How do you use a formula to find the volume of a rectangular prism?

Remember that volume is the number of cubic units $(\text{units})^3$ needed to fill a solid figure.

The volume of the rectangular prism at the right is 72 cubic units.

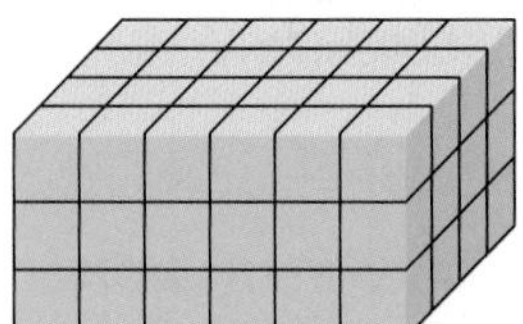

Another Example **How can you find the volume of a rectangular prism when the area of the base is given?**

If a rectangular prism has a base area *B* and a height *h*, use this formula:

Volume = base × height

$V = B \times h$

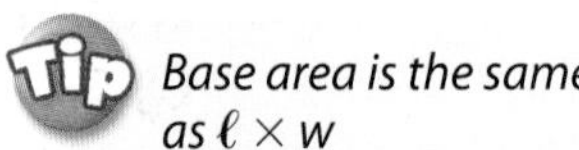

Tip *Base area is the same as $\ell \times w$*

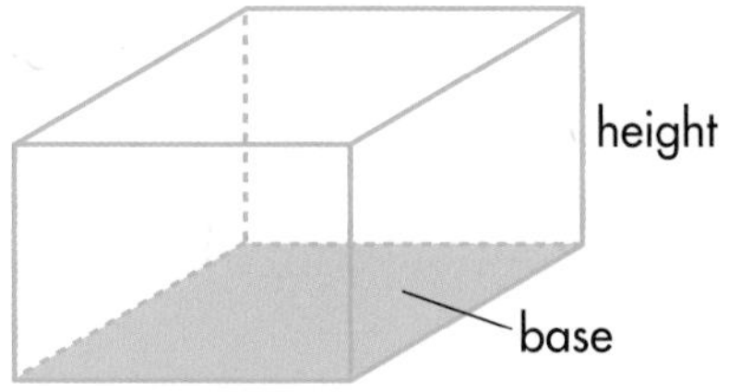

Find the volume of a rectangular prism with a base area of 56 cm^2 and a height of 6 cm.

$V = B \times h$

$V = 56 \times 6$

$V = 336 \text{ cm}^3$

The volume of the rectangular prism is 336 cm^3.

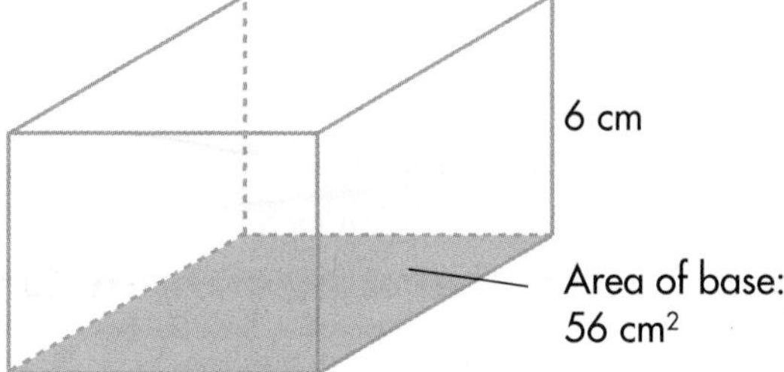

Explain It

1. How is counting cubes related to the formulas for finding volume?
2. How do you know which formula for volume to use?

If the measurements of a rectangular prism are given in length l, width w, and height h, then use this formula to find volume V:

Volume = (length × width) × height

$V = (\ell \times w) \times h$

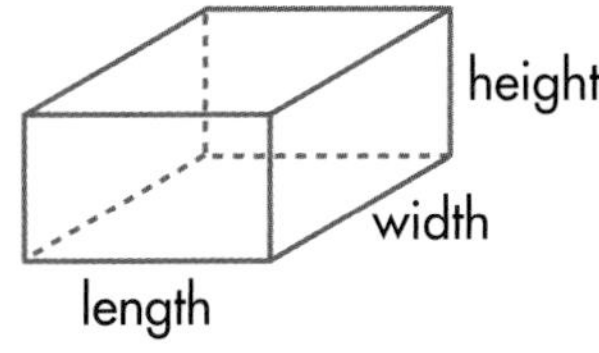

Use the formula to find the volume of the rectangular prism.

$V = (\ell \times w) \times h$

$V = (6 \times 4) \times 3$

$V = 72 \text{ ft}^3$

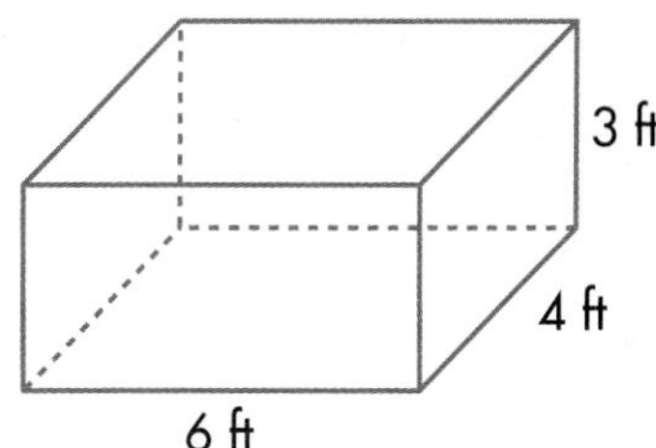

The volume of the rectangular prism is 72 ft^3.

Guided Practice*

Do you know HOW?

In **1** through **3**, find the volume of each rectangular prism.

1.

2.

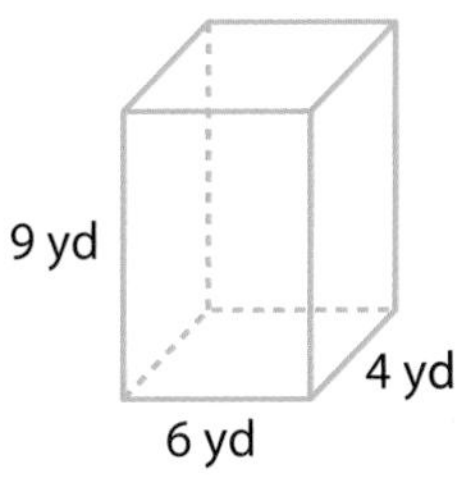

3. Base area: 26 m^2
height: 4 m

Do you UNDERSTAND?

4. In the example above, could you first multiply the height by the width?

5. A cereal box measures 6 in. by 10 in. by 2 in. Draw a rectangular prism and label it. What is the volume of the figure you drew?

6. **Writing to Explain** How can you use different methods to find the volumes of the prisms in Exercises 1–3?

Independent Practice

In **7** through **12**, find the volume of each rectangular prism.

7.

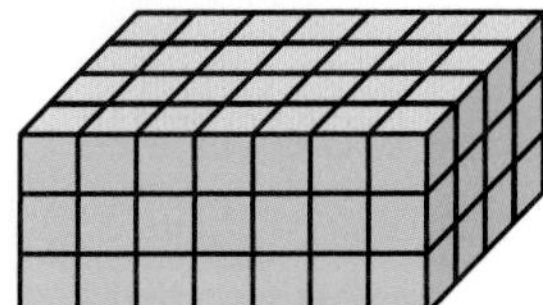

8.

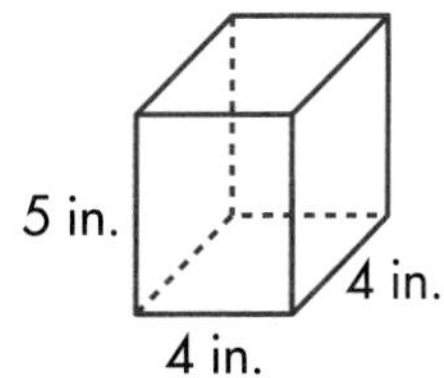

9.

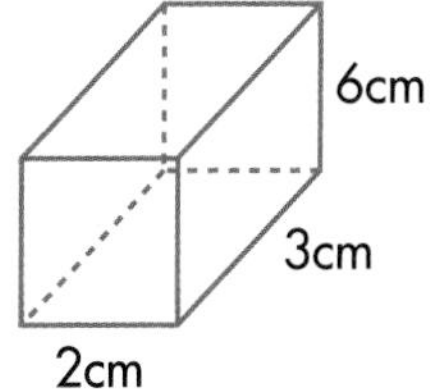

10.

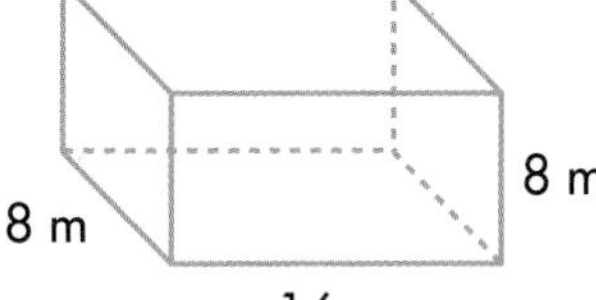

11.

12.

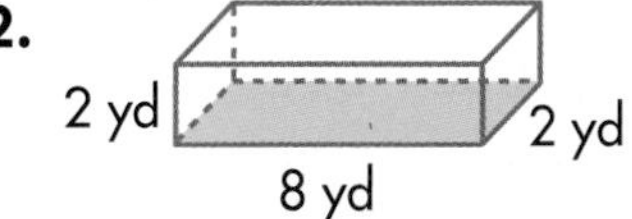

Animated Glossary
www.pearsonsuccessnet.com

*For another example, see Set E on page 339.

Independent Practice

For **13** through **15**, find the volume of each rectangular prism.

13. Length: 8 in., width: 7 in., height: 5 in.

14. Base area: 100 ft^2 height: 17 ft

15. Base area: 72 yd^2 height: 8 yd

Problem Solving

For **16** through **18**, use the information below.

Sixty-four students are planning a field trip to the Art Museum. Each student will pay $9. Each van can hold 7 students and 1 driver.

16. How much money will be collected if all the students attend?

17. How many vans will be needed if all the students travel to the museum?

18. The school pays each driver $50 to drive the van. If the round trip takes 4 hours, how much does each driver make per hour?

19. A refrigerator measures 6 feet tall, 4 feet wide, and 3 feet deep. What is the volume of the refrigerator?

20. Only 3 students per event can win medals at the track meet. If 9 students are competing, what fraction of the students will win a medal?

21. What is the perimeter of this figure?

16 cm
9 cm
11 cm
20 cm

22. Algebra Last week 22 people worked a total of 1,100 hours. Each person worked the same number of hours. Which equation demonstrates this situation?

A $1{,}100h = 22$

B $22 \div h = 1{,}100$

C $h \div 1{,}100 = 22$

D $22h = 1{,}100$

23. Writing to Explain Harry is in line at the store. He has 3 items that cost $5.95, $4.25, and $1.05. Explain how Harry can add the cost of the items mentally before he pays for them.

24. Estimation The Outer Bay exhibit in Monterey, California, has a viewing window that is 56.5 feet long, 17 feet tall, and 13 inches thick. Estimate its volume in cubic feet. HINT: 13 inches is about 1 foot.

25. Think About the Process Which of the following expressions could be used to find the volume of this indoor fish pond?

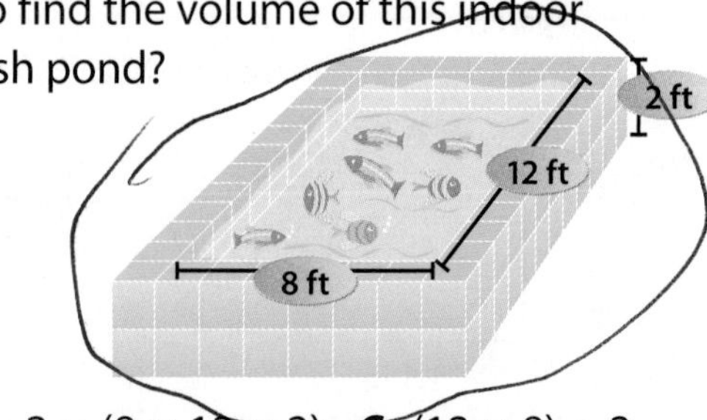

A $2 \times (8 \times 12 \times 2)$

B 8×12

C $(12 \times 8) + 2$

D $(12 \times 8) \times 2$

26. Algebra Find $3c - 17$ if $c = 20$.

Find each quotient. Simplify if possible.

1. $4\frac{1}{2} \div 1\frac{1}{4}$ **2.** $2\frac{1}{2} \div 1\frac{1}{2}$ **3.** $3\frac{1}{6} \div 2\frac{2}{3}$

4. $2\frac{2}{5} \div 1\frac{1}{3}$ **5.** $7\frac{1}{2} \div \frac{1}{4}$ **6.** $6\frac{3}{4} \div 9$

Find each sum. Simplify if possible.

7. $2\frac{1}{2} + 1\frac{3}{10}$ **8.** $4\frac{3}{4} + 2\frac{1}{12}$ **9.** $1\frac{2}{3} + 1\frac{5}{6}$ **10.** $2\frac{1}{4} + 3\frac{3}{8}$ **11.** $\frac{11}{12} + 3\frac{1}{3}$

Find each difference. Simplify if possible.

12. $\frac{5}{6} - \frac{2}{3}$ **13.** $\frac{7}{10} - \frac{1}{2}$ **14.** $\frac{1}{4} - \frac{1}{6}$ **15.** $\frac{4}{9} - \frac{1}{3}$ **16.** $\frac{3}{4} - \frac{1}{12}$

Error Search Find each answer that is not correct. Write it correctly and explain the error.

17. $4\frac{1}{2} \div 2\frac{1}{6} = 2\frac{1}{13}$ **18.** $3\frac{5}{6} + 2\frac{2}{3} = 5\frac{1}{2}$ **19.** $\frac{8}{9} - \frac{1}{3} = \frac{7}{6}$

Number Sense

Estimating and Reasoning Write whether each statement is true or false. Explain your reasoning.

20. The product of 4 and $\frac{3}{5}$ is less than 4.

21. The sum of 14.84 and 13.96 is greater than 27 but less than 29.

22. The product of 20 and 4.89 is closer to 80 than 100.

23. The quotient of 32,480 ÷ 40 is less than 800.

24. The product of 6.12 and 40.32 is greater than 240.

25. The sum of 7.97 + 4.25 is 0.03 less than 12.25.

26. The quotient of 1.87 ÷ 3 is closer to 0.7 than 0.6.

Lesson
14-7

MR 1.2 Determine when and how to break a problem into simpler parts.
Also MR 2.2, MG 2.4

Problem Solving

Use Objects and Solve a Simpler Problem

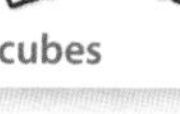
cubes

Shown at the right are 27 cubes that were glued together to form a larger cube. Then, all 6 faces of the larger cube were painted. How many of the 27 cubes have paint on 1 face? On 2 faces? Use cubes to make a model.

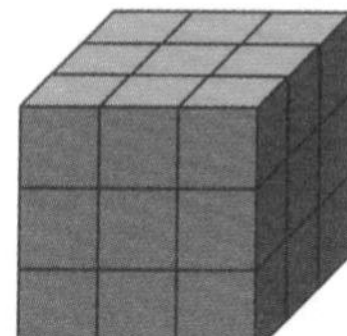

Guided Practice*

Do you know HOW?

1. Use cubes and the example of the simpler problem above to build a larger cube with 4 layers. Each layer will have 4 rows of 4 cubes. How many cubes will the larger cube contain?

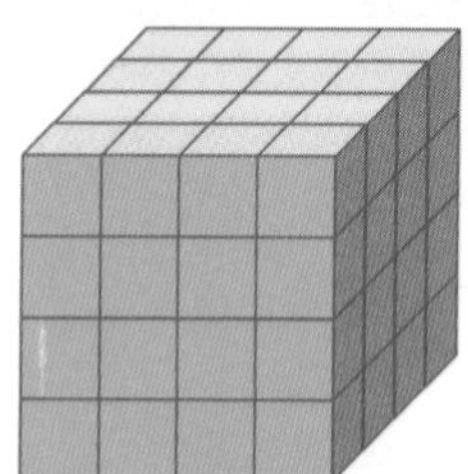

Do you UNDERSTAND?

2. Think of gluing the cubes together for the $4 \times 4 \times 4$ cube you made. Then, think of painting the outside faces. How many cubes will have paint on 1 side? On 2 sides? On 3 sides?

3. **Write a Problem** Write a real-world problem that involves using objects to help solve a simpler problem.

Independent Practice

In **4** through **8**, use objects to help you solve a simpler problem. Use the solution to help you solve the original problem.

4. Alicia uses wood timbers to build steps. The pattern is shown for 1, 2, 3, and 4 steps. How many timbers will she need to build 10 steps?

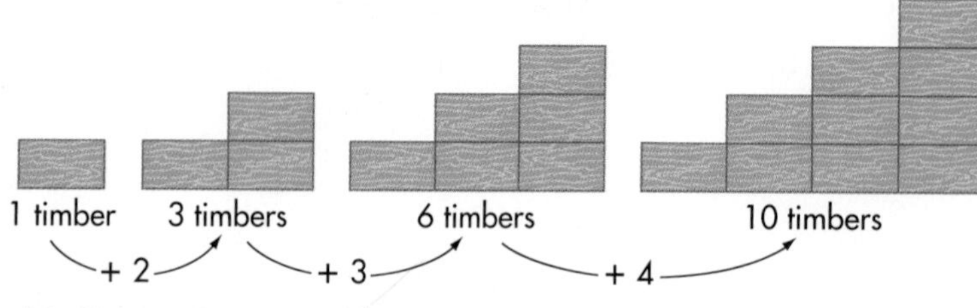

Stuck? Try this....

- What do I know?
- What am I asked to find?
- What diagram can I use to help understand the problem?
- Can I use addition, subtraction, multiplication, or division?
- Is all of my work correct?
- Did I answer the right question?
- Is my answer reasonable?

*For another example, see Set F on page 339.

Plan and Solve

How many cubes have paint on 1 face?

The center cube on each of the 6 faces of the larger cube has paint on 1 face.

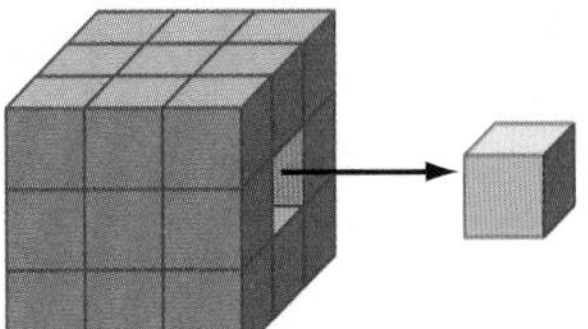

Six of these cubes have paint on 1 face.

How many cubes have paint on 2 faces?

Only 1 cube on each of the 12 edges of the larger cube has paint on 2 faces.

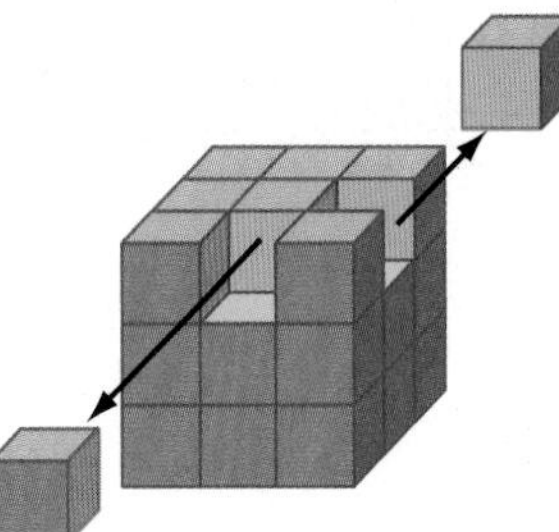

Twelve of these cubes have paint on 2 faces.

5. Four people can be seated at a table. If two tables are put together, six people can be seated. How many tables are needed to make a long table that will seat 20 people?

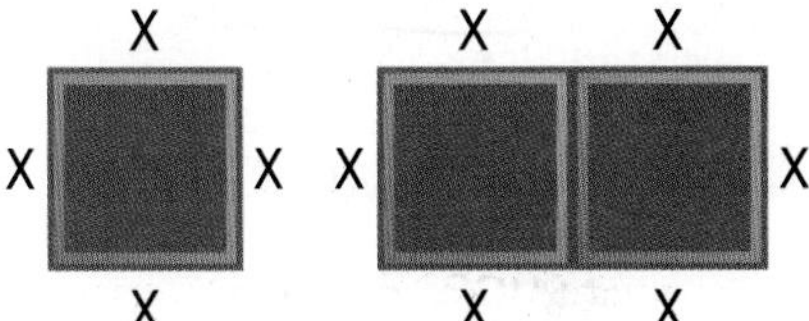

6. Jeremiah wants to make a display of CD boxes. He wants a single box on the top layer. Layers that are below the top layer must form a square, with each layer being 1 box wider than the layer above it. The display can only be 4 layers high. How many total boxes will be in the display? Use cubes.

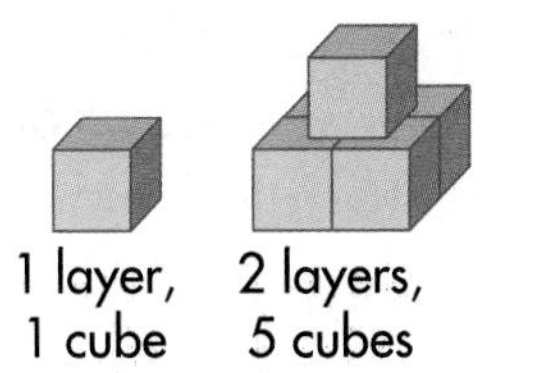

7. Katherine is constructing a patio using the design shown at the right.

a How many total blocks will she need in order to have 5 blocks in the middle row?

b How many total blocks will she need in order to have 6 blocks in the middle row?

c What do you notice about the number of blocks in the middle row compared to the total number of blocks?

2 blocks in middle row

4 blocks

3 blocks in middle row

9 blocks

8. An artist wants to cut 1 flat sheet of copper into 16 equal pieces. Before he cuts, he will draw segments on the sheet of copper showing where to make the cuts. How many horizontal and vertical segments will he need to draw?

9. There are 24 balls in a large bin. Two out of every three are basketballs. The rest are footballs. How many basketballs are in the bin?

Test Prep

1. Which solid has two bases that are parallel, congruent circles? (14-1)

A Cone

B Pyramid

C Cube

D Cylinder

2. What solid can be made with the net shown? (14-2)

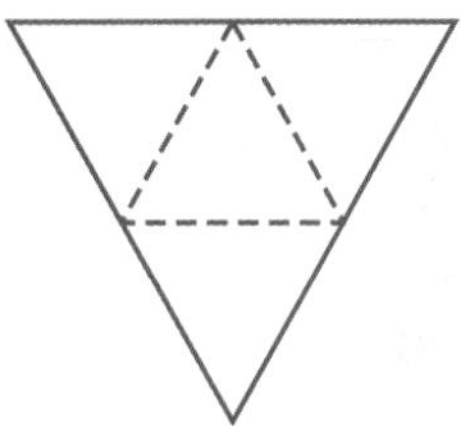

A Triangular Pyramid

B Triangular Prism

C Rectangular Pyramid

D Cube

3. Justin stacked boxes in a closet as shown. How many boxes are in the closet? (14-5)

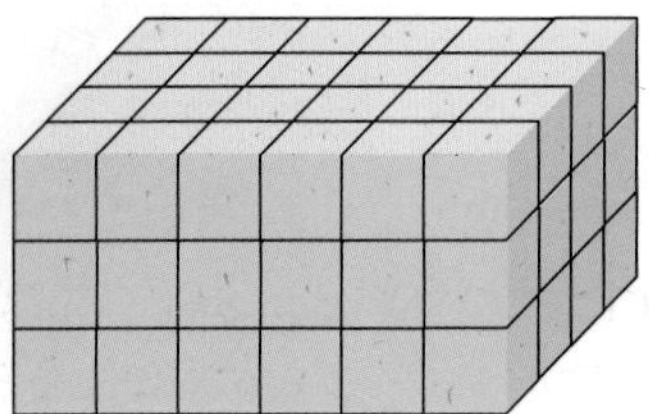

A 18 boxes

B 54 boxes

C 72 boxes

D 108 boxes

4. What is the surface area of the prism formed by the net shown? (14-3)

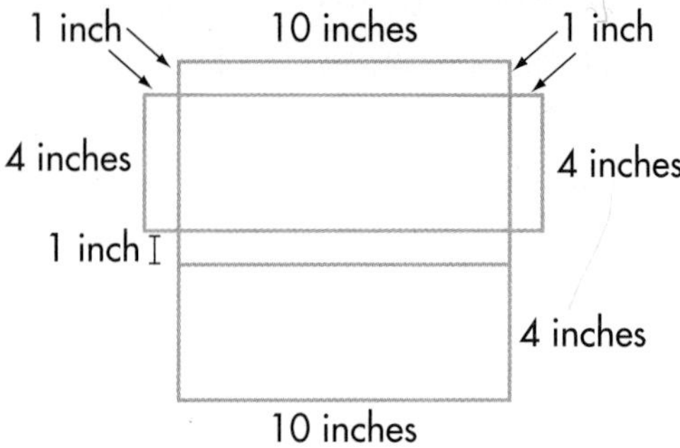

A 44 $in.^2$

B 100 $in.^2$

C 108 $in.^2$

D 120 $in.^2$

5. Nita stacked some crates to make a bookshelf as shown. Which of the following is the top view of the crates? (14-4)

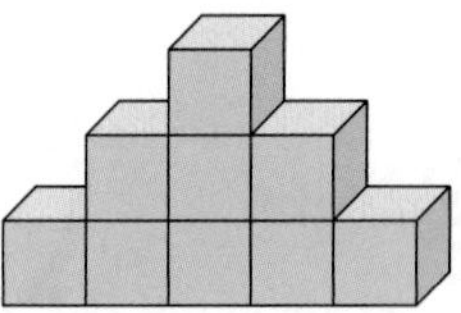

A

B

C

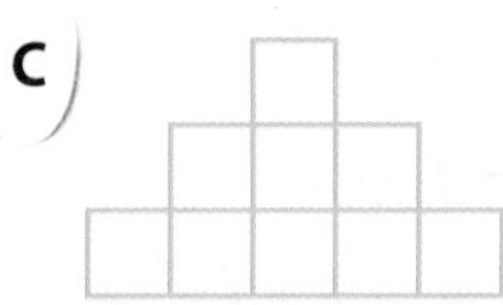

D

Test Prep

6. Todd's mother is setting up a business renting storage units. She is arranging the units in an L-shape. If she puts 3 units on each side of the L, she has 5 units in all, as shown. How many units does she have if she puts 8 units on each side of the L? (14-7)

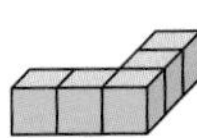

A 13

B 15

C 16

D 17

7. Which trunk has a volume of 30 cubic feet? (14-6)

A

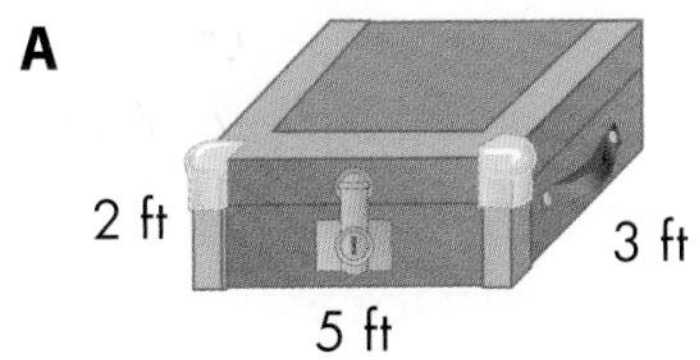

B

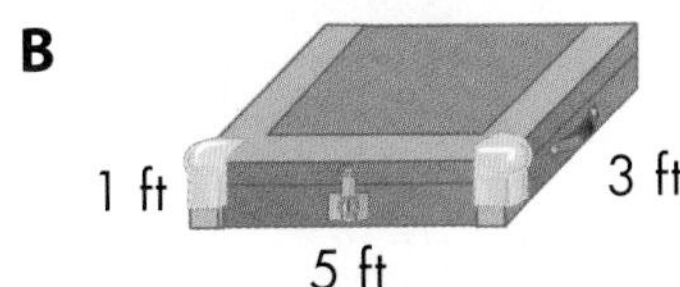

C

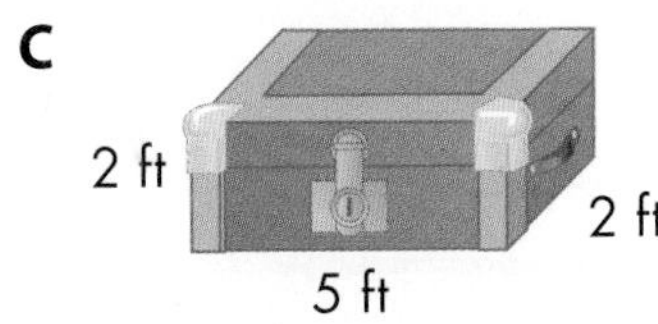

D

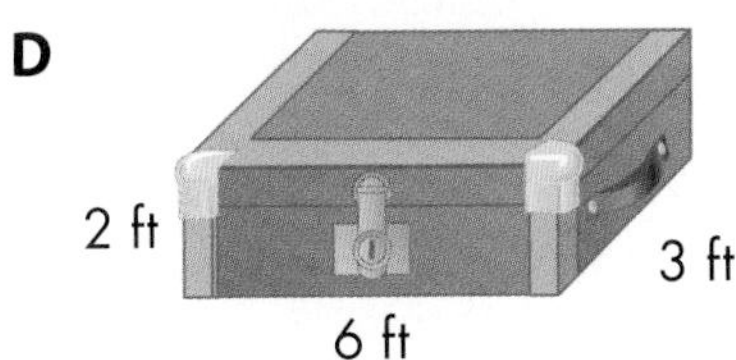

8. What is the surface area of the trunk shown? (14-3)

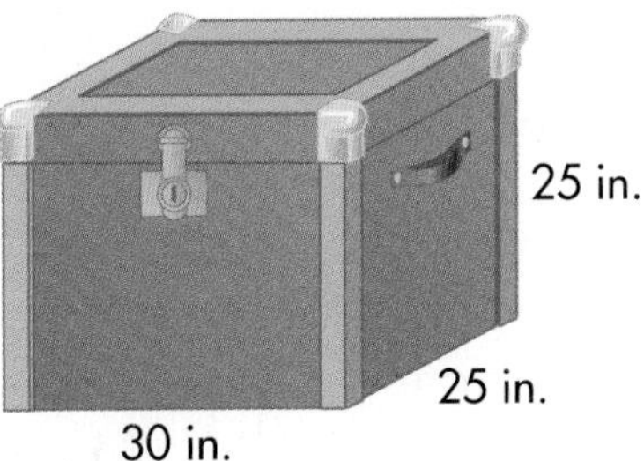

A 320 in^2

B 3,000 in^2

C 4,250 in^2

D 18,750 in^2

9. What is the volume of the bale of hay? (14-6)

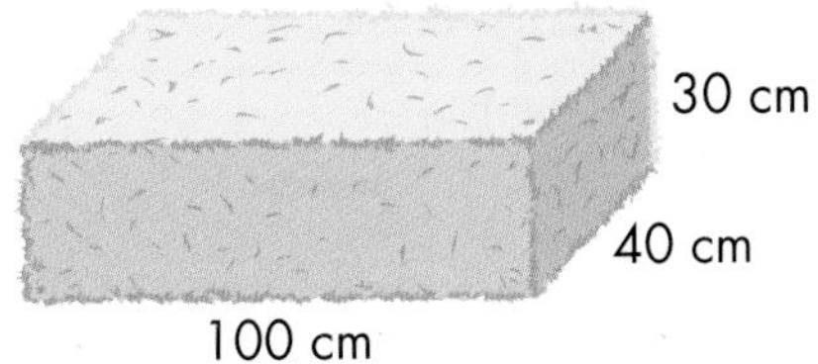

A 120,000 cm^2

B 120,000 cm^3

C 12,000 cm^2

D 12,000 cm^3

10. The rectangular prism shown is made from boxes that are 1 cubic meter. What is the volume of the prism? (14-5)

A 9 m^3

B 12 m^3

C 21 m^3

D 36 m^3

Reteaching

Set A, pages 318–320

Solids are classified by their shape and their faces, edges and vertices. What solid figure is represented at the right?

Faces: All triangles, except for the base. They have a common meeting point not on the base. Therefore, it is a pyramid.

Base: A square, so it is a square pyramid

Remember A prism has two congruent parallel bases, but a pyramid has only one base.

1. Classify the solid. List the edges and vertices.

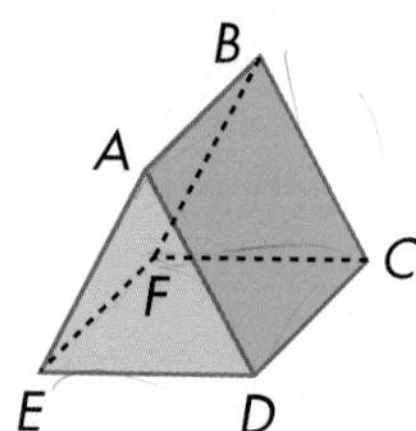

Set B, pages 322–325

A net is a plane figure which when folded gives a solid figure. The net below folds to make a rectangular prism.

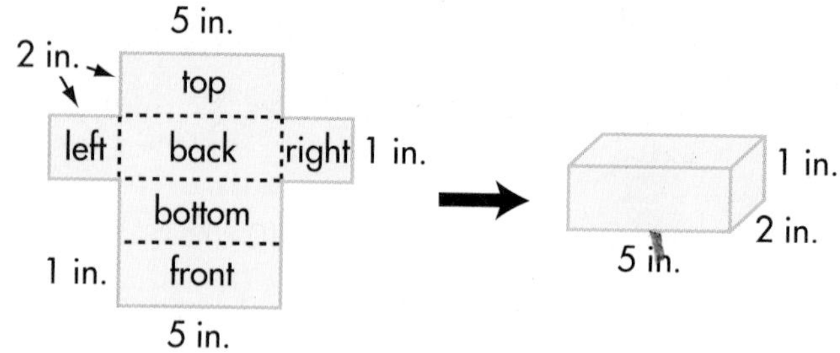

Find the surface area of the prism.

$$SA = (5 \times 2) + (5 \times 2) + (2 \times 1) + (2 \times 1) + (1 \times 5) + (1 \times 5) = 34 \text{ in}^2$$

Remember that surface area is always measured in square units, such as m^2.

1. What figure will the net make?

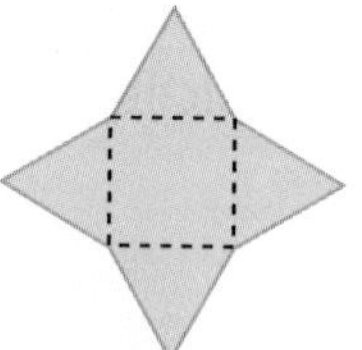

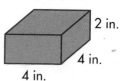

2. What is the surface area of the prism?

2 in.
4 in.
4 in.

Set C, pages 326–327

Draw the front, top and side views of the solid made from stacked cubes.

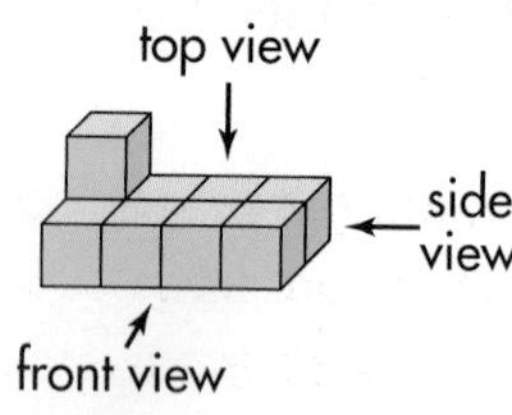

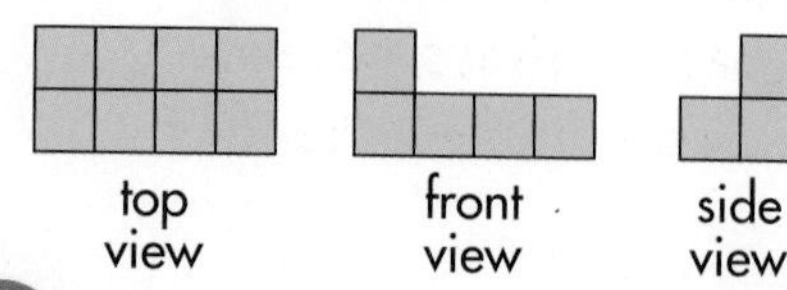

Remember to consider blocks hidden from your view.

1. Draw the front, top and side views of the stacked solid.

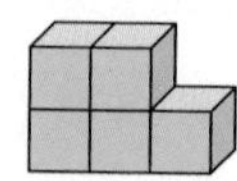

Set D, pages 328–329

Find the number of cubes needed to make this rectangular prism.

There are 3 rows of 5 cubes in the bottom layer. There are 3 layers. So the total number of cubes is $3 \times 5 \times 3$ or 45. The volume is 45 in^3.

Remember that you can find the number of cubes in each layer and then multiply by the number of layers.

Find each volume. You can use cubes or use the drawing.

1. 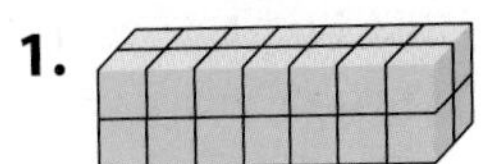

2.

Set E, pages 330–332

Find the volume of this rectangular prism.

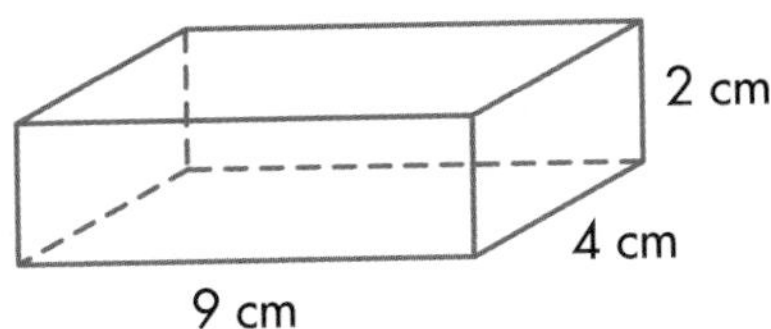

Volume = length × width × height.

$V = l \times w \times h$
$V = 9 \text{ cm} \times 4 \text{ cm} \times 2 \text{ cm}$
$V = 72 \text{ cm}^3$

The volume is 72 cm^3.

Remember If you know the base area of a rectangular prism, use the formula $V = B \times h$, where B is the base area.

Find the volume of each rectangular prism.

1. Base area = 42 m^2, height = 3 meters

2. 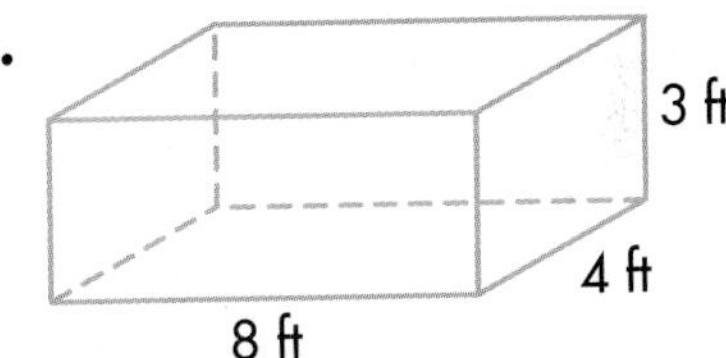

Set F, pages 334–335

To solve a simpler problem, follow these steps:

Break apart or change problem into one that is simpler to solve.

Use objects to solve the simpler problem.

Use the answers to the simpler problem to solve the original problem.

Remember You can use objects to help you see a pattern or relationship between the simpler problem and the original problem.

1. After folding a piece of paper one time, there are two sections. How many sections are there after 2 folds? After 3 folds? If you fold the paper 5 times, how many sections would you have?

Topic 15

Integers

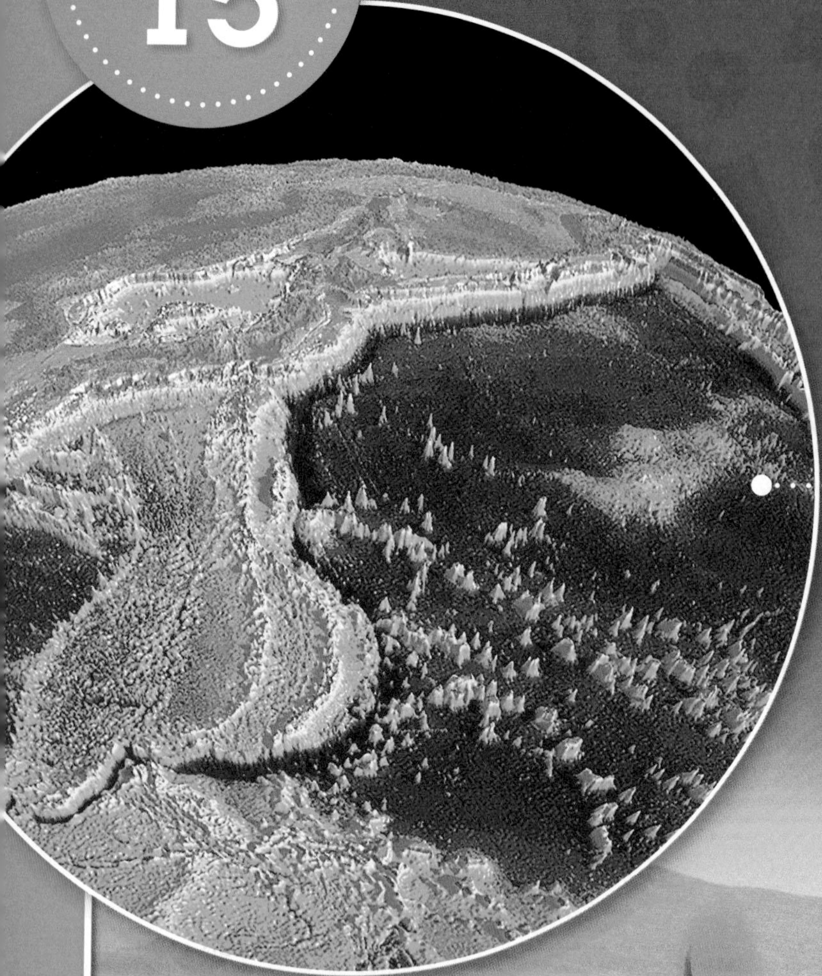

1

The Mariana Trench is the deepest ocean trench in the world. How can the depth of this trench be expressed as an integer? You will find out in Lesson 15-1.

2

Death Valley is located in the Mojave Desert and the Great Basin. This valley has the lowest elevation in the United States. What is the elevation of Death Valley? You will find out in Lesson 15-5.

3 The Colorado Potato Beetle feeds on the leaves of eggplant and potato plants. Do you think the adult Colorado Potato Beetle or the larva of this beetle is smaller? You will find out in Lesson 15-3.

4 The date a state quarter is released is determined by the order in which each state was admitted into the Union. How can you evaluate an expression to find the year California became a state? You will find out in Lesson 15-6.

Review What You Know!

Vocabulary

Choose the best term from the box.

- Associative
- fraction
- decimal
- inverse

1. Two operations that undo each other are called __?__ operations.
2. A number that contains a point to separate the ones place from the tenths place is a __?__.
3. A number used to name a part of a whole is a __?__.
4. The __?__ Property of Addition states that addends can be regrouped and the sum remains the same.

Number Sense

Compare the numbers. Use < or > for each ◯.

5. 512 ◯ 521
6. 0.379 ◯ 0.38
7. $\frac{3}{4}$ ◯ $\frac{1}{3}$
8. $2\frac{1}{5}$ ◯ $2\frac{1}{4}$

Number Lines

Write the number for each point.

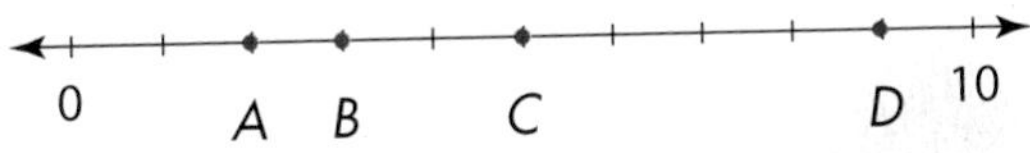

9. *C*
10. *A*
11. *B*
12. *D*

Fractions and Decimals

Writing to Explain Write an answer to the question.

13. What can you do to make comparing $\frac{3}{4}$ and 0.6 easier?

Lesson 15-1

NS 1.5 Identify and represent on a number line decimals, fractions, mixed numbers, and positive and negative integers.

Understanding Integers

What are integers and what situations can integers represent?

The highest point in Louisiana is Driskill Mountain at five hundred thirty-five feet above sea level. The lowest point is New Orleans at eight feet below sea level.

How can you write those highest and lowest points with integers?

535 feet above sea level

Driskill Mountain

New Orleans

Sea level

8 feet below sea level

Guided Practice*

Do you know HOW?

In **1** through **4**, write an integer for each word description.

1. Ten degrees below zero
2. Seventy degrees above zero
3. Two hundred thirty feet above sea level
4. Fifty-two feet below sea level

Do you UNDERSTAND?

5. In the example above, what is the opposite elevation of Driskill Mountain, written as an integer?
6. How far away from sea level is 512 feet below sea level?
7. How would you show sea level represented as an integer?

Independent Practice

In **8** through **12**, use the number line to identify the integer at each point.

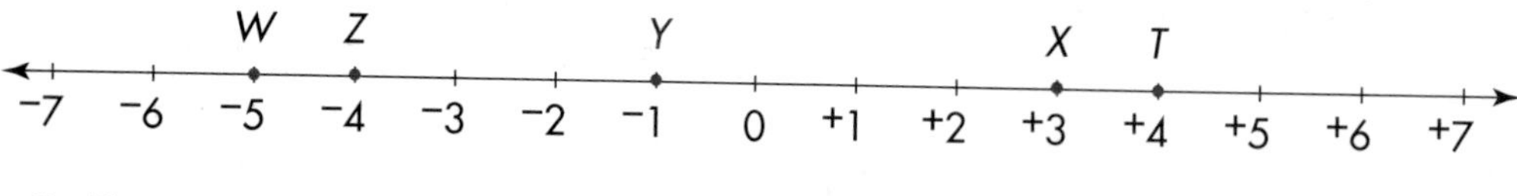

8. *T*
9. *W*
10. *X*
11. *Y*
12. *Z*

In **13** through **20**, write an integer for each word description.

13. A withdrawal of $20
14. A deposit of one hundred dollars
15. A gain of three inches
16. A loss of six yards
17. A loss of 7 pounds
18. A temperature drop of 2 degrees
19. 6 steps forward
20. 10 seconds before blastoff

*For another example, see Set A on page 360.

Distance above sea level is greater than zero. It is represented by a positive integer. $^{+}535$

Distance below sea level is less than zero. It is represented by the negative integer. $^{-}8$

Integers name magnitude (distance) and direction from 0.

0

$^{-}8$ $^{+}535$

The magnitude of $^{-}8$ is 8. The direction is negative.

The magnitude of $^{+}535$ is 535. The direction is positive.

Integers are the whole numbers and their opposites; 0 is its own opposite.

Numbers that are opposites of each other have the same magnitude (distance from 0).

$^{-}5$ and $^{+}5$ are the same distance from 0.

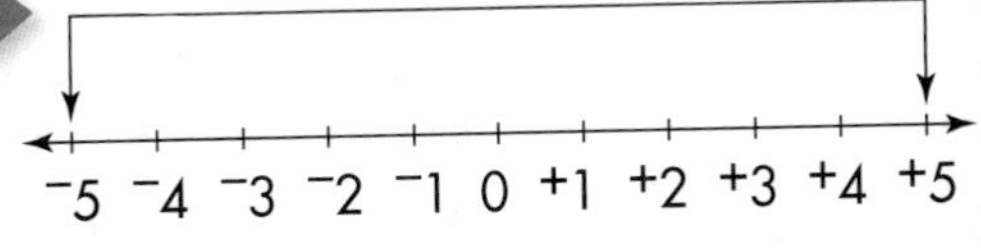

Negative integers are less than zero.

Positive integers are greater than zero.

$^{-}5$ is read "negative five."

$^{+}5$ is read "positive five."

$^{-}2$ is the opposite of $^{+}2$.
$^{+}4$ is the opposite of $^{-}4$.

Problem Solving

21. A football team started at the 20-yard line. In the first two plays, the team lost 4 yards and gained 4 yards. Where did they end up?

22. Adam has $1\frac{1}{2}$ feet of aluminum wire, 1.29 feet of copper wire, and $1\frac{5}{8}$ feet of steel wire. Adam has the most of which kind of wire?

23. A movie company announced that one of its releases lost two million, eight hundred fifty-seven thousand, nine hundred dollars. Write that number in integer form.

24. At midnight, the temperature was 2 degrees. It went down 5 degrees, then it went up 3 degrees, and then dropped 2 degrees. What was the final temperature? Show your answer on a number line.

25. **Number Sense** Julie needs to select an integer that is two less than $^{-}11$. What number should she pick? How did you find the number?

26. The Mariana Trench is located in the floor of the western North Pacific Ocean. It is 35,798 feet below sea level. Express this depth as an integer.

27. **Think About the Process** Pam made \$168.75 at a craft fair. She sold 75 of the 125 book covers she made. Which expression can you use to find the price she charged for each book cover?

A \$168.75 ÷ 75

B \$168.75 ÷ (125 + 75)

C \$168.75 ÷ 125

D \$168.75 ÷ (125 − 75)

28. **Writing to Explain** Describe how to find the surface area of the rectangular prism shown below. Then find the surface area.

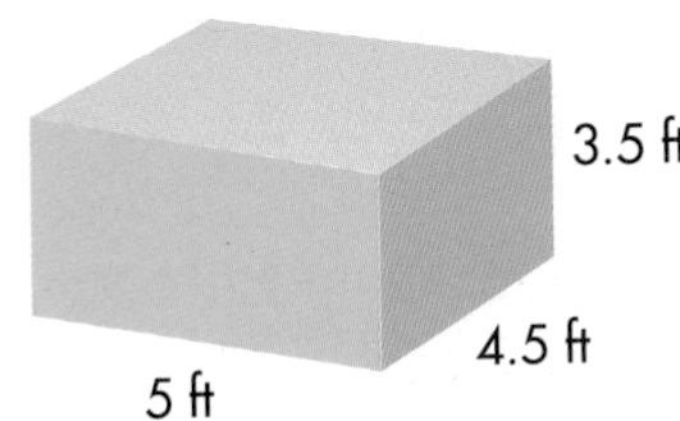

Lesson

15-2

NS 1.5 Identify and represent on a number line decimals, fractions, mixed number, and positive and negative integers.

Comparing and Ordering Integers

How do you compare and order integers?

Alan's family spent a week at a resort in Utah. The resort newspaper listed the low temperature for each night that week.

Which night had a lower temperature, Thursday or Friday? What is the order from least to greatest of the low temperatures?

Data

This week's temperatures (°F)

	Low	High
Monday	6°	30°
Tuesday	0°	28°
Wednesday	4°	21°
Thursday	-7°	17°
Friday	-3°	19°

Guided Practice*

Do you know HOW?

In **1** through **4**, compare. Use $>$, $<$ or $=$ for ◯.

1. $^{+}4$ ◯ $^{+}3$

2. $^{-}2$ ◯ $^{+}2$

3. $^{-}1$ ◯ $^{-}4$

4. $^{-}10$ ◯ $^{-}11$

In **5** and **6**, order from least to greatest.

5. $^{+}8$, $^{-}5$, $^{-}2$

6. $^{-}10$, $^{+}2$, $^{-}3$

Do you UNDERSTAND?

7. Compare $^{-}7$ and $^{-}3$. Use the $>$ sign.

8. In the example above, if the temperature on Wednesday night was $^{-}9$°F, which night would have been colder, Wednesday or Thursday?

9. In the example above, order the week's high temperatures from least to greatest.

Independent Practice

In **10** through **17**, compare using $>$, $<$ or $=$ for ◯.

10. $^{+}1$ ◯ $^{+}3$

11. $^{-}4$ ◯ $^{+}9$

12. $^{+}5$ ◯ $^{-}2$

13. $^{-}11$ ◯ $^{-}10$

14. $^{-}8$ ◯ $^{-}15$

15. $^{+}10$ ◯ $^{+}11$

16. $^{-}7$ ◯ $^{-}6$

17. $^{-}1$ ◯ 0

In **18** through **33**, order from least to greatest.

18. $^{+}1$, $^{-}7$, $^{-}5$

19. 0, $^{-}3$, $^{+}6$

20. $^{-}5$, $^{+}10$, $^{-}1$

21. $^{-}4$, $^{+}11$, $^{-}6$

22. 0, $^{+}8$, $^{-}8$

23. $^{+}3$, $^{+}1$, $^{+}5$

24. $^{-}2$, $^{-}8$, $^{-}1$

25. $^{-}23$, $^{-}50$, $^{-}42$

26. $^{+}15$, $^{-}5$, $^{+}6$, $^{-}2$

27. $^{-}20$, $^{-}1$, $^{-}9$, $^{-}13$

28. 0, $^{-}19$, $^{+}5$, $^{-}4$

29. $^{-}5$, $^{-}20$, $^{-}10$, $^{-}15$

30. $^{+}6$, $^{-}3$, $^{-}2$, $^{+}7$

31. $^{-}18$, $^{-}3$, $^{+}3$, $^{-}8$

32. $^{-}5$, 0, $^{+}1$, $^{-}20$

33. $^{-}6$, $^{-}7$, $^{-}8$, $^{-}9$

*For another example, see Set B on page 360.

Compare the integers $^{-}7$ and $^{-}3$.

Locate $^{-}7$ and $^{-}3$ on a number line. Integers, just like whole numbers, fractions, and decimals, increase in value as you move from left to right.

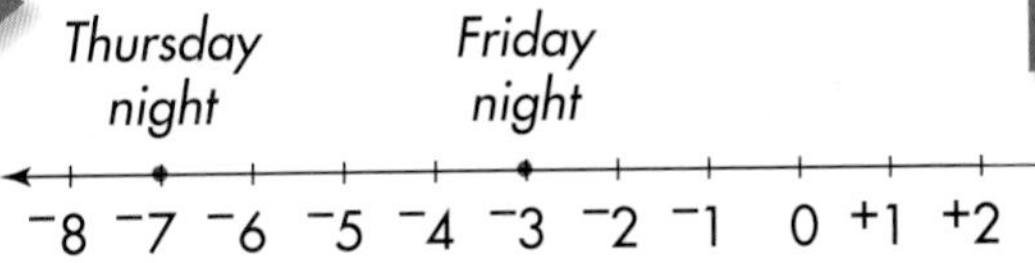

The integer $^{-}7$ is farther to the left on a number line than $^{-}3$. So, $^{-}7$ is less.

$^{-}7 < {}^{-}3$

Thursday night was colder than Friday night.

Order the integers 6, 0, 4, $^{-}7$, and $^{-}3$.

Locate the numbers on a number line.

$^{-}7$ $^{-}6$ $^{-}5$ $^{-}4$ $^{-}3$ $^{-}2$ $^{-}1$ 0 $^{+}1$ $^{+}2$ $^{+}3$ $^{+}4$ $^{+}5$ $^{+}6$

From least to greatest, the week's low temperatures are $^{-}7$, $^{-}3$, 0, 4, and 6.

Positive numbers are often written without the $^{+}$ sign.

Problem Solving

34. Sam's class played a history game. Team A had a score of 200, Team B had a score of $^{-}300$, Team C had a score of $^{-}100$ and Team D had a score of 500. Order the scores, from greatest to least.

35. **Algebra** Write an integer for x to make each statement true.

a $x > {}^{-}3$

b $x < {}^{+}1$

c $^{-}13 < x$

36. **Estimation** What is a good estimate for the value of point C on the number line?

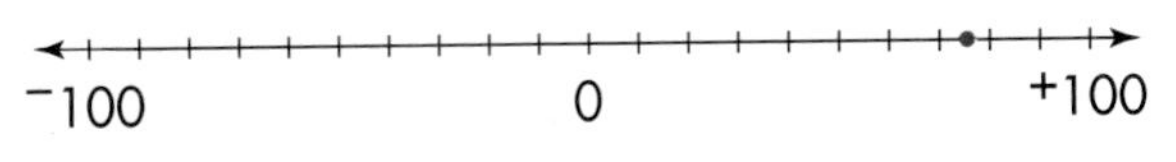

37. **Reasoning** A number, x, is four units to the left of $^{-}5$ on the number line. What is the value of x? Is x greater than or less than $^{-}5$?

38. **Writing to Explain** Is the explanation below correct? If not, tell why not and write a correct response.

$^{-}13$ is less than $^{-}12$ because it is farther to the left on the number line.

39. **Number Sense** Which integer is neither positive nor negative?

In **40** through **42**, use the map at the right.

40. Of the states shown, which had the lowest record temperature?

41. Which state had the warmest record low temperature?

42. List the record low temperatures in order from least to greatest.

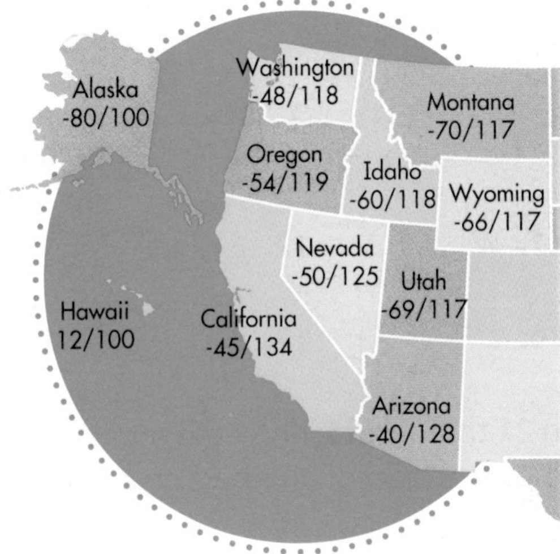

Lesson

15-3

NS 1.5 Identify and represent on a number line decimals, fractions, mixed number, and positive and negative integers.

Integers and the Number Line

How can you name and plot integers, fractions, and decimals on the same number line?

Some points are plotted on the number line below. Write a number to name each of the points *A*, *Z*, *D*, and *W*. Use integers, fractions, mixed numbers, or decimals. Name the points that represent 2.38, and $1\frac{1}{4}$, and $^{-}1$.

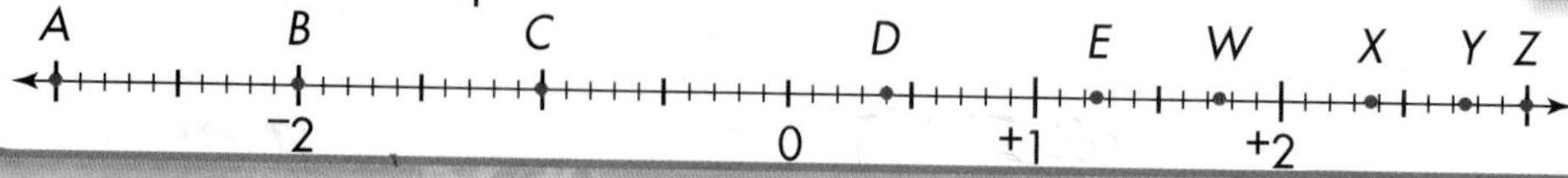

Guided Practice*

Do you know HOW?

In **1** through **4**, use the number line below. Write the number for each point.

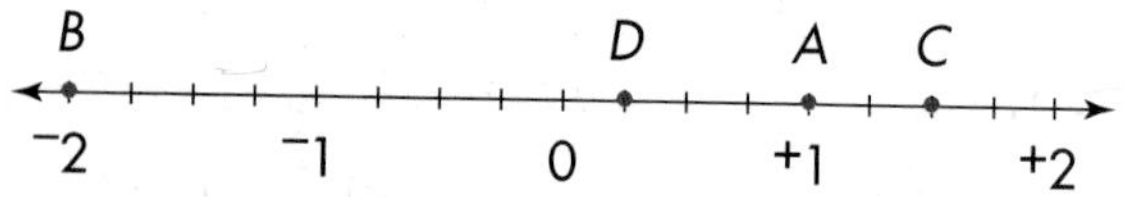

1. *A* **2.** *B* **3.** *C* **4.** *D*

In **5** and **6**, show each set of numbers on a number line.

5. $1\frac{1}{4}$, 0.75, $^{-}1$, $^{-}2$ **6.** $^{-}2$, $1\frac{3}{4}$, 0.5, 0

Do you UNDERSTAND?

7. In the example above, how could you find the points for fractions?

8. In the example above, describe where you would plot $^{+}1.35$.

9. What number is represented by point *B* above?

10. Which point above represents $2\frac{3}{4}$?

Independent Practice

In **11** through **20**, use the number line below. Write the number for each point.

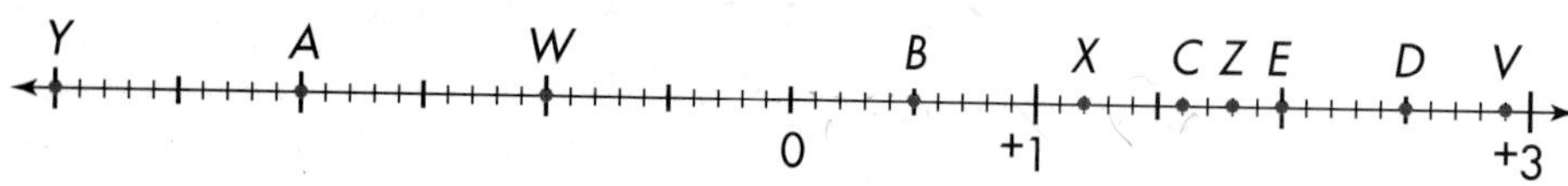

11. *W* **12.** *B* **13.** *E* **14.** *D* **15.** *A*

16. *Z* **17.** *Y* **18.** *C* **19.** *V* **20.** *X*

In **21** through **23**, order the numbers in each set from least to greatest. Show each set of numbers on a number line.

21. $^{-}2$, 1, $\frac{1}{3}$, $1\frac{2}{3}$ **22.** 3, $^{-}3$, 1.5, $2\frac{3}{4}$ **23.** 0.5, $1\frac{3}{8}$, 2.25, $^{-}1$

*For another example, see Set C on page 360.

Write a number to name a point.

The distance between the integers 0 and 1 is divided into 10 equal parts.

Point *A* is to the left of zero. Point *A* is at $^{-}3$.

Point *Z* is to the right of zero. Point *Z* is at $^{+}3$.

Point *D* is at 0.4 or $\frac{4}{10}$.

Point *W* is halfway between 1.7 and 1.8. So, point *W* is at 1.75 or $1\frac{3}{4}$.

Find which point represents a given number.

Since 2.38 is between 2.3 and 2.4 and is closer to 2.4, point *X* represents 2.38.

Since $1\frac{1}{4} = 1.25$ and 1.25 is halfway between 1.2 and 1.3, point *E* represents 1.25.

Since $^{-}1$ is opposite of $^{+}1$, point *C* represents $^{-}1$.

Problem Solving

24. Writing to Explain What might you do to order the numbers $^{-}8$, $^{-}10$, $^{+}8$, and $^{+}5$ without using a number line?

25. Number Sense Kathy owes Marty $\frac{1}{2}$ of a dollar. Mina owes Marty 0.6 of a dollar. Who owes Marty more money?

26. Geometry Find the perimeter of the equilateral triangle below.

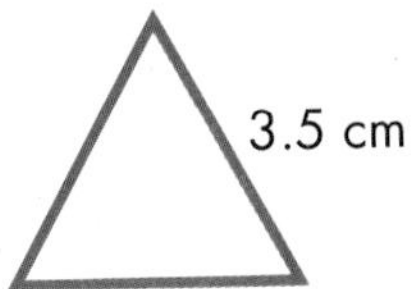

27. The larva of the Colorado Potato Beetle is 0.5 inches long. The adult Colorado Potato Beetle is $\frac{3}{8}$ inch long. Which one is smaller, the adult or the larva?

28. Which number in the following choices makes the statement true?

$$^{-}6 > n$$

A 0 **B** $^{-}5$ **C** $^{-}7$ **D** $^{-}4$

29. Joey got 19 out of 23 questions correct on his Social Studies test. If each question was worth 3 points, how many points did Joey earn?

30. The table below names the lowest points on each continent. Order the points from lowest to highest.

Data

Continent	Height (feet)
Africa	-512
Antarctica	-8,327
Asia	-1,348
Europe	-92
North America	-282
Oceania	-52
South America	-131

31. Which number line shows a point that best represents $^{+}1.6$?

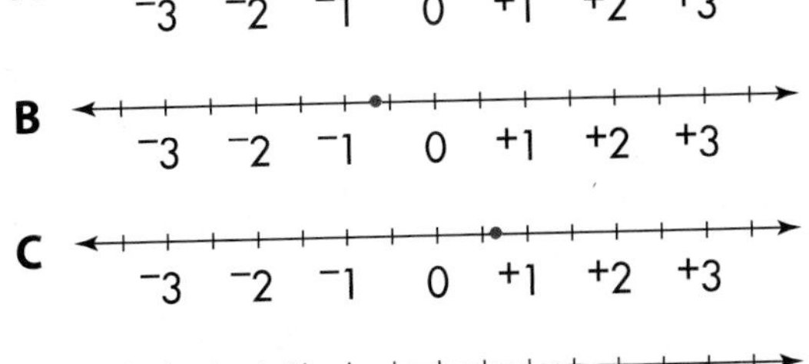

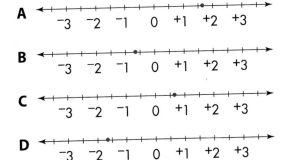

Lesson

15-4

NS 2.1 Add, subtract, multiply, and divide with decimals; add with negative integers; subtract positive integers from negative integers; and verify the reasonableness of the results.

Adding Integers

How can you add two integers?

A football coach keeps a record of the yards gained or lost on each play. What was the total number of yards gained or lost after the two plays shown?

Choose an Operation Add to find the result of joining the two plays.

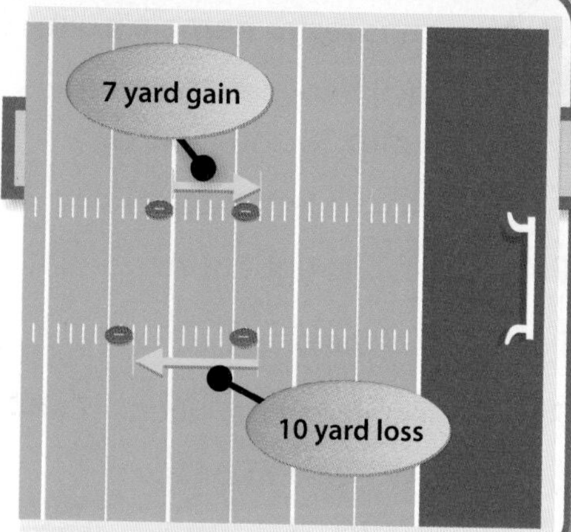

Another Example How can you add two negative integers?

You know how to represent integers on a number line. In this lesson you are using a number line to add integers.

On the next play, the football team lost 4 yards and received a 5-yard penalty. How many yards did the team lose on that play?

Find $^{-}4 + {}^{-}5$.

Start at 0. Face the positive integers. Move backward 4 steps for $^{-}4$.

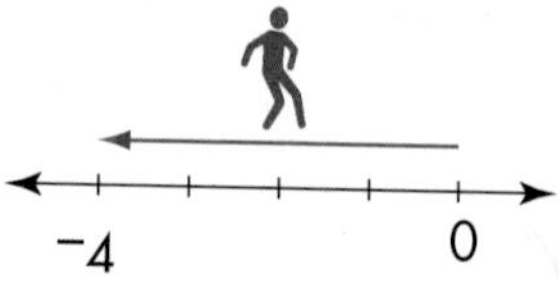

Then move backward 5 steps for $^{-}5$.

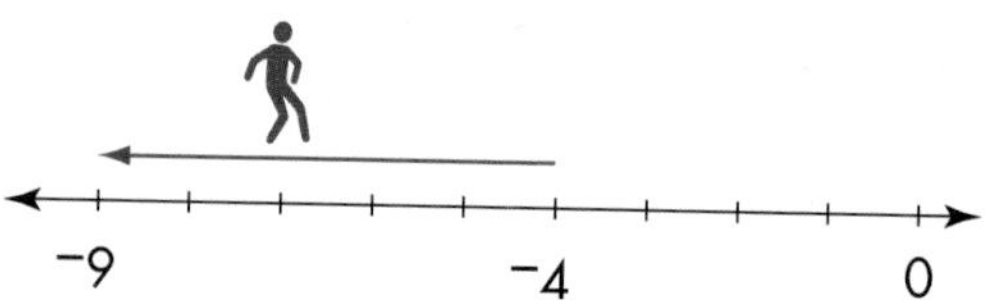

You stop at $^{-}9$. So, $^{-}4 + {}^{-}5 = {}^{-}9$

The football team lost a total of 9 yards on that play.

When adding two integers with the same sign, you move in the same direction on the number line, so you add the magnitude of the numbers. You move in the same direction, so the sign of the sum will be the same as the sign of the addends.

Explain It

1. In the example above, why did you move backwards twice?
2. How would the sum be different if the team had gained 4 yards and the 5-yard penalty was against the other team? How would that sum look on the number line?

Rules for adding integers on a number line:

Start at 0; face the positive integers.

Walk forward for positive integers.

Walk backward for negative integers.

Find $^{+}7 + {}^{-}10$.

Walk forward 7 steps for $^{+}7$. Then walk backward 10 steps for $^{-}10$.

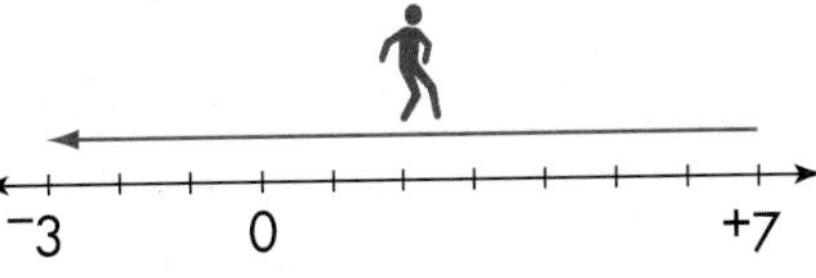

To add two integers with different signs you move in different directions on the number line, so subtract the magnitudes of the numbers. You move farther in the direction of the number with the greater magnitude, so the sign of the sum will be the sign of that number.

$^{+}7 + {}^{-}10 = {}^{-}3$ After the two plays, the team lost 3 yards.

Guided Practice*

Do you know HOW?

In **1** through **8**, use a number line to find each sum.

1. $^{+}2 + {}^{-}7$

2. $^{+}4 + {}^{+}3$

3. $^{-}3 + {}^{-}1$

4. $^{+}5 + {}^{-}9$

5. $^{+}5 + {}^{-}3$

6. $^{-}7 + {}^{+}9$

7. $^{-}4 + {}^{+}7$

8. $^{-}6 + {}^{-}3$

Do you UNDERSTAND?

9. **Number Sense** The integers $^{+}4$ and $^{-}4$ are opposites. What statement can you make about the sum of any integer and its opposite?

10. The football team gained 12 yards on the first play and then lost 9 yards on the next play. How many yards were gained or lost after the two plays?

Independent Practice

In **11** through **31**, use a number line to find each sum.

11. $^{+}2 + {}^{+}3$

12. $^{-}5 + {}^{+}4$

13. $^{+}6 + {}^{-}4$

14. $^{-}8 + {}^{-}5$

15. $0 + {}^{-}4$

16. $^{+}7 + {}^{-}5$

17. $^{-}9 + {}^{+}2$

18. $^{+}7 + {}^{-}6$

19. $^{-}8 + {}^{-}3$

20. $^{+}7 + {}^{+}9$

21. $^{-}4 + {}^{+}8$

22. $^{-}9 + {}^{-}5$

23. $^{-}6 + {}^{-}5$

24. $^{-}8 + {}^{+}7$

25. $^{-}7 + {}^{-}7$

26. $^{-}6 + {}^{+}8$

27. $^{-}9 + {}^{-}8$

28. $^{+}9 + {}^{-}12$

29. $^{-}11 + {}^{-}6$

30. $^{+}14 + {}^{-}5$

31. $^{+}1 + {}^{-}7 + {}^{+}12 + {}^{-}1 + {}^{+}7$

32. In **31**, how can you find the sum without using a number line?

For another example, see Set D on page 361.

Problem Solving

33. Number Sense Mrs. Gomez finds her checking account balance after each transaction. A copy of her check register is shown at the right.

Date	Transaction	Amount
5/1	Beginning balance	$1,230.25
5/3	Check: Cable Co.	$42.50
5/5	Check: Electric Co.	$110.20
5/9	Check: Phone Co.	$74.73
5/14	Deposit	$3,231.36
5/15	Check: Rent	$1,270.30

a Would a check be represented by a positive or a negative integer?

b Would a deposit be represented by a positive or a negative integer?

c Find the checking account balance after each transaction. On which day was the balance the greatest? the least?

d What is the ending balance?

34. Alina is serving juice to her friends. She has $5\frac{1}{2}$ cups of juice. If she gives each friend $\frac{1}{2}$ cup of juice, how many friends can she serve?

35. Xavier did math homework for $\frac{3}{4}$ hour, reading homework for $\frac{2}{3}$ hour, and science homework for $\frac{1}{3}$ hour. How much time did Xavier spend doing homework?

36. Which expression does not have a value of $^{-}5$?

A $^{-}2 + {}^{-}3$

B $^{-}6 + {}^{+}1$

C $^{-}8 + {}^{+}3$

D $^{-}8 + {}^{-}2$

37. Algebra Use a number line to find each missing value.

a $^{-}4 + \square = 9$

b $9 + \square = {}^{-}1$

c $\square + 3 = 0$

d $^{-}7 + \square = {}^{-}13$

38. Think About the Process How would you use a number line to find $^{-}26 + {}^{-}2$?

A Walk forward 26 and backward 2.

B Walk backward 26 and forward 2.

C Walk backward 26 and backward 2.

D Walk forward 26 and backward 24.

39. The sum of Eric's and Gus's heights is $135\frac{3}{4}$ inches. Eric's height is 68.5 inches. How tall is Gus?

40. Writing to Explain How would you find $^{-}19 + {}^{+}32$ without using a number line? What is the sum?

41. What is the prime factorization of 18?

42. Geometry Marcy is making a quilt and cut a triangle from a piece of fabric. What is the measure of the third angle of Marcy's triangle?

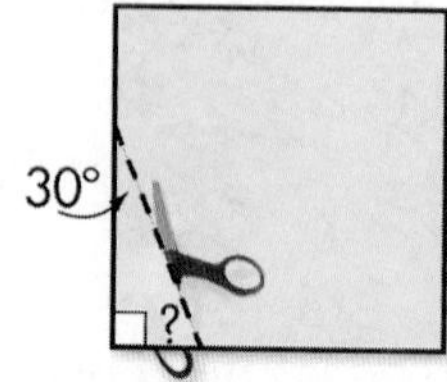

Find each sum.

1. $^{-}14 + {}^{+}10$

2. $^{+}8 + (^{-}6)$

3. $^{-}8 + (^{-}12)$

4. $^{+}9 + (^{-}3)$

5. $^{-}5 + (^{-}5)$

6. $^{-}7 + {}^{+}8$

Find each difference. Simplify if possible.

7. $3\frac{1}{2} - 1\frac{3}{8}$

8. $4\frac{5}{12} - 4\frac{1}{4}$

9. $5\frac{3}{8} - \frac{3}{4}$

10. $4 - 2\frac{3}{10}$

11. $5\frac{5}{6} - 4\frac{11}{12}$

12. $1\frac{4}{5} - \frac{1}{2}$

13. $3\frac{2}{3} - 1\frac{1}{6}$

14. $6\frac{7}{8} - 4\frac{5}{8}$

15. $4\frac{1}{3} - 2\frac{2}{3}$

Error Search Find each sum or difference that is not correct. Write it correctly and explain the error.

16. $^{-}6 + {}^{+}4 = 2$

17. $^{-}3 + (-8) = {}^{-}11$

18. $5\frac{4}{9} - 3\frac{2}{3} = 2\frac{7}{9}$

19. $5 - 1\frac{3}{5} = 3\frac{2}{5}$

Number Sense

Estimating and Reasoning Write whether each statement is true or false. Explain your reasoning.

20. If $a < 0$ and $b < 0$, then $a + b$ is negative.

21. The difference of 29.13 and 17.95 is greater than 11 and less than 13.

22. The sum of $\frac{3}{17}$ and $\frac{5}{17}$ can be simplified.

23. The quotient of 3,746 ÷ 50 has a remainder less than 50.

24. The expression $w - 2.5$ equals 5.5 when $w = 3$.

25. The product of 5 and 2.5 is less than the product of 2 and 5.5.

Lesson
15-5

NS 2.1 Add, subtract, multiply, and divide with decimals; add with negative integers; subtract positive integers from negative integers; and verify the reasonableness of the results.

Subtracting Integers

How can you subtract integers?

On a winter day, George checked the temperature during the afternoon and again at night. How many degrees did the temperature drop?

Choose an Operation Subtract to find the temperature change.

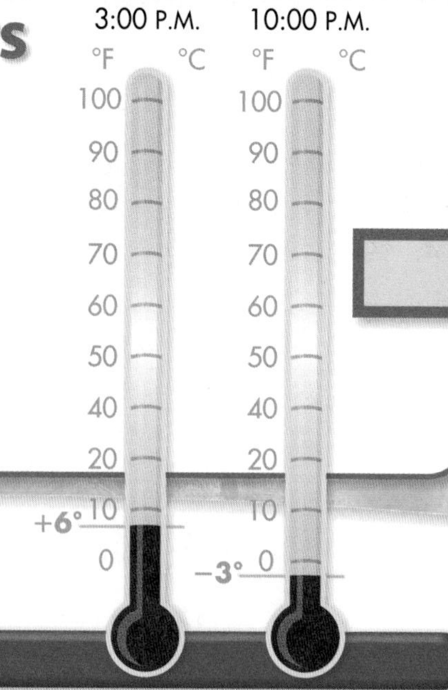

Guided Practice*

Do you know HOW?

In **1** through **6**, rewrite each subtraction problem using addition. Then find the answer. Use a number line to check.

1. $^-1 - {}^+3$ **2.** $^-9 - {}^+4$

3. $^+8 - {}^+5$ **4.** $^+4 - {}^+10$

5. $^-6 - {}^+3$ **6.** $^-10 - {}^+1$

Do you UNDERSTAND?

7. **Reasoning** Why is subtracting an integer the same as adding its opposite?

8. In the example above, suppose the afternoon temperature had been $^+10$°F and the night temperature had been $^-4$°F. How many degrees did the temperature drop?

Independent Practice

In **9** through **32**, rewrite each subtraction problem using addition. Then find each answer. Use a number line to check.

9. $^-1 - {}^+2$ **10.** $^-8 - {}^+3$ **11.** $^-6 - {}^+8$ **12.** $^+3 - {}^+12$

13. $0 - {}^+5$ **14.** $^+5 - {}^+6$ **15.** $^-3 - {}^+10$ **16.** $^-7 - {}^+11$

17. $^-10 - {}^+5$ **18.** $^-12 - {}^+1$ **19.** $^-7 - {}^+3$ **20.** $^+6 - {}^+3$

21. $^+8 - {}^+12$ **22.** $^-4 - {}^+8$ **23.** $^-5 - {}^+2$ **24.** $^-3 - {}^+6$

25. $^-5 - {}^+1$ **25.** $^-2 - {}^+2$ **27.** $^+5 - {}^+7$ **28.** $^-9 - {}^+8$

29. $^+7 - {}^+9$ **30.** $^-5 - {}^+8$ **31.** $^-9 - {}^+6$ **32.** $^+8 - {}^+11$

*For another example, see Set D on page 361.

Step 1

Find $^{-}3 - {}^{+}6$.

Start at 0. Face the positive integers. Walk backward 3 steps for $^{-}3$.

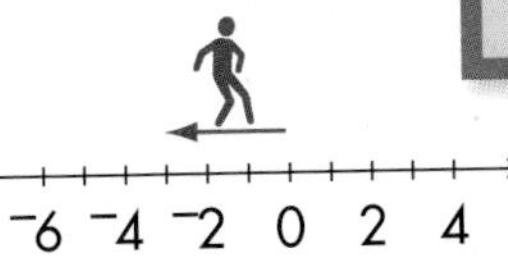

Step 2

The subtraction sign (−) means turn around.

Step 3

Then walk forward 6 steps for $^{+}6$.

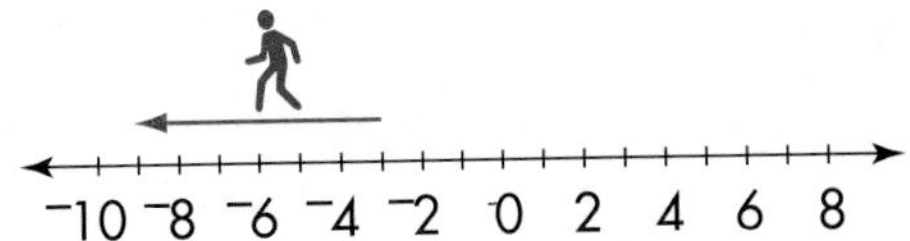

You stop at $^{-}9$.
So, $^{-}3 - {}^{+}6 = {}^{-}9$

$^{-}3 - {}^{+}6$ can be thought of as $^{-}3$ plus the opposite of $^{+}6$.

$^{-}3 - {}^{+}6 = {}^{-}3 + {}^{-}6 = {}^{-}9$

The temperature dropped 9°F.

Problem Solving

33. The temperature rose from $^{-}10$°F to $^{+}15$°F. How much did the temperature rise?

34. Susie cut a blueberry pie into slices. Each slice was $\frac{1}{8}$ of the pie. How many slices of pie were there?

35. Lincoln Elementary students sold school mugs for a fundraiser. They bought the mugs for $3 each and sold them for $5 each. If the students sold 248 mugs, how much money did they raise?

36. The highest elevation in North America is Mt. McKinley, Alaska, at 20,320 feet. The lowest elevation is $^{-}282$ feet in Death Valley, California. What is the difference between the two elevations?

37. Owen has a charge account at the school store. His mom deposited $10 in the account at the beginning of the school year. What is the balance after he purchased the items listed at the right?

Data

Transaction	Amount
Pencils	$1.50
Notebook paper	$0.89
Protractor	$1.29
Pocket dictionary	$4.49
Trail Mix	$1.19

38. **Algebra** Write the integers that could replace *x* to make each statement true.

a $^{-}6 < x < {}^{+}2$

b $^{+}6 > x > {}^{-}2$

39. **Number Sense** The area of California is about 163,696 square miles. What is that measurement rounded to ten thousand square miles?

A 200,000 **C** 164,000

B 163,000 **D** 160,000

40. **Writing to Explain** Describe the steps to find $^{+}4 - {}^{+}7$ on a number line.

41. Finish this sentence "Subtracting $^{+}10$ is the same as adding __?__."

Lesson

15-6

AF 1.2 Use a letter to represent an unknown number; write and evaluate simple algebraic expressions in one variable by substitution.
Also **NS 2.1, AF 1.0**

Simplifying Expressions

How can you evaluate an algebraic expression with integers?

The rules of the game *Number Signs* penalize a player for taking too much time. Greg has a score of 12 points down. What will be his score if he takes too much time on his next turn?

Choose an Operation Subtract to find a score after losing points.

RULES
1. roll
2. move
3. answer
(lose 5 points for exceeding time limit)
SCORES

Another Example How do you evaluate an expression with more than one variable?

When more than one variable is involved, replace each variable with a number. If only addition and subtraction are involved, proceed from left to right, grouping two numbers at a time.

Evaluate $a + b - c$ for $a = {}^{-}8$, $b = {}^{-}6$ and $c = {}^{+}12$.

$a + b - c = {}^{-}8 + {}^{-}6 - {}^{+}12$	Replace a with $^{-}8$, b with $^{-}6$ and c with $^{+}12$
$= {}^{-}14 - {}^{+}12$	Add $^{-}8 + {}^{-}6$.
$= {}^{-}14 + {}^{-}12$	Rewrite the subtraction as an addition of the opposite.
$= {}^{-}26$	Add $^{-}14 + {}^{-}12$.

Guided Practice*

Do you know HOW?

In **1** through **4**, evaluate each expression for $n = {}^{-}5$ and $n = {}^{+}7$.

1. $n + {}^{+}5$

2. $n - {}^{+}9$

3. $n - {}^{+}5$

4. $^{+}8 + n$

In **5** and **6**, evaluate each expression for $r = {}^{-}9$, $s = {}^{-}6$, and $t = {}^{+}8$.

5. $r + s + t$

6. $s - t + r$

Do you UNDERSTAND?

7. a In the example above, what was the opposite operation used to evaluate the expression?

b Use that operation to rewrite the expression in the example.

8. a Write an expression to show what Greg's score would have been if the penalty for too much time was to lose 10 points?

b What would his score have been?

*For another example, see Set E on page 361.

Step 1

Since 5 points are subtracted from the player's score, s, the expression $s - 5$ shows how to find a player's score after getting the time penalty.

Greg's score of 12 points down can be expressed with the integer $^-12$.

Step 2

Evaluate $s - {}^+5$ for $s = {}^-12$.

$s - {}^+5 = {}^-12 - {}^+5$	Replace s with $^-12$.
$= {}^-12 + {}^-5$	Subtracting an integer is the same as adding its opposite.
$= {}^-17$	Add $^-12$ and $^-5$.

Greg's score will be $^-17$, or 17 points down if he takes too much time on his next turn.

Independent Practice

In **9** through **12**, evaluate each expression for $x = {}^+6$ and $x = {}^-8$

9. $x - {}^+3$ **10.** $^+4 + x$ **11.** $x + {}^-9$ **12.** $^+12 + x$

In **13** through **20**, evaluate each expression for $a = {}^-4$, $b = {}^+2$ and $c = {}^-10$

13. $a - {}^+13$ **14.** $c - {}^+15$ **15.** $b - {}^+2$ **16.** $^-18 + a$

17. $c - b$ **18.** $a + b + c$ **19.** $a - b + c$ **20.** $c - b + a$

Problem Solving

21. Which expression names the location of a scuba diver who started at $^-12$ feet and then moved down 3 feet?

A $^-12 + {}^+3$

B $^+3 - {}^-12$

C $^-12 + {}^-3$

D $^-3 + {}^-12$

22. Cory uses red paint and blue paint to make purple paint. How much red paint did he use if he made 9 quarts of purple?

23. **Reasoning** The temperature was $^-9$°F at 6:00 A.M. Write an expression to name the temperature at 3:00 P.M. after it rose 15°F.

24. Barry's CD shelf is 36 inches long. If each CD is $\frac{3}{8}$ of an inch wide, how many CDs can Barry put on one shelf?

25. California was the 31st state admitted to the Union. The expression $1787 + c$ represents the year California obtained statehood. If $c = 63$, what year did California become a state?

26. **Writing to Explain** Jerome says that if you use the LCD when subtracting fractions, you never have to simplify the answer. Do you agree? Why or why not?

Lesson

15-7

MR 2.3 Use a variety of methods, such as words, numbers, symbols, charts, graphs, tables, diagrams, and models, to explain mathematical reasoning. Also MR 2.0, NS 2.0

Problem Solving

Work Backward

Arnie, Brad, Caren, and Danica sold nature photographs to raise money for their hiking club. Brad raised twice as much money as Arnie. Caren raised $100 more than Brad, and Danica raised half as much as Caren. How much money did each person raise?

Guided Practice*

Do you know HOW?

You can solve this problem by working backward. Check your work.

1. The Penguins' hockey practice ended at 7:00 P.M. The team began practice by stretching for $\frac{1}{4}$ hour. Then they practiced skating and shooting for $\frac{1}{2}$ hour. During the last $\frac{3}{4}$ hour, the team played a scrimmage game. What time did practice start?

Do you UNDERSTAND?

2. **Writing to Explain** Describe what you did to check your solution to Problem 1.

3. In the problem above, why is Danica's $110 multiplied by 2 to find the amount that Caren raised?

4. **Write a Problem** Write a real-world problem that you can solve by working backward.

Independent Practice

Solve.

5. On a winter night, the temperature dropped 15°F between midnight and 6:00 A.M. By 11:00 A.M., the temperature had gone up 7°F. By 3:00 P.M. the temperature went up another 9°F, making the temperature 25°F. What was the temperature at midnight?

6. Mel spent $9 at the movies, earned $24 mowing lawns, and bought a magazine for $5. He had $21 left. How much money did he have at the start?

Stuck? Try this....

- What do I know?
- What am I asked to find?
- What diagram can I use to help understand the problem?
- Can I use addition, subtraction, multiplication, or division?
- Is all of my work correct?
- Did I answer the right question?
- Is my answer reasonable?

*For another example, see Set F on page 361.

Read and Understand

I know:

Danica raised \$110.

Danica raised half as much as Caren.

Caren raised \$100 more than Brad.

Brad raised twice as much money as Arnie.

Plan

I know how much each person made compared to someone else.

Arnie → Brad → Caren → Danica \$ 110

× 2 + 100 ÷ 2

Solve

I can start with the amount Danica raised and work backward.

Arnie ← Brad ← Caren ← Danica \$ 110

÷ 2 – 100 × 2

Caren raised $2 \times \$110 = \$220$.
Brad raised $\$220 - 100 = \$120$.
Arnie raised $\$120 \div 2 = \$60$.

7. The numbers show how many shells in each drawer. Meg has a total of 156 shells. She organizes them by size. How many shells are in drawer 1?

8. Mary is knitting a scarf that will be 36 inches long. She knitted 5 inches on the second day, 8 inches on the third day, and 10 inches on the fourth day. She needs to knit 3 inches more to finish the scarf. How much did she knit on the first day?

9. A baby gains about $2\frac{1}{5}$ pounds each month for the first three months after birth. When he was 3 months old, Tyler weighed $14\frac{1}{10}$ pounds. About how much did Tyler weigh at birth?

10. Briana has $1\frac{1}{4}$ cups of sesame seeds left in the bag she bought for baking. She used the sesame seeds to make muffins, bread, and bagels to sell at a bake sale. How many cups of sesame seeds were in the bag she bought?

11. **Geometry** What is the area of a square garden with a side that measures 18 feet?

12. **Reasoning** Donna, Pam, and Mike worked at a school car wash. Donna washed half as many cars as Mike did. Pam washed 9 more than Donna. Mike washed 5 fewer than Pam. If Mike washed 8 cars, how many cars did Pam and Donna wash? What was the total number of cars washed?

13. Workers need 6 weeks to resurface 15 miles of road. They resurfaced $2\frac{1}{2}$ miles the fourth week, 3 miles the fifth week, and $4\frac{1}{2}$ miles the sixth week. How many miles did they resurface during the first three weeks?

A 5 miles
B 10 miles
C 6 miles
D 11 miles

Test Prep

1. The lowest temperature ever recorded in the United States was in Alaska in 1971. It was about $^{-}80°$ Fahrenheit. What is the opposite of $^{-}80$? (15-1)

A $^{-}80$

B $^{-}79$

C $^{+}80$

D $^{+}81$

2. The elevations of some points of interest are given in the table. These elevations are above, at, or below sea level. Which of the following lists the elevations from least to greatest? (15-2)

Data

Location	Elevation (ft)
Potomac River	1
New Orleans	$^{-}8$
Delaware River	0
Lake Champlain	95

A $^{-}8, 0, ^{+}1, ^{+}95$

B $0, ^{+}1, ^{-}8, ^{+}95$

C $^{-}8, ^{+}1, 0, ^{+}95$

D $^{+}95, ^{-}8, ^{+}1, 0$

3. What is the value of $5 - n$ when $n = {}^{+}7$? (15-6)

A $^{-}12$

B $^{-}2$

C $^{+}2$

D $^{+}12$

4. Which of the following can be used to represent a deposit of \$132? (15-1)

A $^{+}132$

B $^{+}1$

C 0

D $^{-}132$

5. Which comparison is true? (15-2)

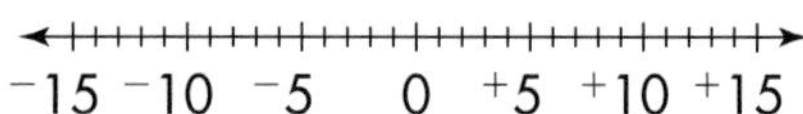

A $^{-}12 < {}^{-}6$

B $^{-}12 > {}^{-}6$

C $^{-}8 > {}^{-}4$

D $^{+}3 < {}^{-}3$

6. Which number line shows Point *F* at $1\frac{4}{5}$? (15-3)

A

F

⁻2 ⁻1 0 ⁺1 ⁺2 ⁺3 ⁺4 ⁺5 ⁺6

B

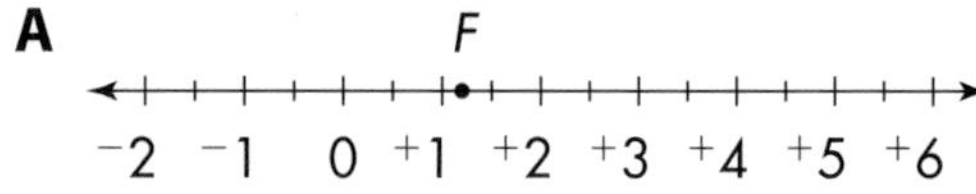

C

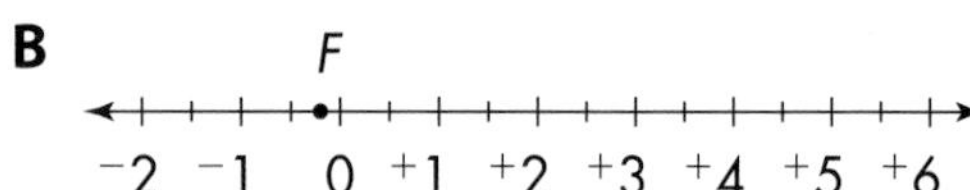

D

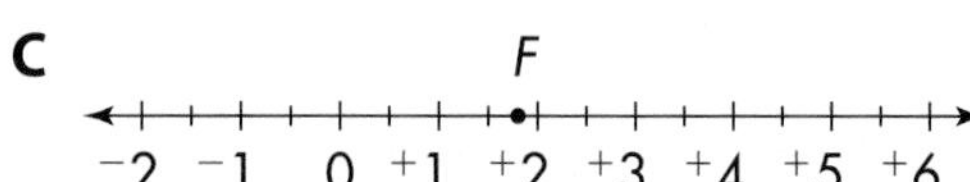

7. What is $^{+}11 + (^{-}18)$? (15-4)

A $^{+}29$

B $^{+}7$

C $^{-}7$

D $^{-}29$

Test Prep

8. What is the integer at Point L? (15-1)

A $^{-}6$

B $^{-}5$

C $^{-}4$

D $^{-}3$

9. What is $^{+}2 + (^{-}8)$? (15-4)

A $^{-}10$

B $^{-}6$

C $^{+}6$

D $^{+}10$

10. Danny had a $^{-}\$30$ balance for an amount borrowed from his parents. Then he borrowed \$20 more. What was his balance then? (15-5)

A \$50

B \$10

C $^{-}\$10$

D $^{-}\$50$

11. After a fundraising dinner, a charity has a balance of \$2,530. They spent \$700 to host the dinner. If they made \$1,400 on the event and another \$300 afterwards from a private donation, how much money did the charity have before hosting the dinner? (15-7)

A \$130

B \$1,530

C \$2,130

D \$3,530

12. Which of the following is equal to $^{-}6 - (^{+}3)$ (15-5)

A $^{-}6 + (^{+}3)$

B $^{+}6 + (^{+}3)$

C $^{+}6 + (^{-}3)$

D $^{-}6 + (^{-}3)$

13. What numbers are represented by Points R and T on the number line? (15-3)

R T

$^{-}15$ $^{-}10$ $^{-}5$ 0 $^{+}5$ $^{+}10$ $^{+}15$

A $^{-}7$ and 8.5

B $^{-}8$ and 8.5

C $^{-}7$ and 9.5

D $^{-}8$ and 9.5

14. On a winter morning, the outside temperature was $^{-}6°$. By noon, it had risen 15 degrees. What was the temperature in the afternoon? (15-4)

A $^{-}9°$

B 9°

C 15°

D 21°

15. What is the value of $a + b - c$ when $a = {}^{-}3$, $b = {}^{+}7$ and $c = {}^{+}1$? (15-6)

A $^{-}11$

B $^{-}10$

C $^{+}3$

D $^{+}5$

Reteaching

Set A, pages 342–343

Write an integer for each point.

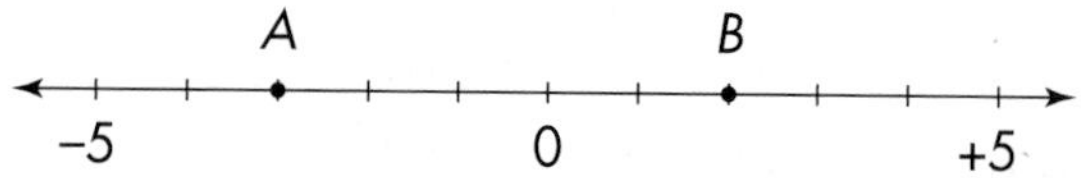

Point *A* is three units from zero and to the left of zero. Point *A* is at $^-3$.

Point *B* is two units from zero and is to the right of zero. Point *B* is at $^+2$.

Remember that the + and − signs name a direction from zero.

Write an integer for each description.

1. Two degrees below zero.
2. Fifty-seven feet above sea level.
3. A loss of three yards.

Write an integer for each point.

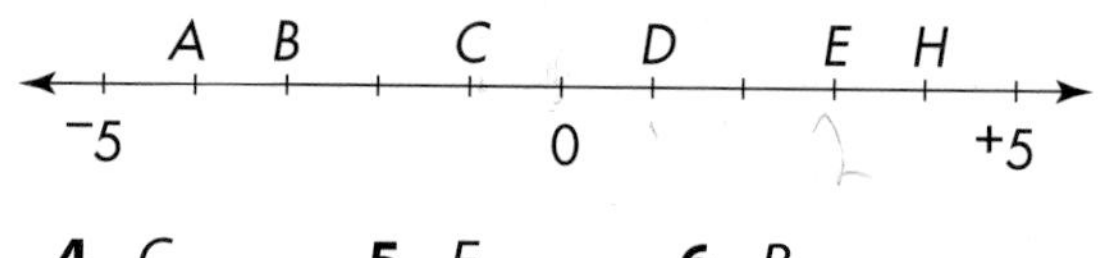

4. *C* **5.** *E* **6.** *B*

7. *H* **8.** *D* **9.** *A*

Set B, pages 344–345

Compare $^-4$ and $^+3$. Use >, < or = .

Plot the numbers on a number line.

$^-5$ $^-4$ $^-3$ $^-2$ $^-1$ 0 $^+1$ $^+2$ $^+3$ $^+4$ $^+5$

As you move to the right from any point on a number line, the numbers increase in value.

$^+3 > {}^-4$ $^+3$ is to the right of $^-4$.

$^-4 < {}^+3$ $^-4$ is to the left of $^+3$.

Remember that numbers increase in value as you move to the right on a number line, and decrease as you move to the left.

Compare. Use <, >, or = for each ◯.

1. $^+3$ ◯ $^-3$ **2.** $^-8$ ◯ $^+2$

3. $^-9$ ◯ $^-7$ **4.** $^+3$ ◯ $^+2$

5. $^+1$ ◯ $^-16$ **6.** $^-14$ ◯ $^-10$

Set C, pages 346–347

Order 4, $\frac{1}{4}$, $^-2$, and 0.5 from least to greatest.

$\frac{1}{4}$ is the same as 0.25. $\frac{1}{2}$ is the same as 0.5.

Plot the numbers on a number line.

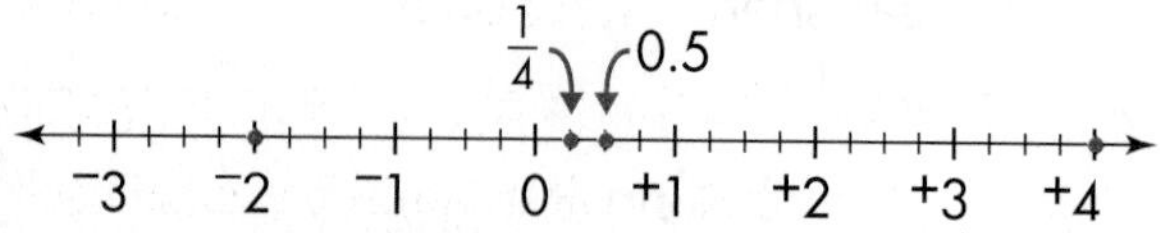

The order from least to greatest is $^-2$, $\frac{1}{4}$, 0.5, 4

Remember to convert fractions to decimals or decimals to fractions to make the comparing easier.

Order the numbers from least to greatest.

1. $^-1$, $\frac{1}{2}$, $^-4$, 1.25

2. 4, 2.5, $^-2$, $\frac{1}{4}$

3. 3.25, $\frac{3}{4}$, 3, $^-1$

4. $2\frac{1}{4}$, $^-3$, 0.68, $^-2$

Set D, pages 348–350, 352–353

Use a number line to find $^+2 + {}^-5$.

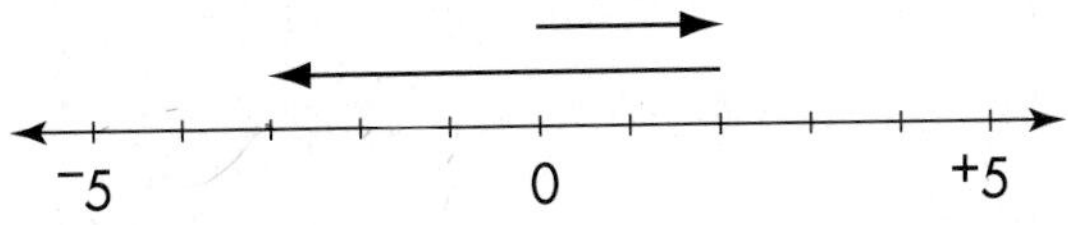

Start at 0 and face the positive integers.
Walk forward 2 steps for $^+2$.
Then walk backward 5 steps for $^-5$.
You stop at $^-3$.

So, $^+2 + {}^-5 = {}^-3$

Find $^-2 - {}^+10$.

To subtract an integer, add the opposite of the integer being subtracted.

$^-2 - {}^+10 \rightarrow {}^-2 + {}^-10$
$^-2 + {}^-10 = {}^-12$

Remember to move to the right on a number line when adding positive integers and move to the left on a number line when adding negative integers.

1. $^+6 + {}^-4$
2. $^-7 + {}^-2$
3. $^-8 + {}^+2$
4. $^+10 + {}^-5$
5. $^-12 + {}^+3$
6. $^-3 + {}^-9$

Remember when using a number line to subtract integers, the subtraction sign means to *turn around.*

7. $^+5 - {}^+8$
8. $^-3 - {}^+2$
9. $^-5 - {}^+8$
10. $^-2 - {}^+4$
11. $^+7 - {}^+9$
12. $0 - {}^+6$

Set E, pages 354–355

Find $a + b - c$ for $a = {}^-4$, $b = {}^+3$ and $c = {}^+5$.

$a + b - c = {}^-4 + {}^+3 - {}^+5$		Replace the variables.
$= {}^-1 - {}^+5$		Add $^-4 + {}^+3$.
$= {}^-1 + {}^-5$		Rewrite subtraction as addition of the opposite.
$= {}^-6$		Add $^-1 + {}^-5$

Remember to replace the variable with the given values.

Evaluate each expression for $x = {}^+3$ and $x = {}^-2$

1. $^+3 + x$
2. $x - {}^+5$
3. $x + {}^+10$
4. $x - {}^+1$
5. $x - {}^+3$
6. $x + {}^+4$

Set F, pages 356–357

To work backward, follow these steps.

Identify the unknown initial amount.

List each change, starting with the initial amount.

Step 3 Start at the end result. Work backward using the inverse of each change.

Remember addition and subtraction undo each other.

1. Jean spent $\frac{2}{3}$ hour on math homework and $\frac{1}{2}$ hour on English. Then she spent $\frac{3}{4}$ hour baking. If she finished baking at 8:00, what time did she start doing her homework?

Topic 16

Solving and Writing Equations

1 One of the tallest trees in the world is a sequoia known as General Grant. How many times taller is General Grant than the height of a typical oak tree? You will find out in Lesson 16-2.

2 How much taller is a full-grown male giraffe than a fifth-grade student? You will find out in Lesson 16-2.

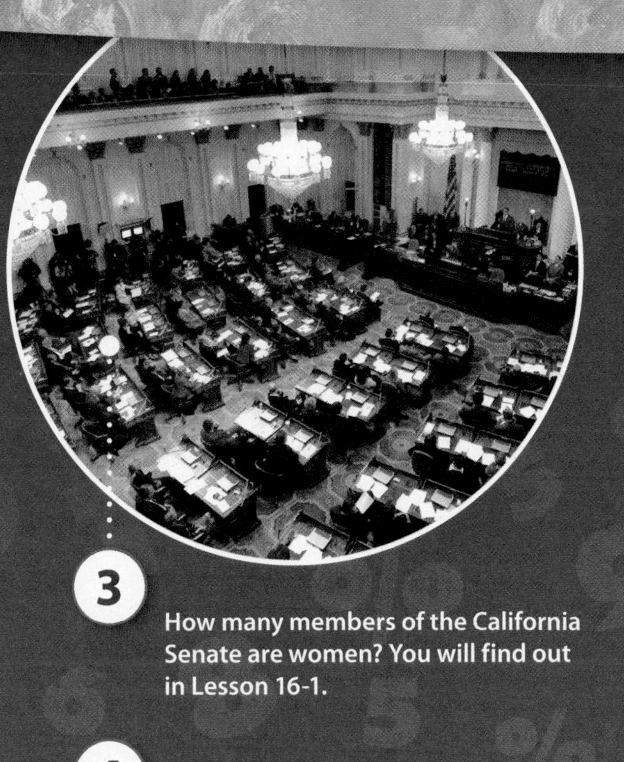

3

How many members of the California Senate are women? You will find out in Lesson 16-1.

4

The area of Lake Victoria, in Africa, is 26,828 square miles. How does the area of Lake Victoria compare to the area of Lake Michigan? You will find out in Lesson 16-1.

Review What You Know!

Vocabulary

Choose the best term from the box.

- equality
- inverse
- operations
- variable

1. Addition, subtraction, multiplication, and division are all __?__.
2. When both sides of an equation have the same value, they have __?__.
3. A __?__ is a letter or symbol that is used to represent an unknown value.
4. Operations that undo each other are called __?__ operations.

Multiplication Facts

Find each product.

5. 8×7
6. 6×9
7. 4×8
8. 3×9
9. 7×4
10. 5×3

Estimation

Estimate each product, sum, or difference.

11. $13 + 24$
12. $81 - 19$
13. 37×3
14. $68 - 31$
15. 27×2
16. $17 + 59$

Problem Solving

Writing to Explain Write an answer for the question.

17. Lin went to the store with $10.00. She bought a toothbrush for $4.59 and a tube of toothpaste for $3.29. Explain what you could do to find out how much change Lin will receive when she checks out.

Lesson

16-1

AF 1.1, Grade 6 Write and solve one-step linear equations in one variable.

Solving Addition and Subtraction Equations

How can you use addition and subtraction to solve equations?

In January 2005, there were 83 women in Congress. How many women were serving in the U.S. Senate?

Data

Members of U.S. Congress	
January, 2005	
U.S. Senate	
Men	86
Women	
U.S. House of Representatives	
Men	367
Women	69

Other Examples

Addition Property of Equality:
You can add the same number to both sides of an equation and the sides remain equal.

Example:
$9 - 4 = 5$
$9 - 4 + 2 = 5 + 2$

Subtraction Property of Equality:
You can subtract the same number from both sides of an equation and the sides remain equal.

Example:
$8 + 6 = 14$
$8 + 6 - 3 = 14 - 3$

Operations that undo each other are inverse operations.
Addition and subtraction have an inverse relationship.

Guided Practice*

Do you know HOW?

In **1** and **2**, what would you do to get each variable by itself on one side of the equation?

1. $x - 45 = 90$ **2.** $n + 23.4 = 36.9$

In **3** through **6**, use inverse operations and a property of equality to solve these equations.

3. $x + 13 = 42$ **4.** $x - 12 = 37$

5. $a + 8 = 37$ **6.** $b - 9 = 25$

Do you UNDERSTAND?

7. What could you do to check the answer in the example at the top of the page?

8. When finding the number of women in the Senate, why must 69 be subtracted from both sides of the equation?

9. Write a subtraction equation for the problem in the example at the top of the page.

 *For another example, see Set A on page 382.

Since Congress includes the Senate plus the House, you can write an addition equation. An **equation** is a number sentence that uses an equal sign to show that two expressions have the same value.

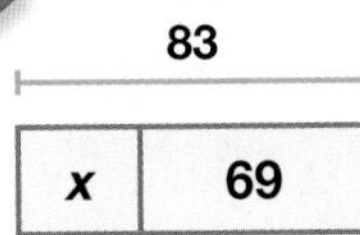

Let x = the number of women in the Senate.

Equation: $x + 69 = 83$.

To solve the equation, get the variable alone.

$$x + 69 = 83$$
$$x + 69 - 69 = 83 - 69$$
$$x = 83 - 69$$
$$x = 14$$

You can subtract 69 from both sides of the equation and the quantities on each side of the equal sign are still equal.

There were 14 women serving in the U.S. Senate in January, 2005.

Independent Practice

Solve each equation.

10. $d - 14 = 13$

11. $p + 31 = 52$

12. $c - 68 = 78$

13. $n + 70 = 265$

14. $y - 28 = 98$

15. $746 + t = 947$

16. $91 = 19 + m$

17. $75 = n - 39$

18. $k + 22.5 = 30$

Problem Solving

19. If there are 57 students in the school band and 29 of them are boys, how many girls are in the band?

20. Writing to Explain Why will the equations $x + 14 = 37$ and $x - 14 = 37$ have different solutions for x?

21. Draw It Draw a diagram to represent the equation $y + 18 = 73$.

22. In 2006, the California Senate had 40 members, of which 29 were men. Solve the equation $29 + x = 40$ to find the number of women in that Senate.

23. Think About the Process Which operation would you use to solve the equation $x - 17 = 23$?

A Add 17
B Subtract 17
C Multiply by 17
D Divide by 1

24. The Johnson family shared a spinach quiche for breakfast. Mom ate $\frac{1}{4}$, Dad ate $\frac{1}{3}$, and Julia ate $\frac{1}{4}$ of the quiche. How much of the quiche was not eaten?

25. The area of Lake Victoria in Africa is 26,828 square miles. The area of Lake Michigan in the U.S. is 22,539 square miles. Solve the equation $22{,}539 + x = 26{,}828$ to find how much larger Lake Victoria is than Lake Michigan.

Lesson

16-2

AF 1.1, Grade 6 Write and solve one-step linear equations in one variable.

Solving Multiplication and Division Equations

How can you use multiplication and division to solve equations?

Keef's scout troop is participating in a Pinewood Derby. The cars are sold by the case. How many cases should the scoutmaster buy for 32 boys?

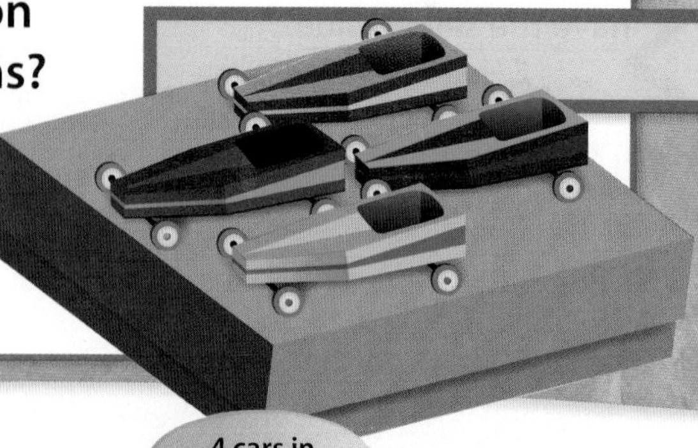

4 cars in each case

Other Examples

Multiplication Property of Equality: You can multiply both sides of an equation by the same nonzero number and the sides remain equal.

Example:

$$\frac{14}{2} = 7$$

$$\frac{14}{2} \times 2 = 7 \times 2$$

Division Property of Equality: You can divide both sides of an equation by the same nonzero number and the sides remain equal.

Example:

$$6 \times 5 = 30$$

$$\frac{6 \times 5}{5} = \frac{30}{5}$$

Operations that undo each other are inverse operations. Multiplication and division have an inverse relationship.

Guided Practice*

Do you know HOW?

In **1** and **2**, what would you do to get each variable alone on one side of the equation?

1. $24n = 120$ **2.** $\frac{b}{7} = 42$

In **3** through **6**, use inverse operations and a property of equality to solve these equations.

3. $y \div 9 = 12$ **4.** $3m = 63$

5. $85 = 17r$ **6.** $24 = \frac{c}{3}$

Do you UNDERSTAND?

7. What could you do to check the answer in the example at the top of the page?

8. Write a division equation for the problem at the top.

9. In the example above, if there were 6 cars in a case, how many cases would the scoutmaster need to buy to be sure every scout had a car?

*For another example, see Set A on page 382.

Let c = the number of cases needed.

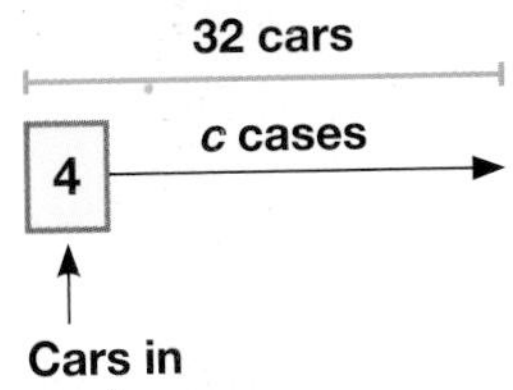

Since each case contains 4 cars, you can write the equation

$4c = 32$

To solve the equation, get the variable alone.

$4c = 32$

$\frac{4c}{4} = \frac{32}{4}$

$c = 8$

You can divide both sides of the equation by 4 and the quantities on each side of the equal sign are still equal.

Remember that $\frac{4c}{4}$ is the same as $4 \times c \div 4$.

The scoutmaster should buy 8 cases of cars.

Independent Practice

Solve each equation.

10. $14d = 56$ **11.** $\frac{c}{8} = 64$ **12.** $45y = 135$ **13.** $184 = 23p$

14. $\frac{m}{5} = 12$ **15.** $8 = \frac{k}{30}$ **16.** $72 = 12t$ **17.** $14 = \frac{w}{7}$

Problem Solving

18. **Geometry** The sides of a pentagon are 11 inches in length. What is the perimeter of the pentagon?

19. **Reasoning** Randy divides 48 by 6 to solve an equation for y. One side of the equation is 48. Write the equation.

20. Martin is going on a 216-mile trip. If his car gets 24 miles per gallon, how many gallons of gas will he need for his trip?

21. **Writing to Explain** How could you use mental math to find m in the equation $279\left(\frac{m}{279}\right) = 72$?

22. Daria measured the length of three ants in science class. They were $\frac{2}{3}$ inch, $\frac{3}{5}$ inch, and $\frac{1}{4}$ inch. Which ant is the longest?

23. **Think About the Process** Which operation would you use to solve the equation $17x = 255$?

A Add 17

B Subtract 17

C Multiply by 17

D Divide by 17

24. Giraffes can grow to about 20 feet tall. Some fifth-grade students can be about 5 feet tall. Solve the equation $5x = 20$ to find how many times as tall a giraffe can be as a fifth-grade student.

25. General Grant, a sequoia tree, is 273 feet tall. A typical Red Oak tree is about 70 feet tall. Solve the equation $70x = 280$ to find about how many times as tall the General Grant is as a typical Red Oak.

Lesson

16-3

MR 1.1 Analyze problems by identifying relationships, distinguishing relevant from irrelevant information, sequencing and prioritizing information, and observing patterns. Also **NS 2.0, MR 3.1**

Problem Solving

Use Reasoning

Laurie has 12 fish in her aquarium. Half of the fish are yellow, $\frac{1}{3}$ of the fish are black, and the rest are orange. How many fish of each color does Laurie have?

Unit cubes can be used to represent the fish and solve the problem.

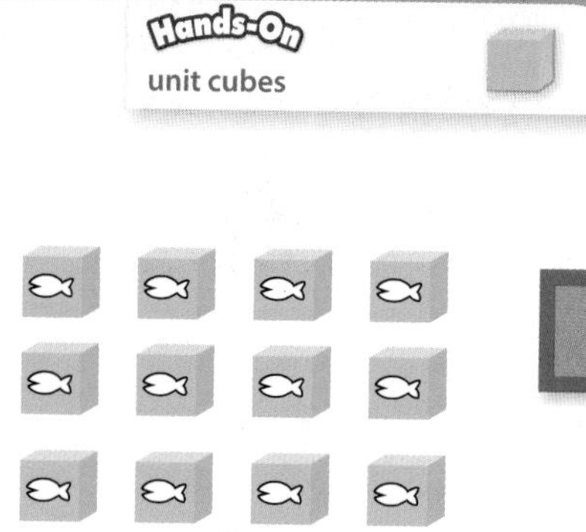

Guided Practice*

Do you know HOW?

1. The Lions soccer team scored 8 goals. Joe scored $\frac{1}{2}$ of the goals, and Carlos scored two fewer goals than Joe. How many goals did Joe score? How many did Carlos score?

2. Percy buys two items that cost a total of \$90. One of the items cost $\frac{1}{3}$ of the total. What is the cost of each item?

Do you UNDERSTAND?

3. In the example above, how can you reason that there are 4 black fish?

4. How many of each color of fish would Laurie have if she had a total of 36 fish?

5. **Write a Problem** Write a real-life problem that involves fractions and can be solved by using reasoning.

Independent Practice

For **6** through **10**, use reasoning to solve.

6. Freemont School tried a new lunch menu for 15 days. For $\frac{1}{3}$ of the days, sandwiches were served. For $\frac{2}{5}$ of the days, hot entrees were served. The rest of the days pizzas were served. How many days for each kind of lunch was served?

7. Mr. Reyes has 24 books. Science fiction makes up $\frac{1}{4}$ of the books, and he has twice as many mystery books as science fiction. The rest are fiction. How many books are science fiction? How many are mystery?

Stuck? Try this....

- What do I know?
- What am I asked to find?
- What diagram can I use to help understand the problem?
- Can I use addition, subtraction, multiplication, or division?
- Is all of my work correct?
- Did I answer the right question?
- Is my answer reasonable?

*For another example, see Set B on page 382.

Plan and Solve

Use reasoning to make conclusions.

Half of the fish are yellow. Half of 12 is 6, so there are 6 yellow fish.

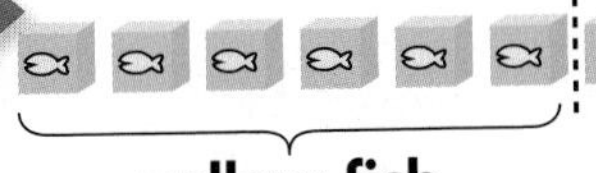

One third of the fish are black. One third of 12 is 4, so there are 4 black fish.

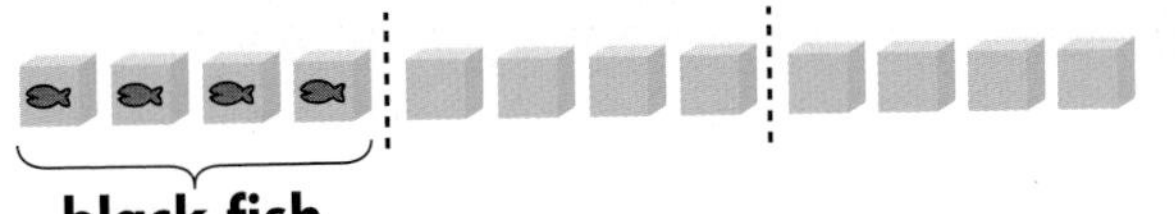

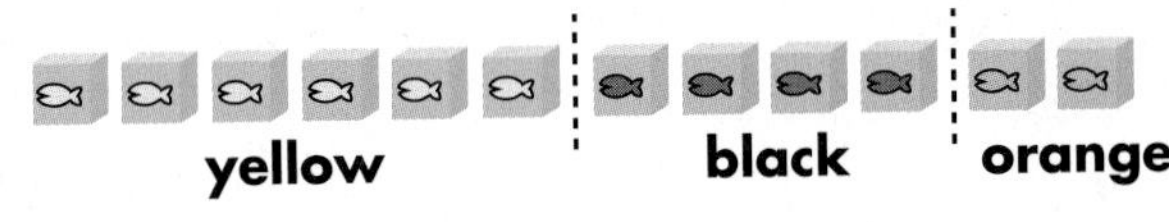

Since $6 + 4 = 10$ and $12 - 10 = 2$, the other two fish are orange.

There are 6 yellow fish, 4 black fish, and 2 orange fish.

Look back and check your answer. Since $6 + 4 + 2 = 12$, the answer is reasonable.

8. Ms. Clark has a box of minerals. In the box there are 4 diamonds. There are also 3 times as many rubies as there are sapphires. The box has 12 minerals in all. How many of each type of mineral are in the box?

10. Kathy, Paul, Sean, and Kelly each play a different instrument. The instruments they play are drums, guitar, bass, and keyboard. Kelly plays the drums, and Paul is not playing the keyboard. If Sean plays the bass, what instrument does each play?

11. **Writing to Explain** Why is the amount of time Cherise spends sleeping more than $\frac{1}{4}$ of her day? What benchmark fraction is this amount closer to?

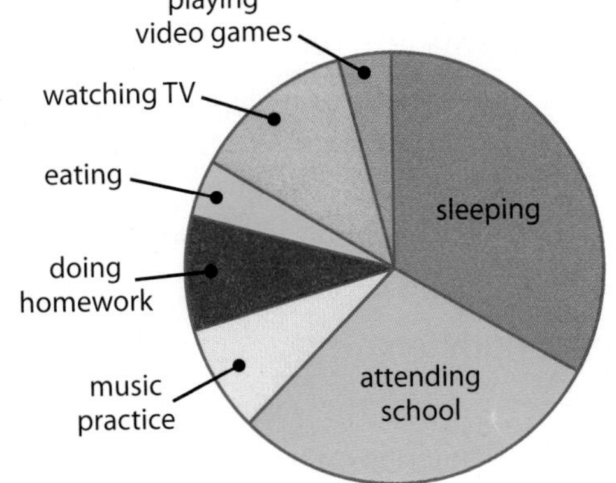

9. Rosie said she did not know how to respond to the following survey question. Explain why.

How old are you?
Circle one.

A Under 10

B 10–12

C 12–15

D Over 15

12. The blue whale is the world's largest animal. An average-sized adult is 80 feet long and weighs about 120 tons. How many pounds does the blue whale weigh? Hint: 1 ton = 2,000 pounds.

13. If a human heart beats 70 times per minute, how many times will it beat in one hour?

14. Two drinking glasses hold the same amount of water. If these two glasses hold a total of 500 milliliters, how many milliliters will three of these hold?

Lesson

16-4

AF 1.2 Use a letter to represent an unknown number; write and evaluate simple algebraic expressions in one variable by substitution. Also **AF 1.5**.

Patterns and Equations

How can you find a rule for a pattern and complete a table?

Dots were used to draw the figures below.

How many dots would be in the 20th figure?

Which figure would have 100 dots?

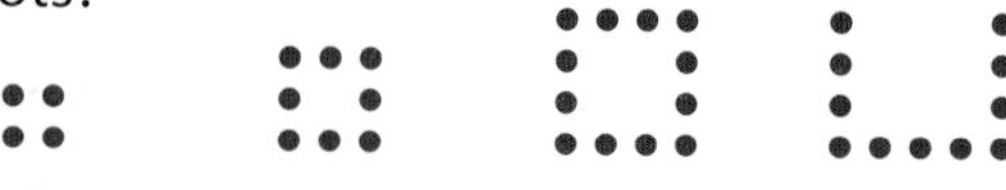

Figure 1 Figure 2 Figure 3 Figure 4

Another Example How can you find a rule?

Which equation gives a rule that states the relationship between each pair of values in the table below?

x	22	34	35	40	
y	11	23	24		47

A $y = \frac{x}{2}$ **B** $y = x + 11$ **C** $y = x - 11$ **D** $y = 2x$

Step 1 State the relationship between the first pair of numbers.
y is half of *x* or *y* is 11 less than *x*.

Step 2 Which relationship is also true for the second pair of numbers?
y is 11 less than *x*.

Step 3 Check that the relationship is also true for other pairs of numbers.

Step 4 The equation for Choice **C** gives a rule for the relationship between *x* and *y* in the table.
$y = x - 11$

Explain It

1. If a rule describes the relationship for one pair of numbers in a table, does it always describe every pair in the same table? Explain your answer.
2. If you know the rule for a table, how can you add pairs of numbers to the table?

Make a table.

Figure number (n)	Total number of dots (d)
1	4
2	8
3	12
4	16
20	
	100

Look for a pattern in the relationship between the figure number and the total number of dots in the figure.

Express the pattern as a rule.

Multiply the figure number by 4

Express the pattern as an equation.

$d = 4n$

4n means 4 × n.

Use the equation to find the missing numbers in the table.

$d = 4 \times 20$

$d = 80$

Figure 20 has 80 dots.

$100 = 4 \times n$

$\frac{100}{4} = \frac{4 \times n}{4}$

$25 = n$

Figure 25 has 100 dots.

Guided Practice*

Do you know HOW?

x	2	4	6	8	
y	14	28	42		70

1. Write a rule for this table in words.
2. Write an equation for the rule.
3. What is a missing y-value?
4. What is a missing x-value?

Do you UNDERSTAND?

5. In the example above, how do you know the table of values is represented by the equation $d = 4n$?
6. If the n-value is 36, what is a d-value?
7. Write and solve equations to find the missing numbers in the table in Another Example.

Independent Practice

In exercises **8** through **11**, find a rule for each table. Write an equation for each rule.

8.

x	y
0	16
20	36
36	52
42	58

9.

x	y
25	17
32	24
46	38
59	51

10.

x	y
6	2
12	4
24	8
33	11

11.

x	y
5	30
3	18
9	54
7	42

*For another example, see Set C on page 383.

Independent Practice

In **12** through **15**, write an equation for each table and find the missing values for x and y.

12.

x	y
12	6
10	4
8	
13	7
	13

13.

x	y
48	96
30	60
25	50
	64
14	

14.

x	y
30	3
80	8
170	17
	25
320	

15.

x	y
3	17
7	21
6	
9	23
	26

Problem Solving

16. **Number Sense** In the equation $y = 12x$, if y is to equal 0, what is the value of x?

17. Write an equation that will give the answer $y = 3$ when $x = 7$.

18. The Autobahn in Germany is known around the world. Along most of the Autobahn, there is an advised speed limit of 130 km/h. How many hours would a car need to travel at the advised speed limit to go 520 km?

19. **Geometry** The triangle below is an isosceles triangle. What is the perimeter of the triangle?

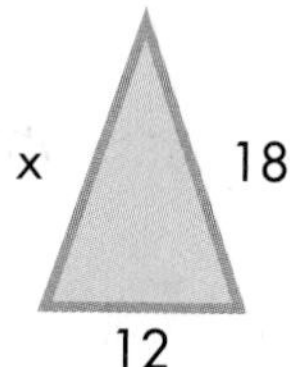

For **20** through **22**, use the table at the right.

20. During which month was the electric bill the highest?

21. During which month was the electric bill the lowest?

22. What was the total cost of electricity for the 12 months?

Data

Month	Electric Bill ($)	Month	Electric Bill ($)
January	58	July	89
February	52	August	88
March	46	September	74
April	47	October	63
May	44	November	63
June	75	December	57

23. **Number Sense** In the equation $y = x - 6$, which positive numbers would you use for x if you wanted $y < 0$?

24. Which pair of values could appear in a table of values for the equation $y = 2x$?

A $x = 2, y = 5$

B $x = 4, y = 6$

C $x = 5, y = 10$

D $x = 0, y = 2$

Find each difference.

1. $^{-}5 - {}^{+}3$ **2.** $^{+}2 - {}^{+}9$ **3.** $^{-}6 - {}^{+}5$

4. $^{-}2 - {}^{+}4$ **5.** $^{-}10 - {}^{+}8$ **6.** $^{-}25 - {}^{+}5$

Solve each equation for z.

7. $25 = z - 22$ **8.** $z - 192 = 24$ **9.** $z - 4 = 312$

10. $z - 19 = 4$ **11.** $150 = z - 225$ **12.** $z - 22 = 222$ **13.** $15 = z - 342$

Solve each equation for c.

14. $12c = 96$ **15.** $10c = 90$ **16.** $8c = 64$ **17.** $5c = 35$

18. $3c = 27$ **19.** $16c = 32$ **20.** $7c = 28$ **21.** $25c = 100$

Error Search Find each value of v that is not correct. Write it correctly and explain the error.

22. $55 + v = 132$
$v = 187$

23. $v - 12 = 111$
$v = 123$

24. $48 = 8v$
$v = 7$

25. $55 = 22 + v$
$v = 33$

Number Sense

Estimating and Reasoning Write whether each statement is true or false. Explain your reasoning.

26. The g in the equation $14 + g = 19$ is equal to 13.

27. The quotient of $45{,}876 \div 32$ is closer to 2,000 than 1,000.

28. The sum of 8,143 and 25,709 is between 33,000 and 35,000.

29. The difference $^{-}3 - {}^{+}8$ is positive.

30. The expression $12 - 8 \div 4 + 6$ equals 16.

31. The product of $4\frac{7}{8} \times 3$ is closer to 15 than 12.

Lesson
16-5

AF 1.2 Use a letter to represent an unknown number; write and evaluate simple algebraic expressions in one variable by substitution.
Also AF 1.5.

More Patterns and Equations

How can you extend patterns given by an equation involving two operations?

How much will a family of four pay for tickets and parking when they go to the Medieval Fair?

Guided Practice*

Do you know HOW?

1. Choose the equation that matches the table.

x	y
0	4(0) + 6
1	4(1) + 6
2	4(2) + 6
3	4(3) + 6

A $y = x + 6$

B $x = 4y + 6$

C $x = 4 + 6y$

D $y = 4x + 6$

2. Write a rule for the table above using words.

Do you UNDERSTAND?

3. In the example above, why is the equation $8.50n + 5 = c$ instead of $8.50n = c$?

4. **Writing to Explain** Tell two ways that you could find the cost for the family of four to go to the fair.

5. A group of 8 people went to the fair in a mini-van. How much did they pay for tickets and parking?

Independent Practice

In **6** and **7**, choose the equation that best matches each table.

6.

x	y
5	6(5 + 4)
6	6(6 + 4)
7	6(7 + 4)
8	6(8 + 4)

A $y = 6x + 4$

B $y = 6(x + 4)$

C $x = 6y + 4$

D $x = 6(y + 4)$

7.

x	y
3	2(3) − 5
5	2(5) − 5
7	2(7) − 5
9	2(9) − 5

A $y = 2x - 5$

B $y = 5x - 2$

C $x = 2y - 5$

D $x = y - 5$

*For another example, see Set C on page 383.

Step 1

State a rule to find how much a family would pay to go to the Fair.

Multiply $8.50 by the number of people, and then add $5.00.

Step 2

Make a table and find a pattern.

Number of people (n)	Cost (c)
1	$8.50 \times 1 + 5.00$
2	$8.50 \times 2 + 5.00$
3	$8.50 \times 3 + 5.00$

Step 3

Write an equation.

$c = 8.50n + 5.00$

For a family of four:

$c = 8.50(4) + 5.00$

$c = 39$

A family of four would pay $39.00 to go to the Fair.

Independent Practice

In **8** through **10**, choose the equation that matches each table.

8.

x	y
2	12
4	16
6	20
8	24

A $x + 10 = y$

B $6x = y$

C $2x + 8 = y$

D $2x + 10 = y$

9.

x	y
1	9
4	21
7	33
10	45

A $y = 9x$

B $y = 4x + 5$

C $y = 5x + 1$

D $y = x + 9$

10.

x	y
5	11
6	14
7	17
8	20

A $x + 6 = y$

B $2x + 1 = y$

C $3x - 5 = y$

D $3x - 4 = y$

Problem Solving

11. Estimation Admission to the skating rink is $4.75 for adults and $2.75 for children. About how much money should Marcy bring to make sure she and her 2 children can get in to skate?

12. Geometry Anji's room is 12 feet by 9 feet. She purchased 95 square feet of carpet for her room. Does she have enough carpet to cover the entire floor in her room? Explain your answer.

For **13** and **14**, use the table at the right.

13. Mario purchased 3 adult tickets and 1 senior ticket. How much did he pay?

14. Joe took his four grandchildren to the movies. Write an equation to find the total cost of the children's tickets plus his senior ticket. How much did he pay?

Data

Cinema Ticket Prices	
Adult Admission	$6.50
Children (under 12)	$4.75
Seniors	$3.75

Lesson
16-6

AF 1.1, Grade 6 Write and solve one-step linear equations in one variable.
Also **MR 2.3, 3.0**

Problem Solving

Draw a Picture and Write an Equation

At an art fair, Dean sold different types of paintings. The price of a portrait is $125 more than the price of a still-life painting. What is the price of a still-life painting?

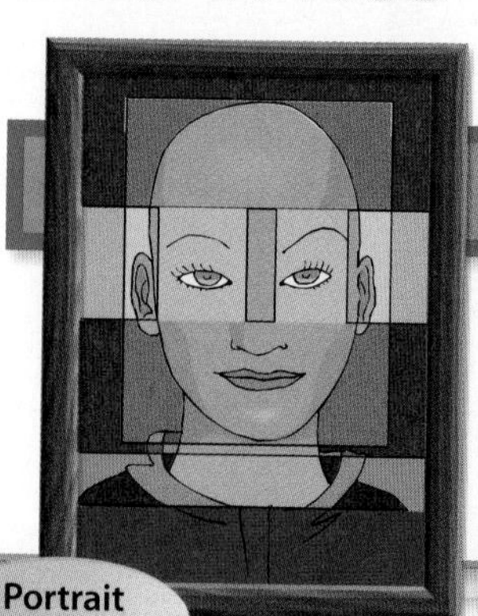

Still Life
$?

Portrait
$210.00

Landscape
$135.00

Another Example

Dean also sold 8 pen-and-ink sketches at the art fair. All the sketches were the same price. He made $196 on the sale of the sketches. What was the price for each sketch?

Read and Understand

What do you know? Dean sold 8 sketches and made $196.

What are you trying to find? The price of one sketch

Plan

What strategy will you use? Write an equation. A diagram can help to picture how the information is related.

Let n = the price of one sketch.

$196

n	n	n	n	n	n	n	n

$8 \times n = 196$
$(8 \times n) \div 8 = 196 \div 8$
$n = 24.50$

Divide both sides of the equation by 8 to get n alone on one side of the equation.

Each sketch was sold for $24.50.

Explain It

1. **Reasonableness** Is $24.50 a reasonable answer?
2. How does the diagram above show the information in the problem?

Plan

Choose a variable for the unknown quantity.

Let p = price of a still-life painting.

Use a diagram to picture the relationship between the prices.

$210	
p	$125

Write an equation.

$p + 125 = 210$

Solve

Solve the equation.

$$p + 125 = 210$$
$$p + 125 - 125 = 210 - 125$$
$$p = 85$$

Subtract 125 from both sides to get the variable alone.

The price of a still-life painting is $85.

Look Back

Estimate to see if the answer makes sense.

Round 85 to 100.

$100 + 125 = 225$, which is close to 210.

The price of $85 is reasonable.

Guided Practice*

Do you know HOW?

1. Use the picture to write and solve an equation.

34	
s	18

Do you UNDERSTAND?

2. **Write a Problem** Write a real-world problem that you can solve by drawing a picture and writing an addition or subtraction equation.

Independent Practice

In **3** through **5**, use each picture to write and solve each equation.

3. Allen read 5 more pages today than he did yesterday. Today he read 42 pages. How many pages did Allen read yesterday?

42 pages	
p	5

4. Dan biked 27 miles yesterday. If he biked 3 times as far as Joe, how far did Joe bike?

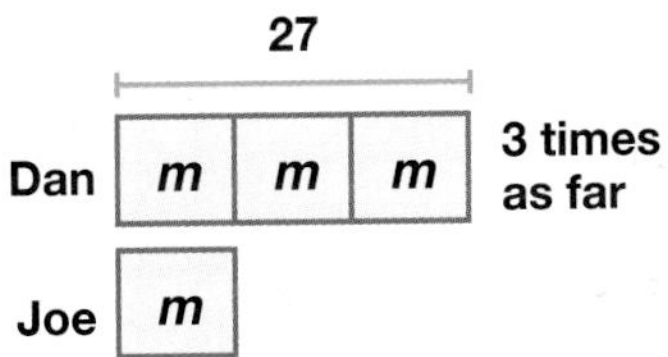

5. Max is saving $15 per month to buy a desk that costs $285. How many months will he need to save?

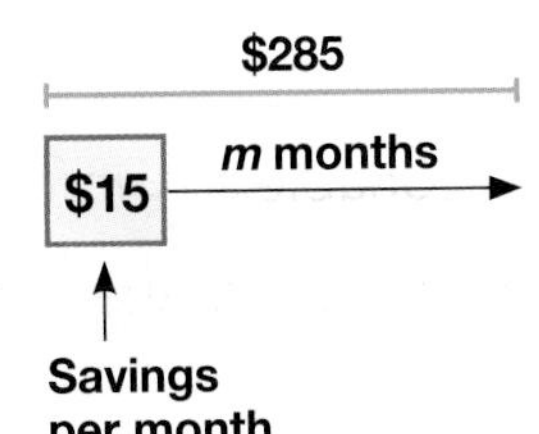

Stuck? Try this....

- What do I know?
- What am I asked to find?
- What diagram can I use to help understand the problem?
- Can I use addition, subtraction, multiplication, or division?
- Is all of my work correct?
- Did I answer the right question?
- Is my answer reasonable?

*For another example, see Set D on page 383.

For **6** through **8**, draw a picture, write and solve an equation to answer the question.

6. Kieko and Linda sold a total of 124 calendars. Kieko sold 57 of them. How many calendars did Linda sell?

7. Carmen has saved \$13 to buy a DVD that costs \$29. How much more money does Carmen need to save?

8. Jonathan loaned his brother \$22 and had \$126 left. How much money did Jonathan have before he loaned the money?

9. **Writing to Explain** Caryn drew this picture and wrote this equation to represent the problem below.

A zoo has 19 more species of fish than birds. There are 152 species of fish. How many species of birds does the zoo have?

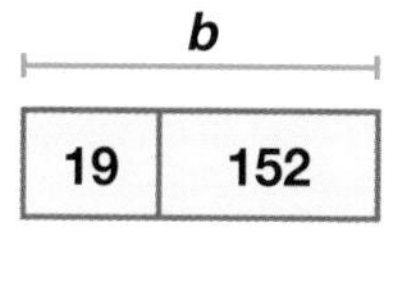

$b - 19 = 152$

Is Caryn correct? Explain your answer.

10. Camille used a coupon to pay for a movie ticket. The original cost of the ticket was \$6.50, but Camille only paid \$4. Write an equation and solve it to find how much the coupon was worth.

11. Orlando saved \$520 in 1 year. He saved \$330 in the last 4 months. Write and solve an equation to find how much Orlando saved in the first 8 months.

12. Dean also does abstract paintings. He charges \$85 less than the price of a portrait. He charges \$210 for a portrait. Write and solve an equation to find the price of one of Dean's abstract paintings.

13. Forests once covered about $\frac{1}{2}$ of Earth's land surface. Today, about $\frac{2}{5}$ of Earth's original forest areas remain untouched and undisturbed. What fraction of Earth's land surface is covered by forests today?

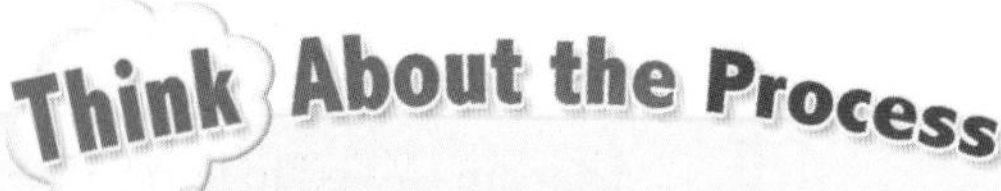

14. A total of 44 adults are going on a field trip with the class. If 14 of the adults are men, how many are women? Which of the following equations gives the number of women?

A $14 + 44 = w$

B $w - 14 = 44$

C $14 + w = 44$

D $w - 44 = 14$

15. Tony is running a 10-kilometer race. He just reached the 4-kilometer marker. Which of the following equations can you use to find out how many more kilometers he needs to run?

A $k - 4 = 10$

B $4 + k = 10$

C $4 - k = 10$

D $10 + 4 = k$

Algebra Connections

Solution Pairs

Remember that an equation is a number sentence that uses an equal sign to show that two expressions have the same value.

When two variables occur in an equation, each variable can be replaced with a different number. When the two replacements make a true equation, the two replacements form a **solution pair**.

Example: Do $x = 12$ and $y = 8$ form a solution pair for $x = y + 4$?

Substitute the given values for x and y into the equation.

Replacing x with 12 and y with 8 gives $12 = 8 + 4$, or $12 = 12$. The equation is true.

So, $x = 12$ and $y = 8$ form a solution pair for $x = y + 4$.

For **1** through **15**, use the table of values at the right. For each equation, determine if the given replacements form a solution pair. Write yes or no.

1. $y + z = 10$ **2.** $b = x + 15$ **3.** $b = a + 15$

4. $a + x = 40$ **5.** $40 - c = x$ **6.** $c - x = 6$

7. $b - y = 43$ **8.** $b = 99 - z$ **9.** $60 - y = b$

10. $63 = b - c$ **11.** $20 + z = c$ **12.** $10 - y = z$

13. $20 = x + y$ **14.** $b + c = 58$ **15.** $a + b = 85$

Table of Values
$a = 30$
$b = 45$
$c = 18$
$x = 12$
$y = 8$
$z = 2$

For **16** through **17**, refer to the table at the right.

16. The cost of an adult ticket is equal to twice the cost of a child's ticket. So, $a = 2 \times c$. Find two different pairs of values for a and c to make the equation true.

17. An adult ticket costs $3 more than a student ticket. So $a = s + 3$. Find two different pairs of values for a and s to make the equation true.

Data

Cost of Museum Tickets

Ticket	Price
Child	c
Adult	a
Student	s
Early Bird	e

Test Prep

1. On average, residents of the United Kingdom have 28 vacation days each year, 14 fewer than the average in Italy. Solve the equation $n - 14 = 28$ to find n, the average number of vacation days in Italy. (16-1)

A $n = 2$

B $n = 14$

C $n = 42$

D $n = 49$

2. Which equation could be used to represent the table shown? (16-4)

n	m
10	0
12	2
15	5
19	9

A $m = \frac{n}{10}$

B $m = 10 - n$

C $m = n + 10$

D $m = n - 10$

3. An African elephant can eat up to 4,200 pounds of food in a week. Solve the equation $7n = 4{,}200$ to find n, the pounds of food it can eat in a day. (16-2)

A $n = 60$

B $n = 600$

C $n = 700$

D $n = 29{,}400$

4. Which equation could be used to represent the table shown? (16-4)

x	y
20	40
13	26
12	24
5	10

A $y = 2x$

B $y = x + 20$

$y = \frac{x}{2}$

$3x$

5. Which equation could be used to represent the table shown? (16-5)

p	q
4	8
6	14
8	20

A $q = 2p$

B $q = 3p - 4$

C $q = 3p + 4$

D $q = 2p + 4$

6. On a trip to the United Kingdom, Kameko exchanged currency as shown in the table. How many British pounds could Kameko get for 38 U.S. dollars? (16-4)

Data

U.S. Dollars	British Pounds
8	4
14	7
20	10

A 19

B 28

C 34

D 76

7. The United Kingdom, Denmark, and Norway have a total of 20 territories. Norway has $\frac{1}{5}$ as many territories as the United Kingdom. Denmark has 2 territories. How many territories does Norway have? (16-3)

A 2

B 3

C 5

D 6

Test Prep

8. What step can be taken to get the x by itself on one side in the equation $x - 13 = 102$? (16-1)

A Add 13 to both sides of the equation.

B Subtract 13 from both sides of the equation.

C Multiply both sides of the equation by 13.

D Divide both sides of the equation by 13.

9. What step can be taken to get the variable m alone on one side of the equation $\frac{m}{5} = 25$? (16-2)

A Add 5 to both sides of the equation.

B Subtract 5 from both sides of the equation.

C Multiply both sides of the equation by 5.

D Divide both sides of the equation by 5.

10. What value will complete the table shown? (16-5)

x	$y = 4x - 23$	y
7	$y = 4(7) - 23$	5
9	$y = 4(9) - 23$	

A 13

B 28

C 36

D 56

11. For his recital, Alberto chose a song with 112 measures. The song was divided into 7 movements, or parts, each with the same number of measures. Which of the following can be used to find, m, the number of measures in each movement? (16-6)

112 measures

m	m	m	m	m	m	m

Measures in each movement

A $m + 7 = 112$

B $m - 7 = 112$

C $7m = 112$

D $\frac{m}{7} = 112$

12. The table shows the total number of lawns, L, that Saul has mowed after w weeks. Which equation could be used to represent the relationship in the table? (16-4)

Number of weeks, w	Number mowed, L
1	14
2	28
3	42

A $L = \frac{14}{w}$

B $L = \frac{w}{14}$

C $L = w + 13$

D $L = 14w$

Reteaching

Set A, pages 364–367

To solve an equation, get the variable alone on one side of the equation.

Solve: $x + 15 = 32$

To get a variable alone, undo what was done to it.

Since 15 is added to x, *subtract 15.*

Solve the equation.

$$x + 15 = 32$$
$$x + 15 - 15 = 32 - 15$$
$$x = 32 - 15$$
$$x = 17$$

To keep the sides of the equation equal, subtract 15 from both sides.

Remember that addition and subtraction, and multiplication and division, undo each other. What operation will get the variable alone on one side of each equation?

1. $a - 17 = 9$ **2.** $3n = 36$

3. $57 + c = 93$ **4.** $\frac{x}{4} = 19$

5. $18b = 108$ **6.** $27 = m - 65$

Solve each equation.

7. $d + 32 = 97$ **8.** $r - 14 = 49$

9. $72 = h - 25$ **10.** $n + 31 = 57$

11. $12b = 144$ **12.** $\frac{m}{10} = 12$

13. $250 = 25x$ **14.** $30 = \frac{w}{6}$

Set B, pages 368–369

Use reasoning to solve problems.

Carlos has 18 marbles. $\frac{1}{2}$ of them are green, $\frac{1}{3}$ of them are blue, and the rest are red. How many marbles of each color does he have?

Unit cubes can be used to show the marbles and solve the problem.

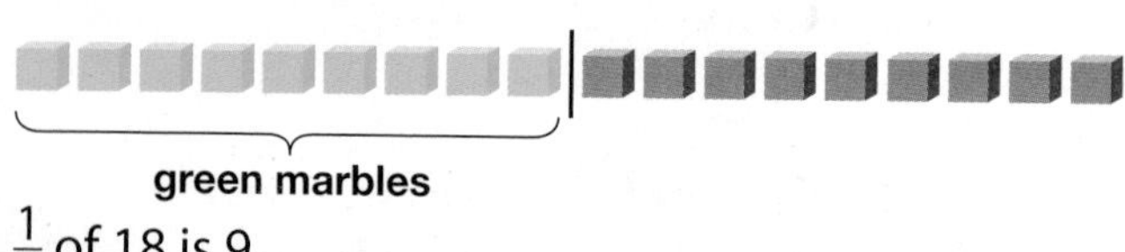

$\frac{1}{2}$ of 18 is 9.

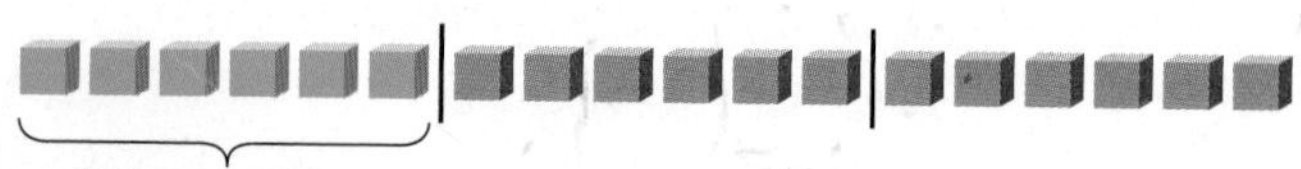

blue marbles

$\frac{1}{3}$ of 18 is 6.

Since 9 marbles are green and 6 marbles are blue, the 3 remaining marbles are red.

Remember that using objects or making a table can help you reason through a problem.

1. Alvin has an insect collection. He has 10 insects in all. $\frac{1}{2}$ of the insects are ladybugs and $\frac{1}{5}$ of the insects are grasshoppers. The rest are crickets. How many of each insect are in his collection?

2. Allie, Tia, and Carla each live in a different city: Los Angeles, Chicago, or Dallas. Tia does not live in Texas. Carla does not live in California. Allie lives in Illinois. In which city does each girl live?

Set C, pages 370–372, 374–375

Write an equation for the table.

x	y
4	12
8	16
12	20
16	24

What can be done to x to get y?

$x + 8 = y$, or $3x = y$

$x + 8 = y$, or $2x = y$

$x + 8 = y$

$x + 8 = y$

The equation $x + 8 = y$ is true for all of the pairs in the table.

Choose the equation that matches the table.

x	y
2	2
3	5
4	8
5	11

A $3y - 4 = x$

B $3x - 4 = y$

C $3(x - 4) = y$

D $3(y - 4) = x$

Replace x with the given values to see which equation gives the correct y-values.

The equation $3x - 4 = y$ matches the table.

Remember that the same equation must be true for each pair of numbers in the table.

Write an equation for each table.

1.

x	y
16	4
20	8
24	12
36	24

2.

x	y
8	1
16	2
24	3
32	4

3. Choose the equation that matches the table.

x	y
2	9
4	13
6	17
8	21

A $2(y + 5) = x$

B $2(x + 5) = y$

C $2x + 5 = y$

D $2y + 5 = x$

Set D, pages 376–378

A flower shop has 98 roses arranged in 7 vases. How many roses are in each vase?

Draw a diagram.

Let r = roses in each vase.

98 roses

r	r	r	r	r	r	r

Roses in each vase

Write and solve an equation.

$$7r = 98$$
$$(7 \times r) \div 7 = 98 \div 7$$
$$r = 14$$

There are14 roses in each vase.

Remember that a diagram or equation can help you.

1. The 5 members of the Wyler family paid \$112.50 for admission to a water park. What was the price of each ticket?

2. Tom gave his sister \$25 and had \$45 left. How much did he have before he gave her the money?

Topic 17

Percent

1

Farmers grow almonds for use in food products such as nut mixes. How can you find the ratio of almonds to walnuts in a bowl of mixed nuts? You will find out in Lesson 17-1.

2

Some of the tallest buildings in the world are located in the United States. What percent of the 20 tallest buildings in the world are located in the U.S.? You will find out in Lesson 17-4.

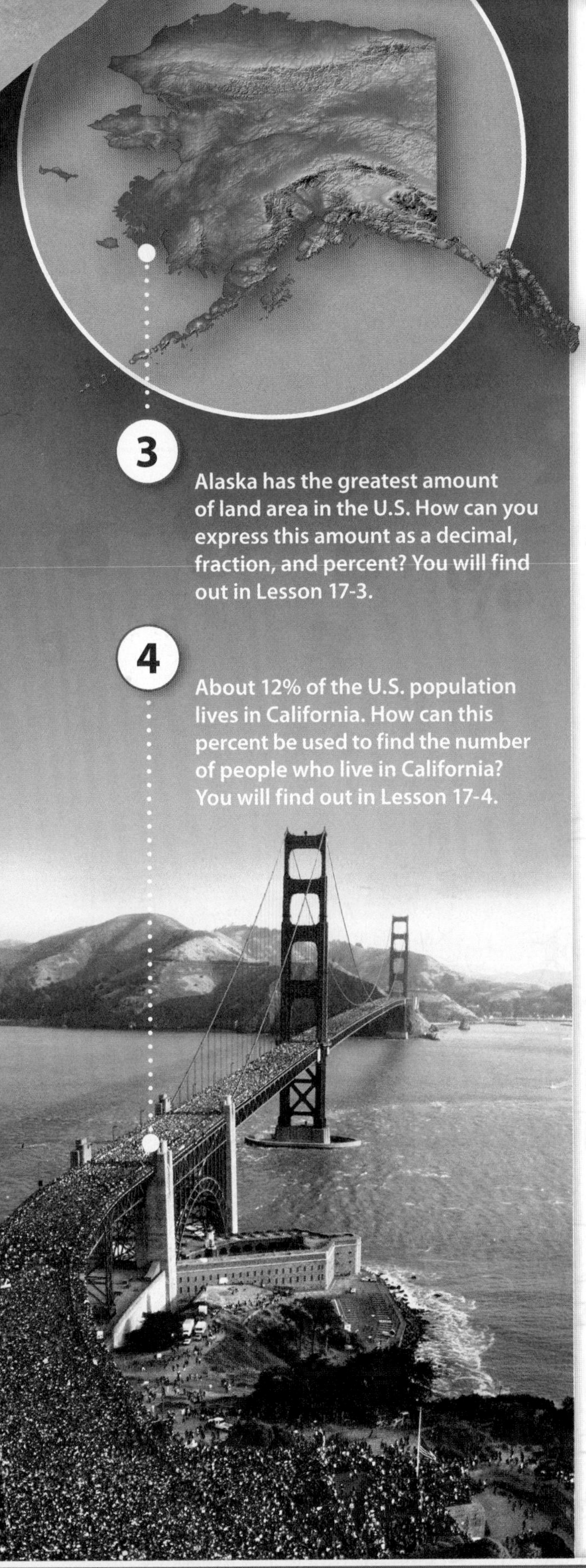

3 Alaska has the greatest amount of land area in the U.S. How can you express this amount as a decimal, fraction, and percent? You will find out in Lesson 17-3.

4 About 12% of the U.S. population lives in California. How can this percent be used to find the number of people who live in California? You will find out in Lesson 17-4.

Review What You Know!

Vocabulary

Choose the best term from the box.

- denominator
- fraction
- equivalent fractions
- numerator

1. The number below the fraction bar is called __?__ and the number above the fraction bar is called the __?__.

2. A __?__ can be used to name part of a whole.

3. Two different fractions that represent the same amount are called __?__.

Simplest Form

Write each fraction in simplest form.

4. $\frac{2}{4}$ **5.** $\frac{16}{4}$ **6.** $\frac{7}{21}$

7. $\frac{5}{25}$ **8.** $\frac{9}{6}$ **9.** $\frac{8}{10}$

Decimals and Fractions

Write each decimal as a fraction or as a mixed number in simplest form.

10. 0.25 **11.** 0.4 **12.** 0.01

13. 0.72 **14.** 4.5 **15.** 2.75

Fractions

Writing to Explain Write an answer for each question.

16. How can you find a fraction equivalent to a given fraction?

17. How can you change a fraction to a decimal?

Lesson

17-1

NS 1.2 Grade 6 Interpret and use ratios in different contexts (e.g., batting averages, miles per hour) to show the relative sizes of two quantities, using appropriate notations ($\frac{a}{b}$, a to b, a:b).

Understanding Ratios

What are ratios and when are they equal?

Todd is using a recipe to make fruit salad. What is the ratio of cups of cantaloupe to cups of apples? Cups of peaches to cups of fruit in the salad?

If Todd has 2 cups of strawberries, how many cups of cantaloupe should he use?

Another Example How can you find equal ratios?

Equal ratios show the same comparison.

You can find equal ratios by multiplying or dividing both terms by the same number.

Use multiplication.

		6 × 2	6 × 3
Cups of cantaloupe	6	12	18
Total cups of fruit	18	36	54
		18 × 2	18 × 3

Equal ratios: $\frac{6}{18} = \frac{12}{36} = \frac{18}{54}$

Use division.

		6 ÷ 2	6 ÷ 3	6 ÷ 6
Cups of cantaloupe	6	3	2	1
Total cups of fruit	18	9	6	3
		18 ÷ 2	18 ÷ 3	18 ÷ 6

Equal ratios: $\frac{6}{18} = \frac{3}{9} = \frac{2}{6} = \frac{1}{3}$

Guided Practice*

Do you know HOW?

In **1** through **4**, write each ratio. Then write two other ratios that are equal to each ratio.

1. circles to squares

2. triangles to circles

3. all shapes to squares

4. circles to all shapes

Do you UNDERSTAND?

5. Writing to Explain Is the ratio 6 to 3 the same as the ratio 3 to 6? Why or why not?

6. If Todd wanted to double the cups of apples, how many cups of cantaloupe would he need to keep the same ratio of fruit?

*For another example, see Set A on page 398.

A ratio is a comparison where for every *x* units of one quantity there are *y* units of another quantity. A ratio can compare a part to a part, a part to a whole, or the whole to a part.

The ratio of cups of cantaloupe to cups of apples can be written as 6 to 3, 6:3, or $\frac{6}{3}$.

The ratio of cups of peaches to cups of fruit in the salad can be written as 3 to 18, 3:18, or $\frac{3}{18}$.

The recipe calls for 4 cups of strawberries to 6 cups of cantaloupe.

For 2 cups of strawberries, 3 cups of cantaloupe are needed.

Todd should use 3 cups of cantaloupe for 2 cups of strawberries.

Independent Practice

In **7** through **16**, give two other ratios that are equal to each ratio.

7. $\frac{3}{4}$ **8.** 5 to 8 **9.** 12:16 **10.** 10:25 **11.** $\frac{5}{1}$

12. 6:9 **13.** $\frac{4}{5}$ **14.** 16 to 6 **15.** $\frac{15}{27}$ **16.** 3:12

Problem Solving

In **17** and **18**, use the survey results at the right.

17. What is the ratio of people who prefer the fresh mint flavor to those who took the survey? Write another ratio equal to that ratio.

18. The report stated that two out of five people preferred the tasty cinnamon flavor. Is that correct? Explain.

Data

Which flavor of toothpaste do you prefer?

Flavor	Number of people
Tasty cinnamon	40
Arctic ice	22
Fresh mint	38

19. In a bowl of mixed nuts, there are 96 peanuts, 34 cashews, 28 almonds, and 35 walnuts. What is the ratio of almonds to walnuts in that bowl of mixed nuts? Write another ratio equal to that ratio.

20. Ms. Graham gathered maps for a geography lesson. She had 8 maps of California, 6 maps of Texas, and 5 maps of Illinois. What is the ratio of maps of Texas to maps of California?

A $\frac{5}{8}$ **B** $\frac{3}{4}$ **C** $\frac{4}{3}$ **D** $\frac{8}{6}$

21. Geometry What is the ratio of the number of sides of a quadrilateral to the number of sides of a pentagon?

22. Number Sense Are the ratios 6 to 20 and 7 to 20 equal? Explain.

Lesson

17-2

NS 1.2 Interpret percents as a part of a hundred; find decimal and percent equivalents for common fractions and explain why they represent the same value; compute a given percent of a whole number.

Understanding Percent

What does percent mean?

The floor plan for a discount store is shown at the right. It is divided into 100 equal parts.

Write the amount of space each department occupies as a ratio and as a percent.

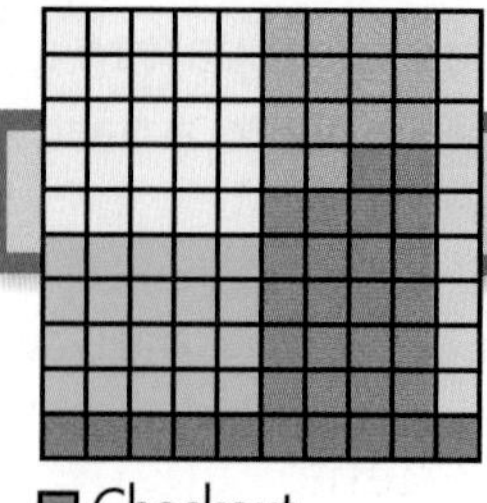

Checkout
CDs & DVDs
Women's Clothing
Men's Clothing
Children's Clothing
Toys

Guided Practice*

Do you know HOW?

In **1** through **3**, write the ratio and the percent that is represented by the shaded part of each 100-grid.

1. 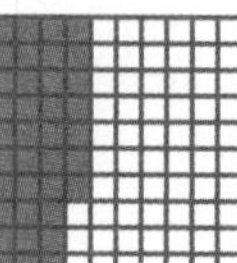 **2.**  **3.** 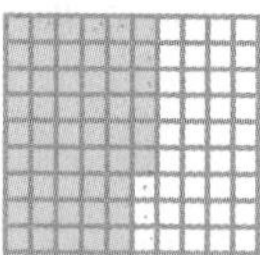

Do you UNDERSTAND?

4. **Number Sense** If all 100 squares in a 10-by-10 grid are shaded, what percent represents the shaded part?

5. Could the floor space in the store be divided this way: Women's clothing 25%, Children's clothing 25%, Men's clothing 25%, Toys 14%, CDs and DVDs 9%, and checkout counter 10%? Explain your answer.

Independent Practice

In **6** through **10**, write the ratio and the percent that is represented by the shaded part of each 100-grid.

6. 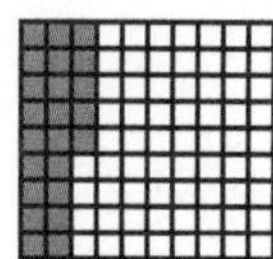 **7.** 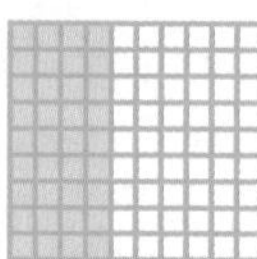 **8.** 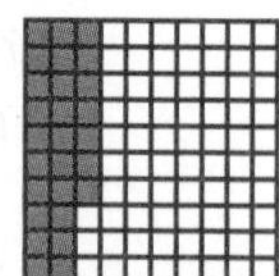 **9.** 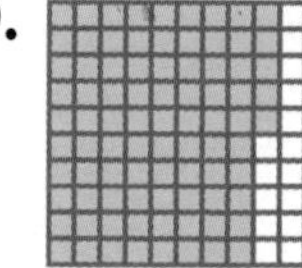 **10.** 

In **11** through **15**, write each ratio as a percent.

11. 47 out of 100

12. $\frac{50}{100}$

13. 76 to 100

14. $\frac{9}{100}$

15. 35:100

16. **Writing to Explain** Is 75% the same as the ratio 3 to 4? Why or why not?

*For another example, see Set B on page 398.

A percent is a ratio in which the first term is compared to 100.

Percent means *per hundred*.

The percent symbol is %.

Toys occupy 14 out of 100 parts, or 14%.

14% is read "fourteen percent."

Written as a ratio, 14% is 14 to 100, or 14:100, or $\frac{14}{100}$.

Floor space occupied by the departments

Women's clothing:	25 out of 100 or 25%
Men's clothing:	20 out of 100 or 20%
Children's clothing:	22 out of 100 or 22%
Toys:	14 out of 100 or 14%
CDs and DVDs:	9 out of 100 or 9%
Checkout counter:	10 out of 100 or 10%

Problem Solving

17. In a group of 100 people, 37 people wear glasses. What percent of the people in the group wear glasses?

18. Both triangles below have 50% of their area shaded. Why are the shaded areas not the same amount?

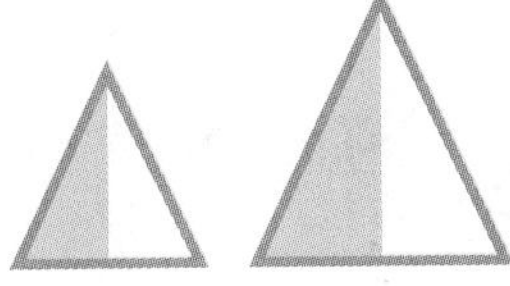

19. A florist is preparing 10 vases of flowers. Each vase will contain 3 roses and 8 carnations. How many of each type of flower will be needed?

20. The Glenview orchestra contains 100 members. The conductor shaded the grid shown below to represent the members in each section. What percent of the members are in each section?

a strings

b woodwinds

c brass

d percussion

e keyboards

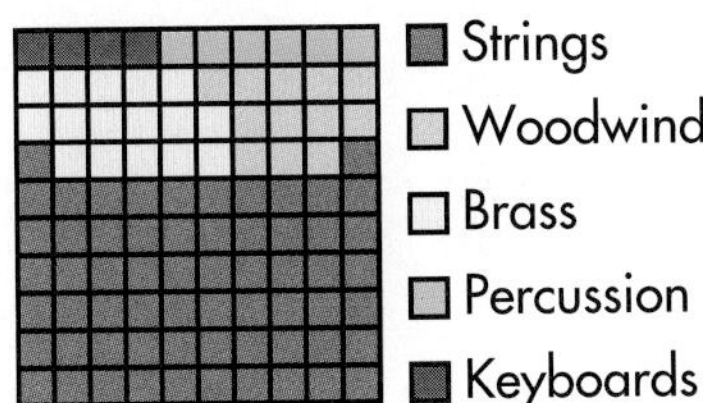

21. **Algebra** What is the value of n in the equation $12n = 180$?

A 12 **C** 20

B 15 **D** 9

22. **Estimation** Some zoo employees gathered data one day and found that 153 people entered the zoo in 10 minutes. Based on that data, estimate the number of people who would enter the zoo in 1 hour.

23. Ashley spent \$5.75 for camera film and \$17.49 for a CD. She also bought lunch. She started the day with \$30. If she had \$2.35 left, how much did she spend for lunch?

Lesson
17-3

NS 1.2 Interpret percents as a part of a hundred; find decimal and percent equivalents for common fractions and explain why they represent the same value; compute a given percentage of a whole number.

Percents, Fractions, and Decimals

How are percents related to fractions and decimals?

Many states charge sales tax on items you buy. Sales tax is often named as a percent. It compares an amount to the 100 cents in a dollar.

How is Indiana's sales tax expressed as a fraction and a decimal?

Indiana sales tax 6%

Guided Practice*

Do you know HOW?

In **1** through **3**, write the percent, decimal, and fraction in simplest form represented by the shaded part of each 100-grid.

1. 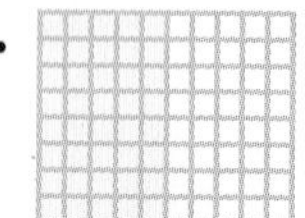 **2.** 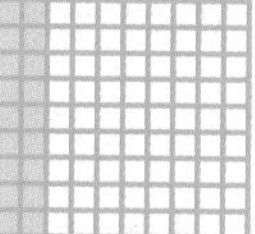 **3.** 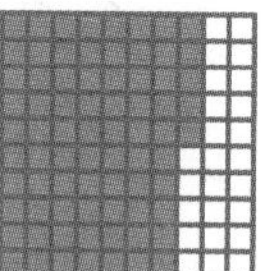

Do you UNDERSTAND?

4. Writing to Explain If $\frac{2}{8} = \frac{1}{4} = 25\%$, then how can you find what $\frac{1}{8}$ is as a percent?

5. The sales tax in Chicago is 9%. Write that percent as a decimal and fraction in simplest form.

Independent Practice

In **6** through **10**, write the percent, decimal, and fraction in simplest form represented by the shaded part of each 100-grid.

6. 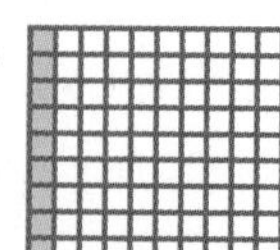 **7.** 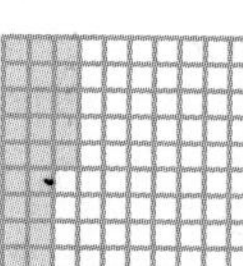 **8.** 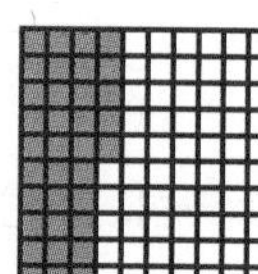 **9.** 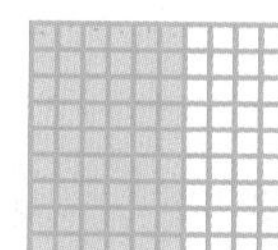 **10.** 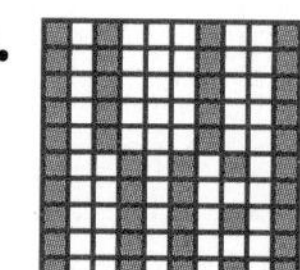

In **11** through **20**, write each percent as a decimal and a fraction in simplest form.

11. 65%	**12.** 5%	**13.** 23%	**14.** 72%	**15.** 1%
16. 2%	**17.** 45%	**18.** 100%	**19.** 125%	**20.** 200%

*For another example, see Set C on page 399.

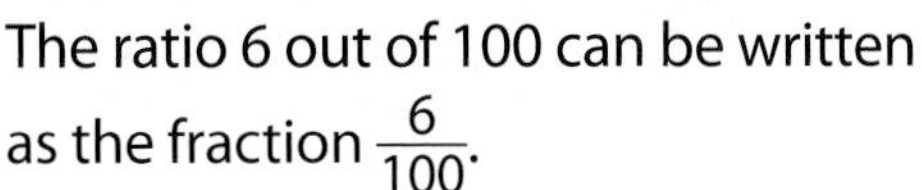

Percent means *per hundred.*

So, 6% means 6 out of 100.

The ratio 6 out of 100 can be written as the fraction $\frac{6}{100}$.

In simplest form, $\frac{6}{100}$ can be written as $\frac{3}{50}$.

$$6\% = \frac{6}{100} = \frac{3}{50}$$

The ratio 6 out of 100 can be written as the decimal in hundredths.

$$6\% = \frac{6}{100} = 0.06$$

Remember to write zeros in a decimal when needed.

Indiana Sales Tax

As a percent: 6%

As a fraction:

$$\frac{6}{100} = \frac{3}{50}$$

As a decimal: 0.06

For every dollar a person spends, an additional $0.06 is paid for sales tax.

Problem Solving

21. Fill in the missing equivalent values.

percent			33%	
fraction		$\frac{19}{20}$		$1\frac{1}{2}$
decimal	0.3			

22. **Think About the Process** What would you do first to order the following numbers from least to greatest?

$25\%, \frac{1}{3}, 0.64, \frac{7}{8}, 0.8$

A Convert the decimals to percents.

B Order the decimals.

C Convert all numbers to decimals or fractions.

D Order the fractions.

23. If there are 4 juice boxes in 50% of a package, how many boxes are in a whole package?

24. About 16% of the total U.S. land area is in Alaska. Write 16% as a decimal and a fraction in simplest form.

25. Only 15% of the class did a science project on birds. What fraction did not do a project on birds?

26. Sally traveled 550 miles on vacation. She traveled 330 of those miles in Nevada. What percent of the trip did she travel in Nevada? (Hint: Write a fraction and find an equal fraction with a denominator of 100.)

27. Melanie counted and identified birds that came near her home. The circle graph shows her observations. Find the ratio of the number of birds of each type to the total number of birds. Write each ratio as a percent, a decimal, and fraction in simplest form.

a Robins

b Wrens

c Cardinals

d Blue Jays

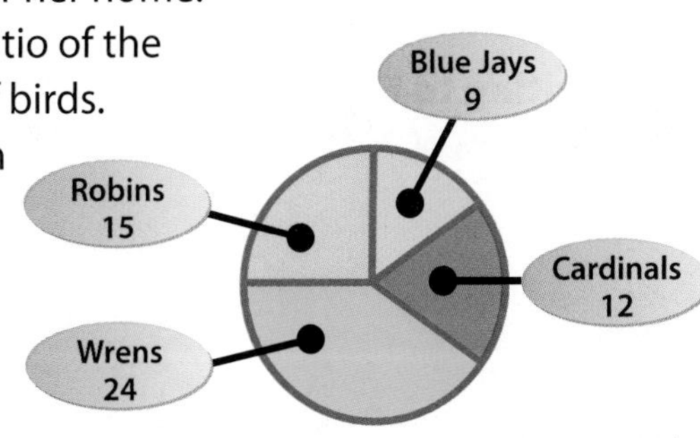

Lesson

17-4

NS 1.2 Interpret percents as a part of a hundred; find decimal and percent equivalents for common fractions and explain why they represent the same value; compute a given percent of a whole number.

Finding Percent of a Whole Number

How can you find a percent of a given number?

Different stores have included a backpack in their back-to-school sale. What is the amount of the discount at each store?

$25

Store	Discount
#1	50%
#2	10%
#3	35%
#4	20%

Guided Practice*

Do you know HOW?

In **1** through **4**, find the percent of each number.

1. 3% of 200 **2.** 25% of 48

3. 90% of 85 **4.** 75% of 44

Do you UNDERSTAND?

5. What is an easy way to find 25% of a number?

6. In the example above, what would the amount of the discount be if the backpack was discounted 40%?

Independent Practice

In **7** through **18**, find the percent of each number.

7. 43% of 350 **8.** 87% of 210 **9.** 5% of 46 **10.** 100% of 37

11. 30% of 66 **12.** 10% of 230 **13.** 20% of 400 **14.** 15% of 90

15. 50% of 75 **16.** 12% of 100 **17.** 33% of 300 **18.** 77% of 10

19. Find 1% of 235. How many decimal places in 235 did the decimal point move to the left in the answer?

20. What is an easy way to find 2% of 660?

21. **Writing to Explain** What is an easy way to find 11% of a number? Use 11% of 70 to explain.

*For another example, see Set D on page 399.

Find 50% of 25.

50% = 0.5

Multiply 25 by 0.5.

$$\begin{array}{r} 25 \\ \times\ 0.5 \\ \hline 12.5 \end{array}$$

Notice that 50% of 25 is the same as 25 ÷ 2.

The discount at store #1 is $12.50.

Find 10% of 25.

10% = 0.1

Multiply 25 by 0.1.

$$\begin{array}{r} 25 \\ \times\ 0.1 \\ \hline 2.5 \end{array}$$

Notice that the decimal point moved one place to the left.

The discount at store #2 is $2.50.

Find 35% of 25.

35% = 0.35

Multiply 25 by 0.35.

$$\begin{array}{r} 25 \\ \times\ 0.35 \\ \hline 8.75 \end{array}$$

The discount at store #3 is $8.75.

Find 20% of 25.

20% = 0.2

Multiply 25 by 0.2.

$$\begin{array}{r} 25 \\ \times\ 0.2 \\ \hline 5.0 \end{array}$$

The discount at store #4 is $5.00.

Problem Solving

22. About 12% of the U.S. population lives in California. If the U.S. population is about 300,000,000 people, about how many people live in California?

23. Marcia had dinner at a restaurant and wants to leave a 20% tip. Explain how she could calculate the tip using mental math.

Use the information from the chart to answer **24** through **26**.

Data

Meat	Ounces	Cost
Ham	14	$5.74
Turkey	11	$4.07
Pastrami	5	$4.85
Roast Beef	8	$6.56

24. What is the cost of 2 ounces of turkey?

25. Which costs more per ounce, roast beef or pastrami?

26. What is the total cost of 14 ounces of ham and 5 ounces of pastrami?

27. Algebra Jordan bought a $35 jacket and a $40 pair of shoes at a 25% discount. Write an equation to find the total amount of discount on the items. Solve the equation.

28. Reasoning Write these numbers in order from least to greatest.

60%, $\frac{1}{4}$, 0.75, 28%, $\frac{1}{2}$, 0.55

29. The price of a computer is $1,450, and a monitor costs $350. The sales tax is 6%. What is the total amount of sales tax on both items?

30. Of the 20 tallest buildings in the world, 20% are located in the United States. How many of the world's 20 tallest buildings are in the U.S.?

31. Critical Thinking The price of a new bike is $90. The store is advertising a 30% discount and the sales tax is 7%. Explain how to find the cost of the bike.

Lesson

17-5

MR 1.1 Analyze problems by identifying relationships, distinguishing relevant from irrelevant information, sequencing and prioritizing information, and observing patterns. Also **MR 1.0, 2.3, NS 1.2**

Problem Solving

Make a Table and Look for a Pattern

Kiesha and Sheryl play on the school basketball team. The statistics from the last game are shown at the right.

If they continue at the same rate, what percent of their shots would each player make?

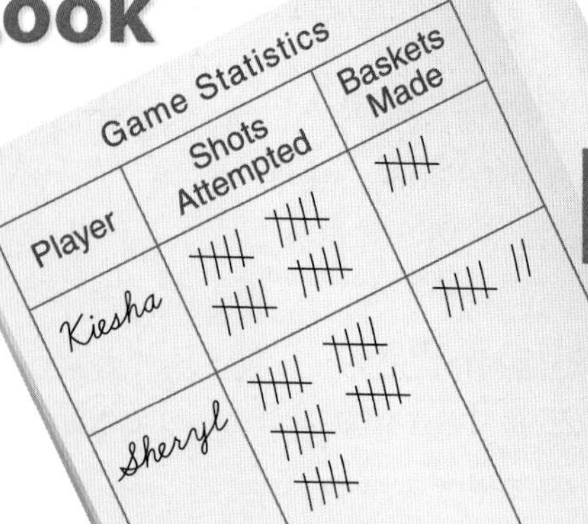

Guided Practice*

Do you know HOW?

Find the percent by completing the table.

1. 4 free throws out of 16 were made

Free throws made	4			
Free throws attempted	16	8	4	

Do you UNDERSTAND?

2. How can a table help you to find a percent?

3. Write a Problem Write a real-world problem that you can solve using a table to find a percent.

Independent Practice

In **4** through **7**, find each percent by completing each table.

4. 8 completions out of 20 attempts

Pass completions	8				
Pass attempts	20	40	60	80	100

5. 6 out of 30 days were cloudy

Cloudy days	6			
Total days	30	10	50	100

Stuck? Try this....

- What do I know?
- What am I asked to find?
- What diagram can I use to help understand the problem?
- Can I use addition, subtraction, multiplication, or division?
- Is all of my work correct?
- Did I answer the right question?
- Is my answer reasonable?

*For another example, see Set E on page 399.

Plan

Make a table and look for patterns to get a comparison with 100. Begin with the numbers you know and find equal ratios.

Kiesha

Baskets made	5				
Shots attempted	20	40	60	80	100

Sheryl

Baskets made	7			
Shots attempted	25	50	75	100

Solve

Complete each table and look for patterns.

Kiesha

Baskets made	5	10	15	20	25
Shots attempted	20	40	60	80	100

Sheryl

Baskets made	7	14	21	28
Shots attempted	25	50	75	100

Kiesha might make 25 out of 100, or 25%, of her shots.

Sheryl might make 28 out of 100, or 28%, of her shots.

6. 30 of the 75 fossils are shells.

Fossil shells	10	▒	▒	▒
Total fossils	25	50	75	▒

7. 54 of the 75 votes were for Fred.

Votes for Fred	54	▒	▒	▒
Total votes	75	150	300	▒

8. Rodrigo wants to wrap a package with paper. Find the least amount of paper he will need.

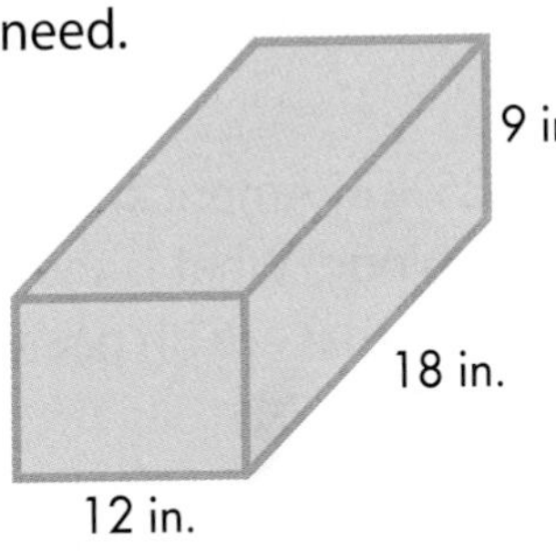

9. Mr. Perez bought 8 souvenir mugs to give as gifts. Mrs. Perez bought 7 souvenir mugs. How much did each person spend? If the tax was 10%, what was their total bill?

10. Draw a net to represent the package Rodrigo is wrapping.

11. Luciana made 45 hits out of 150 times at bat. What is that as a percent?

12. Brett plans to walk 16 miles this weekend. On Saturday, he walked 12 miles. What percent of his goal has Brett walked?

13. Tessa used 24 minutes of an 80-minute CD. What percent of the CD has *not* been used? How many minutes is that?

14. **Writing to Explain** Fran estimated 45% of 87 by finding 50% of 90. Will her estimate be greater than or less than the exact answer? Why?

15. Nicole's digital camera has a 360-picture memory. She has taken 162 pictures. Make a table and find a pattern. What percent of the camera's memory has she used?

Test Prep

1. The table shows the number of animals in an animal shelter. What is the ratio of dogs to total animals in the shelter? (17-1)

Data

Animal Type	Number
Cat	18
Dog	12
Rabbit	3

A 12 : 33

B 12 : 21

C 21 : 12

D 33 : 12

2. What is 61 out of 100 as a percent? (17-2)

A 100%

B 61%

C 39%

D 6.1%

3. Which of the following can be used to find 65% of 80? (17-4)

A Multiply 0.65 by 80.

B Multiply 0.65 by 0.8.

C Multiply 80 by 100.

D Multiply 65 by 80 and 100.

4. Which of the following ratios is equal to 15 to 10? (17-1)

A 10 to 15

B 20 to 15

C 3 to 5

D 3 to 2

5. A football team won 75% of their games. If they played 12 games, how many games did they win? (17-4)

A 7

B 8

C 9

D 10

6. Five out of 25 students are absent. What percent of the students are absent? (17-5)

Students Absent	5			
Total Students	25	50	75	100

A 5%

B 10%

C 15%

D 20%

7. About 85% of Americans have Rh positive blood. What is the ratio of Americans that are Rh positive to all Americans? (17-2)

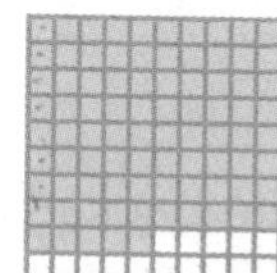

A $\frac{15}{85}$

B $\frac{85}{100}$

C $\frac{100}{85}$

D $\frac{15}{100}$

Test Prep

8. Which of the following represents the shaded area as a percent, a decimal and a fraction? (17-3)

A 21%, 0.21, $\frac{21}{100}$

B 42%, 0.42, $\frac{21}{100}$

C 42%, 0.42, $\frac{21}{50}$

D 21%, 0.21, $\frac{21}{50}$

9. What is the ratio of shaded circles to shaded squares? (17-1)

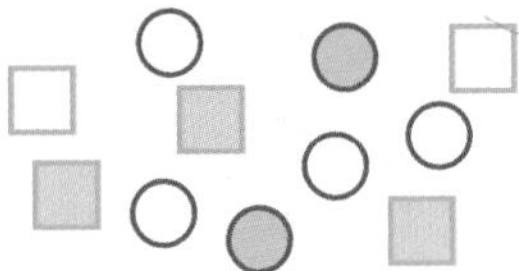

A 3 : 11

B 2 : 11

C 3 : 2

D 2 : 3

10. Which is equal to 20%? (17-3)

A $\frac{2}{100}$

B 20 : 50

C $\frac{1}{5}$

D 2 out of 100

11. Which is 60% written as a decimal and a fraction? (17-3)

A 0.06, $\frac{60}{100}$

B 0.6, $\frac{60}{100}$

C 0.6, $\frac{6}{100}$

D 0.06, $\frac{6}{100}$

12. In a particular hospital during one month, the ratio of the number of girls born to the number of boys born was 24 to 15. Which of the following ratios is equal to 24 to 15? (17-1)

A 5 to 8

B 8 to 5

C 3 to 5

D 19 to 10

13. The United States consumes 27% of all commercially harvested wood in the world. What fraction equals 27%? (17-3)

A $\frac{27}{100}$

B $\frac{73}{100}$

C $\frac{27}{73}$

D $\frac{73}{27}$

14. What percent is represented by the shaded part of the grid? (17-2)

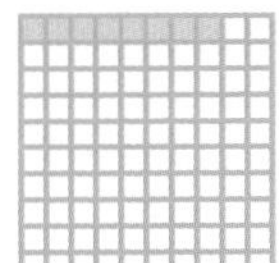

A 0.8%

B 8%

C 18%

D 80%

15. What is 80% of 150? (17-4)

A 80

B 100

C 120

D 130

Reteaching

Set A, pages 386–387

Write the ratio of squares to circles in three ways.

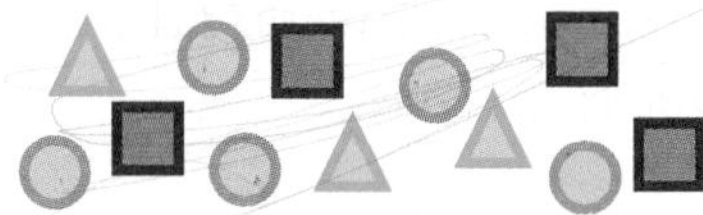

The ratio can be written as 4 to 5, 4:5, or $\frac{4}{5}$.

Write two ratios equal to 4:12.

Multiply or divide both terms by the same number.

$\frac{4 \times 2}{12 \times 2} = \frac{8}{24}$ $\quad$ $\frac{4 \div 2}{12 \div 2} = \frac{2}{6}$

4:12 = 8:24 = 2:6

Remember that the order of the terms is important.

Use the shapes at the left. Write each ratio.

1. triangles to circles
2. all shapes to triangles
3. circles to all shapes

Write two other ratios equal to each ratio.

4. $\frac{9}{12}$
5. 6 to 7
6. 14:28
7. 27:9
8. 15 to 12
9. $\frac{35}{40}$
10. 5 to 3
11. 18:24
12. $\frac{21}{49}$
13. $\frac{15}{21}$

Set B, pages 388–389

Write the ratio that compares the shaded squares to all the squares.

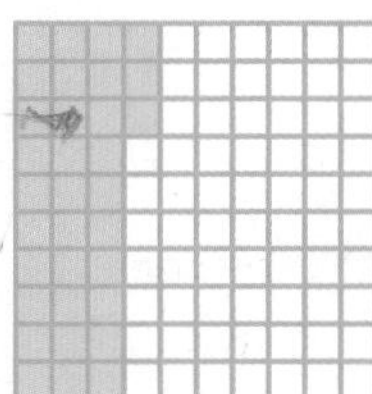

The ratio can be written as 33 to 100, 33:100, or $\frac{33}{100}$.

Write that ratio as a percent.

$\frac{33}{100} = 33\%$

Remember that a percent is a ratio in which a number is compared to 100.

Write the ratio that compares the shaded squares to all the squares for each grid. Write each ratio as a percent.

1\. 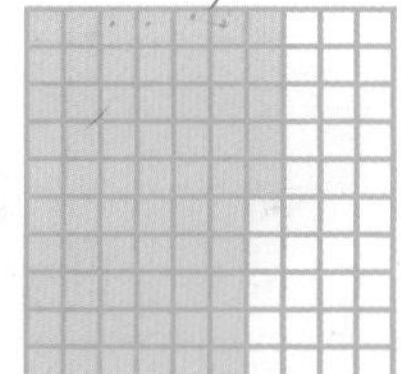

2\. 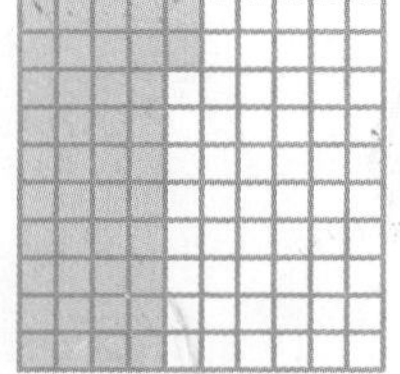

3\. 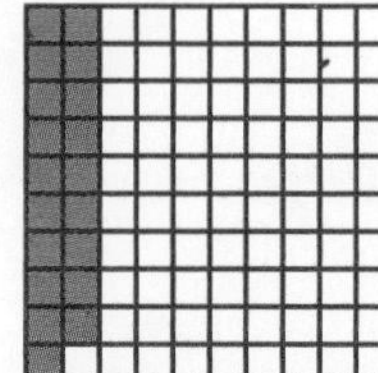

4\. 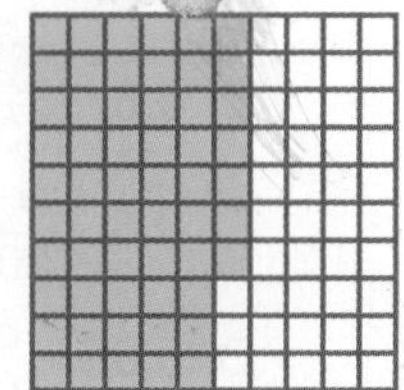

Set C, pages 390–391

Write 24% as a decimal and as a fraction in simplest form.

24% means 24 out of 100.

To write a decimal: Write the ratio as a decimal in hundredths.

24% = 0.24

To write a fraction: Write as a ratio with 100 as second term and find simplest form.

$\frac{24}{100} = \frac{24 \div 4}{100 \div 4} = \frac{6}{25}$

Remember to write zeros when more decimal places are needed.

Write each percent as a decimal and a fraction in simplest form.

1. 50% **2.** 40%

3. 25% **4.** 5%

5. 36% **6.** 70%

7. 94% **8.** 100%

Set D, pages 392–393

Find 40% of 80.

Change 40% to a decimal. 40% = 0.40 or 0.4

Multiply 80 by 0.4.

$$\begin{array}{r} 80 \\ \times\ 0.4 \\ \hline 32.0 \end{array}$$

40% of 80 is 32.

Remember to find the percent of a number, multiply the number by the decimal form of the percent.

Find the percent of each number.

1. 75% of 56 **2.** 10% of 32

3. 50% of 36 **4.** 90% of 60

5. 35% of 40 **6.** 20% of 90

Set E, pages 394–395

A hockey player attempted 15 shots on goal and made 9 goals. What percent of the shots did she make?

Write the ratio in a table. Find equal ratios to get the second term to be 100. Write the percent.

	ratio	÷3	×4	×5
Goals made	9	3	12	60
Shots attempted	15	5	20	100

The hockey player made goals on 60% of her shots.

Remember that to find a ratio equal to another ratio, both terms of the ratio must be multiplied or divided by the same number.

1. A baseball player was up to bat 40 times and got 14 hits. What percent of the times at bat did he get a hit?

2. The weather report stated that rain fell on 9 of the 30 days last month. On what percent of the days last month did it rain?

Topic 18

Equations and Graphs

1 A chess board is set up similar to a coordinate plane. Where on the board are the white knights located at the beginning aof the game? You will find out in Lesson 18-1.

2 Many cities in the United States are laid out like a coordinate grid. How can this be helpful when finding locations in cities such as Los Angeles? You will find out in Lesson 18-1.

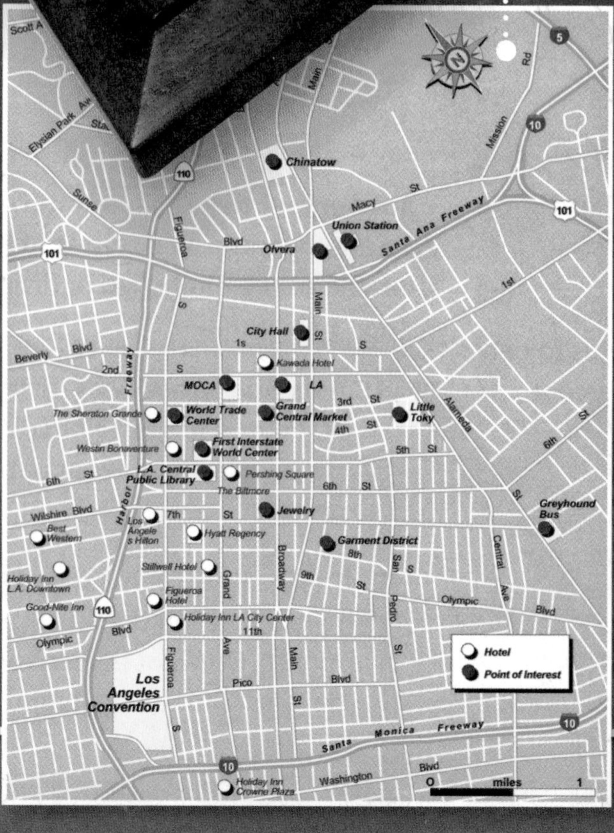

3

Americans spend hundreds of dollars every year on telephone service. How many more dollars did Americans spend on phone service in 2004 than in 2001? You will find out in Lesson 18-2.

4

Cities are located on a globe by using ordered pairs of latitude and longitude. What is city located at the coordinates (30, 30)? You will find out in Lesson 18-2

Review What You Know!

Vocabulary

Choose the best term from the box.

- axes
- ordered pair
- *x*-coordinate
- *y*-coordinate

1. (2, 5) is an example of a(n) ___?___.

2. If you name a point (4, 6), 4 is the ___?___ and 6 is the ___?___.

3. A coordinate plane is made up of two intersecting ___?___.

Basic Facts

Find each sum, difference, or product.

4. 4×5	**5.** 7×8	**6.** 3×6
7. $8 + 6$	**8.** $3 + 9$	**9.** $5 + 7$
10. $16 - 9$	**11.** $8 - 6$	**12.** $12 - 8$

Algebra

13. Evaluate $4x + 8$ for $x = 7$

14. Evaluate $51 \div y - 2$ for $y = 3$

Graphing Ordered Pairs

Writing to Explain Write an answer for the question.

15. Explain the steps you would follow to graph Point *A* (2, 3) on a coordinate grid.

Lesson

18-1

AF 1.4 Identify and graph ordered pairs in the four quadrants of the coordinate plane. Also SDAP 1.0, 1.5

Ordered Pairs

Hands-On
grid paper

How can you locate points on a coordinate grid?

A coordinate grid makes it easy to locate a point on a map. Start at 0. Go 3 blocks east and then 2 blocks north. You will be at the bank.
An ordered pair names a point on a coordinate grid. The bank is at (3, 2).

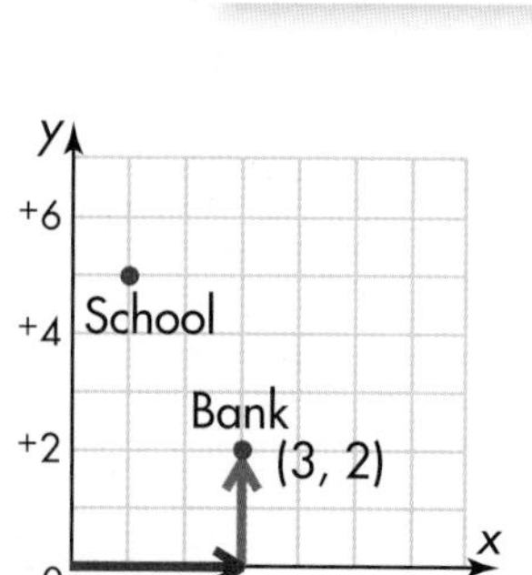

Another Example How do you graph a point on a coordinate plane?

You know that graphs represent data. Now you will see how ordered pairs of numbers can represent points on a coordinate plane.

Graph Point R at ($^-4$, $^-5$)

Step 1 Draw and label the x-axis and y-axis on grid paper.

Step 2 Move 4 units to the left of the origin. Then, move 5 units down.

Step 3 Mark a point and label it R.

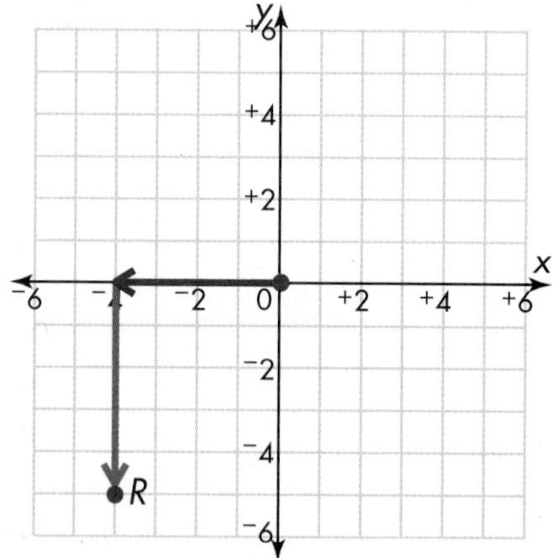

Explain It

1. How would you locate the point ($^+4$, $^-5$) on a coordinate grid?
2. If the location of point R above were changed to ($^-4$, $^+5$), would the point be above or below its current position?
3. Suppose you want to graph the point (0, $^+5$) on graph paper. When you start from the origin, do you move right 0 units or move up 0 units?

A coordinate plane extends to include both positive and negative numbers. It has a horizontal *x*-axis and a vertical *y*-axis. The point at which the *x*-axis and *y*-axis intersect is called the origin.

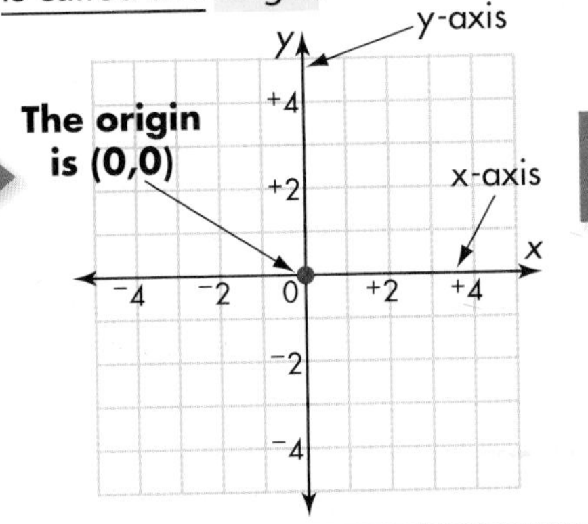

The first number in an ordered pair, the *x*-coordinate, names the distance to the right or left from the origin along the *x*-axis. The second number, the *y*-coordinate, names the distance up or down from the origin along the *y*-axis.

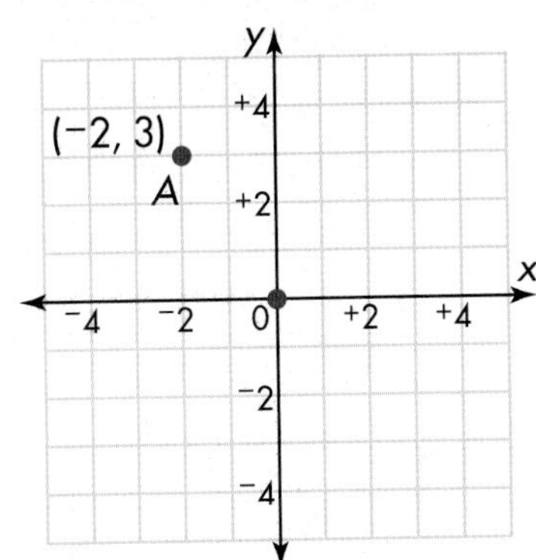

The ordered pair for Point *A* is (⁻2, 3).

Guided Practice*

Do you know HOW?

In **1** through **4**, write the ordered pair for each point. Use the grid at the right.

1. *A*

2. *B*

3. *C*

4. *D*

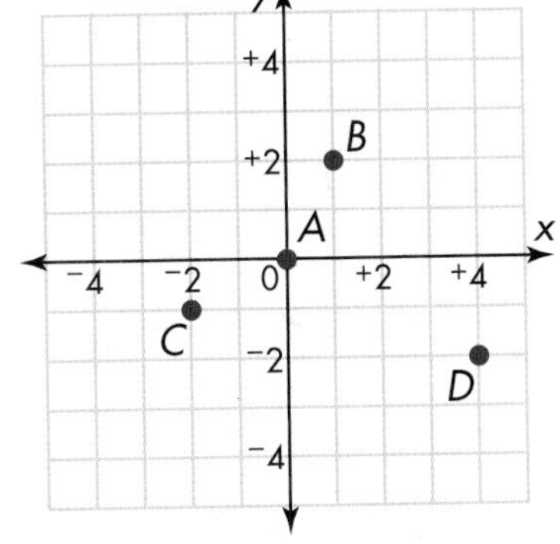

Do you UNDERSTAND?

5. Writing to Explain Describe how to plot the ordered pair (⁻3, ⁺4).

6. What ordered pair names the origin of any coordinate plane?

7. In the example above, name the ordered pair for a point that is 3 units directly above Point *A*.

Independent Practice

In **8** through **13**, write the ordered pair for each point. Use the grid at the right.

8. *M* **9.** *N* **10.** *P*

11. *R* **12.** *S* **13.** *T*

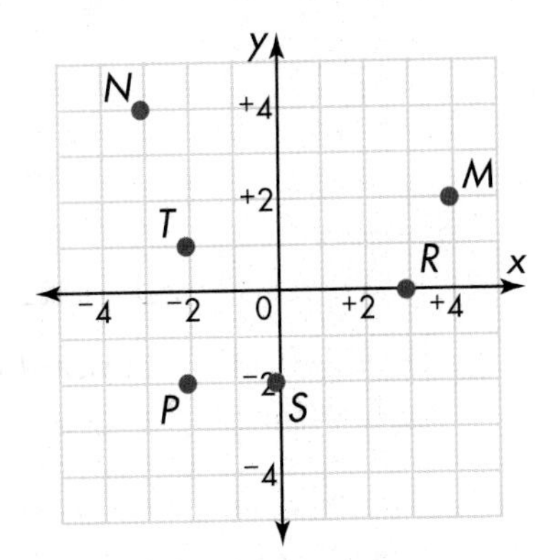

In **14** through **19**, graph and label each point on a grid.

14. *H* (2, ⁺1) **15.** *J* (⁺5, ⁺1) **16.** *K* (0, ⁺5)

17. *E* (⁺1, ⁻3) **18.** *F* (⁺4, ⁻5) **19.** *G* (⁻3, ⁻4)

For another example, see Set A on page 416.

Problem Solving

Geometry For **20** through **24**, complete the table by listing the ordered pair for each vertex of the pentagon at the right.

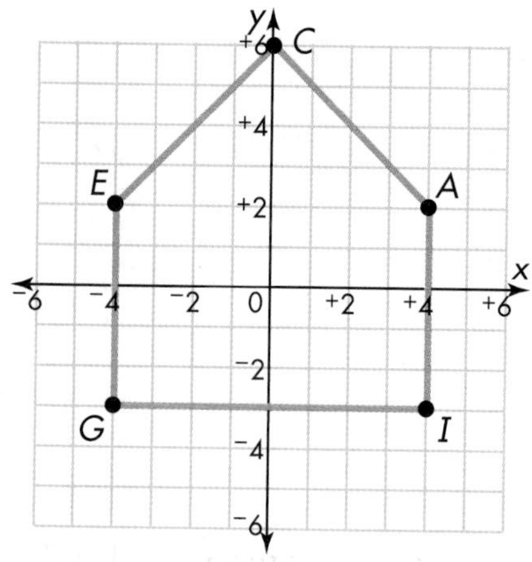

	Label	Ordered Pair
20.	*A*	
21.	*C*	
22.	*E*	
23.	*G*	
24.	*I*	

25. Algebra Which equation shows the relationship of the values in the table?

x	*y*
$^{+}9$	$^{+}6$
$^{-}2$	$^{-}5$
$^{+}5$	$^{+}2$
0	$^{-}3$
$^{+}10$	$^{+}7$

A $y = x + 3$

B $x = y - 3$

C $y = x - 3$

D $y = x$

26. A chessboard is similar to a coordinate grid. The pieces that look like horses are called knights. What letter-number combinations name the locations of the white knights?

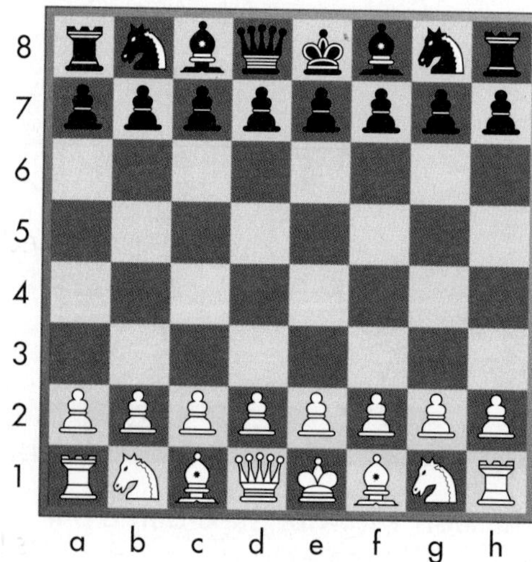

27. Writing to Explain The streets in many cities in the United States are laid out in a coordinate grid. How is this helpful when finding locations in cities such as Los Angeles, California?

28. In a class of 25 students, 15 are girls. Which does NOT show the part of the class that are girls?

A $\frac{3}{5}$

B 0.6

C 60%

D 0.3

Find each difference.

1. 6.7 – 0.921 **2.** 219.2 – 61.3 **3.** 2.5 – 1.054

4. 88.7 – 17.62 **5.** 1.17 – 0.362 **6.** 1.1 – 0.033

In **7** through **13**, solve each equation for *c*.

7. $\frac{c}{8} = 9$ **8.** $\frac{c}{16} = 2$ **9.** $\frac{c}{17} = 5$

10. $\frac{c}{2} = 2$ **11.** $\frac{c}{30} = 3$ **12.** $\frac{c}{10} = 13$ **13.** $\frac{c}{7} = 6$

Find each difference. Estimate to check if the answer is reasonable.

14. $3\overline{)316}$ **15.** 734 ÷ 6 **16.** $5\overline{)98}$ **17.** 723 ÷ 9

18. 10,648 ÷ 39 **19.** $20\overline{)2{,}084}$ **20.** $55\overline{)17{,}932}$ **21.** 6,203 ÷ 43

Error Search Find each sum or difference that is not correct. Write it correctly and explain the error.

22. $\begin{array}{r} 52.03 \\ +\ 21.67 \\ \hline 73.70 \end{array}$ **23.** $\begin{array}{r} 13.7 \\ \times\ 0.95 \\ \hline 130.15 \end{array}$ **24.** $\begin{array}{r} 23{,}061 \\ +\ 48{,}205 \\ \hline 71{,}266 \end{array}$ **25.** $\begin{array}{r} 22{,}114 \\ -\ 36 \\ \hline 22{,}082 \end{array}$ **26.** $\begin{array}{r} 0.116 \\ +\ 0.93 \\ \hline 2.09 \end{array}$

Number Sense

Estimating and Reasoning Write whether each statement is true or false. Explain your reasoning.

27. The sum of $^{-}8$ and $^{+}12$ equals $^{-}4$.

28. The quotient of 5,763 ÷ 8 is between 700 and 800.

29. The difference of 25,980 – 15,980 is less than 10,000.

30. The product of 8 and 5.943 is closer to 48 than 40.

31. The sum of $5\frac{7}{10}$ and $3\frac{3}{4}$ is greater than 9.

32. The *k* in the equation 13*k* = 39 is equal to 3.

Lesson
18-2

SDAP 1.4 Identify ordered pairs of data from a graph and interpret the meaning of the data in terms of the situation depicted by the graph. Also **MR 2.3.**

Line Graphs

Hands-On
metric ruler
grid paper

How can data be represented?

Data is collected information.
A line graph is used to show how data changes over time. It shows a trend, a general direction in data.

This table shows the growth of a plant over a period of several days. The data can be displayed in a line graph.

Plant Growth

Day	Height (cm)
1	4
3	8
5	10
7	11
9	14

Another Example How can you read data from line graphs?

To use data from a graph, locate a point on the graph, and read the values on both axes. To estimate a value not on a graph, interpret the data to determine a trend. The graph below shows Sasha's reading log.

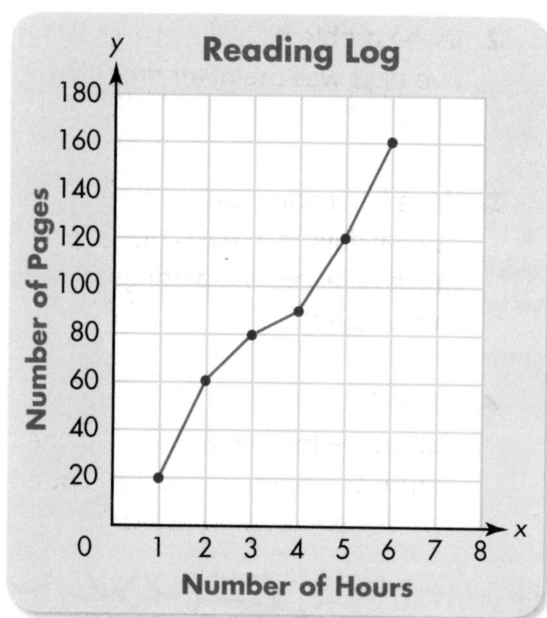

Reading Log

Hours	Pages Read
1	20
2	60
3	80
4	90
5	120
6	160

Explain It

1. Based on the data, how many pages had Sasha read after 2 hours? After 4 hours?
2. If the trend continues, about how many hours will Sasha take to finish a 190-page book?
3. Using the graph, between what two hours was Sasha reading page 140?

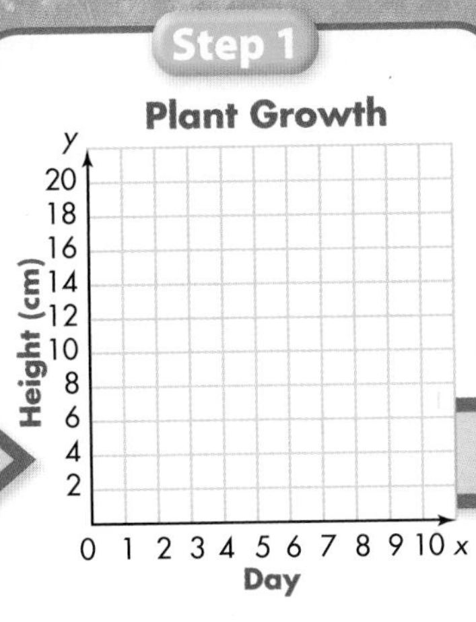

Draw a coordinate grid, use an appropriate scale, and label each axis. Title the graph.

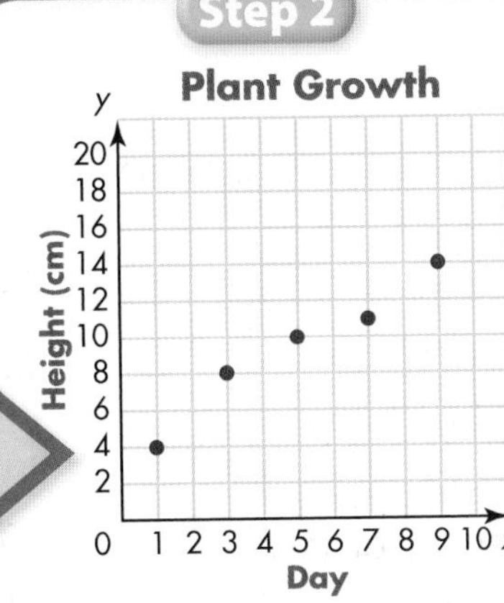

Plot each ordered pair from the table.

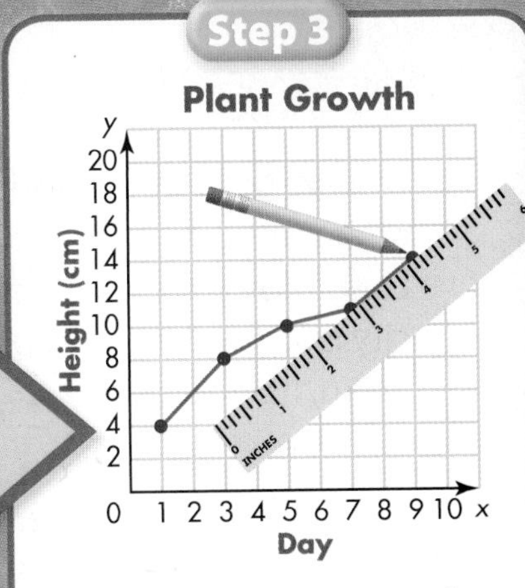

Use a ruler to connect the points.

Guided Practice*

Do you know HOW?

1. Use grid paper to make a line graph. Plot the ordered pairs from the table of values. Use an interval of 2 for each axis. Connect each point with a ruler.

Sam's Reading Log

Minutes	Pages
2	4
4	6
6	10
8	10

Do you UNDERSTAND?

2. In the problem above, between which two days was the plant growth the greatest?

3. If the line connecting the points for several days in a row is horizontal, how much taller did the plant grow during those days?

4. **Writing to Explain** How can you determine information from a line graph for a point that is not plotted?

Independent Practice

For **5** through **7**, use the information from the line graph at the right.

5. When were the most DVDs sold?

6. How many more DVDs were sold during Week 3 than Week 5?

7. Based on the trend, estimate the number of DVDs sold during Week 7.

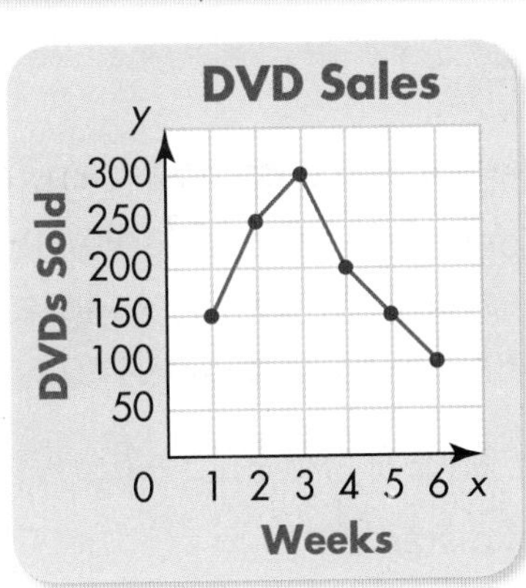

*For another example, see Set B on page 416.

Problem Solving

8. Use the table at the right. On a globe, latitude is the *x*-coordinate. Longitude is the *y*-coordinate. What city is located at (30°, 30°)? Where is Milan, Italy, located?

Data

City	Approx. Degrees Latitude	Approx. Degrees Longitude
Cairo, Egypt	30	30
London, U.K.	50	0
Bordeaux, France	45	30
Milan, Italy	45	10

For **9** and **10**, use the line graph at the right.

9. Look for a trend. How many inches do you predict the plant will have grown by the end of Week 5?

10. How many more inches did the plant grow from the end of Week 2 to the end of Week 4?

Plant Growth

Height (in in.): 0 1 2 3 4 5 6 7 8 9

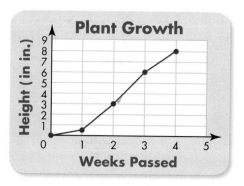

Weeks Passed: 0 1 2 3 4 5

11. Use the table below. How much more did Americans spend on telephone service in 2004 than in 2001?

Annual Household Expenditures for Telephone Service

Year	2000	2001	2002	2003	2004
Amount	$877	$914	$957	$956	$984

12. Think About the Process If a line graph shows an upward trend in population growth for the past five years, what do you know about the population size during that time?

A The population decreased.

B The population inceased and then decreased.

C The population stayed the same.

D The population increased.

For **13** and **14**, use the table at the right. The table shows how far a group of hikers hiked for 4 days.

13. Make a line graph of the data. Use a scale from 0 to 12 and an interval of 2 for the miles hiked. Write a sentence about the trends represented on the graph.

14. During which day did the hikers hike the greatest distance?

Four-day Hike

By End of Day	1	2	3	4
Total Miles Hiked	2	6	8	11

Mixed Problem Solving

Math and Social Studies

The Star Spangled Banner was written by poet Francis Scott Key. Francis Scott Key wrote this poem during the British attack of Fort McHenry in 1814.

1. Francis Scott Key was born in 1779 and lived until 1843. During his life, he worked as a lawyer in Washington, D.C., for many famous politicians. How old was Francis Scott Key when he wrote the Star Spangled Banner?

   A 30 **B** 32 **C** 35 **D** 40

2. The Star Spangled Banner was adopted as the National Anthem of the United States by Congress in 1931. How many years after it was written was Francis Scott Key's poem made the National Anthem?

3. America the Beautiful was written and composed by two different people. Katherine Lee Bates is the author of the poem, *"America the Beautiful."* The poem was published in 1895. Samuel Augustus Ward wrote the melody in 1882. The words and music were first published together in 1910. How many years passed between the publication of the poem and the publication of the words and music?

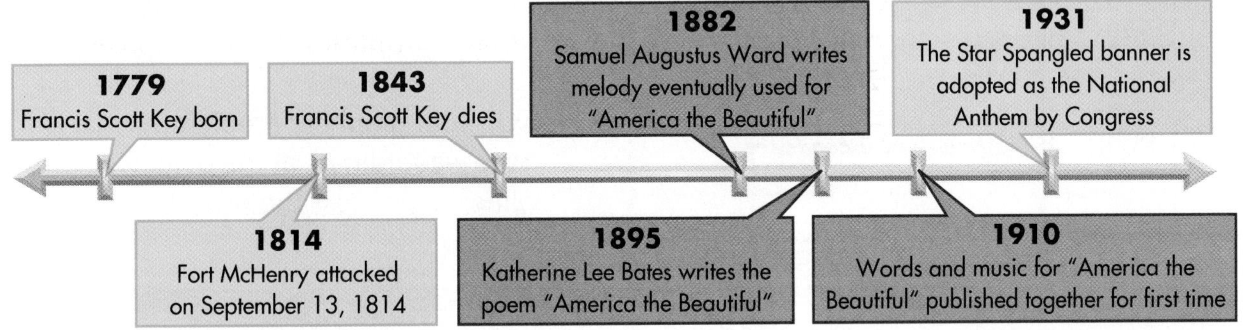
1779
Francis Scott Key born
1814
Fort McHenry attacked on September 13, 1814
1843
Francis Scott Key dies
1882
Samuel Augustus Ward writes melody eventually used for "America the Beautiful"
1895
Katherine Lee Bates writes the poem "America the Beautiful"
1910
Words and music for "America the Beautiful" published together for first time
1931
The Star Spangled banner is adopted as the National Anthem by Congress

4. How many years after the Star Spangled Banner was written was the poem America the Beautiful written?

5. How many years after Samuel Augustus Ward wrote the melody for *"America the Beautiful"* did Katherine Lee Bates write the poem?

6. **Strategy Focus** Solve using the strategy Work Backward.

   Elisa has to be at ballet practice at 5:30 P.M. She has 30 minutes of homework to do and then has to eat dinner, which will take 25 minutes. If it takes 20 minutes to get to the ballet studio, at what time should she start her homework?

Lesson
18-3

AF 1.5 Solve problems involving linear functions with integer values; write the equation; and graph the resulting ordered pairs of integers on a grid. Also **AF 1.4**

Graphing Equations

Hands-On: grid paper

How do you graph an equation on a coordinate grid?

Each day at 7:00 A.M., Tim listed the temperature on his outdoor thermometer and from the radio weather report.

Write an equation to show the relationship between the temperatures and then graph that relationship.

Data

7:00 A.M. Temperature (°F)

	Tim's House	Weather Report
Mon.	2°	0°
Tues.	5°	3°
Wed.	0°	$^-2$°
Thurs.	$^-2$°	$^-4$°
Fri.	4°	2°

Guided Practice*

Do you know HOW?

In **1** and **2**, complete the table of values and graph the equation.

1. $y = x + {}^+3$

x	y
$^+2$	
$^+1$	
0	

2. $y = x - {}^+4$

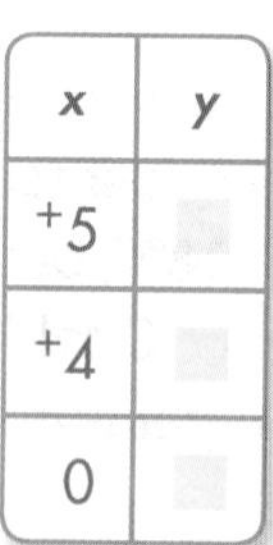

x	y
$^+5$	
$^+4$	
0	

Do you UNDERSTAND?

3. For the problem above, suppose the temperature given in the weather report was 2° F higher than the temperature at Tim's house. Write an equation, make a table of values, and graph the equation.

4. On your graph for Problem 1, what is the *y*-coordinate at the point where the line would cross the *x*-axis?

Independent Practice

In **5** through **7**, write an equation to describe each table.

5.

x	$^-2$	$^-1$	0	$^+1$	$^+2$
y	$^+4$	$^+5$	$^+6$	$^+7$	$^+8$

6.

x	$^-2$	$^-1$	0	$^+1$	$^+2$
y	$^-9$	$^-8$	$^-7$	$^-6$	$^-5$

7.

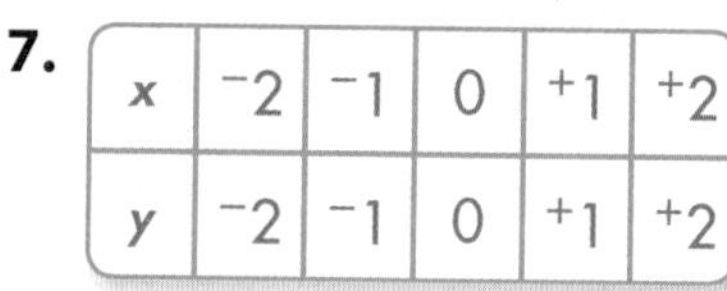

x	$^-2$	$^-1$	0	$^+1$	$^+2$
y	$^-2$	$^-1$	0	$^+1$	$^+2$

In **8** through **10**, complete each table of values and graph each equation.

8. $y = x + 1$

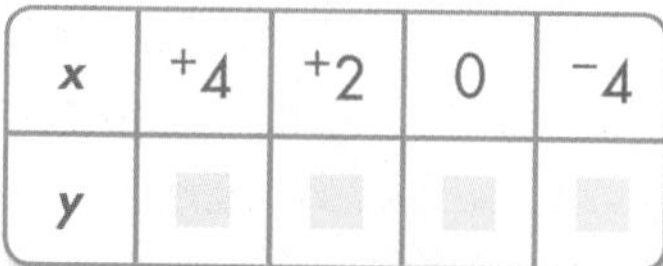

x	$^+4$	$^+2$	0	$^-4$
y				

9. $y = x - 3$

x	$^+5$	$^+1$	0	$^-2$
y				

10. $y = 4 + x$

x	$^+1$	0	$^-1$	$^-2$
y				

*For another example, see Set C on page 417.

Write an equation.

Let x = temperature at Tim's house

Let y = temperature given by the weather report

Each day the temperature was reported as 2° lower.

$y = x - 2$

Use Tim's list to make a table of values.

x	y
$^{+}5$	$^{+}3$
$^{+}4$	$^{+}2$
$^{+}2$	0
0	$^{-}2$
$^{-}2$	$^{-}4$

A table of values shows how x and y are related and lists values that satisfy the equation.

Use the table of values to graph the equation.

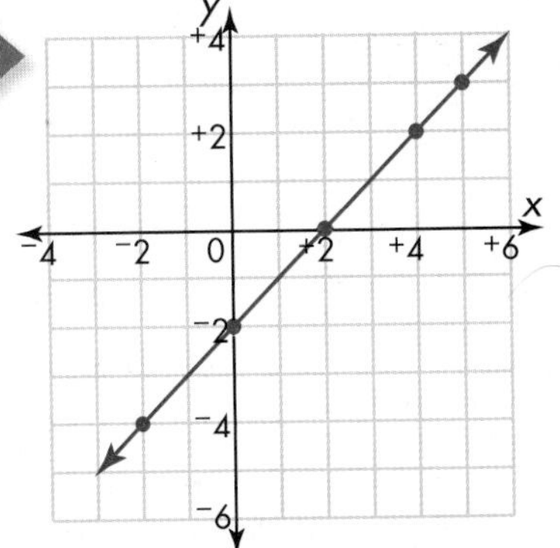

An equation whose graph is a straight line is called a linear equation.

Problem Solving

11. Reasoning If the points ($^{+}1$, $^{+}7$), ($^{+}1$, $^{+}3$), ($^{+}1$, $^{-}5$), and ($^{+}1$, $^{-}9$) were graphed, they would form a vertical line. Do you think the equation for this line would be $x = {}^{+}1$ or $y = {}^{+}1$? Explain.

12. The Clothes Closet was having a year-end sale. Julie bought 2 pairs of jeans. The jeans cost $28 each. Her state charges 7% sales tax. What was the total cost of the jeans?

13. Which ordered pair will be included on the graph for $y = {}^{+}9 + x$?

A ($^{+}6$, $^{+}3$) **C** ($^{+}3$, $^{-}6$)

B ($^{-}3$, $^{+}6$) **D** ($^{+}6$, $^{-}3$)

14. If you were to walk on Mars, the air near your toes may have a temperature of $^{+}18$°C, but the air at your head may be 27°C colder. What would be the temperature near your head?

For **15** and **16**, use the graph below.

15. Make a table of values for the graph.

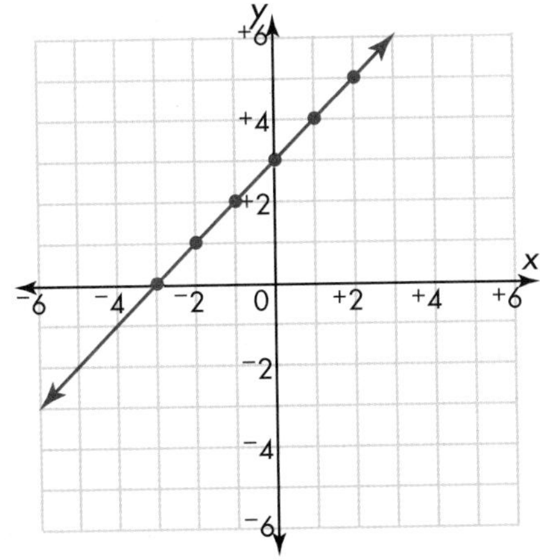

16. Use the table of values to write an equation for the graph.

17. Justin bought a hat for $8.50 and socks for $5.75. He had a coupon for $2 off one item. How much change did he receive if he paid with a $20 bill?

18. Writing to Explain Aaron's graph included the points ($^{+}6$, $^{+}2$), ($^{+}3$, $^{-}1$), and ($^{-}3$, $^{-}7$). Bob's graph included the points ($^{+}7$, $^{+}3$), ($^{+}2$, $^{-}2$), and ($^{-}2$, $^{-}6$). Would all six points be included on the same graph? Why or why not?

19. If two pencils cost $0.25, how much would 12 pencils cost?

Lesson

18-4

MR 1.1 Analyze problems by identifying relationships, distinguishing relevant from irrelevant information, sequencing and prioritizing information, and observing patterns. Also **SDAP 1.5**

Problem Solving

Work Backward

Symbols can show movement of points on a coordinate plane.

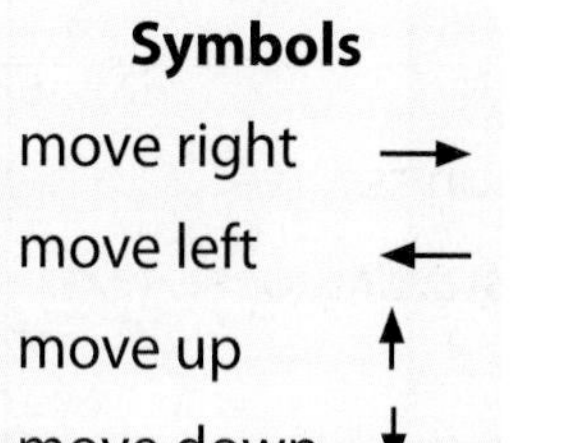

Symbols	
move right	→
move left	←
move up	↑
move down	↓

Starting Position		(2, 3)
5 units	→	(7, 3)
3 units	↑	(7, 6)
4 units	←	(3, 6) **Ending Position**

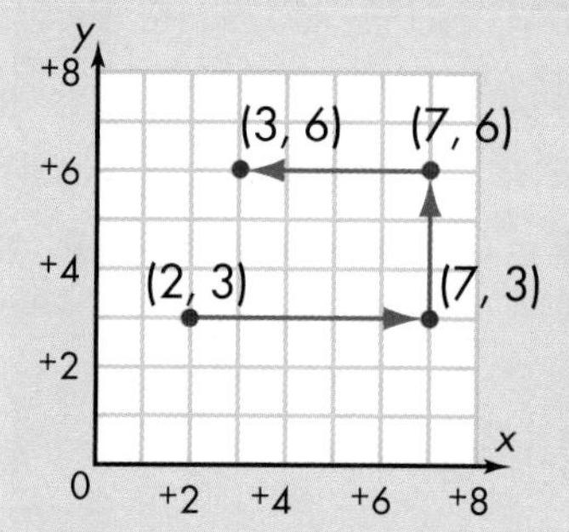

Guided Practice*

Do you know HOW?

1. Work backward to find the starting position.

		Starting (*x*, *y*)
3 units	→	(6, 14)
5 units	↓	(6, 9)
2 units	→	(8, 9) **Ending**

Do you UNDERSTAND?

2. How can you check the starting position in the answer from the example at the top?

3. **Write a Problem** Write a problem involving movement of points on a coordinate plane that can be solved by working backward.

Independent Practice

In **4** and **5**, work backward to find each starting position.

4.

		Starting (*x*, *y*)
4 units	←	
6 units	↑	
2 units	↓	
3 units	→	(3, 9) **Ending**

Tip *Right and left: x coordinate*
Up and down: y coordinate

5.

		Starting (*x*, *y*)
2 units	↓	
7 units	→	
2 units	↑	
14 units	→	(21, 2) **Ending**

Stuck? Try this....

- What do I know?
- What am I asked to find?
- What diagram can I use to help understand the problem?
- Can I use addition, subtraction, multiplication, or division?
- Is all of my work correct?
- Did I answer the right question?
- Is my answer reasonable?

*For another example, see Set D on page 417.

What is the starting position?

If you know the ending position and the motions used, you can work backward to find the starting position.

Starting (x, y)

5 units → (7, 3)

3 units ↑ (7, 6)

4 units ← (3, 6) **Ending**

Plan and Solve

Begin at the ending position. Do the opposite motions and work backward.

Ending (3, 6)

4 units → (7, 6)

3 units ↓ (7, 3)

5 units ← (2, 3) **Starting**

The starting position is (2, 3).

Solve.

6. Pat decided to bake one evening. First, she used a certain amount of flour to make biscuits. Then, Pat used $3\frac{3}{4}$ cups of flour to make bread and $1\frac{1}{4}$ cups of flour to make pretzels. If Pat used a total of $7\frac{1}{4}$ cups of flour for all of her baking, how much flour did she use to make biscuits?

7. The Tigers scored 20 points during a basketball game. The team scored 6 points during the fourth quarter, 4 points during the third quarter, and the same number of points in both the second and first quarters. How many points did the Tigers score in the first quarter of the game? The second quarter?

8. Heather is thinking of a solid that is made up of a couple of shapes. The solid has 5 faces. One of the faces is a shape that has sides of equal length. The other 4 faces are shapes that have three sides. What is the name of the solid Heather is thinking of?

9. Steve, Derrin, Sid, Spencer, and Naji are waiting in line to buy tickets to a movie. Derrin is in front of Spencer and behind Sid. Steve is between Sid and Derrin. Naji is behind Spencer. Who is first in line?

10. Julie kept track of the number of miles she drove over a three-day period. On the first day, she drove 17.25 miles. On the second day, she drove 5.25 miles. On the third day, she drove 24 miles. At the end of the third day, the odometer on Julie's car read 52,607.5 miles. What was the mileage number on Julie's odometer when she began keeping track of her mileage?

11. Philip wants to take the quickest trip to Chicago. Some trains make more stops than others. Which train should he take?

Data

Train Schedule

Train	Leave from Elgin	Arrive in Chicago
A	8:45 A.M.	9:55 A.M.
B	2:35 P.M.	3:50 P.M.
C	3:55 P.M.	5:00 P.M.

Test Prep

1. The map shows the approximate placement of some of the Smithsonian museums located on the National Mall. Which museum is located at $(0, {}^{-}1)$? (18-1)

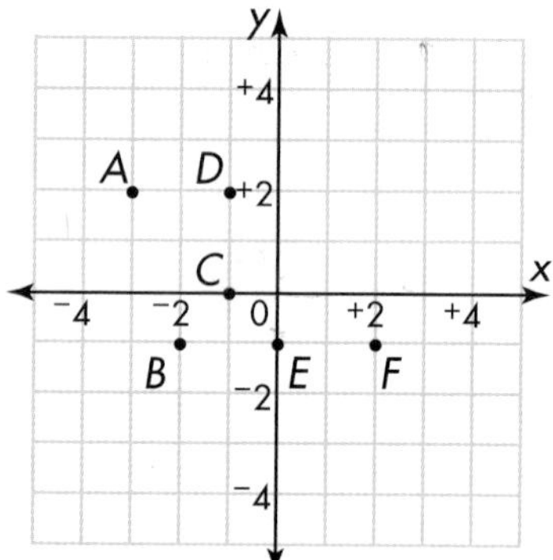

A = American History Museum
B = Freer
C = Smithsonian Castle
D = Natural History Museum
E = Hirshhorn Museum
F = Air and Space Museum

A Hirshhorn Museum

B Freer

C Smithsonian Castle

D Air and Space Museum

2. Complete the table of ordered pairs for $y = x - 5$. (18-3)

x	y
0	$^{-}5$
$^{+}2$	$^{-}3$
$^{+}4$	
$^{+}6$	$^{+}1$

A $^{-}9$

B $^{-}2$

C $^{-}1$

D $^{+}9$

3. The graph shows the Fahrenheit temperature in Old Town taken every hour after 8:00 A.M. What was the temperature at noon? (18-2)

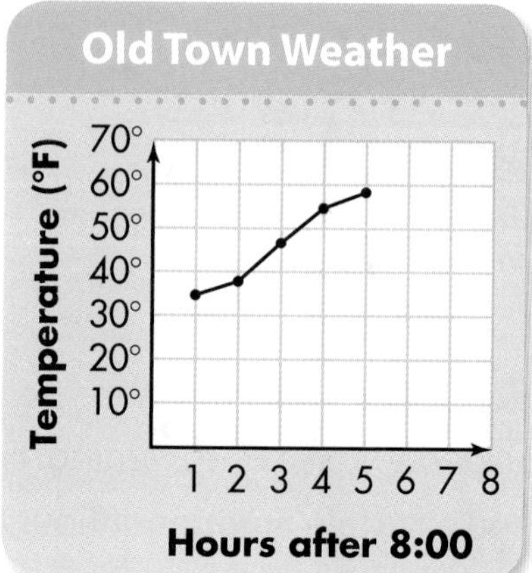

A 58°F

B 54°F

C 47°F

D 45°F

4. Which ordered pair is a point on the line $y = x + 3$? (18-3)

A $(^{+}1, {}^{+}3)$

B $(^{+}2, {}^{+}4)$

C $(^{+}1, {}^{+}2)$

D $(^{-}1, {}^{+}2)$

5. On a map, Todd's school has coordinates $(^{+}6, {}^{+}7)$. From a starting point, Todd walks east (right) 3 blocks, north (up) 5 blocks and ends up at school. What are the coordinates for where Todd started? (18-4)

A $(^{+}9, {}^{+}2)$

B $(^{+}3, {}^{+}12)$

C $(^{+}11, {}^{+}4)$

D $(^{+}3, {}^{+}2)$

6. Which ordered pair is located on the line for the equation $x = 2$? (18-3)

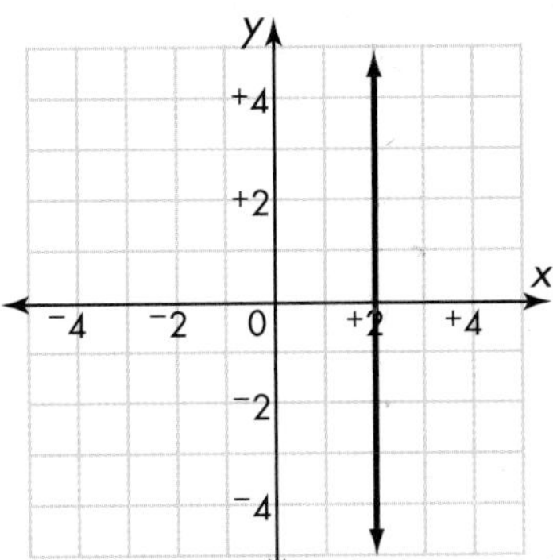

A $(^{+}2, ^{+}3)$

B $(^{-}2, ^{+}2)$

C $(^{+}1, ^{+}2)$

D $(^{+}3, ^{+}2)$

7. Martina drew the graph shown. Which equation did she graph? (18-3)

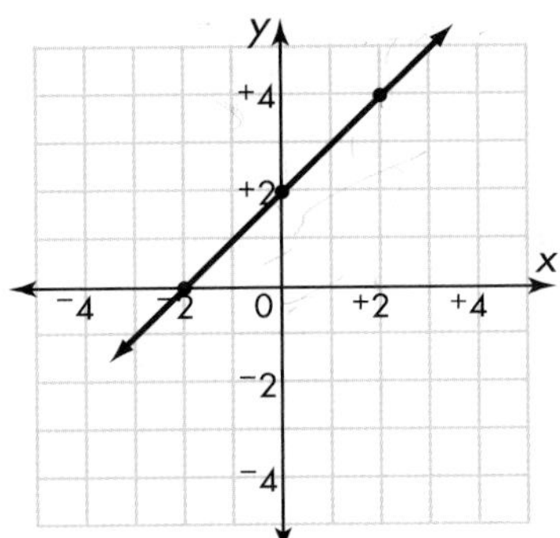

A $y = x + 2$

B $y = x + 1$

C $y = x - 2$

D $y = x - 1$

8. The graph shows the average miles per gallon for vehicles in the United States. Based on the trend, what would be a reasonable estimate of the average miles per gallon for U.S. vehicles in 2010? (18-2)

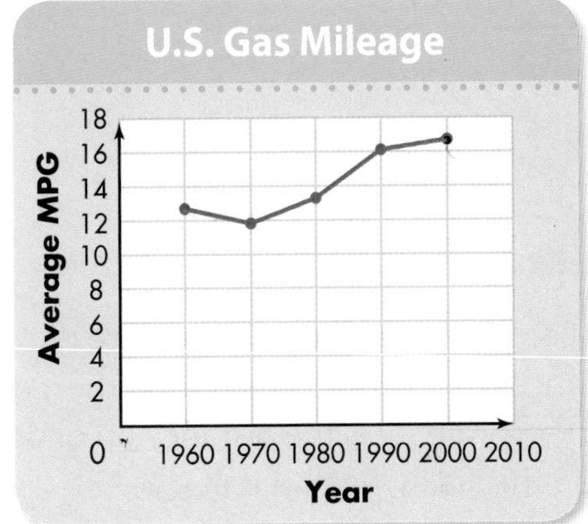

A 11

B 13

C 18

D 25

9. What is the ordered pair for Point X on the graph? (18-1)

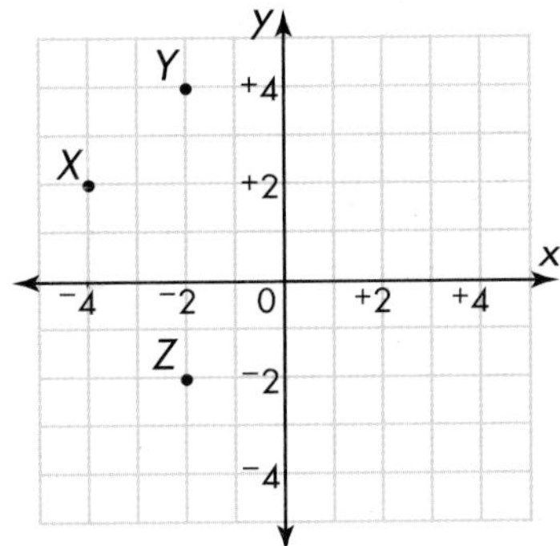

A $(^{+}2, ^{-}4)$

B $(^{-}4, ^{+}2)$

C $(^{+}4, ^{-}2)$

D $(^{-}2, ^{+}4)$

Reteaching

Set A, pages 402–404

What ordered pair names Point *A*?

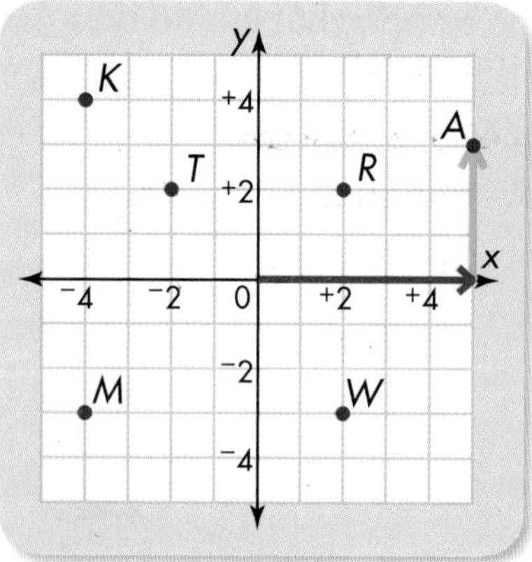

Start at the origin. The *x*-coordinate is the distance to the right or left along the *x*-axis. The *y*-coordinate is the distance up or down along the *y*-axis. Point *A* is at ($^+5$, $^+3$).

Remember to name a point on a coordinate grid, first find the *x*-coordinate. Then find the *y*-coordinate. Write the coordinates in (*x*, *y*) order.

1. Which point is located at ($^-4$, $^-3$)?
2. Which point is located at ($^+2$, $^+2$)?
3. Which point is located at ($^-4$, $^+4$)?
4. What ordered pair names Point *T*?
5. What ordered pair names Point *W*?
6. What is the new ordered pair if Point *A* is moved to the left 5 spaces?

Set B, pages 406–408

Make a line graph for the data.

Day	Newspapers sold
1	6
2	8
3	9
4	10
5	12

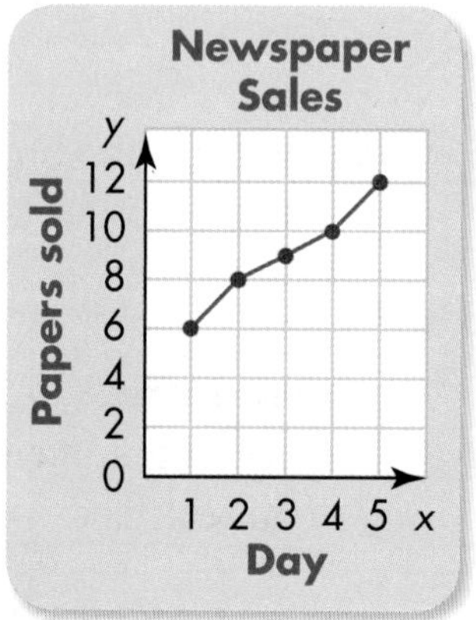

Use grid paper to draw a coordinate grid.

Label the axes.

Number each axis with a consistent scale.

Plot the ordered pairs and connect the points.

Remember that line graphs show data that change over time.

1. Make a line graph for the data.

Week	CDs sold
1	10
2	5
3	20
4	15

2. Describe the trend.

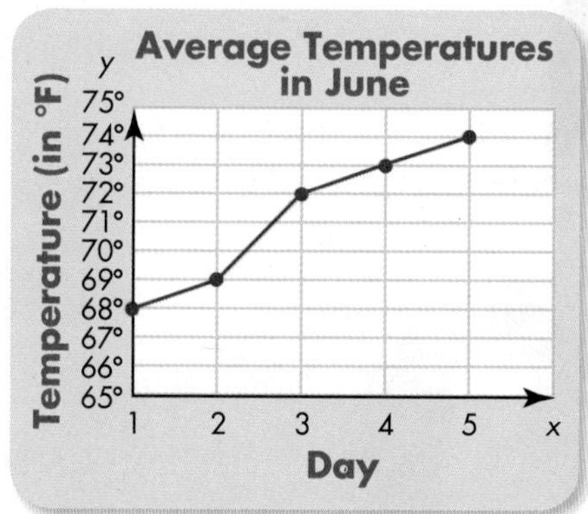

Set C, pages 410–411

Graph the equation $y = x + 2$.

Choose values for x and find the values for y.

x	y	
$^-2$	0	$0 = {}^-2 + 2$
0	$^+2$	$2 = 0 + 2$
$^+3$	$^+5$	$5 = 3 + 2$

Use grid paper to draw a coordinate grid.

Label and number the axes.

Plot the ordered pairs and connect the points.

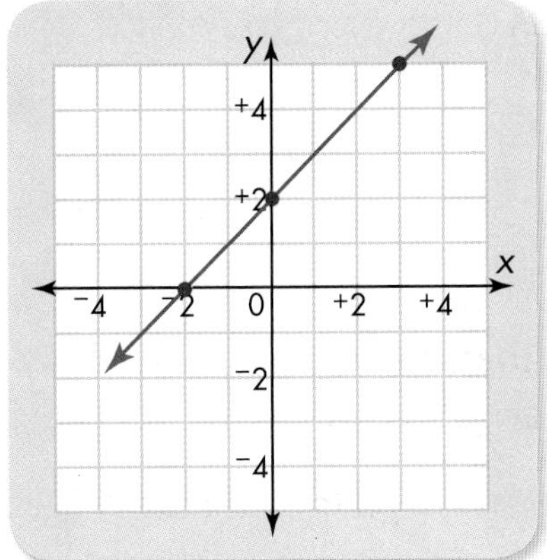

Remember to choose at least three values for x. The values for x and y must satisfy the equation.

Make a table of values for each equation. Then graph the equations on a coordinate grid.

1. $y = x - 4$

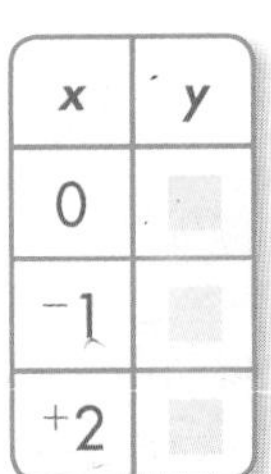

x	y
0	
$^-1$	
$^+2$	

2. $y = 3x$

x	y
0	
$^+1$	
$^+2$	

3. $y = x + 5$

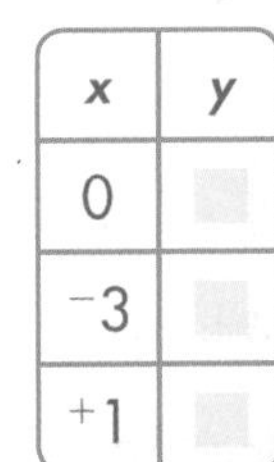

x	y
0	
$^-3$	
$^+1$	

4. $y = x$

x	y
0	
$^-2$	
$^+4$	

Set D, pages 412–413

Franco worked on his science fair project for 35 minutes. Then he spent 20 minutes working on math homework. After that, Franco spent 45 minutes on the computer. If he logged off the computer at 8:10 P.M., what time did Franco begin working on his science fair project?

You can draw a picture to help you work backward. Use an inverse operation for each change.

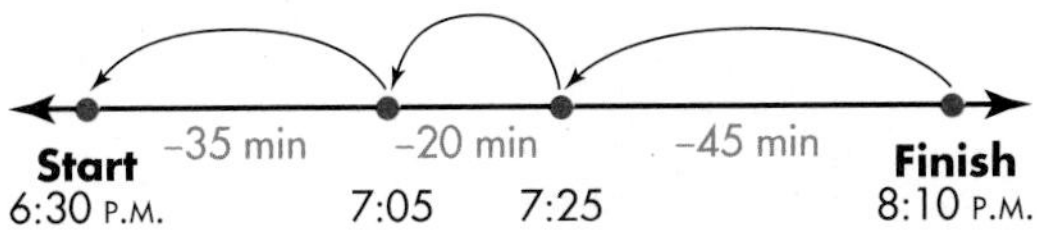

Franco began his science project at 6:30 P.M.

Remember that addition and subtraction have an inverse relationship.

1. Barb has $3\frac{1}{4}$ ft of ribbon left over. She used $2\frac{1}{4}$ ft to wrap a gift and $\frac{3}{4}$ ft to decorate a picture frame. She then used $1\frac{3}{4}$ ft for hair ribbons. How many feet of ribbon did Barb start with?

Topic 19

Graphs and Data

1 More than 4,000,000 people visited the Statue of Liberty in 2005. What was the median number of visitors during May through September of that year? You will find out in Lesson 19-6.

2 Every year, millions of Americans travel to international destinations. How many more U.S. residents visited France than Italy in 2004? You will find out in Lesson 19-1.

3 In 2006, 13,000 rubber ducks raced in the 2006 Rubber Duck Derby in Lake Lanier, Georgia. Other locations across the U.S. had derbies that same year. Which derby had more ducks than the one in Georgia? You will find out in Lesson 19-1.

4 California has some of the most popular beaches for surfing in the world. How many different combinations of a wetsuit and a surfboard could a surfer have? You will find out in Lesson 19-7.

Review What You Know!

Vocabulary

Choose the best term from the box.

- axis
- point
- ordered pair

1. A(n) ___?___ is either of two perpendicular lines in a graph.
2. A(n) ___?___ is an exact location in space.
3. A pair of numbers used to locate a point on a graph is called a(n) ___?___.

Number Lines

Use the number line to answer **4** through **6**.

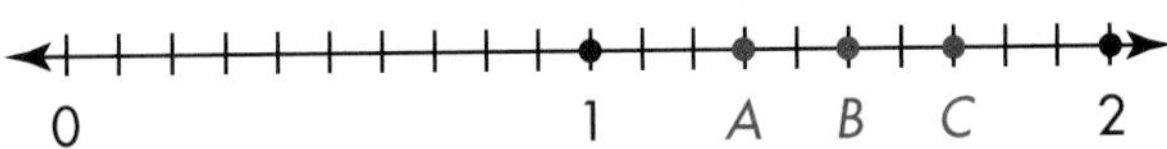

4. Which point is halfway between 1 and 2?
5. Which point is closest to 1 than to 2?
6. Which point is closest to 2 than to 1?

Writing Fractions

7. If 3 out of 6 marbles are red, what fraction, in simplest form, names the red marbles?
8. If 1 out of 5 apples is green, what fraction names the part of the apples that are NOT green?

Division Patterns

Writing to Explain Write an answer to the question.

9. How is the number of zeros in the quotient of 45,000 ÷ 9 related to the number of zeros in the dividend?

Lesson

19-1

SDAP 1.2 Organize and display single-variable data in appropriate graphs and representations (e.g., histogram, circle graphs) and explain which types of graphs are appropriate for various data sets. Also SDAP 1.3.

Bar Graphs and Picture Graphs

How do you display data collected from a count or measure?

Students were surveyed about what they do after school. The results were displayed in a bar graph.

A bar graph uses rectangles (bars) to show and compare data that tells how many or how much.

Data

After-School Activities	
Sports	卌 卌 卌
Homework	卌 IIII
Chores	卌 I
Other	卌 卌 II

Another Example How can you make and interpret picture graphs?

Sonya gathered data about the number of ducks in some of the 2006 rubber duck derbies. Sonya listed the data in a frequency table. Then she made a picture graph to display the data.

Rubber Duck Derbies, 2006				
Location	*Congaree River, SC*	*Lake Lanier, GA*	*St. Louis Riverfront, MO*	*Meinig Memorial Park, OR*
Number of Rubber Ducks	5,000	13,000	15,000	1,000

A picture graph uses pictures or symbols to represent data. Each picture represents a certain amount in the data.

Rubber Duck Derbies, 2006

Location	Number of Rubber Ducks
Congaree River, SC	🦆🦆🦆🦆🦆
Lake Lanier, GA	🦆🦆🦆🦆🦆🦆🦆🦆🦆🦆🦆🦆🦆
St. Louis Riverfront, MO	🦆🦆🦆🦆🦆🦆🦆🦆🦆🦆🦆🦆🦆🦆🦆
Meinig Memorial Park, OR	🦆

Key: 🦆 = 1,000 rubber ducks

Explain It

1. Which is easier to interpret, a picture graph or a frequency table? Explain.

Step 1 List the survey answers along one axis.

Step 2 Choose an interval, the difference between adjoining numbers on an axis. Label both axes.

Along the other axis mark the scale, the series of numbers at equal distances. Begin with 0 and include the least and greatest numbers in the survey results.

Step 3 Graph the data by drawing bars of the correct length or height.

Step 4 Title the graph.

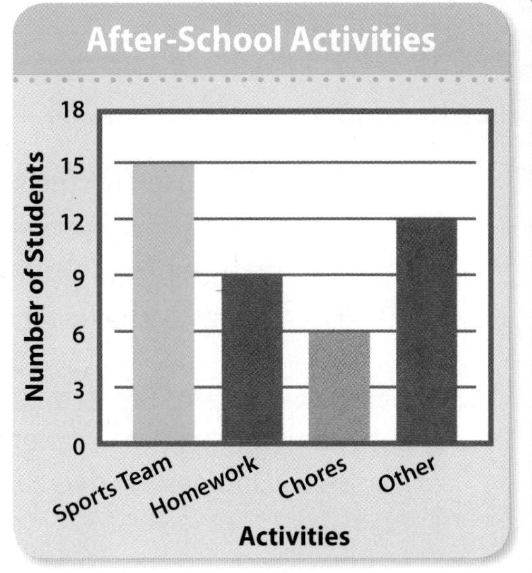

Interpret the Graph

Most students play sports. The fewest number of students do chores.

Guided Practice*

Do you know HOW?

In **1** and **2**, decide if a bar graph or picture graph would better present the data.

1. The number of cats, dogs, and pet birds in a neighborhood

2. The number of cattle on three ranches

Do you UNDERSTAND?

3. Could the data in the example of the bar graph above be presented in a picture graph? Explain.

4. How are bar graphs and picture graphs similar? How are they different?

Independent Practice

In **5** through **8**, answer the questions about the picture graph shown to the right.

5. How many people are represented by each picture?

6. What is the difference in populations between the second most populated city and the least populated city?

7. About how many people live in the two most populated cities?

8. Can this data be presented in a bar graph? Explain.

Top 5 U.S. Cities by Population

New York

Los Angeles

Chicago

Houston

Philadelphia

Key: (picture) = 1 million people

*For another example, see Set A on page 446.

Problem Solving

In **9** through **12**, use the bar graph.

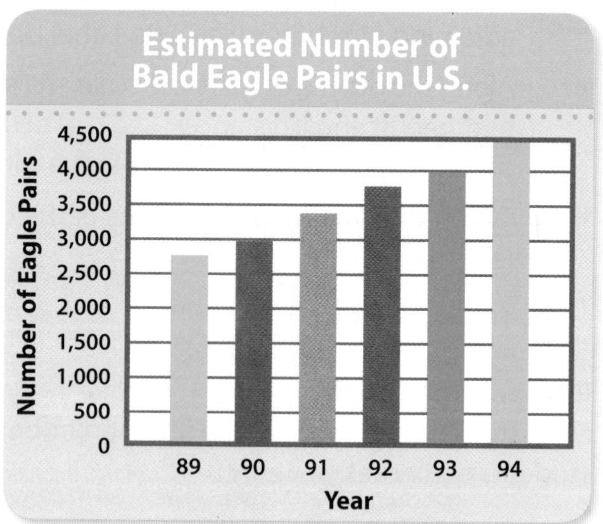

9. What interval was used for the scale?

10. About how many more eagle pairs were there in 1994 than in 1990?

11. **Writing to Explain** Based on the graph, do you think the number of pairs of eagles will increase or decrease? Explain.

12. Between which 2 years did the number of pairs of eagles increase the most?

In **13** through **15**, use the frequency table.

Top 5 Destinations of U.S. Residents, 2004	
Destination	***Number of Travelers***
Mexico	19,360,000
Canada	15,056,000
United Kingdom	3,692,000
France	2,407,000
Italy	1,915,000

13. If you were to draw a bar graph for this frequency table, what scale would you use?

14. How many more U.S. residents visited France than Italy in 2004?

15. **Writing to Explain** Why do you think more residents went to Mexico and Canada than the other destinations?

16. **Think About the Process** Julio bought 3 dozen eggs. He had 13 eggs left after making egg salad for the picnic. Which shows how to find how many eggs Julio used?

A $(13 - 12) \times 3$
B $(12 - 3) - 13$
C $(13 \times 12) - 3$
D $(3 \times 12) - 13$

17. **Think About the Process** A school has 12 soccer teams with 10 students on each team. The school wants to have only 8 soccer teams. Which shows how to find the number of students that would be on each team if there were only 8 teams?

A Multiply 10 by 8.
B Divide 120 by 8.
C Divide 8 by 120.
D Multiply 12 by 8.

18. Point *A* represents which mixed number on this number line?

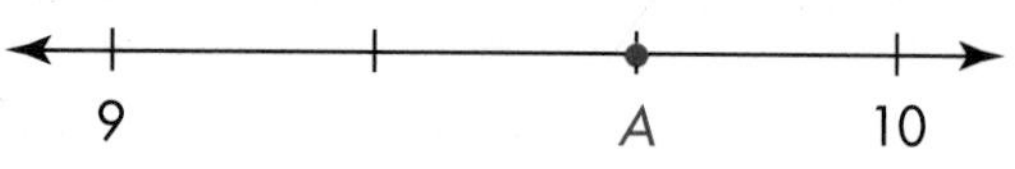

Find each difference.

1. $^{-}5 - {}^{+}6$
2. $^{+}7 - {}^{+}3$
3. $^{-}3 - {}^{+}4$
4. $^{+}8 - {}^{+}9$
5. $^{-}10 - {}^{+}2$
6. $^{-}1 - {}^{+}1$

Find each product. Simplify if possible.

7. $\frac{1}{2} \times \frac{6}{10}$
8. $\frac{2}{5} \times \frac{1}{5}$
9. $\frac{1}{6} \times \frac{3}{4}$
10. $8 \times \frac{5}{8}$
11. $\frac{1}{4} \times \frac{1}{5}$
12. $\frac{3}{8} \times \frac{1}{4}$
13. $\frac{9}{10} \times \frac{1}{10}$
14. $\frac{3}{4} \times \frac{1}{3}$
15. $\frac{5}{6} \times \frac{1}{10}$

Find each quotient. Simplify if possible.

16. $3\frac{2}{3} \div 1\frac{5}{6}$
17. $1\frac{1}{2} \div 1\frac{1}{3}$
18. $6 \div \frac{7}{8}$
19. $1\frac{5}{12} \div 1\frac{5}{12}$

Error Search Find each answer that is not correct. Write it correctly and explain the error.

20. $\begin{array}{r} 5 \\ -\ 3\frac{3}{8} \\ \hline 2\frac{3}{8} \end{array}$

21. $\begin{array}{r} 28{,}403 \\ \times\ \ \ 3 \\ \hline 85{,}239 \end{array}$

22. $\begin{array}{r} 105\text{ R3} \\ 5\overline{)528} \end{array}$

23. $\begin{array}{r} 37.91 \\ +\ 14.23 \\ \hline 23.68 \end{array}$

24. $\begin{array}{r} 50{,}000 \\ \times\ \ \ 40 \\ \hline 200{,}000 \end{array}$

Number Sense

Estimating and Reasoning Write whether each statement is true or false. Explain your reasoning.

25. If $a < 0$ and $b > 0$, then $a - b$ is negative.

26. The product of 25 and 2,002 is 50 less than 50,000.

27. The expression $(64 \div 8) + 2 \times (25 \div 5)$ is 50.

28. The sum of 22,256 and 43,008 is less than 65,000.

29. The product of $6\frac{3}{5}$ and $7\frac{1}{9}$ is greater than 42.

30. The quotient of $13.8 \div 2.1$ is greater than 4 and less than 7.

Lesson
19-2

SDAP 1.2 Organize and display single-variable data in appropriate graphs and representations (e.g., histogram, circle graphs) and explain which types of graphs are appropriate for various data sets.

Histograms

How do you make and interpret a histogram?

A radio station recorded the ages of 25 callers in a phone survey.

This data can be shown by a histogram, a bar graph that groups data into equal intervals shown on the horizontal axis. There is no space between the bars.

Make a histogram to show the frequency of data in each age interval.

Data

Age	Frequency
0–19	6
20–39	12
40–59	5
60–79	2

Guided Practice*

Do you know HOW?

1. The table shows the number of minutes 25 students spent on homework each night. How would the lengths of the bars compare if you made a histogram to show the data?

Data

Amount in Minutes	Frequency
0–29	5
30–59	10
60–89	5
90–119	5

Do you UNDERSTAND?

2. According to the histogram in Exercise 1, what fraction of the students surveyed spent 30–59 minutes on homework each night?

3. In the example above, how can you tell that $\frac{1}{5}$ of the people surveyed were in the 40–59 age group ?

Independent Practice

4. The table shows the results of a class survey about the amount of time students spend on their cell phones each day. Copy and complete the histogram shown at the right.

Data

Amount in Minutes	Frequency
0–9	6
10–19	8
20–29	10
30–39	6

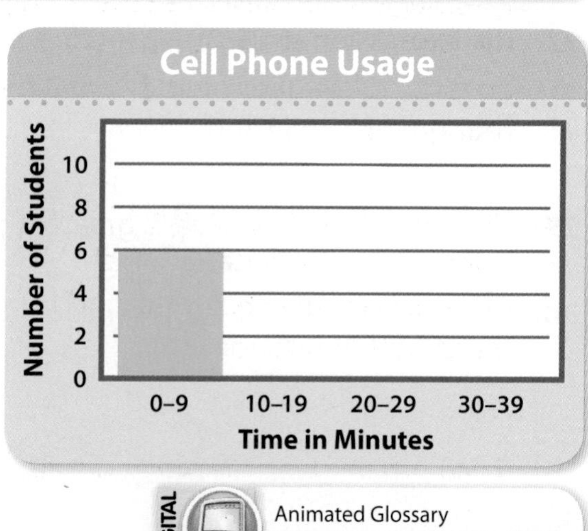

DIGITAL Animated Glossary
www.pearsonsuccessnet.com

*For another example, see Set B on page 446.

Step 1 List the age intervals along the horizontal axis.

Step 2 Along the vertical axis mark the scale. List the greatest and least numbers in the survey results. Choose an interval. Label the axes.

Step 3 Graph the data by drawing bars of the correct height. Title the graph.

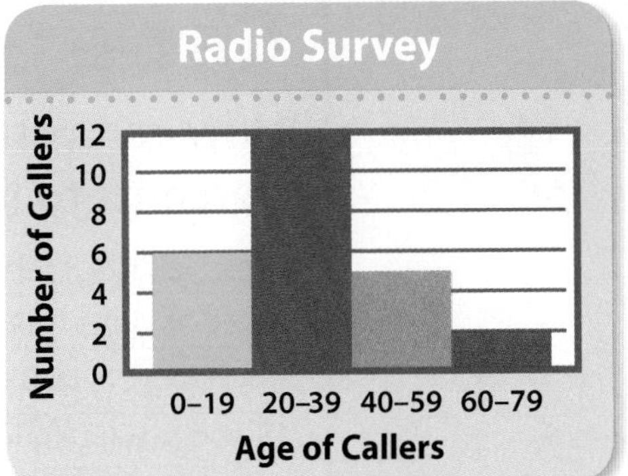

Step 4 Interpret the graph. Twice as many people were in the 20–39 age group as in the 0–19 age group. Most people were in the 20–39 age group.

The group with the least number was the 60–79 age group.

Problem Solving

One class took a survey of the amount of money they spent on CDs over 3 months and made a histogram of the results. The histogram is shown at the right.

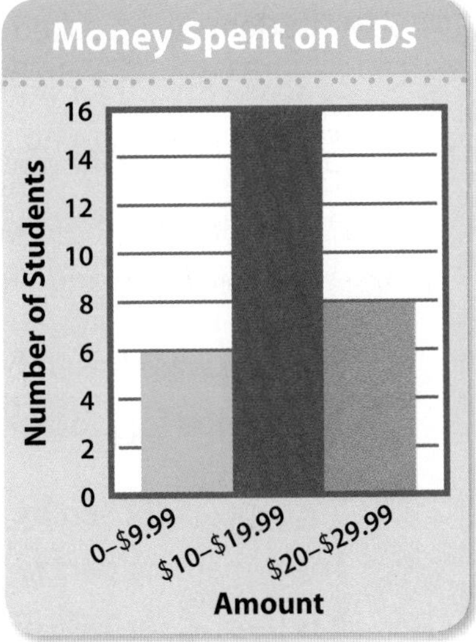

5. a How many students were surveyed?

b What fraction of students spent between 0 and $9.99 on CDs?

c In which range of money spent did twice as many students buy CDs than in the $20–$29.99 range?

6. Reasoning Selma says that a histogram shows that 4 times as many people in the 21–25 age group answered the survey than in the 36–40 age group. How does she know this from looking at the histogram?

7. On a coordinate grid, Sue drew a path starting at (6, 2). She moved 2 spaces to the right and 3 units up. What is the ordered pair for the point where she stopped?

8. On a class trip, Harry spent $28. Nate spent $6 less than Harry. Which expression could you use to find how much both boys spent?

A 28 + 28 + 6 **C** 28 − (28 + 6)

B 28 + (28 − 6) **D** 28 − 28 − 6

9. At 6 A.M., the temperature was ⁻5°F. By noon, the temperature had increased by 12°F. What was the temperature at noon?

A 17°F **C** ⁻7°F

B 7°F **D** ⁻12°F

Lesson

19-3

SDAP 1.2 Organize and display single-variable data in appropriate graphs and representations (e.g., histogram, circle graphs) and explain which types of graphs are appropriate for various data sets.

Circle Graphs

How can you use fractions and percents to label a circle graph?

A circle graph shows how all (100%) of a set of data has been divided into parts. Each part is shown by a wedge (sector) of the circle. What fraction and percent represents the part of each circle that is shaded?

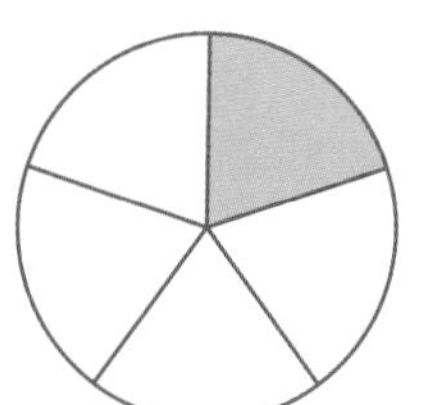

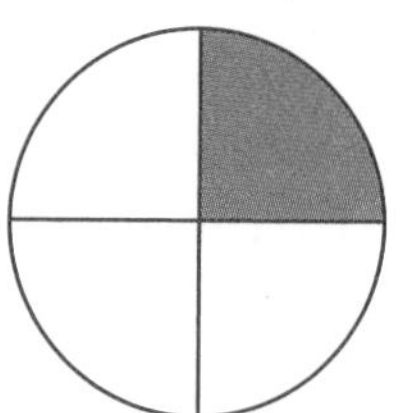

Another Example How can you make a circle graph to display data?

Sixty students were asked to name their favorite sport. How could you use a circle graph to show the results?

Data

Favorite Sport	
Baseball	30
Football	15
Soccer	6
Other	9

Step 1 Use fractions to find what part of the circle should represent each category. Baseball was chosen by 30 out of 60, and $\frac{30}{60}$ is $\frac{1}{2}$ or 50%. The wedge for baseball is half the circle.

Football was chosen by 15 out of 60, and $\frac{15}{60}$ is $\frac{1}{4}$ or 25%. The wedge for football is $\frac{1}{4}$ of the circle.

Soccer was chosen by 6 out of 60, and $\frac{6}{60}$ is $\frac{1}{10}$ or 10%. The remaining part represents students who chose "other". It is $\frac{9}{60}$ or $\frac{3}{20}$ or 15% of the circle.

Favorite Sport

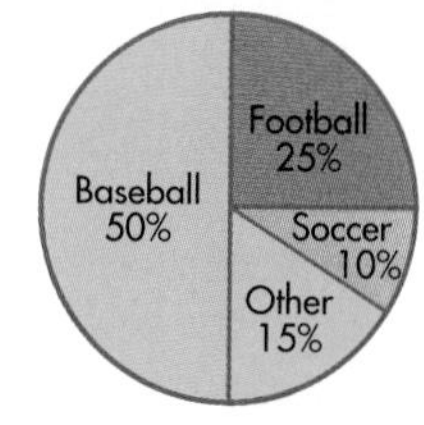

Step 2 Draw a circle with sectors for $\frac{1}{2}$, $\frac{1}{4}$, and $\frac{1}{10}$. The remaining sector represents $\frac{3}{20}$. Label the sectors to show what each part of the circle represents. Often circle graphs are labeled with a percent.

Explain It

1. If 20 out of 60 students in the survey had chosen baseball, what fraction would represent the part of the circle that should be shaded to show the part of the students who chose baseball? What percent is equivalent to the fraction?
2. In the circles at the top of the next page, how many of the 12.5% wedges would it take to equal a $\frac{1}{4}$ wedge?
3. In the circle at the right, how many wedges should be shaded to show 40%?

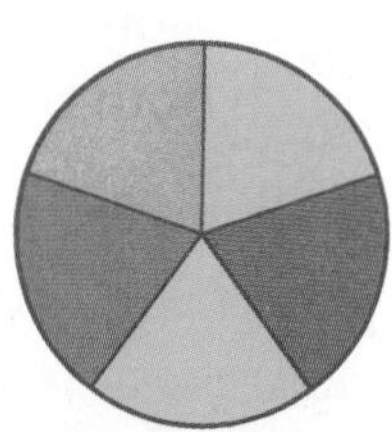

In the first circle graph, $\frac{1}{5}$ or 20% is shaded. In the second circle, $\frac{1}{4}$ or 25% is shaded.

$\frac{1}{5}$ or 20%

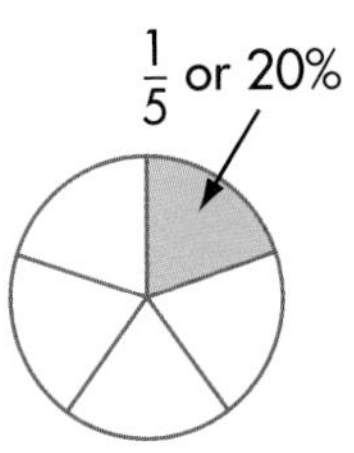

$\frac{1}{4}$ or 25%

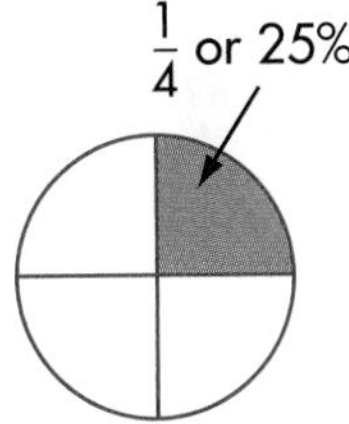

Some other useful fractions for circle graphs are $\frac{1}{3}$, $\frac{1}{6}$, $\frac{1}{8}$, and $\frac{1}{10}$.

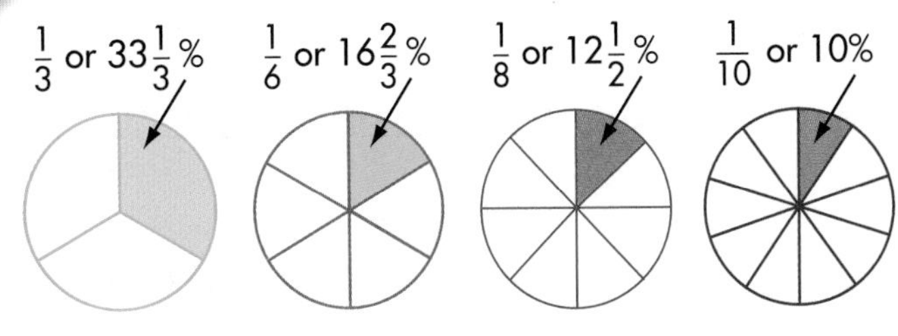

Guided Practice*

Do you know HOW?

Use the circle below to answer **1** and **2**.

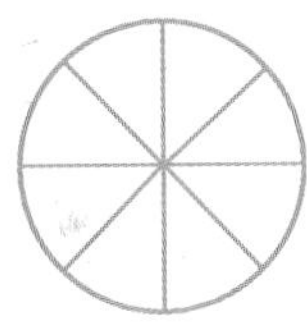

1. If 4 parts of the circle were shaded, what fraction and percent would be represented?

2. If only 1 part were shaded, what fraction and percent would be represented?

Do you UNDERSTAND?

3. In a survey, 20 people out of 80 chose apple. If you made a circle graph, which sector shown in the example above would represent apple?

4. Use the data below. Copy and label the graph. Label each sector with the correct color.

Favorite Color (Data)

Color	Number
Blue	3
Green	3
Red	6

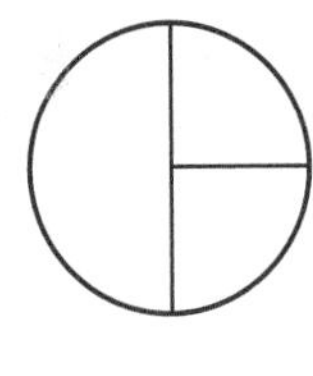

Independent Practice

A restaurant offers four main course choices on their dinner menu. One evening the following choices were chosen by 20 customers: chicken, 10; beef, 5; turkey, 3; ham 2.

5. Copy and complete the table at the right.

6. Copy the circle graph at the right and label each sector with the correct main course.

	Fraction	*Percent*
Chicken		
Beef		
Turkey		
Ham		

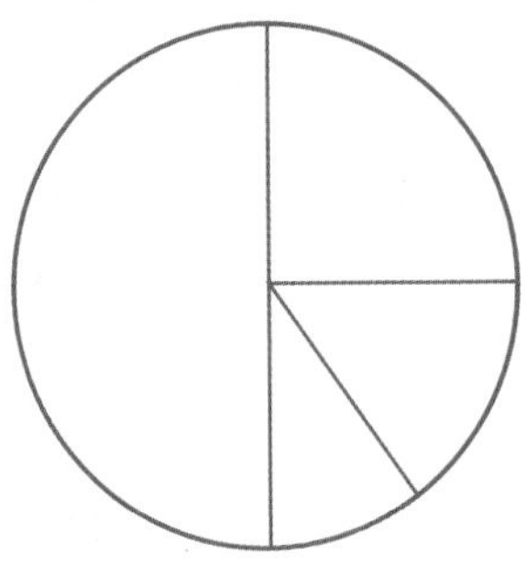

*For another example, see Set C on page 447.

Problem Solving

In two different surveys, students were asked to name their favorite type of movie. The results are shown in the table at the right.

Data

Favorite Type of Movie

	Survey of 50 students	Survey of 100 students
Comedy	10	25
Animated	20	50
Adventure	20	25

7. In which survey did $\frac{1}{5}$ of the students pick comedy?

8. In which survey did 50% of the students choose animated movies?

9. Copy each circle graph and label it with the type of movie and the percent. You can remove the dashed lines in your final graph.

Survey of 50 students

Survey of 100 students

10. **Number Sense** A circle graph is divided into three sections. One section equals 50%. The other two sections are equal in size. What percent of the circle does each of the other two sections represent?

11. A triangle has a height of 16 mm and a base of 6.4 mm. What is the area of the triangle?

A 22.4 mm^2 **C** 51.2 mm^2

B 44.8 mm^2 **D** 102.4 mm^2

12. **Think About the Process** Sonya spent $18 for a book and $22 for a DVD. She paid $2.40 in tax and received $7.60 in change. Which expression shows how to find the amount of money Sonya gave the clerk?

A 18 + 22 + 2.40

B 18 + 22 − 7.60

C 18 + 22 + 2.40 − 7.60

D 18 + 22 + 2.40 + 7.60

13. Renee mixed $\frac{3}{4}$ cup of lime juice, $\frac{7}{8}$ cup of water, and $\frac{1}{2}$ cup of ice to make a limeade. Which is a reasonable total for the amount she mixed?

A Less than 1 cup

B Between $1\frac{1}{2}$ cups and $2\frac{1}{2}$ cups

C More than $2\frac{1}{2}$ cups

D Less than 2 cups

14. A survey asked 200 people to name their favorite type of fruit. The results were as follows: apple, 100; banana, 50; orange, 25; other, 25. Which graph best represents the data?

A

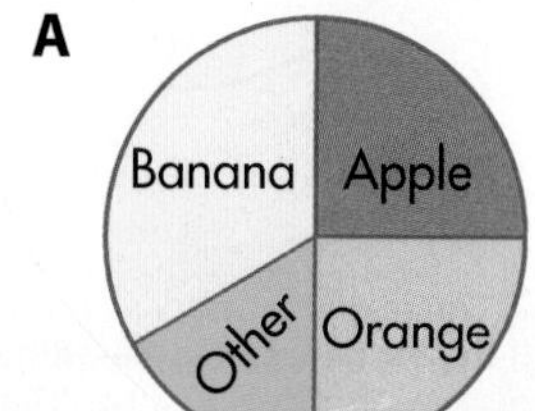

B

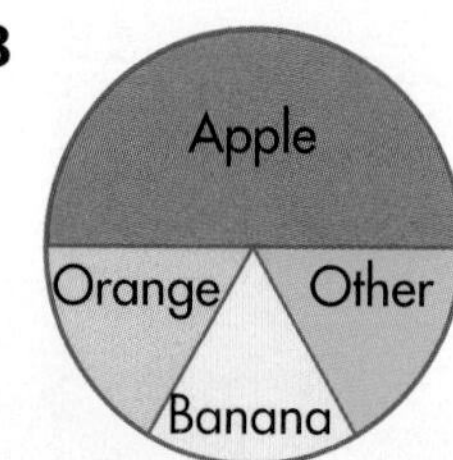

C

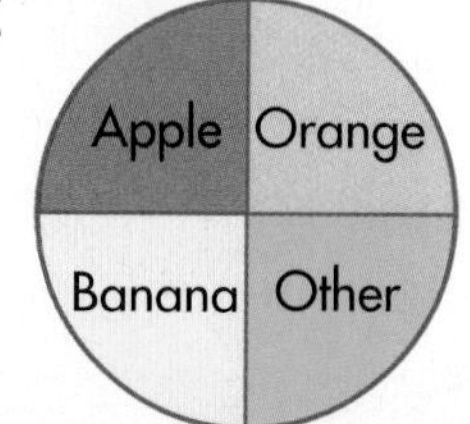

D

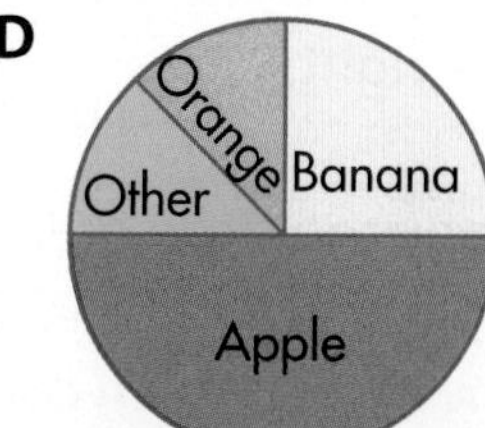

Mixed Problem Solving

Objects on Jupiter weigh about two and a half times as much as on Earth.

1. Complete the table below and then graph the values on the coordinate grid.

Earth weight	50	55	■	■	■	75
Jupiter weight (approx.)	■	■	150	163	175	■

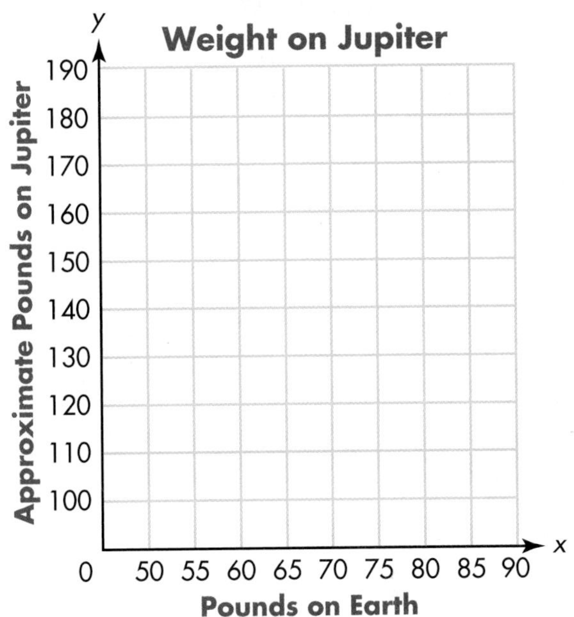

2. If a dog weighs 75 pounds on Earth, about how much would it weigh on Jupiter?

3. If Tyler weighs 120 pounds on Jupiter, about how much would he weigh on Earth?

4. Complete this table using the graph that shows the Big Dipper.

Point	*Ordered Pair*
A	
B	
C	
D	
E	
F	
G	

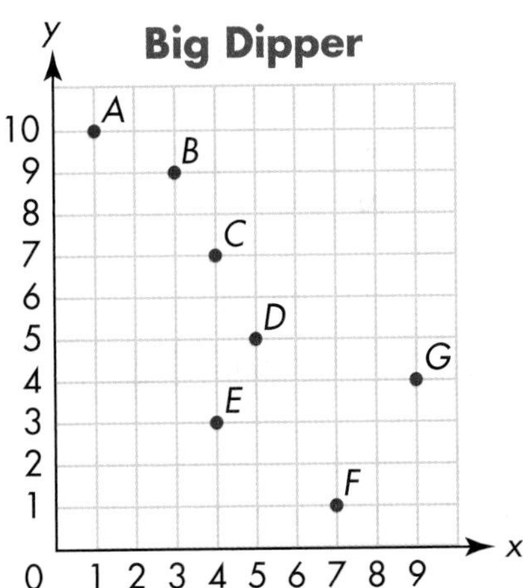

5. If you were to move this drawing of the Big Dipper 3 units to the right on this grid, what would be the ordered pair for point *D*?

6. **Strategy Focus** Examine the ordered pairs for Points *C* and *E*. How do you know that a vertical line can connect those two points? Explain how you decided.

Lesson

19-4

MR 2.3 Use a variety of methods, such as words, numbers, symbols, charts, graphs, tables, diagrams, and models, to explain mathematical reasoning. Also **SDAP 1.2.**

Problem Solving

Make a Graph

Hands-On
grid paper

Data for a company's sales of mountain bicycles and skateboards are shown in the table. Write two statements that compare the sales of bicycles and skateboards.

Make a line graph for each set of data to help you analyze the data.

Data

Year	Number of Bicycle Sales	Number of Skateboard Sales
2003	800	200
2004	900	400
2005	1,000	800
2006	1,000	999
2007	1,100	1,100

Guided Practice*

Do you know HOW?

1. In a survey, students were asked to name their favorite pet. Copy the circle below to make a circle graph to show the data.

Dog	Cat	Bird	Other
12	6	4	2

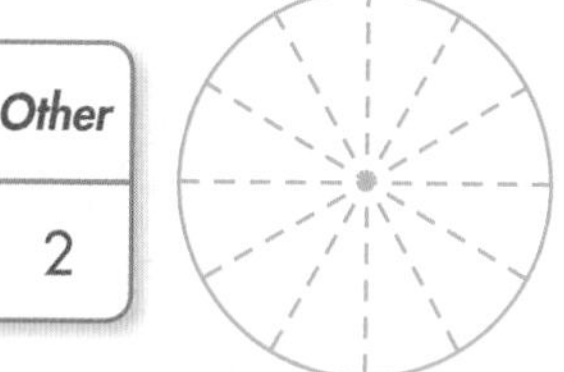

2. Make a bar graph to show the data in Exercise 1.

Do you UNDERSTAND?

3. In the example above, if the trend continues, what can you say about the sales of both bicycles and skateboards in 2008?

4. **Write a Problem** Write a real-world problem that can be solved by making a graph.

Independent Practice

5. Mr. Lauer surveyed his students to find out what kind of field trip they preferred. Make a bar graph to show the data. Which field trip is most popular?

Data

Field Trip	Number of Votes
Zoo	12
Aquarium	9
Musical Play	5
Mystery Play	4

6. Would a line graph be an appropriate graph in Exercise 5? Why or why not?

Stuck? Try this....

- What do I know?
- What am I asked to find?
- What diagram can I use to help understand the problem?
- Can I use addition, subtraction, multiplication, or division?
- Is all of my work correct?
- Did I answer the right question?
- Is my answer reasonable?

*For another example, see Set D on page 447.

Plan and Solve

I can make a line graph for bicycle sales.

Bicycle Sales

Number of Sales: 0, 200, 400, 600, 800, 1000, 1200

Year: '03 '04 '05 '06 '07

Plan and Solve

I can make a line graph for skateboard sales.

Skateboard Sales

Number of Sales: 0, 200, 400, 600, 800, 1000, 1200

Year: '03 '04 '05 '06 '07

The sales for bicycles and skateboards have been increasing over the years.

The difference between the number of bicycle sales and the number of skateboard sales is becoming smaller.

A survey of 16 people recorded the number of books people read in a month. Joe made a histogram and Jean made a circle graph to show the results.

Number of people	8	6	2
Number of books	0–2	3–5	6–8

Histogram

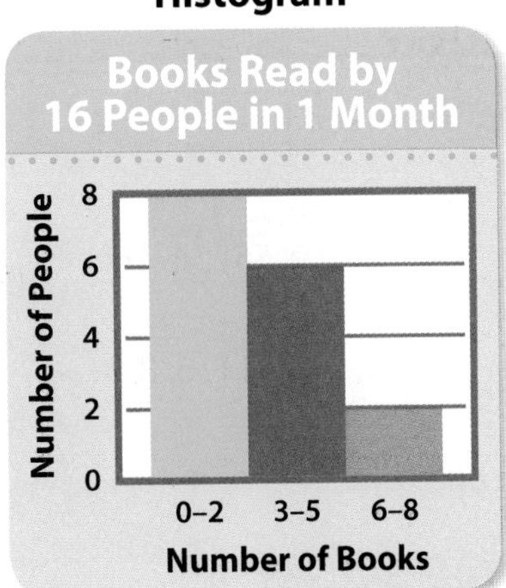

Circle graph

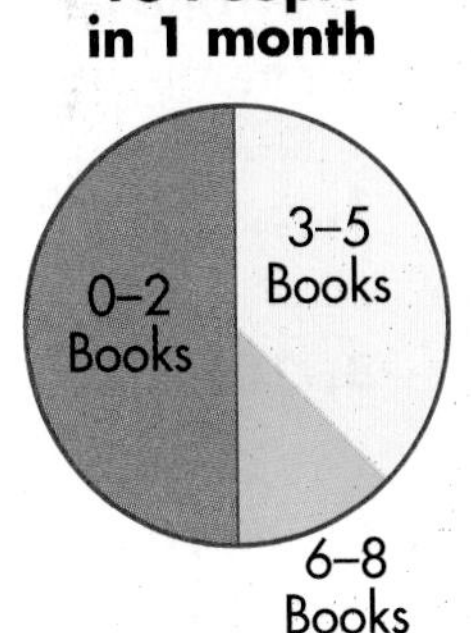

7. Which graph makes it easy to see that $\frac{1}{2}$ of the people read 2 or less books in the month? Which graph makes it easy to tell the number of people in each category?

8. **Writing to Explain** Can you tell from the histogram how many people read 4 books?

9. The data about bicycle sales and skateboard sales at the top of the page could also be shown by a double-bar graph. Part of thengraph is shown at the right. Copy and complete the graph.

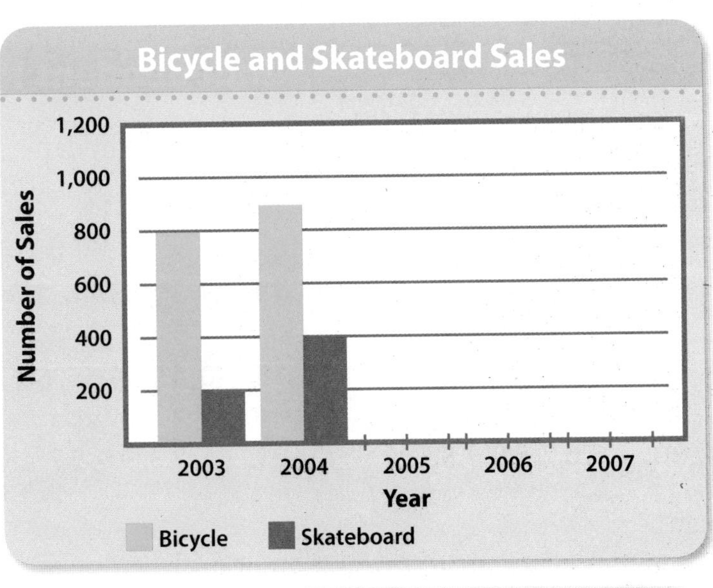

10. A café sells turkey, roast beef, ham, or cheese sandwiches; milk, water, or juice; and yogurt or fruit. How many different meals are possible for a person who wants a sandwich, drink, and dessert?

Lesson

19-5

SDAP 1.1 Know the concepts of mean, median, and mode; compute and compare simple examples to show that they may differ.

Mean

How can data be described by a single number?

How can Carla find the average final score of five bowlers?

The mean, or average, is the sum of all the numbers in a set of data divided by the number of numbers in the set.

9			10				FINAL SCORE
86	7	2	95	6	3	–	95
80	4	2	87	7	0	–	87
77	5	1	84	4	3	–	84
74	2	4	81	5	2	–	81
75	3	3	83	6	2	–	83

Guided Practice*

Do you know HOW?

In **1** through **7**, find the mean for each set of data.

1. 5, 4, 4, 9, 8

2. 19, 55, 34, 16

3. 101, 105, 103

4. 8, 2, 11, 6, 8

5. 85, 70, 84, 91, 88, 92

6. 205, 204, 398, 405, 894, 102

7. 28, 32, 36, 40, 42, 57, 58, 59

Do you UNDERSTAND?

8. Another team had 6 bowlers. Would the mean automatically decrease as the number of bowlers increases?

9. In the example above, how could the mean be raised to 90?

10. **Writing to Explain** Dave said that the mean of 1, 2, 3, 4, and 5 is 8. How do you know this is incorrect without finding the mean?

Independent Practice

In **11** through **22**, find the mean for each set of data.

11. 2, 5, 4, 5

12. 5, 4, 6, 9, 11

13. 6, 17, 12, 11, 4, 6, 7

14. 89, 98, 101

15. 17, 30, 45, 46, 27

16. 13, 16, 19, 21, 26

17. 35, 45, 70

18. 40, 41, 54, 55, 66, 79, 43

19. 164, 198, 301

20. 7.6, 6.2, 6.0, 7.8, 7.4

21. 11, 8.3, 9.0, 3.7

22. 129, 8,002, 1,003, 866

*For another example, see Set E on page 448.

Step 1

Add the final scores in the set of data.

```
   95
   87
   84
   81
+  83
  430 sum
```

Step 2

Divide the sum by the number of numbers in the set.

$430 \div 5 = 86$

```
    86
 5)430
 - 40
    30
  - 30
     0
```

The average, or mean, score for the 5 bowlers is 86.

Problem Solving

Meredith recorded her score for each game of miniature golf she played. Use her scorecard for **23** through **25**.

23. What was Meredith's mean golf score?

24. If Meredith had scored a 50 for the eighth game, how much would her mean score change?

Miniature Golf Scores

Game	1	2	3	4	5	6	7	8
Score	52	56	49	51	54	52	60	58

25. In miniature golf, the lower the score is, the better the game. Meredith wants to find the mean golf score of her four best games. What is this mean score?

26. Geometry Which can be modeled by light beaming from a lighthouse?

A Point
B Plane
C Ray
D Segment

27. Scientists have recorded the lengths of different species of hammerhead sharks. The lengths that have been recorded are 20 ft, 14 ft, 11 ft, and 7 ft. What is the mean length of the hammerhead shark?

A 12.5 ft
B 13 ft
C 17 ft
D 52 ft

28. Estimation What is the approximate mean height of the 7 tallest peaks in Texas listed below?

Data

Peaks in Texas	Height in Feet
Guadalupe Peak	8,749
Bush Mountain	8,631
Shumard Peak	8,615
Bartlett Peak	8,508
Mount Livermore	8,378
Hunter Peak	8,368
El Capitan	8,085

29. Reasoning A data set consisting of 3 numbers has a mean of 24. If two of the numbers are 23 and 25, what is the third number?

Lesson 19-6

SDAP 1.1 Know the concepts of mean, median, and mode; compute and compare simple examples to show that they may differ.

Median, Mode, and Range

How can data be described by one number?

Trey listed, in order, the playing times for the best-selling CD of each music type.

How can he describe the data with one number?

CD Playing Times

Minutes	Music Type
59	Popular
61	Country
63	Blues
63	Soundtrack
64	Gospel
67	Jazz
72	Classical

Guided Practice*

Do you know HOW?

In **1** through **3**, identify the median, mode, and range for each set of data.

1. 5, 7, 5, 4, 6, 3, 5

2. 21, 21, 23, 32, 43

3. 13, 14, 14, 16, 17, 19

For an even number of values, the median is the number halfway between the two middle values.

Do you UNDERSTAND?

4. What operation is used to find the range?

5. In the example at the top, how would the median and mode change if the playing time for the Blues CD changed to 61 minutes?

6. What would the range of playing times be if the 72-minute CD was removed from the list?

Independent Practice

In **7** through **9**, use the table at the right.

7. What are the median, mode, and range for the data?

8. What would happen to the range if the temperature were 82°F on Monday?

9. If the data for Friday were removed from the table, what would the median, mode, and range be?

5-day Weather Forecast

Day	Temperature
Monday	80°F
Tuesday	80°F
Wednesday	82°F
Thursday	84°F
Friday	78°F

*For another example, see Set F on page 448.

Find the median.

List the data from least to greatest.
59, 61, 63, 63, 64, 67, 72

Identify the median, or the middle data value in an odd numbered, ordered set of data.

The median of the number of minutes of playing time is 63.

Find the mode.

59, 61, 63, 63, 64, 67, 72

Identify the mode, or the data value that occurs most often in the data set.

The mode of the number of minutes of playing time is 63.

Find the range.

59, 61, 63, 63, 64, 67, 72

Identify the range, or the difference between the greatest and least values.

$72 - 59 = 13$

The range of the number of minutes of playing time is 13.

Problem Solving

10. Ricardo kept a record of the 7 hottest days of the summer. Use the list below to find the median, mode, and range of the temperatures.

98°F 102°F 100°F 99°F
103°F 98°F 101°F

11. **Writing to Explain** How can you tell the difference between the net for a triangular prism and the net for a triangular pyramid?

12. **Reasoning** For each statistical measure (mean, median, mode, and range) tell whether that number is always, sometimes, or never one of the numbers in the data set.

13. **Think About the Process** One side of a rectangular garden is 13 feet and the other side is 3 feet. Which expression shows how to find the perimeter?

A $(2 \times 13) + (2 \times 3)$

B 13×3

C $2 \times 13 \times 3$

D $3 + 13$

For **14** through **17**, use the table.

14. What was the median number of visitors to the Statue of Liberty from May through September in 2005?

15. What is the range of the data?

16. How many months had over 500,000 visitors?

17. **Writing to Explain** Why do you suppose there had been many fewer visitors in September, than in July or August?

Data

Visitors to the Statue of Liberty

2005	Visitors
May	430,235
June	492,078
July	589,166
August	542,292
September	367,441

Lesson
19-7

SDAP 3.1, Grade 6 Represent all possible outcomes for compound events in an organized way (e.g., tables, grids, tree diagrams) and express the theoretical probability of each outcome.
Also **MR 3.3**

Outcomes

How can tree diagrams help you list possible outcomes?

How many outcomes are possible when spinning a spinner once and then tossing a coin twice?

Use a tree diagram to list all possible outcomes.

A tree diagram is a diagram used to organize outcomes of an experiment.

Guided Practice*

Do you know HOW?

In **1** through **3**, list the possible outcomes.

1. Tossing a number cube
2. Spinning a spinner divided into white, blue, black, and purple
3. Tossing an even number on a number cube

Do you UNDERSTAND?

4. **Writing to Explain** In the example above, how would your tree diagram change if the spinner had 4 colors? How many possible outcomes would there be?
5. Write a multiplication equation to find the possible outcomes of tossing a number cube and spinning a spinner with 4 different colors.

Independent Practice

6. Two spinners are spun. Copy and complete the tree diagram to show the possible outcomes.

Spinner 1

Spinner 2

Spinner 1 **Spinner 2** **Outcome**

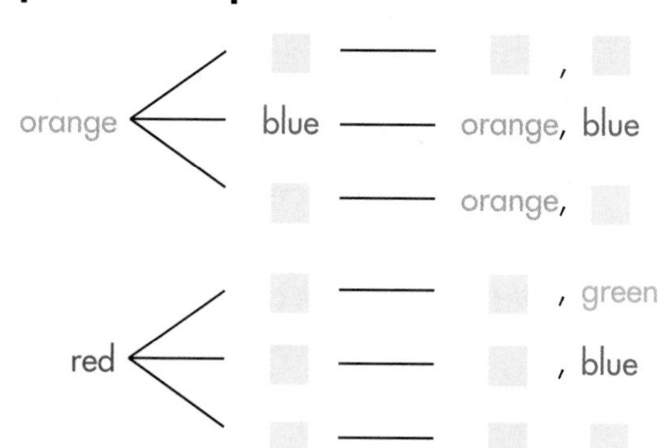

7. Josh and Susan are running for class president. Mark, Maria, Lee, and Eva are running for vice-president. How many possible outcomes are there for electing a president and a vice president?

*For another example, see Set G on page 448.

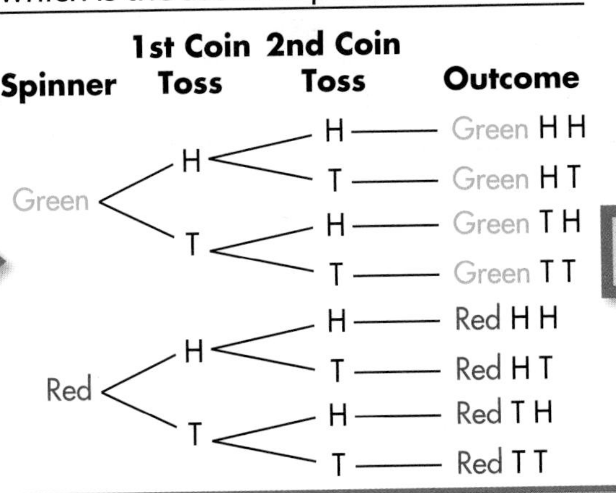

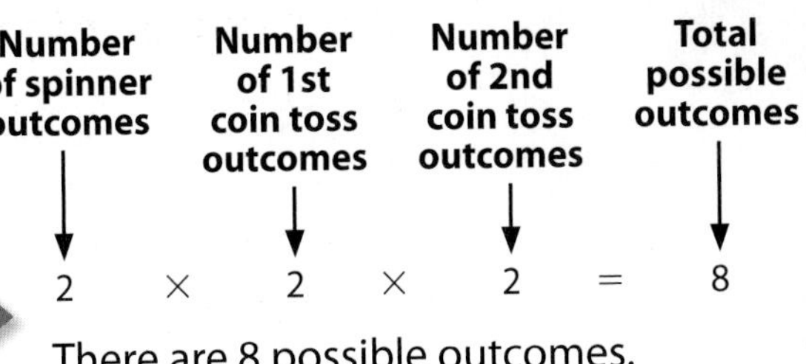

Problem Solving

8. On four tests, Justin scored 90, 85, 90, and 95. What is the mean score of the four tests?

9. Steve's dog is 10 lb heavier than Marsha's dog. Together, the dogs weigh 42 lb. How much does each dog weigh?

10. John, Andy, and Miguel run in the first race. Sharon, Marie, and Mona run in the second race. How many different outcomes are possible for the winning pairs?

A 3 **B** 6 **C** 9 **D** 12

11. Surfers in California often have a variety of wetsuits and surfboards. If a surfer has 3 wetsuits and 6 surfboards, how many different combinations of a wetsuit and a surfboard could the surfer have?

A 6 **B** 9 **C** 18 **D** 36

12. **Writing to Explain** How does a tree diagram make it easier to tell which outcome occurs most often?

13. Lara's ice skating lesson started at 11:15 A.M. and ended at 12:50 P.M. How long did the lesson last?

14. **Think About the Process** Jennifer's paycheck was $314.79. She used $205.75 of that money to pay bills. Then she spent $58 on groceries. Which expression shows how to find how much money Jennifer has left?

A $314.79 + $205.75 − $58

B $314.79 − $205.75 − $58

C $314.79 − $205.75 + $58

D $314.79 + $205.75 + $58

15. How many different outfits consisting of one pair of jeans, one T-shirt, and one jacket can you make if you have three pairs of jeans, four T-shirts, and two jackets to choose from?

16. **Algebra** Find the value of n, if $n \times 400 = 28{,}000$.

Lesson

19-8

SDAP 1.3 Use fractions and percentages to compare data sets of different sizes.

Writing Probability as a Fraction

What is the probability of an event?

Reuben writes each letter of his name on a separate piece of paper and puts them in a bag. He chooses one piece of paper from the bag without looking.

The probability of an event is a number that describes the chance the event will occur.

Another Example What is the probability of two events happening together?

Eva puts the letters of her name into a bag and chooses a letter out of the bag without looking. She puts the letter back into the bag and chooses again without looking. What is the probability that Eva chooses an A both times?

Draw a tree diagram.

First Letter	Second Letter	Outcome
E	E	E, E
	V	E, V
	A	E, A
V	E	V, E
	V	V, V
	A	V, A
A	E	A, E
	V	A, V
	A	A, A

Find the probability.

There are a total of 9 possible outcomes when the two letters are chosen and the first is replaced. One of the outcomes is *favorable* because only one of the outcomes has an A both times.

The probabilty of any event ranges from 0 to 1.

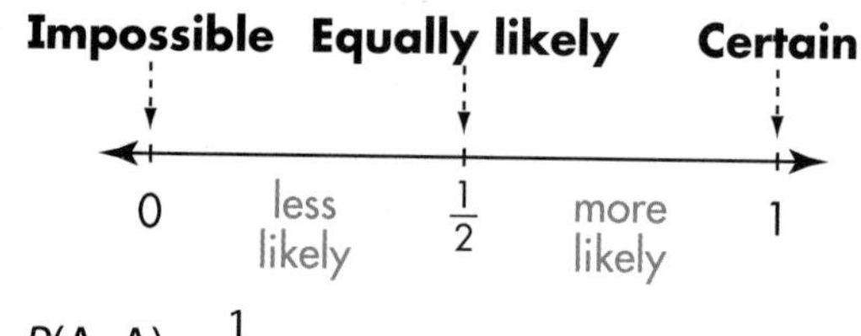

$P(\text{A, A}) = \frac{1}{9}$

The probability that Eva chooses an A both times is $\frac{1}{9}$.

Explain It

1. Use the tree diagram above to find the probability of choosing the same letter twice. Hint: Look for pairs of outcomes with the same letter.

2. If an event has a probability of $\frac{3}{4}$, is it less likely, more likely, equally likely, impossible, or certain to occur?

Probability of an event $= \frac{\text{number of favorable outcomes}}{\text{total number of possible outcomes}}$

What is the probability that Reuben will choose the letter B?

There is 1 favorable outcome out of 6 possible outcomes, R, E, U, B, E, or N. The outcomes are equally likely (have the same chance of occurring). The probability of choosing the letter B can be written as $P(B)$.

$P(B) = \frac{1}{6}$

The probability that Reuben chooses a B out of the bag is $\frac{1}{6}$.

What is the probability that Reuben will choose the letter E?

There are 2 favorable outcomes out of 6 possible outcomes (since E appears twice).

$P(E) = \frac{2}{6} = \frac{1}{3}$

The probability that Reuben chooses an E out of the bag is $\frac{1}{3}$ or $P(E) = \frac{1}{3}$.

Guided Practice*

Do you know HOW?

For **1** through **4**, use the spinner shown.

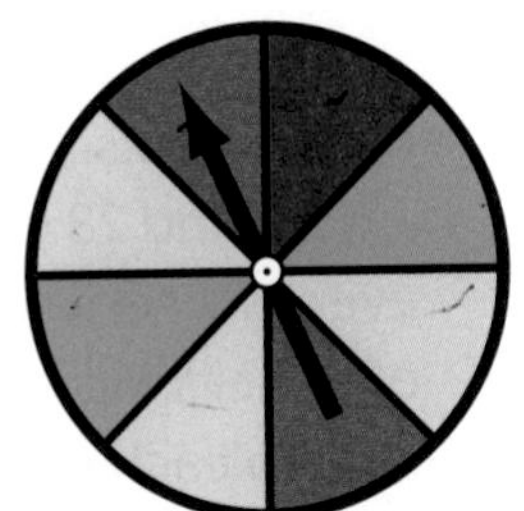

1. Find P(blue).
2. Find P(yellow).
3. Find P(red).
4. Find P(green).

Do you UNDERSTAND?

5. **Writing to Explain** In the example above, is it likely, unlikely, impossible, or certain that Reuben draws a B?
6. What is the probability that Reuben will NOT draw an R?

Independent Practice

7. Write each letter of your first name on a separate small sheet of paper. Put each piece into a box. Do an experiment where you pick one letter and replace it each time. Do this 10 times. Record the number of times you pick each letter, and then write the probability as a fraction.

For **8** through **12**, suppose you toss a quarter and a penny.

8. Make a tree diagram to show the possible outcomes.
9. Find P(one head).
10. Find P(two heads).
11. Find P(quarter heads, penny tails)
12. Find P(no heads)

*For another example, see Set H on page 449.

Independent Practice

13. When a number cube is tossed, there are 6 possible outcomes (1, 2, 3, 4, 5, or 6). If the cube is tossed twice and the outcomes are added, the possible sums are from 2 through 12.

Copy the table and give the probability of each sum.

Sum	2	3	4	5	6	7	8	9	10	11	12
Number of Occurrences	1	2	3	4	5	6	5	4	3	2	1
Probability											

14. Which sum (or sums) has the greatest probability of occurring?

15. Which sum (or sums) has the least probability of occurring?

Problem Solving

16. Geometry Kendra tosses a colored cube. Half of the sides of the cube are red, $\frac{1}{3}$ of the sides are blue, and one side is green. What is the probability that the cube will land on a color other than red when tossed?

17. Mrs. Pierre bought 150 pencils to give to her students. She has three classes with 27, 25, and 23 students each. She wants every student to get the same number of pencils. How many pencils should she give to each student?

18. Think About the Process Jorgé put colored cards into a bag. Two of the cards were green, three were red, one was orange, two were blue, and two were purple. Jorgé wants to find the probability that he will pull an orange card from the bag. What step does Jorgé take to determine the number of possible outcomes?

A Count the number of orange cards.

B Count the number of different colored cards.

C Count the total number of cards in the bag.

D Count the number of cards that are not orange.

19. Carlita buys 3 beanbag throws for $1.00. What is the probability she will toss one beanbag through a hole in the top row of this game? Assume Carlita always throws a beanbag into a hole.

20. How many parts of each color should there be to make sure that it is equally likely this spinner will land on each of 3 different colors?

Algebra Connections

Which Equation is True?

Remember that an equation is a number sentence that uses an equal sign to show that two expressions are equal. Both of the following are equations.

$8 + 2 = 10$

$x + 25 = 100$

The first equation is true. You don't know if an algebraic equation is true or false until you replace the variable with a number.

If $x = 75$, then $x + 25 = 100$ is a true equation.

Example: If $m = 25$, which equation is true?

$2 + m = 30$ $\quad$ $m - 20 = 5$

In the first equation, if you replace m with 25, the result is $2 + 25 = 30$. This equation is false.

In the second equation if you replace m with 25, the result is $25 - 20 = 5$. This equation is true.

Decide which equation is true for each replacement of the variable.

1. If $x = 20$, which equation is true?

$3 + x = 23$ or $\frac{x}{5} = 2$

2. If $y = 100$, which equation is true?

$y - 80 = 180$ or $y \div 2 = 50$.

3. If $x = 50$, which equation is true?

$x + 50 = 75$ or $\frac{x}{10} = 5$

4. If $x = 80$, which equation is true?

$40x = 3{,}200$ or $\frac{x}{4} = 2$

5. If $z = 200$, which equation is true?

$200 - x = 200$ or $x + 100 = 300$

6. If $x = 70$, which equation is true?

$6x = 420$ or $x + 7 = 63$

7. If $x = 0$, which equation is true?

$50x = 50$ $\quad$ $x + 7 = 7$

8. If $x = 1$, which equation is true?

$40x = 40$ or $40 + x = 40$

9. If a teacher has 32 students and divides them into teams of 4, which equation could be used to find how many students will be on each team? Let x represent the number of students on each team.

$\frac{32}{4} = x$ $\quad$ $4 + x = 32$ $\quad$ $\frac{32}{x} = 4$ $\quad$ $4 \times 32 = x$

Lesson
19-9

MR 1.2 Determine when and how to break a problem into simpler parts.
Also **NS 1.0, MR 2.2.**

Problem Solving

Solve a Simpler Problem

books from reading list

Owen needs to read 2 books from a list of 6 books. How many different combinations of books are possible?

Follow these steps to solve a simpler problem.

1. Break apart or change the problem into one that is simpler.
2. Solve the simpler problem.
3. Use the answers to the simpler problem to solve the original problem.

Guided Practice*

Do you know HOW?

1. Draw a picture to show the number of combinations of pairs for 5 books.

2. Think of extending the table at the top to find the number of pairs with 7 books. What number would you add to 15 to find the number of pairs? How many pairs would there be for 7 books?

Do you UNDERSTAND?

3. **Writing to Explain** Is it easier to use the table or to draw a picture as the number of books increases?

4. **Write a Problem** Write a real-world problem that can be solved by solving a simpler problem.

Independent Practice

Solve each problem.

5. Continue the pattern in the book problem above. How many pairs of books would there be for 8 books? 9 books? 10 books?

6. Find the number of degrees in a hexagon. HINT: Divide the hexagon into triangles.

a How many triangles are formed?

b How many degrees are in each triangle?

c What is the total number of degrees in the hexagon?

7. Using the same strategy in Problem 6, what is the total number of degrees in a pentagon? An octagon?

Stuck? Try this....

- What do I know?
- What am I asked to find?
- What diagram can I use to help understand the problem?
- Can I use addition, subtraction, multiplication, or division?
- Is all of my work correct?
- Did I answer the right question?
- Is my answer reasonable?

*For another example, see Set I on page 449.

Use letters to represent the books.

A ——— B

2 books:
1 pair

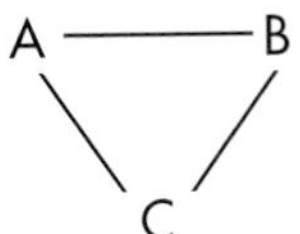

3 books: 3 pairs

A, B, C, D

4 books: 6 pairs

Look for a pattern.

Find the pattern. Continue the pattern to 6 books.

Number of Books	2	3	4	5	6
Number of Pairs	1	3	6	10	15

+2 +3 +4 +5

There are 15 different possible pairs.

8. Juanita tossed 3 number cubes, and these digits came up.

If each of the numbers 2, 1 and 4 is used only once to form a 3-digit number, which shows all the possible 3-digit numbers?

A 214, 421, 142

B 214, 124, 412, 421

C 214, 241, 142, 412, 124

D 214, 241, 142, 124, 412, 421

9. Jill has 3 colored vases to arrange on a shelf.

Let B stand for blue, O for orange, and G for green. Which list shows all the possible arrangements of the vases?

A BOG, OBG, GOB

B BOG, OBG, GOB, GBO

C BOG, OBG, GOB, GBO, OGB

D BOG, OBG, GOB, GBO, OGB, BGO

10. George was choosing his clothes for the next day. In his closet he had 2 ties, 5 shirts, 3 trousers, and 2 belts. How many different ways could George choose a tie, shirt, trousers, and belt?

11. The McMillan family wanted to buy a new vehicle. They could choose a van or a car; a black, silver, or white exterior; and a tan or black interior. How many different vehicles can they buy?

12. After seeing a movie, 2 friends stopped for frozen yogurt. Three flavors were available in small, medium, and large sizes. How many different combinations of flavors and sizes are possible?

13. **Algebra** Draw a picture and write an equation to solve.

Niko had $17\frac{1}{3}$ ft of fencing. He uses $5\frac{2}{3}$ ft to finish a job. How many feet of fencing does Niko have now? Let f = feet of fencing left.

Test Prep

1. The histogram shows the results from a survey asking people how many plays they have seen in the last year. How many people have seen more than 3 plays? (19-2)

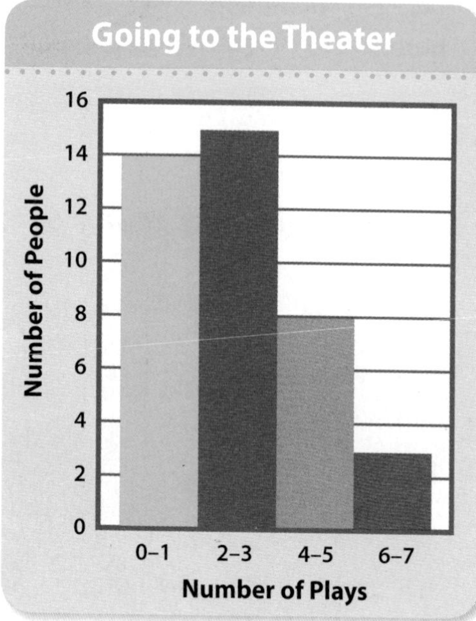

A 26

B 15

C 11

D 8

2. The music teacher is choosing two students out of 10 to sing a duet in the musical. How many different pairs of students must try out if she wants to try every possible pair? (19-9)

A 50

B 45

C 20

D 12

3. James is drawing the picture graph below to show the number of license plates from each state he saw on a recent trip. He saw 15 Arizona license plates. Which picture should he draw for Arizona? (19-1)

License Plates James Saw

State	Number of License Plates
Nevada	000-NNN 000-NNN 000-NNN 000-NNN 000-NNN 000-NNN 000-NNN
Oklahoma	000-NNN 000-NNN 000
New Mexico	000-NNN 000-NNN
Arizona	
Arkansas	000-NNN
Other States	000-NNN 000

000-NNN = 5 license plates

A 000-NNN 000-NNN 000-NNN 000

B 000-NNN 000-NNN 000-NNN 000-NNN

C 000-NNN 000-NNN 000

D 000-NNN 000-NNN 000-NNN

4. The shoe sizes of the starting players on the girls' basketball team are listed below. What is the median of these numbers? (19-6)

7, 6, 5, 6, 8

A 5

B 6

C 7

D 8

Test Prep

5. According to the circle graph below, about what fraction of the t-shirts sold were x-large? (19-3)

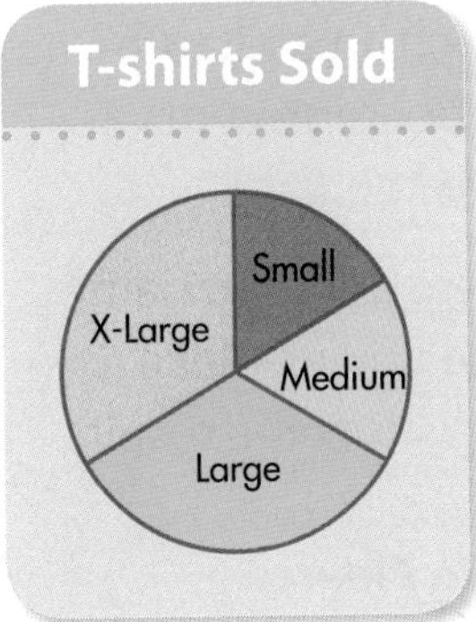

A $\frac{1}{3}$

B $\frac{1}{4}$

C $\frac{1}{5}$

D $\frac{1}{6}$

6. The table shows the heights of a group of friends. What is the mean height of the group in inches? (19-5)

Data

Name	Height (in inches)
Amy	58
Rudy	62
Jessie	55
Pablo	61
Jared	64

A 61

B 60

C 59

D 58

7. A college student plans to take biology, algebra, and literature in the morning. Each letter represents the first letter of each class. Which list below shows all the different orders that these three classes can be taken? (19-7)

A BAL, BAB, LAB

B BAL, LAB, ABL, LBA

C BAL, BLA, ALB, LAB, ABL

D BAL, BLA, ALB, ABL, LAB, LBA

8. The cards shown are placed in a bag and one is drawn without looking. What is the probability Bobby's name is drawn? (19-8)

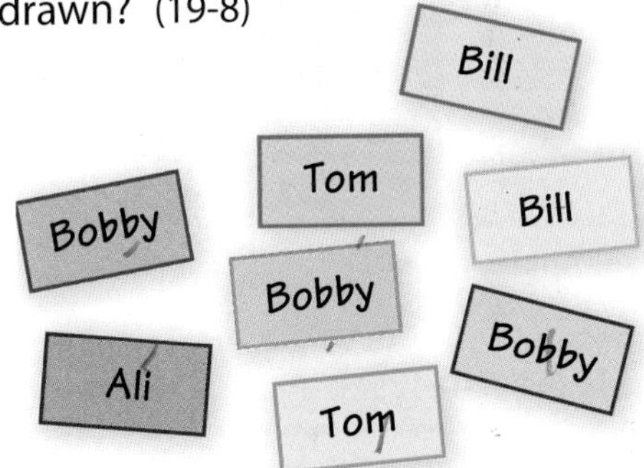

A $\frac{1}{8}$

B $\frac{2}{8}$

C $\frac{3}{8}$

D $\frac{3}{5}$

9. An airline company is making a graph to display the number of each type of ticket they have available on a flight including first class, business class and economy. Which type of graph would be best to display the data? (19-4)

A Bar or picture graph

B Line plot

C Circle graph

D Line graph

Reteaching

Set A, pages 420–422

Students were asked to name their favorite seasons. Make a bar graph to show the results.

Favorite Season	
Summer	8
Autumn	6
Winter	4
Spring	6

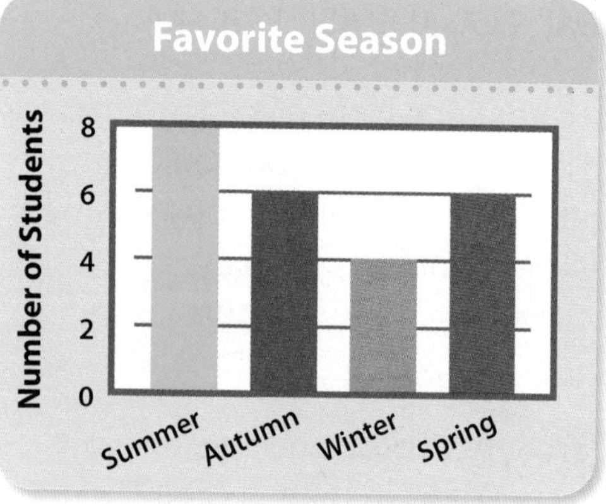

Remember that a bar graph or a picture graph can be used to compare data that shows how many or how much. In a picture graph, each symbol represents a certain amount in the data.

1. Students were asked to name their favorite flower. Make a bar graph to show the results.

Favorite Flower	
Rose	10
Lily	3
Carnation	3
Tulip	6
Daffodil	8

Set B, pages 424–425

David made a histogram to show how many books his class had purchased in the last year.

Using the histogram, find the number of students who purchased 3–5 books. The bar with the 3–5 interval has a height of 8. The number of students is 8.

Remember that histograms are a type of bar graph that has no space between the bars and the bars show equal intervals.

Use the histogram at the left to answer the following questions.

1. How many students were surveyed?
2. How many students had bought more than 5 books?
3. What fraction of the students bought 9, 10, or 11 books?

Set C, pages 426–428

A group of 100 students were asked to name their favorite type of television program. Make a circle graph to show the results.

Favorite Type of Television Program	
Comedy	25
Sports	50
Drama	10
Other	15

Comedy = 25 out of 100 = $\frac{1}{4}$.

Sports = 50 out of 100 = $\frac{1}{2}$,

Drama = 10 out of 100 = $\frac{1}{10}$.

Other = $\frac{15}{100} = \frac{3}{20}$.

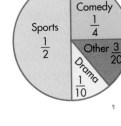

Draw a circle with sectors for $\frac{1}{2}$, $\frac{1}{4}$, and $\frac{1}{10}$ and label those sectors with the program type. The remaining sector shows $\frac{3}{20}$ or Other.

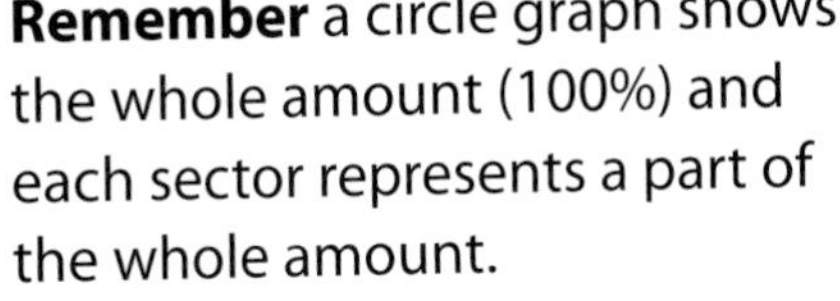

Remember a circle graph shows the whole amount (100%) and each sector represents a part of the whole amount.

Jill spent a total of 30 hours exercising last month: Jogging: 15 hours; Cycling: 10 hours; Swimming: 5 hours.

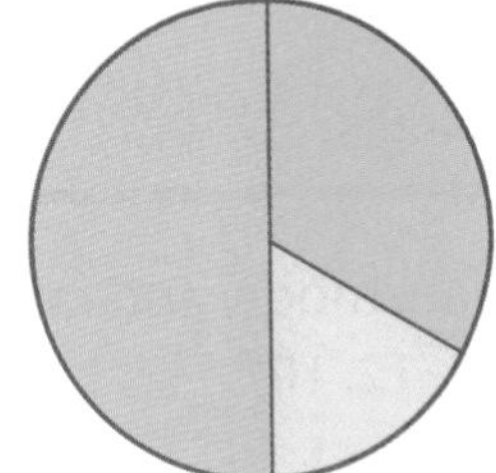

1. Copy the circle graph and label each sector with the activity and fraction.
2. What fraction represents the part of the day Jill spent cycling?

Set D, pages 430–431

Students were asked to name their favorite animal. Make a bar graph to show the results.

Favorite Animal	
Penguin	7
Elephant	6
Lion	3
Monkey	4

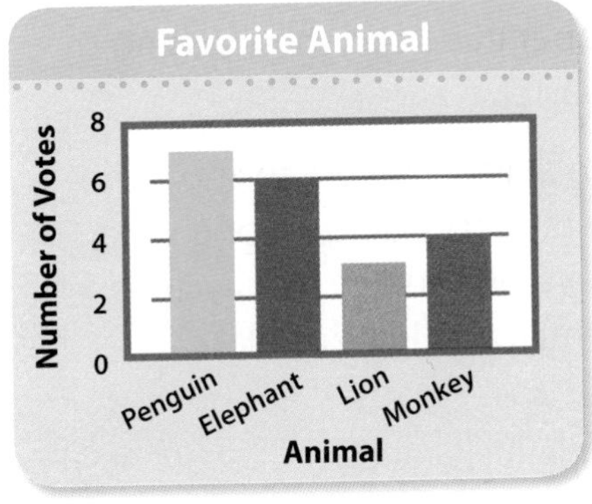

Remember that making a graph makes it easy to visualize data and answer questions about the data.

Monthly Snowfall				
Month	Dec.	Jan.	Feb.	Mar.
Calories	6	12	18	4

1. Make a line graph of the data.
2. Which month has a snowfall 3 times as great as December?

Set E, pages 432–433

Find the mean of this data set:

2, 3, 8, 3, 5, 6, 1

The mean is an average. To find the mean, add the data and divide by the number of data.

$(2 + 3 + 8 + 3 + 5 + 6 + 1) \div 7 = 28 \div 7 = 4$

The mean is 4.

Remember that the mean is an average. You must add the data and divide by the number of addends.

1. 5, 4, 1, 3, 1, 10
2. 6, 9, 5, 2, 8
3. 4, 2, 2, 5, 3, 3, 2

Set F, pages 434-435

Find the median, mode, and range for this set of data: 10, 15, 20, 12, 10

To find the median, list the data in order from least to greatest and find the middle value.

10, 10, 12, 15, 20 **The median is 12.**

To find the mode, list the data in order from least to greatest and find the value that occurs most often.

10, 10, 12, 15, 20 **The mode is 10.**

To find the range, subtract the least value from the greatest value.

$20 - 10 = 10$ **The range is 10.**

Remember that if there is an even number of data, you must add the two middle numbers when the data are ordered from least to greatest and divide by 2 to find the median.

1. Find the median of this data set:
   27.5 27 30 29.5
2. Find the mode of this data set:
   12, 6, 9, 5, 8, 12, 8, 1, 4, 12, 6
3. Find the range of this data set:
   87, 84, 90, 75, 100, 88

Set G, pages 436–437

Judy can pick either a hamburger or a chicken sandwich and then either a coleslaw, potato salad, or a fruit salad. How many different lunch combinations can she have?

Draw a tree diagram.

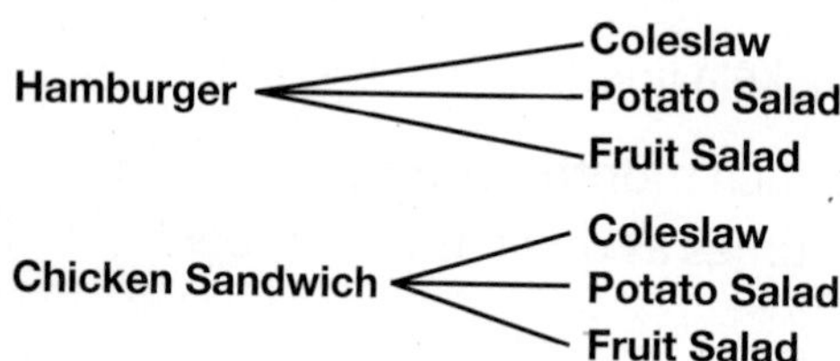

There are 6 possible combinations, so Judy has a choice of 6 different lunches.

Remember that when you make a tree diagram, start with 1 item and list all the possible combinations with it. Continue with all the items.

1. Make a tree diagram to show the sample space for tossing a number cube and then tossing a quarter.
2. Make a tree diagram to show the results of choosing among tuna, cheese, and turkey sandwiches, and milk and juice drinks.

Set H, pages 438-440

You spin the spinner once. Find P (landing in a green section).

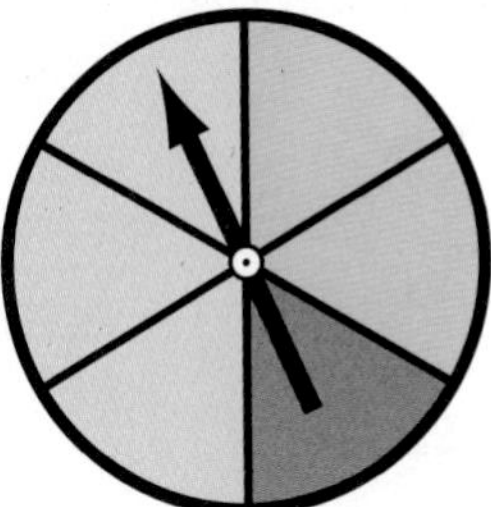

$$\text{Probability} = \frac{\text{number of favorable outcomes}}{\text{number of possible outcomes}}$$

So, $P(\text{green}) = \frac{3}{6} = \frac{1}{2}$

Remember that when you express a probability as a fraction, always write the fraction in simplest form.

Use the letters in MATHEMATICS. Each letter is written on a separate piece of paper and the pieces are put in a bag.

Find the probability of choosing each letter or letters out of the bag.

1. P (a consonant)
2. P (the letter A)
3. P (not the letter A)

Set I, pages 442–443

To solve a simpler problem, follow these steps:

Step 1

Break apart or change the problem into one that is simpler to solve.

Step 2

Draw a picture or use objects to look for a pattern to solve the simpler problem.

Step 3

Use the answers to the simpler problem to solve the original problem.

Four people shake hands with each other once. How many handshakes are there in all?

Use A, B, C, D to represent the people.

AB, AC, AD
BC, BD, CD

There are 6 handshakes.

Remember that you can draw a picture or use objects to look for a pattern in finding the relationship between the simpler problem and the original problem.

1. How many different teams of 2 people can be chosen from 4 people?
2. How many different teams of 3 people can be chosen from 5 people?
3. What is the sum of the angles of an octagon?

Topic 20

Constructions

1

Memorial Coliseum was once the home of the Los Angeles Rams NFL football team. The football field shown inside Memorial Coliseum is in the shape of a rectangle. How can you construct a rectangle? You will find out in Lesson 20-3.

2

Diamond cutters have to be very accurate when cutting angles on diamonds. How can you construct an angle that is congruent to an angle of a facet on a diamond? You will find out in Lesson 20-1.

3

How can you construct a triangle that is congruent to a triangle formed by the roofline of a house? You will find out in Lesson 20-3.

4

The Leaning Tower of Pisa is located in Pisa, Italy, and is one of the most famous buildings in the world. How can you construct an angle that is congruent to the angle that the tower leans? You will find out in Lesson 20-1.

Review What You Know!

Vocabulary

Choose the best term from the box.

- line
- line segment
- perpendicular
- ray

1. A _?_ extends in two directions infinitely.

2. A _?_ has one endpoint and extends in one direction, while a _?_ has two endpoints.

3. _?_ lines intersect at one point and create four right angles.

Identifying Angles

Classify each angle as acute, obtuse, straight or right.

4. 

5. 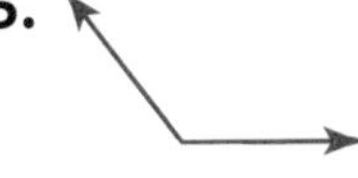

6. 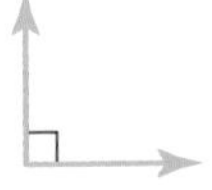

7. ←—•—→

Patterns

Find the next two numbers in each pattern.

8. 1.5, 1.7, 1.9, 2.1, 2.3, ___, ___

9. 26, 21, 16, 11, ___, ___

Shapes

Writing to Explain Write an answer for each question.

10. Can a triangle have two obtuse angles?

11. Is a square always a rectangle?

Lesson

20-1

MG 2.1 Measure, identify, and draw angles, perpendicular and parallel lines, rectangles, and triangles by using appropriate tools (e.g., straightedge, ruler, compass, protractor, drawing software).

Constructing Angles

How can you construct an angle congruent to another angle?

A geometric construction is the drawing of a figure using only a compass and a straightedge. A ruler and a protractor are not used in making a construction.

How would you construct $\angle B$ congruent to $\angle M$?

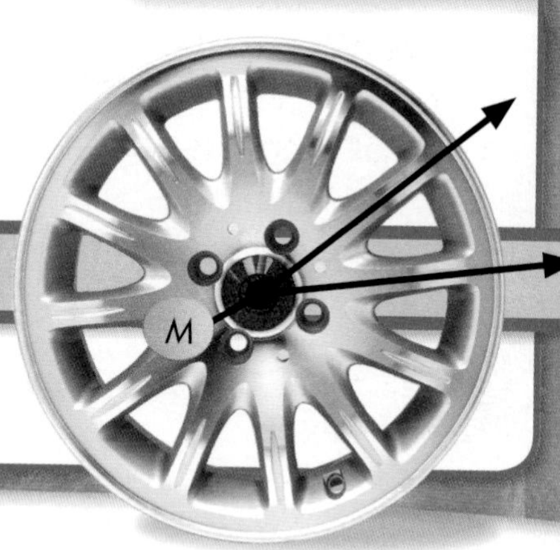

Guided Practice*

Do you know HOW?

In **1** and **2**, trace each angle on a sheet of paper. Then construct an angle congruent to each given angle.

1. 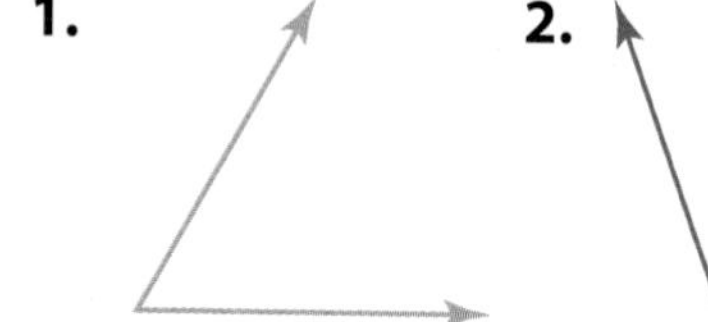

2. 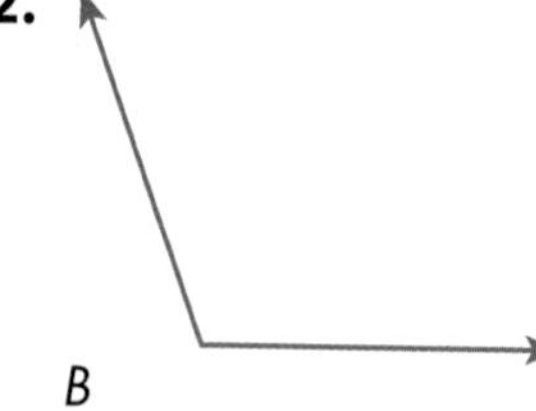

Do you UNDERSTAND?

3. **Writing to Explain** Why is it important to keep the same compass setting in Step 1?

4. How can you tell if a constructed angle is congruent to the original angle?

Independent Practice

In **5** through **7**, trace each angle on a sheet of paper. Then construct an angle congruent to each given angle.

5. 

6. 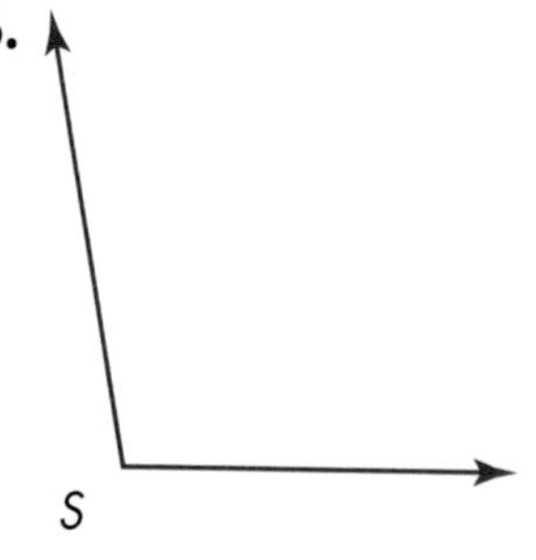

7. 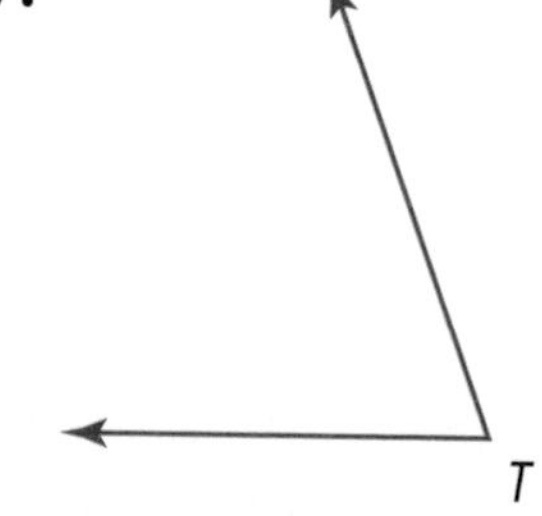

DIGITAL Animated Glossary, eTools
www.pearsonsuccessnet.com

**For another example, see Set A on page 466.*

Step 1

Draw a ray with endpoint B. With point M as center, use your compass to draw an arc that intersects both sides of $\angle M$. Label the points of intersection N and P.

With the same compass setting and endpoint B as center, draw an arc that intersects the ray at point D.

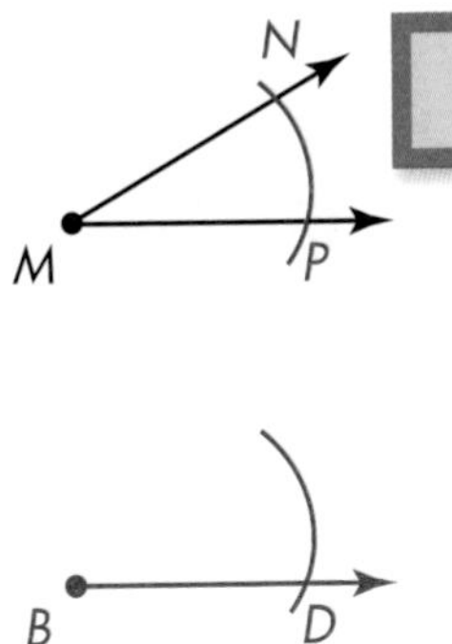

Step 2

Set the compass to the length $\overline{NP}$. Then, with point D as center, draw an intersecting arc. Label the point C.

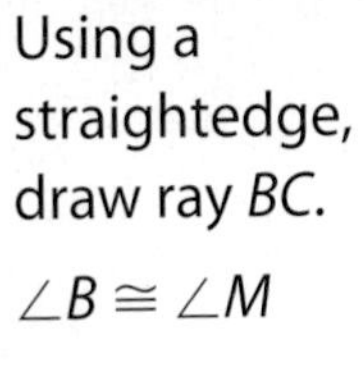

Step 3

Using a straightedge, draw ray BC.

$\angle B \cong \angle M$

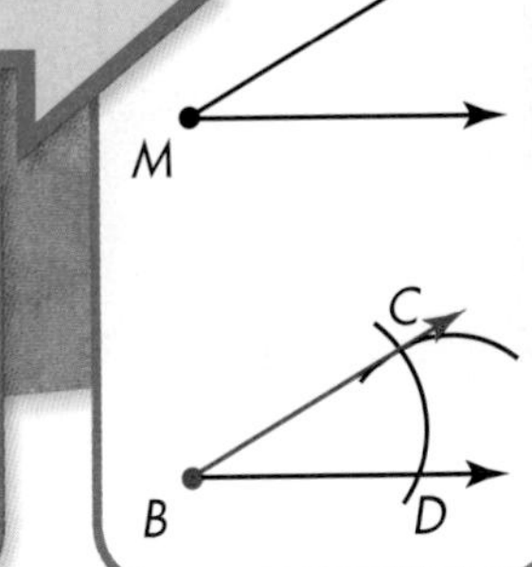

Problem Solving

8. The Leaning Tower of Pisa is located in Italy. It leans to the south at the angle shown in the picture below. Construct an angle congruent to $\angle A$.

12. The high temperatures in a city for 7 days were 87°, 87°, 90°, 90°, 90°, 92°, and 87°. What was the mean temperature for the 7 days?

A 87° **C** 90°

B 89° **D** 91°

9. Mario has saved a number of quarters, nickels, dimes, and pennies. He will use \$3.93 to buy a new toy for his dog. Using the fewest coins, what combination of coins will equal \$3.93?

10. Justin climbed 15 steps to the second floor of a building. Each step is 8 inches high. How many feet higher is the second floor than the first?

11. Diamond cutters must cut angles precisely so that the greatest amount of light is reflected from the facets. Refer to the photo of the diamond below. Construct an angle congruent to $\angle W$.

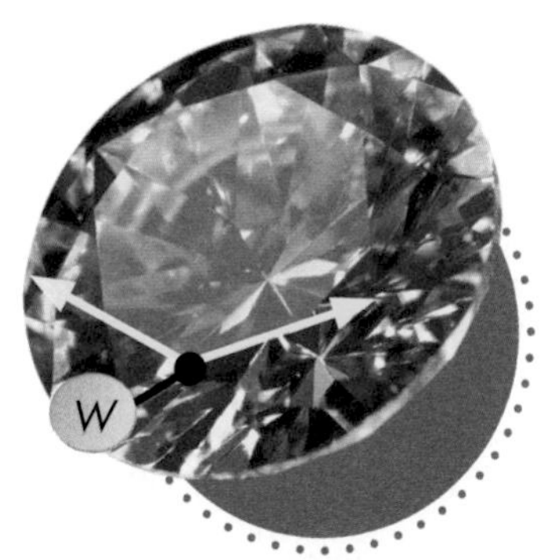

Lesson

20-2

MG 2.1 Measure, identify, and draw angles, perpendicular and parallel lines, rectangles, and triangles by using appropriate tools (e.g., straightedge, ruler, compass, protractor, drawing software).

Constructing Lines

GeoTool

How can you construct perpendicular and parallel lines?

The rails of the track are parallel. The ties are perpendicular to the rails.

Construct a line perpendicular to $\overleftrightarrow{LN}$ and a line parallel to $\overleftrightarrow{LN}$.

Another Example How do you construct a line segment congruent to a given line segment?

Without measuring with a ruler, draw $\overline{JK}$ congruent to $\overline{ST}$.

S T

Step 1 Draw a ray. Label the endpoint *J*.

J

Step 2 On $\overline{ST}$, with point *S* as the center, open the compass so that it lines up with point *T*.

Then place the compass on the ray with point *J* as the center. Without changing the compass setting, draw an arc that intersects the ray. Label the point of intersection *K*. $\overline{JK}$ is congruent to $\overline{ST}$.

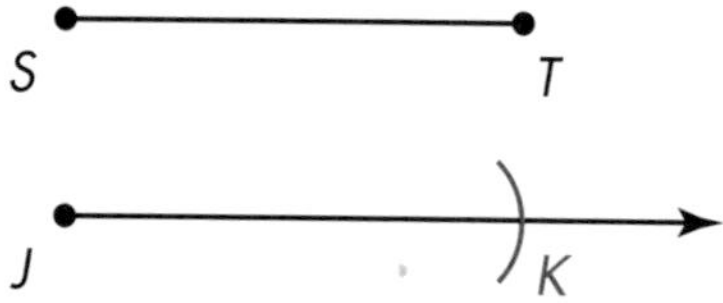

Explain It

1. How is constructing a figure different from drawing a figure?
2. In Step 2, could the ray be any length?
3. Does a line segment need to be horizontal in order to construct another segment congruent to it?

Step 1

Draw a line with points L and N. With L as center, draw two arcs that intersect $\overleftrightarrow{LN}$. Label the points W and X.

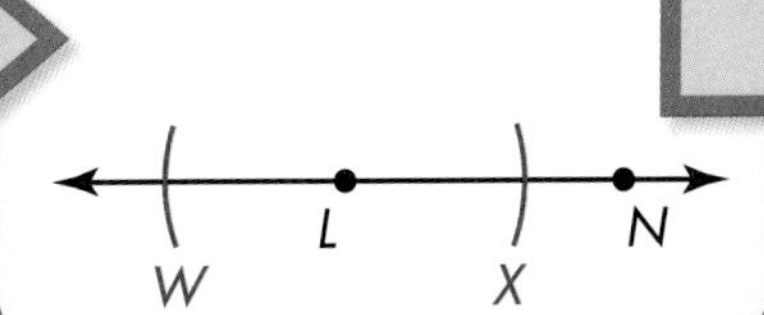

Step 2

Set the compass wider. Using W and X as centers, draw arcs that intersect. Label the point Y. Draw $\overleftrightarrow{LY}$.

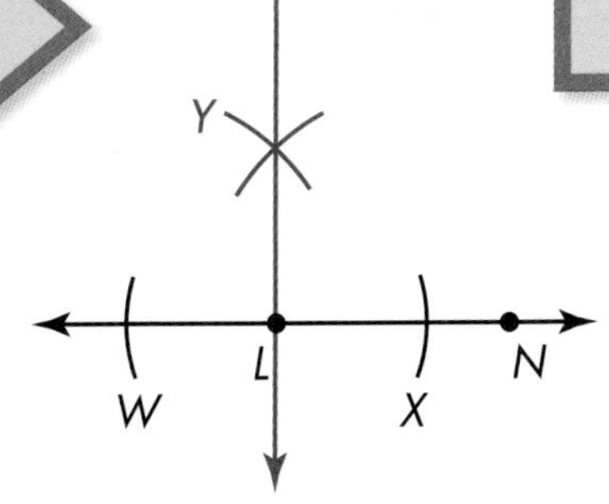

Step 3

Repeat Steps 1 and 2 at Y to find point Z.

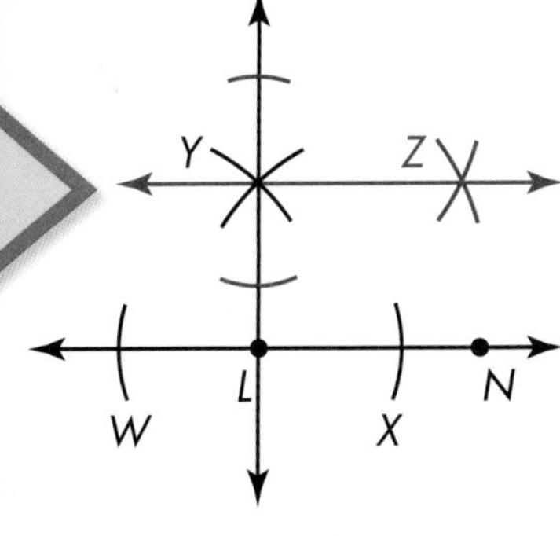

$\overleftrightarrow{LY} \perp \overleftrightarrow{LN}$ and $\overleftrightarrow{LN} \parallel \overleftrightarrow{YZ}$

Guided Practice*

Do you know HOW?

1. Draw a line perpendicular to line CD. Copy $\overleftrightarrow{CD}$ on a separate sheet of paper and construct $\overleftrightarrow{TC}$ so that it is perpendicular to $\overleftrightarrow{CD}$.

2. Draw a segment congruent to $\overline{EF}$. Copy $\overline{EF}$ on a separate sheet of paper. Then draw a ray labeled $\overrightarrow{MN}$. On that ray, construct $\overline{MP}$ so that $\overline{MP}$ is congruent to $\overline{EF}$.

Do you UNDERSTAND?

3. Writing to Explain In Step 2 of the example above, why is it necessary to set the compass wider than the length of segment WL?

4. Look at the line TC you constructed in Problem 1 that is perpendicular to line CD. Use point T and construct a line perpendicular to line TC. How is that line related to line CD?

Independent Practice

In **5** through **7**, copy the figures on a separate sheet of paper and follow the directions.

5. Construct a line perpendicular to line XY.

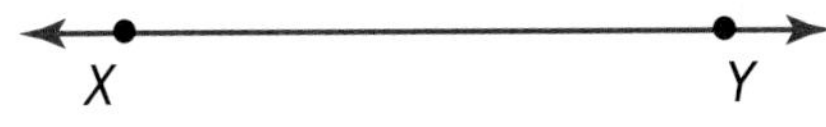

DIGITAL eTools **www.pearsonsuccessnet.com**

*For another example, see Set B on page 466.

Independent Practice

6. Construct a line perpendicular to line *MN*. Then construct a line through it that is parallel to line *MN*.

7. Draw a line segment that is congruent to $\overline{CD}$.

Problem Solving

Engineers are making plans to lay new railroad tracks between cities. In **8** and **9**, use the information in the table.

8. If it costs $155 per mile to construct railroad tracks, how much would it cost to build tracks from San Francisco to Los Angeles?

9. Estimation Railroad ties are set about 2 feet apart. About how many railroad ties are there between Eureka and Sacramento?

Data

	Los Angeles	San Diego	Sacramento
San Francisco	384 mi	502 mi	87 mi
Eureka	647 mi	766 mi	309 mi

1 mile = 5,280 feet

10. If you are comparing two negative integers on a number line, how can you tell which one is greater?

11. Four friends played golf. Their scores were $^{+}3$, $^{-}1$, $^{+}4$, and $^{-}4$ in relation to par. The least score wins. Arrange the scores from best to worst.

12. Algebra Ted has 15 trophies. This is 5 times as many as Harold has. How many trophies does Harold have? Write and solve an equation to answer the question.

13. Writing to Explain Explain how perpendicular lines are similar to intersecting lines.

14. Use the figure to tell whether the statements are true or false.

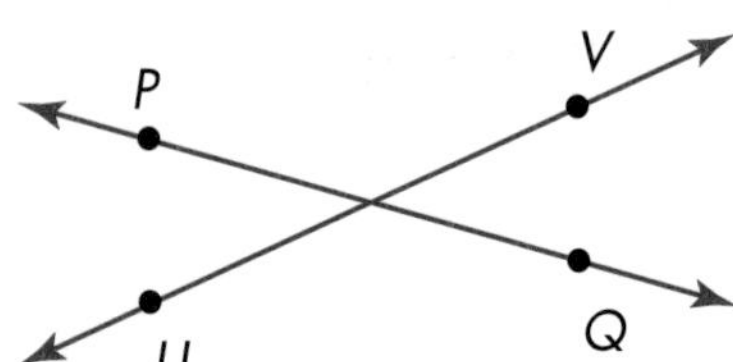

a $\overline{PQ}$ is parallel to $\overline{UV}$

b $\overline{PQ}$ intersects $\overline{UV}$

c $\overline{PQ}$ is perpendicular to $\overline{UV}$

15. Estimation The gas tank in Shondra's car can hold 18 gallons. Her car gets about 22 miles per gallon of gas. On a recent trip, Shondra used about 12 gallons of gas. Which is the best estimate of the distance Shondra drove?

A 120 miles

B 200 miles

C 400 miles

D 1,200 miles

Find each difference. Simplify if possible.

1. $5\frac{5}{8} - 3$

2. $2\frac{2}{3} - 1\frac{5}{6}$

3. $3\frac{1}{4} - \frac{1}{8}$

4. $7 - 3\frac{5}{12}$

5. $6\frac{1}{2} - 2\frac{1}{2}$

6. $5\frac{1}{3} - 3\frac{5}{12}$

7. $8\frac{1}{6} - 2\frac{1}{4}$

8. $4\frac{4}{5} - 1\frac{3}{15}$

Find each product. Estimate to check if the answer is reasonable.

9. 36×36

10. 379×39

11. 405×19

12. 564×50

13. $2{,}705 \times 30$

14. $9{,}191 \times 19$

15. 787×211

16. 904×508

17. 759×196

18. 999×333

Error Search Find each answer that is not correct. Write it correctly and explain the error.

19. $10{,}000 - 5{,}831 = 5{,}169$

20. $12.5 \times 0.75 = 93.75$

21. $14{,}976 + 13{,}867 = 28{,}743$

22. $9.27 \div 9 = 1.03$

23. $3{,}637 \div 36 = 101$

Number Sense

Estimating and Reasoning Write whether each statement is true or false. Explain your reasoning.

24. The quotient of 1,546 ÷ 5 is less than 300.

25. The product of 9.32 and 4.7 is less than 36.

26. The difference of 6,631 and 3,021 is greater than 2,000 and less than 4,000.

27. The sum of 43.04 + 21.56 is 0.04 more than 64.56.

28. When $x = {}^{-}9$, the expression $x + {}^{+}5$ equals ${}^{-}14$.

29. The expression $(4\frac{5}{6} + 3\frac{1}{2} \times \frac{3}{4}) \times 0$ equals 0.

Lesson
20-3

MG 2.1 Measure, identify, and draw angles, perpendicular and parallel lines, rectangles, and triangles by using appropriate tools (e.g., straightedge, ruler, compass, protractor, drawing software).

Constructing Shapes

Hands-On

GeoTool

How can you construct congruent triangles?

Triangles are rigid figures which makes them useful in constructing buildings.

Construct a triangle that is congruent to triangle *XYZ*.

Another Example How can you construct a rectangle?

A rectangle has four right angles and opposite sides that are parallel and congruent. Construct a rectangle *ABCD*.

Step 1

Draw a line *AB*. Construct a line perpendicular to line *AB* at point *A*. Choose a point *D* on the line.

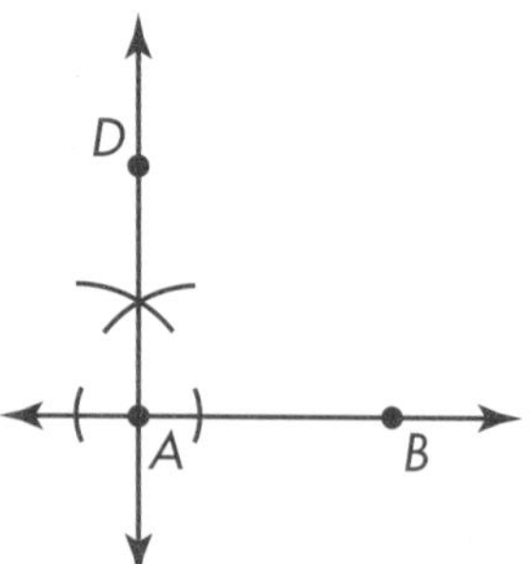

Step 2

Construct a line perpendicular to line *AB* at point *B*.

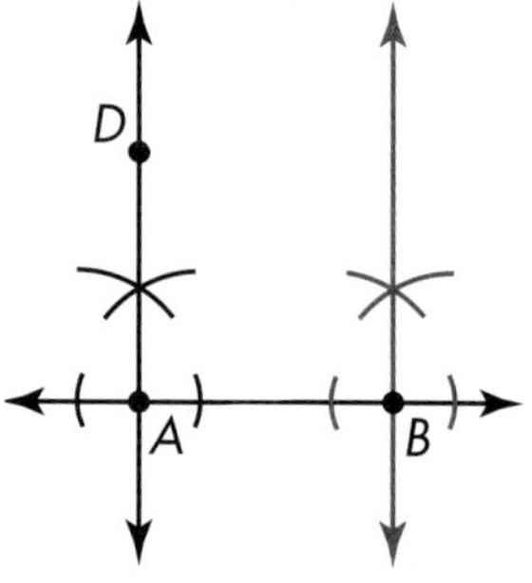

Step 3

Construct a line perpendicular to line *AD* at point *D*.

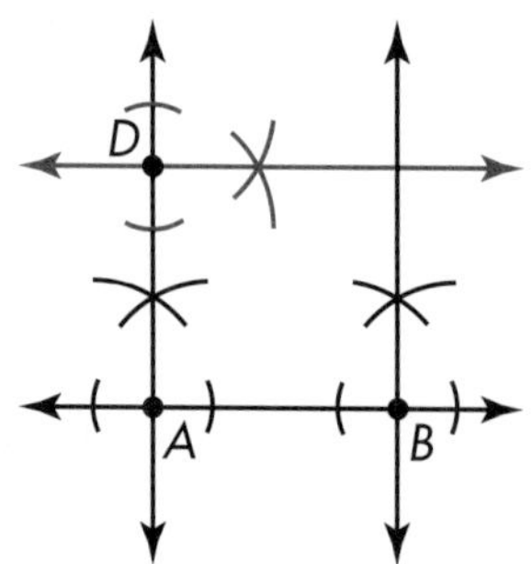

Step 4

The point where the perpendicular lines you constructed in Steps 2 and 3 intersect is point *C*.

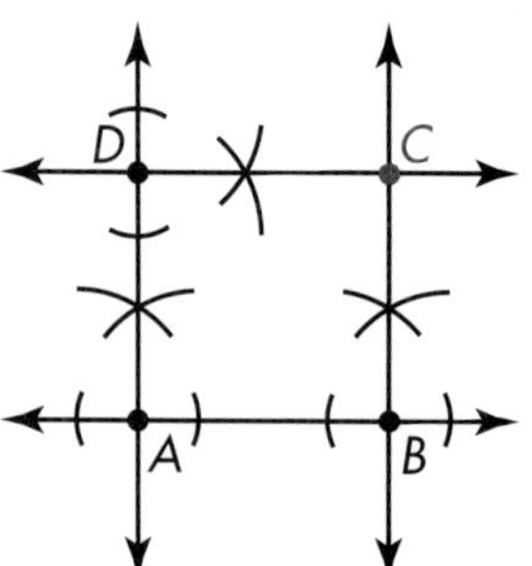

Explain It

1. What are the the four right angles in *ABCD*?
2. Name the two pairs of parallel and congruent sides in *ABCD*.

Step 1

Construct $\angle P$ congruent to $\angle X$.

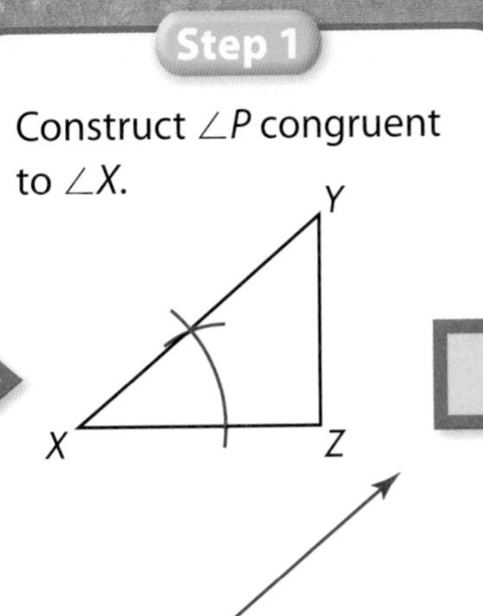

Step 2

On one side of $\angle P$, construct $\overline{PQ} \cong \overline{XY}$. On the other side of $\angle P$, construct $\overline{PR} \cong \overline{XZ}$

Step 3

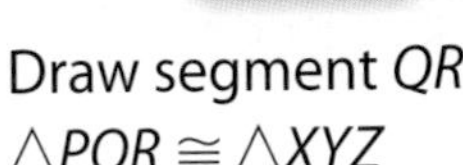

Draw segment QR. $\triangle PQR \cong \triangle XYZ$

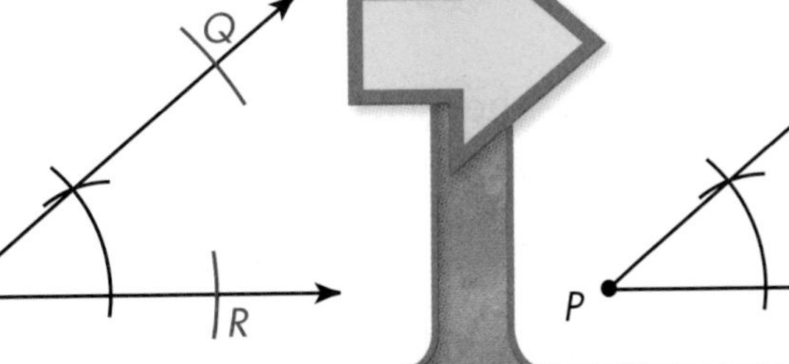

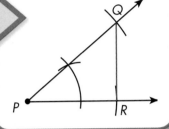

Guided Practice*

Do you know HOW?

1. Copy the following triangle on another sheet of paper. Then construct a triangle congruent to it.

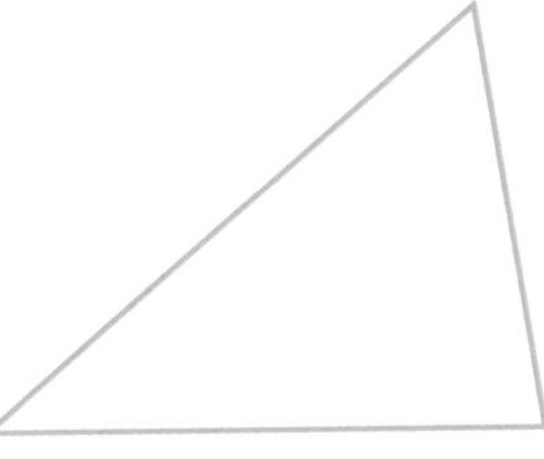

2. Construct a rectangle using a compass and straightedge.

Do you UNDERSTAND?

3. When you construct a rectangle, what is the measure of each angle?

4. How can you be sure that a triangle you construct is congruent to the original triangle?

Independent Practice

Copy each triangle on another sheet of paper. Then construct a triangle congruent to it.

5. 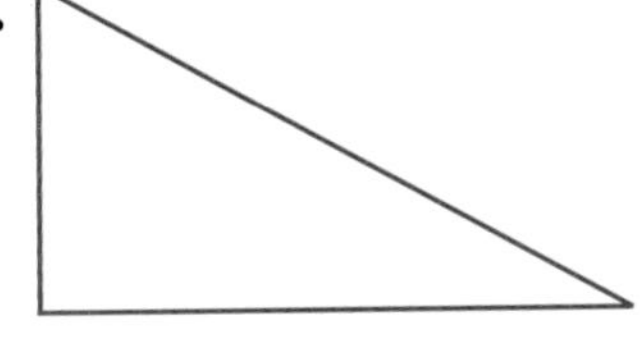

6. 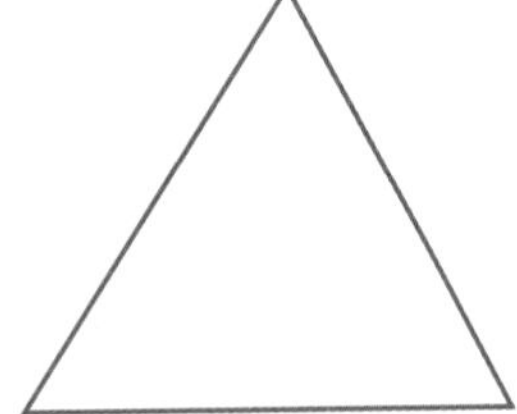

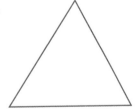

7. 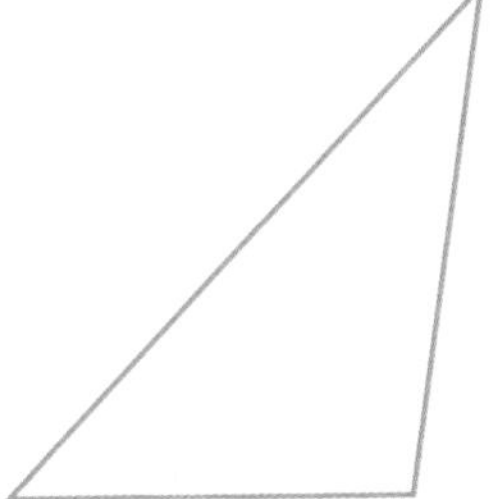

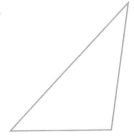

8. Copy the following line on another sheet of paper. Use it to construct a rectangle.

*For another example, see Set C on page 467.

Independent Practice

9. Ellen studied math for $1\frac{1}{2}$ hours, science for $\frac{3}{4}$ hour, and history for $\frac{3}{4}$ hour. How many hours did she study in all?

10. Alan bought 2 packages of tennis balls for \$7.98 each. How much change will Alan get from \$20?

11. **Geometry** What is the measure of the third angle in the triangle?

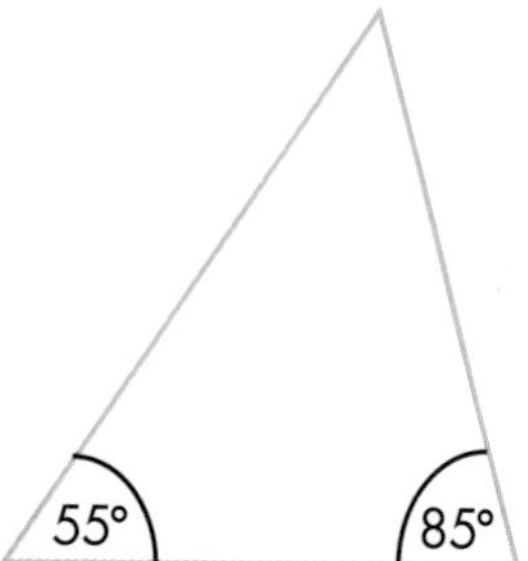

12. **Algebra** Yasmin is 6 inches taller than Burt. If b represents Burt's height, which expression represents Yasmin's height?

    A $b + 6$

    B $b \times 6$

    C $b - 6$

    D $b \div 6$

13. **Reasoning** Terry is arranging furniture and wants to center her 6.5-foot table against a wall that measures 15 feet. How far will the table be from each end of the wall? You can draw a picture to help you.

14. Squares for a quilt are being cut from a piece of material that is 15 inches wide and 20 inches long. The squares are 4 inches on each side. How many whole squares can be cut from the material? Draw a picture to help you.

15. Mr. Smith is redecorating his dining room. Tell if he needs to find the perimeter or area for each the following.

    a the amount of wallpaper border to go around the top of the room

    b the amount of carpeting needed to cover the floor

16. **Writing to Explain** How can you construct a triangle that is congruent to triangle *EFG* formed by the roofline of the house?

17. Let x represent the number of miles Gina ran. Paul ran 3 more than $\frac{1}{2}$ as many miles as Gina. Which expression represents the distance Paul ran?

    A $\frac{1}{2}(x + 3)$

    B $\frac{1}{2}x + 3$

    C $3x + \frac{1}{2}$

    D $2(x + 3)$

Mixed Problem Solving

1. How many Kemp's Ridley sea turtle nests were found in 2002?

2. How many more Kemp's Ridley nests were found in 2004 than in 2001?

3. Is there a trend in the data for Kemp's Ridley sea turtle nests? Explain.

4. Between which two years did the number of Kemp's Ridley nests increase the most?

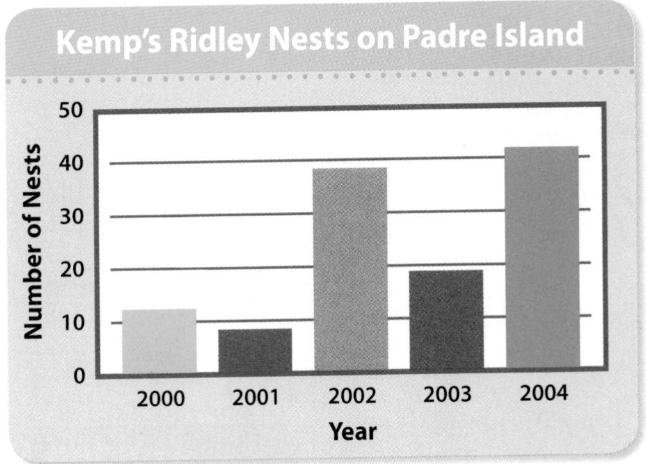

5. On a picture graph that shows the number of participants in rubber duck derbies, one picture equals one thousand participants. How many participants are represented by 3.5 pictures?

6. **Strategy Focus** Solve using the strategy Use Reasoning.

   Greg, Rick, and Tom like either math, science, or art best. Tom dislikes art. Rick is not the student who likes art or math best. Which student likes each subject best?

7. What was the high temperature on August 4?

8. On which date was the high temperature the lowest?

9. What was the difference between the greatest and least high temperatures for the week?

10. A scientist is studying the types and number of plants in a small area. What kind of graph should the scientist use to present his data?

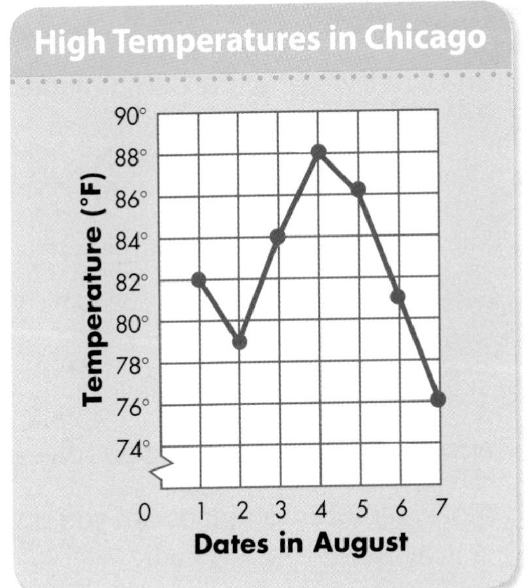

Lesson
20-4

MR 2.3 Use a variety of methods, such as words, numbers, symbols, charts, graphs, tables, diagrams, and models, to explain mathematical reasoning. Also **MR 2.6, MG 2.0**

Problem Solving

Use Objects

Hands-On
square tiles

A pentomino is an arrangement of 5 identical squares in a plane. The squares must be attached to one another edge to edge.

This is a pentomino.

This is not a pentomino.

Using 5 identical square tiles, how can you build 3 more pentominoes that have 3 squares in a row?

Guided Practice*

Do you know HOW?

1. Is the following a pentomino? Explain.

2. Are these two pentominoes the same or different? Explain.

Do you UNDERSTAND?

3. In the example above, how many more pentominoes can you find with 3 in a row?

4. **Write a Problem** Write a real-world problem that can be solved by using objects.

Independent Practice

In **5** and **6**, tell whether the pentominoes in each pair are related by a reflection or a rotation.

5.

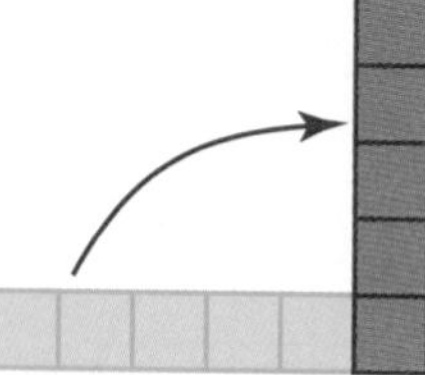

6.

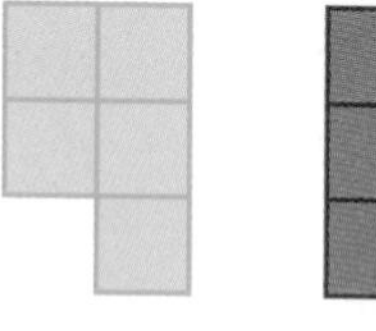

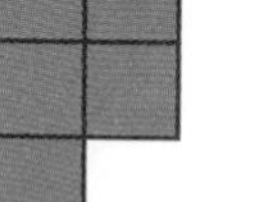

In **7** and **8**, use objects to help you solve the problem.

7. How many pentominoes can you build with 5 in a row?

8. How many pentominoes can you build with 4 in a row?

Stuck? Try this....

- What do I know?
- What am I asked to find?
- What diagram can I use to help understand the problem?
- Can I use addition, subtraction, multiplication, or division?
- Is all of my work correct?
- Did I answer the right question?
- Is my answer reasonable?

*For another example, Set D on page 467.

Read and Understand

What am I asked to find?

Three more unique pentominoes that have 3 squares in a row

Two pentominoes are the same if they can be matched together by rotating or reflecting.

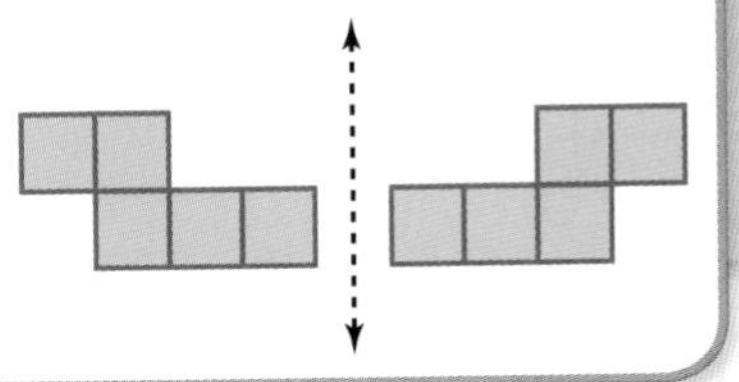

Plan and Solve

I can use objects to build 3 more pentominoes with 3 in a row.

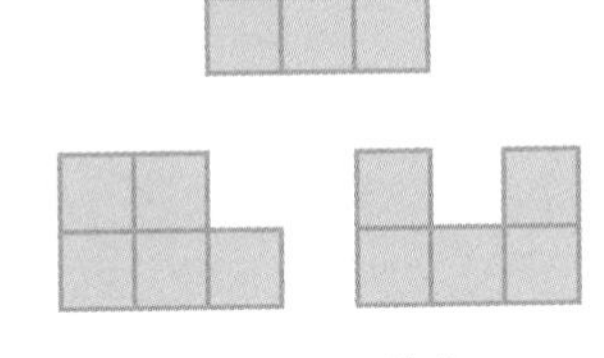

Here are 3 possible solutions.

Look Back and Check

- All are attached edge to edge.
- All can be rotated and reflected. None are repeated.

The 3 pentominoes I've made are all unique.

9. Suppose each square in a pentomino is a table that seats one person on a side. Find a table arrangement (a pentomino) that can seat 12 people.

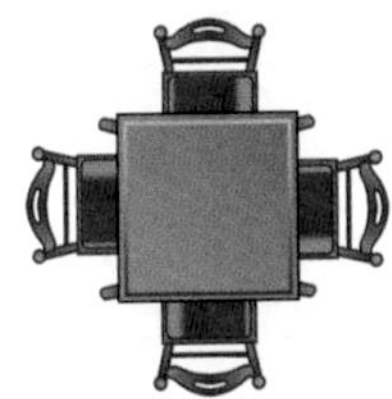

10. The figure below can be folded to form a box. After it is folded, which face will be parallel to Face *ABDC*?

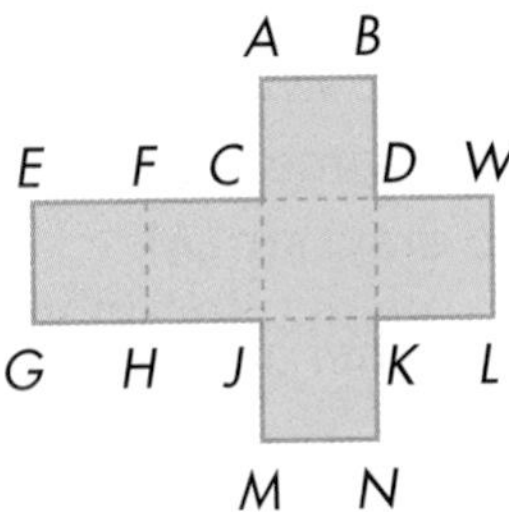

11. Maureen is buying a game that is priced at \$15. She has a coupon worth \$2.50 off the regular price. After Maureen gives the clerk a \$20 bill, how much change does she receive?

12. James and Kurt were paid \$176 for landscaping a yard. James worked 9 hours and Kurt worked 13 hours. How much is Kurt's fair share of the earnings? James's share?

13. Use objects to build pentominoes with 2 squares in a row. How many of these kinds of pentominoes can be built?

14. Make an organized list. How many different combinations of coins can make \$0.42 if one of the coins is a quarter? One possible combination: 1 quarter, 17 pennies.

15. At the concert, Mischa, Jordan, and Elijah are sitting together in a row. Make a list of the possible orders the three could be sitting.

16. **Estimation** A great white shark can weigh 4,400 lbs. A dolphin can weigh 440 lbs. About how many times as heavy is the shark as the dolphin?

DIGITAL Animated Glossary, eTools
www.pearsonsuccessnet.com

Test Prep

1. Teresa is constructing $\angle C$ congruent to $\angle A$ for her drafting class. What is the next step that Teresa should take to complete the construction? (20-1)

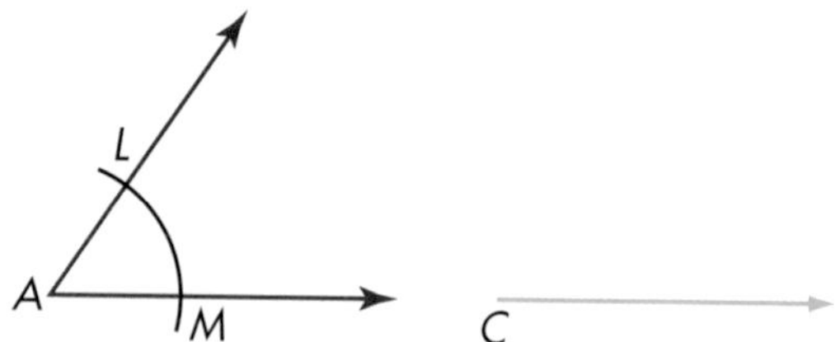

A Measure the opening of arc *LM* with a compass.

B Measure the opening of arc *LM* with a protractor.

C Draw an arc with center at point *C* using the same compass setting used to draw arc *LM*.

D Draw another arc that intersects arc *LM*.

2. Mrs. Bradley is an architect who needs to construct $\overline{ST}$ congruent to $\overline{LM}$. She has drawn a ray with endpoint *S* as shown. What is the next step she should take? (20-2)

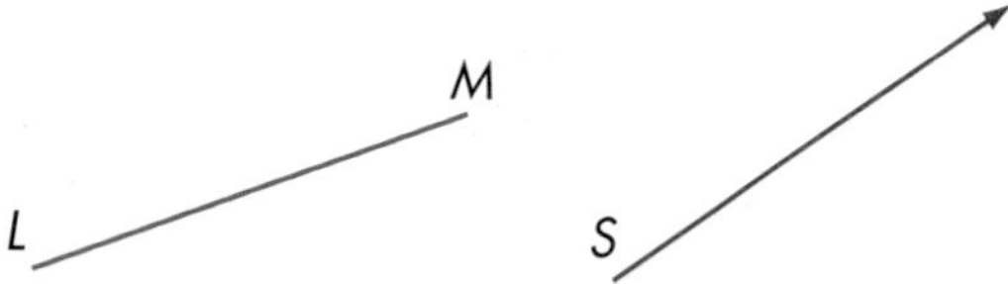

A Draw an arc above $\overline{LM}$.

B Draw an arc above and below $\overline{LM}$.

C Draw an arc on $\overline{LM}$.

D With point *L* as the center, open the compass so it lines up with point *M*.

3. What is the next step in constructing a line parallel to $\overleftrightarrow{AB}$? (20-2)

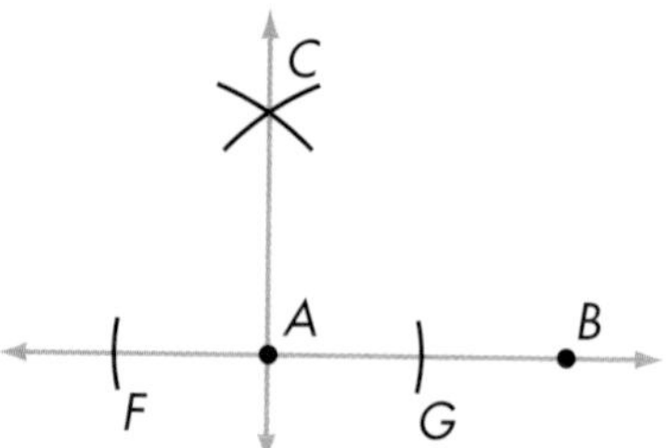

A Draw segment *BC*.

B Construct a line perpendicular to line *AC*.

C Construct a line segment congruent to line segment *AB*.

D Draw a line through point *G*.

4. Angelo is constructing *LMN* so that it is congruent to *ABC*. He has constructed $\angle M$ congruent to $\angle B$ and $\overline{ML}$ congruent to segment $\overline{BA}$.
What is the next step? (20-3)

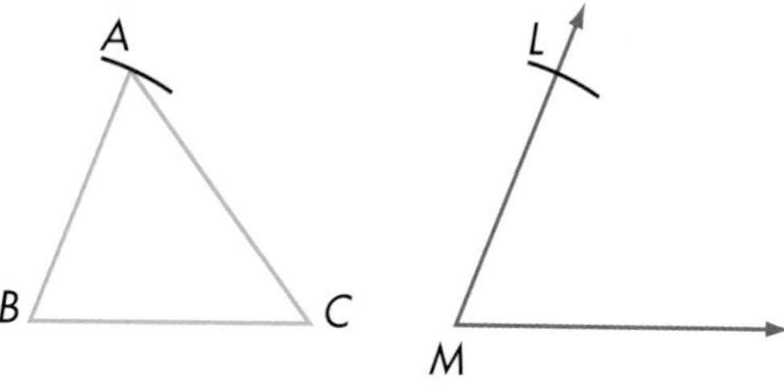

A Measure the length of $\overline{BA}$ with his compass.

B Measure the length of $\overline{BA}$ with his protractor.

C Construct $\overline{MN}$ congruent to $\overline{BC}$.

D Connect point *L* with $\overrightarrow{MN}$.

Test Prep

5. What is missing from the construction of a line perpendicular to $\overleftrightarrow{DE}$? (20-2)

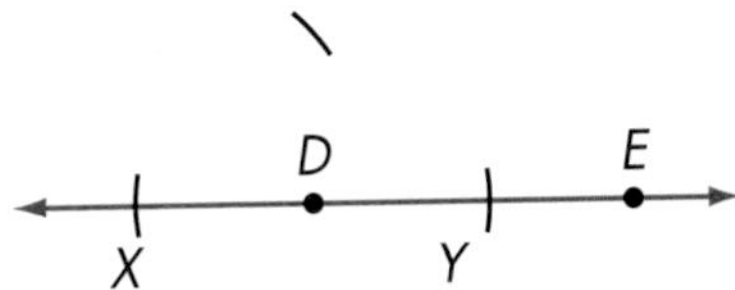

A Arc above $\overleftrightarrow{DE}$ with center at point *E*.

B Arc above $\overleftrightarrow{DE}$ with center at point *D*.

C Arc above $\overleftrightarrow{DE}$ with center at point *Y*.

D A line parallel to $\overleftrightarrow{DE}$.

6. The first step in constructing a rectangle *ABCD* is to draw line *AB*. Which of the following choices could be the next step? (20-3)

A Construct two lines that are parallel.

B Construct a line segment that is congruent to segment *AB*.

C Construct two angles that are congruent.

D Construct a line perpendicular to $\overleftrightarrow{AB}$ at point *A*.

7. Suppose each of the 6 squares in a hexamino represents a table which can seat one person on a side. Which arrangement of 6 tables can seat exactly 12 people? (20-4)

A

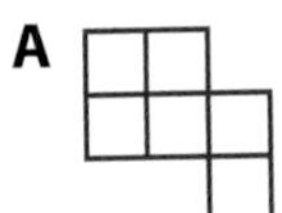

B

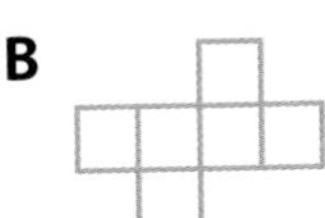

C

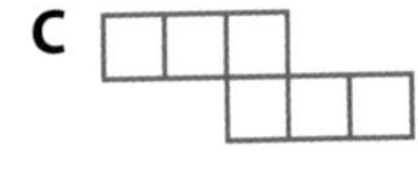

D

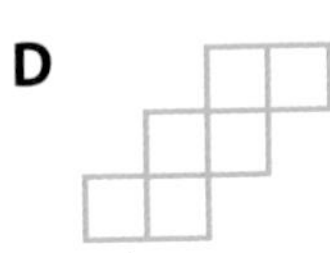

8. What two tools are used to construct geometric figures? (20-1)

A ruler and straightedge

B straightedge and compass

C ruler and protractor

D compass and protractor

9. Aidan is a graphic designer and needs to construct $\angle S$ congruent to $\angle T$ for one of his projects. What is the first step in the construction? (20-1)

A Draw a ray with endpoint *S*.

B Draw a ray with endpoint *T*.

C Draw an arc with endpoint *S*.

D Draw an arc with endpoint *T*.

Set A, pages 452–453

Construct an angle congruent to angle *A*.

Draw a ray with endpoint *E*. With point *A* as center, use your compass to draw an arc that intersects both sides of angle *A*. Label the points of intersection *R* and *S*. With the same compass setting, use point *E* as center and draw an arc that intersects the ray at point *D*.

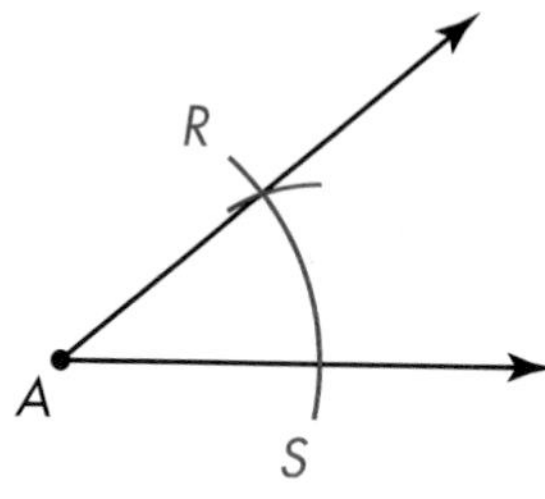

Open the compass to length *RS*. Then, with point *D* as center, draw an intersecting arc. Label the intersection *F*. Use a straightedge to draw ray *EF*.

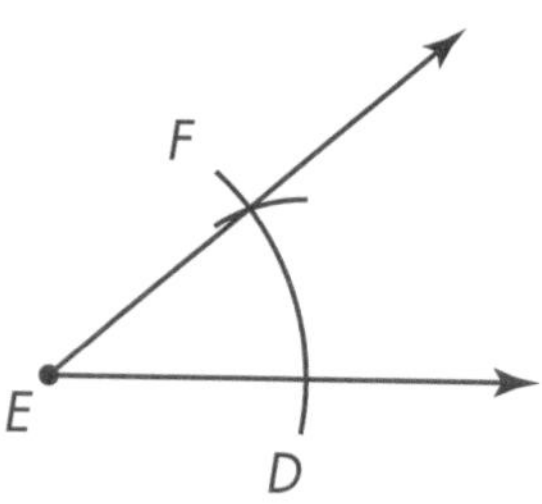

Angle *E* is congruent to angle *A*.

Remember that a construction uses only a compass and a straightedge.

Construct an angle congruent to the given angle.

1. 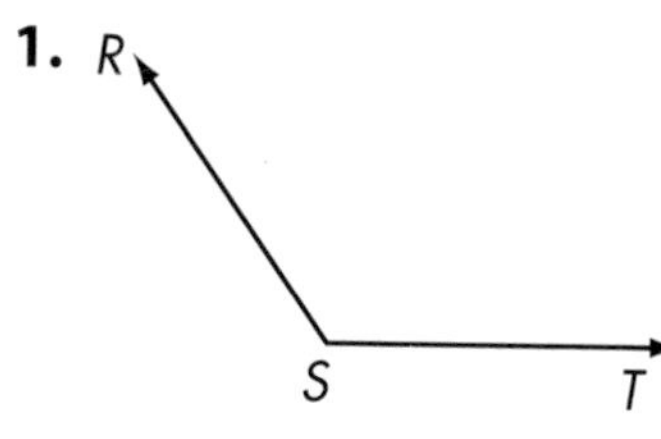

2. 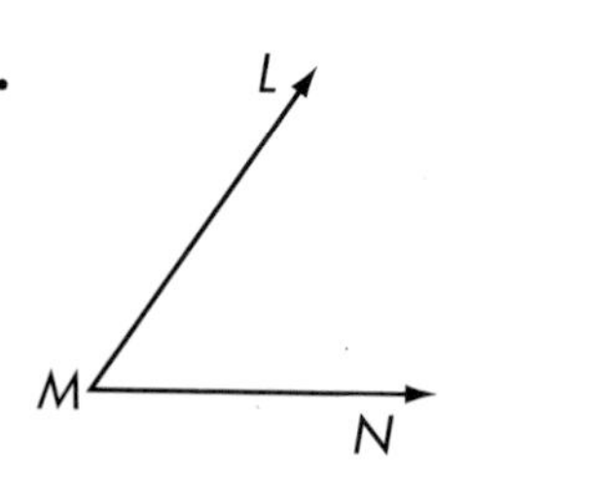

Set B, pages 454-456

Construct a line perpendicular to another line.

Draw line *AB*.

With *A* as center, draw two arcs that intersect line *AB*. Label the points of intersection *D* and *E*.

Open the compass wider.

Using *D* and *E* as centers, draw arcs that intersect. Label the intersection *C*.

Draw Line *CA*.

Line *CA* is perpendicular to line *AB*.

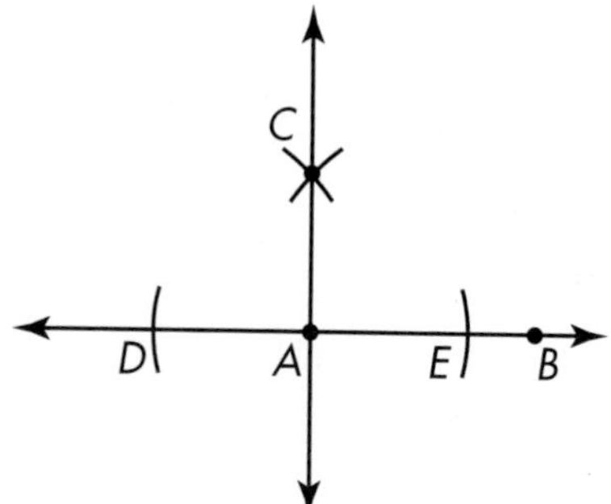

Remember to keep the compass open to the same setting when drawing the arcs with *D* and *E* as the centers.

1. Construct a line perpendicular to another line.

2. For the construction started below, what is the next step to construct a line perpendicular to line *XY*?

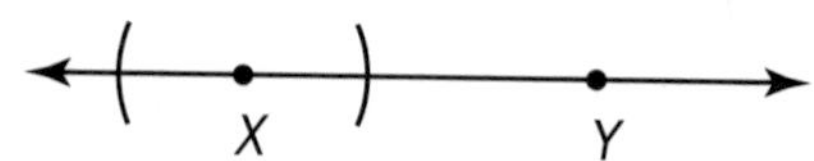

Set C, pages 458–460

Construct a triangle congruent to triangle *DEF*.

Draw a ray with endpoint *G*.

Construct angle *G*. Congruent to angle *D*.

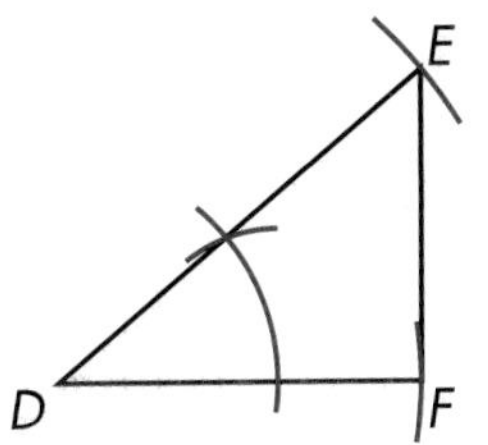

Construct segments *GK* and *GL* on the sides of angle *G* so that they are congruent to segments *DE* and *DF*.

Draw segment *KL*.

Triangle *GKL* is congruent to triangle *DEF*.

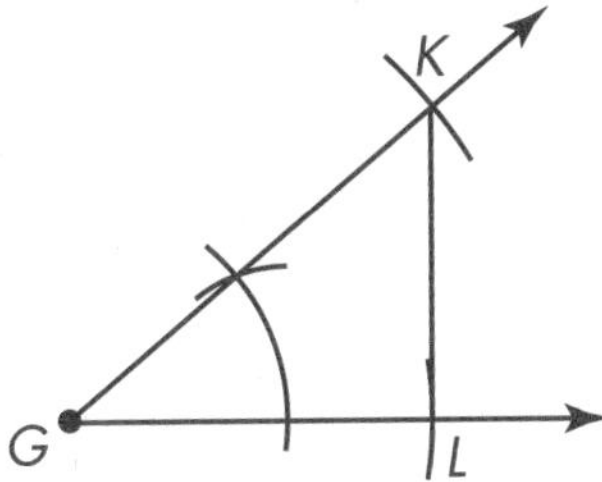

Construct a rectangle *ABCD*.

Draw line *AB*.

Construct line *DA* perpendicular to line *AB* at *A*.

Construct line *DC* perpendicular to line *DA* at *D*.

Construct line *CB* perpendicular to line *AB* at *B*.

Lines *DC* and *CB* intersect at *C*.

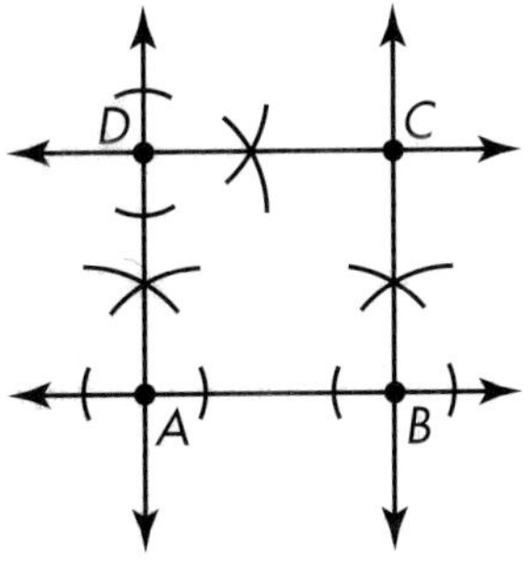

Remember to use the compass to measure the length of the original line segments by placing the point on one endpoint and the slider on the other endpoint.

1. Construct a triangle congruent to triangle *XYZ*.

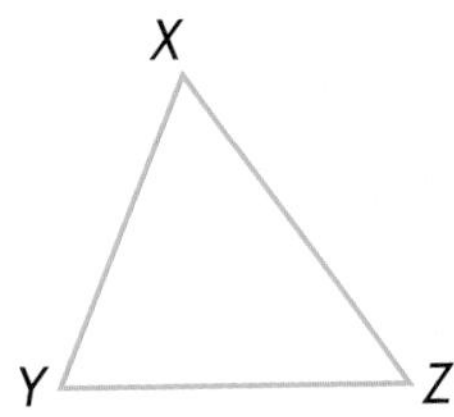

2. Construct a rectangle *KLMN*.

Set D, pages 462–463

When you use objects to solve problems, follow these steps.

Step 1 Choose objects that can best model what is described in the problem.

Step 2 Use the objects to make a model of what you know.

Step 3 Use the objects to act out the action in the problem. Look for patterns.

Step 4 Find the answer in your model.

Remember to state clearly at the beginning what your objects represent in the problem.

1. How many total bricks are needed if the pattern extends to 4 bricks in the middle row?

ssary

acute angle An angle that measures less than 90°.

acute triangle A triangle in which all three angles are acute angles.

Addition Property of Equality The same number can be added to both sides of an equation and the sides remain equal.

algebraic expression A mathematical phrase involving a variable or variables, numbers, and operations.
Example: $x - 3$

angle Two rays that have the same endpoint.

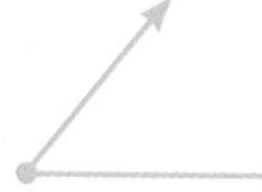

area The number of square units needed to cover a surface or figure.

array An arrangement of objects in rows and columns so that each row has the same number of objects and each column has the same number of objects.

Associative Property of Addition The grouping of addends can be changed and the sum remains the same.
Example: $1 + (3 + 5) = (1 + 3) + 5$

Associative Property of Multiplication The grouping of factors can be changed and the product remains the same.
Example: $2 \times (4 \times 10) = (2 \times 4) \times 10$

average The number found by adding all the data and dividing by the number of data. Also, called the *mean.*

axis (plural: axes) Either of two lines drawn perpendicular to each other in a graph.

bar graph A graph that uses bars (rectangles) to show and compare data that tells how many or how much.

base (in arithmetic) The number that is multiplied by itself when raised to a power.
Example: In 5^3, 5 is the base.

base of a polygon The side of a polygon to which the height is perpendicular.

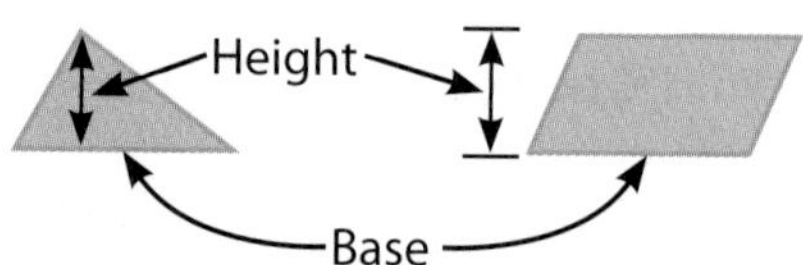

base of a solid The face of a solid that is used to name the solid.

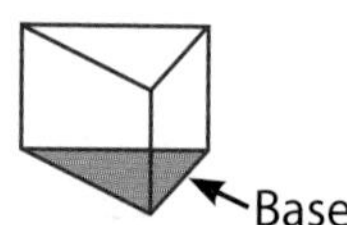

benchmark fractions Fractions such as $\frac{1}{4}, \frac{1}{3}, \frac{1}{2}, \frac{2}{3}$ and $\frac{3}{4}$ used for estimates of actual fractional amounts.

capacity The volume of a container measured in liquid units.

center The point from which all points in a circle are equally distant.

centimeter (cm) A metric unit of length. 100 centimeters equal 1 meter.

certain (event) An event that will always happen.

circle graph A graph in the shape of a circle that shows how all (100%) of a set of data has been divided into parts.

common denominator A number that is the denominator of two or more fractions.

common factor A number that is a factor of two or more given numbers.
Example: 1, 2, and 4 are common factors of 4 and 8.

common multiple A number that is a multiple of two or more numbers.

Commutative Property of Addition The order of addends can be changed and the sum remains the same.
Example: $3 + 7 = 7 + 3$

Commutative Property of Multiplication The order of factors can be changed and the product remains the same.
Example: $3 \times 5 = 5 \times 3$

compatible numbers Numbers that are easy to compute with mentally.

compensation Adjusting one number of an operation to make computations easier and balancing the adjustment by changing the other number.

composite number A whole number greater than one that has more than two factors.

cone A solid figure with one circular base; the points on the circle are joined to one point outside the base.

congruent figures Figures that have the same size and shape.

construction The drawing or copying of a figure using only a compass and a straightedge.

coordinate grid A grid that makes it easy to locate points in a plane using an ordered pair of numbers.

coordinate plane A coordinate grid that extends to include both positive and negative numbers.

coordinates The two numbers in an ordered pair.

cube A solid figure with six flat surfaces called faces. All the faces are squares.

cubed A name for a number to the third power.

cubic unit The volume of a cube 1 unit on each edge.

cup (c) A customary unit of capacity. 1 cup equals 8 fluid ounces.

cylinder A solid figure with two circular bases that are congruent and parallel.

data Collected information.

degree (°) A unit of measure for angles and temperature.

degree Celsius (°C) A unit of measure for measuring temperature in the metric system.

degree Fahrenheit (°F) A unit of measure for measuring temperature in the customary system.

denominator The number below the fraction bar in a fraction.

diameter Any line segment through the center of a circle and that connects two points on the circle.

difference The number that results from subtracting one number from another.

digits The symbols used to write numbers: 0, 1, 2, 3, 4, 5, 6, 7, 8, 9.

Distributive Property Multiplying a sum (or difference) by a number is the same as multiplying each number in the sum (or difference) by that number and adding (or subtracting) the products.
Examples: $3 \times (10 + 4) = (3 \times 10) + (3 \times 4)$
$3 \times (10 - 4) = (3 \times 10) - (3 \times 4)$

dividend The number to be divided.

divisibility rules Rules that are used to find if a number is divisible by numbers such as 2, 3, 4, 5, 6, 9, or 10.

divisible A whole number is divisible by another number when the quotient is a whole number and the remainder is zero.

Division Property of Equality Both sides of an equation can be divided by the same nonzero number and the sides remain equal.

divisor The number used to divide another number.

edge A line segment where two faces meet in a solid figure.

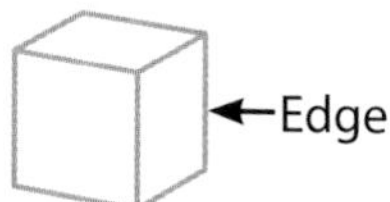

elapsed time The difference between two times.

equally likely (outcomes) Having the same chance of occurring.

equal ratios Ratios that show the same comparison.

equation A number sentence that uses an equal sign to show that two expressions have the same value.
Examples: $9 + 3 = 12$, $x - 5 = 10$

equilateral triangle A triangle in which all three sides are the same length.

equivalent decimals Decimals which name the same amount.
Example: $0.7 = 0.70$

equivalent fractions Fractions that name the same part of a whole region, length, or set.
Example: $\frac{1}{3} = \frac{2}{6}$

estimate To give an approximate value rather than an exact answer.

event A collection of one or more outcomes.

expanded form A way to write a number that shows the place value of each digit.
Example: 3,562 can be written as
3,000 + 500 + 60 + 2

expanded form (numbers with exponents) A way of writing a number involving exponents that shows the base as a factor.

exponent A number that tells how many times the base is used as a factor.
Example: $10^3 = 10 \times 10 \times 10$
The exponent is 3 and the base is 10.

exponential form A way to write a number using a base and an exponent.

face A flat surface of a polyhedron.

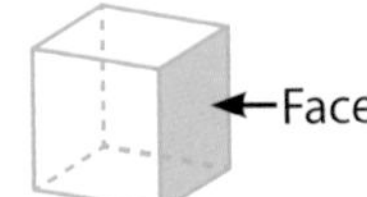

factor pair A pair of whole numbers whose product equals a given whole number.

factors Numbers that are multiplied to get a product.

factor tree A diagram that shows the prime factorization of a composite number.

fluid ounce (fl oz) A customary unit of capacity equal to 2 tablespoons.

formula A rule that is stated with symbols.

fraction A symbol, such as $\frac{2}{3}$, $\frac{5}{1}$, or $\frac{8}{5}$, used to name a part of a whole that is divided into equal parts. A fraction can name a part of a region, a part of a set, a location on a number line, or a division of whole numbers.

frequency table A table used to show the number of times something occurs.

front-end estimation A method of estimating by changing numbers to the place-value of their front digit and then finding the sum or difference.

gallon (gal) A unit for measuring capacity in the customary system. 1 gallon equals 4 quarts.

generalization A general statement.
Example: A generalization about rectangles applies to all rectangles.

gram (g) A metric unit of mass equal to 1,000 milligrams.

greatest common factor (GCF) The greatest number that is a factor of two or more given numbers.
Example: The GCF of 6 and 15 is 3.

height The length of a segment from one vertex of a polygon perpendicular to the base.

hexagon A polygon with six sides.

histogram A bar graph that groups data into equal intervals shown on a horizontal axis. There is no space between the bars.

hundredth One part of 100 equal parts of a whole.

Identity Properties The properties that state the sum of any number and 0 is that number, and the product of any number and 1 is that number.

impossible (event) An event that can never happen.

improper fraction A fraction whose numerator is greater than or equal to its denominator.

input/output table A table of values which shows one output value for each input value.

integers The whole numbers and their opposites; 0 is its own opposite.

intersecting lines Lines that pass through the same point.

interval (on a graph) The difference between adjoining numbers on an axis of a graph.

inverse operations Operations that undo each other.

isosceles triangle A triangle with two sides of the same length.

kilogram (kg) A metric unit of mass equal to 1,000 grams.

kilometer (km) A metric unit of length equal to 1,000 meters.

least common denominator (LCD) The least common multiple of the denominators of two or more fractions.

least common multiple (LCM) The least number, other than zero, that is a multiple of each of two or more numbers.

line A straight path of points that goes on forever in two directions.

linear equation An equation whose graph is a straight line.

line graph A graph that connects points to show how data changes over time.

line of symmetry The fold line in a symmetric figure.

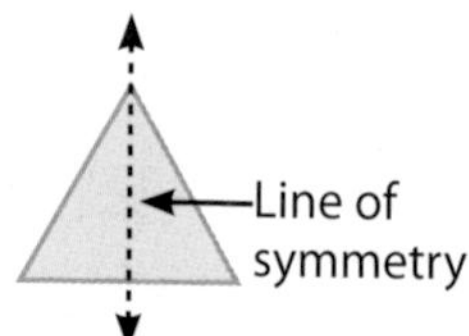

line plot A display of responses along a number line with x's recorded above the response to indicate the number of times the response occurred.

line segment Part of a line having two endpoints.

liter (L) A metric unit of capacity equal to 1,000 milliliters.

mass The measure of the quantity of matter in an object.

mean The number found by adding all the data and dividing by the number of data. Often called the average.

median The middle data value in an ordered set of data.

meter (m) The basic unit of length in the metric system.

milligram (mg) A metric unit of mass. 1,000 milligrams equal 1 gram.

milliliter (mL) A metric unit of capacity equal to 0.001 liter.

millimeter (mm) A metric unit of length. 1,000 millimeters equal 1 meter.

mixed number A number written with a whole number and a fraction.
Example: $2\frac{3}{4}$

mode The data value that occurs most often in a set of data.

multiple The product of a given whole number and any other whole number.

multiple of 10 A number that has 10 as a factor.

Multiplication Property of Equality Both sides of an equation can be multiplied by the same nonzero number and the sides remain equal.

multiplicative inverse Another name for reciprocal.

net A plane figure which, when folded, gives a solid figure.

numerator The number above the fraction bar in a fraction.

obtuse angle An angle that measures between 90° and 180°.

obtuse triangle A triangle in which one angle is an obtuse angle.

octagon A polygon with eight sides.

order of operations The order in which operations are done in calculations. Operations inside parentheses are done first. Then exponents are calculated. Then multiplication and division are done in order from left to right, and finally addition and subtraction are done in order from left to right.

ordered pair A pair of numbers used to locate a point on a coordinate grid.

origin The point at which the *x*-axis and *y*-axis of the coordinate plane intersect. The origin is represented by the ordered pair (0, 0).

ounce (oz) A customary unit of weight. 16 ounces equal 1 pound.

outcome A result in an experiment.

overestimate The result of using numbers greater than the actual numbers to estimate a sum or product. The estimate is greater than the actual answer.

parallel lines In a plane, lines that never cross and stay the same distance apart.

parallelogram A quadrilateral with both pairs of opposite sides parallel and equal in length.

partial products Products found by breaking one of two factors into ones, tens, hundreds, and so on, and then multiplying each of these by the other factor.

pentagon A polygon with five sides.

pentomino An arrangement of 5 identical squares in a plane. The squares must be attached to one another edge to edge.
Example:

percent A ratio in which the first term is compared to 100.

perimeter The distance around the outside of any polygon.

period A group of 3 digits in a number. Periods are separated by a comma and start from the right of a number.

perpendicular lines Two lines that intersect to form right angles.

picture graph A graph that uses pictures or symbols to represent data. Each picture represents a certain amount in the data.

pint (pt) A customary unit of capacity equal to 2 cups.

place value The position of a digit in a number that is used to determine the value of the digit.
Example: In 5,318, the 3 is in the hundreds place. So, the 3 has a value of 300.

plane An endless flat surface.

point An exact location in space.

polygon A closed plane figure made up of line segments.

positive integers Integers greater than zero.

pound (lb) A customary unit of weight equal to 16 ounces.

prime factorization Writing a number as a product of all of its prime factors.

prime number A whole number greater than 1 that has exactly two factors, itself and 1.

prism A solid figure with two congruent parallel bases and faces that are parallelograms.

probability (of an event) The ratio of the number of favorable outcomes to the total number of possible outcomes. The ratio describes the chance that the event will occur.

product The number that is the result of multiplying two or more factors.

protractor An instrument used to measure and draw angles.

pyramid A solid figure with a base that is a polygon and whose faces are triangles with a common vertex.

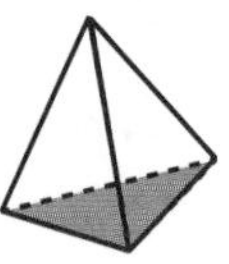

quadrilateral A polygon with four sides.

quart (qt) A customary unit of capacity equal to 2 pints.

quotient The answer to a division problem.

range The difference between the greatest value and the least value in a data set.

ratio A relationship where for every *x* units of one quantity there are *y* units of another quantity.

ray Part of a line that has one endpoint and extends forever in only one direction.

reciprocal A given number is a reciprocal of another number if the product of the numbers is one.
Example: The numbers $\frac{1}{8}$ and $\frac{8}{1}$ are reciprocals because $\frac{1}{8} \times \frac{8}{1} = 1$.

rectangle A parallelogram with four right angles.

regular polygon A polygon that has sides of equal length and angles of equal measure.

remainder The number less than the divisor that remains after the division is complete.

rhombus A parallelogram with all sides the same length.

right angle An angle that measures 90°.

right triangle A triangle in which one angle is a right angle.

rounding A process of replacing a number with the nearest multiple of 10, 100, 1,000, and so on.

sample A representative part of a larger group.

sample space The set of all possible outcomes.

scale (in a bar graph) A series of numbers at equal distances along an axis on a graph.

scalene triangle A triangle in which no sides have the same length.

sides (of an angle) The two rays that form an angle.

similar figures Figures that have the same shape. They may or may not have the same size.

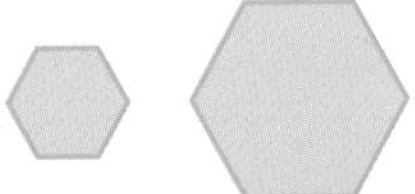

Similar hexagons

simplest form A fraction in which the greatest common factor of the numerator and denominator is one.

solid figure (also: solid) A figure that has three dimensions and volume.

solution The value of a variable that makes an equation true.

sphere A solid figure with all points the same distance from the center point.

square A rectangle with all sides the same length.

squared A name for a number to the second power.

standard form The most common way of writing numbers. It uses digits and place value.
Example: 3,458

standard form (numbers with exponents) The common way of writing numbers without any exponents or operations.

straight angle An angle that measures 180°.

Subtraction Property of Equality The same number can be subtracted from both sides of an equation and the sides remain equal.

sum The number that is the result of adding two or more addends.

surface area (SA) The sum of the areas of all faces of a polyhedron.

survey A question or questions used to gather information.

symmetric figure A figure that can be folded into two congruent parts that fit on top of each other.

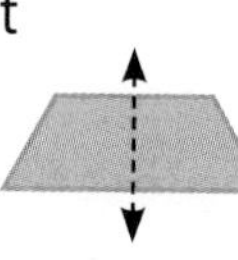

table of values A table used to show how one quantity is related to another.

tablespoon (tbsp) A customary unit of capacity equal to 3 teaspoons.

teaspoon (tsp) A customary unit of capacity equal to $\frac{1}{3}$ tablespoon.

tenth One out of ten equal parts of a whole.

thousandth One out of 1,000 equal parts of a whole.

ton (T) A customary unit of weight equal to 2,000 pounds.

trapezoid A quadrilateral that has exactly one pair of parallel sides.

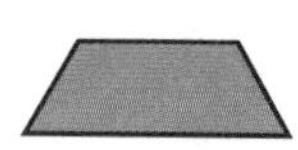

tree diagram A diagram used to organize outcomes of an experiment.

trend The general direction in a data set.

triangle A polygon with three sides.

underestimate The result of using numbers less than the actual numbers to estimate a sum or product. The estimate is less than the actual answer.

value (of a digit) The number a digit represents, which is determined by the position of the digit. See also *place value.*

variable A letter, such as *n*, or a symbol that represents an unknown amount that can vary, or change in an expression or an equation.

vertex (plural: vertices) **a.** The common endpoint of the two rays in an angle. **b.** The point at which three or more edges meet in a solid figure. **c.** The point of a cone.

volume The number of cubic units needed to fill a solid figure.

weight A measure of how light or how heavy something is.

whole numbers The numbers 0, 1, 2, 3, 4, and so on.

word form A way of expressing numbers by using words.

***x*-axis** A horizontal line that includes both positive and negative numbers. It is used to locate points in a coordinate plane.

***x*-coordinate** The first number in an ordered pair. It names the distance to the right or left from the origin along the *x*-axis.

***y*-axis** A vertical line that includes both positive and negative numbers. It is used to locate points in a coordinate plane.

***y*-coordinate** The second number in an ordered pair. It names the distance up or down from the origin along the *y*-axis.

Zero Property of Multiplication The product of any number and 0 is 0.
Example: $8 \times 0 = 0$

Scott Foresman • Addison Wesley

enVisionMATH™ California

Cover

Luciana Navarro Powell

Illustrations

Neil Stewart 4, 6, 52, 118, 174, 223, 262, 300, 305, 319-320, 374, 394; Joe LeMonnier 32, 95, 224, 342, 345; Dick Gage 41, 60, 113, 296, 298-300, 307, 310, 312, 332, 348, 420, 432; Leslie Kell 64, 78, 128, 138, 215-216, 233, 239, 248, 254, 259, 285, 354, 356, 366, 376

Photographs

Every effort has been made to secure permission and provide appropriate credit for photographic material. The publisher deeply regrets any omission and pledges to correct errors called to its attention in subsequent editions.

Unless otherwise acknowledged, all photographs are the property of Scott Foresman, a division of Pearson Education.

Photo locators denoted as follows: Top (T), Center (C), Bottom (B), Left (L), Right (R), Background (Bkgd).

Front Matter: xvi ©Bob Mitchell/Corbis

2 (B) ©Eddie Gerald/Alamy Images, (TL) ©George D. Lepp/Corbis, (TC) Getty Images; 3 (TL) NASA, (BL) ©Scott T. Smith/Corbis, (TL) Getty Images; 5 ©George D. Lepp/Corbis; 8 NASA; 12 (TR) ©Barbara Strnadova/Photo Researchers, Inc., (BR) ©Raymond Mendez/ Animals Animals/Earth Scenes, (T) ©Holt Studios International Ltd/Alamy Images; 22 (CR) ©Janice Wolf/Rocky Ridge Refuge, (B) ©Felix Stenson/Alamy Images; 23 (BL) ©Joe Caveretta/AP Images, (TL) Getty Images; 40 ©Royalty-Free/Corbis; 50 (B) ©J.D. Griggs/Corbis, (TL) ©Alan G. Nelson/ Animals Animals/Earth Scenes; 51 (B) ©Oliver Eltinger/Corbis, (TL) ©Marianna Day Massey/ Corbis; 55 ©Douglas Peebles/Corbis; 76 (B) David Peart/©DK Images, (TR) ©Machteld Baljet & Marcel Hoevenaar/Alamy Images, (TL) ©Joel Sartore/Getty Images; 77 ©Dennis di Cicco/Corbis; 98 (B) ©IT Stock Free/Jupiter Images, (C) ©DANI/JESKE/Animals Animals/ Earth Scenes; 110 (TL) ©Cosmo Condina/ Getty Images, (B) ©VEER/Gib Martinez/Getty Images; 111 (BL) ©AP Images, (TL) ©Michael Patrick O'Neill/Alamy Images; 134 (B) Jupiter Images, (TL) ©imagebroker/Alamy; 135 (TL) Acc. #I-20828/Phoebe A. Hearst Museum of Anthropology, (BL) Getty Images; 143 ©Photos Select/Index Open; 144 ©Merlin D. Tuttle/Bat Conservation International; 146 ©photolibrary/Index Open; 152 (B, CL) Getty Images, (TR) ©Bill Ross/Corbis; 153 (TL) David Sanger/Alamy Images, (BL) ©Royalty-Free/Corbis; 172 (T) ©Dallas and John Heaton/Corbis, (B) ©Mitchell Funk/Getty Images; 173 (TR) ©Frank Greenaway/Dorling Kindersley/Getty Images, (BL) Courtesy of the Dresden Village Association, (TL) ©Perennou Nuridsany/Photo Researchers, Inc.; 174 ©Peter Pearson/Getty Images; 179 ©David R. Frazier Photolibrary, Inc./Alamy Images; 180 Jupiter Images; 181 (C, CR) Jupiter Images, (BR) Ingram Publishing, (CL) ©Dallas and John Heaton/Corbis; 183 ©Mitchell Funk/ Getty Images; 192 (B) ©Joe McDonald/Corbis, (CL) ©2007 Faber-Castell Aktiengesellschaft; 193 (TL) Courtesy of the Rick Hansen Man in Motion Foundation, (BL) ©Kristin Siebeneicher/AP Images; 212 (CL) ©Prof. Yves Roisin/Museum des Sciences Naturelles, Bruxelles, Belgium, (B) ©Johner Images/Getty Images; 213 (TL) ©Bruce Coleman Inc./Alamy Images, (BL) Courtesy of the American Sport Art Museum & Archives, Division of United States Sports Academy, Daphne, AL; 232 (C) ©Barbara Strnadova, (BL) Colin Keates/©DK Images; 246 (C) ©Martin Harvey/Corbis, (BL) ©Dr. Merlin D. Tuttle/Photo Researchers, Inc.; 247 (BL) ©Lindsay Hebberd/Corbis, (TL) ©Austin Hargrave; 255 ©Lindsay Hebberd/Corbis; 260 ©Image Source/Jupiter Images; 265 (CR) ©photolibrary/Index Open, (BR) ©AbleStock/Index Open, (TR, C) Getty Images; 268 (CL) ©DK Images, (B) ©Clay Jackson/AP Images; 269 (TL) ©DAJ/Getty Images, (C) ©Rubberball/Jupiter Images; 294 (B) Steve Perlstein/Courtesy of Mohawk Resources, Ltd., (TL) ©Joseph Sohm/ChromoSohm Inc/Corbis; 295 (TL) ©Mandel Ngan/AFP/Getty Images, (B) Jupiter Images; 306 ©Christie's Images/Corbis; 307 ©Christie's Images/Corbis; 309 Getty Images; 316 (B) ©Michele Falzone/Alamy Images, (T) ©Cosmo Condina/Alamy Images; 317 ©Randy Wilder/Monterey Bay Aquarium; 320 ©Michele Falzone/Alamy Images; 340 (B) ©Harald Sund/Getty Images, (TL) ©US Geological Survey/Photo Researchers, Inc., (B) Getty Images; 341 ©John T. Fowler/Alamy Images; 362 (TL) ©Richard Packwood/Oxford Scientific/Jupiter Images, (B) ©Martin Harvey/ Alamy Images; 363 (TL) ©Rich Pedroncelli/AP Images, (BL) ©Michael Lewis/Getty Images; 384 ©John Scheiber/Corbis; 385 (TL) Getty Images, (BL) ©Baron Wolman/Getty Images; 400 (C) Stockdisc, (BL) ©MAPS/Corbis; 401 Getty Images; 418 (L) ©Louie Psihoyos/ Corbis, (R) Corbis; 419 (TL) ©Rab Harling/ Alamy Images, (BL) ©David Pu'u/Corbis; 450 (B) Jupiter Images, (CL) ©Douglas Slone/ Aerial Photography Services, (TR) ©Royalty-Free/Corbis; 451 ©Westend61/Alamy Images; 453 ©Westend61/Alamy Images; 460 ©Todd Korol/Getty Images

Index

Acute angle, 178, 183

Acute triangle, 183

Act It Out, 128–129

Addition
- Associative Property, 24–25, 197, 341
- Commutative Property, 24–25, 197
- decimals, 38–39
- estimation, 30–31
- evaluating algebraic expression, 114–115
- fractions
  - with like denominators, 248–250
  - with unlike denominators, 254–255
- Identity Property, 197
- integers, 348–350
- mental math, 24–25
- mixed numbers, 258–259
- order of operations, 125
- solving equations of form $y = x + a$, 364–365
- translating words into expressions, 113
- whole numbers, 34–35

Addition Property of Equality, 364–365

Algebra, 8, 137, 141, 145, 155, 158, 161, 200, 250, 257, 261, 274, 307, 309, 320, 323, 332, 345, 350, 389, 393, 404, 437, 443, 456

Algebra Connections
- Changing Words to Expressions, 71
- Completing Number Sentences, 121
- Completing Tables, 159
- Number Patterns, 33
- Which Equation is True?, 441
- Properties and Equations, 197
- Shape Patterns, 321
- Simplifying Numerical Expressions, 89
- Solution Pairs, 379
- What's the Rule?, 217

Algebraic expressions, 173
- changing words to, 71
- distributive property for writing and solving equations, 122
- evaluating addition, 114–115
- evaluating division, 114–115
- order of operations, 124–125
- simplifying, 354–355
- translating words into, 112–113, 118–120
- writing and evaluating with variables, 118–120

Angles
- acute, 178, 183
- congruent, 452–453
- constructing, 452–453
- drawing, 179
- measuring, 179
- obtuse, 178, 183
- right, 178, 183
- straight, 178

Area
- parallelograms, 306–307
- rectangles, 304–305
- squares, 304–305
- surface, 324–325
- triangles, 308–309

Arrays, 194–195

Assessment
- Test Prep, 18–19, 46–47, 72–73, 106–107, 130–131, 148–149, 168–169, 188–189, 208–209, 240–241, 264–265, 290–291, 312–313, 336–337, 358–359, 380–381, 396–397, 414–415, 444–445, 464–465
- Review What You Know!, 3, 23, 51, 77, 111, 135, 153, 173, 193, 213, 247, 269, 295, 317, 341, 363, 385, 401, 419, 451
- Stop and Practice, 17, 37, 45, 63, 85, 99, 117, 167, 177, 201, 229, 275, 303, 333, 351, 373, 405, 457

Associative Property
- Addition, 24–25, 197, 341
- Multiplication, 53, 197

Axes, 401

Axis
- *x*-, 403
- *y*-, 403

Bar graphs, 420–422

Base
- cone, 318
- cylinder, 318
- exponent, 67
- prism, 318
- pyramid, 318

Benchmark fractions, 239

Centimeter, 299

Charts
- place-value, 4–5

Circle graphs, 238, 426–427

Classifying
- angles, 178–179

Common denominator, 247, 269

Common factors, 204–205

Common multiples, 252–253, 269

Commutative Property
- addition, 197
- multiplication, 52, 197

...ring
...cimals, 12–13
...ractions, 224–225
integers, 344–345
mixed numbers, 224–225
whole numbers, 6–7

Compatible numbers
estimation, 31, 54, 96, 140–141

Compensation in estimation, 24–25

Composite numbers, 198–199, 202
writing as product of prime factors, 198

Cones, 318

Congruent angles, 452–453

Congruent triangles, 186–187, 308–309

Connections to earlier lessons, 60, 96, 114, 140, 156, 348, 402

Coordinate grid, 402–403
movement of points, 412–413

Critical Thinking, 53

Cubic unit, 330

Customary units
length, 296–297

Cylinders, 318

Data
finding mean, 432–433
median, mode, and range, 434–435
outcomes, 436–437
reading from line graphs, 406–407
trends, 406–407

Decimal place value, 10–11

Decimals, 341
addition, 38–39
comparing and ordering, 12–13
division
by 10, 100, or 1,000, 154–155
by decimals, 162–163
by whole numbers, 156–157, 160–161
equivalent, 10–11
estimation, 140–141
multiplication, 136–137, 142–143
of whole numbers by, 138–139
on number line, 236–237
place value, 10–11
relation of fractions to, 234–235
relation to percents, fractions and, 390–391
rounding, 28–29
subtraction, 40–41
writing fractions as, 230–231

Denominators, 214–215, 221, 247, 269, 385
common, 247, 269
like
addition of fractions, 248–250
subtraction of fractions, 248–250
unlike
addition of fractions, 254–255
subtraction of fractions, 256–257

Diagrams
drawing, 84, 126, 365
tree, 436–438

Difference, 23. *See also* Subtraction

Digits, 3

Distributive property, 122–123, 197

Divisibility rules in finding factors, 194–195, 199

Division
decimals by
decimals, 162–163
10, 100, or 1,000, 154–155
whole numbers, 156–157, 160–161
estimation, 80–81, 160–161
evaluating algebraic expression, 114–115
fractions, 278–280
fractions to show, 218–219
greater numbers, 100–101
mixed numbers, 286–287
modeling, 82–84
1-digit numbers, 86–88
order of operations, 125
patterns in, 78–79
translating words into expressions, 113
2-digit numbers, 92–93, 96–98
whole numbers by fractions, 276–277

Division Property of Equality, 366–367

Divisors, 153, 295
1-digit, 86–88
2-digit, 92–93, 96–98

Draw a Picture and Make an Organized List, 310–311

Draw a Picture and Write an Equation, 42–43, 102–104, 288–289, 376–378

Edges, 318
pyramids, 318

Endpoints, 174

Equality, 363
Addition Property, 364–365
Division Property, 366–367
Multiplication Property, 366–367
Subtraction Property, 364–365

Equations, 51, 173
addition, 364–365
graphing, 410
patterns and, 370–372, 374–375
solving of form $y = x + a$, 370–372
subtraction, 364–365
writing and solving, 122–123

Equilateral triangles, 182

Equivalent decimals, 10–11

Equivalent fractions, 135, 193, 222–223, 385

Estimation, 88, 123, 257, 277, 345, 375, 456, 463
addition, 30–31
compatible numbers, 54, 96, 140–141
division, 80–81, 160–161
greater numbers, 64–65, 100–101
multiplication, 54–55, 140–141
rounding, 55
subtraction, 30–31

Exponents, 66–67

Expressions. *See* Algebraic expressions; Numerical expressions

Faces, 318–319
prism, 318

Factor pair, 194

Factors, 51, 135, 193, 194–196
common, 204–205
greatest common, 204–205

Factor tree, 202–203, 204

Fibonacci numbers, 33

Formulas
area, 304–305
parallelogram, 307
triangle, 309
defined, 300
perimeter
rectangle, 300
square, 300
volume, 330

Fractions, 341, 385
addition
with like denominators, 248–250
with unlike denominators, 254–255
benchmark, 239
changing to percent, 390
comparing and ordering, 224–225
defined, 214–215
denominator, 214–215, 221, 247
division, 278–279
whole numbers, 276–277
equivalent, 222–223
improper, 220–221
multiplication, 270–271, 272–273
on number line, 218, 236–237
numerator, 214–215, 221, 247
precise measurement, 296
relation to decimals, 234–235
relation to percents, decimals and, 390–391
to show division, 218–219
in simplest form, 226–227
subtraction
with like denominators, 248–250
with unlike denominators, 256–257
writing as decimals, 230–231

Generalizations, 186
making, 186–187
testing, 186–187

Geometry, 65, 126, 143, 257, 259, 261, 274, 287, 347, 350, 357, 367, 372, 375, 387, 404
angles, 452–453
basic concepts, 174–176
lines, 454–455
measuring and classifying angles, 178–179
polygons, 180–181
quadrilaterals, 184–185
triangles, 182–183

Graphing equations, 410

Graphs
bar, 420–422
choosing appropriate, 430–431
circle, 238, 426–427
line, 406–407
picture, 420–422

Greater numbers
division, 100–101
estimation, 64–65, 1
multiplication, 64–6

Greatest Common F
204–205
fractions in simplest form, 226

Hexagons, 181

Histograms, 424–425

Hundredths, 230–231

I

Identity Property
addition, 24, 197
multiplication, 53, 197

Improper fractions, 220–221

Integers, 342–343
addition, 348–350
comparing and ordering, 344–345
number line, 346–347
subtraction, 352–353

Intersecting lines, 174

Inverse operations, 341, 363
addition and subtraction, 34, 364–365
multiplication and division, 159, 366–367

Isosceles triangles, 182

Kilometers, 299

Large numbers
writing, 4–5
expanded form, 5, 11, 66–67
exponential notation, 66–67
standard form, 4, 5, 11, 66–67
word form, 5, 11

Least common denominator, 269

Least common multiples, 252–253, 269

Length
customary units, 296–297
metric units, 298–299

Like denominators
addition of fractions, 248–250
subtraction of fractions, 248–250

Line graphs, 406–407

Line segments, 174

Lines, 175
constructing, 454–455
intersecting, 174
parallel, 174
perpendicular, 174

Look for a Pattern, 14–16, 262–263, 394–395

Make a Table, 394–395

Make an Organized List, 310–311

Make and Test Generalizations, 186–187

Math and Literature, 59

Math and Music, 127

Math and Science, 27, 233, 429, 461

Math and Social Studies, 9, 95, 281, 409

Mean, 432–433

Measurement
customary units
length, 296–297
metric units
length, 298–299

Measuring angles, 178–179

Median, 434–435

Mental math, 24–25

Meter, 299

Metric equivalents, 298

Metric units
length, 298–299

Millimeters, 299

Missing or Extra Information, 282–283

Mixed numbers, 135, 220–221
addition, 258–259
comparing and ordering, 224–225
division, 286–287
multiplication, 284–285
subtraction, 260–261

Mixed Problem Solving, 9, 27, 59, 95, 127, 233, 281, 409, 429, 461

Mode, 434–435

Models/modeling
connecting with symbols, 82–83
division, 82–83
volume, 328–329

Multiples
common, 252–253, 269
least common, 252–253, 269

Multiple-Step Problems, 68–69, 164–165

Multiplication
Associative Property, 53, 197
Commutative Property, 52, 197
decimals, 142–143
decimals by 10, 100, or 1,000, 136–137
Distributive Property, 122–123
estimation, 54–55, 140–141
fractions, 270–271, 272–273
greater numbers, 64–65
Identity Property, 53, 197
mixed numbers, 284–285
by 1-digit numbers, 56–57
order of operations, 125
translating words into expressions, 113
by 2-digit numbers, 60–61
whole numbers, 270–271
whole numbers by decimals, 138–139
zero in product, 144–145
Zero Property, 53, 197

Multiplication Property of Equality, 366–367

Net, 322–323

Notation
exponential, 66–67

Number lines
decimals on, 236–237
fractions on, 236–237
integers, 346–347
to represent fractions, 218

Numbers
comparing and ordering whole, 6–7
composite, 198–199, 202–203
Fibonacci, 33
finding prime factors, 202–203
mixed, 220–221
prime, 198–199
whole, 195
writing large, 4–5

Numerators, 214–215, 221, 247, 269, 385

Numerical expressions
order of operations, 124–125
simplifying, 89

Obtuse angles, 178, 183

Obtuse triangles, 183

Octagons, 181

One-digit numbers
division, 86–88
multiplication, 56–57

Operations, 363. *See also* Addition; Division; Multiplication; Subtraction

Ordered pairs, 401, 402–403

Ordering
decimals, 12–13
fractions, 224–225
integers, 344–345
mixed numbers, 224–225
whole numbers, 6–7

Order of operations, 124–125

Origin, 403

Outcomes, 436–437

Parallel lines, 174

Parallelograms, 184, 318
area, 306–307

Patterns
division, 78–79
equations and, 370–372, 374–375
looking for as problem-solving strategy, 14–15, 27, 33, 137, 262–263, 394–395
shape, 321
showing relationships, 114–115

Pentagons, 181

Pentominoes, 462–463

Percents, 388–389
changing to fraction, 390
finding of whole number, 392–393
relation to fractions, decimals and, 390–391

Perimeter, 300–301
rectangle, 300
square, 300

Period, 3

Perpendicular lines, 174, 451

Picture graphs, 420–422

Place value, 3, 4–5, 153, 295
decimal, 10–11

Place-value charts, 4–5

Planes, 175

Points, 175

Polygons, 180–181
perimeter, 300–301
regular, 180

Prime factorization, 198, 202
finding greatest common factor, 204

Prime factors
finding for number, 202–203
writing composite numbers as product, 198

Prime numbers, 198–199

Prisms, 318
rectangular, 319
triangular, 319
volume, 330–331

Probability, 438–440

Problem Solving
Act It Out, 128–129
Draw a Picture and Make an Organized List, 310–311
Draw a Picture and Write an Equation, 42–43, 102–104, 288–289, 376–378
Look for a Pattern, 14–16, 262–263, 394–395
Make and Test Generalizations, 186–187
Make an Organized List, 310–311, 463
Make a Table, 115, 116, 137, 394–395
Missing or Extra Information, 282–283
Multiple-Step Problems, 68–69, 164–165
Reasonableness, 146–147
Solve a Simpler Problem, 334–335, 442–443
Try, Check, and Revise, 9, 183, 206–207
Use Objects, 334–335, 462–463
Use Reasoning, 128–129, 368–369, 461
Work Backward, 356–357, 412–413
Writing to Explain, 238–239

Products, 51, 135, 193

Property
Associative
addition, 24–25, 341
multiplication, 53
Commutative
addition, 24–25
multiplication, 52
Distributive, 122–123
Identity
multiplication, 53
Identity
addition, 24
Zero
multiplication, 53

Protractor, 179

Pyramids, 318
triangular, 319

Quadrilaterals, 181, 184–185, 317
finding missing angle measure, 184

Quotients, 153, 193, 295
estimation, 80–81
zeros in, 90–91

Range, 434–435

Ratios, 386–387

Rays, 174

Reasonableness, 146–147

Rectangles, 185
area, 304–305
perimeter, 300

Rectangular prism, 319
surface area, 324–325

Regular polygon, 180

Relationships. *See* Patterns

Remainder, 153

Reteaching, 20–21, 48–49, 74–75, 108–109, 132–133, 150–151, 170–171, 190–191, 210–211, 242–245, 266–267, 292–293, 314–315, 338–339, 360–361, 382–383, 398–399, 416–417, 446–449, 466–467

Rhombus, 184, 185

Right angles, 178, 183

Right triangles, 183

Rounding, 51
decimals, 28–29
estimation, 54–55
whole numbers, 28–29

Scalene triangles, 182

Shape patterns, 321

Shapes
relation to solids, 322–323

Simplification
numerical expressions, 89

Solids, 318–319
edges, 318–319
faces, 318–319
relation to shapes, 322–323
vertices, 318–319
views, 326–327

Solution pairs, 379

Solve a Simpler Problem, 334–335, 442–443

Squares, 184, 185, 317
area, 304–305
perimeter, 300

Straight angles, 178

Stop and Practice, 17, 37, 45, 63, 85, 99, 117, 167, 177, 201, 229, 275, 303, 333, 351, 373, 405, 423, 457

Subtraction
across zeros, 34
Associative Property, 24–25
Commutative Property, 24–25
decimals, 40–41
estimation, 30–31
fractions
with like denominators, 248–250
with unlike denominators, 256–257
integers, 352–353
mental math, 24–25
mixed numbers, 260–261
order of operations, 125
solving equations of form $y = x + a$, 364–365
translating words into expressions, 113
whole numbers, 34–35

Subtraction Property of Equality, 364–365

Sum, 23. *See also* Addition

Surface area, 324–325

Symbols
completing number sentences, 121
connecting with models, 82–83

Tables, 217
completing, 159

Tenths, 230–231

Tests. *See* Assessment

Thousandths, 234–235

Trapezoids, 184

Tree diagrams, 436–438

Trends, 406–407

Triangles, 181, 182–183, 317
acute, 183
area, 308–309
congruent, 186–187, 308–309
equilateral, 182
finding missing angle measure, 182
isosceles, 182
obtuse, 183
right, 183
scalene, 182

Triangular prism, 319

Triangular pyramid, 319

Try, Check, and Revise, 206–207

Two-digit numbers
division, 92–93, 96–98
multiplication, 60–61

Unlike denominators
addition of fractions, 254–255
subtraction of fractions, 256–257

Use Objects, 334–335, 462–463

Variables, 112–113, 173, 363
- writing and evaluating expressions with, 118–120

Vertex, 318

Vocabulary. *See under* Assessment
- volume, 330–331
- models, 328–329
- prism, 330–331

Whole numbers, 195
- addition, 34–35
- comparing and ordering, 6–7
- division by fractions, 276–277
- division of decimals, 156–157, 160–161
- estimation, 140–141
- finding percent, 392–393
- multiplication by a fraction, 270–271
- multiplication by decimals, 138–139
- rounding, 28–29
- subtraction, 34–35

Words
- changing to expressions, 71
- translating, into expressions, 112–113, 118–120

Work Backward, 356–357, 412–413

Writing to Explain, 238–239

***x*-axis,** 403

***x*-coordinate,** 401, 403

***y*-axis,** 403

***y*-coordinate,** 401, 403

Zero(s)
- as placeholder, 40
- in product, 144–145
- in quotient, 90–91
- subtraction across, 34

Zero Property of Multiplication, 53, 197

Scott Foresman · Addison Wesley

enVisionMATH™

California